100 NIGHTS OF FUN & FROLIC! *Monte Proser's*
DANCE CARNIVAL
in **MADISON SQUARE GARDEN**
OPENING FRIDAY, MAY 30
CONTINUOUS DANCING EVERY NIGHT TO THESE **3** FAMOUS ORCHESTRAS
BENNY GOODMAN
LARRY **CLINTON** ★ **BARNET** CHARLIE
WORLD'S LARGEST DANCE FLOOR
THOUSANDS OF SPECTATOR SEATS
NO EXTRA CHARGE FOR DANCING **66¢** INCLUDING TAX
SAT. SUN. HOL. & HOL. EVE. **88¢**

SIMON SAYS

The Sights and Sounds of the Swing Era

1935-1955

SIMON SAYS

The Sights and Sounds
of the Swing Era

1935-1955

GEORGE T. SIMON

ARLINGTON HOUSE   New Rochelle, New York

Contents

A PREFACE — with some apologies

This book was Neil McCaffrey's idea. Neil is the man who, during his days with the Macmillan Company, suggested to them that they get me to write *The Big Bands*. For that, I will be eternally grateful to him. Then, after he formed his own publishing company, he suggested to me that I compile this book of selected pieces written during my generation with METRONOME Magazine. This time, after having re-read some of those pieces, I'm not exactly sure just how grateful I'm going to be.

Naturally, I'm honored that Neil decided to publish this book. And I'm delighted that you decided to read it. I hope you will share the enthusiasm and excitement that Neil and I had as we put it together. It's a big book, but still it contains only a small portion of the pieces I wrote during those twenty happy years with METRONOME. And, as I've already intimated, it does contain some things I now wish I'd never written—or, at least, wish I could have rewritten.

Yes, some of those earlier pieces not only amuse me and sometimes amaze me, but they also disturb me. For they reflect, perhaps too accurately for comfort, the style, the spirit, and the foibles of a youthful, enthusiastic, naive, at times quite immature young writer, who obviously loved very much the music about which he was writing, who admired many of the people who made it, and who, in turn, seemed, sometimes too obviously, to want to be loved and admired by them. For those early pieces do reveal a good deal of hero worship, of that "Gee whiz, isn't he one swell fellah!" idolatry. Those are some of the things I'd just as soon Neil hadn't convinced me—"for accuracy's sake and because some are so nice and campy"—should be reprinted here.

Neil kept pointing out that personal attitudes, social values, writing styles and conditions in general were quite different two generations ago, and that I really shouldn't be so hard on myself now. Still, some of my early comments, especially a few about black bands and black musicians, do embarrass me. They sound naive and at times even condescending. I don't think I was a racist then, though anyone who'd write like that today could be branded as one. I just didn't know any better then. I'd been brought up in a society that was almost totally insensitive to the conditions, problems and values of other races—or at most didn't bother to do much about them. Thank goodness, it finally listened—and learned—and changed. And so did I.

Something else I'd like to point out: throughout my METRONOME career, I preferred the music and the company of some musicians more than those of others. It shows in this book, and for this I offer no apologies. Strictly commercial and sterile bands and singers bored me as much then as they do now and so what little I did write about them wasn't especially inspired and certainly doesn't warrant inclusion in this book. On the other hand, jazz musicians and musicianly popular music creators, including some whose careers I could report from their inception, have always intrigued me. That's why this book does contain an abundance of material about people like Glenn Miller, Woody Herman, Benny Goodman, Dinah Shore, Frank Sinatra, Ella Fitzgerald, Louis Armstrong,

Tommy Dorsey, Artie Shaw and the Bob Crosby band. For some of you, there may be too much. If so, I'm sorry—but not terribly so. After all, this book is primarily a personal reflection of what one well-ensconced and deeply interested writer saw and heard, and what he thought about it all, not now, but then. It also includes some rather revealing and quite current comments from those whom I was writing about, in which they point out how right or wrong they think I was. My thanks go to all those who contributed them. And thanks, also, to two very kind gentlemen, Bob Asen and Milton Lichtenstein, owners of METRONOME and its assets, for their permission to reprint all the articles in this book, and for the majority of its photos. Additional pictures came from various other sources, as listed in the photo credits, for which, still more thanks.

But, of course, in the final analysis, I should and I do thank most of all the magnificent collection of people who appear in the pages that follow. Without them and their contributions, there just wouldn't have been any Swing Era and, least of all, this book. So thank you, ladies and gentlemen, very much!

—GEORGE T. SIMON

May, 1971

8

INTRODUCTION

Metronome celebrated its sixtieth year of publication in 1943 via a large October issue. My contribution was the article that follows, one of a series of pieces I wrote under the heading of "Simon Says" that began during my years in the army. Though, as the opening lines suggest, my arithmetic wasn't too accurate, it traces the development of the music of the swing era, from the time I joined Metronome, which was when the swing era began (1935), to the time the article appeared. As such, it serves fairly well as an introduction to much of what follows it in this book.

October, 1943

The last ten years of jazz started nine years ago, so far as I'm concerned. It started in studio 8H of NBC, and, thanks to some strong urging by John Hammond, I was lucky enough to be in on most of it.

The last ten years were started nine years ago by Benny Goodman and that great "Let's Dance" band, which spotted Krupa and Berigan and Erwin and Mondello and Schertzer, and Lacey and Helen Ward, in addition to Benny and Henderson arrangements.

Don't get me wrong. I don't mean that Benny Good-

man started swing. Sure, Ellington and Henderson and Redman and Goldkette and others had been there first, but so far as swing's acceptance and, in many ways, its greatness go, it's all pretty much Benny.

Casa Loma

The public had had somewhat of a taste of it. Casa Loma had presented swing in a modified form, modified mostly because it had a rhythm section that didn't swing. In those days I was never too sure how much Casa Loma swing was being accepted generally, though. I got my answer at a dance one night when a very pretty girl told me she was terribly interested in bands. "How do you like Casa Loma?" I asked, pushing the conversation along in the vein of the day. "I don't

Bandleaders Teddy Wilson, Count Basie, Cootie Williams, Gene Krupa, Don Redman, Benny Goodman, Tommy Dorsey, Lionel Hampton and Coleman Hawkins with Steve Ellis (front center), m.c. of an all-star bash

know," she replied. "How does it go?"

I used to hang around the Glen Gray Gang in those days, listening with one open ear while college professors tried to cram knowledge into the other semi-closed one. I admired the outfit more for its sweet and its ability to create moods, than I did for its swing. I'll never forget a short talk I had with Sonny Dunham one eve. The band I had at college used to feature *China Boy*, because we had a trumpet player who memorized Red Nichols' chorus pretty well. I asked Sonny if the band played it. "Well, we have an arrangement of it," he said, "But we've only had it for three weeks and I don't think the guys know it well enough yet."

Which made me feel that maybe Casa Loma didn't like swing after all.

In the spring of 1934 I heard a new band play the best organized swing I'd heard up to that time by a white group. It was a sleeper. Nobody had heard much about the Dorsey Brothers, but a few of us musicians went out to hear it at Nuttings-on-the-Charles, near Boston, and were knocked for several loops. Being a drummer in those days, I was especially impressed with a dead-panned guy who kept the most marvelous time I'd heard yet, and who got a beaut of a tone from his drums. He was Ray McKinley.

Hammond tried to convince me that Goodman had a better man a few months later, but though I admired Gene tremendously, Mac still stuck in my mind. I got to know Krupa at that time, too, and found him to be one helluva swell guy, very intense, terribly eager to make himself an outstanding, all-around drummer. I remember he used to have a xylophone set up in the middle of his living-room, and if he'd had room, I know he'd have had some tympani there, also. What's more, Gene used to make those faces, the kind that have made lots of stupid people think wrong things, even when nobody was looking, like at rehearsals. That's no affectation with Gene. With a lot of other imitators, it is, though, just the way imitation itself is an affectation.

Benny's band, as it became famous after its Elitch's Gardens engagement in Denver, garnered its share of imitators, too, of course. But none of them ever sounded as good. It wasn't overnight success, of course. The band had tried breaking in at the Roosevelt, since rechristened "Fort Lombardo," and had laid such a huge egg that the band could have eaten omelettes for days. For all I know, it did. Benny acted worried for a time, but Hammond and Willard Alexander, the MCA gent who pulled so hard for him and who's still his closest adviser, kept his spirits and bookings up, respectively, and so the inevitable came along.

The success of Benny as a business venture spurred others to hop onto the (literally speaking) band wagon. MCA, which so far had had pretty much of a monopoly in the band business, found itself with just one man (Alexander) who had any idea of what this swing was all about, and he was concentrating pretty much on Goodman. So other bookers, like Rockwell and O'Keefe and later on Joe Glaser and Moe Gale and Si Shribman, jumped in and started to do something with bands that didn't merely drool.

Swing as an art and swing as a business began to grow together. One helped the other, for as more people got to hear the better and more exciting type of dance music, more money came in, and as more money came in, other leaders and backers were encouraged to push their bands along.

Norvo

One outfit I'll never forget in those early days. That was Red Norvo's group, which at its first New York Commodore Hotel and its only Syracuse Hotel engagements played more consistently exciting music than any band I've yet heard. It was exciting not only because it was rhythmic, but because it had some amazing arrangements by Eddie Sauter (Glenn Miller recently told me that Sauter was so far ahead of his time then, he wonders if the guy realized how great he actually was), and an over-all feel and esprit that,

Glen Gray (center) surrounded by Guy Lombardo, Lennie Hayton, Seger Ellis and Jan Savitt

Red Norvo's soft, subtle swing band of 1936: pianist Joe Liss, vocalist Lew Hurst, drummer Maurice Purtill, bassist Pete Peterson, Norvo, trumpeters Stewie Pletcher, Bill Hyland, Eddie Sauter, trombonist Leo Moran, saxists Slats Long, Frank Simeone, Herbie Haymer

so far as I'm concerned, hasn't been matched by any other outfit since. Even Duke, if you hear him through a long evening, will have occasional let-downs, especially when he tries to play a pop tune. I can't remember a single let-up in the Norvo brand of soft, subtle swing.

The pace didn't last. Red enlarged the band (it had just ten men in its best days) and Mildred joined and the band went into the Blackhawk in Chicago. Mildred and the Blackhawk management and crowd didn't blend—I'll never forget the night some square offered her a dollar for a tip—and the wonderful feel of the band was gone—for good.

The Crosby band started coming along right after that, also playing thrilling stuff. But, whereas the Norvo beat had been subtle, the Dixieland Dispensers' was as obvious as a BMT Express roaring into the station. It didn't do too well financially for a while, but later on, as swing business grew, the band's exchequer grew too and everybody was happy.

While all this was going on, the greatest of 'em all, measured in time and achievement, was still lingering in the background. Duke Ellington was doing well, all right, but it wasn't until several years later, when a new development in jazz, so far as the public went, was receiving general approbation, that everybody started talking about the Duke.

As jazz improved, so did the bands, naturally.

Cab Calloway, who had confined himself merely to shouting in front of an average outfit, gradually whipped a top-notch crew into shape. "It's something I'd always wanted to have," he told me recently. "Now that it's here, though," he added, "it's not really mine. It belongs to the guys, themselves, for they're the ones who really built it into something."

That Cab is a very modest fellow.

The public's acceptance of jazz didn't hinder Jimmie Lunceford one bit, either. He had started a few years before Benny and had received some measure of acclaim when he had played the Cotton Club in New York, but he never did start getting known and paid for on a national scale until Goodman had paved the way.

Same goes for other bands. Count Basie came roaring into town and soon proved a huge success. The late Chick Webb, who'd been banging it out at the Savoy, came through and started making so much money (in part, thanks to Ella), that he used to have his own chauffeur. I was once driven home in very grand style by the duo. That was before gas rationing.

Wilson

A couple of Johns in Chick's band got together with a pianist on the opposite stand in Willie Bryant's band. He brought along the drummer and a trumpeter from the outfit when he had a chance to make some records for Brunswick. John Hammond had fixed that up and, just to make the first Teddy Wilson date a success, he had friend Goodman come along to play too. Those first sides with bassist Kirby and guitarist Trueheart from Webb's band and trumpeter Roy Eldridge, drummer Cozy Cole and Wilson from Bryant's bunch, as well as tenor man Ben Webster, to me constitute some of the really great swing sides of all time.

Little bands, though, didn't cut much figure then. Kirby came along and clicked in his own little way, and Farley and Riley achieved some success for the music going around, but on the whole it was a big band business.

Bookers get more commission out of big bands.

The results saw lots of outfits starting up, and the great majority of them were good, certainly above the standard of music of the preceding era.

One of the shrewdest of all band businessmen, Tommy Dorsey, raided Bert Block's band [as well as Joe Haymes's] and opened at the Lincoln, where Isham Jones had recently closed. Wise-owl Dorsey, however, never tried to compete completely with Goodman. He knew BG had the jump, so TD started concentrating upon sweet just as much as he did on swing. He had two big helps: his trombone and Jack Leonard.

Tommy's band turned out to be one big happy family for a while. Dorsey bought a big estate in New Jersey and the whole bunch used to go out there week-ends. When things are going right, there's nobody like Dorsey, and things were really going right then.

Brother Jimmy, on the other hand, was doing not quite so well. A less aggressive character, he had taken his bunch to the coast, where it did fairly well for itself on the Crosby radio show, but it didn't get much national acclaim. Bob Eberly helped him, but that comes later.

Shaw

The business grew and grew. Benny was still very much king. Naturally, rival bookers wanted to find a threat. Rockwell and O'Keefe found Artie Shaw, and he really pressed Goodman. But Benny was still the original, and it's awfully hard to improve on the original, as you know, and especially difficult when the original happens to be Benny Goodman.

There were others, too. Charlie Barnet, who has more guts than almost any other leader in the business, arose intermittently, with various bands and ideas.

Larry Clinton, thanks to some great record plugging and consistent assignment of pop tunes, came up fast. Les Brown came up from Duke and Bob Chester came in from Detroit.

Tommy was very big at the time, so a new vogue of trombone-leaders came along. Willard Alexander pulled Will Bradley out of a hat with a Schwichtenburg hat-band in it, and Ray McKinley out of Jimmy Dorsey's band to put forth a strong group. Bobby Byrne left Jimmy too. Jack Teagarden left Whiteman. Jack Jenney left the radio studios.

Another trombonist started a band about this time, but he didn't play trombone with it. "I can't see this imitating stuff," he told me back in 1937. "After all, Tommy is the big thing right now. I certainly can't cut him on his own horn, so why should I get up front and try it?"

That's when Glenn Miller started concentrating on the new reed section sound. In those days I thought Tommy was smart. But then I began to know Miller really well. He is THE man in that department.

Later in the swing era, Goodman started receiving competition from some of his own men. Gene Krupa started his band and at times did really top-notch business. Lionel Hampton, a less direct competitor, got going several years later. So did Bunny Berigan and Vido Musso.

James

Harry James left Benny. He didn't go well for quite a while, though his band rocked like mad. One night at Roseland he took me aside. "I've got a great idea," he told me, excitedly. "I'm going to add strings."

"You're absolutely out of your head," I retorted quickly.

Several years later I realized I must have been referring to myself.

Harry's success as a sweet band is a logical segue to another part of the last decade in bands which I haven't mentioned much so far. That's the sweet music side of it.

Before the present era, there were very few good sweet bands—very few good bands, for that matter. Top-notcher, of course, was Paul Whiteman, but Leo Reisman also used to put forth some pretty tasty material on records. Otherwise, there were just bands like those of Jack Denny, Bernie Cummins, Johnny Hamp, George Hall, all about as musical as a submerged submarine.

Two good musical bands came to the fore at about the same time that Benny did. I don't think there's any correlation between them and Goodman, but it's at least interesting to note that public taste began to improve at the same time in both divisions, so that Hal Kemp and Ray Noble began to enjoy their due success at about the same time.

Kemp, in case you never knew it, used to have a fine jazz band. For quite some time he featured a top-notch trumpeter. His name was Bunny Berigan.

But Kemp changed his style. It bordered on mickey, but it had lots of musical qualities. Not the least was a first trumpeter named Earl Geiger. Hal

Old friends Charlie Barnet, Gene Krupa, Glenn Miller, Tommy Dorsey (whom Glenn, by his own admission, was smart enough not to imitate) and Dick Stabile

The Hal Kemp band on tour in England. Kemp is second from right. Moving toward left: drummer-vocalist Skinnay Ennis, trumpeters Mickey Bloom and Bunny Berigan, trombonist Gus Mayhew and (with hat) pianist-arranger John Scott Trotter

built many of his arrangements around this muted king. Earl, however, was a problem child and he and the band parted. When Skinnay Ennis, around whom much of the rest of the stuff was built, left to start his own band, the top Kemp days, musically speaking, were gone. Hal tried to switch to swing. That was a mistake.

Noble

Noble had a thrilling band. At the same time Hammond was trying to convince me about Benny—and succeeding, I was trying to convince him about Noble—and failing. But to me, for sheer good taste and all-around smart dance music, that was the band of the times. And why shouldn't it have been, with men like Glenn Miller, Charlie Spivak, Claude Thornhill, George Van Eps, Delmar Kaplan, Will Bradley, Peewee Erwin, Bud Freeman, Johnny Mince, Milt Yaner and Al Bowlly?

So far as I'm concerned, it's to Ray that we owe the good taste and the good sound that pervades today's good sweet bands—to Ray, and, to some extent, to Paul Whiteman, too.

Sweet music should sound good. A few bands in the middle thirties tried hard to make pleasant noise. Will Osborne's was one. He had what I thought was a crack outfit at the Lexington Hotel, one which featured awfully pretty arrangements, built around trombones, and a good piano player with a funny name: Ruppert Biggadike. Will, too, is one of the funniest guys in the business—and finest, too.

Other outfits, like the very smart Hudson-DeLange group, which should have been even greater, and could have been if Will and Eddie could have gotten along better, and the late Orville Knapp's (now Leighton Noble's), also deserve special mention here.

But then, around that time, came the era of bad bands, bands that made unmusical sounds via a host of ickey tricks. Up until then, music as an art and as a commercial product had progressed pretty much together.

It took Sammy Kaye and Blue Barron and Lawrence Welk and the Tucker lads and the McFarland twins (since reformed, by the way) to shunt aside musical notes for bank notes. I will say that they did all right by themselves. But as for some of us, who have a little pride in our profession, these lads acted pretty badly.

Kaye and Kyser featured their singers a great deal. Kyser turned his bunch into a musical outfit eventually, but he still emphasized vocals. He was and is a very smart man.

For vocalists were coming to the fore more and more. Even Benny's Helen Ward had received more notice than you'd expect the lone romantic interest in a rhythmic unit to get. But whereas Helen embellished Benny's band, several other singers helped to make other bands.

Most obvious of all is the effect of Bob Eberly and Helen O'Connell upon an otherwise not overly successful Jimmy Dorsey band. So far as I can figure out, it took Billy Burton, who these days is making a

Two very effective Jimmy Dorseyites: Helen O'Connell and Bob Eberly

specialty of singers, to capitalize upon those two when he first came in to manage Jimmy.

Brother Tommy did right well, first by Jack Leonard and less so by Edythe Wright, which proved the public wasn't completely gullible, and later on with Sinatra. Woody Herman, who had done pretty well with his first dixieland, then combination band, since leaving Isham Jones, started to feature himself more and more. Success came faster and faster.

Other bands, thanks to their singers, hopped right along. An obvious example is Vaughn Monroe. The King Sisters helped Alvino Rey; Eugenie Baird made Tony Pastor's music especially palatable, and, of course, a good deal later on, Helen Forrest did an awful lot for Harry James.

Forrest

I remember Helen from way back—way back in 1935 when I happened to tune in on a corny program on WNEW. Suddenly, out came this glorious voice, singing so much more in tune, with so much more real musical feeling than other singers of the time. That was Helen Forrest. I raved about her, but she passed from earshot.

Next time I ran across her, she was with Artie Shaw at the Lincoln. I remember going to the Lincoln to hear the band and Helen came over to our table.

The girl I was with was also a singer and I thought a pretty good one. But, after Helen left the table, the girl turned to me.

"Gee, she's wonderful," she exclaimed, "I sure'd like to sound as natural and good as that!"

The girl was Dinah Shore.

Dinah, so far as I'm concerned, has raised the level of singers a lot. I wrote about that about a year or so ago in pretty great detail, as I recall. Dinah pays strict attention to good taste and good delivery. The combination, especially when coming from such a gifted and intelligent person, is unbeatable.

Bing, the greatest of them all, is also the most natural of them all. It's interesting to note that Dinah not only thinks he's the greatest singer; she also considers him just about the greatest guy on earth—as do all who know him.

Sinatra, too, is exceedingly natural and sincere-sounding. That is why, I think, he has stolen the spotlight from Eberly and Como and all the rest. For naturalness, providing it's musical, has won the favor of more and more of the public. Which, so far as I'm concerned, is really a major victory for popular music.

Public acceptance of music in good taste has helped the cause tremendously during the past decade. Its acceptance of a good beat, of good tones, of good intonation and musical phrasing are really something.

And what's happening now? It's beginning to accept them all, not so much individually, as collectively.

The Future

Popular music is making tremendous strides. Now that it has established melody, which it actually established long before the past decade, and good rhythm, it now reaches ahead one more step and is attempting to establish really good harmony.

The leader in that direction, has, obviously enough, been the Duke. He was bringing out interesting chords and changes long, long before the rest. And now that bigger commercial names are doing the same thing, many more people are starting to notice Ellington, and the greatest of them all is slowly achieving some of the glories he deserves.

Glenn Miller, who started off with a band that he wanted to sound like Basie, is primarily interested in harmony now. All of his disciples, Claude Thornhill, Hal McIntyre and Charlie Spivak, have the same leanings, though with Charlie, his wondrous horn has had a lot to do with his success.

Teddy Powell's simple, relaxed style was an effective contrast to these fellows' stuff, an absolute tops in taste.

In the cases of Thornhill and McIntyre, too much praise cannot be heaped upon them for the musical daring and good taste each has displayed.

Bands that already achieved success as swing units have also made the change. Artie Shaw added strings, Tommy Dorsey added strings, Jan Savitt added strings. And (though only to prove that Simon doesn't know what he's talking about) James added strings and immediately became the biggest thing in the country.

Ten years ago, popular music was primarily melody.

Five years ago it was primarily melody and rhythm.

Today it is melody, rhythm and harmony, with each striving to improve. There's no doubt about it, swing, jazz, popular music, or whatever you want to call it, has come a long way during the past ten years.

And from the looks of things, it's going to come a long way more!

Things to come: the sounds of bandleaders Stan Kenton, Woody Herman, Dizzy Gillespie

Sinatra with Gloria DeHaven, one-time Jan Savitt vocalist, and Sammy Kaye

July, 1935

This was my first interview with a major bandleader. Written just four months after I'd joined *Metronome,* it deals with a type of music I outgrew shortly thereafter but for which I had a good deal of empathy because of the style of music I'd been playing with my band at college and on club dates thereafter. Hopefully, my writing style began to improve with my taste.

DUCHIN LED PIANISTS OUT OF RHYTHM RUT

B. D. (Before Duchin) Piano Players Pounded Out Common Chords in Dance Orks All Night Long—Then Along Came Eddy Duchin

Plays Up Melody and Figures

Uses No Arrangements

Once upon a time there was a piano player in a dance orchestra who did practically nothing but hammer out basic chords behind saxes, brass and fiddles. In fact, once upon a time there were a lot of piano players in a lot of dance orchestras who did practically nothing but hammer out basic chords. But that was all B. D.

"B. D." (for the benefit of you readers who haven't already caught on) means "Before Duchin." And that was a sad, sad era for piano players in orchestras; in those days they were just part of the rhythm section; they just sat there all night and hammered out chord after chord in tempo with little chance to express themselves via the keyboard. They were repressed individuals, indeed.

But along came Eddy Duchin! It was in 1928. Before then nobody except his family and friends knew that he had been born on April 1, 1909, in Cambridge, Mass., or that he didn't like to practice piano as a youngster, or that he was attending the Massachusetts College of Pharmacy and studying piano under Felix Fox of Boston.

But then came 1928, Eddy Duchin, and the emancipation of all repressed piano players. Leo Reisman was looking for a piano player. He held an audition at the old Waldorf-Astoria in New York. A tall, nineteen-year-old youth with dark, wavy hair, and with only two years experience, was selected. Eddy Duchin, of course.

It was then that the new style of dance band piano began. Duchin had little experience but lots of ideas. Had he had more of the former, he probably would have stuck to the prevalent oom-pah style of piano.

Eddy Duchin, mid-forties vintage, with two other famous style-setters, Nat "King" Cole and Bing Crosby

But he was a comparative youngster, unrepressed, and at a very impressionistic age—impressionistic because one is likely to be greatly impressed by one's own ideas.

Reisman's new piano player's ideas were revolutionary. To him a pianist was more than a rhythm man; he was a melody man as well. The combination gave him the freedom of the entire keyboard to play rhythm, or melody, or whatever figures he happened to feel.

That, incidentally, is the essence of Duchinesque piano playing—"whatever he happened to feel." Duchin's piano is one of moods. As he puts it: "I close my eyes, hum to myself, and then play whatever I happen to feel inside of me. I think it's the first time that any dance orchestra pianist has adopted that formula—playing what he feels rather than what he sees. It's inspirational rather than mechanical."

That conception, though much copied since 1928, was something entirely new. It struck Reisman's fancy; struck it with such force that Duchin not only won the audition but soon became a feature of Reisman's band at the Central Park Casino. But it took phonograph recordings to introduce Duchin to the general public and to musiciandom. Such discs as *Moanin' Low*, *What Is This Thing Called Love*, *You've Got That Thing*, and *You Do Something to Me* made people listen again and ask: "Who is that guy who plays melody in the bass and all that stuff?"

Gradually these people began to discover that it was Eddy Duchin—his fame spread all over. Reisman's recordings became terrific sellers and folks came to the Central Park Casino just to hear "that piano-player with Reisman." The "with Reisman" part was omitted, though, in September, 1931. The band at the Casino became Eddy Duchin and his Orchestra, with maestro Duchin the first leader to direct from the keys.

Duchin's band was, and still is, essentially a society dance orchestra. The ritzy crowd at the Casino made that imperative. But it wasn't completely of that ilk; Duchin realized the importance of contrast—that had always been evident in his piano playing. He incorporated that into his orchestra. It wasn't just a strictly fox-trot band, playing all its tempos fairly up. "My idea of a good dance orchestra," said Duchin, "is one that can play to whatever type of dancer is on the floor. You know what I mean; preponderance of faster tempos for the older people; mixed tempos for the college kids with emphasis on extremes, and so on. After all you must remember all the time that your dance music is for dancing primarily. If the crowd finds your music easy to dance to, you're a success."

That formula is pretty evident in the type music Duchin dishes out. Notice the rhythm, especially.

There's tremendous emphasis of beats—a good example is drummer Harry Campbell who plays about the loudest off-beat cymbal in dancebandom. And notice, too, the tempos. Duchin is continually changing them in an endeavor to play to the moods and feet of the dancers. That's the main reason he doesn't go in for arrangements. Any arrangement, to be effective, must be played at a definite tempo. But it's impossible for Duchin to stick to any one tempo and to his formula at the same time. Ergo, no arrangements.

"And when you don't have to bother about a lot of complicated arrangements you're free to do other things," explained Duchin. "We can concentrate completely on such finer points as phrasing. You've probably noticed that yourself when listening to the band—the way the saxes will crescendo and diminuendo together—you can just feel them feel. And, as I've explained before, it's the same way with my piano. I hum whatever song we're playing, and I can just feel what I'm going to play. You know, I hardly ever play a tune the same way twice. Of course, there are a few choruses I've worked out, but otherwise it's all done on the spur of the moment."

Once upon a time there were a lot of piano players in a lot of dance orchestras who did practically nothing but hammer out basic chords. But along came Eddy Duchin! Now there are a lot of piano players in a lot of dance orchestras who play all over the piano. And when a leader stops one of them and says, "Here, here, enough of that," the pianist invariably comes back with his argument invincible: "Duchin does it!"

But the piano player overlooked just one point—there is only one Eddy Duchin!

Artie Shaw was sensitive to pressures from some of his jitterbugging fans. In this interview he confesses about other aspects of leading a band that bugged him—bugged him so much that, a few weeks after this interview, he gave up his band and flew away to Mexico.

'I STILL DON'T LIKE JITTERBUGS'

Artie Sticks by Guns That Rocked Music World; Defines Terms; Unhappy in Business

"Sure, I don't like jitterbugs! I don't like the business angles connected with music. I can't see autograph-hunters. I thought the Old Gold commercial was lousy for my music. And I don't like prima donna musicians!"

So spake Artie Shaw in his hotel room exclusively to METRONOME's reporter the day after his sensational opening at the Hotel Pennsylvania.

But Artie went further, and what he had to say amplified greatly that all-important interview he had given New York *Post's* Michal Mok early in October; an interview which caused anti-Shaw clubs to spring up, bitter resentment in the music business, and continual rumors that he lost his Old Gold commercial because of his expressions, that his band would break up, and that he would never open at the Pennsylvania.

"Everything I said, I feel. Frankly, I'm unhappy

Artie Shaw and his Jitterbug Glare

in the music business. Maybe I don't even belong in it. I like the music part—love and live it, in fact—but for me the business part plain stinks!

Misquoted

"I told Mike (Mok) that, only he amplified it greatly and got me wrong in a couple of places. He got me on a tough day; I was so tired that I didn't even want to talk with him, but he felt that I'd let loose more that way. I guess I did," grinned Artie.

In that *Post* article Artie attacked jitterbugs with vehemence. "But," he now explains, "I didn't mean those out on the floor. I meant the ones who continually yank at your coat and who keep shouting at the band all night long so that you can't concentrate on music and the folks in front can't hear.

"There's only one in a hundred in any group of dancers, and if they're the ones who are sore at me, I don't care. They should be told off, both for music's sake and for the other ninety-nine dancers who know how to act."

As for the music business in general, Shaw explained that he was still an idealist, that when he first started his band he had pictured getting to the top and then playing the kind of music he wanted to.

"But it's not like that at all," he said. "Two years ago we used to love playing; we made up tunes on the stand. Now it's all business. I'm a musician, not a business man. If I wanted to go into business, I'd enter Wall Street and at least keep regular hours!"

Shaw was quoted in the *Post* article as calling all autograph seekers "morons," saying that he often let his valet sign his name for him. "Kids, maybe," he explains, "but why should grown-ups want my signature? As for that valet business, I just mentioned to Mok that one time somebody asked my valet for his autograph after getting mine. That business he ran about his signing my name is the bunk."

Artie is glad to be off the Old Gold show, despite the financial loss. "The show was built all wrong for me," he declared. "When I auditioned for it, I had a definite musical formula, but it gradually turned into a comedy which didn't do the band any good.

"Besides, it was on a weak network, thus killing its rating, and the new schedule called for a west coast show at 11 o'clock Saturday nights and I couldn't leave the Penn for that. And so when I asked for a one-week vacation because I was so tired, and they wouldn't give it to me unless I quit the show entirely, I quit the show entirely."

The question of future plans came up, as it does in all interviews. "I'm going to pay strict attention to music," Shaw asserted. "The band's morale is still high, thank God, though there are a couple of guys who feel they're too important. That'll have to change. No prima donnas in this band!

"You know," mused Shaw, in summation, "I'm not sorry this has happened. There's been some tough publicity—in fact I'm sick of being asked what I really think of jitterbugs—but it puts me straight with the world. I want everybody to know that all I'm interested in is making good music. If they like it, they can have it; if they don't they can keep away from it. But let 'em concentrate on my music and not on me!"

October, 1946

To some, Benny Goodman was no longer King of Swing when I talked with him in his Bedford Village, N.Y., home in 1946. Obviously, I didn't agree with those "some," despite the fact that Benny was not then leading one of his most inspired editions. And some writers insist that Goodman is just about impossible to interview. Here again I disagree, and offer what follows as ample evidence.

BENNY GOODMAN

Swing can thank Benny Goodman and Benny Goodman can thank Swing. Swing can thank Benny Goodman for making possible its acceptance in a world which, before the advent of the King's reign, thought that the best swing hung between two trees in a backyard and that a beat was reserved exclusively for cops and reporters. Benny Goodman can thank Swing for making possible his attaining a huge house, a swimming pool, a tennis court, a wife, two daughters, a slew of managers and the security that allies itself with a million cabbage leaves, all autographed either by Vinson or Morgenthau.

Today, though Goodman and Swing are no longer considered monopolistically synonymous by the public, each still has an important influence upon the other. There are the newcomers who insist that Benny is no longer the King of Swing, that Herman or Kenton or Raeburn have succeeded him on the throne . . . that's the way things happen in a kingdom where rulers are whims and fads combined.

Ask Benny himself, and though he won't come right out and swat himself on the chest and shout "I am still King," he will give you the impression that he still considers himself to be right up there and that nobody's going to shove him off with any tricks, especially with any that don't swing. "There are different types of swing," he says. "It's silly to try to compare them. If they swing, they swing, and if they swing, they're good. There's no point in making it out as something complicated. It's really very simple. Some musicians are stiff and awkward and don't swing; others are relaxed and play free and easy and so they swing. It's either in them or it isn't."

Swing has been in a lot of guys who have been in and out of Benny Goodman bands. That's because if they can't swing, Benny doesn't want them. One of his favorite tricks is to rehearse his band without the rhythm section. "That's a sure way of finding out whether or not a musician swings. If the band can make a thing move without the lift a good rhythm section gives, then it can swing. But if it can't move it, provided, of course, the arrangement is movable, then something's wrong." Discovery of the wrong thing usually results in the focusing of the famous Goodman Ray (the only well-known look of contempt produced solely by the eye without any curling of the lips) on said wrong thing with said wrong thing usually finding himself out of the King's good graces and eventually out of his band.

Most of the good swing men left Goodman of their own accord, among them trumpeters Harry James, Cootie Williams, Ziggy Elman, Bunny Berigan, Chris Griffin, Billy Butterfield, Jimmy Maxwell, Peewee Erwin; trombonists Lou McGarity, Vernon Brown, Murray MacEachern, Miff Mole, Joe Harris; saxists Vido Musso, Dick Clark, Arthur Rollini, Bud Freeman, Jerry Jerome, Toots Mondello, Hymie Schertzer, Les Robinson, Skippy Martin, Dave Matthews, Babe Russin; pianists Teddy Wilson, Mel Powell, Johnny Guarnieri, Jess Stacy; guitarists Charlie Christian (who left because of illness), George Van Eps, Allen Reuss, Benny Heller, George Rose; bassists Artie Bernstein, Sid Weiss; drummers Gene Krupa, Dave Tough; vibraphonist Lionel Hampton.

With a few exceptions, Goodman is the guy who

really started these fellows to fame, the man who took them as nobodies and nurtured them into swing successes. His was the first of the really popular bands to feature individual jazz stars, and it was because of the opportunities he gave them that men like James, Berigan, Wilson, Stacy, Krupa and Hampton achieved enough fame to be able to go out on their own. And Benny was able to give them those opportunities because in 1935 he was brave enough to go out into a comparatively swingless world and get it to accept the kind of dance music in which he honestly believed.

It wasn't easy for Goodman at first, just as his earlier life, during which he was the primary earning power for a large and underprivileged Chicago family, was a tough struggle. Despite the build-up afforded by his Saturday night radio commercial, he failed miserably on his first location spot in the Spring of 1935, the Roosevelt Grill in New York, where he followed Guy Lombardo and where he lasted just two weeks because the band was too loud. But he plugged hard and made it, as you've probably read many times in various success stories, one of which this isn't.

And while making it, he also literally made a great number of swing stars. Why so many have left him has always been the cause of much tongue-wagging. Benny explains it rather simply and thusly: "I'll never be satisfied with any band. I guess I just expect too much from my musicians and when they do things wrong I get brought down." And when Benny gets brought down, anything's liable to happen. Suffice it to say that the down-bringer does not lead a very happy existence. Benny doesn't curse or rant or rave, but he makes it so obvious via a passive approach that he's no longer happy with the person in question, that said p. in q. has no difficulty in catching on, gets brought down himself, and soon the relationship draws to a close. Benny seldom actively fires a musician, but his perfectionist tendencies and his varying moods have resulted in a tremendous passage of stars in and out of Goodman organizations.

About his band today, a band which many musi-

A post-Swing Era Goodman with the other three-quarters of his famed Quartet: Lionel Hampton, Gene Krupa, Teddy Wilson

cians rate inferior to earlier Goodman groups and musically below Benny's level: "There are very few good musicians today. By good musicians, I mean men who can play everything, including, of course, men who can swing. I've got a few, yes, especially this kid drummer, Louis Bellson, who to me is a helluva musician any way you look at it. But too many of them don't know their instruments and so you can't depend on them.

"I've been listening to some of the rebop or bebop musicians. You know, some of them can't even hold a tone! They're just faking. They're not real musicians.

"What do I think of bebop? Well, from what I've heard, bebop reminds me of guys who refuse to write a major chord even if it's going to sound good. A lot of the things they do are too pretentious. They're just writing or playing for effect, and a lot of it doesn't swing."

About certain accusations from the more modern-minded musicians that Benny's own playing is harmonically limited: "That's easy. I could play a lot of weird notes if I wanted to. But I don't want to. That's just my own personal taste. I still like Mozart and Brahms. If somebody else prefers Stravinsky, that's his privilege, but if I want to continue preferring Mozart and Brahms, well, that's my privilege, isn't it?"

About the feeling of certain musicians, beboppers especially, that the beat doesn't have to actually be put down but can be just as effective if it's only implied: "There are various types of swing, I guess, but some of this so-called relaxed style gets so relaxed that it just about collapses. So far as I'm concerned, if it swings, it swings, and that's that.

"You know what I like? That record Ella and Louis Jordan made of *Patootie Pie*. To me that's the best jazz record in the last ten years. And it's relaxed, too. I've been playing it every morning now for about six weeks, almost as soon as I get up, and I still think it's great. That's a good test, isn't it? Ella's not one of those *sub gum* singers and Louis's little band really swings.

"There's a relaxed style in all music. In classical clarinet you can take a man like Reginald Kell. He's very relaxed. Some others are much stiffer. But, as I said, when it comes to swing, though you've naturally got to be relaxed to a degree, you can still carry it too far."

Benny's new band is less relaxed than a good many other swing outfits. Often it seems to be trying too hard, pressing. There's a plausible reason: "I'm sick and tired of rehearsing. I've had enough of that stuff. I guess I've just passed the stage where I want to knock myself out. For what? If we wanted to have everything just the way I want it, I'd have to rehearse

all the time, and even then I'm not sure that I'd get it." Which should explain why the current Goodman Gang is less clean than earlier groups. When a musician reads unfamiliar stuff, he can't play too well and he certainly can't relax a great deal.

Goodman no longer wants to do it the hard way, that's obvious. He likes to spend as much time as possible on his big estate in Bedford Village, N. Y., with his very charming wife, Alice (John Hammond's sister), his two daughters and his three step-daughters, whom he sometimes calls simply "Pops," because he's absent-minded and doesn't remember their names too well. He plays tennis, golf, and bridge and keeps company with other wealthy folk. He has had his kicks and now he wants his contentment, too. Which may explain his willingness to capitalize on the popularity of his boy singer, Art Lund, a capable performer, who has resorted to an old-fashioned style for identification and who has caught on. "To me, all boy singers are bad. They're not musicians. You can't take even the best of them seriously. How often do you listen to a record by a good band just for the vocal? I know I never do. It's just something you've got to add because the public wants it, and if I've got to have a boy singer with me I might as well have one the public likes. And they certainly seem to like Art. So more power to him!"

It's a peculiar phenomenon. Benny doesn't think much of boy singers, but he's willing to permit one to become the selling point of his current band. Benny doesn't want to spend a lot of time rehearsing and yet he'll admit that he's by no means completely satisfied with his band today. Benny can plainly hear other bands advance beyond his, musically, and he admittedly wants to get some new, smart arrangements, and yet he doesn't seem to be devoting much effort to finding a new, smart arranger for his band. Instead he plays a lot of Henderson-ish, Sampson-ish things which jump all right, which are fine in small doses, but which, in the field of arranging, are not swing kings by any means.

Many explanations have been offered, some going as far as the ragtime pianist who insists that Benny can't play with feeling because he's not poor! There is no doubt about it, Goodman enjoys his easier life. He has worked hard and he wants to enjoy some of the fruits of his labor before he gets so old that his teeth won't be able even to dent an apple skin. Undoubtedly, he closes his eyes and ears to a great many things that he doesn't want to see or hear so that he won't be tempted to return to his inbred, perfectionist way of musical living, a way of living that leaves little or no time for a Country Gentleman's existence.

But don't think for a minute that Benny doesn't know what's going on, or that Benny, if he really wanted to, couldn't get ahead and build himself a truly magnificent swing band. He might tell you that he can't find the musicians he wants or that he can't get the type of arrangements he wants, but you can bet your last bottom buck that if he really wanted to, he could.

Me, I've got a feeling that he doesn't really want to right now. And me, I can't altogether blame him, either. But to me, he's still the most thrilling instrumentalist in jazz today. And for that, and for all that he has done to bring it into the wide open spaces, where everybody can breathe it and where all the musicians in the world can get a chance to play it, for that, to me, Benny Goodman is still King of Swing!

December, 1946

He may never have made it quite as big as some of the other bandleaders; yet Les Brown always had a good band and he always had the respect of his musicians. This interview reveals a bright, nice guy, who actually *did* retire (as he said he would) right after this article appeared, but who un-retired shortly thereafter and has been leading a band almost ever since.

LES BROWN

The heat was really on Les Brown about six years ago. His band was just beginning to grab some of the "renown" that radio announcers always mention whenever they do his broadcasts. For the Brown band was clean, modern, exciting; it was creating a lot of talk, and it had, in addition to leader Les, a hunk of fine sidemen who were helping its cause mightily.

Six years ago was also the height of the raiding season. Musicians would fluctuate from band to band faster than today's price of a pound of steak. So it was only natural that guys like Wolffe Tanenbaum, Billy Rowland, Si Zentner, Butch Stone, Steve Madrick and Don Jacoby, stars of the Brown unit in those days, should get offers from bands that had already reached the top and which, in several instances, offered some of the men much more than twice the amount they were getting from Les.

Any of them go?

You can bet your life they didn't.

For Les Brown was then, as he is today, one of the really great, if not the greatest of leaders in the

A thinking man's Les Brown

world to work for. Les is not only a musician's musician, he's also a musician's gentleman, and that, gentlemen, is one helluva combination in this business! No, they could have wooed Wolffe with a thousand gross of fresh reeds (no man ever had reed trouble like his in those days), or they could have offered Butch a half-share of the home plate in Yankee Stadium (it's rumored he spends all his vacations in the Stadium grandstand, even if there isn't a game being played), but none of those guys would have left Les in those days. They liked him much, much too much.

The band, playing the Log Cabin in Armonk and the Astor Roof, really started to hit in 1940 and '41. It had been a pretty tough struggle for Les, too, because he had come out of Duke University with his Blue Devils in 1936, fully expecting to set the band world on fire. The Devils made some records for Decca, about which Mr. Brown prefers to remain quite silent these days, but that was in Summer and when Fall rolled around again the parents of most of the guys in the band insisted that their sonny-boys return to Duke to finish their educations. Since Les had just been graduated, that left him stranded.

His records having caused some comment, and being gifted with a great deal of arranging talent, Les didn't find it too difficult to find work around New York. He arranged for the bands of Larry Clinton, Isham Jones, Ruby Newman and Don Bestor, and finally a few years later, in 1938, organized a twelve-piece group that sounded pretty good in the Hotel Edison. This was sort of the beginning of the present group.

The beginning of Les himself took place in Reinertown, Pa., on March 14, 1912. His Dad, an accomplished musician, led a saxophone quartet called "The Four Brown Brothers," not to be confused with the more famous "Six Brown Brothers." Papa Brown, primarily a trombonist, also played soprano sax in the act, which may be the psychological factor governing Les's apparent insatiable desire to include that instrument in all of his reed sections.

Mr. Brown taught all his three sons. Les learned the reeds, but Warren, who is two years younger, and "Stumpy," who's eleven years Les's junior, took up the parental instrument, the trombone. Both brothers are in the current Brown trombone section, Warren having recently returned after a sojourn in the Navy and a fling at music publishing.

This current Brown band is the best in Brown history, both musically and commercially. Its musical qualifications are yours to hear for yourselves, on the air, in theatres, on locations, and most easily and most important, on Columbia phonograph records. As for the commercial qualifications, let Les explain:

"It has been records—no doubt about it. Any success we've had can be laid directly to them. I don't feel we have arrived in the Miller or Dorsey class for the simple reason that we haven't had a record as big as their big hits. But what we have done is produce a variety of records during the last five years that has helped to keep us right up there, cause comment and make money.

"You can put our records into five different classes. There's the swinging of the classics, like *Mexican Hat Dance* and *Bizet Has His Day;* there's the straight swing stuff, like *High on a Windy Trumpet, Lover's Leap* and *Leap Frog;* there are the novelties, such as *Frim Fram Sauce, A Good Man Is Hard to Find* and *Joltin' Joe DiMaggio;* then there are the commercial ballads of the schottische type, such as *You Won't Be Satisfied, My Dreams Are Getting Better All the Time* and *I Guess I'll Get the Papers and Go Home;* and then finally there are pretty things like *'Tis Autumn* and *Sentimental Journey*. You know, I think *Journey* could have been THE record for us if we could have gotten enough pressings, but there was a war on then and Columbia was having its troubles. Still, I'm sure that over a period of years it'll be by far our most important record.

"Also, I can't give enough credit to the people who have helped so much, to Butch and Doris Day and now Jack Haskell—watch him, by the way—and to Joe Glaser and Manie Sacks, and, of course, to all the guys in the band, those who have been with us for years and the late additions, too. Guess I'm a pretty lucky guy!"

Les has plans for retiring soon. He'll continue to record, but he wants to concentrate more on radio and movies. In any case, musically he plans to stick pretty close to his current format. "Our stuff may not be as adventurous or as involved as some of the things other bands are doing, but at least I think the boys play what they do play really well, and, though we never play down to a crowd, I think everybody knows what we are doing—or at least they seem to—and they all keep dancing, too."

Les isn't as knocked out by the ultra-modern school of jazz as a lot of other musicians are. Sure, he's a Stravinsky enthusiast and he spends a great deal of time listening to modern composers in his sumptuous home, but a lot of what he calls "overarranged stuff" doesn't move him. Maybe it's because he has always been a perfectionist (when he was still an unknown he used to get very excited because the musicians in Jimmy Dorsey's band didn't give the proper value to quarter notes) that a good deal of the sloppiness in these bands irks him. Maybe, too, it's because he doesn't think all of the writing is sincere, that it's too much an attempt just to make an impression, to draw attention, without having proper musical merit. Maybe, too, it's because he likes jazz very much, likes to hear it played with a beat, and, as he says, "I've never yet heard any be-bop that had a *real* beat." Despite what some of the younger, hipper fans might

Les and young vocalist Doris Day admire saxist-vocalist Butch Stone's proboscis

think or say, he's not at all ashamed to admit that he also likes dixieland, providing of course, that it's good dixieland. "But you don't hear much that's good nowadays," he says, "which is too bad, because I don't know of any really happier jazz than dixieland."

Not that Les Brown needs too much outside stimulus to make him happy. For not only does he have his awfully pretty wife, Claire, but the two of them also have son Butch and daughter Denny, two of the prettiest kids in captivity. What's more, Les now has security, a handsome Hollywood house where he can play bridge all day long, a music-publishing firm where he could play gin-rummy all day long if he wanted to, and a band that is not only tremendously successful, but a band whose members still swear by their leader even as they taste the success that has come his and their ways after a lengthy, often cheerful, but at times a very sentimental journey.

24

Everyone may not always have agreed about Stan Kenton's music, but every writer found him about the most cooperative, provocative and, at times, most verbose leader to interview. This piece celebrates his band's selection as "The Band of 1946." It also offers a good insight into the man, his musical theories, and his persistent enthusiasm.

STAN KENTON
BAND OF THE YEAR

The band of the year is Stan Kenton's. All through 1946, the brilliant, exciting, almost frightening music of this band from the Far West has caused musical chills to tingle the spines of dance band lovers throughout the land; has created in their souls first an awe, then an appreciation of a new kind of dynamic music, a kind of musically manic state in a land of music lovers whose tastes are as wild and as varied as the violently opposite reactions of any manic-depressive can be.

Stan Kenton has literally overpowered his public, has rammed relentlessly into its ears a kind of music that will never take "no" for an answer, has forced it by the very impact of his startling, two-fisted attack to accept this kind of music, the kind he himself likes to refer to as "progressive jazz." All over America, wherever he and his men have played, he has left in his path a host of converts, every one of whom swears by his band, calls it "the greatest," votes for it in all polls, and even refers to Kenton as "The Saviour of American Music."

Stan Kenton's is obviously the band of 1946. Whether you like its music or not makes little difference, counts not at all, in fact, for it is so clear to everyone whose musical eyes and ears have been wide open during the past year, that this is the band that has taken the biggest strides and has achieved a greater proportion of success than any other band in the land during 1946.

Success came comparatively suddenly to Stan Kenton, the son of an auto mechanic and a piano teacher. His band had been in operation since 1934, but at the end of each year, Stan realized that his hopes had far exceeded his achievements once more. Only a year ago, when he was playing in New York's Paramount Theatre, he was ready to call it quits. "I felt I didn't have it, musically speaking, to reach the top. Our music seemed out of tune with the people; we just had no common pulse. I guess I just had the wrong goddam feel for music. Yes, some people with lots of nervous energy could feel what we were doing, but nobody else could.

"But, you know, somehow the Lord always gets with you in desperation, for I remember one morning in Boston, right after we had left the Paramount, I woke up and I said to Gene Howard (then the band's singer, arranger and Kenton's room-mate), 'Gene, I think the Lord must have spoken to me last night. The clarinets are out. We need a mood—a JAZZ mood.' "

At that time Stan had been toying with the idea of having a really commercial band, one that played a lot of sweet as well as jazz, the kind of band that his bookers wanted him to have. "Bookers know less about music than anybody in the music business, but they're always shooting off their mouths to all young band-leaders, giving 'em the stuff about how they've been in the business for so many years and they know what the public wants and just listen to them and you can't help being a success. If we become a really big success, and I sure hope we do, because I feel I owe music something and the best way I can repay it is to help raise its standards, I feel that we'll have become a success despite all the things the guys in the office tried to straighten us out on." (It should be made very clear in this connection that Stan does not include in his overall condemnation of the "swivel-chair leaders" a fellow named Carlos Gastèl, who is his present manager, and who, Kenton readily admits, is one of the big reasons for his band's sudden skyrocketing to fame.)

Practically everything Stan has done, he has done because HE wanted to do it and not because somebody else wanted him to. Take, for example, his interest in piano. His mother tried to get him to play at home in Bell, California, the suburban Los Angeles town to which the Kenton family had moved shortly after Stan had been born (Wichita, Kansas, February 19, 1912). But Stan "didn't want to know from nothin' about piano. I wanted to play ball." He still knew from nothin' about piano two years later when cousins Art and Bill, both musicians, stopped in at the house for a few weeks and began to play jazz. "That's when the bug hit me." Stan decided for himself that he wanted to play piano; his mother helped him, and there it was.

Nobody tried to talk him into arranging, either, but a year later he was picking that up too. In addition to working in a hamburger joint, he used to play jobs at Bell High School and he studied some more under Frank Hirst, an organist. The bug hit him so hard that he used to run into L.A. Saturday afternoon and hang around the Majestic Theatre Building, "just hoping to see musical celebrities." By 1930 he was earning thirty dollars a week in San Diego on a summer job, "but I got homesick and I kept hoping the job would blow up so I could go back home. It did. I went home."

In 1934, Kenton joined Everett Hoagland, "who was a big man at the Rendezvous Ballroom in Balboa." Stan played piano and wrote arrangements. Vido Musso and Bob Gioga, who's in Stan's band now, also worked for Hoagland. And a gal named Violet Peters used to come to the dance on Saturdays. By 1935 she was Mrs. Stan Kenton. And several years later, Mr. Stan Kenton was leading his own band at the Rendezvous in Balboa, where it started to cause an awful lot of comment.

Success after Balboa was by no means instantaneous. West Coast musicians got on the band, and a few articles appeared praising it. But the public wasn't ready to accept. Nor were the promoters. Nor were the bookers. When the band laid a lot of eggs on its first Eastern trip that was studded with bad luck, everybody started giving Stan advice. He took all he could and things got even worse and worse and worse. And then came that morning in Boston with Gene Howard.

Stan

Stan immediately set back for Hollywood. "I realized that my style had become antiquated . . . there was nothing really new . . . no new sounds, just a lot of rhythmic accenting. Today, all styles that concentrate on accenting beats are through. Now it's the manner in which you phrase. Every tone must have a pulse.

"Anything stiff has got to go today. That's what was wrong with my band; it was much too stiff. I have learned, I have felt that music today is a natural, human, pulsating sound. It's no longer mechanical. . . .

"We don't care if people don't understand what we're doing, just so long as they feel a thrill, a throb, a pulse. . . .

"We can't have just 'fine' musicians in our band. They're no good unless they play with jazz sounds, with jazz feeling. They won't fit, unless they have a common pulse. You've got to have that for a whole band to create a mood, and I want, above all, always to create a mood through jazz. And that's one of the things that's so great about the stuff Pete Rugulo writes for us. It always creates a jazz mood. What's more, the guys in the band, all of them, are getting to feel what Pete's after and they're all beginning to loosen up like mad. That's something my band never had: a good, loose feel, the kind you get from a common pulse."

It's strictly artistry in rhythm for Kenton. Rhythm plays an important part, a terribly important part in what he's trying to do. But other things count as well. Stan can't stomach Dixieland, because there's nothing to it except a dull rhythm. He can't see be-bop, either, because it never gets down to a real, rock-bottom beat. "We're in the last stages of an era in jazz. Now we're moving into an era of new rhythms. We've got to get away from the OLD beat, the old sameness. But we've still got to retain that four-four motion.

"Rhythmically, the Cubans play the most exciting stuff. We won't copy them exactly, but we will copy some of their devices and apply them to what we're trying to do. The guys in our rhythm section are doing just that. So were the guys in Woody's. And while we keep moving toward the Cubans rhythmically, they're moving toward us melodically. We both have a lot to learn.

"Jazz is progressing rapidly; much faster than most people think. Soon there'll be no more 'in the middle' bands, no more of those that try to play something new for a few minutes and then settle back into the old way because it's more commercial. The pace is much too fast for that sort of thing. Duke and Woody are putting themselves in a class by themselves. That's the kind of music that's going to be IT from now on. The rest of the bands will have to make up their minds whether they want to be plain, commercial dance bands or whether they want to be progressive, musical bands. Quite frankly, I think that if the commercial bands try to compete with the more modern type of bands, they'll wind up making asses of themselves.

"What are we trying to do? We are trying to present a progressive form of jazz. We've got that common pulse now, we know what we want, we know what we are going to do and we know how to do it. We want to make our contribution to real music and we want to make it a really worthwhile contribution. So, my friends, this is it, and you can take it or leave it, because from now on in we're not going to change, we're not going to listen to anybody else. We've found what we've wanted, what we believe in. For we've found that common pulse at last!"

September, 1947

Ted Weems had been an important bandleader before the Swing Era began. Then he faded away as one of the second line of leaders. But in 1947, a North Carolina disc jockey uncovered an old Weems recording of *Heartaches* and played it so often that it soon became a national hit. Ted's reactions and hopes, many of them uncomfortably bitter, permeate this interview, which reveals some of the depressing problems that face a very veteran bandleader.

TED WEEMS

The musical heartaches of Ted Weems, as expressed on Decca and Victor Records, have become familiar to many millions of Americans, some of them music lovers, most of them mere *Heartaches* lovers. But the headaches of Ted Weems are known only to Ted himself, to a few intimate friends, and to those of you who read this article.

It's the headaches that are predominating these days within the well-rounded, balding noggin of the man who looks more like the ticket agent his family wanted him to be than like the successful, veteran bandleader he turned out to be.

"I appreciate what has happened to me," Ted told me at lunch a few weeks ago. "I know I was getting to be strictly a territorial band around the Midwest, though we weren't doing exactly bad out on the Coast, either. But then that disc jockey down in Charlotte (North Carolina) started his one-man campaign on *Heartaches* and before we even had much chance to

do any thinking, our price went sky-high and we were wanted everywhere.

"That was great. It seemed like a real gold mine for me and I guess everybody thought I was really pulling in the dough. Well, we did all right on the road and, knock wood, we still are, but you know, yourself, where we should have made the big haul was on that Decca record, the one that started everything all over for me. We should have, all right, but do you know that I haven't received a single, red cent from Decca for that record since we made it, and that was ten years ago. You see, I had no royalty contract with them at the time. Everything we made was strictly on a flat basis, so that Decca and the writers and the publishers are the ones who benefit. But we don't!"

Ted does have a royalty agreement with Victor, but since the Decca record was the big hit, outselling Victor's almost three to one, Weems doesn't cash in as much as folks suspect. And to show you one of the unpleasant facets of the music industry, nobody at Decca has even contacted Ted since the record began

Ted Weems with boy singer Perry Como. Guitarist is ex-Goodmanite Allen Reuss, who, at about the time this photo was taken, phoned George Simon from Chicago to tell him that Como was leaving the band, and to ask him if he would try to help him out when he arrived in New York

to sell; in fact, according to Weems, everybody up there has been strictly non-communicative, which is not the way things used to be when Ted was just one of their fairly successful artists. And, to top it all, Decca is re-releasing several more sides by Weems, primarily because of the furore created by *Heartaches* and also because they figure there's an added gimmick in the name of the vocalist whom Weems featured on these sides, Perry Como.

So Decca is doing right well off Weems, but not vice versa. The same condition holds true for Ted and the writers of *Heartaches*, Al Hoffman and John Klenner. "You should have heard those guys complain the first time I played their tune on the air. We were working in Chicago—this was around fifteen years ago, I guess—and the publishers had been begging us to put the tune on the air. So one night we introduced it. We played it just the way you hear it on the record, with that corny, sort of half-rumba rhythm and with all those effects. After the broadcast, the writers and the publishers called me up on the phone and they really let me have it. They claimed I was ruining their song, that we were giving it the wrong interpretation and all that. We never heard much from them after that. Now, though, they're raking in all the dough from the record and from other performances, but do you know that I still haven't heard a single word from them, nothing at all to say that maybe, after all, I wasn't such a complete idiot and that maybe the way we played their song didn't ruin it after all."

Weems, as you must have gathered, is far from being an idiot. He's not a great musician and makes no claims in that direction. He used to play violin, then switched to a mediocre trombone, which he doesn't bother about anymore, and he has written a few novelty hits like *The Martins and the Coys* and *Egyptian Ella*. He has also been a good picker of tal-

ent, having produced Como, Elmo Tanner, who still whistles with him, and a couple of successful novelty salesmen, Parker Gibbs and Country Washburn. His has never been a great band, musically, but it has always remained within the realm of good taste and acceptable musicianship. Its appeal has not been directed at any one segment of the public and it has never developed a conscious style. Weems has been smart enough to focus attention on his talented members, like Como and Tanner, and, unlike other less talented leaders, he hasn't pushed himself into the spotlight too much.

"But now I have a real problem," admits Ted. "I know I can't continue to get these prices just on the strength of *Heartaches*. I have a chance to re-establish myself all over the country right now, but the question is what's my next move?" And therein lies the big Weems headache.

Ted thinks he might dig up a follow-up for *Heartaches*, using exactly the same format, though the idea is pretty repugnant to him. He has certain musical scruples, and he can't quite see or hear himself carrying on in a style that he labels "strictly a freak." And, also, how many times can you repeat that formula without having the public tire of it? Chances are that even a second *Heartaches* wouldn't be too acceptable.

Ted could, on the other hand, feature Elmo Tanner, whose whistling helped sell the record, even more often, though the chances of a band retaining its popularity because of a whistler seem pretty slim. Weems right now is also featuring his latest discovery, singer Bob Edwards, of whom he expects great things.

What Ted would like to do more than anything else is to develop a really great musical style, but he realizes that he'd be taking a tremendous risk. He's not a vain guy; he's a pretty modest, clear-thinking businessman and smart enough to realize that he'd have to invest a great deal of money to create something startling, that he'd have to increase the size of a band that has always been able to capitalize on its low overhead, and, what's more, that he's no dashing spring chicken any more and that it's pretty difficult for a man of his age to create a sensation in a field that's becoming more and more the property of the younger generation. He smiles when he says it: "Funny how surprised a lot of the kids are when they see me in person. Lots of them are so young that they'd never heard of me till they heard *Heartaches*, and so they naturally think that I'm some young upstart."

Ted smiles when he says it, but he's not completely happy about the idea. He'd like to be a young bandleader again, just starting out, with lots of time to experiment, with no feelings of bitterness about record companies or about writers of songs that he helped to make famous. It's all a little sad. For Ted Weems, though he seems to be happy and enjoying some of his recent success, really has his headaches in addition to plenty of real heartaches that have never and will never be found on wax.

Louis

March, 1948

Anyone who thinks that Louis Armstrong is purely a happy-go-lucky, eye-rolling entertainer need only to read this interview to find out how utterly wrong he can be. Herein Louis, hounded by all sorts of pressures, including the emergence of bop, reveals in no uncertain terms the troubles that nobody seems to know he's been seeing—and feeling!

LOUIS ARMSTRONG

Satchmo sat himself down before his dressing-room mirror and tied the handkerchief around his forehead in such a way that the cloth covered the top of his head completely. Immediately sweat began to seep through, soaking the kerchief just the way it had soaked the shirt on his back. Funny, but it didn't seem that he had worked that hard down there on the stage. No, it didn't seem that he had, that is until you stopped to think of what had gone on, the way he not only blew his trumpet, but the way he sang and mugged and hopped up and down and encouraged every guy in his little band as he took his solos. And you began

to realize something you had almost forgotten, that Louis Armstrong is not only a great artist, but also a wonderful, hard-working performer, always giving his all.

Now here he was in his dressing room, tired and bothered about something, his trumpet lying on the floor in its case next to the dressing table, his most potent means of expression silent for the moment. Managers and flunkies milled around the little room. There was confusion and yelling, do this and do that, where is he and where is she, and suddenly Louis had disappeared. By the time he returned from the bathroom, most of the noise had gone down the hall, into other dressing rooms and out into the street.

Satchmo seemed a bit more relaxed in his clean underwear and his dark blue corduroy dressing gown. Then came the word "bebop" and once again the troubled look returned. "They're always misquotin' me so I don't like to discuss it no more." He walked over to a stack of letters and pulled forth one of those four-page hot club bulletins. "Read this. I never said that. They're always addin' words. What do they want to do that for, anyway? You know, one trouble with the beboppers is that they can give it, but they can't take it! They tear you down, but if you say somethin' against them, they yell you're oldfashioned and you don't know nothin' about jazz any more."

Pops didn't want to talk any more about bebop, not yet anyway. Well, then, how about the trumpeters who play the way Louis likes to play? "The best of them? That's easy. It was Bunny. But, you know, you can't talk too much about ONE style. Note for note, you'll never find no two trumpeters who play the same. It's impossible. When a guy copies somebody, he only copies what he heard on that one performance. Maybe the first guy'll never play the thing the same way again, so you can't really say the second guy is copying his style, can you? Anyway, what difference does it make who you blow like, just so long as you blow good!"

Other trumpeters who blow the way Louis likes to? "You know who's real good? That's Billy Butterfield. Ever hear what he played on that record Ella and I made together, that *I Won't Be Satisfied*? Listen to it, man; that's what I think is real good. He don't fake a lot of little notes just because he can't hold a long one. He knows how to blow his horn right.

"This blowin' a trumpet's not easy. Some folks think all you gotta do is hold it to your lips and blow. I'm tellin' you, them babies get so sore sometimes, you can't even touch a powder puff to 'em. And I learned how to play a trumpet right, just the way Bunk and the others did. Trouble today is most of the kids start right off blowin' them real high ones. In a couple o' years they won't have no chops left at all, blowin' the way they do. They'll be all wore out. I started blowin' all them high notes to impress folks but I never intended to keep it up."

Louis looked into the mirror and patted his lips lightly, affectionately. They were his way of expressing himself, much more so than just mere words. "I play what I feel, what's inside of me. I don't expect to please everybody. You know a lot of the new cats say 'Armstrong, he plays too many long notes.' They want me to change, but why should I go ahead and change just to please a lot o' cats who are way ahead of themselves, anyway. I listen to what I play, and if it pleases me it's good. That's the only way to judge what you're doin'. I'm my own best audience.

30

"I'd never play this bebop because I don't like it. Don't get me wrong; I think some of them cats who play it play real good, like Dizzy, especially. But bebop is the easy way out. Instead of holding notes the way they should be held, they just play a lot of little notes. They sorta fake out of it. You won't find many of them cats who can blow a straight lead. They never learned right. It's all just flash. It doesn't come from the heart the way real music should."

The music business has really changed, so far as Satchmo is concerned. "They do such silly things nowadays. Like the time the man from some newspaper calls me up at home, wakes me up out of a sleep, to tell me that Erskine Hawkins challenges me to see which one of us can hold a note longer. How silly can you get? That's not music and I told the man I didn't want to have nothin' to do with anything like that. 'I'm a musician,' I told him, 'and not an acrobat.' He said he guessed I was right at that and the whole thing was called off.

"I've been blowin' this horn a long time and you'd think by now I'd know what it was all about. But the people in the business like to treat me like a child.

Louis and interviewer Simon

There's hardly a one among the bookers and managers who knows anything at all about music and it shows in the things they do, too. They get guys to blow tricks on the trumpet and they push those trick records and all the freaks go ahead and make a lot of money. I play the kind of music I feel is right and what do I gotta do but sometimes even scuffle to get a week's work when all those other guys are makin' thousands and thousands of bucks. It's gettin' so that I'm gettin' ready to pack this horn away and go back to hitchin' up my mule . . . What'cha laughin' at? I'm serious, and you can put that in your paper, too!"

Those were real tears in the big, round Armstrong eyes, tears of despair, of frustration, tears from a man who had always tried to do what he felt was right, in his relations with people and in relation to his music, tears from a man whom everybody loved, who wanted to harm no one, but who wanted to be free to blow his horn the way he wanted to blow it, without interference from bookers, from managers, from people so warped that they could look up at a blue note but down at a brown skin, even from people in his own profession who closed their ears to much of the musical beauty behind them so that they could concentrate better on the involved manipulations that they were trying to create, a new sound with which they wanted to supplant the kind of music which Louis and Joe Oliver and others had created and lived.

"I've been blowin' a long time now. My chops get mighty tired sometimes. But I wish they'd let me blow the way I want to. No, I didn't make records when that big rush was on at the end of the year. They didn't give me anything to play that I felt was right, and I'm not goin' ahead and makin' records just for the sake of makin' records. Not me. Not ol' Satchmo. If I can't blow right, I don't want to blow at all, and that's final!"

Louis bent over and picked up his horn, patted it gently, then held it to his lips, very lightly. The next show was coming up. He blew a few warm-up notes. The spit seeped out of the side of his mouth. He reached over for the top handkerchief on a big pile and wiped the spit away. He blew some more, and more saliva started dripping down his chin. The handkerchief again. And a curious thought hit you: how much liquid can the man hold? It comes out of all his pores when he comes off the stage; it comes out of his eyes when he talks about things that mean so much to him, and now, even before he even starts to work, it pours forth from his lips!

What was that he said about the boppers? "They can give it, but they can't take it." They can give it, sure they can, with words. But when it comes to giving of himself, giving what he feels inside, giving warmth and feeling to music and to the world, giving with his body, his spirit, and with his horn, even when "them babies get so sore you can't even touch a powder puff to 'em!"—I'll *take* Louis Armstrong and *give* you the rest!

Harry James on Louis Armstrong (August, 1941)—

Armstrong is the daddy of them all. Everybody's playing his stuff, and until a greater creator comes along, that's the way it'll be—for me, anyway.

August, 1949

Claude Thornhill was one of my favorite people in the world. Warm, witty, vague, terribly talented, he led at least two of the greatest bands of all time. Today, many musicians realize that few outfits displayed such magnificent musicianship. And yet, Thornhill never achieved the national acclaim accorded his close friends, Glenn Miller, Artie Shaw, Benny Goodman and Tommy Dorsey. Why? Maybe this interview will explain. Then again, maybe it won't, because Claude was really terribly vague. Or was he?

THE THORNHILL MYSTERY

Of all the bands in the business, the one that has always struck me as Most Likely to Succeed has been Claude Thornhill's. In fact, it has struck me so often that it's almost beginning to look as if I'm stuck with it. Which wouldn't be too bad, because I can't think of a pleasanter band I'd rather be stuck with—or struck with!

But seriously, or at least more seriously, I still can't quite figure out why Claude Thornhill isn't bigger than he is, why his isn't one of the one, two or three top bands in the country. To me, his outfit, right from the very beginning almost ten years ago, has had just about everything that a successful commercial band should have. And, in addition, it has played the prettiest music of any band in the business and has recently come across with a fine brand of modern big band jazz.

The guy most able to ease my insatiable bewilderment should be Claude Thornhill, and so I cornered him the other day behind a gigantic glass of iced coffee. After I had confessed both my admiration and my problem to him, Claude meditated for a while, swallowed some coffee, inserted a cigarette into a cigarette holder, lighted same, inhaled, exhaled, looked at me, took another swallow of coffee, meditated, and then replied with utmost sincerity: "I don't know."

From then on the conversation was quite simple. Since we were both on the same completely uncertain footing, we both listened avidly and clung tenaciously to what the other had to say and, with one or two minor exceptions, agreed perfectly. In fact, at one point we thought we had the whole problem solved. That was when Claude said, "There's nothing that a hit record wouldn't cure." Of course, when we started discussing how Claude was going to get that hit record, we returned to almost the same point from which we had started, with one exception. That was, we started to figure out just what ingredients, in addition to the ever-prevalent hit song, Claude needed to get that hit record. And if you think we're going to tell you the results of those findings, you're crazy, because if anybody is going to get a hit record as a result of our skulduggery, it's going to be Claude Thornhill. And, what's more, if we did tell you everything, and Claude still didn't come across with that hit record, wouldn't that make us both look sort of silly?

We can tell you, though, that we did discuss in great detail several problems that have been bothering Claude. (Here I started out to be the guy with the problem and now it turns out he's got his too!) For example, one thing that has been worrying Claude a great deal is whether he is featuring his piano enough. He points to the successes of Carle, Cavallaro and Duchin and then starts wondering if he shouldn't ape them a little bit more. Then he realizes that he shouldn't ape and I reassure him that a man of his musical ability should not stoop to such tactics. Not that he couldn't do it, mind you, because Claude is a far more accomplished pianist than his light noodlings would lead you to suspect. Before he started his band late in 1940 he was one of the top men in radio circles, playing with, among others, Andre Kostelanetz, and before that having been an integral part of a group of top musicians that included Glenn Miller, Artie Shaw, Tommy Dorsey, Will Bradley and so forth.

The question of tempos, too, has bothered Claude. Has he been making too much of an effort to create a romantic mood and by so doing has he sacrificed danceability by playing too slowly? And how about his singers? Have they been up to the calibre of his band? Claude was a little kinder on this point, for I insisted that he has never had a male singer who

could measure up to the band's musical standards. He defended some of the lads who have sung for him, especially his current singer, Russ McIntyre, who, Claude thinks, is improving steadily and could amount to something. On the subject of current Thornhill singers, I was very much impressed, while listening to the band a few weeks ago at Glen Island Casino, with his new girl, Nancy Clayton, a very slight little miss who looks as if she couldn't dent a mashed potato but who sings with much authority and heart, somewhat like Fran Warren, with good control plus a tone worthy of the Thornhill band. The band itself, though not as startling from the standpoint of jazz soloists as previous Thornhill units, still manages to be just about the most pleasing dance band of them all. Bad news for many METRONOME readers, though, for it's not playing as much jazz as Claude's previous unit did.

Claude likes jazz and likes to hear it played around him. His was one of the first of the hotel bands to play bop and he still gets his kicks dropping into jazz joints. His favorite recent listening was the George Shearing Quartet that played at the Clique, the one that had Buddy DeFranco, John Levy and Denzil Best. But he can't see the stuff commercially and so "what's holding us down is the small item of wage earning. That may be keeping me in check to some extent. My number one concern is keeping a band in operation fifty-two weeks a year. And so from now on I plan to play music that the majority can understand.

"Lots of bop and progressive jazz leaves people disturbed. They can't get it and so naturally they're bothered. If progressive jazz could be presented so that people could enjoy it and not be annoyed with it, then it can survive. And also, a certain amount of it has been played from a purely selfish viewpoint. The musicians play just for themselves. They have a point, of course, because they are evidently happy playing that way and derive a tremendous amount of satisfaction from it. But others don't."

This sort of thinking, of course, only deepens the Thornhill mystery, though here the unraveling becomes pretty simple. "I definitely prefer to be understood!" exclaims Claude with a minimum number of concessions and a certain amount of generalization. "The music that has held up, like Bach, for example, has been understood by the masses. It has been based on pure, simple form. Of course I realize there's simplicity and there's simplicity. Take the average Tin Pan Alley songs: they're simple but without foundation. After all, there's good steel and then there's good steal. And that pun is purely intentional!"

And YOU think YOU'VE got worries!

This business of having a band has never been a

pushover for Claude, though contrary to most other name band leaders, he's making money these days. But, oh what a tussle he had getting started! Take his first job, at a swank spot in Virginia Beach. The band was all primed, all ready to set everybody within earshot on, of course, his ear. But the night before the band was to open up the place burned down. There followed a bit more East Coast panic and then the band went out to play at Balboa Beach on the West Coast. Sounded like a great job, except that when they got out there the manager decided that he'd stay open only a few nights a week. But at least the guys got themselves a sunburn and later on moved up to San Francisco and a swank hotel job. There they became thoroughly unpopular because they didn't sound like Henry King. Or was it Joe Reichman? What's the difference? So they headed East again, this time for a club in Hartford, Connecticut.

The first thing Claude did when he got to Hartford was to hop a cab for the new job. Jolt No. I: the cab driver hadn't even heard of the place! After a lot of asking, he finally found it. Jolt No. II: after having played the job for two nights and really doing well, the band went back for the third night and found the place not only closed but padlocked. The boss had run away with all the money. So back to the hotel in a bread truck that the band had been using for transportation where Claude, already as depressed as a guy could be, received what he considers the greatest humiliation of his life. Let him relive it. "We were walking into the hotel lobby feeling about as low as any gang could feel. Here we'd come all the way across country for that job and look what happened! No job. No money. But then came the *real* blow! As we walked by the desk in the lobby, the room clerk called out, 'Say, aren't you Mr. Toe-nail? We have a message for you.' Imagine that. Mr. Toe-nail! I've been called just about everything else, starting with Clyde Thornton, but that was the worst. Claude Toe-nail and his Orchestra. Wow! What a name!"

But, as all of us know, Claude Toe-nail managed to weather the mental and the financial depression that seemed to envelop all his early efforts and now he has emerged a successful bandleader, not quite as successful, though, as he hopes to become and certainly not as successful as many of us feel he should become. Which brings us right back to the Mystery Department. Claude, as easygoing, relaxed and natural as the night he walked into the swank Rainbow Room in his undershorts to show his disapproval to leader Ray Noble for having to play overtime, is still trying to figure out ways of becoming more of a national music hero. But he's not getting frantic about it. He just sits there, sips glass after glass of iced coffee, smiles, listens, nods, often looks vague. But he knows what's going on all the time and, because he's so much more intelligent than nine-tenths of the top bandleaders, he has a pretty fair idea of what to do about it. All of which heightens the mystery just that much more.

Eight years ago this spring I picked Claude Thornhill's as the Coming Number One Band. You'd think by this time that I'd give up. But no, because after listening to what Claude's band has to play and what Claude himself has to say, I still think he's going to make it. But why is it taking so long? That question is, to me at least, the REAL Thornhill Mystery.

Benny Goodman on Bop (August, 1948)—

I don't like to listen to a lot of bop. It seems that everyone is trying to see just how much he can put in. It's nervous more than exciting music. It seems that they're all trying to outdo and outstartle each other. And as for some of those chords they're using, they're just pretentious tripe. Modern writers did that years ago. How can you compare that with something like Bartok's *Contrast Suite*? . . . And yet, you know, I think something good will come out of all this. But one thing that bothers me most of all is the morals of those guys. Before you can give some of them a job in your band, you've got to screen them, like the FBI.

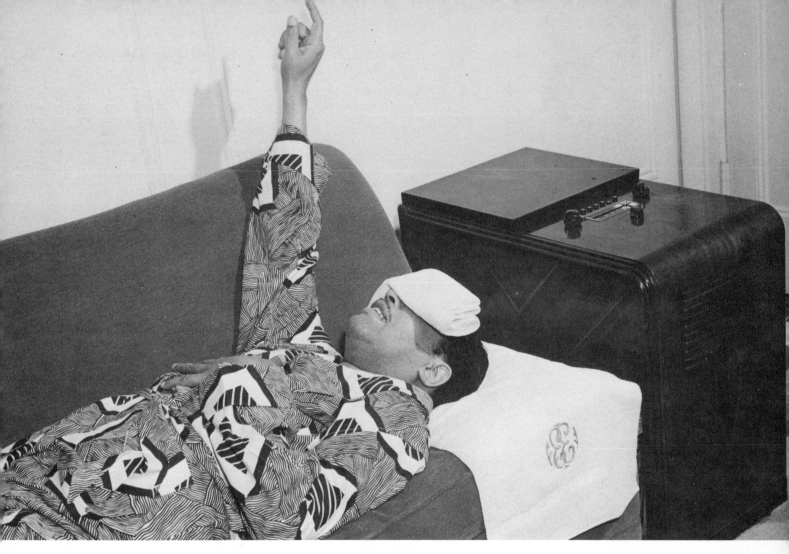

"I see pretty little white germs with pink wings," etc., etc.

September, 1952

Interviewing the great Duke Ellington is always a joy. In fact, just about everything concerning the man is a joy. This interview reveals the Duke's colossal looseness, his delightful imagination and his perennial ability never, but never, to take himself too, too seriously.

THE NEW DUKE ELLINGTON

He now has a great jumping band and he also has some new and colorful germs

"I see pretty little white germs with pink wings and violet blue polka dots. They have kissy-pink mustaches, they're wearing golden spats, and they have multi-colored tails. They attain a velocity of ten thousand miles a minute and they make great sounds while they're flying. I can hear them. Now I've got to capture them and put them in their right places!"

Duke Ellington was describing his next concert venture. It was still in a pretty nebulous state, as you no doubt can guess, but as he puts it, "I have the germ of an idea, and the germs of my idea are quite elaborate but amazingly elusive. You never catch them like other germs, but their perfumed wake creates a maze of sound facets, with unlimited dramatic intangibilities. (Fly, man!)" Nothing has been written yet and there's a good chance that not too much will be written until immediately before Duke's next concert series. "I don't know why I take such a disadvantageous position, but you know most of the time the programs for my concerts are written before the music!" (Ellington concertgoers who have had difficulty following the music on the basis of the concert notes should now have faith in themselves once more. Chances are what they had been reading and what they were listening to didn't have too much relation to each other.)

Regardless of what the Duke and/or his right hand pen, Billy Strayhorn, write(s) for the next concert series, the rendition will doubtlessly be tremendous. Why? Because Duke Ellington has a tremendous band these days.

I sat in on its latest Columbia recording session and it was really colossal! The excitement, the big, round sounds, the fantastic chords, the full-bodied drive, and all the other typical Ellington trimmings were there, but there were great new additions also. The saxes now have Hilton Jefferson on lead alto. His fluid, flowing, superbly assured style has made him a favorite of mine for years, and so it was a big kick to hear Duke rave about him and how "Jeff's got a helluva sound!" Clark Terry, whom I first heard (and raved about in these pages at the time) one morning at six in an after-hours club in St. Louis back in 1947, is leading the trumpets along with Cat Anderson. As Duke raves, "Terry just does everything!" He blows great lead, plays fine, modern jazz, etc. There's an even newer trumpeter in the band, too. His name's Willie Cook and Duke praises him highly for "his great taste. He plays good, melodic licks with a slight bop touch."

The band has two new singers, and it's a pleasure to be able to report that Duke finally has two really good singers again, instead of some of those pretty miserable turkeys he was carrying with him. Actually, one isn't new to the band, because Betty Roche used to sing with Duke ten or so years ago. She is still one of the most emotional singers I've ever heard, who does a tremendous job on blues, and whose recording of *Take the A Train* should convince you of her greatness. The other vocalist is Jimmy Grissom, who has a great, natural sound-box and who uses it in tune, with good taste and with none of the affectations that have sounded so ludicrous when coming from past Ellington singers.

The rest of the band is as it has been for quite some time. Carney, Hamilton, Procope and Gonsalves are the other saxes. Ray Nance is still with the trumpets. The trombones have Tizol, Jackson and Woodman, while Wendell Marshall is still on bass and Louie Bellson continues to spark everything with his scintillating drumming.

The band has been playing a good many one-nighters. So far as dance music is concerned, Duke asks, "It's getting to be more a business than an art, isn't it? 'Dance music' is now little more than what we have always called 'the business man's bounce.' We're constantly getting instructions on how to play for dances from the heads of college prom committees. They like medium dance tempos . . . not too loud. At least it's a change for us and that's fine. Sometimes, though, our followers want to hear some of the things with which we have been associated. I refer them back to the committee. Usually some compromise is effected."

Duke, though, continues to get his kicks from his concerts. "It's a funny thing," he says, "but people think that if you've heard one jazz concert, you've heard them all. *That's just not true!* Most of those concerts are just jam sessions, with guys screeching and trying to cut one another. People often don't realize what they'll get at our concerts; that they won't be hearing just another one of those blowing things; that they'll be hearing a period of prepared pieces. Take what happened to us recently out in Denver. Some people came to hear us quite by accident; some friends just dragged them along. But they became very attached to our *Harlem Suite* and now they are going to do it with the Denver Ballet.

"And then out in Hollywood," he adds with considerable pride, "there's a great dance group called the Lester Horton Dancers, and they've been giving our *Liberian Suite* a really good-sized run out there."

Unlike some other leaders with great musical bands, Duke has no qualms about the future. "Actually, my ambitions extend no farther than what we have. The other bands are more concerned with the styles of the times and we've hit a period now when everything becomes confused. We've had bop and progressive and wilder types of things and we've also had a tremendous drive on Dixie. Our band, though, is sandwiched in between. You see, we're more concerned with *who's* playing it. I'm more of a primitive artist in that I only employ the materials at hand. I always write for the men in the band. That has sustained us throughout. I'm not so much concerned with what the styles of the times are as I am with the styles and the capabilities of the men in our band.

"Right now I think I've got a helluva great band, and so naturally I think we've got a great period ahead of us. Stimulating soloists have always made me want to write, and we certainly have a lot of them in our band today. It's when I have men like these to write for that I get a germ of an idea and these germs are different. They are the ones with pink wings and violet blue polka dots and kissy-pink mustaches and golden spats and multi-colored tails. They're the germs of the ideas that I'm going to put into music. I think our next concert series should really be something!"

Interviewing Buddy Rich can result in almost anything. You can wind up with a first-rate story, with nothing at all, or even with a punch in the nose. Actually, this piece is less of an interview and more of an appraisal of the talents and character of one of the most talented, driving and at times troubled characters ever to lead a band. But there's still enough of Buddy's own opinion to warrant its inclusion here.

BUDDY RICH

A sensitive, intense musician with a colossal technique, fine singing and dancing talent, and beliefs as strong as his beat, Buddy Rich appreciates good jazz as much as good jazz appreciates his drumming . . . but most of all he appreciates good people

Every once in a while there comes in a writer's life a tremendous urge to write about something or somebody. Usually, if he looks back, he finds that it's something he has wanted to say for a long time. And usually it takes some special incident to set his typewriter keys in motion.

The special occasion for this two-fingered attack on my Royal portable took place a few weeks ago when I caught Buddy Rich with his own group down at the Bandbox. Harry James's band had opened that night; there was excitement and cause for playing, and Buddy was really on. He played drums like I've never heard them played before: astounding technique; scintillating, propelling drive; colossal imagination and humor. He did things that made me want to scream, and for a guy who's been writing about music and musicians for close to twenty years, such an emotional outburst is a rarity. But scream I did. It was just too much!

A few days later I talked with Harry James. He told me with great glee that Buddy, who had been sitting in down at the Bandbox, was going to join his band. "It's something I've always wanted," said Harry. "And I knew the other night that I just had to get him, because for the first time in all the time that I've had the band, I had a drummer who was driving *me*.

Up till then I'd always felt *I* had to carry the band. But now Buddy will do it."

A few days ago I talked with Harry again. He couldn't rave enough about Rich. Everything he had told me earlier now went double.

There's another great band blowing some mighty fine jazz these days. Buddy doesn't play with it, but its leader, the Count of Basie, told me an amazing story about Buddy that ties in with all this. It seems that Jo Jones took sick one night out on the coast and Count asked Buddy to play with his band for a couple of nights. There's no conversation to report about how the guys felt about Buddy's playing, just this reaction, as related by Basie: "They were so excited about playing with Buddy that the next night they all showed up *early* for the job. And if you know our band, we've never been accused of showing up early!"

Such admiration is reciprocal. Today as always Buddy's favorite band still is Basie's. His favorite drummer still is Jo Jones, with Rich's ex-assistant, Stanley Kay, mentioned as his nomination for the best all-around drummer.

I first started admiring Buddy's talents one hot summer's day when, for lack of anything better to do, I took a boat ride up Long Island Sound. Like all those excursion boats do, this one had a floor show. Its m.c. was a talented, curly-haired youngster of about fifteen or sixteen, who danced excellently and introduced the various acts with smart quips. The acts were so bad that I started walking out. To do so, I had to pass the back of the bandstand. Sitting there, with a pair of drumsticks in his hand, and beating out some fancy, fast paradiddles to amuse himself was this fast-talking, fast-stepping young m.c. Having been a drummer myself, I stopped to talk with him, and he told me among other things that his name was Buddy Rich. I wish I could say right now that I immediately started to write raves about him. But, alas, I can't say I discovered Buddy Rich, though I did watch him with one of those "I-knew-him-when" attitudes, as he played around town with Joe Marsala and Bunny Berigan, and later hit the big time with Artie Shaw and Tommy Dorsey.

Buddy's improvement was tremendous. A combination of entertainment experience (his family started him off years before I first saw him) and great natural abilities helped him develop into the tremendous drummer and showman that he is.

His drumming, of course, is the thing that has always knocked me out, and which has inspired me to write this sort of article. I doubt if there has ever been a single musician anywhere who has been able to spark a band all by himself the way Buddy has. The men with whom he has played invariably remark about that quality. Some admit that he has a tendency at times to play too loud. You can chalk that up to overexuberance. Because of his early training, Buddy is a great extrovert. It shows in everything he does. It shows in his personal relationships. To some people he is just a cocky kid, sometimes overbearing, at times unnecessarily arrogant. That's because they have only the outward, extroverted exuberance to go by. Calm Buddy down, show him that he doesn't have to spark every gathering the way he sparks every bunch of playing musicians, and you've got one of the warmest, most sensitive gents you've ever met.

Singer Buddy Rich

Buddy's very intense. He has strong beliefs. In music, he clings to the theory that a drummer should set and hold the beat, that it's up to him to keep the band going. Consequently he has great disdain for most bop drumming. To him a drummer has no right to break up the rhythmic flow with constant explosions and extraneous back beats that most of the time do nothing but interfere with what's going on. Notice Buddy's drumming. He may throw in extra riffs or explosions, but never does he sacrifice the rhythmic continuity. "I don't know what some of those guys think a left hand is for," he says. Notice Buddy's. He keeps his going all the time, playing rhythm, instead of just slapping away with it now and then. The same goes for his foot. His bass drum is a rhythmic, moving percussive instrument; he doesn't use it merely to augment brass explosions.

Rich's kind of drumming requires good technique. It requires, above all, a good left hand. Few drummers possess that attribute. And no drummer, so far as I am concerned, can begin to compare with Rich when it comes to all-around technique. The same goes for his beat. The more I hear him play, the harder it is to believe. It's just fantastic stuff!

Buddy feels he has never been recorded properly. "Too many things are going against a drummer. He has to hold back most of the time. Usually everybody is unfamiliar with the arrangement and so naturally it's hard to swing." If you want to hear some of the best recorded Rich, try Herbie Haymer's *Laguna Leap* and the METRONOME All-Stars' *Nat Meets June*.

There's another Rich record I'm especially fond of. It was made by his own band and it's called *Baby, Baby All the Time*. But here's the twist. Buddy doesn't play on it. He sings it!

Not many people know how well Buddy sings. Those who have heard him are usually knocked out. And that really pleases him, because he has a tremendous yen to do more of same. He's quietly waiting for the day when Harry James asks him to sing a number. And Harry, who thinks that Buddy doesn't want to be bothered with singing, is waiting for the time when Buddy asks to do so. He even has a couple of tunes all ready for him!

The James relationship is the happiest, with the possible exception of a short stay with Les Brown's band, that Buddy has ever had. To him, those two are easily the greatest guys he has ever worked for. "Their attitudes are so great!" he says. "To them it's 'Let's play and have a ball!' It shows up in their music, too. They *sound* happy." What's more, Buddy appreciates anybody who treats him like a human being, rather than like an employee. That's true not only in his relationships with his bosses, but with the world in general. For here is basically a sensitive, talented human being, who, because of long years in show business, has learned that you just can't trust everybody immediately. It's an unfortunate commentary, but when a guy has been kicked around a lot (and young, cocky performers usually get plenty of that in their early days), he often finds that the best defense is an offense. Show him, though, that there's nothing to defend himself against, and you'll find the real person. And they don't come much more real, and certainly not much more talented, than Buddy Rich. It's my feeling that when jazz history is set down, this tremendously inspiring, swinging drummer will go down, along with Davey Tough, as THE man on his instrument. So far as I'm concerned, he's already that today.

September, 1953

Artie Shaw was always interested in much more than merely music. In this interview, he offers a course in semantics and common sense, beamed primarily at playing music, but applicable to the partaking of all sorts of other forms of enjoyment. So, as you read this, try applying Artie's advice to aspects of your own life. You'll find the guy has a lot to offer.

THE SAME MUSIC ISN'T ALWAYS THE SAME!

Artie Shaw offers a course in semantics and in common sense to help make life more livable for dance band musicians

Semanticist Shaw

Dance band musicians have double troubles these days. They have to try to keep alive physically, by making enough money to eat, and they have to try to keep alive spiritually, so that they won't completely lose their appetites for playing music.

Artie Shaw, who has experienced both of these problems, doesn't have any special solution for the former, but he does have a tip which he thinks will help a lot of musicians through the latter problem.

"It takes a lot of discipline," he says, "self-discipline. A guy can go out of his head repeating the same phrases night after night. But if he can prove to himself that they're not the same, then he's really got a chance.

"Let me illustrate with an example in semantics. You say 'Cows give milk.' True. Cows give milk. All cows give milk. But narrow that down at each milking to one cow and each time you've got a different situation. Each time it's 'This cow gives milk.' But cow #1 gives milk in varying quantities. And so does cow #2, and cow #3, and so on.

"Now, carry that over to playing an arrangement. Each time you play it, it's another numbered version of that arrangement. Try to think of it each time as a new version, one you've never heard before, instead of the same arrangement that you've been playing night after night. Each time it's a new situation in itself. Try to convince yourself, even if you're only doing so during the playing of the particular piece, that 'this is the first time I'm playing this.' In other words, forget all the other times. Don't play from habit. Read the notes and try to think that they are fresh and new. If you're playing in a section, listen to what you and the guys next to you are playing as though you hadn't heard it or played it before. Try each time to see how well you can blend and play together. Don't make it a comparative thing. Don't see whether you can do it better this time than you did last time. That's not the point. Instead, try to see how well you can play it, period. Use it as a challenge to your ability in itself.

"To me one of the most spontaneous-sounding groups in the music business is the Mills Brothers. Every time they sing a song, they sound as if they're doing it for the first time. I heard them do *Paper Doll* recently, and I could have sworn that they had just started doing the thing. The reason it sounds that way is because they feel it, and the reason they feel it is because they approach each performance as though it's the first time they're doing the song.

"One thing that impressed me tremendously occurred a few years ago. I was on the same bill with Smith and Dale. Now you know they've been doing that Dr. Kronkite routine for about fifty years. And yet, when they came off the stage, they were arguing, because one of them complained that the other was stepping on his lines. 'You've got to wait more there,' he was saying. You see, it was still a new, different performance for them, even after all those years!

"The same thing holds true to an even larger extent if you're a soloist. Naturally you're even less limited because you're not dependent as much upon other musicians. But even being a soloist has its limitations. I know that after having played *Begin the Beguine* I don't know how many thousands of times, I've long passed the stage where I can find something new to play. There just aren't that many combinations of notes that fit the chords. But I find that if I don't think of any of the other times that I've played

it before, I get much more of a kick out of it. Each version is a new one to me. I may play it in Dallas in 1953, and that's the Dallas 1953 version. Then I may play it in Hartford a month later, and that becomes the Hartford 1953 version. You know, I still like to play the thing, and only because I've been rather successful in adopting that attitude. I can really make believe and convince myself that 'this is the first time I'm playing this.' And it shows both in my playing and also in my attitude toward my audiences. I can sense that they feel that I'm happy in what I'm doing, and so I've licked the problem not only of pleasing myself, but the more important one of pleasing them as well.

"I know this can sound mighty vague to a lot of you. It did to me when I first thought about it. I gave it a lot of thought, and then I gave it a lot of tries, and for a long time I couldn't develop the necessary self-discipline to establish the necessary attitude. But after a while it came, and now it's all quite simple. And, believe me, I'm having much more of a ball playing with my band, even though we repeat an awful lot of numbers, than I've had in years!"

Touring Thoughts

Artie recently completed a lengthy tour of one-nighters. He's not at all sure how happy the guys in the band were playing the same things night after night. He suspects not as happy as he was. "Today's musicians need something to make them want to play. They're farther advanced harmonically than they were ten or fifteen years ago, but their ears aren't as good, because most of them depend on their knowledge of chords, and thus they tend to depend less on their ear. They can't find new chords for themselves as easily, and so they find it harder to fulfill requests. And bands should be able to play reasonable requests, despite what some crusading leaders may believe, even though they may be pretty frightening. On our last trip we played stocks of *April in Portugal* and *Moulin Rouge*, and *Ruby* and a samba and everybody loved it. Those and some of the standards in our book like *Beguine* and *Back Bay Shuffle* and *Traffic Jam* and two or three others.

"It didn't surprise me. I'd expected it. Four years ago I started off with a great band, as great a band as I've ever heard, with a book full of modern things by Johnny Mandel and Tad Dameron and Eddie Sauter and really fine arrangers like that, but by the time we finished the tour in New York, I had to break up the band because hardly anybody wanted to hear those great things we were playing. They wanted the standards I mentioned and the popular tunes of that era.

"This time before I started out I told the booker

in Texas, where we played most of our dates, that I wanted to bring down a good band, like the one I had started out with last time. I figured—or hoped—that tastes had improved since then, because everybody seemed to be talking about bands and good music coming back. He told me that if I did he wouldn't guarantee me a successful trip, because what the promoters wanted was my old recorded stuff. So I dug out the 1938 book and bought some stocks and we did have a terribly successful trip!"

Fun for Artie

"I didn't expect to reincarnate the spirit and the playing of my original band. I know that you can't do that. I think another bandleader we know discovered that recently too. Mine wasn't a bad band, but it wasn't a topflight one by any stretch of the imagination. The guys did what they had to do well enough. It was a job for them and that was that. And I must say that they were good and willing workers.

"It's too bad, though, that they couldn't have had as good a time as I did. I know I'm older and more mature than they are, and maybe I've done a bit more reading and studying, but I wish that at least some of them could have adopted that attitude I've been talking about. I think that they would have felt much more satisfied, both with their music and with themselves. And it's quite possible that both they and the audiences would have heard better music and had a lot more fun. I know I certainly did!"

Upcoming Bandleader
Glenn Miller on Style (May, 1939)—

It's pretty much of an accepted fact that if you want to have a successful dance band, you've got to have something that's different. There's a danger in that theory, though. That's making your style too stiff. And that's why so many of these styled bands have such a short life.

By a stiff style, I mean constructing all your arrangements so much alike that the public gets fed up on them. You'll notice that today some bands use the same trick on every introduction; others repeat the same musical phrase as a modulation into the vocal. They may be effective as identifying features, but after awhile they get mighty monotonous. And even worse than that, they hamper you terribly when making arrangements.

We're fortunate in that our style doesn't limit us to stereotyped intros, modulations, first choruses, endings or even trick rhythms. The fifth sax, playing clarinet most of the time, lets you know whose band you're listening to. And that's about all there is to it.

BAND REVIEWS

One of the reasons I got the job with *Metronome* was because I suggested that they run dance band reviews, which had never been published on a regular basis in any music magazine. They liked the idea enough to offer me twenty-five dollars a month, which I immediately accepted. During the next twenty years, I wrote hundreds of such reviews (later Barry Ulanov and Leonard Feather also wrote some), of which those that follow are among the most significant. Alphabetical ratings indicate musical qualities; numerical ratings, in some of the later reviews, stand for commercial appeal.

April, 1935

HAL KEMP

(*A minus*)

Hal Kemp and His Ork. Manhattan Room of Pennsylvania Hotel, New York. NBC and WOR wires. Saxes: (1) Harold Dankers, (2) Ben Williams, (3) Saxie Dowell. Trumpets: (1) Earl Geiger, (2) Russell Case. Trombones: (1) Gus Mayhew, (2) Eddie Kusborski. Guitar: Phil Fent. Bass: Jack Shirra. Drums: Skinnay Ennis. Piano: John Trotter. Vocalists: Maxine Grey, Bob Allen, Skinnay Ennis and Saxie Dowell. Leader (and sax): Hal Kemp.

Background

Kemp first received recognition when down at the University of North Carolina, where he organized in the middle twenties. In 1930 came a highly successful European tour with engagements in Paris, London and Ostend. Then on to the Blackhawk Restaurant in Chicago and even greater success.

At Present

Down in the Manhattan Room of the Pennsy, Kemp has built up a fine following. It's almost entirely the young collegiate bunch, whose moods and style of dancing are made to order for Kemp's type of dansapation, and vice versa. When spotted on a Tuesday eve, the place was doing just about capacity biz to a preponderance of school kids.

The famed Madhattan (originally Manhattan) Room, down in the basement of the Hotel Pennsylvania, has since been transformed into a coffee shop down in the basement of the Statler-Hilton Hotel.

The kids really dressed up for this band—perhaps because its music was so basically romantic and polite. Many evenings prom-type clothes (tuxedos and evening gowns) would outnumber the less formally clad dancers.

Leader Kemp and trombonist Kusborski

Type of music is, for the most part, slow and dreamy—mostly cupped brass and sustaining clarinets with a minimum of rhythm.

Standing out in the band is the brass with special credit to first trumpeter Earl Geiger. The boy's solo work, with its slurring, is about the neatest stuff this reviewer has heard in a long time. Rest of the section strings along nicely, too, with Kusborski sliding along smoothly on his own now and then.

Saxes are well-toned and phrase prettily, Dankers does a sweet job on lead and all three have had enough practice to become experts on sustained clarinets. Kemp uses that trick to excess, if anything. Section is not as brilliant as formerly, chiefly because Kemp's style is becoming more and more subdued. Once in a while, though, the boys show their flash, and here special credit goes to their maestro, whose lead alto is truly brilliant.

Rhythm section, by comparison, is the weak spot of the outfit. Kemp's style calls for subdued rhythm, but it's carried to an extreme. There's no accenting at all, to speak of, which makes it tough to dance to. Shirra, on bass, could come out more, and Ennis could make all his beats sharper and more distinct.

Geiger, the ideal lead trumpeter for the Kemp style, left shortly after this review appeared, apparently because of a drinking problem, and the band never sounded as intimate again. Successor Clayton Cash was probably a better all-around trumpeter, but neither he, nor any other trumpeter I've heard since, had Geiger's unique delicacy.

Vocalists all click plenty. Ennis, long a fixture with the band, is great with his sentimental vibrato. Maxine Grey, who's been with the band on and off for quite a while, displays plenty of personality on her hep tunes. Bob Allen, a soft, well-modulated baritone, takes care of the heartaches in nice fashion, and ditto for Saxie Dowell on the comedy end.

Band plays only manuscript for which not enough praise can be heaped upon modest Johnny Trotter and quiet Gus Mayhew. They've helped Kemp plenty in developing a distinctive style that certainly has brought him close to the top.

Simon says A minus.

John Trotter later gained a middle name, "Scott," plus many, many pounds. But he always remained modest and Mayhew never did turn into a gabber.

Van Johnson on Wanting to Make It as a Singer
(July, 1947)—

Musicians scare me. I used to go to hear bands all the time and I'd stand in front of the bandstand and look at those guys, and put them on a pedestal. And I'd look at the singer and wish I could be up there, singing with the band, not with any spotlight or anything, but just singing for the people who were dancing by.

But me, I'm strictly a bathtub singer. When you take singers like Dinah and Lee Wiley and Lee Morse—remember her and her Blue Grass Boys?—well, then you'll see what I mean. And whatever happened to Loretta Lee?

You know, I often thought that just about the biggest kick any singer could get would be to walk into a spot that has a jukebox and hear his own record being played. But, you know, I'm a little frightened to think about my record in one of those contraptions. I wonder, do you think people will laugh when they put mine on?

CASA LOMA

(*A minus*)

Glen Gray and the Casa Loma Orchestra. Colonnades of Essex House, New York. CBS wire.

Saxes: (1) Glen Gray, (2) Frank Davis, (3) Clarence Hutchinrider, (4) Arthur Ralston, (5) Kenneth Sargent. Trumpets: (1) Robert Jones, (2) Henry Watts, (3) Elmer Dunham. Trombones: (1) William Rauch, (2) Walter Hunt, (3) Fritz Hummel. Violin (and leader): Melvin Jensen. Piano: Howard Hall. Guitar: Jacques Blanchette. Bass: Stanley Dennis. Drums: Anthony Briglia.

Background

The band, originally the Orange Blossoms, booked by Jean Goldkette, took the Casa Loma monicker in memory of the Canadian night club they were scheduled to play, but which never opened. Mostly one-nighters, with a preponderance of college dances, until 1933 when they began their Glen Island-Essex House routine.

A co-op enterprise consisting of most of the boys in the band plus booker O'Keefe. Gray is prexy; Davis is secretary-treasurer.

The Colonnades (still in existence) was and is a lovely ground floor room right across the street from Central Park.

Somebody fed this cub reviewer some overly-of-ficial-sounding first names. We all knew Frank Davis as Pat Davis, Henry Watts as Grady Watts, Elmer Dunham as Sonny Dunham, and Walter Hunt as Peewee Hunt. Oh well, at least their mothers recognized them.

Kenny Sargent of the bedroom voice with Glen Gray and Peewee Hunt

It's a characteristic of band boys in general to praise a new, good individual band to the skies; then when it's made the grade and the boys have heard it for a while, they turn right around, pick on every minor flaw, and say that the band is lousy, that it's pulling the same stuff all the time. For them the novelty of something new (that's good too) has worn off; they want something else in place of what they used to think good, and, if they hadn't heard it a lot, would still think good.

That's the kind of deal the Casa Loma boys have been getting in many circles. This reviewer feels it's unjustified. The band is still all there, in fact much better than when it first reached the top. The boys work together nicely; they're clean, accurate and they're danceable.

Main drawback of the band is, and always has been, that they're "arrangement conscious." You've got to give the boys (especially Gene Gifford) credit for starting a subtler ballroom style of music, but they should realize that by overemphasizing that aspect they're harming themselves. Paying so much attention to arrangements, playing everything just as writ, tends to make the boys stale. They have to spend so much time and energy concentrating on the finer points of the intricate arrangements that they're unable to do themselves justice on the less mechanical and more imaginative aspects, such as phrasing and hot choruses.

The brass, more than any other section, has put the band across. Jones sticks to a pretty lead, while Grady Watts takes most of the hot. Sonny Dunham (an arranger) goes off now and then with a bite that puts him ahead of Watts in this reviewer's estimation. Rauch plays the pretty trombone (e.g., *Smoke Rings*) while singer Hunt takes the hot. Hummel, new to the outfit, sticks pretty close to paper.

Gray, a tone-specialist, plays lead sax. Pat Davis plays the most discussed tenor in musical circles: nobody, including the boys in the band, knows what's coming out—at times it's brilliant, at times it's awful. The rest of the hot reed work is taken by "Hutch," who besides a hot, dirty clarinet, lets go on alto and baritone. He also sings. Ralston, a recent addition, adds color, via bassoon, oboe, etc., while Kenny Sargent, between high C's and pretty smiles, finds time enough to push an adequate sax into his mouth.

There's a fiddle section growing up in the band, consisting of Jenssen, Blanchette and Hummel, the latter also taking care of the hot choruses.

Tops in the rhythm section is Tony Briglia, one of the country's most imitated drummers. Dennis plays almost too much bass, while Hall flashes at times and Blanchette keeps going nicely. A tendency here for

> A pretty pertinent observation for a young writer. This being-taken-for-granted attitude later plagued such subsequent headliners as Benny Goodman, Glenn Miller, Nat Cole and Frank Sinatra.

> How my tastes and standards eventually changed! Tony Briglia "tops"? After listening more to Krupa, Webb and McKinley, I began to realize it was Tony's drumming that kept this band from ever achieving a relaxed, swinging beat. But he was a nice gent.

46

the four boys to go too heavy on the four-four, especially on the faster tunes, making it difficult for the dancers. This is due, also, to the tempos, which often are too extreme for even the collegiate bunch; they should be modified.

The boys are good musicians, though probably not a one would rate on those mythical all-star bands. No doubt they have been hampered by their own over-emphasis of arrangements; that goes for their development and their opportunities to show what they can really do. As a finished product, though, they can do enough to really rate. Simon says A minus.

Al Jolson, at the Age of 60, on His Ambition (July, 1947)—

You know what would be absolute heaven to me, something I still hope to do one of these days? It's to sing for a whole evening with the Goodman Sextet behind me! That to me is the greatest thing of all. They play so relaxed and easy and they never get in your way like so many of those overarranged groups do. Yeah, that'd really be heaven for me!

Al Jolson with Dick Haymes, Dinah Shore and Margaret Whiting

BENNY GOODMAN
(A)

Benny Goodman and His Orchestra. Hotel Roosevelt, New York City. Saxes: (1) Toots Mondello, (2) Arthur Rollini, (3) Hymie Schertzer, (4) Dick Clark. Trumpets: (1) Ralph Muzzillo, (2) Peewee Erwin, (3) Jerry Neary. Trombones: (1) Jack Lacey, (2) Sterling Ballard. Piano: Frank Froeba. Guitar: Allen Reuss. Bass: Harry Goodman. Drums: Gene Krupa. Vocalists: Helen Ward and Ray Hendricks. Leader (and clarinet): Benny Goodman.

Background

Goodman has played for almost every famous leader in the country; as a leader himself, though, he's confined his activities to three groups: (1) the Charleston Chasers, a bunch of all-star musicians which recorded for Columbia records; (2) his Music Hall band, and (3) his present outfit, organized for his recent Let's Dance commercial.

At Present

This is the band about which all the musikers have been raving—raving plenty, and rightfully so. Even with one or two minor defects, the outfit is the closest to perfection this reviewer has heard in many moons.

Heard first on their Saturday night commercial, the boys proved right off that they were a ranking hot band; plenty of sock and swing via superb arrangements and astounding ensemble and individual execution. But it was when they got down into the subdued and none too large Roosevelt Grill that they proved their real worth. It was a difficult transition; many of the experts called it boneheaded booking. But Benny and the rest of the boys adapted themselves beautifully; they produced a subdued type of swing music that was a credit to the profession and which clicked immediately with all the varied ages the grill down there draws. All in fine taste; the melody instruments showed very pretty tones (and that's unusual for an ace hot band), while the rhythm lifted without exploding.

Top section honors must be divided between the saxes and the rhythm with the brass a plenty close third.

The reed section is a prettily rounded group. The boys blend nicely on ensemble; the usual instrumentation being Mondello and Schertzer on altos, Rollini

The same Roosevelt Grill in which Guy Lombardo greeted thousands of customers and dozens of New Years.

It probably was. The band got its two-weeks notice on opening night. Too loud for the room, complained the management. Re this engagement, Benny recently told me, "We sort of looked at the job as a place to rehearse. It was a pleasant place to be and people came in to hear us. But we were busy playing and getting the book into shape. I had my eye on other things at that time." Why does Benny wear glasses? Far-sighted, obviously.

and Clark on tenors. Plenty of variety, too, for all four double or triple and so on. Mondello plays an outstandingly good lead, while Clark and Rollini both get off. And, of course, it's absolutely impossible to overlook Goodman's magnificent clarinet; it's featured often, but then you can never get enough of the best.

The rhythm section keeps swinging both on the pretty and the hot stuff, yet it's never obnoxious. Plenty of credit to Gene "Hall-of-Fame" Krupa, who has that rare combination of terrific swing and technique. Ditto for Frankie Froeba, who's especially adept in the latter department. Harry Goodman (yes, a brother) and Allen Reuss (a newcomer) are easily sufficient on the rhythmic strings.

The brass works together nicely. Muzzillo plays first trumpet on the sweet tunes, while Erwin, besides playing all the hot choruses (and they're good) takes over the lead on the faster numbers. Jerry Neary is talented enough to deserve a better build-up. Lacey and Ballard are good sliders, though neither is especially astounding on either smooth or hot.

Helen Ward warbles most of the rhythm tunes, while Hendricks emits on the ballads. La mademoiselle is quite o.k., but Ray, though technically adequate, could sing with a lot more imagination. Plenty of bouquets here to Frankie Froeba for the best backing of vocals ever heard.

The band plays well, but you've got to give much credit to the arrangers who give them what they play. Hats off to Fletcher Henderson, Spud Murphy and Deane Kincaide.

Chief defects of the band can be attributed to its concentration on radio. It all boils down to a lack of personal showmanship. On the air, of course, there's no need to try to fit in personably with the crowd; to show off on the personality angle. A band, judged solely by musicians on a purely musicianship basis, doesn't have to worry about that either. But in order to reach the absolute heights, judged from every possible basis (and that's how this reviewer judges), the showmanship angle must be included.

This doesn't mean that Goodman's boys are a bunch of mugs who merely play their instruments well. Quite on the contrary, they're all great chaps. But there's nothing there to convince the crowd that they are. Each set (not each tune) is too mechanical; there seems to be no attempt to create any sort of mood for the crowd, either by contrast of tunes or by visual showmanship. And that's an important item that can't be overlooked.

It's merely a matter of time and thought to clear up the defects; Goodman and the boys have been around long enough to appreciate their own shortcomings and to know how to overcome them.

In retrospect, the good points far overshadow the poor. Simon says A.

Goodman today: "That's a funny word, 'sliders,' for trombone players. But I guess they used a lot of words like that in those days, didn't they?" Yes, and I think I managed to create some of the worst of them.

This write-up doesn't do Helen justice. She was an exceptionally good band vocalist with a terrific beat. And what a sexy-looking chick! She still is, too!

A new and recent observation by Goodman on Henderson: "He was just a marvelous arranger. After I heard one or two of his arrangements, I just couldn't get enough of them. Each one was a little classic, especially the ones he *wanted* to arrange. If you asked him to arrange things he particularly didn't like, you might not get such a good job."

Goodman today: "Nothing like a hit band to be a showman, is there? Talent, I believe, is the greatest showman in the world. Look at Barbra Streisand, she's not beautiful either."

CHICK WEBB

(B plus)

Chick Webb and His Orchestra. Savoy Ballroom, Harlem, New York City. NBC wire.

Saxes: (1) Peter Clarke, (2) Elmer Williams, (3) Edgar Sampson, (4) Wayman Carver. Trumpets: (1) Mario Bauza, (2) Robert Stark, (3) Taft Jordan. Trombones: (1) Fernando Arbello, (2) Sandy Williams. Piano: Joseph Steele. Guitar: John Trueheart. Bass: John Kirby. Drums: Chick Webb. Vocalists: Ella Fitzgerald and Charles Linton.

Background

Chick Webb's orchestra has been at the Savoy long enough to be an accepted institution within an accepted institution. Chick himself, a by-word in dance-band-drumdom, has had numerous offers to join more famous bands, but, as he puts it, "I'd rather be assured of this here good, steady job, than take my chances on being way on top for just a while."

At Present

Chick Webb's band is a neatly rounded outfit, concentrating on swinging everything within the walls of the famous Savoy. And when those darksters start swinging things up there, they really swing.

Plenty of rhythm. Chick, as a drummer, belongs in a class with Gene Krupa and Ray McKinley; his lift and technique and showmanship are wonderful. He's ably assisted by bass-man John Kirby, who's considered by many to be the best in the business. Steele and Trueheart help to keep the pendulum moving.

Melody sections join right in, not only because of the natural swing that any colored musician feels, but also because of the beautiful arrangements turned in by Edgar Sampson. His rhythmic figures are truly extraordinary. Especially effective with the saxes (for whom they are mostly written); the reed boys get right into the swing of them both as a unit and as individualists. In the latter department, don't miss Sampson's hot alto. It's all there.

Brass clicks too, especially on the hotter tunes. Stark and Jordan get off often and in sizzling fashion that isn't just a lot of notes. Former has lot of bite, while latter's choice of phases, a la Armstrong, is a thing of beauty. His imitations of the great Louis are

The Savoy, known to its regular customers as "The Track," was a very wide, not very deep, second-story room that stretched the length of the block between 140th and 141st Streets on the east side of Lenox Avenue. There were two shallow bandstands connected in the middle of one of the long walls; Chick's band occupied the one on the left, and Ella Fitzgerald used to stand between the two bandstands, watching the musicians with rapt attention and obvious joy as she semi-directed the brass and sax sections through their arrangements, catching all the cues and just having herself a ball.

Ouch! "Darksters?" Back in 1935, many of us weren't as aware or as sensitive to the racial situation as we are today. But even then, dark was beautiful.

Krupa, years ago, admitted that Chick, "when he felt like it, could cut down any of us." More recently he stated without equivocation: "Chick was my all-time idol." And even today, McKinley adds, "Chick was the best then, but that was *pre*-Buddy Rich. And I know, because I used to play opposite him when I was with Milt Shaw's Detroiters at the Roseland in New York. Sometimes I'd even sit in for him." (Insiders point out that Webb used to refer to McKinley as "*my* boy.")

Another "ouch!" But many of us succumbed to that "they've got that certain rhythm" nonsense in those days—a generation ago. I'm sorry.

Edgar, a quiet, shy, schoolteacherish-looking gent, also wrote instrumentals like *Don't Be That Way*, *Stompin' at the Savoy* and *Blue Lou*, which Chick played before Goodman helped make them famous and put his composing name to the first two.

about the finest in captivity. Trombones work nicely, Williams getting off nicely now and then. The five men are easily adequate on tones and sweet tunes.

Vocalists, both recent additions, suffer from a poor p.a. system. Miss Fitzgerald should go places, while Linton, with a little more seasoning, should arrive.

It's all very good hot music and certainly deserves every bit of the fine rep it's got in Harlem.

Simon says B plus.

Miss Fitzgerald did go places. But I guess Mr. Linton never did attain the necessary seasoning.

Chick

The Ray Noble Orchestra in the Rainbow Room. In back: Glenn Miller, Will Bradley (*né* Schwichtenberg), Charles Spivak, Peewee Erwin, Bill Harty, Jimmy Cannon, Delmar Kaplan, Johnny Mince, Milt Yaner, Bud Freeman. In front: Al Bowlly, Fritz Prospero, Nick Pisani, Danny D'Andrea, George Van Eps, Claude Thornhill, Noble

52

RAY NOBLE

(A)

Ray Noble and His Orchestra. Rainbow Room. Rockefeller Center, New York. NBC wire.

Saxes: (1) Milton Yaner, (2) Bud Freeman, (3) Johnnie Mince, (4) Jim Cannon. Trumpets: Charles Spivak and Peewee Erwin. Trombones: Wilbur Schwichtenberg and Glen Miller. Violins: (1) Nick Pisani, (2) Fritz Prospero, (3—and 5th sax) Dan D'Andrea. Piano: Claude Thornhill. Guitar: George Van Eps. Bass: Delmar Kaplan. Drums: Bill Harty. Vocalist: Al Bowlly.

Background

Noble made a name for himself when, as director of Light Music for H.M.V. (British Victor), he assembled an all-star band for recording dates, fed them some of his magnificent arrangements, and turned out record after record that made the majority of our own bands sound pretty mediocre. Prospects over here being brighter, Noble laid plans to come over and produce his stuff in person instead of in wax. Politics delayed him at various stages, but, finally, last fall he arrived in America, went to Hollywood to write tunes, and then came back east to front his own band. And here he is.

At Present

There's that theory that our friends, the English, have it all over us when it comes to good taste and refinement. With Ray Noble used as a standard of English dance music, the theory holds up beautifully, for there's not a leader in this country who has approached Ray Noble's exquisite taste.

You have to remember that it wasn't until Noble settled down in the Rainbow Room (if it's possible to settle down sixty-five floors above the ground), that he was given a free hand and allowed to produce just what he wanted to, exactly as he wanted to. Before that (on his commercial program) he had been hampered by all sorts of ad agency men, who in turn had been hampered by sponsors, and so on. More simply, another case of pure commercial pfui.

But back to Noble and what he's been doing on his own hook.

To describe good taste in dance music is like trying to describe the effect in toto of any masterpiece of art—it's not possible, and, what's more, any attempt

That Rainbow Room was the swankest I'd ever seen—crystal chandeliers, windows around three of its four sides, "sixty-five stories nearer the stars," as they used to say on the radio broadcasts, overlooking not merely the southern, eastern and western parts of Manhattan Island but also New York's harbor, plus parts of New Jersey and Long Island. Formal dress was obligatory and the prices were also sixty-five stories nearer the stars.

Wilbur was to become Will Bradley. Glen didn't warn me about the second "n" in his first name. But that was really quite some line-up!

to do so strikes this reviewer as being in pretty poor taste. The only thing to do is to see or hear the original or an exact reproduction of it; if you fail to receive the effect—well, that's unfortunate.

To describe the component parts which make up the total effect is a different matter, however.

Noble has assembled another all-star band, which, though rough at first, is finally smoothing out and rounding into shape beautifully. When you take some men from one band, others from another (e.g., there are three ex-Dorsey Brothers, two ex-Benny Goodmen, two ex-Joe Haymesites, etc.), and so on, it's pretty difficult to make them all sound like something right away. Like wines, they take time to blend—right now they've reached the beginning of a truly good stage— pretty tones on smooth; plenty of bite on the hot, with melody section and rhythm fitting in neatly.

The saxes have taken longest to round into shape; as a unit they don't yet rate as high as some others (including Noble's English section). The improvement has been phenomenal, however, compared to what they were when the band first started. And they couldn't have been so bad then, when you realize that the department contained such outstanding individualists as Bud Freeman, the ace recording tenor man, and Johnnie Mince, who subbed on clarinet for Jimmy Dorsey for a month with very few of the wisies any the wiser. No doubt Noble's fine work on his English section makes the standard plenty high for these U. S. boys.

Ditto for the brass, though right now they're just about on a par with Noble's original hornmen. This bunch is very neat, both tonally and torridly. On the smooth it's Spivak who leads; on the hot it's Peewee Erwin (recently with Benny Goodman) who dittoes and also gets off. Schwichtenberg, a recent addition to the band, plays very pretty trombone, while Glen Miller, of Dorsey Brothers, Red Nichols and all sorts of other fame, slides into the hotter places.

Three fiddles work nicely together; playing what they have to play very prettily, and having sense enough to shut up when all they could do would be to overlap.

The rhythm section is one of the few on the face of the earth that knows how to swing quietly. It's a difficult thing to make the dancers want to dance and the rest of the band want to play and yet be scarcely audible yourself. A section that can do that is outstanding. This one is. Plenty of credit to drummer Bill Harty (Noble's manager and the only man in his English band playing over here), who's become infected with his leader's good taste. The two rhythm stringsters, Van Eps and Kaplan, have always rated high on their respective instruments; the work they're turning in now easily justifies that. Claude Thornhill

I'd like me to explain the logic of that to me sometime. Sounds like a 1935 cop-out.

has a tough assignment in trying to emulate Harry Jacobson of Noble's old band—rhythmically he's easily his equal, if not better, but honors go to Jacobson (over practically any other pianist, for that matter) when it comes to phrasing and choice of figures.

Al Bowlly, the South African lad who's been a symbol of the great majority of Noble's recordings, sings nicely. He hasn't got much of a voice, technically speaking, but he has an uncanny sense of pacing, plus lots of feeling, which make him rate plenty.

You can't overlook the arrangements. Most of the hot is turned in by Glen Miller in the style in which he put over the Dorsey Brothers last season. Fred Van Eps does a few, too. But it's Noble himself who does most of the arrangements, and certainly those that typify his style. When he sticks to straight stuff, either slow and sweet (e.g., *Time on My Hands*, *The Very Thought of You*, etc.) or legitimate hot (e.g., *Sally on Sunday*, *Brighter Than the Sun*, etc.) he's magnificent. But he should forget some of the trash he's been turning out—mush like fast fox-trot arrangements of *I Love You Truly*.

Visually the band is all there, too, with Mr. Noble doing a neat job up front. He has that combination of refinement and warmth that's not usual; needless to say it clicks with the dancers, who are always around him either as he's waving the baton or else sitting down at the piano for an occasional fill-in.

America should feel proud to have Ray Noble—not only for his cultured music but also for his own cultured self. Without hesitation Simon says A.

Without hesitation, Simon sounds snobbish.

Elliot Lawrence on Pleasing Critics (October, 1947)—

For a long time just about the only thing I'd think of when making a score was, "I wonder how the critics are going to like this." Then it dawned on me that even all the critics don't think alike, so why not do what I felt inside was best?

ISHAM JONES

(B plus)

Isham Jones and His Orchestra. Blue Room of Hotel Lincoln, New York. CBS wire.

Saxes: (1) Victor Hauprich, (2) Maynard Mansfield, (3) Don Watt, (4) Tommy Macey. Trumpets: (1) John Carlson, (2) Clarence Williams, (3) Chelsea Quealey. Trombones: (1) Mark Bennett, (2) Russ Jenner. Violins: (1) Nick Hupfer, (2) Vincent Allora, (3) Eddie Stone. Piano: Howard Smith. Guitar: George Wartner. String bass: Walter Yoder. Tuba: Joe Bishop. Drums: Walter Lageson. Vocals: Eddie Stone and Woody Herman. Arrangements by: Gordon Jenkins, Jiggs Noble, Nick Hupfer and Joe Bishop.

Background

Isham Jones has been famous as a name dance band leader for such a long time now, and so much has been written about him, that a discussion of his background would not only be impossible in the space allotted here, but would be superfluous as well. Suffice to say that most recently he's been at the Steel Pier in Atlantic City; the Claridge Hotel in Memphis, and Elitch's Gardens in Denver.

At Present

Ever since this reviewer can remember, Isham Jones has had a very good band. That impression dates from all the way back when he made such Brunswick records as *It Had to Be You* and *After the Storm* to the present day when he is playing at the Hotel Lincoln. As a matter of fact, not being able to rank Isham Jones' orchestra in the exceptional class is quite a bit of a personal disappointment for your correspondent. But unfortunately there are a few weak spots in the outfit which keep it from reaching the heights and attaining the same admiration and perfection of the previously reviewed Benny Goodman, Ray Noble, Al Kavelin, Hal Kemp and one or two other orchestras.

Where Jones does rank head and shoulders above all the rest, and that includes any dance band that has ever been in existence, is in the department of ensemble phrasing. Never has this reviewer heard a dance orchestra phrase as prettily as a complete unit as Isham Jones's outfit does. The crescendos and diminuendos, the intonations, and the tonal balance are well

Ish

The band's chief arranger, Gordon Jenkins, writes: "This was not the good band of the era 1930–1936. Outside of Mansfield and Bishop, Howard Smith, and, of course, Woody, the good players were all gone. The real Isham Jones band of my time had George Thow, Jack Jenney, Red Ballard, Milt Yaner, conspiciously among the missing here. The band in Atlantic City during the summers of '32, '33 and '34 was a real gas and will never be heard again, for the simple reason that I doubt there are that many good tones left in our amplified world today."

More from Jenkins: "What made our band great was the combination of Carlson's phrasing and Jones's conducting of some pretty good arrangements. Jones wasn't much as a show conductor, with tempo changes, etc., but he was a giant in a nice, slow tempo. He just physically *made* the guys go along with him, literally molding them around John [Carlson]."

nigh perfect when the whole band gets together on ensemble. Credit here can go to various departments: to Jones himself, for all he gets out of his men as a conductor: to the arrangers, for their really beautiful instrumentating; and to the various men themselves, for their individual musicianship.

Much credit in this last department must go to the brass. And within the brass just as much credit must go to first trumpeter Johnny Carlson.

The section itself is a very prettily blended unit; the men work well together; their tones match and there is some outstandingly fine phrasing. The good performance is all the more noteworthy when the fact that there have been some recent brass additions is taken into consideration.

Johnny Carlson himself is terrific as a lead man. His intonations and his taste in phrasing as he leads are truly works of dance musical art that have seldom been approached. So far as hot trumpeters are concerned, though, the band has been comparatively weak since the respective departures of George Thow (now with Jimmy Dorsey) and Peewee Erwin (now with Ray Noble). The absence of Sonny Lee's hot trombone is much less noticeable for Jones has uncovered a lad with all sorts of possibilities as a hot man in Russ Jenner.

And while on the subject of hot men, there is, of course, the justly famed Saxey Mansfield in the sax section. One of the truly great hot tenor men of the day, though it's a bit upsetting to find Mansfield foresake his unique rhythmic style of hot tenor, at times, in favor of a more flowery and perhaps a bit more melodic style (somewhat along the lines of Hawkins and Chu)—a style which is not nearly so well suited to Saxey's lighter tonal qualities.

The sax section, as a whole, is good enough, though it is not exceptional. At times the boys work together very prettily, but there are other times when there is an unbelievable amount of raggedness—unbelievable when coming from an outfit of Jones's caliber. Not only are the boys often not together, in those instances, but there's some pretty poor balance as well. And, surprisingly enough, it's Mansfield, more than anyone else, whose harmony part busts through too loud most often. The fact that there have been a few recent changes in the section excuses the boys to some extent.

The fiddles are a good section. The men have good tones and the arrangers have made use of them sensibly. The unit comes through especially well on ensemble work at medium and slower tempos.

Like the saxes, the rhythm section is good though it's not exceptional. The two bass idea gives plenty of solidity, and both bassists are good. Lageson plays solid drums, in fact they're a bit too solid and heavy along with a tuba and string bass. A bit more light

Jenkins agrees. "Carlson was always the big man; all the arrangements were written around him, even to his weaknesses, such as his inability to double-tongue. You had to be careful about giving him too many eighth notes in a row, and many's the time I would just leave him out a few bars and let George [Thow] do it."

I blush a bit when I read this. Saxey wasn't really that great.

More agreement from Jenkins: "Mansfield was always too loud in the section, partly due to the giant, fat tone that he got, and I used to keep him on the lead whenever possible for just that reason."

From Jenkins: "In my opinion, we never had anything more than a sweet band. Lageson was real good-looking and a wonderful society drummer, but almost a total loss on getting a beat going. However, on a good ballad, and with good players, we were hard to beat."

57

lift would help no end. Wartner is good, while the little-heard-of Howard Smith's piano lives up to his excellent reputation.

Eddie Stone, with his impish style of singing, is as great as ever. His is a personality voice that throughout a period of many years has never tired. Herman delivers his vocals sincerely, though not sensationally. In front of it all, Jones, if only because of his veteranship, creates an appearance of respect.

Finally, don't overlook the excellent arrangements turned in by the four arrangers. They've done plenty towards creating Jones's fine reputation.

In toto, it's a very good band, really exceptional in many ways, but with a few weak points that keep it from reaching its greatest heights. Perhaps those weak spots will be smoothed out soon, and Isham Jones's orchestra will attain those heights which, for some other reason or other, it justly deserves. As it is, Simon says B plus.

Jenkins' conclusions: "I think most of this review is a very true picture of that particular band. . . . If memory serves, the band broke up not too long after this review. Jones was tiring and having trouble getting the men he was accustomed to." Gordy was correct: within a year the band did break up and some of its better musicians reformed with Woody as their leader.

Oscar Peterson on a Foundation, Faith and
Juvenile Delinquency (October, 1954)—

I think it's *so* important for a musician to have that firm base, a foundation. A family is the greatest thing of all. You can trace all kinds of delinquency, juvenile and the kinds we come across in our field, to lack of any firm foundation. I think a good home life is the firmest asset anyone can have. The trouble with most young musicians these days is that they have no roots. They leave home for New York and they get detoured from a normal life. They're like a hanging string, and they can wind up on either side of the line. But if they have faith in something, in addition to their music, they'll probably turn out all right.

Oscar Peterson

The Bob Crosby band: (front row) Gil Bowers, Eddie Bergman, Nappy Lamare, Crosby, Gil Rodin, Eddie Miller, Noni Bernardi (who replaced Deane Kincaide), Matty Matlock; (back row) Bob Haggart, Ray Bauduc, Yank Lawson, Andy Ferretti, Ward Sillaway, Mark Bennett (who replaced Art Foster)

April, 1936

BOB CROSBY

(A)

Bob Crosby and His Orchestra. Hotel New Yorker, New York. CBS wire.

Saxes: (1) Gil Rodin, (2) Eddie Miller, (3) Matty Matlock, (4) Deane Kincaide. Trumpets: (1) Andy Ferretti, (2) Yank Lausen. Trombones: (1) Ward Sillaway, (2) Art Foster. Violin: Eddie Bergman. Piano: Gil Bowers. Guitar: Hilton Lamare. Bass: Bob Haggart. Drums: Ray Bauduc. Vocals: Bob Crosby and Frank Tennille.

Background

Most of the men in this outfit are from the fine Ben Pollack band of a few years back, leader Crosby, brassmen Ferretti, Sillaway and Foster, and bassist Haggart being the only replacements. In its present form this Crosby Crew has performed at the Netherlands Plaza in Cincinnati, the Adolphus in Dallas, and the Biscayne Kennel Club in Miami.

This Bob Crosby band is not only one of the swing greats of the country today, but it's one of the smartest and neatest all-around performing units heard in a long, long time. Primarily a group of exponents of the most undefinable of arts, jazz, the boys can turn right around and turn in both swell, soft schmaltz, and nutsy, nutty novelties.

The type of swing is, for the most part, enlarged dixieland that swings right out with a sock, and which, though arranged, bears no resemblance to the harnessed kind of stuff that so many bands nowadays unfeelingly call, and think is, swing. There's a great freedom of attack, credit for which can be divided between arrangers Kincaide, Matlock and Haggart, the great rhythm section, and the various individuals in the outfit who are so adept at instrumentally conveying their feelings.

That rhythm section keeps socking it at you with grand gusto, never letting up on you till you feel plenty high, and then just keeping you in that state. Much credit, of course, to the manner in which the four men work together, but whatever you do, don't miss the individual efforts of bassist Bob Haggart and drummer Ray Bauduc. The former, playing in his first name band, displays colossal tone, technique and guts in exquisite taste, while Bauduc's dixieland, slam-bang way of drumming is the height of inspired, percussionistic swing—much technique and push here, too, in a style which might be considered in poor taste in any other band, but which fits in perfectly with the entire Crosby attack.

And on the subject of individualists, be sure to get all you can of Eddie Miller—and even then you won't be getting enough. Here's a man who's absolutely the last word in tenor saxing—a grand swing stylist who achieves such glorious results because he seems to know just what he's doing all the time, with the resultant splendidly patterned passages: because he's such a master of his instrument that he doesn't have to resort to an unmusical lack of tone to achieve effective intonation, and because he's a man who not only can feel swing, but who's fortunate enough to be able to convey all the grand stuff that he feels.

Miller's three reed compatriots are plenty fine and combine with him to form a splendid sax quartet. Fine blending, phrasing and execution in combinations ranging all the way from two flutes and two clarinets to two baritones and two tenors. Note the fine leading of backbone-of-the-band Gil Rodin and Miller, the very neat clarineting of Matty Matlock and the versatile musicianship of Deane Kincaide.

The four-man brass team suffers only from comparison with the other sections. The newly-formed unit is quite sufficient, but lacks the finesse of its two

Later I was to realize that Bauduc actually didn't have very much technique and that the push came just as much from the trumpet of Yank Lausen (later he became Lawson). But Ray did fit the band admirably. Today he's pushing even less hard in Texas, where his wife, Edna, inherited a huge bundle.

For consistent beauty, I can't think of many musicians who have worn as well as Miller. I heard him a couple of years ago when some of the Crosby guys played in New York and the sound and style were as pure and gorgeous as ever. He's now the father of a very successful doctor, a very proud grandfather, and at this writing is back in New Orleans, playing with Pete Fountain's group.

riper associates. Comparatively speaking, the balance and blending of this section is not up to par: for example, Ferretti's pretty lead seldom cuts through as it should, while the muted work of the four men does not display the tonal uniformity of an older section. Note, however, the individual efforts of trumpeter Yank Lausen, whose open hot horn is definitely worthwhile. Art Foster displays a pleasing, easy attack, though neither trombonist is too impressive on smooth or hot solo passages.

What's extremely gratifying is to hear a swing band like this calm down and produce some of that aforementioned swell, soft schmaltz. Some grand tonal blending all around (note Eddie Miller's pretty tenor lead), plus soft, light-lift rhythm, combine with medleys of old favorites at intelligent tempos to produce that goose-pimply, relaxed atmosphere, all the more effective because of the contrast with what's preceded. This is where the very pretty fiddling by Eddie Bergman and the nice piano touch of Gil Bowers show off to best advantage. Ditto for the effective tenoring by handsome Frank Tennille.

The band's novelties make its stock soar even higher. Bauduc, Tennill, Miller and Lamare display some screwy dancing; Bob Haggart's bass choruses and accompanying antics are stitch-worthy; the vocal background harmonics of the band rate as does the impish personality of scatter Nappy Lamare. And on the subject of personality, give much credit to the fine poise of comparatively inexperienced leader Crosby—apparently he knows what it's all about—he warbles effectively and puts up a neat front before a band that must be a pleasure, indeed, to lead. Simon says A.

> Bob handled himself handsomely from the start and succeeded very well in becoming socially accepted by a group of older, more experienced men who'd already paid their dues before he was hired (out of necessity because the group needed a front man) to stand in front of them.

Bobby Hackett on Playing Guitar Instead of Trumpet in Glenn Miller's Band (September, 1941)—

Glenn has me down in front, playing guitar. You might think I don't like it. I do, though, because it gives me a chance to hear all that's going on behind me.

TOMMY DORSEY

(*A minus*)

Tommy Dorsey and His Orchestra. Blue Room of Hotel Lincoln, New York. CBS wire.

Saxes: (1) Noni Bernardi, (2) Sid Block, (3) Joe Dixon, (4) Clyde Rounds. Trumpets: (1) Ralph Muzzillo, (2) Joe Bauer, (3) Maxie Kaminsky. Trombones: (1) Tommy Dorsey, (2) Ben Pickering, (3) Red Bone. Piano: Dick Jones. Guitar: Bill Schaeffer. Bass: Gene Traxler. Drums: Dave Tough. Vocals: Edythe Wright, Jack Leonard, and the Three Esquires (Leonard, Bauer and Odd Stordahl).

Background

Tommy Dorsey has been known and heard for years as one of the modern greats on trombone. About a year ago he started his first solo flight as a band fronter when he took over Joe Haymes' outfit. First he changed its style, and then, just to make a complete job of it, gradually changed the personnel until now there's little left of the original Haymes mortgage. Most of the time the band has been on the road; only about a month ago it moved into the Lincoln for its first steady spot.

At Present

Dorsey has succeeded in whipping into shape a really formidable unit which, in time, should become one of the really rating bands in the country. Because of Dorsey's personal preferences, as well as the current trend in dance music, emphasis is upon swing, and it's as a swing unit that the band should eventually cop the most glories.

It's a modern type swing, made so by arrangers Odd Stordahl, Paul Wetstein, Fred Stulce and Dick Jones, as well as by the natural feel of swing quite obviously possessed by the instrumentalists in the band. There are only special arrangements but there's enough faking of old pops to relieve any possible monotony. The specials are smartly done (for which you can doff your cap four times to the scribbling quartet) and give much opportunity for leader Dorsey to exhibit his slide-of-hand tromboning.

What comes out of Dorsey's horn is truly magnificent stuff. As a master of the instrument, Dorsey definitely rates tops; his tone is exquisite, his phrasing and technique are superb, and his newly-developed hot style makes him one of the two or three great sliding swingers in captivity.

Half-right, it also made it as a sweet band. Jack Leonard writes that in his opinion, the style was "sweet swing."

Odd Stordahl became Axel Stordahl and Paul Wetstein, who was Catholic, not Jewish, became Paul Weston. Leonard said he was the one who called Odd "Axel."

Slightly unnecessary enthusiasm; Tommy wasn't that good as a jazz trombonist. He knew it too.

The rest of the brass, especially the trumpets, aid Dorsey nobly. Ralph Muzzillo, until recently with Benny Goodman, plays a really solid lead, while Maxie Kaminsky's open hot style, besides being in fine taste, really sends you.

The saxes as a section—and this goes for the trombones as ditto, too—are good but not as good as they might be. Undoubtedly that can be attributed to recent changes in personnel. The intonation of the reeds in general can be greatly improved; there's definite indication that each man isn't quite sure just what and when the horn next to him is about to emit, though that isn't bad enough to be noticed by the uncritical observer—i.e., the dancers.

Two individuals within the section are worth noting. Noni Bernardi plays a very pretty lead with much guts, while Joe Dixon's clarinet work is worth watching (cf. November METRONOME, review of Bill Staffon's band). Sid Block's tenor tone is fine; with the aid of a few more ideas, achieved through experience, his performance in a swing band should really rate.

The rhythm section is not only plenty steady, but achieves plenty of lift from bassist Gene Traxler and drummer-man Dave Tough. The former's steadiness and fine tone are exceptional, while Tough's natural swing coupled with a flair for good taste puts this ex-Chicagoan right up there as a rating beater.

Edythe Wright, an attracting lass, emits on most of the up tunes in a husky voice that can really send you. Jack Leonard is a vastly improved vocalist (cf. September METRONOME, review of Bert Block's band) who uses a mike intelligently, sings pleasantly, and makes a fine appearance, though his performance could be improved by the avoidance of affectations in enunciation.

From the dancers' viewpoint the band has much to offer besides its musical ability. Dorsey's setting of tempos and choice of tunes to suit the prevailing mood are rhythmically and psychologically excellent. The contrast of ensemble arrangements and frequent trombone solo passages is pleasing while Dorsey's personality and screwy gags help out too.

Once the sections, especially the reeds and trombones, become definitely set in personnel the band should rank as one of the country's swinging greats. As it now stands it has enough to offer to warrant its inclusion in the exceptional class. Simon says A minus.

The latest change in personnel, effective April 15, has the famed Bud Freeman joining the band on tenor sax.

Kids Jack Leonard in reviewing this review: "I like Davey as a rating beater."

Again from Leonard: "Me affected? Hell, no! . . . Was the A minus rating because I was affected? We could have had an A."

Throughout the years, this remained one of Tommy's top attributes. Unlike other leaders, he'd sustain moods, especially pretty ones, with long medleys.

After Bud joined, the band started playing more jazz. And when Bunny Berigan replaced Maxie Kaminsky a few months later, the band really began to jump!

SHEP FIELDS

(B plus)

Shep Fields and His Orchestra. Hotel Pierre, New York. NBC wire.

Saxes: (1) George Kraner, (2) Charles Prince, (3) Mel Lewin. Trumpet: Lou Halmy. Violins: (1) Max Miller, (2) Seb Mercurio. Accordion: Jerry Shelton, Piano: Sal Gioe. Guitar: Charles Chester. Bass: George Rodo. Drums: Sid Green. Vocals: Mary Jane Walsh and Charles Chester.

Background

Fields has been leading his band around New York for sometime, but he never really jumped into prominence until he began stylizing and hooked up with the Veloz and Yolanda dance team. His most recent engagements, at the Palmer House in Chicago and the Cocoanut Grove in Los Angeles, have really brought him into the spotlight.

Shep

At Present

Shep Fields has attempted the pretty difficult thing of stylizing a society band; difficult if for no other reason than that society bands are supposed to dish out very simple, and almost as boring, dance music with little style, while adhering strictly to melody with a fiddle-sax type combo.

Using basically society instrumentation, playing society tempos, and sticking closely to the melody most of the time, Fields has still developed a style band. He calls it "rippling rhythm." Though it's not musically very exciting, it's attracting. In its simplest form it merely amounts to reeds, fiddles and sharply muted trumpet playing a very staccato melody with either an accordion, piano or sometimes a muted viola filling in for contrast—more or less the old stop-chorus idea. Or else it may be one or more of the melody sections playing a much triplitized chorus. In any of its stages it can hardly be considered the latest in hep dance music, but it is, nevertheless, very good commercial style that still keeps within the bounds of society's repressing limitations.

Sometimes, but not very often, the boys play straight stuff, and those are the times when they show off to best musical advantage. Messrs. Kraner, Prince and Lewin phrase their prettily matched tones to produce a very fine, soft, schmaltz sax sound. Trumpeter Halmy, even though he persists in using a very sharp

Shep writes: "Your comment that society music at its best was pure and simple and usually a bore is true. For that reason, there really never was an internationally popular society bandleader other than Eddy Duchin, and he, like myself, developed a definitive style of music from the basic society brand that you refer to."

mute that doesn't blend at all well on ensemble, exhibits some finished horn-blowing via some neat phrasing and a good all-around attack. Fiddlers Miller and Mercurio phrase very prettily too, and don't overlap. The former's muted viola is used nicely over a p. a.

Accordionist Jerry Shelton plays some very lovely stuff by himself, and is one of the few push and pull men heard so far who really knows how to fit into a rhythm section. He has an extraordinarily light touch (his manipulation of the bellows is excellent) that fits in very neatly with the light, society lift imparted by the four other rhythmsters.

The band, as a whole, produces such nice music when it's playing straight, society style, that it seems a pity not to hear more of it. The cute, mickey-mouse-like style that Fields has adopted definitely has its commercial merits, but there's a feeling that he's carrying it just a bit too far. After listening to it for more than an hour or so at a time you feel like getting up and, hopping very daintily all around the room on tip-toe, squeaking in a very high falsetto, "O-o-o-h, lookie, don't you think I'm a cutey iddy-biddy thing too?" Almost all of the arrangements are simply cut-up stocks, and practically every one of them is cut up exactly like the next one. Too much of that continual repetition is too much; it strikes this reviewer that more good straight dance music would make the Fields style stand out much more, if for no other reason than that of contrast.

Shep has since admitted that his arrangements *were* doctored stocks, i.e., printed arrangements altered to suit the band's style. He agrees that his programs "were very repetitious and, to a music critic such as yourself, could conceivably be monotonous. However, in order to achieve immediate success in those days, you had to have a brand of music that was instantly recognizable anytime anyone tuned in a radio program. The repetition and high stylization of Rippling Rhythm was calculated. . . . About six months after your article was written, we had reached the heights that I had dreamed of and it was then, having accomplished what we had set out to do, that I reduced the stylization of Rippling Rhythm arrangements from 80% to 25%."

All in all, however, the performance is very good. When it sticks to straight stuff the band rates really high as a musical aggregation, while its new style still adds color, if nothing else. More is added, too, by the vocalists, with midwestern Mary Jane Walsh really exceptional: she sings as if she knows what it's all about in a clear, accurate voice, while Chester's efforts, though not as unusually fine, are still very pleasing.

Even though his enthusiasm for his newly developed style may cause him to overemphasize it, Fields, nevertheless, deserves much credit for the very good performance he and his band turn in. Simon says B plus.

I took quite some razzing for having given a mickey mouse band such a good rating. But it did play that particular style very well chiefly because the guys were polished musicians. Otherwise it could have been a catastrophe.

Don't let the "G G" on the lapels fool you—this is not the Glen Gray Orchestra, but the original Shep Fields band!

ARTIE SHAW

(*A minus*)

Artie Shaw and His Orchestra. Silver Grill of Hotel Lexington, New York. CBS wire.

Tenor sax: Tony Pastor. Trumpets: (1) J. D. Wade, (2) Lee Castaldo. Trombone: Mike Michaels. Violins: (1) Jerry Gray, (2) Ben Plotkin. Viola: Sem Persoff. Cello: Jim Odrich. Piano: Joe Lippman. Guitar: Gene Stone. Bass: Ben Ginsberg. Drums: Sam Weiss. Vocals: Peg La Centra, Tony Pastor, Gene Stone. Leader and clarinet: Artie Shaw.

Background

Though he's only in his middle twenties, Artie Shaw has already created much of a rep for himself as a clarinetist. A New York and New Haven (no Hartford) lad, he broke into big time with Roger Wolfe Kahn; then on to the middle west as leader of the really fine, but apparently unappreciated, Austin Wylie band. Then back east and tooting for practically every popular radio commercial outfit. Commercialism palled; swing called, and Shaw hauled out this band of his.

At Present

The instrumentation of the Shaw outfit is pretty unorthodox, as you'll notice if you look at the line-up above. The whole idea is a bit of Artie Shaw beanwork, and a clever bit of thinkage it all is, too.

What Shaw has done is to build himself a style band that can do a neat job on both swing and schmaltz and at times even combine some of the elements of each. It's a unit which can give a boot to those swingsters who have come to hear and to dance, as well as soothe the nerves of the schmaltzier who have come mostly to be soothed.

The basic instrumentation is, of course, largely responsible for the fortunate combination. Via the three brass, tenor sax, and clarinet Shaw can deliver a quite adequate brand of dixieland, while just the presence of the strings helps to appease, and even satisfy, those folks who have drifted into the room, but who don't care much for "this newfangled thing that you young, wild folks call swing music, by cracky!"

And even for the less icky patrons those strings are pleasing for they lend to the general effect a soothing, sort of syrupy quality, which makes it quite pleasant when you want to sit down and talk a bit, or just relax

The Silver Grill, an oval-shaped room with tables on tiers, was one of the greatest rooms in which to hear a band. It was intimate and had fine acoustics. Later it became more famous as the Hawaiian Room, catering to out-of-town and tired businessmen.

Artie says: "Read 'totally' for 'pretty' and you're closer."

From Shaw: "This little passage sure dates things a bit, eh, George? 'Icky'? Hey, there!"

and forget about everything completely. You know, the background sort of stuff that helps a lot when you're feeling jumpy.

Of course, it's not only the style that helps to make this Shaw outfit a good one. The execution of the basically Shavian principle is nobly attended to by arrangers Joe Lippman and Jerry Gray who have turned in some really high class manuscripts—neat scoring throughout that makes good use of the brass and reeds, putting them mostly in the foreground, and which supplies much depth via much sustained harmony from the wide range of strings. And, after all, there's nothing like a string section for sustained harmony.

Much credit, too, must go to the men in the band who, in the short space of about three weeks, have managed to form a very neat blending unit playing a surprisingly small number of clinkers. Outstanding among the melody men is, of course, Shaw himself. His clarinet style, similar in some respects to Goodman's, but displaying definitely original ideas as well, is much fun to listen to, and, when the man does get inspired, can really send you pretty far. In the rhythm section honors can be divided by Joe Lippman (mentioned in last November's review of Bill Staffon's band as "a lad worth watching") and Sammy Weiss. The former possesses a wealth of original ideas plus a very neat touch, while the latter's slam-bang way of drumming, though a bit overbearing every once in a while, lifts the rhythm section, as well as the entire band, plenty.

The other soloists deliver some neat stuff, too. Bluesmongers should get a terrific kick from Mike Michaels' easy, mournful trombone style, as really low-down and insinuating as any style could possibly be. The other hot brass man, Lee Castaldo, delivers via a clear crisp horn; he certainly is one of the city's most improved musicians. J. D. Wade's lead trumpeting is quite adequate, while Tony Pastor, heralded by some writers as truly sensational, displays a somewhat limited number of ideas but a fine facility for sending himself; he's a born showman.

The strings, whose emphasis upon background work doesn't give much of a scope for being sensational, should nevertheless be given much credit. The four men are quite obviously finished musicians, experienced in heavier music, but who have fitted their qualifications to dance music style. Standing out in the section is first violinist Jerry Gray (Bostonians will remember him as hot fiddler Jerry Graziano) whose inflections prove beyond a doubt that he's got a pretty fine feel for the Shaw type of music.

The band satisfies, too, from a showmanship angle. Shaw, a clean-cut looking chap, presents a pleasing, reserved front. Quite obviously he knows what the

Lippman had been arranging before this for Benny Goodman. And before *that* he had been playing piano with George Simon and his Confederates in and around Cambridge, Mass.!

I doubt if Artie liked this comparison with Benny. Just read his comments on this subject in the review of his 1939 band.

Jerry was one of the first hot jazz fiddlers to knock me out. I used to listen to him during the earlier thirties in some joint underneath the El up in Boston. He also played good jazz accordion. A real nice gent, who later became my Army roommate in the Glenn Miller band.

To anyone who has watched Artie on those TV talk shows, "reserved" is sure a misnomer.

69

dancers want for not only does he contrast his tempos nicely, but he also sets tempos that are thoroughly danceable. Showmanship credit too to Peg La Centra who sings for the crowd, rather than at it, and who does it well. And don't overlook the aforementioned Tony Pastor, whose kidding around and screwy faces help bring the mob up to the bandstand.

It's going to be interesting to hear how this outfit will sound in about a half year from now. Naturally, affairs aren't running as smoothly now as they will be; blend and balance will probably be improved upon, the library of specials will be much enlarged, and, all in all, things should be running even more smoothly than they are now—not that there are many catches at present, at that.

Not only because he's accomplished so much in such a short space of time, but also because what he has accomplished is in the exceptional class, does Artie Shaw deserve much credit. Simon says A minus.

Peg had a unique style of singing—a thin voice, but an infectious vibrato and a very musical way of phrasing. She later married actor Paul Stewart, who was then a radio announcer.

According to Artie: "It was out the window, down the drain—kaput. And the resultant band was the one you reviewed later as the *numero uno* swing band in the U.S." (Did I ever review it as that? It's news to me.)

Harry James on Pleasing Critics (July, 1948)—

They call me old-fashioned, huh? Those critics are really going off the deep end. You know what a lot of them are doing nowadays? They're criticizing jazz for what it isn't, instead of for what it is. They've got so many fixed opinions of the way they want something to sound that unless you do it their way, you're just no good.

What's that you say? Some critics think that getting a real good beat is simple, that anybody can do it? Listen, any of those guys who say something as stupid as "anybody can swing" have just plain flipped their lids. They're so wrapped up in chords and new sounds and stuff like that that they've lost all sense of proportion when it comes to feeling jazz and feeling a good beat. Believe me, it's not that easy, and if any of these guys (most of 'em never played in bands in the first place, anyway) tell you different, they just don't know what they're talking about and shouldn't be jazz critics.

Woody at Roseland with trombonist Neal Reid and trumpeter Kermit Simmons

January, 1937

WOODY HERMAN

(*A minus*)

Woody Herman and His Orchestra. Roseland, New York. MBS and WNEW wires.

Saxes: (1) Murray Williams, (2) Saxey Mansfield, (3) Jack Ferrier, (4) Bruce Wilkens. Trumpets: (1) Kermit Simmons, (2) Clarence Willard. Flugelhorn: Joe Bishop. Trombone: Neal Reid. Violin: Nick Hupfer. Piano: Norman Schermer. Guitar: Chick Reeves. Bass: Walter Yoder. Drums: Frank Carlson. Leader, clarinet, and vocals: Woody Herman. Arrangements by: Bishop, Hupfer, Reeves, Gordon Jenkins, Horace Diaz, and Dave Torbett.

Background

When Isham Jones' band disbanded several months ago, a bunch of the boys organized under Woody Herman. There was much gardening, such as weeding out the corn, until the men (Herman, Mansfield, Bishop, Hupfer, and Yoder) found what they wanted. What they wanted and found has been organized for a bit over a month, is entrenched in a New York ballroom, managed by Rockwell-O'Keefe, and scheduled to remain in town with a Mutual wire for some time to come.

Looking back at it, Woody describes the batch of arrangers as "an excellent staff, especially in view of the fact that we could not afford to pay for arrangements." This was during the band's scuffingest period.

It's a smart band, this Woody Herman outfit. It shells out and gives in a manner that convinces you thoroughly that the boys know just what swing is and how to express it musically, and it produces tone and intonation that convinces you too that the boys know how to express other stuff musically as well.

What makes the band stand out so is the body and solidity of both the tonal and rhythmic instruments. Credit for the former must go to a great extent to the fine manuscript turned in by the arrangers, and to the general good, all-around intonation and blending. Credit for the latter goes to a steady rhythm section that really gives in a free and easy sort of way. The melody men are all there—they're good musicians who get the most out of the fine arrangements that can be gotten by a band organized for such a short time. The blend of the sax section is commendable: Jumbo Murray Williams plays a fine lead alto; Saxey Mansfield not only blends much better than he did with Jones' section about a year ago, but plays solo stuff that convinces he's much more inspired than he was in those days; and Jack Ferrier plays clarinet that isn't far behind Herman's—and that, in itself, is going some.

The saxes are good; comparatively speaking, the brass are excellent. Simmons and Willard split first and second parts—quite frankly it's too difficult to decipher just who's playing what when to make any definite comparison between the two men's work. Suffice to say that they're both good. Joe Bishop plays a flugelhorn, and that's what really makes the section. That instrument, pitched as it is between a trumpet and a trombone, adds plenty to the band—not only because of its freak range (talking about freaks, you ought to get a look at the instrument) but because of its very broad tonal qualities. Needless to say the experienced Bishop (he used to play tuba for Jones, you'll remember) handles the instrument beautifully in a right-cheek embouchurish sort of way. And he plays an easy, lazy sort of hot, too. But it's trombonist Neal Reid whom hot fans will go for. This lanky lad's been around town for quite some time but for some reason or other nobody's paid too much attention to him. But there's no doubt that everybody will from now on. The man plays a really great swing trombone; there's terrific boot in his style, grand inflections, and he has a good tone besides. He and Mansfield are the ranking get-off men in the band.

That rhythm section, as intimated before, is plenty fine, too. As stated here at various times, no rhythm section can really swing out unless it has a good drummer. This section not only has a good drummer; it has a terrific drummer. Frankie Carlson, the young

Willard, who sounded a lot like Johnny Carlson of the Isham Jones band, played the beautiful lead on the ballads, many of them arranged by Gordon Jenkins, another Jones alumnus.

Says Woody: "I think Joe Bishop was probably the person who influenced the band most. Later we became 'The Band That Plays the Blues' and that was Joe Bishop all the way."

As I recall it, not many people did pay too much attention to Neal, though Woody recalls that "Neal made the excitement." Still, I wonder how Woody felt, ranking behind Mansfield and Reid in this review.

According to Woody, "Frank Carlson did play with gay abandon. It was real. He now was out of the clutches of Clyde McCoy! As for Walt Yoder, he was THE father confessor of the band."

southpaw cowhide puncher, just sits up there in back of the band and plays, swinging away like hell, solid and steady as they come. There's much punch, too, in Chick Reeves' guitar, and Walter Yoder's bassing is much better than it was in later Jones days, caused no doubt by greater inspiration from the drums.

The Herman routine is diversified enough. Woody sets tempos that are danceable and never too extreme. The library consists almost entirely of specials. Because the band is new, there's much emphasis on standards; the arrangers are just beginning to catch up with the great flock of tunes whose insertion is needed to make any new and modern library complete.

The newness of the band is reflected, too, in the blending between sections and the contrast between tunes in general. Obviously the men have not yet felt each other out completely, and so they all go ahead pretty much along an accepted plane. That's not at all unusual in new bands and is quite forgivable. In time, for example, the rhythm section will know instinctively just how far to tone down when the melody men play softer stuff, etc. And as for that softer stuff, the band as a whole should reach a more relaxed, softer plane. Of course, playing in a ballroom it's not too important, but it's certain niceties like that which make a good band stand out from the rest when it comes to radio and hotel work. When you stop to consider the age of the outfit, though, you've got to give it much credit for presenting as many niceties as it already does.

Undoubtedly the aim of the outfit is to go into smarter spots. In that respect the boys have much in their favor; they make a good appearance, and they possess an excellent fronter and contact man in Herman. He's a clean-cut looking lad with a nice smile that should attract the dancers; he sings very nicely and plays good clarinet, both attributes that command musical respect; and he's very much of a gentleman and real all-around nice guy whom you'd like to know even better off the stand.

This Herman outfit bears watching; not only because it's fun listening to it in its present stages, but also because it's bound to reach even greater stages. Simon says A minus.

Quips Woody: "I haven't changed a bit. Want to bet?" The answer: no. Woody hasn't changed a mite —maybe a hair or two or several thousand—but not a mite.

It did, at that, didn't it?

Basie's Lester Young and Jo Jones

February, 1937

COUNT BASIE

(B)

Count Basie and His Orchestra, Roseland, New York. MBS wire.

Saxes: (1) Cauche Roberts, (2) Lester Young, (3) Jack Washington, (4) Herschel Evans. Trumpets: (1) Joe Keyes, (2) Carl Smith, (3) Buck Clayton. Trombones: (1) George Hunt, (2) Dan Minor. Piano: Count Basie. Guitar: Claude Williams. Bass: Walter Page. Drums: Jo Jones.

Background

Basie is well known in Kansas City where he used to entertain many musikers with his smaller band at early morning jam sessions. Of the present personnel, Young, Washington, Keyes, Smith, Hunt, Minor, Page, and Jones were with him at that time. A few months ago some influential admirers took Basie from his home-town hangout and presented him with a few more men to help him set the country afire. The first selected timber box was the Grand Terrace Cafe in Chicago, which is still standing. Then came Roseland. The William Penn Hotel in Pittsburgh is the next mark.

The terrific fuss and ballyhoo made by the Count's sponsors has created a psychological handicap that is difficult for him to overcome. Heralded as "without any doubt the greatest band in the country" by some advertising men and publicity agents, who may have been shouting in memory of Basie's small-band Kansas City days, the outfit had something terrific, stupendous, and super-colossal to live up to right at the start. Its inability at that start to play in anything even resembling tune was a bitter disappointment to an audience that was anxiously waiting to hear the country's greatest, and left a bad taste in its mouth that won't be washed out too easily.

To the Count himself must go much credit for keeping a level head. He used it, too, and, looking through the ballyhoo, saw that his newly organized band was not yet a bunch of world-beaters, and, what's all the more to his credit, admitted as much. So, instead of basking in the glory set by his publicity agents, he silently withdrew into the shade, gathered his men about him, and saying: "Boys, we're not as good as all that. Let's try to be, though," started upon an intensive rehearsing campaign.

The result of the Count's tactics is vast improvement in the band. That's especially obvious in the outfit's weakest department, intonation. Though the men still suffer from an inability to sustain notes on the same, even pitch—a fault that crops up mostly in slow tunes—they do sound in tune when it comes to biting off notes or even playing some smartly written figures on faster numbers.

Right now it's those written figures that make the band stand out and show promise of really amounting to something in the future. There's some brilliantly conceived stuff there: figures that not only swing in their own right, but which also fit into some cleverly worked out swing patterns. The men are beginning to feel them more than they did at first; they're relaxing more, and consequently, deriving greater benefits from them.

One part of the band that has been consistently fine from the very beginning is that rhythm section. The four men really do swing out in no mean fashion; they give in every sense of the word. Much credit goes to drummer man Joe Jones, one of the finest hide sockers heard in many a moon; the man not only swings as steady as a rock (if you can picture a rock swinging!), but he plays in excellent taste, filling in, etc., just at the right times. Basie is, of course, an outstanding pianist whose frequent solo passages are a delight to listen to; they're as original in conception as are his orchestrations, and that's saying plenty. Claude Williams quite obviously gets much of a kick out of his guitar, and, besides turning in really fine

A month earlier, after having heard the Basie band over the radio, I'd blasted it with: "That sax section is so invariably out of tune. And if you think that sax section sounds out of tune, catch the brass! And if you think the brass by itself is out of tune, catch the intonation of the band as a whole! Swing is swing, but music is music, too. Here's hoping the outfit sounds better in person." It did.

The famed Freddie Green hadn't even joined the band, so you can imagine how green it must have been.

work on that instrument, comes through with some good hot fiddle passages. Not much could be heard of Walter Page's bass.

The two melody sections, as mentioned before, are responsible for holding back the band. Intonation and blend are not yet good. In colored sax sections that's sometimes overlooked, but it can't be in brass units. There are as compensation a few outstanding soloists. In the brass the only new man, Buck Clayton, sends you with interesting stuff obviously played with much feeling. Lester Young and Herschel Evans both carry off their share of hot tenor passages adequately enough.

The selection of tempos by Basie is highly commendable: they are at all times thoroughly danceable, besides enabling the men to get in as deep a groove as possible. Unfortunately not as much can be said for the selection of tunes; here the Basie library is woefully weak. The band plays very few current pops, and those it does play it plays very badly. There's no getting away from the fact that it's dependent almost entirely upon its limited selection of specials.

Judged entirely from pure swing angles, and that's the only way it can be judged, the band is good, Simon says B.

Page was actually great, but the Roseland acoustics stank.

That's true: black sax sections often did play out of tune, often because the men could afford only cheap, inferior horns. But as for terming Evans and Young merely "adequate enough"—well, now I wonder what I was doing that night!

What did remain to be seen, also, was how wrong I was. The band, by the way, was playing Roseland opposite Woody Herman's, which I did like. At least I wasn't 100% wrong during that period.

Chick Webb on Swing (February, 1936)—

It's like loving a gal, and having a fight, and then seeing her again.

ANDY KIRK

(A minus)

Andy Kirk and His Clouds of Joy. Reviewed at Savoy Ballroom, New York. NBC wire.

Saxes: (1) John Williams, (2) Dick Wilson, (3) John Harrington, (4) Buddy Miller. Trumpets: (1) Harry Lawson, (2) Paul King, (3) Earl Thompson. Trombone: Theodore Donnelly. Piano: Mary Lou Williams. Guitar: Ted Brinson. Bass: Booker Collins. Drums: Ben Thigpen. Vocals: Pha Terrell and Ben Thigpen. Leader (and sax): Andy Kirk.

Background

The history of the Kirk men appeared in story form on page nineteen of the January, 1937, METRONOME. Since that time the band has put in a successful appearance at the Trianon in Cleveland and a ditto repeat engagement at Harlem's Savoy. Leader Kirk has left his sax chair to concentrate upon leading, while Pha Terrell acts as featured vocalist.

At Present

The swing shower that drops from the Clouds of Joy is definitely one of heaven's greatest gifts to dancebandom. It drenches you with a light, easy, relaxed lift that convinces you once and for all that this is one of the country's finest colored aggregations.

There are four clouds especially that drop some of the greatest swing you've ever heard, and which, more than anything else, succeed in really sending you. They comprise the rhythm section. What a colossal light lift that quartet propels! It's completely relaxed: there's no fancy Krupian drum beating; no involved Stan Dennis bass slapping; nothing sensational like that. Instead it's simple stuff done in wonderful taste by four rhythmsters who quite obviously not only feel what they're doing but who are also finished enough musikers to do everything they do with great polish and finesse.

Of the four who deserve special mention, two deserve super-special commendation. Number one is the little girl with the earrings who plays piano, Mary Lou Williams. Undoubtedly you've heard some of her work on the band's Decca records. Most of that has been excellent. But it's when she's in surroundings a bit more inspiring than bare recording studios that

Kirk

Kirk recently pointed out that despite my "no fancy Krupian drum beating" observation, "on many occasions Thigpen stopped the show with his showmanship." One generation later, his son, Ed, was to stop many shows as Oscar Peterson's drummer.

the gal really gets off. She has terrific ideas of figuration, employing an extraordinary feminine technique to put them across. Many of those ideas, you'll note, are employed at some time or other by both the reed and the brass sections: in other words she turns in some fine arrangements, too!

The other recommended rhythm man is drummer Ben Thigpen. Obviously his theory is that repetition of a good, basic beat produces the maximum of swing, and it's in his choice and clean execution of those basic beats that he really shines. On the subject of basic beats, note the colossal bass drum beats the man employs; his use of the foot pedal puts most ranking drummers to shame.

The repetition angle holds good not only for Thigpen, but for the two melody sections as well. What strikes you more than anything else in those units are their background figures. They really send you! If you pay attention to them, you'll note that they're not at all involved; that for the most part they're merely basic figures repeated over and over again. And it's the monotony of that repetition that really gets you after a while.

That doesn't detract one iota from the section's execution. Given those same figures, the chances are that most reed or brass quartets couldn't make nearly as much out of them. But both Kirk units have the happy quality of being able to relax completely, of feeling and producing certain undefinable inflections that make those figures really swing.

Sometimes those background figurations come to the fore and become the predominating melodic theme. When they serve such a purpose one of the sections, the brass, gets the decision over the other, the reeds, chiefly because the straight horn men achieve a better blend and truer intonation. On top of that they possess a fine lead man in Harry Lawson who can hit notes right on the button and phrase them intelligently as well. The sax section isn't bad; for some reason or other, though, colored sax sections, especially when playing forte, never do sound completely in tune (Duke Ellington's foursome excepted). It may be an inability to tune together; inability to get together on ideas of phrasing (cf. Lunceford's quintet), or inability to match vibratos perfectly. In the case of the Kirk men the problem apparently lies in the vibrato situation; leadman Johnny Williams, for all of his fine qualities, possesses a slow vibrato that must be pretty difficult to match and to have sound completely in tune at all times. The situation, however, isn't bad enough to warrant too much worrying on anybody's part: it crops up only when the band is playing slow ballads or the sax section is bellowing forth, and that's not very often.

On the subject of the reedmen, don't overlook the

What I was trying to say was that Mary's piano style often sounded like that of a full band.

I was having a great deal of trouble with my own foot pedal during those days; maybe that's why Thigpen's technique impressed me so much.

One of Johnny's finest qualities was his wife, Mary Lou.

individual efforts of tenor man Dick Wilson, whom you've probably also heard on records. Though the man is not the most consistent hot tenor man in the world, he certainly is one of the very best when he gets off on the right track. He has good technique that stands him in fine stead when applied to some of his really fine ideas.

Two other instrumentalists who deserve individual mention: Ted Donnelly plays some fine trombone stuff easily, and Booker Collins promotes plenty of solid punch from his bass.

Missing in the band is a really outstanding hot trumpeter. King, the feature get-off man, is good enough: Thompson, featured less, has more bite, but neither one is an A plus man. Fortunately, the Kirkian type of swing doesn't actually call for the use of any blower whose screeching will absolutely chill ya on the spot, so that both Thompson and King are easily adequate in their chairs.

An item that shouldn't be overlooked is the band's fine appearance. They're all clean-cut, well-built lads, and they're fronted by one of dancebandom's most pleasing personalities, Maestro Kirk, who possesses that happy faculty of immediately winning all the dancers over to him. The same holds true, in a more boyish sort of way, of vocalist Pha Terrell, who not only looks well but who sings a very nice song.

They say that black clouds are storm clouds. Forget it. Kirk's black clouds are happy, swinging clouds of joy whom you should try to seek out at your earliest convenience. Rating clouds is an entirely new phenomenon, but, not overawed one bit, Simon says A minus.

Kirk to the rescue! "Dick was a stylist," he explains, "a fine section man, musician and soloist."

Donnelly later developed into an outstanding soloist, reminiscent of J. C. Higginbotham with his wild and woolly style.

"You seemed to realize," writes Andy, "that the band was built primarily for dancing. This was the reason that during those days when everyone was dancing, we never sacrificed the 'dance beat' for sensationalism."

Gene Krupa on Classifying Himself (September, 1948)—

I'm sick and tired of being classed as just a noise-maker. I like to think of myself as a creator of sounds!

April, 1937

KAY KYSER

(B)

Kay Kyser and His Orchestra. Trianon Ballroom, Chicago. MBS wire.

Saxes: (1) Armand Buissaret, (2) Morton Gregory, (3) James Barger, (4) Sully Mason. Trumpets: (1) Robert Guy, (2) Merwyn Bogue. Trombones: (1) Charles Probert, (2) Harry Thomas. Piano: Lyman Gandee. Bass: Lloyd Snow. Drums: Muddy Berry. Vocals: Nancy Nelson, Bill Stoker, Arthur Wright, Sully Mason, Merwyn Bogue, and Bobby Guy.

Background

Kyser organized his band at the University of North Carolina in 1926. Since then he's played such spots as the New Yorker in New York, the Black-hawk in Chicago, the William Penn in Pittsburgh, the Gibson in Cincinnati, and the Bal Tabarin in San Francisco. He's now doing a repeat engagement at the Trianon. He records for Brunswick.

A band like this Kay Kyser outfit really becomes a reviewer's enigma. Admittedly it's a luscious ear in the field of corn, but it's mighty tough to examine all the kernels thoroughly enough to discover just how much of the icky stuff is done for effect and how much of it creeps out because the Kyserians just don't know any better. There's so much kidding going on most of the time that when the boys do settle down to a ballad or such you begin to wonder whether or not they're still in the fooling stage.

One fact, though, can't be lost sight of. The Kyser Krew is definitely out to make a name for itself as a novelty band. Most of the stuff it does is along those lines. Therefore judged solely upon such a basis, it really does turn in an excellent piece of work. Dancers are continually hanging around the bandstand not only keenly interested in what's going on, but also in anticipation of what's coming next. The Kyser brand of novelty, though by no means the last word in subtlety or originality, is so well paced and rehearsed that it never fails to come off. And in that respect the patrons are definitely well satisfied. Kyser's great popularity in his main stomping ground, the midwest, affords ample proof.

Forgetting the novelty for a moment, and judging the outfit primarily from dance musical standards, its rating is not nearly so high. And that's why it's tough for any reviewer to make dogmatic statements about the band's ability. The obvious, corny novelty can be overlooked for the time being; the discussion now centers upon the organization's musical ability.

If you're a Lombardo Lover you're probably a Kyser Kraver. Musically the two are pretty synonymous. Lead saxist Armand Buissaret possesses a slightly modified Carmen Lombardo vibrato; Robert Guy bastardizes a muted trumpet tone in true Liebert Lombardo fashion; Muddy Berry plays a little more and better drums than that which belongs to that school, but Lloyd Snow's concentration upon the tuba succeeds pretty well in creating that stiff, oom-pahish rhythmic effect. If you like Little Jack Little's twiddlings on the piano, you'll like Lyman Gandee's fill-ins. If you like swing, with plenty of men who can really get off, you'll hate this band.

True, there are some legitimate musical effects that are noteworthy; they certainly should not be overlooked. There's a fine blend among the brass men, and Merwyn Bogue really plays a very pretty lead trumpet. There's blend among the saxes, too, though it's not as startling as that of the straight horn men. Both of those ensemble qualities prove conclusively once more that the Kyser band is well drilled. Nobody can ever accuse it of being the least bit sloppy.

Shortly after this engagement, the Kyser band did set out to make a national name for itself with the introduction of its coast-to-coast radio show, "Kay Kyser's College of Musical Knowledge."

Guy switched from Liebert's style as the band's music improved; eventually he wound up as an outstanding lead man, very big in the Hollywood studios.

Gandee, like Guy, also got much better, once the band did.

This bit about Bogue is a pleasant surprise. I'd always recalled him as primarily a dead-pan comedian. But apparently he also had a live lip.

81

As mentioned before, the band's fine discipline is most apparent in its presentation of its novelties. There's never any hesitation; everything is done like clockwork. Most amusing in that category are the poker face "Ish Kabibble" antics of Merwyn Bogue who really sends himself and his audience plenty with his interpretations of the country's super-icky man. Most commercial are the singing of all tune titles by Bill Stoker and the quite pleasant glee club. Most relaxing are the vocal efforts of Sully Mason and Stoker. Most eye-filling are Nancy Nelson's renditions. Most annoying (though well received) are the corny antics of Kyser in front of the band—though with all due respect to him he seems like too intelligent a chap to mean them seriously.

A word, too, about the band's appearance. The word: good.

In toto, then: as a commercial band of dance music the work of the Kyserians is excellent; as a musical bit of dance music it's dubious. Averaging the two, Simon says B.

Kay, now a Christian Science Reader in North Carolina, summarizes the review: "For the time it was written, your critique was quite accurate—and unique in that it reviewed the baby chick, so to speak, just before it burst out of its shell!" Later on, during the forties, the band developed into a superb musical outfit featuring such outstanding musicians as tenor saxist Herbie Haymer, lead saxist Noni Bernardi and trombonist Joe Howard, playing thoroughly musical, non-mickey mouse arrangements, and spotting really good singers like Ginny Sims, Harry Babbitt, Lucyann Polk and Michael (Mike) Douglas. By then, it certainly wasn't kidding anymore.

Ray McKinley on Modern Jazz (December, 1948)—

I don't think that anybody, including a Kenton, can wed jazz to modern composition. Eddie Sauter has come closest, but to me you just can't go ahead justifying jazz on the grounds of a strictly intellectual art form. So much of the stuff that they are writing violates the fundamentals of controlled sound. They seem to forget that an instrument is supposed to be a vehicle of pleasant and beautiful sounds.

And as for the idea that all the guys in the past are just a bunch of bums, that's a lot of hooey.

DUKE ELLINGTON
(A)

Duke Ellington and His Orchestra. Cotton Club, New York. MBS wire.

Saxes: (1) Otto Hardwick, (2) Barney Bigard, (3) Johnny Hodges, (4) Harry Carney. Trumpets: (1) Artie Whetsol, (2) Cootie Williams, (3) Rex Stewart. Trombones: (1) Lawrence Brown, (2) Juan Tizol, (3) Joe Nanton. Piano: Duke Ellington. Guitar: Freddy Guy. Basses: Bill Taylor and Hayes Alvis. Drums: Sonny Greer. Vocals: Ivy Anderson.

Background

You all know Duke's background, so, after reading the part about this being his first lengthy New York engagement in years, you can just omit the rest of this paragraph—of which there is no more.

At Present

The Ellingtonians are one of the, if not THE, most outstanding and astounding bands of any century! That's saying an awful lot, but year in and year out the men have produced such consistently fine grade A dance music, that such a rave can hardly be considered amiss. True, they have probably never achieved the national popularity (and, judging from a current band poll, musicians' acclaim) that, say, Goodman, Casa Loma, and Lombardo have, but that's so chiefly because they have never received the same kind of a terrific, super-stupendous, ballyhoo build-up. Suffice to say that this reviewer will forget the ballyhoo stuff and will be content merely to deposit Duke and his Disciples into that "terrific, super-stupendous" class. In fact, he'll even add "colossal," just for good measure. And so much for motion-picture-trailer jive.

You all must know pretty well the stuff for which Duke's famous among musicians: slow blues, and fast blues, and all that great stuff that he's cut into wax. Swing critics have raved about it pretty unanimously. But every once in a while, one or more of them have taken a round-house swing at Duke for some of the commercial things he's been dishing out. This reviewer does a right-about-face to his colleagues, though, and publicly goes on record as commending Ellington for his commercial work; not commending the principle in the abstract, mind you, as much as commending the Duke for making the best out of prevailing circumstances.

"What I find especially interesting now, in 1970," Duke remarked after reading this review, "are the references to 'dance music.' Of course, that is what most of it was then, music created with the intention of accompanying or inspiring dancing, amateur or professional. The inspiration that came *from* dancers is another matter, one that merits much consideration when the period is under review."

The Cotton Club draws many ickies who pester Ellington to play pop tunes that were hardly intended for him to attack. He plays them, and the fact that he plays them well enough to satisfy those ickies, and even to draw their applause, should be added to the plus rather than to the minus side when computing Duke's total score. Versatility, even when it doesn't emphasize your personal preference, is still an asset, after all.

Harlem's Cotton Club was patroned largely by whites, and, judging from the way Duke tried to adapt to some of their tastes, his bandstand could have been named the Concession Stand. But even then, some people didn't realize when Duke was putting them on.

Of course, from a hepper musical point of view, Duke's forte is the kind of stuff that he likes to play and that has made him famous. For sheer originality, interest, and structure his orchestrations (though, often, merely extemporaneous) have yet to be equalled in the field of dancebandom. And their interpretations are in a similar class. Ellington himself is largely responsible, but you must give plenty of credit to all the men in the organization. Here is perhaps the classic example of a group of good musicians who have played and lived together so long that each one knows and feels just what the others are going to do when, why, and how. A condition like that can't help bringing great results, per se.

The condition has continued to prevail for more than thirty years since.

Speaking less in general platitudes, and a bit more analytically, brings the subject of sectional and individual ability to the fore. The first point, and the one that has struck most people most strongly, is Duke's really great sax section. As a combination of phrasing, shading and tonal blend it has yet to be equalled. On top of that it possesses by far the best intonation of any colored section in the business. Credit goes of course to all four men, but, speaking in terms of ensemble playing only, you must slap on an extra scoop of whipped cream for Messrs. Hardwick and Hodges, who share the lead.

The brass, though also a fine section, is not as consistent. Phrasing and shading are good, but tonal blend, and intonation, especially, are not as close to perfection. But then, when you consider how free and relaxed the group plays, and how much is left at all times to individual interpretation, you can forgive and forget somewhat, at least, any prevailing sloppiness. Certainly the section's good points are in abundance.

The rhythm is good. The two basses (both of them are fine musicians) aid not only because of the expected added lift, but also because they fill in partially the empty spots prevalent when Duke is not at the keys, and help to steady the section and the band as a whole when Sonny Greer gets off into one of his unsteadier and show-offy moods. That Greer man is a much underrated drummer in many circles. When he really feels like settling down into a groove and feeding his cohorts, he turns in an excellent brand of drumming. It's only when he puts on his commercial exhibition that he turns out to be just a mediocre percussionist.

Sonny's peculiarly jerky way of playing seemed to suit the band perfectly, and it never sounded quite the same after he left in 1951—better sometimes, worse sometimes, but still never the same.

84

Duke with trumpeters Artie Whetsol, Cootie Williams and Rex Stewart

Don't forget that the quintet is aided no little by the general rhythmic structure (note all the background figures) of the arrangements, and by the general rhythmic freedom of its ten melody men. There's fine cooperation there between the five and ten.

From all of which you must have gathered by this time that there's a fine bunch of musicians in the band. Among them, though, there are five who stand out as most consistent and exceptional soloists. You've heard them all so often by now that there's no need going into the subject of why each one of the following is so good: (1) little Johnny Hodges and his alto—probably the most famous soloist in the band; (2) studious-looking Barney Bigard and his clarinet—who

Ellington saxists Johnny Hodges, Otto Hardwick, Barney Bigard and Harry Carney. (Hardwick was featured on alto, not bass sax, and Carney on baritone, not alto sax, as pictured here)

never does seem to get his due share of acclaim; (3) boyish Harry Carney and his baritone—the best of the lower register hot reed men and a fine clarinetist; (4) rotund Cootie Williams—plunger player par perfection and able open horn blower, too, and (5) even-more-rotund Rex Stewart—whose relaxed Beiderbeckian style is the height of being sent in good taste, and who's also capable of some mighty potent screeching.

Much like Rex, in that she's at her best when she's relaxed rather than when she's shouting, is the band's attractive and only vocalist, Ivy Anderson. The inconsistency of her various performances is due mostly to her not capitalizing on her better qualities. She herself must know why and when she sounds good and

Carney was still looking boyish on his 60th birthday, April 1, 1970.

For an excellent example of how much Rex could sound like Bix, listen to the Duke's 1936 recording of *Kissin' My Baby Goodnight*.

86

when she sounds indifferent. Intelligent concentration should make her a more consistent performer, for when she's good, she's great.

And finally, you mustn't overlook the entire motivating force behind the entire organization: the Duke himself. He's probably the greatest exponent of modern dance music: not only has he blessed it with his musical genius, but just by being in the field, he has embellished it with one of the most gracious (and whacky, too, for that matter) characters on the entire earth. And this isn't from any press agent, either!

With many thanks to Duke and his cohorts for giving him the opportunity to do so, Simon says A.

There's that reference to dance music again that Duke was talking about. Wonder why I just didn't go all out and use the word "jazz." I'll have to ask myself sometime.

Duke remarks: "When George refers to its being 'embellished' by one of the most 'gracious' and 'whacky' characters, he means, CRAZY, BABY!"

Count Basie on Duke Ellington (November, 1948)—

He's definitely a statue in American music. He doesn't have to move an inch; he's great as he is.

BUNNY BERIGAN

(B plus)

Bunny Berigan and His Orchestra. Pennsylvania Hotel, New York. CBS and MBS wires.

Saxes: (1) Sid Perlmutter, (2) George Auld, (3) Joe Dixon, (4) Clyde Rounds. Trumpets: (1) Steve Lipkins, (2) Irving Goodman. Trombones: (1) Morey Samuel, (2) Sonny Lee. Piano: Joe Lippman. Guitar: Tom Morganelli. Bass: Arnold Fishkind. Drums: George Wettling. Vocals: Ruth Bradley. Leader, trumpet and vocals: Bunny Berigan.

Background

This is Berigan's second dance band since his departure from CBS studios. The first one wasn't much.

Bunny is also well noted as a trumpeter, not only because of his CBS house work, but also because of his blowing with the bands of Benny Goodman and Tommy Dorsey. For more complete details, see the Hall of Fame in the June, 1936 METRONOME.

At Present

Bunny Berigan's band is coming along nicely. When it started off there were some inherent weaknesses, especially within the sax section, that didn't bode too well for the musical success of the organization. But then came some changes in personnel, much rehearsing, and now the Berigan bunch is in a class bordering on the exceptional.

Outstanding in the band is just what you'd expect: Bunny's trumpet. It's unnecessary to go into details about his style—it should suffice to state that it's mighty thrilling at almost all times, and that it serves as an inspiration not only for the listeners, but for the boys in the band as well. Which is plenty.

About the boys themselves: On the whole they play the manuscript, supplied mostly by Joe Lippman (cf. this month's special METRONOME orchestration of *Listen to the Mocking Bird*), well. There's good solidity in the band, patterned on the Tommy Dorsey style (they're both managed by Arthur Michaud), backed by a pretty hefty kick from the rhythm section. On the whole the band digs a lot, and plays pretty loud, all of which is accentuated a lot by the arched acoustics of the Pennsy Roof.

The sax section is certainly the most improved—in fact it has now turned into a good all-around unit. Much credit must go to recently-added leadman Sid

Very few trumpeters have worn as well as Berigan. He had a warm, broad tone that didn't cool off or thin out when he went into the upper register and he played with tremendous heart and fire. It's a tragedy that he didn't take better care of himself. We lost him and thus his music much too soon.

Possibly I may have been rooting extra-hard for Joe, because he had played piano in my band at college. But he did become very successful, first with Jimmy Dorsey, later with Perry Como and in television. (I still remember his old phone number in Boston: Blue Hills 0434. He MUST have made quite an impression!)

Perlmutter, a thorough musician who phrases well, and possesses both excellent tone and intonation. Clyde Rounds (formerly with Tommy Dorsey) makes a fine all-around fourth man with a lovely baritone tone. Joe Dixon (cf. last month's review of Gus Arnheim) is still a good clarinetist and third man. If there is any fault to be found with the section, you'd probably find it in the proximity of young George Auld, who, probably because of lack of experience, doesn't blend with the rest as well as he might. However, the lad supplies much visual interest as he gets off on tenor via his flat-footed stance and his screwed-up face. He'll be mistaken for a traffic cop one of these days. His playing, though forced, shows promise.

Georgie may have sounded rough, but I doubt if he EVER was mistaken for a cop—not Georgie, of all people. Obviously, the promise was eventually realized.

Bunny

The brass is also turning out to be a good section. When Bunny makes the quartet a quintet, it's obviously at its best. But even without Maestro Mustachio it's plenty o.k. Steve Lipkins plays a strong lead; Irving Goodman (Benny's younger brother) is beginning to prove pretty conclusively the theory that good musicianship can be an inheritance; Morey Samuel still possesses a pleasing tone (cf. Lennie Hayton review in May, 1937 METRONOME), while Sonny Lee is playing every bit as good as, if not better than, he did in his Isham Jones heydays. This reviewer, by the way, never realized until the last few weeks what colossal rhythmic lift Sonny does propel when he gets off. That's unusual in trombone players, and, therefore, all the more noteworthy.

Probably the weakest of the three sections is the rhythm. That shouldn't be, either, because it's comprised of some pretty good men. But, as they say, there's not complete rhythmic integration, and, surprisingly enough, the fault lies with the man who by reputation is the best musician of the four. That's drummer George Wettling (formerly with Jack Hylton), who makes the mistake of trying to fit small jam-band drums into the rhythmic scheme of a full-sized thirteen-piece outfit. As a result, Wettling plays too many wrong things at the right time. It just doesn't jibe with the rest of the section, so that you get much pulling and pushing, no groove, and few steady tempos. All of which is an unfortunate mistake for such a really fine drummer as Wettling. Judging the rest of the rhythm section is pretty difficult, then, because you can't tell when the men are playing what they want to play and when they're trying to compensate for the inherent unsteadiness.

However, don't let all that lead you to think that the Bunny Berigan band isn't danceable. It is. Moreover, it's pleasing to listen to, especially when you get to the Berigan solo passages. Dixon's and Lee's are also fun. And the vocals of Ruth Bradley (a fine hot clarinetist in her own right) mustn't be overlooked—despite a weak lower register, her pleasing voice and appearance make her easily the best of the many recent Berigan femme warblers.

All in all, the presentation is very good. In time, say by the end of the summer, it can quite easily become excellent. Meanwhile, Simon says B plus.

Sad to state, but the band never did get much better. Bunny was just not a born leader.

Horace Heidt and the entire entourage. The four gals at the left are the King Sisters. Alvino Rey is the guitarist in front; the guitarist behind him is Dick Morgan

August, 1937

HORACE HEIDT

(B)

Horace Heidt and His Brigadiers. Moonlit Terrace of Hotel Biltmore, New York. CBS and MBS wires.

Saxes: (1) Frank De Vol, (2) Robert Reidel, (3) William Tieber. Trumpets: (1) Sidney Mear, (2) Norman Kingsley, (3) Jerry Bowne. Trombone: Ernie Passoja. Violas: (1) Paul Lowenkron, (2) Herbert Hagenah, (3) Jimmy Wood. Piano: Eugene Knott. Guitar: Alvino Rey. Bass: Art Thorsen. Drums: Bernie Mattinson. Vocalists: Lysbeth Hughes (harpist); Alyce, Donna, Louise and Yvonne King; Bowne, Thorsen, Larry Cotton, and the Glee Club: Bob McCoy (soloist), Charlie Goodman (soloist), Jack Millard, Myron Ernhardt, Rollin Butts, L. L. Smith, Ray Berrington, Lee Throm.

Background

A synopsis of Heidt's history was contained in last month's issue. Suffice to say, he used to front a stage band, but of late has been making much of a name for himself on the air and at the Biltmore. His is the first aggregation that has really done big business in that hostelry since its Paul Whiteman days some years back.

Final Score: Singers 16, Musicians 14.

Horace Heidt's Brigadiers are the greatest spectacle in dancebandom today. You can't get away from that. In fact, if you happen to be in the Moonlit Terrace of the Biltmore, you'll find that you can't get away from them. They're all over the place. When they're not playing dance music, they're singing and playing harps and cocktail shakers. Any minute you expect one of them to come swooping down at you from the ceiling on a flying trapeze or something. It's the greatest bit of diversified entertainment ever put into a hotel room by one musical aggregation; never a dull moment; always something doing, and always something different. You don't even have the opportunity to pick up your hat and say, "Come on, let's go; here's where we came in."

You've got the Glee Club with its soloists singing all the tunes every glee club sings; Lysbeth Hughes harping and singing pretty much in tune at the same time; the very attractive King Sisters, all of whom seem to be capable of soloing in a different style; Larry Cotton, a fine tenor who used to be an even better crooner, and things like that to keep you amused between sets. And you've got a fourteen-piece dance orchestra to play for you during sets.

About the dance orchestra—were it not for the superb bit of showmanship put on by Heidt and his troupe, it's pretty obvious that the aggregation could not rate in the higher brackets for too long a time. True, there is a style, as exemplified by Alvino Rey's electric guitar, Ernie Passoja's high trombone, the triple-tonguing trumpets, and the Lombardo-like saxes. But tricks like that are always dangerous: unless they're done exceptionally well, there's always a chance of their becoming tiresome. And so Heidt has very wisely interspersed them with all the other trimmings of which his vast entourage is capable.

Taken entirely upon their own merits, the instrumentalists are adequate, but no more. They keep a steady tempo and they play their flashy arrangements. The triple-tonguing of the trumpets draws attention, despite the fact that triple-tonguing of one note is known by brass men to be one of the simpler tricks. Speaking strictly along musical rather than flashy lines, the section would be much more impressive if it paid more attention to intonation. A typical example of how much the brass men try to appeal to the public rather than to musicians is the high-note slurring contributed by Ernie Passoja, who only at times plays those high notes in tune.

The other section of horns is good if you enjoy saxes with vibratos of their ilk. The blend is good, and the men play in tune, but that saccharine style of schmaltz is something this reviewer can't stomach.

The King Sisters are now the King Mothers and sometimes Grandmothers of the King Family.

Cotton had been an outstanding crooner in Jimmy Grier's band, but apparently Heidt wanted more high tenor dramatics. Show-wise the switch may have been for the better—not music-wise, though.

According to Alvino Rey, Fred Waring was one of Heidt's idols. Another (see a few lines later) was Guy Lombardo. Some alumni think Napoleon may have been a third.

By far the most adequate of the sections is the strings. The three men blend together beautifully, their intonation is by far the best of any group in the band, and they phrase their parts very prettily.

As stated before, the rhythm section is steady, but it is awfully stiff. When it comes to dishing out straight hotel-room tempos for the older folks, it's quite adequate, but whenever the quartet tries to swing out, its basic deficiencies hit you right on the head. With the exception of Alvino Rey, whose rhythmic strumming of the Spanish guitar is, musically speaking, far and away superior to his flashy work on the singing box, there isn't a really flexible rhythmster who can "give" in the section. Rey beats out some good lilt, but the other three men are so hopelessly stiff and old-fashioned in their conception of modern rhythm that Alvino's contributions are pretty hopelessly submerged. Heidt would be wise to stick closely to hotel tempos and forget swing under present rhythmic conditions. Even with the Glee Club in the background helping the quartet by much shaking of cocktail containers filled with metal, the rhythm is not what it should or could be.

That bit of background rhythmic work is typical of the Heidt brand of showmanship. Apparently Horace believes that as many people in the organization as possible should be working as much as possible. That formula has been highly successful. But it obviously requires much rehearsal and a healthy esprit de corps. And to obtain both of those it is necessary to have a fine leader. In Horace Heidt the Brigadiers have just the man; not only a fine leader but a fine m.c. and mixer with the patrons.

Obviously the basic aim of the Brigadiers is to entertain as well as to provide music for dancing. Any rating would have to be based upon a combination of the two. And so, though the work of the instrumentalists is only adequate, the excellent commercial entertaining of the entire group does a mighty neat job of compensating. Averaging the two, Simon says B.

Very obviously, Heidt thought as a showman—and as a businessman, too—as per the friendly letter in a reply to my request for his comments on the preceding, hardly glowing review and the far more complimentary one in September, 1943, reprinted later on. Heidt's letter follows in its entirety because. To me, it's a classic example of the philosophy of the pragmatic, businessman's approach to leading a band, as opposed to the era's more idealistic, musician's approach of the swing band leaders.

July 6, 1970

Dear George:

I certainly was happy to hear from you and it was very interesting to read the reviews back in the days when big bands were popular. You asked me to include any comments, so I would like to bring out a phase of my orchestra which very few people have ever spoken about. This is the part which has to do with doing greater business. One cannot expect to stay for six or seven years at any hotel unless they

93

have an organization force which handles this particular feature.

At the Biltmore Hotel in New York I had a personal mailing list of over 10,000 people. We would get this list by asking for birthdays or wedding anniversaries and, of course, it took quite a few years to compile it, but we would mail a postcard to this list once a month. If we were on the road, we perhaps would show our bus or the city that we were playing, or maybe an automobile accident on the road that we could have been involved with, or anything that would be interesting to these people that were good friends of ours. Then we would mention the date of our opening at say the Biltmore Hotel, and hoped that they would be there. We were always assured of a big opening. Then we would send pictures of celebrities who were visiting the room. This particular end of my organization was handled by Art Thorsen.

Later on, we got into our Youth Opportunity Program, where every Monday afternoon we would audition people at the Hotel, then have these people invite their friends down and organize parties on the night of their appearances. Not only did we pick up good talent, but it increased business. My hotel managers could not figure out how when we left, the business would stop like it was cut off with a knife, and then the day that we opened the room would be packed, but this was our secret, and we kept it as one for many, many years. We never depended upon the actual draw of the band as much as we did the personalities in the band and the friends that they had throughout any given city.

This was later followed into radio and television, when to protect ourselves against a rating decline, we had a sales force on the road of 15 to 20 men, who would merchandise in supermarkets the product we were advertising. We would ask for a preferred location in markets due to the fact that we were helping the youth of their city, and almost everyone came through with nice displays. At the same time it increased our sponsor's business tremendously to the extent of the networks being unable to cancel us if they wanted to. The sponsors would simply show them a chart of our sales results and that is all there was to it. In this way the sales of Philip Morris jumped tremendously as they did with the American Tobacco Company, and later on Swift Company had the largest sales in their history in the year that we merchandised from city to city for them. These business activities of our organization were what I really think kept us going for so many years. The tour from city to city would naturally help us while playing in Chicago or New York, as people from these cities who were visiting would always drop in to say hello. It became very personalized and, as you know, very successful.

In later years, I had to make a very serious decision—whether to stay at our home at the Biltmore in New York City or whether to come to California with my family and simply play occasional dates, maybe going out for two or three months a year. This was really the starting point of the decline of the Musical Knights, but as I was getting on in age and had not known my children as well as I should, although it was a sacrifice, in another way it was one of the best things I did.

At the present time, I am trying to start Horace, Jr., who is 24 years old and gets out of the Army in September. I am trying to build the same entertainment features into his orchestra as I had in mine—a band that can play good dance music and also do a good show. This would be for young people, and I think that he has a chance if I can find a place for him to play. The band will be modern, composed of five pieces, and then I will put talent around him as I formerly did. At any rate, it is going to be an interesting experiment to see whether in the next five or six years he can catch on. He has one decided advantage in his favor over myself—he has a very beautiful voice and handles himself well on the floor. As I started in a gasoline station to work my way through college I was never quite able to adapt myself to the sophistication necessary in the band era.

Again, it was a pleasure hearing from you, and any more information that I can give, please be so kind as to drop me a note. I sincerely feel that you have done a lot for the band, and everyone should be very thankful that you showed the interest you did in helping them get ahead with your good, frank comments. If you ever get to California let me know as I would certainly enjoy having dinner with you.

Kindest personal regards,
Horace Heidt

KRUPA'S BAND KILLS CATS AT ATLANTIC CITY OPENING

Felines Howl, Then Purr, As Gene's New Gang Blasts Forth at Initial Siege . . . Brass, Rhythm, but Not Sax Section Feature Powerful Attack

In the neighborhood of four thousand neighborhood and visiting cats scratched and clawed for points of vantage in the Marine Ballroom of Atlantic City's Steel Pier on Saturday, April 16, and then, once perched on their pet posts, proceeded to welcome with most exuberant howls and huzzahs the first public appearance of drummerman Gene Krupa and his newly-formed jazz band. The way the felinic herd received, reacted to, and withstood the powerful onslaughts of Krupa's quadruple "f" musical attacks left little doubt that Gene is now firmly entrenched at the helm of a new swing outfit that's bound to be recognized very shortly as one of the most potent bits of catnip ever to be fed to the purring public that generally passes as America's swing contingent.

If Gene had any cause for worry, that cause was completely submerged before his band's musical history was even one set old. Right from the opening strains of his theme (*Apurksody*—read the first five letters backwards) and on through the colossal arrangement of *Grandfather's Clock*, which officially opened proceedings, it was as obvious as the hair that had already fallen into Gene's face that his band would satisfy the most belligerent cat's meow. Throughout the evening the kids and the kittens shagged, trucked, jumped up and down and down and up, and often yelled and screamed at the series of solid killer-dillers that burst forth from the instruments of the Men of Krupa. When the proceedings started, they were lined forty-five deep around the huge bandstand, and when at one-thirty the band led its limp lips and limbs from the field of battle, at least one-third of that number of rows remained in an up-

right position—as thrilling a tribute as any opening bandleader could possibly hope for.

Louder Than Benny

Krupa's band is a loud edition of what Goodman's Gang used to be, pulling its punches even less and presenting for the most part a solid, two-fisted attack that varies more in tempo than it does in volume or intense drive. Paced by a powerful six-man brass section, it maintains a pace that at times is almost punishing in its fierceness, in the way it pelts your ears, and leaves them ringing, and even more so in its ability to hold your musical interest while varying little in musical format.

Of course, the very fact that Gene's Genesis was something new made its first public appearance exceedingly exciting. That, and Gene's remarkably sincere showmanship, were the motivating forces that first caused the assembled cats to howl with glee. But it took a good deal more to keep them purring for the rest of the long evening, and it's in the purring department, in its ability to sustain interest, that the young band really exhibited its true merits.

Gene with tenor saxist Vido Musso, trumpeter Davey Schultze and alto saxist Murray Williams

The merits consisted of, in the first place, sixty or so great arrangements supplied by Jimmy Mundy, Chappie Willet, Fletcher Henderson, Dave Schultze, George Siravo, and a few other members of the band. Then there was a truly remarkable brass sextet that had colossal drive, fine intonation, and a brilliant ensemble attack. The rhythm section, paced by Gene and a great bassist named Horace Rollins, kept swinging out all night at a remarkably steady pace and all the time doing much to propel the other sections as well as the hot soloists right out into very high and elated space.

Top Soloists

Of those soloists, four stood out especially far. On tenor sax, Vido Musso blew forth a tone and licks that were even improvements over what he used to play with Goodman—which is probably enough praise in itself. On trombone, Bruce Squires, though still exhibiting a tendency to overdo his lip trills, really emitted some rhythmic, almost gutbucket riffs that stamp him as one of the few sliphorn artists today who play an effective hot style on that instrument.

However, the two hot trumpeters, Tommy Goslin and Dave Schultze, really supplied the most exciting hot passages of the night. The former is a high-note screecher whose blunt, remarkably consistent "hit-'em-on-the-nose" attack has a telling effect. The latter is a bit more subtle: his choice of prettier phrases played with a magnificent, ringing tone, comprise the most thrilling bit of soloing within the entire Krupa entourage.

The third trumpeter in the section, Tommy (Tummy) Di Carlo, is also a remarkable musician who combines a marvelous intonation and attack with as brilliant and piercing a tone as has been heard in these parts since Charlie Spivak left for Chicago. And the remaining members of the brass section, trombonists Chuck Evans and Charles McCamish, deserve much commendation, if only because they round out a fine brass sextet. The latter also plays some good hot passages.

Weak Points

Looking at the performance from a purely musical point of view (which is what you're doing now), the band did fall down in one section, and that was the saxes. True, the acoustics within the shell of the Marine Ballroom have always been tough, but compared with the rhythm and the brass, the reed men were definitely the weak sisters of the evening. Their phrasing at times was very good, but their intonation was far below par, and their work as an ensemble unit often very sloppy. Gene has a good lead man in

The original Krupa rhythm section: pianist Milt Raskin, bassist Horace Rollins, guitarist Remo Biondi and Gene himself

Murray (Jumbo) Williams, and the other men also possess good tones, but some more serious rehearsing and cooperation on individual conceptions of pitch are very much in order. The causes for the band's rough spots, that many critics during the course of the opening evening excused, and ascribed to the short time which the band has played together, can be traced directly to laxity—yes, almost inexcusable laxity —on the part of the sax section alone.

However, what could be excused, and ascribed to the short time, was the singing of Jerry Kruger, the tall showgirlish lass who joined the band the day before the opening. Fine things can be expected from her, but on the opening night she was overcome by (1) the excusable lack of knowledge concerning her material, and (2) the less excusable and apparently insatiable desire to sing everything in the style of Billie Holiday. More time and originality will help Miss Kruger a lot, for she has the basic stuff.

Time, of course, is going to help Krupa's band a lot too—that is, from a musical aspect. From a commercial point of view, the band already has just about everything: colossal drive and swing, marvelous Krupa showmanship, some novelties in which the entire band plays tom-toms attached to the attractive music stands; all in all, an approach to the younger and shaggier dancing element that, with Krupa's aid, had proved so successful to the Goodman Gang, and which, even without the aid of the Gang, will quite conceivably help Krupa's band to become a huge financial and social success.

(Undated; c. March, 1971)

Dear George:

You said it!

Have no comments, only an anecdote you might find amusing.

Following that initial engagement in Atlantic City, I was driving back to New York with Ethel and a few of the sidemen and, en route, turned on the car radio. It warmed up and began playing just as the Benny Goodman band, which was playing in Philadelphia at the time, was swinging into one of its big standards. We all listened and I, obviously lending a closer ear than the others, began picking the drumming to pieces, passing along observations of the new man's faults on this remote broadcast.

You can imagine my embarrassment when, at the conclusion of the number, the announcer informed us we'd been listening to a recording of Benny Goodman and his orchestra—with, of course, Gene Krupa on drums.

Best personal regards and all good wishes for the success of the new book.

Cordially,
GENE

BENNY GOODMAN

*Marvelous Band
With a Style*

(A)

Benny Goodman and His Orchestra. Manhattan Room of Hotel Pennsylvania, New York City. CBS and Mutual wires.

Saxes: (1) Dave Matthews, (2) Bud Freeman, (3) Milton Yaner, (4) Arthur Rollini. Trumpets: Harry James, Ziggy Elman, Chris Griffin. Trombones: (1) Vernon Brown, (2) Red Ballard. Piano: Jess Stacy. Guitar: Ben Heller. Bass: Harry Goodman. Drums: Dave Tough. Vocals: Martha Tilton. Leader and clarinet: Benny Goodman.

Previous Review

Benny was first reviewed in this department when he was at the Roosevelt Hotel (New York) in June, 1935. At that time he received a straight A rating—which meant less in those days than it does now when the musical standard of bands is much higher. Outside of Benny himself, the only present members of the band at that time were Rollini, Ballard, and brother Harry. A history of the Goodman doings since then is unnecessary.

At Present

Benny's band swings more now than it ever did. It's looser and less mechanical than at any time in its history. It settles into deeper grooves from which it is jerked much less quickly and abruptly; there's more personal expression of feeling, and there's less sensationalism than ever before. Apparently in that Carnegie Hall Concert, Benny and the boys reached a climax in the art of playing to the public, and after it was all over, experienced a reaction that must have left them saying: "Aw, to hell with all this blasting to lift them off their seats—let's just settle back and swing as purely as possible—and give ourselves the kicks for a change." That attitude, combined with his differences with Krupa, must have convinced Benny that the time for housecleaning, so far as style and men were concerned, was at hand.

The new style is more simple and brilliant. And, to put it briefly, since simplicity is the keynote of good swing, the Goodman Gang now has good swing.

The arrangements (mostly by Edgar Sampson) are less involved, and rely much more upon the method of building towards one climax instead of achieving various climaxes during the course of one number. As a result, and speaking figuratively, the Gang settles down into one deep, wide groove and remains pretty far down in that groove until the final climax lifts it right out. The Jim Mundy arrangements, which Benny used to play before the change, had a different approach: playing them, the band was not so much lying in a groove and achieving momentum within that groove, as simply pushing straight along on top and punching its way to a series of climaxes.

Stated less figuratively and more technically, today's Gang relies once more on simple background rhythm figures, repeated over and over again until the background is really rolling and serving as in inspiration for the featured men. This is combined with much simpler beating from the rhythm section. And for this type of swing, a simple rhythm is the most effective because it never clutters up other rhythmic effects, and, at the same time, gives the rest of the band (which is at times almost playing pure rhythm) a solid, basic, rhythmic foundation upon which to impose its own rhythmic structure. Stylistically, this can best be described as a shift to a more definite colored swing—the old Goodman band was more like Chick Webb (who plays almost a white, intricate swing), while the new Goodman band is more like Count Basie's.

So much for the shift in style—listen to any of Goodman's radio programs nowadays (especially his sustainings) and compare them with his records of four or five months ago and you'll get the general idea, anyway.

The new style has left the brunt of the attack to the undisturbed brass section. You can't give enough credit to trumpeter Harry James, who embodies more natural rhythm in his playing than any other melody instrumentalist does today. This is reflected not only in his thrilling solo passages, but also in his magnificent leading of the section. His bite, his inflections, his attack are almost superhuman—there probably isn't another white trumpeter in the world (including Berigan) who could kick the Goodman brass, and therefore the entire Goodman band, the way James does. The comparative letdown when either Griffin or Elman lead (and they are both excellent trumpeters and leaders, mind you) serves as additional proof of Harry's value.

Credit too, must go to the trombonists: to Vernon Brown for his fine hot work, and to Red Ballard for his pretty tone and for his uncanny ability to blend and phrase with others so perfectly. Little wonder

I loved Cab Calloway's description of a Jimmy Mundy arrangement: "Man, he comes on like Gang Busters and goes off like the Good Will Hour."

Couldn't I just have easily just called them "riffs," which is what they were?

Somewhat Confusion Dept.—The new Goodman band may have sounded more like Basie's than Webb's, but Edgar Sampson, who's been drawing all the raves here, had been Webb's arranger for years.

Benny must have loved this superlative. Actually, nobody ever swung more than Goodman.

99

that this modest man is considered by most musicians as the best second trombonist in the business.

Dave Tough has made an entirely different kind of a rhythm section out of Benny's beaters. To be sure, gone is the driving pressure, the brilliance, and the sensationalism of the Krupa regime, but in its stead there is a steadier, freer section which, instead of changing beat and working with every brass figure, is content to remain more in the background while repeating basic beats, and serve as a solid rhythmic pattern for the rest of the band to work against. And, as mentioned before, such simple rhythm is much better suited for the new, looser Goodman style.

The new sax section (in a transitory state, if one is to believe reports prevalent at the time of writing) phrases more loosely than the old one, but is not as good a unit. There aren't major difficulties such as intonation and really bad tones, but there are certain subtleties such as matching of vibratos that will have to be ironed out before the quartet can rate with the one it replaced. Dave Matthews' phrasing is marvelous and more inspiring than Hymie Schertzer's was, but he has neither the tone, the intonation, nor the general all-around solidity of the man whose place he took. And Freeman and Yaner still haven't gotten the feel of things in general. The former is a vastly improved section man, but still not the best.

100

However, Bud has imbued a spirit into the band that has been a tremendous help spiritually. There is little in swing that's more inspiring than a Freeman solo when Bud is feeling right, and fortunately Bud has been feeling the nuts lately. As a result, he's been emitting some astounding stuff that's so contagious that it's even affected Benny himself. It's hard to imagine Goodman playing like Freeman, but Benny is emitting more inspired stuff nowadays than he has in years—and you can bet your last reed that Bud's been the cause!

Benny, Bud, and Harry are the three outstanding soloists in the big band, but there are other swell get-off men too: Jess Stacy at the piano; Vernon Brown on trombone; Ziggy Elman on trumpet; Matthews on hot alto, and Arthur Rollini on tenor. And, of course, when you come to the trio and quartet, you have the marvelous Teddy Wilson and Lionel Hampton, who besides his vibre work, is turning in some sensational drumming nowadays.

No comment on soloists is complete without mention of the fine and vastly improved vocals of Martha Tilton, a personality who's a distinct personal credit to the music world. For that matter, the same can be said of Benny himself, one of the least understood personalities in dancebandom, who seems to be thoroughly sincere in his display of his newfound kicks. And appraising those same kicks, and at the same time getting his own kicks, Simon says A.

Still true; few do. After 35 years, I think I'm just beginning to know him and to appreciate some of the personal qualities about which Glenn Miller used to tell me with such unbridled enthusiasm for Benny Goodman, the man.

Ziggy Elman

GLENN MILLER

(*A minus*)

Glenn Miller and His Orchestra. Raymor Ballroom, Boston. NBC wire.

Saxes: (1) Hal McIntyre, (2) Gordon Beneke, (3) Wilbur Schwartz, (4) Stanley Aaronson, (5) Sol Kane. Trumpets: (1) Bob Price, (2) Gasparre Rebito, (3) Johnny Austin. Trombones: (1) Al Mastren, (2) Brad Jenney. Piano: Chummy MacGregor. Bass: Rolly Bundock. Drums: Bob Spangler. Vocals: Gail Reese and Ray Eberle. Leader and trombone: Glenn Miller.

Background

Miller, a Colorado Collegiate, has been around for a long time both as a trombonist and as an arranger. He served in those capacities on many of the Red Nichols' Five Pennies dates, and after a sojourn in the radio studios, played an important part as organizer, arranger, and instrumentalist in the Dorsey Brothers' and Ray Noble's orchestras. This band, organized a few months ago, is his second, his first having been the chief sufferer in a bit of managemental disagreement.

This was the band's second appearance at the Raymor, a rather desultory ballroom just down the block from Symphony Hall, but a holding spot for Miller during his band's early struggles.

Glenn rehearses his early 1938 brass section of trombonists Brad Jenney and Al Mastren, trumpeters Gasparre Rebito, Bob Price and Johnny Austin

At Present

Quite definitely this is one of the very best of the newer outfits. It's blessed with magnificent arrangements, a peach of a sax section, a fine rhythm trio, good brass, some swell soloists, and a healthy esprit de corps that's reflected in a young, comparatively inexperienced group of musicians sounding like a much more mature and prettily polished musical aggregation.

Credit in the first instance goes to Miller, not only because he's the leader, but also because he's responsible for practically all of the manuscript. He's one of the few arrangers today who jots down consistently pretty selections of sweet notes and ditto rhythmic series of swingy black dots. Note, for example, his unique style of scoring for one clarinet and four saxes, and then some of the moving background figures he writes for the brass to play into hats, and you'll get a pretty good idea of the swell, set style upon which he and his men are working.

To those men goes loads of credit also, for they do especially nice things with the manuscript with which they're confronted. The total ensemble achieves a pretty blend, phrases neatly together, and, with a few exceptions, always sounds extremely in tune.

Of the three sections, the most attracting is the sax quintet. There's a tonal solidity and a blend within this group that's seldom been duplicated by any other of its kind. Here, again, credit goes to *what's* being played as much as to *how* it's being played. The *what* having been discussed a few paragraphs ago, the emphasis now shifts to the *how*. In that category give much credit to lead man Hal McIntyre, possessor of a fine tone, good execution and grand conceptions of phrasing. On some of the dreamier tunes, the lead shifts over to tenor man Stanley Aaronson, who, though less experienced in Millerian Mannerisms, achieves remarkably satisfactory results via an extremely pretty tone and relaxed phrasing.

The "fine rhythm trio" mentioned a little while ago is just that. It's solid, steady, plays behind the sweet in good taste, and, in most instances, achieves a fine lift behind the band's swingier attempts. Rolly Bundock is a solid bass player with a fine tone; Bob Spangler, when he's not trying too hard, really kicks on drums, while Chummy MacGregor's value to the band is increased via his ability to arrange and even to compose.

The brass section's a better than average unit. All five men phrase together, attack together, possess good tones, and play pretty well in tune. There's a certain lack of consistency within the quintet which can in the final analysis be attributed to the comparative inexperience of trumpeter Johnny Austin and trombonist Brad Jenney. However, when Miller

They called Stan "The Moose." Why, I don't know. He was a good musician and an exceptionally likable guy. He played lead tenor because Miller was not yet using too much of his clarinet lead style. When he did, the Moose usually doubled the melody with Willie Schwartz's clarinet.

Today Bundock is one of the west coast studios' top bassists, a member of Les Brown's band, among others.

changes the group into a sextet with his frequent sojourns into the land of lead trombone, you quite naturally find a more solid and more satisfactory brass section, one that can be classified as potentially excellent.

However, the brass does contain the two outstanding soloists within the entire band. Number one is Johnny Austin, one of the most inspiring hot trumpeters to hit dancebandom in a long, long time. The lad blasts forth in a free, voluble style that's bound to electrify you and even make you duck your head so that you won't hit it too hard as you're lifted toward the ceiling. Few white men have ever played with such thrilling abandon.

The second soloist is Miller himself, a consistently fine hot trombonist, who seems to have the happy faculty of knowing just what he's going to do next—and of doing it, too! There are other instrumentalists, too, who shine when the spotlight's shifted to them. Wee Willie Schwartz plays a fine, original clarinet, while Tex Beneke, though lacking somewhat in consistency, reaches truly brilliant heights on some of the tenor passages alloted him. And the two lead men, McIntyre and Price, both get off nicely every now and then on clarinet and trumpet respectively.

And finally, when discussing individuals, there are the two vocalists. The improvement in Gail Reese's singing (remember her with Bunny Berigan, Charley Barnet and Carl Ravel?) is almost unbelievable: now, besides still being an extremely attractive lass, she's a mighty fine warbler. Ray Eberle (younger brother of Bob who sings with Jimmy Dorsey) sings quite adequately, and should sound even better as soon as he settles down into a more relaxed and subdued groove.

All in all, then, with the exception of a few weak spots that time should be able to strengthen rather quickly, this is an exceptionally fine outfit. Through the efforts of its leader, it has achieved a style that's not only unique, but what's a great deal more important, is extremely musical. You can recognize some bands a mile off by their style—even if you don't want to—but as soon as you hear this outfit, you'll know it's Glenn Miller's—and you'll be glad to know it, too! True, style isn't everything, but, in this instance, the men who produce it are above average musically and personally. The latter adverb becomes exceptionally important when you commence to think in terms of the future, as Miller and his Men must be doing nowadays. Glenn is possessed with a young, eager, and exceptionally clean-cut appearing group, while this group, in turn, is fortunate in being led by a man who's considered by other well-known leaders as well as by his own men as being not only one of the finest musicians in the business, but also one of the most thoroughly respected personalities within the en-

Willie had been playing lead alto and jazz clarinet in Julie Wintz's band when a reviewer (me) heard him and told Glenn about him. After awhile Glenn used Willie's clarinet almost exclusively as a lead horn. Few imitators have been able to match that full, rich Schwartz sound.

While in Boston during this engagement, Glenn heard Marion Hutton with the Vincent Lopez band and soon hired her. A Boston song plugger named Jack Philbin, whom Glenn liked very much, soon fell in love with Marion and they were married. Philbin is now Jackie Gleason's executive producer.

For me, that relaxed groove never materialized.

tire musical profession. Such a complete combination can hardly help reaching truly great heights.

But, even forgetting the future and looking only at the present afford one a keen musical thrill. Simon says A minus.

Ray Eberle and Gail Reese

LARRY CLINTON

(B plus)

Larry Clinton and His Orchestra. Glen Island Casino, New Rochelle, N. Y. NBC and MBS wires.

Saxes: (1) Fletcher Hereford, (2) Tony Zimmers, (3) Leo White, (4) George Dessinger. Trumpets: (1) Rickey Traettino, (2) Jimmy Sexton, (3) Walter Smith. Trombones: (1) Joe Ortolano, (2) Jack Bigelow. Piano: Sam Mineo. Guitar: Jack Chesleigh. Bass: Walter Hardmann. Drums: Henry Adler. Vocals: Bea Wain, Dick Todd and Jack Chesleigh. Leader, trumpet and trombone: Larry Clinton.

Background

Despite the current popularity of Clinton's band, it's still a comparatively new outfit. Larry, who suddenly sprang out of the realms of mediocre 802 trumpeting three or four years ago via his sensational arranging for Casa Loma and Jimmy Dorsey, originally organized his band about nine months ago to record for Victor and be featured on that company's commercial. His instant success, aided no little by his writing such tunes as *Dipsy Doodle*, *Satan Takes a Holiday*, *Study in Brown*, etc., made it pretty obvious that he'd have to be put into a spot. Bookers Rockwell-O'Keefe wisely kept him on college dates with the idea of springing him with much gusto upon the kids when they came home for vacation in Westchester. Their bit of springing has worked most successfully, because Clinton has smashed all records at the Casino. Chances are you'll find him in the Lincoln Hotel (New York) next winter.

Clinton writes: "I remember my first thought on these lines . . . 'Surely, this is the most unkindest cut of all!' " Its basis: Larry and I had played one or two pick-up dates together. I had emerged as a critic out of the realms of sub-mediocre Local 802 drumming.

An even better chance: Artie Shaw would be in the Lincoln; Clinton would be in the New Yorker.

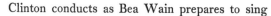

Clinton conducts as Bea Wain prepares to sing

At Present

The biggest danger in reviewing this band is putting too much emphasis upon Larry Clinton's arrangements and not enough upon the basic musicianship of the orchestra. For it's the former, rather than the latter, that the general public seems to take into consideration when discussing the merits of this organization. Clinton now has almost as much of a definite style as Lombardo and Wayne King have. And since this is a dance band review, emphasis should not be put too much upon whether the style, per se, is good, any more than (or perhaps even as much as) whether the musicians themselves turn in good jobs in portraying that style.

Good Beanwork

One thing is certain, and that is that Clinton does a magnificent job of playing directly into the hands (and feet and young hearts, too) of the shagging adolescents who make periodic trips to the Glen Island shrine to worship their idol of 1938. Following pretty closely the psychological technique employed by Glen Gray when he played the spot for two seasons, Larry uses the art of contrast to great advantage, jumping intelligently from soft, slow, "hug-me-tight" musical insinuations to fast, raucous, "look-at-me-shag" blasts—thus giving the kids opportunities for romancing and dancing on the same spot—all for one price.

Strangely enough, despite the fact that Clinton's is usually referred to as a swing band, it's the sweeter stuff at which he excels. That's due both to the arrangements and to the musicians.

Clinton: "True, true. If my college was Casa Loma, my guru was T.D., whose fundamental precept was that a dance band leader's first and most important job was to get people on the dance floor."

The Arrangements

Larry's pen and ink, when applied to ballads, produce exceedingly pleasing and danceable results. His use of clarinets and of unison, his chord changes, modulations and, for the most part, his voicing are good, and, what's every bit as important, are really excellent when applied as mood creators. His attempts at arranging swing are not as uniformly fine; they're inclined to be monotonous and, what's even more detracting, they often become cumbersome. Chalk up that last deficit to Clinton's basic weakness when it comes to swing: his stereotyped and almost soggy way of writing for saxes. His scoring for the brass (note the rhythmic figures—and also the fact that Clinton himself is a brass man) is excellent and results in a swing, but his reed manuscript has a dull, dampening effect that acts very much toward swing as a governor on the accelerator of an auto does towards speed. It's interesting to note, too, that one of the reasons the Casa Loma crew has never achieved

Clinton: "In this review I think George came not to praise Clinton but to bury him." Come to think of it, it is surprising that Larry and I *have* remained on such good terms through the years. I must have written something better later on.

107

any freedom and truly relaxed swing that springs therefrom is because its sax section is also too much of a burden to overcome.

The Musicianship

The comment concerning *what* the saxes play carries over to *how* the saxes play. The tones, intonation and blend of the quartet are exceedingly good, and that goes for both its saxophone and its clarinet work. But its phrasing, especially when trying to play swing, is dull, unimaginative and devoid of any rhythmic inflection. To be sure, Clinton's reed men don't have to go to the extreme of phrasing as loosely as Lunceford's or Norvo's saxes, but there's an awful lot of room between that style and the stiffness that characterizes Larry's lads. Fundamentally it's lack of rhythm —an absence of a certain, almost undefinable feel that's usually exemplified by little subleties in attack and release of notes and phrases.

The brass, on the other hand, are less stiff. As mentioned before, they're blessed with much more rhythmic parts to play, and that's basically the difference in the two sections when it comes to a matter of swinging. When it comes to sweet, the horn men are certainly no better than the reeds—in fact, so far as balance and blend go, they're not always as consistent. Still, they're a good section, made so in part by first trumpeter Rickey Traettino, one of the best lead men in the business, and by two far-better-than-average trombones. Clinton's doubling on trumpet and trombone adds a valuable depth and variety of tonal coloring.

The rhythm section, not always the steadiest in dancebandom, is easily adequate. Jack Chesleigh plays a powerful guitar and Sam Mineo a tasty piano. Walter Hardmann's bass tone is excellent; his conceptions border a bit too much on the "see-how-fast-I-can-slap" school to be classified as completely brilliant. Henry Adler's a vastly improved drummer (compared with his Red Norvo days) who plays intelligently in his soberer moments, but who, when he attempts to swing, is hampered by a passion for playing monotonously on a tinny-sounding set of high-hats.

Good Performers

Swing, as Irving Kolodin of the New York *Sun* so aptly put it, is performance. It follows that any good swing band must have good performers. The get-off men in Clinton's crew are good, but they're seldom brilliant. And that's one reason for not being able to classify Larry's band as an exceptional swing band. The dearth of any exciting soloists keeps you waiting continuously for something to happen—it's like waiting on a street corner for a friend who never shows up.

Larry doubled so that he wouldn't be caught too often waving a baton. For him only one leader, Paul Whiteman, looked good conducting, and that was almost pure show. Larry was talented, but no extrovert, he.

Clinton: "However, I categorically deny that Henry Adler was ever a lush!" Adler, by the way, is now one of New York's most successful teachers with a whole studio of instructors working under him.

Leo White plays a good clarinet, Tony Zimmers' tenor style, though inclined to be repetitious, presents some interesting notes, and Walter Smith emits a refined style of hot on both trumpet and mellophone —so conservative, in fact, that you could almost present it at court to Queen Elizabeth. How wonderful it would be, though, to hear a Fazola, or a Barnet, or a Berigan suddenly emerge from the midst of the Clinton organization! How much more inspiring it would be! And what a lifting effect it would probably have upon the rest of the boys!

But then, maybe Clinton's idea is to build a style; one that won't be overshadowed and possibly even spoiled by brilliant but temperamental soloists. If his ultimate goal is only a good, commercial, style band —well, Mr. Clinton, you have arrived. But if he wants to reach truly great heights as a leader of a swing band, he must enlist the aid of musicians whose individual performances (as well as whose conceptions within sections) can produce the excitement that's part of this thing called swing. Simon says B plus.

Later listening to Tony convinced me I was way wrong here. The guy had a lovely way of phrasing and a gorgeous tone, and he could swing, too. Larry agrees: "I still consider Tony Zimmers one of the fine tenor jazz stylists of our time, and you might be surprised at how many latter-day savants and studio jazz men agree. Unfortunately, Tony was only with me for a few months, and never seemed to find a niche for his inventiveness before the war intervened." Zimmers was one of the first top musicians drafted and later erroneously reported killed in action.

Larry never did aim to scale the swing band heights, but he sure reached his goal of a tremendously successful all-around band, especially after his hit records of *My Reverie* and *Deep Purple*, featuring Bea Wain. How come I never mentioned her, such a fine singer, and Dick Todd, such a nice guy, though then not a very good singer, in this review?

Shelly Manne on Playing Drums on
Commercial Radio Shows (April, 1949)—

The thing that got me was if I ever hit a rim-shot on a program like Manhattan Merry-Go-Round, forty musicians would turn around at once and wonder what happened!

JIMMIE LUNCEFORD
(A)

Jimmie Lunceford and His Orchestra.

Saxes: (1) Willie Smith, (2) Joe Thomas, (3) Ted Buckner, (4) Earl Carruthers, (5) Dan Grissom. Trumpets: (1) Eddie Tompkins, (2) Paul Webster, (3) Sy Oliver. Trombones: (1) James Young, (2) Russell Bowles, (3) Elmer Crumbley. Piano: Edwin Wilcox. Guitar: Albert Norris. Bass: Mose Allen. Drums: James Crawford. Vocals: Smith, Thomas, Grissom, Tompkins, Oliver and Young.

Background

This band, composed almost entirely of college graduates, was organized some years back in Memphis. Since then it's been one of the country's most consistently successful road bands. In September it opens at the Southland, in Boston, for eight weeks with three NBC shots per week.

A previous review appeared in these columns just two years ago. At that time the band was playing in manager Harold Oxley's Larchmont Casino spot. Hindered by sloppy playing of ballads and far too many displays of unnecessary screeching, it rated a B plus then. Now—well, read on:

The Jimmie Lunceford band: (front row) Sy Oliver, Paul Webster, Eddie Tompkins, Eddie Wilcox, Lunceford, Willie Smith, Dan Grissom, Joe Thomas, Earl Carruthers; (back row) Russell Bowles, Elmer Crumbley, Eddie Durham, Jimmie Crawford, Al Norris, Mose Allen

At Present

When that Jimmie Lunceford band is right, there isn't an outfit in the land that can outswing it—or perhaps even swing as high. Lately it's been just right and on three separate occasions has handed this scribe three of the year's biggest boots.

Occasion number one was in New York's Loew's State, where one morning the Lads of Lunceford put on such a colossal stage show that it occasioned occasion number two that same evening. The third "Place de Sending" was up in South Norwalk, Conn., in Leo Miller's Roton Point spot, where Jimmie's boys settled into a groove so deep that they had to be chiseled out with pick and shovel and shipped home.

For combined spirt, enthusiasm and swinging musicianship, the Lunceford band had no equal. I can't remember any other band swinging as high and with as much fun as this one did. No wonder I kept following it around that month.

Potentialities Realized

Nobody (not even this supposedly harsh reviewer) has ever denied the great potentialities of Lunceford's band. What had been lacking heretofore, though, was consistency—the boys would wind you way up and then let you way down with sad displays of out-of-tune slop. Such a reactionary condition doesn't exist any more in Jimmie's regime, it seems, for the men now shell out consistently great swing.

Amusing. Whoever supposed I was a harsh reviewer? Maybe I did. My harshest critics have accused me of being too easy.

One of the main reasons for the improvement is the arrangements. All of them—not just a few—swing in some way or other—it may be very slow or very fast, but it's still swing. Jimmie has veered from both the bad ballad stuff that used to bring everybody down, and the very unnecessary and equally ineffective series of screeching killer-dillers that used to kill nothing except the brasses' lips. Now he patterns his manuscript more or less upon a Sy Oliverian model (remember *Four or Five Times* and *My Blue Heaven?*) with simple, offbeat rhythm and wonderful background figures supplying the momentum.

Sy Oliver disagrees about the "slop." "Give me a for instance," he writes.

Unnecessary to everyone except, perhaps, Irving Mills, who helped the band get going. Mills Music published those screeching killer-dillers.

Great Improvement

Another great, almost astounding, improvement is in the sax section. Formerly this used to be a unit in which Willie Smith led as he pleased and the others followed as they pleased, with all of them tuning up as nobody pleased. But that system has been relegated to the ranks of the "we-know-better-now" species, with the result that Lunceford now has a sax section which phrases all those marvelous figures well together, and which plays in tune. Credit for such an improvement must go to the men themselves, of course. Joe Thomas on tenor, whose previous efforts would have qualified him for the presidency of the "To-hell-with-what-how-and-when-the-first-man-phrases" Society, now blends nobly, while Ted Buckner, a comparatively recent addition on alto, proves himself not only an able section man, but also a truly thrilling soloist on his horn.

From Oliver: "George—at this point I get the feeling that you have your bands confused. The state of affairs you describe simply never existed. Of course, you were young then (and clever with words?)."

111

Leadman Willie Smith has aided the general condition by kindly omitting many of the flowers he used to incorporate in his lead overphrasing, and, moreover, has made remarkable strides in the development of a truly beautiful alto tone. And finally, as you go down in the section, there's Earl Carruthers deep on his baritone: one of the most rhythmic of all sax men, and a truly great trucker and poser in his own right.

Not So Great

Another great, almost astounding, improvement isn't in the brass section because (1) the brass section two years ago was better than the saxes, and (2) the brass section just hasn't improved much, anyway. It's still a great sextet, mind you. Eddie Tompkins is even a more brilliant and ingenious first trumpeter than he used to be, and James Young's trombone has aided the tonal qualifications no end, but (and this is a great big "BUT") the six men are inclined to be slightly sloppy. That condition is exemplified mostly in the most obvious way: weak intonation. The night the band was caught in Connecticut, for example, Young played consistently flat and Paul Webster just as sharp. True, swing implies variations on the conceptions of the tune, but not of the "in-tune!" The section is potentially too sensational to permit carelessness to interfere as much as it does. In its phrasing, in its brilliancy, and in its showmanship it has too much to give.

The Lunceford rhythm section needs no verbal emulation. Hear it and marvel! Here's complete rhythmic simplicity supplying a swing that few rhythm sections have ever achieved—and supplying it consistently, as well. As John Hammond would say, this is "complete rhythmic integration." Each man knows and feels instinctively what his compatriots are doing and are about to do. The result is tremendous lift, either in an easy, offbeat style, or in a more intense drive. Heaps of credit go to drummer Jimmy Crawford—as one member of the band put it: "man, sometimes before the job I feel beat, but just as soon as I feel Jimmy behind me, I'm right in there again swingin'!" The energetic and personable Mose Allen on bass adds plenty both rhythmically and spiritually, while Al Norris and Ed Wilcox aid nobly if only because of their impeccable taste.

Swing bands have their exciting soloists and Lunceford's is no exception. The aforementioned Ted Buckner is one. Equally as thrilling, and sharing honors in this reviewer's estimation, is Sy Oliver's trumpet: rhythmic, mean, dirty with a mute, and then again, when open, pretty, delicate, and clean.

There are others worthy of much mention. Among the brass take trombonist Elmer Crumbley for his hot and Jimmy Young for his sweet. Among the saxes

The spirited Carruthers was one of the few musicians who actually seemed to be dancing while he was seated and playing. He infected both his fellow bandsmen and the kids out front.

Oliver: "The brass was *never* better than the saxes."

At this time he wasn't known as "Trummy" Young—or at least nobody told me.

Oliver: "Surprisingly perceptive for such a young critic(?)."

Wilcox should also have been cited for his great arrangements. Sy Oliver, who has pointed out that he often gets credit for things Eddie wrote, calls Wilcox the band's unsung hero.

Kids Oliver: "Here you begin to show signs of your coming maturity and good judgment."

there's Willie Smith's oft-heard alto and Joe Thomas' tenor, while from the rhythm section every now and then spring some screwy guitar passages from Albert Norris.

Vocal Department

Solo proficiences extend to the vocal department with the trio, composed of Tompkins, Oliver and Smith, copping top honors. Oliver himself sings far too few solos: he's easily the most exciting vocalist in the band. Smith's novelties are cute without ever becoming too cute; Dan Grissom has improved greatly and will undoubtedly continue to do so once he overcomes more affectations, while Joe Thomas and Jimmy Young are easily adequate along more scaterian lines.

No appraisal of the band's work can be complete without much favorable mention of its showmanship. Few bands seem to have as much fun on the stand as do Lunceford's Lads. They're sending themselves as much as they're moving the watchful cats, and when a band does that, it can't help winning over the crowd. Moreover, there are plenty of visually colorful but never corny effects. Add those to smart selections of tunes and a decidedly winning smile from Leader Lunceford, and you can see why promoter after promoter wants to get the band back and why it's been so consistently successful on the road over a period of years with practically no build-up whatsoever on the usually much coveted airwaves.

Yes, Lunceford's band has made grand strides within the past two years. From a band that was truly great at times, it's developed into an outfit that's thrilling all the time. Such talent can't be denied. With great gusto, the September, 1936 ante is upped, and Simon says A.

Repeats Oliver: "Here you begin to show signs of your coming maturity and good judgment."

A polite way of saying I didn't like him. In fact, I thought he was terrible, especially when compared with Henry Wells, who had been singing ballads with the band.

Manager Harold Oxley and Lunceford found there was more money to be made on one-nighters and so the band was seldom booked into any spots with radio wires. There weren't many in which black bands could play anyway. But after awhile the guys began to get so fed up with the constant traveling that they started to leave. That was the beginning of the end, because few of the replacements could match the spirit and musicianship of the originals. They were one uniquely talented group!

RED NORVO

(A)

Red Norvo and His Orchestra. Hotel Pennsylvania, New York, and The Meadowbrook, Cedar Grove, N.J. CBS and MBS wires.

Saxes: (1) Frank Simeone, (2) George Berg, (3) Hank D'Amico, (4) Maurice Kogan. Trumpets: (1) Johnny Owens, (2) Jack Palmer, (3) Barney Zudecoff. Trombones: (1) Wes Heins, (2) Al George. Piano: Bill Miller. Guitar: T. Allen Hanlon. Bass: Pete Peterson. Drums: George Wettling. Vocals: Mildred Bailey, Terry Allen. Leader and xylophone: Red Norvo.

Background

Norvo started his band as a sextet in New York's Famous Door two and a half years ago; first started adding more men, then wife Mildred Bailey, and then still more men. Of the original group only Pete Peterson remains. The band's most important spots have been the Syracuse Hotel (guess where!), the Blackhawk in Chicago, the Palomar in Los Angeles, the Sir Francis in Frisco, and the Commodore and Pennsylvania Hotels in New York.

Norvo was reviewed in his septet stage in the March, 1936 issue, receiving an A rating.

Red Norvo leads his band of (front row) vocalist Lew Hurst, saxists Slats Long, Frank Simeone, Herbie Haymer, (back row) drummer Maurice Purtill, bassist Pete Peterson, trumpeters Stewie Pletcher and Bill Hyland, (behind palms) trumpeter-arranger Eddie Sauter and trombonist Leo Moran. This was the band that played even softer and subtler swing than the later edition that is reviewed on these pages

At Present

This band used to be noted for its "soft, subtle swing." Remember? Well, during the past couple of years the "soft" has disappeared almost completely, the "subtle" has been minimized, but the "swing" still remains—and how!

The softness and the subtlety were wonderful stuff and it's too bad that Norvo had to lose them. He could keep them, and did keep them, so long as he played in hotel room spots, but once he started hitting the road, he found out that he had to bang it out to convince the ickies out front that his was truly a swing band. And Norvo, like at least half the bandleaders, is not a millionaire, and therefore had to succumb to the ickies' demands.

Those Arrangements!

Thanks to arranger Eddie Sauter, though, Red has still been able to retain a definite style and a definite swing. Not enough praises can be heaped at one time upon the shoulders of that brilliant manuscripter: he can arrange the most marvelous swing that really kicks out and then turn right around and produce some of the most knocked-out, gorgeous sweet arrangements you've ever heard. He's responsible for the style of the band and in more ways than one for its success.

Of course, Eddie couldn't do so well if he didn't have some great artists to build his arrangements around. Most of his sweet works are written with Mildred Bailey's voice in mind—which must be an inspiration to any arranger! As Mildred explained recently: "When I hear a new song, I immediately get definite ideas of how I want to sing it and how the entire arrangement should sound. And without fail, Eddie comes through with just the kind of an arrangement I'd been dreaming of—only better!" Which must be an inspiration to la belle Bailey, whose vocals, in turn, are such an inspiration to so many of us.

That Band!

There always has to be a band to play arrangements, and no matter how good the manuscript may be, if the band isn't good the result is likely to be exceedingly nebulous. Right now Red has, musically speaking, the best band he's ever had. It doesn't swing as much as it did in its subtler days at the Famous Door or even in Syracuse, but it's capable of producing much finer music—and it does!

There isn't a bad section in the band. Not even a mediocre one. The saxes, upon whom there's an unusual amount of emphasis, achieve a fine blend, and largely through the free and easy phrasing of Frank Simeone (who just returned to the band after a long absence) produce a fine swing almost by themselves.

At its swinging softest, the Norvo band used to insinuate itself very subtly into your conscious (and subconscious) with its light, airy drive. It was almost hypnotic and was the perfect example for those of us who fought the cliché of the day, namely that swing was nothing but a lot of noise. As samples of what the band sounded like then, listen to (if you can locate them) some of its late 1936 and early 1937 Brunswick recordings, especially *A Porter's Love Song to a Chamber Maid, It Can Happen to You, I Would Do Anything for You* and *Remember*. Especially *Remember*.

All the guys in the band looked up to Mildred. They were pretty scared of her, too, because in addition to her tremendous singing talent, she could come on awfully strong. A warm, spirited woman, unhappy because of a chronic weight problem, she was one of the very few singers of her era who sounds every bit as good now as she did then. Which is some kind of a true test of talent.

Simeone, a short, squat Italian who looked like a waiter in a beer joint, blew a soft, sensuous, almost jug-toned sax lead. Without him the band never achieved its full subtlety.

115

The brass isn't as easy but is much more powerful. Both number one men, trumpeter Johnny Owens and trombonist Wes Heins, have brilliant tones. Unlike the saxes, though, the brass hits you directly with direct punches, whereas the saxes, with their sliding into and off notes and phrases, insinuate themselves into your very being. Both have their good points, though the reed section fits more closely into the pattern of Norvo's basic swing style.

Simple Rhythm

Backed by all this is a rhythm section that's steady and unobtrusive, sticking mostly to a pretty simple and straight four-four. Drummer George Wettling is a miraculously improved musician: it's almost impossible to believe that this clean, tasty percussionist is the same man who about a year ago used to wreak havoc with Bunny Berigan's band. Pete Peterson is still the same fine bassist he was in March, 1936, with a much better bass and consequently improved tone, while you'd never think from looking at him that Allen Hanlon could produce such a strong, solid guitar. But he does!

There are other men in the band deserving of much individual commendation. Foremost is leader Norvo himself, who's proved conclusively that xylophonic prowess should not be measured by how fast you can play with the greatest number of hammers. Originally the subtlety of the band was built pretty much around the highly original stuff he used to hammer out. More than any other musician in the band he retains just those qualities—he's a man of whom you'll never tire: his imagination and rhythmic delicacy put him in a class with only one or two others (per example, Teddy Wilson) in the world of swing.

Those Soloists!

There are other soloists who are far above swing par. Hank D'Amico plays a brilliant clarinet that's rivaled only by his alto work. Newly discovered George Berg produces some tenor stuff that comes directly from a heart that must have a swing beat all of its own. Trumpeter Jack Palmer (another recent addition) emits dirty, original passages with sort of a pretty, mudpie-slinging effect, while Wes Heins gets off nicely within the scope of a truly phenomenal range.

The two vocal soloists deserve much space too. Mildred Bailey's singing is so well known and so universally appreciated that any further comment here is superfluous. You don't have to be told how good she is. However, you might have to be told how good Terry Allen is. This west coast lad sings with fine feeling, possesses a strong, mellow, well-trained voice, and all in all is heads and shoulders above almost

Terry had a great voice, very masculine-sounding, but, even though he phrased nicely, he never could seem to loosen up completely. His singing sounded as if he were taking himself too seriously, which sometimes he did.

116

every one of the band vocalists today. It's just because he has had to buck up against comparisons with the established Mildred Bailey that he doesn't achieve more national recognition.

Those Faults!

Don't think from all this that there's nothing wrong with Norvo's band. It has its weak points. The brass, for example, is not yet settled: the section plays much too loud a good deal of the time and because of its forcing doesn't achieve the freedom in phrasing necessary for the completion of the Norvo style. The rhythm section, though it is the oldest in the band, is not yet completely integrated, while Wettling's wood-block and bass-rim stick work behind most of D'Amico's passages is much more suitable for a Dixieland band —something which Norvo's outfit definitely is not.

But the dancers don't notice those things, so maybe they don't matter too much. What Norvo does very successfully, so far as the hoofers are concerned, is offer contrast. Mildred Bailey's singing and the magnificent arrangements create most of the mellow moods, while the band, when left alone, shells out in accepted shock troop formation. Even within the blastier arrangements there is contrast, for there's almost always a soft xylophone passage from Norvo. Red, by the way, is missing a big bet by not featuring himself more. Musically speaking and commercially speaking his work is tops and there's no reason in the world why he shouldn't emphasize it much more than he does. Moreover, he has a helluva swell personality up front, which he could employ successfully much more often. He should be just as much an identifying feature, even more so, of the band as are the Bailey vocals and the Sauter arrangements.

But even with Red in the semi-background, Simon says A.

Red was, and still is, a pretty shy, retiring guy, with a pixieish sense of humor that only sometimes got across to his public. Maybe if he'd been a little more aggressive, people might have noticed him more. But how much can a guy be noticed behind a xylophone set? It wasn't like blowing a horn. And besides, Mildred came on so strong that there wasn't room for two aggressive personalities.

SAMMY KAYE

(B minus)

Sammy Kaye and His Orchestra. Palm Room of Hotel Commodore, New York. CBS and MBS wires.

Saxes: (1) George Brandon, (2) Charlie Wilson, (3) Andy Russett, (4) Jimmy Brown. Trumpets: (1) Frank O'Blake, (2) Lloyd Gilliom. Trombone: Ozzie Resch. Piano: Ralph Flanagan. Guitar: Tommy Ryan. Bass: Paul Cunningham. Drums: Ernie Rudisill. Vocals: Wilson, Brown, Ryan and The Three Barons. Leader and clarinet: Sammy Kaye.

Background

Kaye's band broke into prominence about a year ago via its work at the Statler in Cleveland. Since then it's been turning in highly successful stands, both one-night and much longer, in the eastern part of the country mostly and has recorded for Vocalion and Bluebird. It made its New York debut at the Commodore late in September and is scheduled to remain there until the first of next year, at least.

The following comments are all Sammy Kaye's:

"B Minus—That's better than I did at Ohio U. getting my Civil Engineering Degree. Thanks."

"Pretty good cast. Ralph Flanagan became a pretty famous bandleader and Jimmie Brown became and still is very big singing jingles."

The Ohio University band that helped Sammy Kaye get his engineering degree

With the aid of some beautifully poetic lines, some already accepted Kyserian tricks, and fair musicianship and some good beanwork on his own part, Sammy Kaye has become a sudden commercial success. Good for him! But how about a bit of analyzing of those points:

Those poetic lines—ah!

"Swing and Sway
With Sammy Kaye!"

The "swing" of Sammy Kaye, it can truthfully be described as follows:

End of description of Sammy Kaye's swing.

The "sway" of Sammy Kaye is best exemplified by the weaving of jitterbugs who gather in front of the bandstand and watch. The band itself doesn't sway. Come to think of it, what is meant by a band's "sway?"

But let's stop analyzing the poetry for a while and, leaving the public's point of view, dwell a bit upon the musical aspects of the organization.

Soft and Mellow

It's effective dance music. It's soft, unobtrusive, and capable of producing a fairly mellow mood upon the majority of its listeners. The rhythm is simple and easy to keep time to. Both the melody sections are obviously well-rehearsed, phrasing and blending very neatly among themselves. What's more, the band is excellently routined: like a group of West Point cadets, each one seems to know just what the other is going to do. Not a thing is left to imagination or inspiration, the total result being a magnificently trained and exceedingly unoriginal group of musicians.

The Kay Kyserian influence has been noted often in many places. Suffice to say that Kyser's is much the older organization. It's interesting to note, too, that Kyser's style has become more musical and less tricky lately. Take that for what it's worth to you.

The fair musicianship has been touched upon two paragraphs ago. Of course, you can't pass final judgment upon musicians who are forced to play only one definite and very limiting style any more than you can pass upon the intelligence of some underling in an organization (say the Navy) who's permitted absolutely no leeway in the carrying out of certain definite instructions.

"Many Kyserian tricks preceded both of us, like the high trombone of Henry Theis on *Sometimes I'm Happy*, I believe his theme song. 'Swing and Sway with Sammy Kaye'—*Variety* once mentioned that phrase as a million dollar phrase. The phrase is not broken down into two components, as you did. Swing and Sway flows together."

"Thanks for the 'excellently routined' and 'magnificently trained' compliments. In that category I place Hal Kemp, Glenn Miller, Benny Goodman (outside of jazz choruses), etc."

"Singing song titles came at Ohio U. when we copied a record by Gus Arnheim of 'I'm doing that thing, getting that swing, falling in love.' That's not the title, but the whole band sang it in the intro. After we saturated the public with our stereotyped style, we also modified. Three of our biggest hits were not at all in that style, *Daddy, It Isn't Fair, Harbor Lights*."

"On musicianship, our motto has been, 'The tone is greater than the technique.'"

Therefore, if, like this reviewer, you can't stomach the clichés in overphrasing, the exaggerated vibrato of the first trumpet, the continual glissing of the trombone, or the stiff, crunchy rhythm, don't go ahead and classify the musicians as lousy. After all, they're not being given a chance to exhibit *musical* talents— like a pup in a vaudeville dog-act they're told to go through their tricks, and when they're finished showing off for the folks, as they've been told to, they'll receive a nice tidy sum of money. Like the well-trained canine, they're well fed. Yet, 'tis said that in many cases the poorer mongrel is often a much more satisfied animal. It's quite conceivable that such an analogy can be carried over to musicians, too.

Don't blame the unnatural phrasing and vibratos on the musicians themselves, then. They're probably very excellent within the limits of the style. But they're not perfect, because they exhibit certain deficiences that would be obvious in any style. For example, the rhythm rushes many modulations, and when the band is playing loud and fast (swing?), almost drowns out the melody section. What's more, drummer Rudisill slaps a set of high-hats monotonously and ineffectually, resulting in noise more than rhythm, while bassist Cunningham treats his string bass (he plays mostly tuba) in pretty similar fashion. Then, Frank O'Blake's trumpet tone suffers very much in comparison with Lloyd Gilliom's, though to the former go most of the first parts. In fairness to him, though, it should be noted that he phrases with more sensitivity than Gilliom does. The individual efforts of each to play hot trumpet deserve less mention than this sentence.

Where the band does fall down lamentably is on the showmanship angle—and you'd think that Kaye would capitalize on that. It has little to offer to the patrons other than a vocal trio and three good singers. In that connection, note that Tommy Ryan is a really fine vocalist, a swell combination of a pleasing personality and a sweet tenor voice.

But for some reason or other the band runs through everything very mechanically with long faces, never seeming (even) to enjoy its own music. The general formality is accentuated by the boys' wearing stiff mess jackets, which this reviewer had always thought had gone out of smart bands and spots along with the laughing saxophones. Kaye himself is an effective medium between dancers and band and deserves commendation for his compliance with and renditions of requests.

In toto, then, Sammy Kaye plays fairly well an unoriginal style, which was not musical even when it was new. His appeal is definitely not to lovers of music nearly so much as it is to just plain lovers. For, to the

"You must have been a poor soul, George, 'listening in the dark.' Had you seen the potential, and then perhaps taken part of the action, like Jim Peppe did with me and the Schribmans [sic] and Michaud and Marshard did with the others, instead of being an oracle of 'what?'" [Note: Sammy never did complete the sentence, but I presume he meant I'd now be as rich as he is. Which would be nice. He's worth millions, they tell me. And taking part of some band's action wouldn't have been hard for an influential critic and editor to get. Maybe some did. But I chose to remain that "poor soul," that "oracle of 'what.'" And so now I'll still let Sammy pick up all the dinner tabs.]

120

average ear, his music is soothing, and you don't have to be told what a bit of soothing music can do to help along your romance. Kaye should thank the guy who invented love.

And so, because of the band's emotional appeal and its almost military discipline (which from certain standards must be admired), the Kaye Krew must be judged better than merely adequate. Accordingly, Simon says B minus.

"The band you criticize went on to making two Hollywood movies, playing every major hotel, theatre and ballroom in the country, had its own radio show (Sunday Serenade) for about 12 years, its own TV show (So You Want to Lead a Band), plus other TV shows, one on which you worked with me (before I saw this review—joke). Not bad for B minus."

Lionel Hampton on Racial Equality (March, 1938)—

A man can be pink, white, black or orange. But as long as his stuff is what the doctor ordered, he's got something. But definitely.

121

ARTIE SHAW KICKS WITH "SEABISCUIT GUSTO"

Fine Arrangements and Spirit Aid "A" Outfit . . . Simplicity A Keynote . . . Saxes Sometimes Sloppy . . . "Garages" Pop Up in Rhythm

(A)

Artie Shaw and His Orchestra. Blue Room of Hotel Lincoln. NBC wires.

Saxes: (1) Les Robinson, (2) Tony Pastor, (3) Hank Freeman, (4) George Auld. Trumpets: (1) Bernie Privin, (2) John Best, (3) Chuck Peterson. Trombones: (1) Les Jenkins, (2) George Arus, (3) Harry Rodgers. Piano; Bob Kitsis. Guitar: Al Avola. Bass: Sid Weiss. Drums: Buddy Rich. Vocals: Helen Forrest and Pastor. Leader and clarinet: Artie Shaw.

Background

Shaw, who used to clarinet in all the big radio stations, started his first band almost three years ago. It was a fine dixieland-string quartet outfit that wasn't loud enough for the ickies but which rated (musically) a strong A minus (cf. Oct. '36 Band Reviews). A bit over a year ago, Artie changed to the brass-sock style, captured a lot of air time and attention from Boston, and gradually started a climb to greater national prominence.

An early photo of the Artie Shaw band with trombonists Harry Rodgers, George Arus and Russ Brown, drummer Cliff Leeman, saxists Tony Pastor, George Koenig and Hank Freeman, plus Artie's left hand

At Present

Shaw's is a great band—a great band not only because it really kicks out freely with Seabiscuit gusto when it trots out its swing, but also because it can play much prettier stuff than just about any of the ranking swing outfits (don't count Tom Dorsey). What makes those pretty tunes especially effective is their not getting away from the general motif of the unit. The slow music (dinner sets as contrasted with supper stuff) is prettily scored and played but still retains a good swing.

Credit, in the first place, the arrangers, notably Jerry Gray, Rodgers and Shaw. Credit the men too, of course. And if you get your kicks from Shaw's music, you can even go so far as thanking the Lord that you've caught the boys when they're still fresh and coming up. For there's nothing like the impetus and inspiration of feeling that you're arriving someplace rather than that you've already arrived, to give a band a verve and consistency of performance that'll seldom find it NOT swinging. It makes you stop and wonder whether this band will sound as fresh and happy when it's as old as Goodman's. Looking over the top white swing bands, you'll find just one *veteran* outfit that kicks with as much abandon as it did when it first started out, and that's the Bob Crosby crew. When you stop to analyze that, you'll find out that the reason is the healthy esprit de corps that continues to pervade in everything this group does. If Shaw can maintain that, he'll be swinging years hence too.

Simple

There's nothing fundamentally new in Shaw's style. It's simple, and because of its very simplicity it swings. There's not a lot of cluttering up of parts. Instead there are easy rhythm figures, modern innuendoes, and so forth, that make the boys feel the manuscript. And when you've got the guys in your band feeling the stuff they're playing, then you're more than half-way there.

In this connection, note too that everything is made simple for the dancers as well. For Shaw, unlike many swing band leaders, doesn't hit a lot of killer-diller tempos in which it's just a matter of the musicians or the dancers pooping first. Instead, Artie really beats out fine time. He does what few white leaders do and that is beat out a number of measures to himself until he hits just the right tempo, and then passing it on to his men. There's another reason for the band's sounding natural.

Faults

Strictly upon a musical basis (leaving style and inspiration out of the picture for the moment) the band's

Writes Artie: "Who am I to argue with this, at this late date?" Seabiscuit, for those of you who didn't listen to Clem McCarthy, was the top racehorse of the times. Clem McCarthy, for those of you who didn't ride Seabiscuit, was the top racehorse broadcaster.

To quote Artie: " 'Simplicity is the single most difficult thing to achieve.'—Shaw—not G. B., but A.S."

good too, though it's not perfect. Its greatest assets are its ensemble phrasing and its intonation. The tones are almost as good. But there are a few weaker spots:

(1) The saxes, though often brilliant, are inclined to be sloppy. It's true not so much in attacking and phrasing as it is in the holding of notes. If you listen closely you'll notice that the men don't always follow Robinson; one or more may release or hold on longer than their leader. As a result there's not the consistent homogeneity you'd expect in a group of this sort.

Too Rich Rhythm

(2) The rhythm section is apt to play too much. The recent advent of Buddy Rich is probably the main cause. Buddy is a brilliant percussionist: he has tremendous technique, he's steady, and he gets a fine swing. But like so many drummers who have grown up in the Krupa era, he's cursed with the misconception that a drummer's supposed to do much more than supply a good background. As a result Buddy, in his enthusiasm, plays too much drums, consequently breaking up the general rhythmic effect. If you'll recall a few paragraphs back, one of the highlights of Shaw's style and swing is its simplicity: that's the main reason for drummer Cliff Leeman's (now ill) fitting in as well as he did. But with Rich building garages, beautiful as they are, a lot is taken from the style and the swing too. That's true not only because

A Shavian (A.S. not G.B.) complaint: "How about this for nit-picking, George? That was, and records prove it, probably the finest 4-man sax *section* that ever came down the pike—and I truly mean that!" Simon (G.T. not Simple) wants to know how to prove a probability. Opines A.S.: "Oh well, maybe you caught us on an off night . . . ?" As I recall it, the band was off on Sundays. I think I reviewed it on a Thursday.

A Shaw reaction: "Maybe, but Buddy was, in my opinion, perhaps the single greatest (white) drummer that ever hit the American (whole wide world?) jazz scene. . . . Extravagant? . . . Nevertheless, I firmly believe it." I concur completely with Artie. I'll even eliminate the "white" qualification. It's interesting to note, though, that I was reviewing the band right after Buddy had joined it, and it's quite conceivable that he hadn't yet achieved the simplicity that Artie admits is so difficult to achieve. Certainly, Buddy soon did settle into a tremendous groove and the Shaw band began to swing as it never had with any of its previous drummers.

ARTIE SHAW'S 1939 BAND: (left to right) Chuck Peterson, Georgie Auld, Harry Rodgers, Bernie Privin, Hank Freeman, Les Jenkins, Johnny Best, Les Robinson, Shaw, Tony Pastor's shoulder, Buddy Rich, Al Avola, Sid Weiss

too much drums clutter up everything in general, but also because the rest of the rhythm section, appreciating Buddy for the truly fine technician that he is, have come under his spell (probably only temporarily). And in trying to keep pace with his brilliance, they are playing too much. But that can be remedied quite easily—as can the too loud bass drum.

Solos

Returning to the more inspirational side, you'll get your boot from a number of soloists in the band. First of all there's Shaw, rightfully picked the second greatest clarinetist in the world today (cf. results of contest last month). Then there's Tony Pastor, a vastly underrated hot tenor man with a splendid tone and a simple but pleasantly rhythmic style. Contrasted with him is the more brilliant Georgie Auld, who's improved greatly since he first started out with Berigan. He has many new melodic ideas and still retains his typical rhythmic drive. Once his tone improves, he should be even greater.

Blessed Brass

The brass is blessed with two fine blues-blowers and two men who play a more sensational hot. Southerners Johnny Best and Les Jenkins play just the lazy, beautiful hot you'd expect them to. Describing their fine work (which, incidentally, those of you who aren't schooled in the blues style might not appreciate) is easiest by drawing comparisons with men more familiar to you: Best's with Yank Lausen's and Jenkins' with Jack Teagarden's. Tommy Dorsey, by the way, has often moaned to this writer: "Oh, if I could only play jazz like Jenkins!" The other two more brilliant men are trumpeter Bernie Privin, the lad with the biting tone and prolific conceptions, and trombonist George Arus, a reformed violinist, who plays an almost shockingly barrelhouse horn—but really good!

Other Solos

Three more soloists are worth your attention: Bob Kitsis, the Harvard grad who just joined the band, and who in his few featured spots plays some fine piano; Helen Forrest, the very best of the name band girl singers who phrases marvelously and definitely sings in tune; and Tony Pastor, whose amusing scat vocals (especially when you see him) are chawming, indeed.

Other credit should be given to Les Robinson for his fine conceptions of phrasing; to Chuck Peterson, who occasionally leads the brass and very brilliantly, too; to Al Avola, a strong, steady guitarist who's very much responsible for the solidity of the rhythm section; to Sid Weiss, an all-around fine, steady bassist,

"Wha?" notes Artie. "*At that time*, I was playing second to nobody—says he, modestly! As for who could maybe *now* be second best or first best clarinet player in the world, I should in any case be excluded from consideration—even as third, fourth, fifth, you name it—since, as you know, I have not been a clarinet player at all for the last sixteen years . . . . Could be that maybe now I'm the first, second, third, fourth of fifth best *non*-clarinet player in the world?"

Les used to play in Tommy's band, and late at night, Tommy would feature Jenkins, instead of himself, on a series of jazz trombone passages.

and to Hank Freeman, whose outstanding contribution is his baritone work.

And that just about covers the entire band. Quite a bit of coverage it is. Pleasant coverage, too. Here's hoping it'll remain as pleasant for a long, long time. Musically, the band is bound to improve, but if it is going to improve in its entirety, the enthusiasm that's prevalent now will have to remain. That'll be tough, but Shaw has overcome tougher obstacles. Simon says A.

Hank later wound up as lead alto saxist in the Glenn Miller AAF Band.

Unfortunately, the man who soon lost his enthusiasm completely was Artie himself: later that year he junked the band and ran off to Mexico.

Count Basie on Bop Musicians (November, 1948)—

If a guy is gonna play good bop, he has to have sort of a bop soul. It's not good, even on paper, unless you have the feeling for it.

JIMMY DORSEY SWINGS TO HIGH HEAVEN!

And Makes You Think You're There When He Plays Sweet, Finds Simon While Re-Reviewing "Most Underrated Band"

(A)

Jimmy Dorsey and His Orchestra. Reviewed at Hotel New Yorker, New York.

Saxes: (1) Milton Yaner, (2) Herbie Haymer, (3) Sam Rubinwitch, (4) Charles Frasier. Trumpets: (1) Ralph Muzzillo, (2) Shorty Sherock. Trombones: Bobby Byrne, Sonny Lee, Don Matteson. Piano: Fred Slack. Guitar: Roc Hillman. Bass: Jack Ryan. Drums: Ray McKinley. Vocals: Helen O'Connell, Bob Eberly, Matteson, McKinley. Leader, sax and clarinet: Jimmy Dorsey.

Background

Jimmy's been leading his own band ever since he and brother Tommy decided that water's thicker than blood in the summer of 1935. He's played spots all over the country; he's been on the Kraft radio commercial, and he's recording for Decca. The outfit was reviewed in these columns only last May, when it received an A minus.

At Present

Jimmy Dorsey's is definitely the most underrated band in the land. Not only that, it's also the most improved. And, to go one step further, it's one of the very few great dance orchestras in the world!

Some of you, who took seriously a serious review of the outfit in last May's METRONOME, may remember that at that time it possessed one glaring weakness. Summed briefly, it was a lack of consistency. The review went on to state that unless that lack were obviated, the band would never realize its potentialities. Well, the boys finally have mastered a consistency—and thus the raves that follow:

The band not only swings to high heaven, but it's capable of producing a brand of sweet that'll make you think you're there. A year or so ago it could do

Ray McKinley recently described the earlier edition of the band as "kind of a patchwork band. I guess you'd say 'heterogeneous' was the word to describe it." Notes Bob Eberly: "I think the Kraft radio show with Bing deterred and slowed its growth in spite of its being in Big Time. Accurate criticism, though, George."

127

neither too well, chiefly because of arrangements that (1) had no definite swing pattern, and (2) were none too interesting or mood-creating when it came to sweet. Now, though, thanks to Toots Camaratta and in a lesser degree to Don Redman, it's blessed with magnificent manuscript which finally permits the musicians in the band to show their true worth.

Not only has that manuscript improved, but the sax section too has taken remarkable strides. It has achieved a fine blend, good intonation, and phrases with far greater feeling and imagination. Much credit goes to leadman Milt Yaner on that last score. And both tenor men, Charlie Frasier and Herbie Haymer, have blossomed into fine section men, with the latter still blowing some thrilling solos.

Trumpets Caught Short

The brass, though still handicapped by its abbreviated setup, remains every bit as good as it was. Workhorse Ralph Muzzillo's leading is prodigious. Shorty Sherock's turning into one of the truly great hot trumpeters of our day. And trombonist Bobby Byrne, who plays as pretty a horn as you'd ever expect to hear, is also turning in some good hot.

The rhythm section is great. Last year, this reviewer went into ecstasies over Ray McKinley's drumming. That goes double this year. The extra bouquets aren't his fault entirely, though. Here, once more, heave petals upon the arrangers. Last year the rhythm was seldom permitted to settle into a groove (pardon the trite expression). Emphasis was continually shifting from four to two beats in a measure and back again. Today, however, the band has pretty much forgotten the dixieland stuff and is concentrating more upon a four-four drive. Just listen to it once to see how much it kicks.

Yes, Jimmy's band has developed a style. But it's not limited just to swing tunes. For the Dorseyites play their pop ballads as if they mean something too. Almost any swing band going today puts little emphasis upon the tunes that the country's humming. You know yourself how boring the music of Goodman, Shaw, and very often Tommy Dorsey, gets when it struggles through a pop tune. Apparently to them it's just a necessary evil, through which they dash with little or no effort in a mad endeavor to get to their killer-dillers. Jimmy Dorsey's gone a step further, though, by trotting out arrangements of pops that are really interesting. That goes not only for the chord structure and sequences, but even more so for the structure of the arrangements as a whole.

Loud and Soft

And one thing more that's extremely important, and which almost all bands overlook, is dynamics.

Toots Camaratta later became Tutti Camarata and finally just Camarata. He'd been playing lead trumpet in the band, but Jimmy must have decided he'd be more valuable arranging full-time.

Even having two trumpets in place of the usual three or four must have been some sort of concession on Jimmy's part. Originally the band had just one trumpet! Says Eberly: "Ralph Muzzillo needed help over a mental 'mouthpiece disease'—potentially regal but blinded by a persistent idea that mouthpieces were his enemy."

The reason young Byrne began playing better hot was because Ray McKinley kept insisting that he listen to old Louis Armstrong and Jack Teagarden records. "He even threw in some of Louis' licks now and then," McKinley recalls.

Bob Eberly: "Ray McKinley was my idea of the perfect drummer."

A plausible explanation from Bob Eberly: "Instead of individuals striving for standout performances aimed at their own 'stardom,' it seemed that each, instead, became a voluntary contributor of rich, good taste that would not make ugly ripples in the main product—the sound of music. Blueprinted by Camarata, even the vocalists had their paths guarded and lit by well-thought-out voicings and flute, bass and treble passages."

Jimmy greets friend and movie actor Bob Taylor

Bob Eberly and Helen O'Connell on the Dorsey bandstand with tenor saxist Herbie Haymer and trombonist Sonny Lee

Jimmy puts tremendous emphasis upon them. Consequently you'll seldom find any of his listeners or dancers bored. You don't begin to appreciate the importance of delicacies like these until you get a chance to compare bands directly. Recently, this reviewer caught a Dorsey broadcast and a Shaw broadcast in quick succession. Right then and there he began to realize again how much more there is to listen to when a band pays strict attention to the finer points of dance music, making an effort to sustain interest throughout the thirty minutes, than there is in listening to a band which, building up to two or three killerdillers, reaches high points only a few times during a program.

Well, this is turning into quite a rave for Jimmy Dorsey's band. Obviously, that's because there's so much to rave about—all the way from its best swing arrangements that are paced so marvelously by McKinley and feature such outstanding soloists as Jimmy (especially on alto), Haymer, Sherock and Freddy Slack, to the extremely pretty, soft passages that feature vocalist Bob Eberly and trombonist Byrne. The raving doesn't mean that the band hasn't any faults, however. The men do hit some bad notes at times. And there'll continue to be plenty of them until such a time when another trumpet is added and less emphasis is put upon Ralph Muzzillo's weary lips.

But, all in all, the good points mentioned in May are even more apparent, and most of the poor points have vanished. A recent addition, in the person of Helen O'Connell, can well be added to the asset column: the lass, besides being unbelievably pretty, sings well, features a pretty upper register, but would do herself more justice if she worked a little less hard with her eyes and dimples. With her, and with Bob Eberly, one of the greats in male vocaldom, Jimmy certainly needn't bother much about his vocal department. In fact, for the first time since he's started his band, Jimmy really needn't worry too much about anything. Simon says A.

Jimmy certainly was more impressive on sax than on clarinet, except, as McKinley points out, "when he played slow ballads on clarinet in the low register." McKinley wishes Jimmy had featured himself more on trumpet. "He played the horn great—much better than Tommy played trumpet—but he had no chops."

Those same eyes and dimples remain Helen's trademarks more than thirty years later as she does television shows and commercials. A nice gal who, I understand, never has really forgiven me for some of the uncomplimentary things I used to write about her singing. And she could really look mad, too!

From Eberly: "Really sincere account. . . . Diagnosis really good and time-consuming . . . How would you like to try to be a critic with today's 38,741 groups all aiming at something? Thanks, George."

"KILLER" SAVITT BLASTS

Jan's Top Hatters Play "Loud But Good"; Sax and Singers Star As Outfit Impresses

(B plus)

Jan

Jan Savitt and His Top Hatters. Blue Room of Hotel Lincoln, New York City. NBC wire.

Saxes: (1) Gabe Gelinas, (2) Ed Klausen, (3) Frank Langone, (4) Sam Sachelle. Trumpets: (1) Jimmy Campbell, (2) Johnny Austin, (3) Jack Hansen. Trombones: (1) Fred Ohms, (2) Robert Cutshall, (3) Norman Sipple. Piano: Jack Pleis. Guitar: Guy Smith. Bass: Morris Raymond. Drums: Bob Spangler. Vocals: Carlotta Dale and Bon Bon. Chief arranger: Johnny Watson.

Background

Savitt, who arrived in this country some twenty-odd years ago (when he was two), received his musical training at Philadelphia's Curtis Institute and abroad, dwelling upon arranging and composition as well as upon violin. Several years ago his broadcasts from station WCAU began to draw much attention. Whereupon another Philly station. KYW, caught on, and made him its musical director. Came so many lucrative offers that Savitt decided to forsake the studio for the open road. However, most of his men didn't feel like breaking up their happy Quaker homes, so Jan came into the Lincoln in March with Gelinas, Hansen, Watson and the vocalists as the only holdovers and a batch of new men to break in. At the time of writing, he's planning to make a few more personnel changes.

At Present

There's a trite little phrase among musikers that runs, "He may not play good, but he sure plays loud." Merely take out the third word ("not"), and you've given a pretty fair description of Jan Savitt and His Top Hatters.

For the Savitt band does play good dance music—very good, in fact. It possesses some swell orchestrations, and some fine musicians to play them. In fact, your first impression of the Top Hatters, after listening to them for a short time in person, will quite likely be that it's one of the finest dance bands in existence.

But first impressions aren't infallible—and that's where the second half of that trite little phrase comes in. For Savitt's band throws its music at you with such gusto that after a while you find yourself backwatering (possibly along with your first impression) towards the general direction of the room's farthest wall. Either you'll be backwatering under your own steam, or else under the blast emanating from the Savitt instruments.

That Shuffle!

Jan has a style. If you've ever danced to the band, that style has probably been impressed upon you via a feeling of somebody pushing you from the rear in an attempt to make you dance just twice as fast as the band is actually playing. Actually there's nobody there—it's just Savitt's shuffle rhythm, a doubling of the basic beat (only the piano does it) in what resembles six-eight time but which really is still good old four-four.

Maybe it's the influence of that unnatural forcefulness, or maybe it's a too-conscious attempt to satisfy the jitterbug element that has caused Savitt to drive his melody men as hard as his rhythm section. The result is an almost continual brass barrage that causes the kids to cheer wildly for a while (perhaps even for the length of a broadcast) but which, because of its intensity and lack of contrast, actually becomes quite aggravating by the end of an evening.

There's too much music in the Savitt band to be hidden behind those screeches—too much good music, at that. There's a fine sax section, a quite good brass sextet, and an excellent rhythm section. And there are two wonderful vocalists. All of them are lucky enough to be faced with some mighty musical arrangements.

Sectional Discussion

The saxes are blessed with a great lead man named Gabe Gelinas, who also plays a whale of a hot alto. Their intonation is very good; the blend, except once in a great while when a tenor becomes a bit too self-assertive, is far above average.

The brass, still in semi-formative stages, carries the brunt of the attack. If it's power you want, the six men have it; tonally, they aren't given much of a chance to show off. It might possibly be that their screeching hides a multitude of musical sins. The intonation is fair; the boys, possibly because of the continual pressure, showing a tendency to play sharp. Jimmy Campbell's lead has plenty of punch. Johnny Austin's hot trumpet is still as exciting as it was in its Glenn Miller days, while trombonist Robert Cutshall also gets off some pretty fair hot.

Sounds as if the band was playing in a goldfish bowl, maybe. Or was I confused between shuffle rhythm and rippling rhythm? Anyway, pardon that mixed metaphor.

That's the beginning of "Cutty" Cutshall, who later played for Goodman and starred at Eddie Condon's for years.

132

The rhythm is the strongest of the three sections; credit Morris Raymond for his prodigous bassing, Jack Pleis for his tasty piano, and Bob Spangler for his steady drumming in the face of terrific tempos. (At the time of writing, Guy Smith, a fine guitarist, was just breaking in.)

Fine Vocalists

No dance band has two better singers than Carlotta Dale and Bon Bon. The former is great; she phrases as prettily as any lass in the business, possesses fine timbre, and really sings in tune. Her dusky compatriot, besides singing ballads well in an accustomed Crosbian manner, lets loose some fine vocal jive.

And in front of the large organization stands Savitt, an exceedingly likable chap who seems to be getting a big kick out of all that's going on. His violin professor at Curtis might be a bit shocked to see his protégé bouncing before those blasts, but Savitt, apparently, has found a new and happy way to glory. Simon says B plus.

Pleis later became a successful arranger-conductor.

Jan used to remind me of a kid with a brand new, big, frightfully expensive toy. His enthusiasm was immense, and yet at times he seemed to be overawed by famous jazz musicians and name leaders. Maybe if a set of instructions had come with that brand new toy of his, his band would have sounded even better. Jan knew what to do; what he didn't know as well was what *not* to do, and, perhaps least of all, how to fix little things that would have made his toy run better.

Count Basie on Stan Kenton (November, 1948)—

He has the most fantastic ideas of all. He's thinking right all the time.

133

MR. T's BAND AMAZES!

Magnificent Trombone by Leader Teagarden Inspires Young Outfit To Spiritual Heights

(A minus)

Jack Teagarden and His Orchestra. Reviewed at Roseland, New York. Now at Blackhawk Restaurant, Chicago. Mutual wire.

Saxes: (1) Ernie Caceres, (2) Hub Lytle, (3) Clint Garvin, (4) Johnny Van Eps, (5) Art St. John. Trumpets: (1) Charlie Spivak, (2) Lee Castaldo, (3) Karl Garvin. Trombones: (1) Jose Gutierrez, (2) Charlie McCamish, (3) Mark Bennett. Piano: Johnny Anderson. Guitar: Allen Reuss. Bass: Artie Miller. Drums: Clois Teagarden. Vocals: Linda Keene. Trombone, vocals and leader: Jack Teagarden.

Background

Teagarden's tromboning has been known the jazz-world-over for years. Brought up in the blues-blowing tradition of the southwest, he brought just that style of horn playing to Red Nichols' Five Pennies, the bands of Ben Pollack and Paul Whiteman, the Cloverdale Country Club Orchestra, and all sorts of outstanding recording units. This past February, at the expiration of his Whiteman contract, he went into the leading business in a big way, retaining John Gluskin, Tommy Dorsey's manager, as his adviser, and shelling out a financial as well as managing interest to Charlie Spivak. After breaking in at Roseland for almost two months, the outfit moved on to Chicago's Blackhawk for a twelve-week stay. MCA manages. Brunswick records.

Jack with Ernie Caceres

At Present

The musical rise of the Teagarden Troupe is really amazing. Only a bit over three months old, it already plays with the poise, the sureness, and the finesse that far older outfits try for years to achieve. Tonally, it's beautiful. Rhythmically, it's highly danceable. Spiritually, it offers bits of rare inspiration.

The style of the band is built around Teagarden, and for this reviewer at least, whose favorite of all jazz instrumentalists has always been Jack Teagarden, you couldn't find a greater musical hub. Jackson is

Jack was one of the very few jazz musicians whose talents defied time. In the mid-sixties, trombonists the world over still marveled at his facility and style. His recordings today still sound wonderfully fresh and spontaneous.

primarily a blues-blower, with a soul that expresses through his horn that undefinable feeling of beauty that goes with the complete release of pent-up emotions. As contrasted with much of the jazz you hear today, this is a melodic rather than a rhythmic means of expression. Instead of creating the tense feeling caused by modern killer-dillers, it achieves a more mellow mood—still exciting, but far more relaxing, and in many ways, a great deal more musical.

Passive Rhythm

Don't gather from this that rhythm isn't important. It's not as predominant, to be sure, for this style of jazz doesn't call for the usual insistent four-four beating. But it's still swing, a two-four, dixieland swing, with the intensity relieved by greater emphasis of the second and fourth beats. And with that intensity gone, the melody men are freer to phrase melodically (rather than with a rhythmic drive), thereby expressing as a group the true feeling of the blues style.

All this, of course, is portrayed in the first place by Teagarden's trombone with its beautiful and subtle phrasing, its broad and natural tone. But already, despite its youth, the band is catching on to the lead of its leader, and is achieving a similar ensemble style.

Active Tone

Great credit for the beautiful sound of the band goes to the brass with its clear tones, its magnificent dynamics. And at least half of the credit therein goes to first trumpeter, Charlie Spivak, whose brilliant tone, phrased as if he were literally singing through his horn, gives such beautiful shading and phrasing not only to the brass, but to the ensemble work of the entire band. There probably isn't another trumpeter in the world today who could supply to the Teagarden Troupe what Spivak has given it.

The blend of the saxes, too, is noteworthy, though, as in most two-beat, non-killer-diller bands, their work is not as strongly emphasized. Ernie Caceres makes a fine section leader, and though the quintet has not yet achieved the ultimate in tonal blend, it's still a unit that can be classified as great. Here, again, it's the ensemble phrasing of the group as a whole that makes you marvel most.

Like the saxes, the rhythm is emphasized less than in most swing bands. It's unobtrusive, yet it offers a solid foundation. Its lack of self-attraction never permits it to interfere with the all-important phrasing of both individuals and ensemble. Its backbone, young Clois Teagarden, is the most vastly improved musician in the band. When first imported from Oklahoma by his older brother, he was unreliable, both in tempo and taste. Now after some valuable

Spivak was terribly important to the band. It never sounded as brilliant or as exciting after he left.

experience, he is far more rockbound and never juts into the scope of his fellow instrumentalists.

Stop That Four-Four!

Once in a while the rhythm section, and the band as a whole, tries to shift to a four-four Goodman-Basie style of jazz, and this is without any doubt the outfit's biggest failing. Playing stuff like *One O'Clock Jump* effectively requires an entirely different kind of feel—the rhythm section must lead the attack itself with a forceful drive of which the Teagarden quartet is incapable, while the melody men must phrase much less directly, sliding in and out of phrases instead of meeting them head-on, with complete frankness, a la the open Teagarden style. What's more, killer-diller stuff like that calls for way-up tempos, and though Jack does beat off some fast times, the band, especially the rhythm section, just doesn't feel right and consequently plays with little or no swing. The band's basic style won't permit it to do whatever justice can be done to flag-wavers. Medium swing tempos are obviously the outfit's forte.

The soloists, too, falter at the shift. For, with the possible exception of trumpeter Castaldo who just joined the band, their individual jazz efforts are of the lazier, more melodic variety. And as such many of them are more than just notable. Teagarden's need no further discussion. But both tenor-men (Van Eps more so on slower tempos) phrase with great feeling in the style of the blues. Ernie Caceres, a deep Texan, plays some really thrilling clarinet passages, while young Clint Garvin from Nashville is responsible for some keen clarinet competition within the organization. The latter's seventeen-year-old brother, Karl, over in the trumpet section is probably the youngest budding star in all of dancebandom. When called upon, he plays some truly gorgeous jazz, though right now hot trumpet emphasis is upon the lips of the more driving and experienced Castaldo.

More Good Soloists

The rhythm section offers two additional and equally fine soloists. One is the flashy Johnny Anderson, whose weird and varied conceptions are cause for much admiration. The other is the Benny Goodman veteran, Allen Reuss, who once in a while is permitted to prove to the world that he can play some fine guitar solos, besides banging out a steady rhythmic lift.

Vocal efforts are divided between Linda Keene and Teagarden. The former, a lovely looking lass, has some good ideas but is prone to lapse into unnatural and affected ideas of phrasing. Jackson sings the blues type of number wonderfully, but nowadays is biting off a bit too much with flings at romantic numbers.

I can't remember her singing too well, but what a sexy-looking dame!

136

Featuring himself less on vocals, and then only upon those numbers suited to his lazy, "I-don't-give-a-damn-about-enunciation" style of emoting, would be far more effective, if only because the bad wouldn't detract from the good.

As for the band as a whole, there's hardly any bad to detract from all the good. There are a few things that time undoubtedly will correct, especially the unnecessary attempts to play a different style, but so far as the standard of dancebandom as a whole is concerned, the Teagarden Troupe has definitely arrived in its highest brackets. Already it's great music—and pure music too—and there are chances that one of these days it will be the greatest musical group jazz has ever known. Until that day Simon says A minus.

Jack never looked the romantic part either. His demeanor was rather phlegmatic. He seemed ill at ease in his role of a front man who had to socialize with the dancers. Probably simple shyness prevented his genuineness and warmth from passing beyond the confines of a bandstand.

Another Simon prediction that didn't come true. It was pretty much downhill for the band after this, even though Jack stuck it out with various editions for several more years before returning to the small group set-up. Some of his Columbia recordings, like *Red Wing* and *Somewhere a Voice Is Calling*, show the band at its best.

Benny Goodman Again on Bop (October, 1949)—

The bop musicians I've known have been fine musicians. They can read anything. [But] I wouldn't try to play bop. I'd rather listen to Bunny Berigan's *I Can't Get Started*.

BARNET'S—BLACKEST WHITE BAND OF ALL!

Charlie Spark Plug of Band That Plays Deep, Intricate Jazz; Nursing Necessary

(B plus)

Charlie Barnet and His Orchestra. Reviewed at Playland, Rye, New York. NBC wires.

Saxes: (1) Don McCook, (2) Kurt Bloom, (3) Gene Kinsey, (4) Jimmy Lamare. Trumpets: (1) Johnny Owens, (2) Bob Burnet, (3) Billy May. Trombones: (1) Ben Hall, (2) Bill Robertson, (3) Don Ruppersberg. Piano: Bill Miller. Guitar: Bus Etri. Bass: Phil Stephens. Drums: Ray Michaels. Vocals: Judy Ellington and Larry Taylor. Leader, alto and tenor sax: Charlie Barnet.

Background

Barnet hails from New Orleans, member of a socially prominent family, grandson of a former New York Central director. Still in his twenties, he's been famous in New York as a tenor saxist for years. Strangely enough, he's seldom played for other leaders, almost always fronting his own combination, though he has recorded with numerous name bands. He organized this present outfit less than a year ago to show the world that white men can play Ellingtonian music too. The bunch records for Bluebird and is now playing at the Meadowbrook in New Jersey and airing over NBC.

At Present

Charlie Barnet's band is Charlie Barnet. Take Billy Rose away from his Aquacade, John L. Lewis away from his CIO, or Mickey Mouse away from Walt Disney and you'd have about as little as Barnet's band without Barnet. For Charlie, one of the Real Greats of Dancebandom, is the sole sparkplug of a band that could be good enough without him, but which, with him, is capable of reaching glorious swing heights.

The band's style is distinctly negroid. It's easily the blackest white band in existence. The men make no bones about the fact that they're aping Duke Ellington, copying many of his arrangements, adapting standards and some pops to his style, using his sax

The band recorded *Cherokee* while at Playland. Charlie claims Lyman Vunk was playing fourth trumpet. I don't remember seeing him then. I think he joined soon thereafter, though.

Charlie had always been so thoroughly jazz-oriented and talked with anything but an eastern accent, so I fell for somebody's data that he came from New Orleans. Actually, he was born and raised in New York, and educated at some of its finest private schools.

Writes Barnet: "Jazz is the product of the black man. Why not pattern your music after the most inventive contemporary and try to go on from there? The sax section setup was not original with Ellington and was used by many bands before the Goodman band's success with Henderson arrangements." (Note: I knew of no other band except Ellington's that used two altos, one tenor and one baritone. Goodman and others were using two altos and two tenors.)

section set-up of two altos, tenor and baritone and his growling trumpet and trombone.

But there the similarity ends. Barnet's band also has Charlie's tenor: the most forceful, driving reed instrument in the world. Charlie's mad conceptions and apparent complete mastery of his horn are very much like Harry James' handling of his trumpet. He just kicks and kicks and kicks, dashing madly through the deadliest of chord changes only to come out musically unscathed and diving fearlessly into another exciting pattern. It's all quite chilling and at the same time thrilling.

Difference in Time

But, whereas Charlie's band has his tenor and his almost as effective alto, it doesn't possess the homogeneity of Duke's group. Time, of course, makes a lot of difference here. Ellington's men have been playing together for years; Barnet's only for months. And, what's more, the white boys are trying to master in one jump what it took the colored lads a long, long time to develop. The Barnet manuscript is extremely interesting, but just as intricate. Even a bunch that had been playing as a unit for years would have difficulty cutting it.

That's why you don't hear the clean attack and ensemble phrasing that you hear in other new bands such as Miller and Teagarden and James these days. But, then, nobody expects you to hear them—yet, anyway.

Weak Rhythm

However, there is one important thing lacking in Charlie's band that other bands do have and which you'd expect the Boys of Barnet to possess. That's a good rhythm section. It seems the outfit's been suffering in that department ever since its inception. There have been some personnel changes, but they haven't done much good. Right now the weakness is in the percussion department. Ray Michaels is a fine legitimate drummer, but so far he hasn't adapted his playing to Barnet's style. Consequently his work is stiff and liftless, with the other rhythmsters, especially bassist Stephens and guitarist Etri, and sometimes Barnet himself carrying him through. When you've got a drummer who's being led instead of leading the band through its rhythmic stream, your outfit won't kick as it should. It can go full steam ahead in second, but it can't shift into high!

The band swings most when it's playing easier manuscript at middle bounce tempos. At such times the inflections of the brass and saxes help tremendously to create more typically Lunceford than Ellington bounce swing; the men don't have to pay so much attention to reading difficult passages, in which weird

Charlie's direct explanation: "We drank a lot in those days."

Barnet: "The arrival of Cliff Leeman, shortly after this review was written, helped the rhythm section considerably. Good drummers were always a problem, as was the bass chair."

Barnet: "I thought the band was very talented in getting high."

Those must have been Billy May's arrangements. Said Charlie years later: "Billy's charts gave our band its identifiable sound."

139

Charlie Barnet greets
his favorite inspiration

Trumpeter Bobby Burnet and admiring leader
Charlie Barnet

chords are continually getting in their eyes, and so can phrase more freely and naturally. Charlie would be wise to ease up a bit on some of the manuscript, feeding the lads more stuff of this type, until he gets greater cooperation between the various sections.

Other Soloists

The lack of an inspiring rhythm section may be the cause for the dearth of exciting solo passages (Barnet's excluded). Featured trumpeter Bob Burnet plays some great stuff, but too often goes into passages out of which he doesn't come too easily. It may be in an effort to push the band himself that he goes after notes that fit neither his best style nor his technique. Billy May, the other hot trumpeter, tries less hard to lead the attack, consequently emitting passages that make more melodic sense, even though they may not reach the sensational heights of Burnet's. While mentioning trumpeters, don't overlook Johnny Owens' fine lead, especially his free phrasing and good tone.

Outside of Charlie, there isn't a really exciting soloist among the reeds. Don McCook plays good clarinet, though he's not Barney Bigard, while Jimmy Lamare's mighty effective baritone is confined mostly to ensemble passages. In the rhythm section Bill Miller plays some light piano that really swings, while Bus Etri, though seldom heard by himself, is one of jazz's great guitar soloists.

The Chirpers

Then there are two more individuals who are featured quite often. They're the vocalists, both of them good. Miss Ellington has a fine flair for phrasing, especially a ballad, though her "super-southern-style" on rhythm tunes gets in your hair. Mr. Taylor sings easily and naturally, as band vocalists should, but he'd do well to watch his flatting of low notes.

Routining of the band is good. For a while Barnet selected too many killers. Now, with the addition of more middle-groove manuscript plus a few more commercial ballads as sung by Taylor, he gives out a well varied set. And, strangely enough, almost all his flag-wavers are danceable. He himself makes a good front, his appearance and natural manners helping greatly.

Barnet's band is biting off an awful lot. It can't expect to reach perfection in one chew and swallow. But the longer Charlie keeps feeding his lads the kind of stuff he's giving them, the better they're going to digest it. Right now he should watch his step and make sure not only that each man in his group is capable of digesting that food, but also that he doesn't feed the band too much at one time. For with a modified diet it's very likely to develop into the strongest white swing band of all time. Judging it in its still-growing stages, Simon says B plus.

"At this stage," notes Barnet, "we were not getting big money, so good soloists and sidemen were hard to come by, although I thought Bob Burnet was a very exciting soloist. We started using Etri on solos during this period."

Barnet: "No comment other than the fact that I would never use any vocalist except for public demand."

Barnet: "We were born in the Famous Door—listening, no-dancing policy."

Another of those enthusiastic predictions that didn't quite come true.

JAMES JUMPS

Harry's Trumpet, Band's Arrangements, Rhythm, Tempos Share Honors

(A minus)

Harry James and His Orchestra. Reviewed at Roseland, New York. CBS and Mutual wires.

Saxes: (1) Dave Matthews, (2) Claude Lakey, (3) Drew Page, (4) Bill Luther. Trumpets: Claude Bowen, Jack Palmer, Jack Schaeffer. Trombones: Russell Brown, Truett Jones, Dalton Rizzotti. Piano: Jack Gardner. Guitar: Bryan Kent. Bass: Thurman Teague. Drums: Ralph Hawkins. Vocals: Margie Carroll and Frank Sinatra. Leader and trumpet: Harry James.

Background

Born in Georgia, raised in Texas, introed into music as a drummer, Harry James hit big time only a few years ago when Ben Pollack summoned him out to the coast. Came the jump to Benny Goodman and consequent, well-known fame. He started his band last January, including mostly fellow Texans, ten of the lads being Lone Rangers. The outfit's played the Pennsylvania in New York, Philly's Benjamin Franklin, the Steel Pier in Atlantic, and Roseland three times. It opens in Chicago's Sherman Hotel the ninth of this month. If you don't live there, catch it on Brunswick records.

The Harry James band in Atlantic City a few months before its Roseland date. L. to r., saxist Bill Luther, bassist Thurman Teague, pianist Jack Gardner, trumpeter Jack Schaeffer, drummer Ralph Hawkins, guitarist Red Kent, saxist Drew Page, vocalist Connie Haines (who later joined Tommy Dorsey's band), James, vocalist Frank Sinatra (who later joined Tommy Dorsey's band), saxist Dave Matthews, trumpeter Claude Bowen, trombonist Truett Jones, trumpeter Jack Palmer, saxist Claude Lakey, trombonist Russ Brown

If it's sheer swing kicks you're looking for, stop right here in front of Harry James' band! Stop, and let it drive some of the most inspired blasting of all time onto those eardrums of yours. In a few seconds, you'll find yourself rocking all the way down to your heels; rocking as you've seldom rocked before, while catching a band that kicks as few have ever kicked before!

The entire Harry James band is Harry James personified. All of you must know his sensational, intense style, the most rhythmic that's ever come out of any white trumpeter. Well, the James band is just about the most rhythmic white band dancebandom has yet known.

Credit deserves to be spread. There's Harry, of course—not only his blowing, but also the magnificent tempos that he sets. There's the extraordinarily solid rhythm section, topped by Ralph Hawkins' ultra-clean drumming. There's the rhythmic push of the saxes led by Dave Matthews. There's the ensemble bite of the brass. And finally there are the rhythmic virtues of Andy Gibson's fine arrangements, with their inspiring backgrounds. All of these combine to push the entire James band into swing grooves out of which it won't budge until it sees the end of the road, marked "Coda."

Often, after it passes those "Coda" signposts, the James bunch switches to ballads. Surprisingly enough it does a very acceptable job on them too. Jack Mathias' arrangements are interesting without ever becoming too involved. Featured throughout many are the very pleasing vocals of Frank Sinatra, whose easy phrasing is especially commendable, and the less frequent but also good efforts of Margie Carroll, an extremely recent addition to the band. Mathias is also making background-hummers out of the entire band: an extremely effective effect.

However, there's no getting away from the fact that the band has weak points, and they become most noticeable on its slower tunes. Most glaring is the sloppiness of the saxes. Dave Matthews is an extremely imaginative lead alto man, but whether it's because he imagines and interprets the same passage differently each time he plays it, or because the rest of the men can't seem to remember just how he does phrase it, the section often does not sound as one. Such a situation should not exist among top-notch men such as these.

There are individual bright spots, however, that more than offset the deficiencies. One is the same Dave Matthews' great alto solos, considered by many to be second only to those of Johnny Hodges. Then there are, of course, the works of two men discussed before, Harry and drummer Hawkins, the latter with

Harry was a good drummer, who'd sit in occasionally. That could be why his tempos were always so good.

It was while I was leaving Roseland, after having listened to the band all evening, that Harry's road manager, Jerry Barrett, ran after me to ask me please to "give the new boy singer a good write-up because he wants it more than anything and we want to keep him happy." Maybe I would have written more enthusistically without such pressure. By the way, whatever happened to Margie Carroll?

Later Matthews switched to tenor. He sounded great there. Maybe that's what he should have been playing in Harry's band and letting somebody else blow a more consistent lead alto.

143

his fine taste, neat technique, tremendous lift, and uncanny steadiness ranking him as one of the country's drumming greats. Back again to the saxes, and you'll hear Claude Lakey's soulful tenor, which probably reminds you, too, of the late Herschel Evans. None of the trumpeters gets a chance to blow much on his own, though Bowen takes over some of Harry's parts now and then in fine fashion, while among the trombones, Dalton Rizzotti emits in an exciting, plunger-mute style. The exceedingly fine rhythm section, definitely one of the best in the world, lets loose Jack Gardner in a Jess Stacian manner—perhaps not quite as crisp, but certainly mighty inspiring. That leaves a hot clarinet as the only solo instrument unaccounted for, and it'll continue to remain unaccounted for until such time as Harry decides to feature one. Suffice to point out that its absence does cause an aural void.

However, Harry's band possesses some attributes usually not found in swing bands. Most surprising is its ability to play rumbas and tangos, as well as waltzes. And there are the two unusually good vocalists. Palmer does some scat singing, but his work doesn't fall into that classification.

All in all, it's a well-rounded swing band that Harry James fronts, and fronts with a pleasing personality that shows that he's having just as much fun playing for you as you might have listening to him. It's sincere stuff in the exceptional class. Simon says A minus.

There was no law that said a band had to have a good jazz clarinetist. Guess I was more of a conformist than Harry was. Good for him.

Those rumbas, tangos and waltzes weren't Harry's doing, however. The Roseland management made the band play them. Can you imagine what might have happened if a less flexible guy, like Artie Shaw for instance, had been asked to follow such orders?

Responds Harry: "To the best of my knowledge, this is the first favorable review I received when I started my band. In 1939, there were quite a few struggling bands trying to get started, and a few encouraging words like these helped to pass the time on those 400- and 500-mile one-nite stands by bus . . . and they also helped to forget the hunger pains caused by the lack of time, and lack of money. So . . . James sez, 'SIMON A-1'."

Benny Goodman on Stan Kenton (August, 1948)—

I wouldn't go out of my way to hear the band, though I must admit that what they're doing, they're doing violently!

WILL BRADLEY'S BAND BEST OF 1940 CROP

Outfit Has Rookie's Fire, Veteran's Poise; Arrangements, Leader, Rhythm Impressive

(A minus)

Will Bradley and His Orchestra. Famous Door, New York. NBC wire.

Saxes: (1) Artie Mendelsohn, (2) Peanuts Hucko, (3) Jo-jo Huffman, (4) Sam Sachelle. Trumpets: (1) Steve Lipkins, (2) Joe Weidman, (3) Herbie Dell. Trombones: Jimmy Emert and Bill Corti. Piano: Freddy Slack. Guitar: Steve Jordan. Bass: Felix Giobbe. Drums and co-leader: Ray McKinley. Vocals: Carlotta Dale, Jordan and McKinley. Leader and trombone: Will Bradley.

Will Bradley, Ray McKinley and Freddy Slack perform some press-agent exercises in the Paramount Theatre's upstairs gym

If Will Bradley's bookers or publicity men should try to tell you that his is the outstanding new band of 1940, don't argue with them. Either just believe them, or better still, go and hear the Bradley Boys in person. The former way is easier, but the latter is far more convincing proof that they're absolutely right.

If you should happen to catch the band on one of the many nights when it's really clicking (it's impossible for new outfits to be consistently sublime night after night), you'll hear one of the most musically thrilling units in all dancebandom. It possesses a freshness and crispness found in practically no veteran groups, plus a sureness, based on musical accuracy, that's startling for an outfit as young as this.

The freshness and crispness, reasons for the more obvious excitement, are attributable to the original manuscript and to the brilliant play of the rhythm section, and of a few melodic men, as individuals. The arrangements by Leonard Whitney, Freddy Slack, Bert Ross, and Fred Datz, are exciting not only because of their thoroughness and impeccable taste, but also because of the novel way they present what usually are trite phrases.

Back-Slapping Department

Slap Ray McKinley on the back for that wonderful rhythm section—but save enough strength to pat the rest of the boys gently on their heads, too! Quite frankly, after five years of raving, this reviewer has just about run out of superlatives for Mac's drumming. When it comes to the playing of actual drums (snare and bass, omitting high-hat cymbals)—well, there's just nobody else who shows such gorgeous taste in playing under a band, who sounds and feels so solid, and who is blessed with such a sense of originality! (End of rave.)

As for the lads whom you're supposed to pat: a couple of months ago these columns remarked about bassist Felix Giobbe in the review of Teddy Powell's band. Those complimentary phrases about his beautiful tone and his good beat are reiterated now, with superlatives added for the masterful way in which he also handles the bowing parts of the complex Bradley bass book. Freddy Slack remains the brilliant, original pianist you probably knew when he was featured with Jimmy Dorsey, while young Steve Jordan gets a strong, healthy beat out of that guitar of his.

Featured most often among the other individuals offering excitement is leader Bradley. Here's a trombone player who has everything: a real, legitimate brass tone, pretty conceptions of phrasing sweet tunes, and a solid, rhythmic punch to his jazz efforts. Little wonder that Glenn Miller once remarked in these pages that Will is the country's number one all-around trombonist.

One reason the band sounded exciting, according to Bradley, was "because many of the arrangements were played in brilliant keys; instead of the usual B flat we'd play a thing in B natural, or instead of the usual key of F we'd go into F sharp. This could be tough on the jazz soloists, who weren't used to faking in those keys, but it sure kept all the guys on their toes."

Today McKinley wonders why he never played better high-hats "because I used to sit opposite Walter Johnson in Fletcher Henderson's band at Roseland, and he really played them right!"

146

One of the warmest of all band vocalists, Carlotta Dale also sang with Jan Savitt's band

Other Excitement

He's not the only soloist worthy of much note, though. Most exciting get-off man, so far as this column is concerned, is "Peanuts" Hucko, a tenor-man with a gorgeous tone applied to consistently fine, melodic passages, which instead of just honking unintelligibly, actually say something musically. It's the Eddie Millerian quality that so few new hot tenorites seem to be capable of producing.

Somewhat similar in style, in that his successions of phrases weave a fairly definite pattern, is hot trumpeter Joe Weidman, who, when he is at his best, is an interesting as well as exciting artist. There's also an extremely original hot trumpeter in the section, Herbie Dell, who exhibited all sorts of original ideas in his days with Bob Chester, but who, for some reason or other, is given no opportunities with his new compatriots. And there's also another ad lib man, clarinetist Jo-jo Huffman, who has a sure style of playing, which, however and unfortunately, is too often lacking in any signs of inspiration.

And now for the "sureness, based on musical accuracy" referred to in the second paragraph.

Credit for that quality must be divided many ways. Primarily it goes to all the men, for with no exceptions

But Peanuts couldn't play clarinet well enough, so they finally fired him. Today he's one of the world's greatest jazz clarinetists.

McKinley: "I guess you could have called Jo-jo the Julius Boros of the clarinet."

147

they're real musicians who really know their instruments. There's not a knocked-out, hot-mad youth in the group. Proof is ample: their tones as reflected in the rich tonal quality of the band; their intonation as exhibited by the outfit's never sounding out of tune; and their ability to play together, which accounts not only for the tonal blend and balance, but also for their phrasing so well as a unit.

Credit also goes to the leadmen: to Bradley, who has done such a fine job of rehearsing the men thoroughly; to Steve Lipkins, the consistent, well-schooled lead trumpeter, and to Art Mendelsohn, the steady lead saxist with the fine intonation and tone.

The musical consistency is a reflection of Bradley's many years in radio. But, unfortunately, so is the band's major defect. That is its inability to create a really mellow mood when playing popular ballads. Musically, like most large radio orchestras, it plays them just about flawlessly. But radio groups are liable to be a bit frigid, and so is Bradley's.

One of the chief causes is the tempos set for the pretty tunes. Too many of them are just a shade too fast. As such they move, never dragging, which is one of the aims of all radio groups. But when you're playing for dancers, and especially for the younger element, the idea is to play pretty tunes not only prettily (musically speaking), but also to create a definite, mellow mood. There's still a medium between a bright tempo and a dragging tempo that the band has overlooked. It's that undefinable, intimate, simple way of playing which too many dance orchestras, in an effort to impress musically, overlook these days.

There's good ammunition for creating mellow moods in the Bradley band. Will's fine trombone has already been mentioned. But Carlotta Dale's voice hasn't, and here is one of the finest ballad singers of all time. She's good as she is, but that soft, cozy way she has of singing would be even more effective if given more of an intimate atmosphere.

While on the subject of singers, don't let McKinley's magnificent drumming allow you to overlook his singing—he has a completely whacky style that is responsible for a great deal of the showmanship the band possesses. Visually, of course, his drumming attracts also, as does leader Bradley's appearance; as clean-cut and handsome a front as there is in the business.

Yes, the Will Bradley bookers and publicity men have something here—something great too—certainly the most exciting and most polished band yet produced by 1940. What's going to happen to it from now on—well, at the rate it's going, and with continually improving consistency and a bit more concentration on the creation of moods, there's no apparent reason why it shouldn't turn out to be just about the finest outfit in all dancebandom. Right now Simon says A minus.

148

Bradley, found this review "amazingly accurate except for that part about the tempos. You know, I'm no Arthur Murray, but I'll be damned if I could dance to anything as slow as some of those things that Tommy and Glenn played. How do you slow yourself down that much?" Maybe Will didn't realize that the kids weren't exactly *dancing* to those extra-slow tempos.

Perhaps the reason wasn't apparent then, but soon thereafter, Will and Ray started disagreeing about the direction the band should take. Ray wanted more emphasis on their boogie-woogie novelties and jazz, Will more on ballads. Will carried on for awhile after Ray left, but the band was never the same.

DUCHIN BAND REFRESHING

Eddy's New Band Less Mournful Though Piano Is Out of Place; Melody Good; Rhythm Heavy

(B)

Eddy Duchin and His Orchestra. Reviewed at Roton Point Casino, South Norwalk, Conn.

Saxes: (1) Marty Oscard, (2) Stewie McKay, (3) Tony Leonard, (4) Johnny Drake. Trumpets: (1) Jimmy Troutman, (2) Lew Sherwood. Trombone: Jap Harris. Pianos: Eddy Duchin and Al Giroux. Guitar: Gene Baumberger. Bass: Sid Rhein. Drums: Harry Campbell. Vocals: June Robbins, Drake, Sherwood and Leonard.

Background

You've heard of Duchin for years and have probably always classified him as strictly a society-type bandleader. So he was, achieving his greatest glories in New York's defunct Central Park Casino and its Plaza Hotel. Recently, though, in an apparent effort to up his one-nighter intake, he shelved that style, substituting a group that played more conventional, public-minded dance music.

At Present

Musically speaking, Eddy Duchin's new outfit is a happy one compared with the band he used to have. For in place of the Mournful Moaners, who used to be led by depressing tenor sax tones that clashed so acridly with an unhealthy-sounding, Harmon-muted trumpet, he now presents a group with bright, legitimate tones, playing music that's more on the refreshing than the depressing side.

The instrumentation is now orthodox: a four-way sax section consisting of two altos and two tenors; brass composed of two trumpets and a trombone; all backed by a five-man rhythm section. And when you've got orthodox instrumentation, you can play orthodox dance music. Which Duchin does.

There are good musicians in the band, so that its blend and its intonation are just about flawless. The brass is especially clean, with Jimmy Troutman playing an intelligent lead. Tonally, the trio is big, compensating somewhat for its abbreviated size, and making the entire band sound much fuller than most outfits that sport just three straight-horn men.

The same tonal compliment can be tossed at the saxes, with ditto phrases for Marty Oscard's lead phrasing. The quartet is new, so that the blend is not quite as consistently excellent, but even in its worst moments, it's a unit far cleaner than you'll find most places.

Noteworthy Men

There are good soloists in both those sections. Troutman plays most of the jazz trumpet in a Texan manner, while McKay is capable of playing some great Hawkinsian tenor. Drake's pretty tenor tone deserves all the spotting it gets. Most featured individual is, as you'd suspect, Duchin himself, whose piano-playing interests the folks out front more than any one single component of the band. Appreciation of his style of playing is, of course, purely a personal matter, but it has certainly satisfied enough tastes in past years to warrant every bit of spotlight it gets.

However, that "I'll-run-ahead-for-a-couple-of-measures-and-see-what-it-looks-like-up-there-and-then-wait-for-the-rest-of-the-rhythm-section-to-catch-up-to-me" style of piano doesn't fit the type of music Duchin's band now plays nearly so well as it did his previous, more informal pattern. For playing arrangements, even when they're as dull and uninspiring as most of Duchin's are, calls for much greater rhythmic exactness. Nonconformity with what the rest of the fellows are doing is prone to spoil the entire effect that the arranger originally had in mind.

Rhythmically Stiff

Maybe it's because of Eddy's explorations into measures-to-come that his rhythm section retains a splint-like stiffness, a holdover from its society days. There's a heavy crunch effect that implies a "we'll-hold-that-tempo-till-the-last measure-or-die-in-the-attempt" that's all very noble on the part of Messrs. Giroux, Baumberger (who can't be heard to advantage when hidden behind a bass), Rhein and Campbell, but it's sacrificing nobility for danceability. The tempos, too, don't fit the arrangements too well, many of them, especially on ballads, being better suited for society's demands than for those of the dancers who attend one-nighters, and making relaxation on the part of the rhythm section all the more difficult.

There are some good men in that rhythm section, bassist Rhein especially, and there's no getting away from the fact that once the pressure is off, they'll probably impart a much lighter and less intense lift.

Be Some Changes Made?

All this rhythmic criticism presupposes, of course, that Duchin wants to change the style of his band, a bold move which may prove to be quite disastrous in the end. For his forte is, and always has been, his style of piano, and that definitely fits a society-type band much better than it does a more conventional, and perhaps more musical, outfit. Couple that roaming, informal type of playing with Duchin's informal and pleasant personality, and you've got the perfect set-up for a smart intimate hotel-room maestro—much more so than for one-night stands, where Eddy might cash in for a short period, but where he runs much less of a chance of making the name for himself that he has within bluer-blooded boundaries.

One section so far has received no comment, and that's the vocal group. It's a good one, versatile and musical. Miss Robbins phrases nicely, though she still slurs a little too much, looks good and is a vastly improved singer since her early days with Gus Arnheim. Johnny Drake is the most impressive of the men, though the veteran Lew Sherwood and the tenoric Tony Leonard add pleasant variety.

Taken all in all, Duchin's band in its present form is a good one. The biggest vote of thanks goes to the men themselves, a group of fine musicians who do as much as they can with unexciting arrangements and a style that still has to progress beyond its present, formative stage. Eddy right now is half-way between a society and a swing band, and once he makes up his mind which road he's going to take, and then concentrates upon his choice, chances are his outfit will be even better than the good one it is right now. Simon says B.

Gene Krupa on Judging Musicians (July, 1954)—

The thing to consider when judging a musician is not what you think of the type of music he is playing, but rather how well he is playing whatever type he is attempting to play.

One thing that I don't think many of the young musicians give the older jazz musicians credit for is the fact they they were the ones who conceived things, and they didn't just listen to a lot of records and copy and perhaps make a few changes.

LES BROWN 99% PURE

Cleanliness, Intelligence, Good Tones and Intonation Produce Great Results

(A minus)

Les Brown and His Orchestra. Arcadia, New York and Glen Island Casino, New Rochelle, N. Y.

Saxes: (1) Steve Madrick, (2) Wolffe Tanenbaum, (3) Tony Martell, (4) Eddie Scheer. Trumpets: (1) Bob Thorne, (2) Eddie Bailey, (3) Joe Bogart. Trombones: (1) Si Zentner, (2) Ronnie Chase, (3) Warren Brown. Piano: Billy Rowland. Guitar: Joe Petrone. Bass: Johnny Knepper. Drums: Eddie Julian. Vocals: Doris Day and Chase. Leader, sax and clarinet: Les Brown.

Background

Those of you who saw page 12 of the July, 1940 METRONOME must know all about what has happened to Les and his boys since they first got together, and what a tremendously well-liked fellow the young leader is. Since that lengthy story appeared, Les and band have appeared at the World's Fair Dancing Campus and Glen Island Casino, and have been signed to a healthy contract by Columbia-Okeh records.

At Present

Les Brown has himself a band that has just about everything. And just about everything it has is good. For this vastly underrated outfit possesses amounts of musical ability, danceability and commercial appeal which in the aggregate should be the envy of 99 per cent of the bands in captivity. Why it hasn't achieved the national acclaim accorded to others among that Ivory Soap figure remains one of dance-bandom's hugest mysteries.

Musically, this is one of the purest, one of the cleanest bands of all. The men phrase together with understanding and intelligence; they play in tune; there's not a bad tone in the group; there are some imaginative soloists, and there's a rhythm section that steadily backs some extremely musical arrangements.

Those manuscripts, mostly by Brown himself, are for the most part pretty straightforward, though they achieve some unusual tone colorings from the reeds

Steve Madrick has been audio engineer on NBC's "Today" show for many, many years.

Ira Mangel, now Louis Armstrong's road manager, booked all the bands into the World's Fair Dancing Campus. "Of all of them, Les's was the best," he recently told me.

Not a mystery to Les. "It takes time, George!" he explained, after seeing this review.

151

with their two soprano saxes and other doublings. The saxes form an especially joyous blend, with heaps of credit going to little Eddie Scheer for his consistency on the various reeds. The section also produces one of the two outstanding hot men in the group. That's Wolffe Tanenbaum, whose soaring tenor often reaches truly thrilling heights. Leader Les plays some interesting clarinet on occasion, giving you the feeling that he'd play even better if he played more.

Spreading Credit

The brass sextet matches the reeds in musical splendor, though on the whole it's a more conventional unit. The Credit Department in this instance is headed by first trombonist, Si Zentner, a great musician, and Bob Thorne, a sympathetic first trumpeter. The accuracy of the others makes these two shine all the more, with Eddie Bailey's bopping of high notes particularly noteworthy. As for hot passages, Joe Bogart and Ronnie Chase are quite satisfactory in their genteel ways.

The phrasing of these two sections, plus the almost uniformly good tempos, and the steadiness of the rhythm section combine to create the band's danceability. That propelling quartet contains an excellent bassist named Johnny Knepper, possessor of a fine tone and an ability to anchor the rhythmic ship whenever it shows any signs of wavering. Pianist Billy Rowland is the other outstanding soloist within the band, his crisp solos being uniformly interesting, rhythmic, and in superb taste. Joe Petrone plays a powerful guitar, and Drummer Eddie Julian supplies much lift; as soon as he relaxes more (something which you can't do when you're straining your face and wondering how Gene would look if he were playing that particular passage), the rhythmic stiffness that occasionally hampers the band should become even less apparent. Another method of making it disappear completely would be for Brown to forego some of his extremely fast, one-steppy tempos. They're definitely becoming a thing of the past, thank goodness, and nowadays no longer serve even to bring the dancers around the bandstand.

Visual Appeal

As a matter of fact, there's enough visual commercial appeal within the organization to attract the folks out front. There's the exceptionally clean-cut appearance of the entire group, starting with its well-mannered leader and ending no place. And there's Doris Day, who for combined looks and voice has no apparent equal: she's pretty and fresh looking, handles herself with unusual grace, and what's most

152

Les: "The late Eddie Scheer had the prettiest tone I've ever heard on soprano sax!"

Les: "Wolfie's tenor was very imaginative!"

Les began to play less, instead. Too bad.

Les: "What ever happened to Si?"

Later, Bogart's music became far less genteel—for years he was music director of WMCA, New York hard rock radio station.

Billy went on to a 20-year radio and TV career with Perry Como.

"At the Arcadia," Les points out, "they were still one-stepping!"

"What ever happened to Doris Day?" asks Les. Who knows?

important of all, sings with much natural feeling and in tune. Only when she lets out too much are all these superlatives inapplicable. Male vocalist Ronnie Chase also sings nicely (he plays good jazz trombone—see above) and should become even more effective once he learns how to relax his spine before a mike.

"Bend Your Spine"

The band's one real drawback (and this may be why it hasn't received its due national acclaim) also lies within the unrelaxed spine category. Perhaps there is too much emphasis upon musical perfection and upon interesting ensemble arrangements—perhaps the cause may lie somewhere else—whatever it may be, the fact remains that the band lacks intimacy. Only at times does it ever get really close to the dancers. Novelties, of course, would help, though they are by no means necessary. Chances are that less emphasis upon ensemble and more upon musical intimacy, as achieved by mere frequent spotlighting of soloists (if only for contrast), would bring the dancers and listeners closer to Les Brown's band and make them notice it more. As matters now stand they hear it and like it, but they don't go home at night feeling as if they really *know* it. Getting the public to know and to remember his music is obviously Les's most important problem. He has solved all the others and has done a superb job in the bargain. Simon says A minus.

"Butch Stone supplied the spark and novelties when he joined us in 1941," writes Les. Butch has remained with Les for a generation and a half.

One of the most expressive of band vocalists, Doris Day also sang with Bob Crosby's band

153

ALVINO REY'S BAND

And Its Fine Saxes and Good Rhythm Make It a Good Musical Group Too; Novelties and King Sisters Help

(B-1)

Alvino Rey and His Orchestra. Reviewed at Rustic Cabin, Englewood Cliffs, N. J. Saxes: (1) Skeets Herfurt, (2) Charlie Brosen, (3) Jerry Sanfino, (4) Kermit Levinsky. Trumpets: (1) Frank Strasek, (2) Danny Vanelli, (3) Paul Fredericks. Trombones: (1) Bill Schallen, (2) Wally Baron. Piano: Buddy Cole. Guitar: Dick Morgan. Bass: Sandy Block. Drums: Eddie Julian. Vocals: The Four King Sisters, Herfurt, Schallen, Morgan. Leader and guitars: Alvino Rey.

This Alvino Rey band is really a kick! Not only is it fine musically, but it's also the most entertaining, informal big band this reviewer has ever had the pleasure of spending his evenings with. Chalk it up then as the No. 1 "never-a-dull-moment" aggregation of dancebandom.

It's not only the many novelties, all of them non-kernelic, that make this band so much fun. It's the pervading atmosphere and attitude of the entire entourage. They're out to have fun, and at the same time to give you a good time. In all departments, they succeed handsomely without ever showing the slightest strains of too much self-conscious effort. As a result, you feel as if you've busted into a big family, composed completely of kids who are just awfully happy to have you in with them.

Responsible for this informal social atmosphere are the boys themselves. So are the much-at-ease King Sisters. Ditto for the novelties, many of them spotting whacky antics by Dick Morgan and Skeets Herfurt that are amusing enough to stand as an act in themselves.

There are various reasons for the remarkable esprit de corps. The personal calibre of all involved, from leader through subleader through sisters to the rest of the musicians, is mighty important. You can't get

The Alvino Rey band, several months after this review, with a few personnel changes. Alvino is at far left. The King Sisters are Alyce, Louise (Mrs. Rey), Donna and Yvonne, who married pianist Buddy Cole. Saxes are Charlie Brosen, Jerry Sanfino, Skeets Herfurt and Mike Sabol. Dick Morgan is on guitar. Bill Schallen and Charles Lee are the trombones. Eddie Julian is on drums. Danny Vanelli, John Fallstich and Paul Fredericks are the trumpets

just an ordinary bunch to work and play as hard as this one does. The pervading faith that the band has something unusual and that it will click is also important. And finally, and in many ways most important of all, is the music itself.

It's interesting, all of it. Besides the unique novelties, there's some fine jazz manuscript as supplied by Bud Estes, there are some marvelous, mellow moods, and there's a worthwhile assortment of Latin rhythms. And besides being interesting, it's all done well.

Stylistically you'd think the band would be built around Alvino's guitaring. It is—to some extent. There's always terrific danger of overdoing something like that, and it's to the band's everlasting credit and advantage that its leader doesn't go overboard. As it is, his strumming and sliding is discreetly confined to intros (thus letting folks know whose band they're listening to), to a limited number of bars per arrangement, and to out-and-out novelties.

That leaves much room for the rest of the band to show off, and show off it does—well. Most impressive of the three sections is the sax quartet. This is a really solid group, splendidly blended and coordinated, and blessed with some fine, free-phrasing leading by Skeets Herfurt.

The brass is slightly less good. Its chief asset is its consistency, and therein it's also blessed with a good leader, Frank Strasek, who seldom, if ever, misses and who is also able to express what he feels the same way every time. Its blend isn't quite as good, however, and when it comes to playing jazz numbers it lacks a definite punch and attack. The fault there is lack of tonal as well as lack of rhythmic guts. As a result too much of the burden on swing attempts falls upon the rhythm section.

That rhythm section can take it, though, because it's far above par. Of course it does strain too hard here and there when the brass drops a burden on it, but for the most part it lets loose handsome beats. Dick Morgan, whom most folks know as a comedian, is also a splendid guitarist: strong, steady, and letting loose a real beat. Buddy Cole is an exceptional pianist —here's a lad who fills in behind a band tastily and without ever losing sight of the fact that he's still basically a rhythm man. Sandy Block is a strong bassist with a fine tone and much imagination, while Eddie Julian, when not emphasizing the second and fourth bars too much on his snare (that makes things chunky), is a discreet, well-disciplined drummer with a good beat.

That section is ample cause for inspiring the band's hot men, who, though not scintillating, are quite adequate. Most impressive is Herfurt, who plays good alto and ditto clarinet. Charlie Brosen's tenor is both interesting and motivating, while trumpeter Danny Vanelli finds his best medium when he's not straining. Bill Schallen gets off some good, almost two-beatian trombone bits. And then, of course, there's the aforementioned pianist Cole, who's every bit as brilliant on his solos as he is on ensemble—he's not only a rare find but a real musician as well.

There are plenty of fine soloists in the non-jazz category too. There's Alvino himself, whose single string work on Spanish guitar impresses this reviewer from a musical standpoint more than anything else the man does. And then there are the clear-enunciating Four King Sisters, who as a unit not only sing good novelty stuff, but also come through with some really fine harmonics and dynamics on ballad choruses. And to top it all, they unleash two good soloists: Alyce, who takes care of ballads with much true warmth, and Yvonne, who takes care of light rhythm tunes with much cuteness.

The whole band is constantly unleashing stuff. It's got a whole bagful more of surprises, musical and novel, which are much better to hear and see than to be told about. Ditto for everything else concerned about the happy group, too, for carefree joy is something that's even more joyous when participated in than when told about. Which brings this review to a close with the almost anti-climatic remark that Simon says B-1.

THORNHILL BEST POTENTIAL POPULARITY BET

Claude's Group, Most Unique in Years, Gives Forth Gorgeous Arrangements, Mellow Moods And Scintillating Solos

(A-1)

Claude Thornhill and His Orchestra. Reviewed at Glen Island Casino, New Rochelle, N. Y. Saxes: (1) Dale Brown, (2) Hammond Russum, (3) Johnny Nelson, (4) Ted Goddard. Clarinets: (1) Irving Fazola, (2) George Paulsen. Trumpets: (1) Conrad Gozzo, (2) Rusty Diedrick, (3) Bob Sprintall. Trombones: (1) Bob Jenney, (2) Tasso Harris. Guitar: Allen Hanlon. Bass: Harvey Cell. Drums: Gene Lemen. Vocals: Betty Claire, Dick Harding, Bob Jenney. Leader and piano: Claude Thornhill.

Chalk up Claude Thornhill's as the band of 1941 with the highest P. P. rating. "P.P." stands for "Potential Popularity." Which means that of all the new bands this year, and, so far as this writer is concerned, for all years since the advent of Glenn Miller, Claude Thornhill's stands the greatest chance of turning out to be the nation's No. 1 dance orchestra.

Truly, it's an amazing aggregation! For not only has it struck upon a style that's musically unique and thrilling, but it also shows a flare for commercialism that's lacking even in most bands whose only claim to fame is kowtowing to the public's demands.

Hearing this band for the first time was one of my biggest musical thrills. It may never have attained No. 1 ranking commercially, but few bands ever matched this edition or later editions of Claude's for sheer musicality. Its music still stands up beautifully today. (Sorry about still another of those No. 1 predictions. I just couldn't stop myself, could I?)

The Claude Thornhill band on the Glen Island Casino bandstand. Claude is at the piano. Vocalists Dick Harding and Betty Claire flank saxists (l. to r.) Hammond Russum, Johnny Nelson, Dale Brown and Ted Goddard. Middle row: trombonists Tasso Harris and Bob Jenney, guitarist Allen Hanlon, clarinetists Irving Fazola and George Paulsen. Back row: trumpeters Bob Sprintall, Conrad Gozzo (who married Betty Claire) and Rusty Diedrick. Gene Lemen is the drummer and Harvey Cell is the bassist

The style, the first really new one to emerge in recent years, and one that often borders on modern classical music, is a Thornhill creation. Fundamentally, it revolves around the six-man reed section; more obviously around a clarinet sextet that often plays in unison in the upper register. To the casual observer, the voicing of the varied reeds (the range is from baritone to flute), by themselves and with the brass, is less obvious, but it constitutes just as important a part of the musical scheme of things as does the clarinet ensemble.

Incorporated in the Thornhill style is Claude's piano, played neither in the Wilsonian nor the Duchinesque manner. It's distinctly Claude Thornhill: few notes, often just melody notes, played with a light, intimate touch that's a stupendous contrast with the fullness and stolidness of the band's ensemble.

That ensemble is a joy to hear. Claude's arrangements and those of Bill Borden are responsible in part. But so is the expert musicianship of the entire group, with its powerhouse brass section, its well-blended reeds, and the tasty, potent rhythm section.

The brass is headed by an excellent young trumpeter named Conrad Gozzo, whose brilliant tone and fine control thereof have much to do with the band's extremely effective dynamics. There isn't an emasculated hornblower in the quintet, for that matter, all the men being quite capable of blowing "ff" without ever sacrificing tonal quality. In fact, so exuberant do certain members become that the blend of the brass sometimes becomes disrupted by too much tromboning, and ditto for the attack, which in some exciting times leans towards the disrupted side.

In some ways the reeds form a more polished unit. Though there is more stylistic emphasis upon them, there is also less physical strain, for lots of those brass parts are extremely tough. Like the brass, though, the reed sextet must pay strict attention to dynamics, and also like the brass it does so with both precision and intelligence. Theirs is not an easy task, especially when you consider the extremes in range with which they are presented, and so if perfect intonation is not always present, they have more than an adequate excuse.

The rhythm section, extremely tasty and quite capable of carrying the band, is, along with wise tempos, largely responsible for its danceability. It's well coordinated, and unlike most rhythm sections, it doesn't try to do too much. As a result, the beat is always there, even though during certain exciting passages, it permits itself to be rushed by an overzealous brass section. Self-assertion during such emergencies is mighty important.

Claude was the only piano-leader I can recall who specialized in touch.

Borden, chairman of the board of the Manhattan School of Music, continues to give us Thornhill recordings through his Monmouth-Evergreen label, all of them previously unissued performances. But Columbia doggedly refuses to make the band's music available. What crass commercial obstinacy!

The same Gozzo who became the idol of so many other trumpeters, including Al Hirt, and who was soon to marry vocalist Betty Claire, Dorothy's kid sister.

Thornhill's Piano

Within the rhythmsters is Thornhill's piano, the band's most featured solo instrument. It's not as effective on the air, chiefly because over the wireless Claude and Cohorts are unable to create the moods that they do in the room. Those moods form an integral part of the outfit's routine, and also play, and will continue to play, an important factor in the band's future success. The mellowness achieved when Claude plinks lightly on the keys, while the rest of the boys hover in a subdued background, and then the contrast achieved when the entire group bursts forth in that tremendous ensemble—that's something that no other band within this reviewer's memory has ever been able to carry off, and something that creates a stupendous, emotional reaction on all the customers within the room, the hall, or wherever Claude happens to be playing. It's unfortunate that he doesn't make more of an attempt to build those moods and that contrast over the air, instead of playing so much out-and-out jazz.

Not that the band's jazz isn't good, mind you. It has to be, if only because you hear brilliant passages from the ever-soulful Fazola; the potent, rhythmic Bob (yes, Jack's brother) Jenney trombone; the definite, full-bodied, Beriganesque trumpet of Rusty Diedrick's; the booting tenor of Hammond Russum, and the ingenious altoing of Ted Goddard. And, too, there's the drive of Allen Hanlon's guitar, a brilliant strummer, and of Harvey Cell's bass.

But the public shouldn't get the idea that Claude Thornhill's is primarily a jazz band. It isn't. It's primarily a musical band, as reflected even more by its rendition of ballads than of swing numbers. And don't think for a minute that Dick Harding's rich and sincere singing doesn't help the former plenty, too.

More of a Room Band

Perhaps it might be even more accurate to say that now, in its kindergarten condition, it's more of a room band than an air band. Its mood creation, though the paramount, is not the only reason. Its versatility is another, as reflected by its ability to play rumbas, congas and waltzes as well as it does fox-trots. Ditto its young, clean-cut appearance. The vocal duets of young Betty Claire and Bob Jenney form still another. And the fact that Claude has made many beautiful scorings of ASCAP tunes, which either stand alone or comprise effective medleys, is an extremely important reason for the band sounding even more impressive in person than it does over the air.

Chances are that once the radio music battle is

> The shadings of the band were so subtle that probably the remote engineers on broadcasts would have destroyed them because they always tried to keep everything at one level. So maybe Claude was right in broadcasting the more obvious.

> ASCAP tunes were banned from radio during this period. Those medleys were truly gorgeous—warm, musical and very sexy for dancing.

settled, the country in general is going to hear even more thrilling Thornhillisms than it has to date. And when you stop to consider what it's been hearing already, you can probably see why this aggregation captures the highest "P. P." rating of any new group in the business. Simon says A-1.

MONROE MORE IMPRESSIVE THAN HIS BAND

Vaughn the Vallee of New Generation; Dull Arrangements, Lack of Finesse No Aid to Leader's Personality

(B-2)

Vaughn Monroe and His Orchestra. Reviewed at Frank Dailey's Meadowbrook, Cedar Grove, N. J. Mutual and CBS wires.

Saxes: (1) Andy Bagni, (2) Frank Levine, (3) Don Falco, (4) Ziggy Talent. Trumpets: (1) Benny West, (2) Bobby Nichols, (3) Dino Digeano. Trombones: (1) Joe Connie, (2) Al Diehl, (3) Art Dedrick. Piano: Arnold Ross. Guitar: Guy Scafati. Bass: Jimmy Athens. Drums: Irving Rosenthal. Vocals: Marylin Duke and Talent. Leader, vocals and trumpet: Vaughn Monroe.

Vaughn Monroe is being sent by young trumpeter Bobby Nichols

"The Rapid Rise of Vaughn Monroe," or "A Press Agent's Dream," is certainly the current phenomenon of dancebandom. Seldom has any band come up so quickly, with so much attendant ballyhoo, and clicked so heavily with the audiences it has had to face.

The primary cause is obvious. For, despite all managerial push and tremendous pressure from press agents, the group would never have had a chance to score so brilliantly, were it not for that one cause—Vaughn Monroe himself.

His is a dynamic personality. It's around him, not his band, that the girls flock. It's when they hear his voice, not the band's playing, that they go girlishly ga-ga. His smile sends romantic, not musical, shivers down spines that are just beginning to harden. Here is the modern generation's Rudy Vallee.

Rudy never had a brilliant band, and, sad to relate, neither has Vaughn. It's a good enough group, and maybe it's just as good that it's not good enough to take any of the play away from its leader. But were it to stand strictly upon its own musical merits, chances are it would never have done much better than remain a territorial favorite. Thanks to Vaughn, it has now captured the fancy of northeastern United States, and runs a good chance of winning over the other three-quarters of this country before Monroe begins to lose either that voice, that smile, or perhaps even a few locks of that wavy hair.

The reason the band could never go far on its own merits is that there's nothing distinctive about its style, and, though it's good in some spots, the boys don't perform any brilliant instrumental feats.

On the whole, the arrangements are amazingly trite and dull. That goes both for the hackneyed swing and the unsympathetic ballad material. You get the idea that poor Johnny Watson is being frightfully overworked; that they're hounding him all the time for manuscript, and that all he can do is to turn out one work after another as fast as he can, without being able to give any time to use initiative. (Or is Johnny Watson getting too much credit?) For the Monroe library is a very complete one, and, to use a phrase as overworked as those arrangements, what it lacks in quality it makes up in quantity.

Faced with uninspired manuscript, the boys don't ever sound too inspired. Sad to relate, but the Monroe group too often suffers from mechanical neurosis, an apparent inability to put much feeling into the things it plays. For a band that has gained the popularity that this outfit has, it pays surprisingly little attention to the finer points of producing good dance music. Dynamics and shading are delicacies that are greatly underexploited. Tone quality is apparently not considered a necessity, while ensemble phrasing and

If the band had been twice as good, it still would have only been about half as good as its press agents claimed it was. Monroe had been a big hit in the Boston area, and since Boston then proudly claimed itself to be "The Hub of the Universe," all outlying areas would naturally be expected to follow its flow. But, as somebody once pointed out, the universe keeps going while the hub stands still.

Johnny had been a partner in the Watson-Sears band that had impressed many of us when it played in Yoeng's Chinese-American Restaurant, the same place that had housed Paul Tremaine and his Lonely Acres Band, in New York's Times Square. This was the band that spawned tenor sax star Herbie Haymer.

balance also seem to be relegated to the "maybe-we-get-it-maybe-we-don't" class.

To say that the Monroe band is bad when it comes to all those niceties of dance music would be going overboard. And yet it certainly isn't strong on any one of them. For there's an overall sameness that commences to pall after a few sets; there's nothing pretty or rich to arouse your musical emotions, and there's no brilliant cohesion of musical forces to awaken your appreciation of good musical mechanics.

If a band is going to be a really good sweet band, it has to have excellent men in key positions (notably sectional first chairs), consistent men capable of leading men who are flexible enough to be led. And if a band's going to be a really good swing band, it has to have a rhythm section with a real beat, an ensemble with a ditto, at least a few good soloists, and arrangements that can be swung.

Good enough in all these departments, the Men of Monroe are never outstanding in any one of them. The trumpets, powerful enough when their lips are holding out, possess neither fullness of tone (they pierce all right here and there) nor richness of phrasing. The saxes, blowing loudly most of the time, are more flexible, but there's no ensemble tone that'll ever thrill you. The same goes for the trombones. And the rhythm section, steady enough, becomes monotonous because of a drummer who sticks solely to high-hats on rhythm numbers, and which, as a unit, is too content to stick methodically to four stiff beats to the bar on everything it does.

There's the Vaughn Monroe band at its worst for you, and were it to be left at just that, there'd be just cause for wondering at, and perhaps even questioning, its sudden and phenomenal success.

Monroe Dynamic

But it's not just that. Of course, there's Monroe himself. He's dynamic, and the fact that this reviewer's tastes won't permit him to become impressed with a popular singer who sings through a tightly closed throat, instead of producing more informal and pleasing head tones, can't alter the conclusion one bit that here is a really big and important man in the music business.

He has another singer, Marylin Duke, a very stately-looking lass, who sings with far more assurance than most girls do, with more natural feeling, a clearer tone, and with far fewer affectations. In other words, a truly fine vocalist. Ziggy Talent turns in comedy performances here and there that amuse the kids out front, but which could be far more effective if the fellow mugged less intensely.

As for other individual talents, Monroe has uncovered a real find in Bobby Nichols, a seventeen-

Later, Bagni proved to be an outstanding lead saxist, especially when he blew softly and subtly, as not too many lead men could or would.

year-old Boston trumpeter, who blows rhythmically and whose passages possess a musical cohesion which many men, far older in experience and years, would be proud to attain. There's also a tenor-man named Frank Levine, who has many ideas of pretty phrasing which he gets across, and a talented pianist, Arnold Ross, whose simple, tasty passages are very worth listening to.

These are the three men Vaughn features most in the many jazz arrangements the band plays. How much of this attempted swing is necessary is conjectural. Some of it serves a commercial purpose, for it is played at such breakneck tempos that the kids out front can't dance and so crowd around the bandstand and gape. At which point, Mr. Monroe can simply follow up with a ballad featuring his voice, and the little girls will go more ga-ga than ever, while romantic shivers race up and down their young, supple spines.

From all of which you can gather that without its leader, the Vaughn Monroe band, both musically and commercially, is just another band. For proof, catch it any time Vaughn's not on the stand. As soon, then, as it masters some of the finer points of producing fine dance music, it will become a far greater musical unit than it is today, and will be able to hold the interests, emotional and others, of its entire audience. Judging the group in its present entirety, Simon says B-2.

Nichols and Ross both developed into really top-notch jazz players. Bobby later starred in the Glenn Miller AAF Band and, after the war, in Ray McKinley's and the Sauter-Finegan outfits. Arnie was with the Miller unit for awhile, but couldn't or wouldn't take the tough discipline and was finally shipped out after telling Glenn he didn't have time to finish any arrangements because he was too busy getting GI haircuts. After his army discharge, he contributed swingingly to the Harry James rhythm section and to several all-star jazz recording groups.

CAB CALLOWAY BAND BRILLIANT

More Precision, Kicks Dent Program

Hotel Sherman, Chicago, NBC-Blue, June 16, 12:00 midnight, E.D.S.T.

Who ever thought Cab had a band as wonderful as this! This airshot was one of the year's top surprises, for Cab and Cohorts produced just about everything a great swing band can produce in one-half an hour!

I never did have the opportunity of reviewing Cab's band in person. It was so good and deserves recognition so much that I'm inserting herewith this review of one of its radio programs.

Cab

What drive; what brilliance; what moving arrangements! And, above all, what surprising cleanliness and in-tuneness!

Starting off with *No. 10 Lullaby Lane*, the lads proceeded to kick out like mad. Right off that powerful rhythm section, led by steady, scintillating Cozy Cole, took command as a rhythm section should, and the boys were off.

The drive of the brass was brilliant; ditto solo passages such as Chu Berry's on *Lane*, *Boy I'm Happy*, and a jazz tune, third on the program, whose title slips memory, and Dizzy Gillespie's trumpet choruses on *My Sister and I*, that jazz tune, and on *Geechy Joe*.

Only drawbacks on the program were the band's being too loud behind Cab's jive vocal of *Lullaby Lane*; not enough first sax on *My Sister*, and Cab's terribly poor taste in his rendition of the latter lyrics. He should confine his singing to joyous songs, such as *Boy I'm Happy*, and get himself a good ballad singer to take care of the pretty tunes. Then there was also the poor balance on the lost trumpet solo in that third jazz opus.

But the band itself! What virility! It's seldom that you hear a broadcast as inspired and as inspiring as this was; seldom does any band relax as much as this on the air.

Besides showing that Calloway has one of the most vastly underrated bands in the business, the half-hour proved once again that Cozy Cole is the rarest of drummers: a man with an exceptionally wonderful beat, impeccable taste, and a keen perception of how to play drums for a microphone. Drum solos on the air usually are dull, but his work on *Rhapsody in Drums*, a brilliant composition, by the way, was a masterpiece of rhythmic cohesion. Milton Hinton's bass helped mightily throughout the program, as did the guitar (Danny Barker?) and the billed but unsoloed Benny Payne piano.

NBC is to be congratulated on a masterpiece of engineering; the ensemble balance was excellent throughout and the rhythm cut through mightily and still never too much. This Calloway Crew must have inspired even mechanical genius!

I was wrong. Cab has done some very good ballad singing, such as his recording of *You Are the One in My Heart* that had recently been released.

LAWRENCE WELK
(C-2)

LAWRENCE WELK and His Orchestra. Reviewed at the Rustic Cabin, Englewood Cliffs, N. J.

Saxes: (1) Freddy Worrel, (2) Roger Cozzi, (3) Everett Olson, (4) Bud Riffle, (5) Shirley Grundy. Trumpets: (1) Leo Fortin, (2) Dave Kavitch, (3) Bill Kaylor. Piano: Tommy Sheridan. Organ: Jerry Burke. Bass: Parnell Grina. Drums: Johnny Reese. Vocals: Jayne Walton, Jo Anne Hubbard, Olson, Kaylor and Grina. Leader, accordion and solo-vox: Lawrence Welk.

It isn't easy for an urban easterner to tell just how much of the time a rural westerner is kidding. Their senses of humor aren't exactly the same. And, apparently, neither are their musical ideals. Therefore, a lot of what is to follow might well be taken with a grain of salt—instead of with just a well-known grain—for, frankly, this reviewer isn't too well-versed on the subjects of square-dances, polkas, rural gags, and corn.

Accordionist-leader Lawrence Welk

Undoubtedly, Welk's band has a tremendous commercial appeal in the middle west. Its showings there have proven that. And it's easy to see why. The band is entertaining constantly, giving forth all sorts of novelties, including tunes that you haven't heard in a generation. Its trotting out less than a half a dozen current pops during the course of an evening *might* also be construed as a novelty. On top of that unique approach, it also booms the old personal contact idea, with Lawrence making sure, via much smiling at and talking with the customers, that the folks out front are thoroughly conscious of what's making the WELKin ring.

The actual ringing is what's likely to puzzle the average easterner. At times, the Welk band produces some downright fine music; at other times it puts forth a plethora of stuff in true Schnickelfritz fashion —so much of it and done with so little exaggeration, that you're not sure whether the men are doing it as a gag or whether they actually mean it. In fact, by the end of the evening, you find yourself wondering if the boys themselves are sure.

Saxes Standout

From a strict, musical point of view, the obvious standout group is the sax section. It's a clean, legitimate quintet, capable of producing good tone colorings, playing in tune, and giving the impression of a good, modern unit. It's blessed with a fine lead man, Freddy Worrel, whose excellent conceptions and clear tone give the band a finished sound it might otherwise never achieve. What's more, his alto choruses are easily the best hot solos contributed by any member of the entourage.

Doublings within the sax section help the Lyle Davis arrangements, too. An especially pretty effect springs from Everett Olson's shift to fiddle with the other four men playing clarinets. Shirley Grundy's trombone doubling helps for a fuller brass section, a unit, by the way, which is not as impressive as the reeds.

What's written for the boys and the general style of phrasing makes it just about impossible for the brass to portray any musical legitimacy. It's either rickety-tickety stuff of the triple-tonguing school, or else it's super-schmaltzy phrasing led by a Leo Fortin vibrato that reminds you of the temperature graph of a pneumonia patient. Fortin adds to the generally confused impression by playing some pretty muted solos as well as the rankest corn any side of North Dakota. Dave Kavitch, in his few spotted appearances, seems to be a trumpeter worth watching. He has both good tone and good conceptions.

From a musical point of view, by far the worst part of the band is its unsteady, outmoded, wrangling

Writes Welk: "TV has broadened our horizons. . . . You may now include the entire U.S."

Re the "fine music," Welk writes: "I trust this still holds true."

From Welk: "Key words are 'clean,' 'legitimate,' and 'playing in tune.' Excellent qualities in *any* band."

Grundy now arranges for Welk and is associated with his music publishing firm.

Re the "pneumonia patient" bit, Welk writes: "*Wonderful* line!" Thanks.

167

rhythm section. It rushes and drags and crunches in a liftless, listless, plodding manner that couldn't satisfy even the least discriminating polka devotee. The boys obviously don't seem to have the same conception of what constitutes the correct tempo or a rhythmic beat, with only pianist Tommy Sheridan, at times an interesting soloist, displaying any symptoms of modernity. This section isn't kidding, either.

Included in the rhythm on most numbers is Jerry Burke's organ, used as tastefully and possibly as effectively as an organ can be used in a dance orchestra. The instrument has too many natural limitations, however, ever to make it a definite asset in a modern dance orchestra.

Girl Deserves Billing

Burke gets billing above the other men, though it's hard to tell just why. Jayne Walton also gets her name plastered about. She deserves it, for she sings well—in tune, with a good sense of phrasing, but hampered by too many visual gymnastics. Jo Anne Hubbard does a few numbers in semi-concert style and also sings with three men from within the band. Of those three, all of whom do solo stints, Bill Kaylor is especially impressive. He sings pleasantly, easily and effectively, three compliments which you can't toss at many male vocalists these days.

Pleasant, also, is Lawrence Welk, as a front man, though he's not the last word when it comes to being at ease. Pleasant, as well, are his accordion interludes. Far less so are his solo-vox attempts, his instrument producing a grating, unmusical tone, not far removed from the sound you get when you blow across a blade of grass.

All in all, the Welk band is a good commercial group. You may never be able to relax to it, what with its tempos and continuous tricks and obvious attempts to make you notice what's happening on the bandstand. And, if you happen to be an urban easterner or a musician at heart, you might not (to use a noncommittal verb) *understand* everything that's going on. But, in any event, despite confusing appraisals, you're going to notice it and you're going to remember it, and, after all, those are two highly important factors within the field of commercial dancebandom, aren't they? Simon says C-2.

Welk: "Hope we have overcome this weakness in the past 29 years."

Welk disagrees: "Properly used, it has proved to be a *very definite asset*."

Welk: " 'In tune . . .' Glad to see this phrase used again."

Re his front-man abilities, Welk notes: "Some current TV critics would be quick to disagree."

Welk, re his interludes: "Far more pleasant are those by Myron Floren," his current accordionist.

Welk: "Solo-vox has gone the way of the musical saw. Looks like you were right in this case." I was even more right in the paragraph that followed: he surely was noticed!

For Welk's reaction to criticism of this sort, criticism in general, and other things, please note his charming letter reprinted here:

July 10, 1970

Dear George:
It was good to hear from you, and to learn about your forthcoming book. It sounds like an interesting project, and I'm sure you are well equipped to handle the subject. I wish you the best of luck.

Further comments in addition to the marginal notes follow and you are welcome to use any of them.

Needless to say, our band has been the subject of countless reviews during a career of some 45 years. They have been both flattering and derogatory, witty and dull, friendly and hostile. I guess it's just as well I developed a thick skin early in life.

Regardless of the nature of some of the reviews, I think I can truly say that I have never really been offended. This was because I found that by analyzing the criticism, I could always learn something.

I also discovered that the reviewers' opinions did not necessarily reflect those of the paying public, and I could always console myself with this thought when the notices were especially bad.

I was a pretty naive farm boy when I first started leading a band. Part of my education in the music business came when I learned about sending a bottle of champagne to the more influential critics. Suddenly we began to receive much better reviews.

George, this is not to imply that you were ever the recipient of such bribes. Judging by the tone of the review reprinted here this would seem quite unlikely.

In general I believe your comments are very fair, well stated, and indicate an excellent knowledge of your subject.

The closing sentence of your review strikes me as rather prophetic, and bears out my long-held opinion of your good judgement.

Warmest regards and all good wishes.

Sincerely,
Lawrence Welk

FREDDY MARTIN

(B-1)

Freddy Martin and His Orchestra. Reviewed at Cocoanut Grove of Ambassador Hotel, Los Angeles. Mutual wire.

Saxes: (1) Reed Christensen, (2) Russ Klein, (3) Clyde Rogers. Trumpets: (1) Norman Bailey, (2) Harry McKeehan. Trombones: (1) Glen Hughes, (2) Charlie Probert. Violins: (1) Eddie Bergman, (2) Charles Bilek, (3) Eddie Stone. Piano: Jack Fina. Bass: George Green. Drums: Bob White. Vocals: Rogers and Stone and a quartet (Christensen, Rogers, Hughes, Probert). Leader and sax: Freddy Martin.

Freddy Martin gazes fondly at photos of two composers he helped make famous, Peter Ilich Tchaikovsky and Edvard Grieg

This Freddy Martin outfit's about as fine a hotel room band as you can possibly find. It has everything to satisfy the casual customer—plenty of charm and finesse, versatility and danceability. It's never too dull and it's never too loud, maintaining at all times an aura of musical complacency that'll keep happy both the young kids who have come for the romance as much as for the dance, as well as the older folks who just happened to drop in because they'd heard that the Cocoanut Grove was the place to go.

Throughout the evening, Martin maintains a mellow musical mood. That's achieved by the tonal quality of the band—the richness of the tenor lead and the full-bodied tone of the brass quartet. For variation, there's an extremely tasty violin section that phrases unusually well together, while for a basis there's an unobtrusive rhythm section that maintains thoroughly danceable tempos. Besides keeping a steady, lifting beat, the trio also spots an outstanding soloist in Jack Fina, whom you shouldn't judge solely upon his jazzing of the classics, but rather upon his tasty background work and modulations on both ballads and rhythm numbers. Drummer Bob White, too, is unusual, for playing in a band that borders on the society style, he never produces that stiff chugginess characteristic of most of those drummers. Instead he gets a light, effective lift which, along with Fina's pianistics, and George Green's good bass tone, makes this an unusually good rhythm section.

The arrangements, by Ray Austin, are more interesting than those you usually find in a hotel-room, tenor-sax-led aggregation. They're not brilliant, in the sense that, say, Claude Thornhill's are, for the Martin type of band doesn't call for that. In fact, this kind of an orchestra does limit an arranger's scope (as well as its own musical possibilities), for its very formula calls for a direct, "let-'em-know-at-all-times-what-the-melody-is" interpretation. That Austin, therefore, does manage to bring in moments of real musical beauty (especially his scorings for the fiddles) is all to his credit and all to Freddy Martin's advantage.

The stringsters' interpretations of the manuscript of course help plenty. Ditto that of the other two melody sections. The brass is a strong unit: it's led by a trumpeter, Norman Bailey, who not only can lead ensemble with a pure, rich tone while employing fine shading, but who can also play some mighty pretty muted solos. The tone of the entire brass section, as a matter of fact, is far above average.

Not that much can always be said of the saxes. Here's an extremely effective section, especially when it's playing by itself. Then the men usually employ subtones, creating not only a good blend, but a fine, intimate effect. Martin himself comes through with pleasant passages too, this way. But when the lads let out in more legitimate proportions, they're not as effective. True, Martin's getting away from that bovine tremolo that used to characterize most of his blowing, but the section still doesn't get a perfect blend. Somebody gets an awfully thin tone on alto, which, when you consider the preponderance of tenors and their inherent heaviness, doesn't round out the section as it should. Fortunately, the saxes don't blow out often, so that this failing isn't too obvious.

Deemphasized presentation also helps you to forget two other failings noted on the night the band was caught. One was poor intonation among the reeds when doubling on clarinets (quite possibly an oversight, for the saxes always play in tune); the other was the not too good blend of the trombone quartet (both trumpets double). The latter, by the way, is a fine idea in itself, which in time should prove a valuable asset to the band.

Other assets emanate from the vocal department. Eddie Stone, whom you may recall for his years of service with Isham Jones, is still one of the most infectious singers in the business. That "happy imp" delivery of his gets you grinning inside, while his mugging at the mike entices the folks out front. Less personable, but quite adequate as a balladeer, is Clyde Rogers. You have the feeling, though, that this lad is holding back in an attempt to achieve a style. His phrasing, alone, proves that he's too good a singer to allow affectations to interfere.

The Martin band, as a group, still has a few minor affectations that hurt it musically, though not commercially. One is a holdover of the corny, trombone "wah-wahing," a trick which Martin promises he's going to shelve. Another is the degrading of the classics, sometimes tastefully done and thus not offensive, but at other times done with much pomp and very little circumstance.

A third is an exaggeration of dynamics, as exemplified by a sudden burst of brass into a dulcet sax or fiddle passage. Less intense shading would be less jarring and more convincing.

Freddy himself makes a convincing front man. He smiles pleasantly and sincerely; he keeps dancers happy by fulfilling requests quickly and accurately, and he uses much intelligence in his routining of sets. He's definitely a man who knows what the hotel-room audiences want, so that it is not at all surprising to find him breaking all sorts of records at the famous Grove and creating tremendous west coast talk. Yes, he not only knows what they want, but he's also giving it to them. What more can you ask? Simon says B-1.

171

Rather than comment on the review of his band, point by point, as some other leaders did, Freddy chose to reply with a letter answering some of my comments, but concentrating more on the effects of his having popularized the classics. His letter follows:

Dear George:

It was tremendously interesting to me to read your 1941 review of my orchestra at the Cocoanut Grove. It really turned back the pages of time to an era that many of us wish could return.

I can't recall what I thought of your review at that time but re-reading it some 29 years later I'd say you analyzed perfectly my philosophy concerning what I was trying to do then—and that was to create a mood for the romantic Cocoanut Grove by playing listenable as well as danceable music and never to intrude upon the conversationalists. I must have succeeded in that respect because I've heard it thousands of times from people—"You're the reason we married" or "I romanced my wife at the Grove"—ad infinitum.

Some of your criticisms were valid, in that at that time I sometimes sacrificed a little musicianship to get a man who sang—and that applied to all the men who vocalized (four). I'll take issue on the "degrading" of the classics, however. I could provide you with statistics (from my scrapbook) that prove my popularization of most of these classic recordings in dance tempo automatically caused a tremendous increase in album sales of the original.

It was particularly so in the case of the *Tchaikovsky Concerto*. The London Philharmonic (RCA) with Artur Rubenstein was the only album I could find at the time I decided to do my recording of it. When my record, in a few weeks time, became the number one seller in the country, the sales for the Rubenstein album boomed, so much so that the great artist Artur Rubenstein asked to meet me and thanked me for bringing this music to the attention of the masses—and, incidentally, bringing surprising monetary returns to him. It also prompted RCA to re-record it that same year with Toscanini and Horowitz. Jose Iturbi also thanked me for giving him the greatest encore he ever had while playing for troops overseas. The G.I.'s kept asking for Freddy Martin's *Concerto* (laugh).

There were many other incidents, too (some not so flattering), but I think I'll save them for my own book. Don't we all have a book?

As to the wah-wah trombone—as you know I did get rid of it. It was a holdover from the time Russ Morgan played for me. But—when people started accusing me of copying Russ—that did it!

All in all, George, I believe your valuation of the band at that time was just and valid. (I made sure the clarinets tuned up constantly.) Coming from you, whose deep affection was for jazz and the swing bands, it was a most gratifying review.

Warmest personal regards,
Freddy Martin

15th July 1970

STAN KENTON BAND DRAWS RAVES

Young Coast Crew Packs Wallop; Arrangements and Beat Point Towards Sensational Future

(A-3)

Stan Kenton and His Orchestra. Reviewed at the Casino, Balboa Beach, California.

Saxes: (1) Jack Ordean, (2) Red Dorris, (3) Bill Laney, (4) Ted Romersa, (5) Bob Gioga. Trumpets: (1) Frank Beach, (2) Chico Alvarez, (3) Earl Collier. Trombones: (1) Dick Cole, (2) Harry Forbes. Guitar: Al Costi. Bass: Howard Rumsey. Drums: Marvin George. Vocals: Terry Harlyn and Red Dorris. Leader and piano: Stan Kenton.

A young Stan Kenton urges on saxists Stan Getz (?!) and Bob Gioga

It's little wonder that this Stan Kenton band has been causing such tremendous talk in the far west— talk that has finally begun to filter through to the east with so much pressure that managers of places like the Famous Door and Meadowbrook are already beginning to tell you what great business this young outfit's going to do for them.

But it isn't all "talk" that's done all this, either. It's music, darned good music. More specifically, it's jazz, and great jazz at that. For within the Stan Kenton band nestles one of the greatest combinations of rhythm, harmony and melody that's ever been assembled under one leader.

Kenton himself is chiefly responsible. He's the lad who has arranged for the band's distinction. That distinction revolves around the unique manuscripts that have poured from his pen and around the consequent interpretations thereof, they also being guided by Stan.

Besides producing some astounding voicings (which, one arranger admitted, scared the wits out of him), the Kenton saxes provide a great part of the tremendously energetic boot this outfit gives just about everything it plays. The attack of the reeds, their slight anticipations, their infinitesimal sharp-shooting at the true value of notes—modern conceptions like that make for a rhythmic barrage (and a style, too) that's likely to knock you clear into the next room.

The reed quintet, of course, is aided immeasurably by the powerful three-piece rhythm section, which spots a tremendous bassist in Howard Rumsey, who plays an electric instrument, by the way, a strong guitarist in Al Costi and a potent drummer in Marvin George. It's an even more formidable section when abetted by Kenton's piano, but that abettation thereto takes place very seldom. More of that later, though.

The brass, too, is a brilliant section. It has a terribly tough book to play, for just about everything in the Kenton library is written in scintillating keys. And that's hard on any man's lip. Stan's extremely fortunate in having a sensational first trumpeter, a young lad named Frank Beach, who leads everything with a shrilling, thrilling tone backed by a real feel for rhythmic jazz. Surprisingly enough, the rest of the section keeps up with him, so that you don't get the preponderance of lead trumpet that you might expect. However, because of the effervescent blasting, you sometimes do get a sharpness in intonation, something which you also do expect to hear from any section blowing and overblowing as consistently as this one is forced to do. There's only one real soloist in the quintet, Chico Alvarez, who plays some interesting stuff, but usually behind the beat, causing excitement to lag.

The scared-witless arranger was Ralph Yaw, the first man to tell me about the then brand new Kenton band.

Could be that Rumsey played an electrified bass in self-defense. (See later, re the band's volume.) Afterwards, Howard became one of the west coast's foremost jazz promoters. His Lighthouse presented top jazz names even after it wasn't fashionable to do so.

174

It's interesting to note that the saxes don't keep up with their leadman the way the brasses do. It's not a matter of the amount of volume, either, though Jack Ordean does blow a powerful alto. It's a thrilling alto, too: one of the surest and yet most exciting in its series of solos to hit jazz in many a moon. This Ordean is one man whose conceptions you're going to hear plenty of from now on!

The saxes conceive fundamentally the same way; they obviously have the same rhythmic feel, and, as stated before, the result is rhythmically moving. But dynamically they're not always consistent, so that at times you'll not hear the rest of the saxes shading the way leader Ordean does. The cause quite possibly could be the setup of the section, for Jack sits far at the left instead of in the middle. Little wonder, then, that the man at the farthest right might have a bit of trouble hearing just what is going on.

Maybe Ordean could hear only out of his right ear!

Come to think of it, lots of the men must have that same difficulty at various times. For the Kenton band, judged upon its Balboa showing and also upon a witnessed studio broadcast basis, is the loudest band in captivity. How the men themselves can stand that volume throughout a full evening is amazing. If the future audiences are able to take it, also, that will be even more amazing. As a matter of fact, that continual blasting is the one major deficiency that may keep this Kenton outfit from really hitting the top. It's great to screech with complete abandon, but you've got to screech at the right time. When you do it all the time, even in a place as huge as the ballroom at Balboa, you're going to scare the folks—but scare them the wrong way.

Stan *was* a trail-blazer all right—right into rock, maybe?

Easy Medicine

Fortunately, Kenton has a simple remedy for this very major commercial deficiency. That's simply the matter of adding softer numbers to his library. Right now (and remember, this is criticism from a commercial rather than a utopian point of view) he plays far too many originals and jump numbers and not nearly enough popular tunes. As it is now, some of the hepper minority might be able to take an all-night barrage, such as Kenton offers, but more than likely it'd be only a minority among an already existent minority. Add that up and see how much business you could do over a period of time! Yes, soft, mellow, and still musical treatments of pops are definitely the remedy here.

For complete achievement, Kenton also needs a good male singer. Red Dorris, who also plays quite adequate tenor, is acceptable only on rhythm numbers. Terry Harlyn does her bit with a broad vibrato that helps, along with her phrasing, to convince you of her sincerity, but a well-rounded band can't depend entirely upon one girl these days, even if she does look good enough.

As a matter of fact, most of the visual showmanship comes from Stan himself. He's a tremendously elongated fellow with a thin face and long locks, who bounces madly up and down in front of the band, gesticulating for brass figures by extending his long fingers, and calling for sax shadings via a huge spread of his arms. It's all extremely sincere stuff, but you don't find out that fact until you've talked with Stan afterwards. And unless you're able to do that, chances are you'll leave at the end of the evening either laughing at the continual antics or perhaps believing (falsely, of course) that Stan's a terrific show-off.

"Please Play More!"

From which you can gather that Kenton would do well to curb his gesticulistic enthusiasms. There's another reason for that, too. For Stan is a brilliant pianist, one who can not only play great solos, but who's one of the finest section men in the business. The boys in the band know that, and they feel that, too. It's obvious in the improvement in the beat and in the greater steadiness of tempos (the trio rushes at times) whenever Stan gets weary enough to sit down and pound out beats on the keys instead of into the air.

Yes, greater restraint is probably the keynote to the ultimate success of this thrilling new band. Not a depressing type of restraint, either, for nobody in the world would want to curb this group's remarkable, refreshing enthusiasm. However, all its brilliance will be tremendously enhanced once it is framed in a soft, contrasting frame. For Kenton himself must realize, the darker the night the brighter the star. And those stars are potentially brilliant. Simon says A-3.

Writes elongated, thin-faced, long-locked, madly-bouncing, gesticulating Kenton: "Dear George: As I read this and recall the first band, I'm forced to admit that this was one of the most perceptive pieces you ever wrote about the music. Time has proved that all you heard and saw was valid. I wish I could argue, but my honesty prohibits doing so." Some years ago, Stan admitted that he needed to make himself into a personality to take him and his band along the road to success. So maybe he really was a show-off after all! See how naive I was!

And the lousier the writer, the cornier the prose.

GOODMAN GREAT

Benny Fires New-blooded Band;
McGarity, Powell, Both Singers,
Rhythm Section Also Stand Out

(A-1)

Benny Goodman and His Orchestra. Hotel New Yorker, New York. CBS and Mutual wires.

Saxes: (1) Skippy Martin, (2) Vido Musso, (3) Clint Neagley, (4) George Berg, (5) Chuck Gentry. Trumpets: Billy Butterfield, Jimmy Maxwell, Al Davis. Trombones: Lou McGarity and Bob Cutshall. Piano: Mel Powell. Guitar: Tommy Morgan. Bass: Sid Weiss. Drums: Ralph Collier. Vocals: Peggy Lee and Art London. Leader and clarinet: Benny Goodman.

One thing about Benny Goodman—he *can't* have a bad band. He may not always have the greatest band in the country, and he may not always be leading the greatest group of his career. But still, he's too great a jazz personage ever to have a bad band.

All of which has little or nothing to do with what's immediately to follow.

For Benny Goodman *has* a great band. It's a band that packs a tremendous punch; that plays brilliantly-scored arrangements; that reaches thrilling rhythmic

This band, considered by many to have been the best of all Goodman groups, was recently described by Benny as "a different cup of tea. By this time I was making my fourth comeback."

Benny Goodman fronts his band at the New Yorker. Art Lund (originally Art London) and Peggy Lee are the singers. Mel Powell is the pianist, Sid Weiss the bassist, Tommy Morgan the guitarist and Ralph Collier the drummer. The saxists are Vido Musso, Clint Neagley, Julie Schwartz, George Berg and Chuck Gentry. The trombones are Lou McGarity and Cutty Cutshall. The trumpets are Jimmy Maxwell, Billy Butterfield and Al Davis

heights, and that, contrary to what you might believe because of previous Goodman editions, can and does create wonderful, soft, mellow moods.

The keynote, of course, is Benny himself. Reams have been written about him. Among musicians, he's probably the most talked-of man of all. Even crackpots take potshots at him. As for this reviewer, he'd like to go on record as saying that to him Benny Goodman is the greatest instrumentalist not only in jazz today, but the greatest the field has ever known—and that includes Louis, Bix, Teagarden, Shaw, Hodges, in fact, anybody else you can mention, even down to your last Kid Ory. Benny has everything: imagination, feeling, tone, technique, rhythmic drive, plus an ability to inspire others to reach heights they might never otherwise attain.

That's why Benny'll never have a bad band. And that's one of the main reasons for Benny's newest band sounding as fine as it does. For it's Benny the clarinetist and Benny the leader who's constantly making the men play as high as their heads and at times even over them.

Of course, there are more reasons than just that. Benny couldn't achieve such results with a group of mediocre musicians. Meaning that he has a group of fine men now.

Take the brass section, for example. Besides a trumpet section that spots blowers as brilliant as Billy Butterfield and Jimmy Maxwell, there's a two-man trombone team that has no equal. In Lou McGarity, Benny has one of the real finds of jazz's younger generation, a man who blows with a bounteous boot, who not only has a feel for jazz and an ability to express it, but who also gets a fine, legitimate tone from his horn. Were it not for McGarity's exceptional prowess, Goodman would probably be featuring his other trombonist, Bob Cutshall, who possesses most of Lou's attributes, if to a slightly less degree.

Those aforementioned trumpets are worth more mention. Butterfield is a magnificent all-around trumpeter. He has a gorgeous tone, feels and expresses a powerful beat as well as his accepted beautiful phrasing, and has the range and power to make him the great leadman that he is. His tone may not possess the sharp brilliance of a James, Elman, or even an Alec Fila, but it makes up for that in part with the warmth that its inherent broadness lends to the Goodman ensemble. As for Maxwell, he's also a fine all-around man who's capable of playing much more hot than he's given a chance to, or credit for, and who, now that Cootie Williams has left and Butterfield is seriously considering ditto, will undoubtedly be given more opportunities to prove his worth. Al Davis is the third man in the section, and, though he isn't featured, he's been doing his bit in making the trio sound as fine as it does.

As for the saxes, they're in a state of flux right now. Skippy Martin has fine conceptions and not quite as fine a tone, plus a current plan to join Glenn Miller's band. How the section will sound without the Martin drive as well as without the Martin tone depends, of course, upon Benny's choice of a permanent replacement. Whoever the man is will have four good compatriots. Vido Musso, as you know, is a brilliant soloist who's not quite as strong in a section. Clint Neagley, who can play fine jazz alto but doesn't, is an excellent little musician, with both good tone and good conceptions. Unfeatured George Berg and Chuck Gentry both are extremely able sectionmen.

Benny's real prize and pride right now is his rhythm section. Ever since B.G. started this new band a little over a year ago, he's been plagued by a quartet which in some instances was all right in itself, but which never actually fitted the Goodmanic driving school. This one does.

Credits

Credit goes all over. It goes to Ralph Collier, the young coast drummer, who's given the band the most typical Goodman drive since the days of Krupa. For one thing, the lad knows how to play high-hats, an extremely important phase of drumming-for-Benny, and he's content to sit back and keep a real beat going instead of showing off tastelessly with a lot of clanging top cymbals. And besides, he succeeds in getting a strong beat and keeping it. Much aid comes from Sid Weiss, an excellent, experienced bassist with a strong punch and a fine tone, and from Tommy Morgan, who has similar attributes.

But the greatest rhythmic inspiration of all comes from Mel Powell. Maybe it's because he hasn't heard as much of him as he has of other pianists, that at this particular writing this reviewer is getting more kicks out of Mel's playing than from that of any other pianist in the business. Naturally, the newness has something to do with that. But so has Mel's colossal beat; his aggressive touch; his facile technique; his great ideas, and (and this is where he differs from so many pianists who always border on the great) his magnificent taste that results in his always doing the right thing at the right time, never overplaying, never underplaying his instrument. As for this lad's future —well, remember that he's only eighteen years old, and that, besides playing all that wonderful stuff, he's also contributing some fine arrangements for the band.

Most of the manuscript, as you probably know, comes from Eddie Sauter. Here's a truly unique arranger, one who in many ways is so far ahead of his field that you often just sit back and wonder. It's both Sauter's chords and his voicings that send chills down your back while acting as an identification tag for

Skippy followed his plan shortly hereafter. See next band review.

And, according to a recent talk with Benny, "Mel got better and better and better by the day."

Benny demurs: "Mel did very few arrangements. He liked composing those days better than he did arranging."

Benny's band. No other outfit has arrangements approaching these.

Sauter's stuff is what makes the band's ballads so much more interesting than they used to be. You remember what they were like: saxes taking melody and brass punching figures, and then the other way around, with everything as rhythmic and mechanical as any ballad wasn't ever meant to be. Eddie makes much more out of them, setting appropriate moods, besides supplying all the technical interest. And if he goes overboard once in a while, putting in so much that it's difficult to follow (especially the beat on rhythm numbers), you can still excuse him on the grounds that here's a man who's truly going forward in the field of dance music.

Benny's ballad stock is further enhanced by two fine vocalists. Peggy Lee, who wasn't too impressive till she got over the shock of finding herself with Benny's band, is slowly turning into one of the great singers in the field. The lass has a grand flair for phrasing—listen to her on those last sets at night, when the band's just noodling behind her (at which time, thanks also to Benny's and McGarity's solos, it creates its most mellow moods) and when there aren't any complicated backgrounds to sing against, and you'll get the idea. That she gets a fine beat, that she sings in tune, and that she's awfully good-looking are more self-evident. Art London, who's a very recent addition, doesn't seem to be at all overcome by his rise. An impressive-looking lad, he takes it all in stride, emoting naturally, also with much feeling and good quality, and never resorting to the clichés that have come to plague most boy singers of today. Benny's lucky in this department.

But then, he's lucky all the way around. That is, if you consider any guy who has a great band, both musically and commercially, lucky. There's, of course, more behind it than that. Which should, by all rights, send you straight back to the beginning of this review. And which, in the final analysis, is the most important part of it all. It's Benny Goodman. Simon says A-1.

Benny recently told me: "Eddie was and still is a great arranger. I was really taken by the new style and by the different kind of sound that he gave to the band. I don't know how the public took to it . . . it was not as good for dancing as Fletcher's. But we didn't quit playing the other kind of arrangements; we had a combination of both."

When Benny discovered Peggy in Chicago, he "was struck by her sound and interpretation. After she joined us, she was quite nervous for six months, or we hadn't picked the right material for her at the beginning, and a lot of people were not taken with her singing. But she certainly caught on after that when she came out with *Somebody Else Is Taking My Place* and *Why Don't You Do Right?*." I can still see Peggy on the stand, casting nervous glances at Benny, to make sure she was doing right. Lovely lass then, vague and sensitive and very bright. Hasn't changed very much since then, either.

180

January, 1942

GLENN MILLER PRECISE

Billy May Has Added Freshness To Stylized Group; Instrumental Soloists Better Than Vocalists

(A-1)

Glenn Miller and His Orchestra. Reviewed at Cafe Rouge of Hotel Pennsylvania, New York City.

Saxes: (1) Skippy Martin, (2) Tex Beneke, (3) Ernie Caceres, (4) Al Klink, (5) Willie Schwartz. Trumpets: Dale McMickle, Billy May, Johnny Best, Bobby Hackett. Trombones: Jim Priddy, Frank D'Anolfo, Paul Tanner. Piano: Chummy MacGregor. Guitar: Bill Conway. Bass: Doc Goldberg. Drums: Maurice Purtill. Vocals: Marion Hutton, Ray Eberle, Beneke, The Modernaires. Leader and trombone: Glenn Miller.

There's no getting away from the tremendous precision and appeal of Glenn Miller's band. For here is probably the most excellently drilled dance orchestra of all time—drilled not only in all the fine points of instrumental production, but also of instrumental presentation. And that goes all the way from the most subtle tonguings and shadings of musical phrases to the least subtle wavings of brass hats and screeching of theatrical codas.

Credit goes primarily to Glenn himself. For of all the leaders in dancebandom today, he possesses the greatest combination of knowing just what he wants and knowing just how to get just what he wants. Many bandleaders know one or the other well; Glenn knows both perfectly.

The result is the precise Glenn Miller band that sticks to the basic stylized formulas that have brought it to its No. 1 niche, and which, with enough variations to add a certain amount of freshness, have kept it up there for a long time.

Technically, the band's heretofore impeccable ensemble may not be at its peak right now. But it does contain more exciting musicians than it used to, which, to some, especially jazz purists, is more than merely compensation.

Bobby Hackett, for example, is a welcome addition. His cornet solos, infrequently spotted, are gorgeous bits of music. But from a technical point of view

> I find that I kept writing that same phrase over and over again. But it was true.

> The band did start swinging more along in here.

(and Miller has always laid much emphasis upon that technical point of view), his pretty but weak blowing doesn't fill out the trumpet quartet the way it should.

The same goes for the saxes. Skippy Martin's almost tenor-toned lead alto has added a rhythmic guts to the section that it never had before. But the quintet doesn't achieve the faultless, fluid blend it had when Hal McIntyre used to sit in the first chair. To technicians, that's all too bad, but for purists, who are basically rhythm, or, as they say, "inspiration" conscious, that's all to the good.

Neither of these two changes, however, has made an appreciable difference in the Miller music. For of paramount importance are the arrangements. Within the last year or so, the addition of one man has made a tremendous difference in that department. That's Billy May, whose inspiring manuscripts have fired a feeling for jazz which before his arrival in the band was very close to the ember stage. Ditto Billy's trumpet.

That the band still doesn't play great jazz, in the true sense of the word, isn't May's fault. It's not any one individual's fault, for that matter, though it can be traced pretty directly to an incapable rhythm section. If you ever listen to the band, evening after evening, and pay strict attention to the rhythm quartet, chances are you'll come away, too, feeling that there's only one man in the quartet who's thoroughly capable of transmitting a consistent beat. He's Doc Goldberg, one of the really fine bassists of jazz. The other three men are good instrumentalists within limitations, but those limitations don't seem to include the type of jazz that May writes.

Little Jazz

Glenn, self-admittedly, doesn't care too much about out-and-out jazz, though there's too much of a feel for that sort of music within the man to lead one to believe that he doesn't care about it at all. But if the kids out front like it—and Lord knows, they do—that's probably enough.

They like his ballads, also. They're presentations that you can't help admiring. Not only are they played without mistakes, but they also show gorgeous sectional and ensemble shading, precise attacks, perfect intonation, and beautiful tonal effects. Their arrangements are highly imaginative, though at times they do become repetitious.

But they're still not as mood-setting as they might be. The heavy emphasis upon a four-to-the-bar rhythmic attack produces a stodginess that makes complete relaxing an impossibility. The oft-featured Pied Pipers get a sensational blend, but their phrasing, or lack thereof, is far too self-conscious for spiritual comfort. And Ray Eberle, for all of his fine personal

182

Bobby hadn't recovered completely from major tooth surgery. Steve Lipkins soon came in, and the section perked up greatly.

For those who want to hear what the civilian band might have sounded like with a really good rhythm section, listen to some of the recordings of the AAF band.

For years I sensed this ambivalence in Glenn. He loved jazz; he had developed and lived with some of its great musicians. And yet, leading a band was a business with him, a project with which he was determined to be successful and remain successful. It must have been hard on the man.

Glenn and I argued about the heavy, stiff four-four emphasis for years. He always won, though I think Billy May influenced him a little in my direction.

Funny how that typo slipped through. I should have said the Modernaires, of course. They wrote me a letter to tell me how dumb I was!

The Glenn Miller brass, rhythm and vocal sections in the movie *Sun Valley Serenade*.

FRONT ROW: trombonists Paul Tanner, Jim Priddy, Frank D'Anolfo, Miller and singer Paula Kelly.

MIDDLE ROW: trumpeters Ray Anthony and Mickey McMickle; singers Ray Eberle, and Hal Dickenson, Chuck Goldstein and Bill Conway of the Modernaires

BACK ROW: trumpeters Johnny Best and Billy May, part of guitarist Jack Lathrop, drummer Maurice Purtill and bassist Trigger Alpert

qualities, will never become a first-rate singer until he learns how to open his mouth and his throat sufficiently to overcome that Strangulation Style of Singing that has afflicted various young baritones of our day.

Personalities

Individuals, however, aren't too important in the Glenn Miller scheme of things. That he has good soloists like Hackett, May and Martin, as well as trumpeter Johnny Best, whose warm-toned style often reaches thrilling heights, and two extremely able tenor-men like Tex Beneke (who can be sensational on slow stuff) and Al Klink (who's more exciting than Tex on faster jazz) and Ernie Caceres, who's a fine jazz clarinetist—that Miller has all these, isn't too important in a general appraisal of his band's abilities. That he even has a trombonist named Glenn Miller who can, upon occasion, play truly sensational horn, doesn't cut too much ice. For Glenn Miller, the trombonist, doesn't fit too completely into the schemes of the Glenn Miller, the bandleader. Soloists like the Pied Pipers and Eberle and Marion Hutton, who still adds as much to a bandstand (and somewhat less to a broadcast) as any girl singer has, and Tex Beneke, who does nobly when emoting blues—they're the ones who add more to the general Miller scheme of things.

Twice as dumb, yet!

To repeat—Glenn Miller knows just what he wants. And he has gotten just what he wants. If you might want something a little purer, that's up to you. But you've still got to admit that though Glenn Miller has gone as commercial as any man could possibly go, he has never, like so many other commercial bandleaders have, forsaken the realm of good taste in music. For here's one of the few really rich bandleaders who can still go to sleep any night without fear of being kept awake by his musical conscience. For an honest leader, who knows what he wants honestly, has gone ahead and honestly produced a great all-around dance orchestra!

Here I go again!

LOMBARDO COMMERCIALLY GREAT!

Guy's Group Treats Its Dancers With Respect and Intelligence; Danceable, If Not Too Musical

(C-1)

Guy Lombardo and His Royal Canadians. Grill Room of Hotel Roosevelt, New York. Saxes: (1) Carmen Lombardo, (2) Fred Higman, (3) Merton Curtis, (4) Victor Lombardo. Trumpet: Liebert Lombardo. Mellophone: Dudley Fosdick. Trombone: Jack Miley. Pianos: Fred Kreitzer and Frank Vigneau. Guitar: Francis Henry. Bass: Bernard Davies. Drums: George Gowans. Vocals: Kenny Gardner, Carmen Lombardo, Victor Lombardo and (sometimes) Rosemarie Lombardo.

Taking potshots at Guy Lombardo's music has been a pet pastime of writers in this field for many years. There are many reasons. It's easy. It's a lot of fun. It gives a guy a chance to let off steam, while knowing that he's not going to hurt anybody. And it makes a guy a big-shot in the eyes of a lot of people who don't happen to appreciate the kind of music Lombardo plays.

This reviewer belongs in that last, unappreciative class. He just doesn't like that style. To him the exaggerated sax vibratos, the clippety brass phrases with their illegitimate tones, the little use made of five rhythm instruments, and the style of singing that lets you hear all consonants and no vowels—all of them comprise a type of music that he'd prefer to do without.

But that doesn't condemn Guy Lombardo forever and ever. Lombardo's band, for example, is a wonderful band to dance to. It hits superb tempos, and though it doesn't produce a rhythmically inspiring beat, it produces a succession of steady, unobtrusive beats that make it a pleasure to take your girl out on the floor and move around to the best of your ability. If you can dance at all, you can dance to Lombardo's music.

Lombardo's band is also a wonderful band to talk to. It never plays so loudly that you've got to say "What?" whenever somebody asks you a question. If you catch it at dinner-sessions, you can even hear a mashed potato drop.

And Lombardo plays wonderful tunes to listen to. Disregarding the subject of how he plays them, you've got to admit that the songs he selects are, on the whole, exceptionally pretty. And that goes not so much for the current tunes as it does for the revivals. For the Lombardo band, with its years and years of experience, knows how to select songs that create a mood, an intimate cozy mood. Such a creation is mighty important in appraising the commercial appeal of any sweet band.

So far as the public is concerned, therefore, it's little wonder that Guy Lombardo's band has lived as long as it has lived. And it's not entirely inappropriate to mention that so far as people in the music business, especially the song-pluggers, who have to

Liebert, Carmen, Guy and Victor Lombardo

185

take such a beating from most bandleaders, are concerned, there's not a nicer group of fellows in the entire music industry than the Lombardo brothers. This reviewer, because of his inability to enjoy their music, has never had the opportunity of spending much time with the Lombardos, but he's willing to abide by the completely unanimous verdict of everyone who knows them that they personally deserve every bit of the commercial success that has so long been theirs.

It is unfortunate, in a way, that the Lombardos are resting so very completely on their laurels. True, they have made one or two changes recently, such as adding their sister to their radio shows and letting Kenny Gardner sing choruses in a pleasant, if not inspiring, tenor. But it strikes this reviewer that the Lombardos are now so firmly ensconced that they would have nothing to lose if they tried experimenting a bit more musically, and would, at the same time, have a great deal to gain, possibly not only for themselves but also for the cause of the production of popular music as a field.

Legitimatizing their music, for example, so that it would grate less upon an even slightly trained ear, would be one way. There's no doubt about the fact that the dancing public today knows more about the finer points of music than it did when the Lombardos first reached the heights—more than at any other time in this country's history, for that matter. Consequently, there are more dancers, especially kids, repelled by the most extreme Lombardo mannerisms, such as Carmen's vibrato (vocally as well as saxophonically) and drummer Gowans' almost complete refusal to do anything but tap the shell of his bass drum with the tip of his stick (except on the famed codas, of course), than there ever were before.

Of course there are still plenty of folks in the older generations who'll always flock to hear Lombardo: because he brings back memories; because he plays songs they know; because he's easy to dance to, and because they can talk when they don't feel like dancing. If Guy is perfectly content, as he well might be, to go along, merely satisfying them—well, then all this talk is thoroughly irrelevant.

But if, on the other hand, he does have some pride about his musical integrity and about the advancement of his own band's musical level, and, very indirectly, that of dance music in general, then this is the time to stop resting on his well-earned and now completely impregnable commerical laurels, and to try to go one step further. He might, for example, try fuller harmonies and less stereotyped voicings. He might make use of his two-piano team, instead of having both men oom-pahing most of the evening. He might add a trumpet to give more depth to his brass section, and he might add another, deserving singer who undoubtedly would get recognition from just being associated with such a well-known organization. He might even let Gowans hit his snare drum every now and then.

There are many things he *might* do. There are even more that he has already *done*. For Guy Lombardo, as a leader, has carved for himself a great name in the field of thoroughly commercial dance music. As a true person he has done every bit as well. Here's hoping that before it's too late he will try to see what he can do about achieving just as high a standard in the field of actual music. For then Guy Lombardo will be the complete credit to the field of dance music that some people already think he is and everybody wants him to be. Simon says C-1.

Twenty-nine years and one month later, Lombardo sent this communique from the Tropicana in Las Vegas:

"Your review in 1942 was absolutely ridiculous. To prove that fact, 100,000,000 records and almost 30 years later, our band is still the Number One Band in the country, and all the reviews throughout the country, including those from the Las Vegas papers of our current stand, also prove that fact.

"Last year we had the biggest year in the history of the Royal Canadians. This year we're off to an even bigger start—upwards of 35,000,000 people viewed our show this past New Year's Eve on TV in the United States as well as in Australia, which further suggests that your observation in 1942 was an individual opinion which had nothing to do with the public vote. As Leo Feist, the publisher, once told me, 'Whatever you do, be the best. And, Guy, you are the best. Do not change, ever!'

"And so, despite some of your negative observations in 1942, everything in our career thus far has been absolutely positive, because we have continued to please our most important commodity—the public—and we will continue to play for lovers, not for acrobats."

Obviously, Guy and I agree about his "completely impregnable commercial laurels" which I wrote about in the next to the last paragraph and for which I gave him a "1" rating, the highest commercial rating obtainable. As for his band's musicianly qualities, obviously we don't agree—or, come to think of it, maybe we do, because Guy never touched on that aspect. And, of course, he is dead right: the public does consist more of lovers than of acrobats—thank goodness!

HAMPTON BAND RATES RAVES

Lionel's Lads Really Kick Like Mad, While Playing in Tune and Together and Spotting Showmanship and Soloists

(A minus-1)

Lionel Hampton and His Orchestra. Savoy Ballroom, New York City. Saxes: (1) Marshall Royal, (2) Illinois Jacquet, (3) Ray Perry, (4) Dexter Gordon, (5) Jack McVea. Trumpets: (1) Karl George, (2) Ernest Royal, (3) Joe Newman. Trombones: (1) Fred Beckett, (2) Sonny Graven, (3) Henry Sloan. Piano: Milton Buckner. Guitar: Irving Ashby. Bass: Vernon Alley. Drums: George Jenkins. Vocals: Rubel Blakely. Leader, vibraphone and vocals: Lionel Hampton.

The Hampton band in action. Directly behind Lionel is saxist Illinois Jacquet. Next to him is Marshall Royal. Two chairs away is Dexter Gordon. Milt Buckner is the pianist, Ernie Royal the trumpeter next to the drummer

A more serious Hamp listens to a plea from Lena
Horne. The song: *You Go to My Head*

That guy who said you can't play arrangements
accurately and in tune and still get a mammoth beat
is just plain crazy. Or, maybe, he just hasn't heard
Lionel Hampton's new band. In either case, he's an
unfortunate character.

Lionel's band is tremendous. Not only does it swing
like mad, but it shows some amazing precision, and
it plays more in tune than any other colored crew,
except the Duke's of course and the Count's (less "of
course").

Focal point of the band isn't, as you might suspect,
completely Hampton. Lionel does get and give his
share of the play. But so does everybody else in the
outfit, for it's the combined as well as the individual
efforts of all members of this crew that give you some
really great thrills.

Each section is strong in itself. Take the trumpets.
This is a brilliant trio. They don't make first men
any finer than Karl George. The man has a wonderful tone, marvelous conceptions, fluent range, and
plays right in tune. In some ways, young Ernest
Royal is even more amazing. He's consistently bopping
off high "C's" and "F's" with what appears to be no
effort whatsoever. He doesn't go through a lot of

Young Royal went on to the bands of Basie, Herman, Barnet, Ellington and Kenton, and is currently
one of New York's most sought-after studio men.

facial grimaces and he doesn't miss. The visual and aural effects are stupendous. Both George and Royal play jazz, but so does Joe Newman, and in lots of ways his is the most thrilling. For besides getting a great beat, the man produces some highly satisfactory constructions to his passages. The section's fine collectively, too, with all three men playing in tune and blending tones and phrases expertly.

Though not as brilliant as the trumpets, the trombones are also impressive. Fred Beckett is an accurate, warm-toned first man, who plays pretty solos and can also take some quite good hot. Sonny Graven, a happy-looking fellow, plays some amusing plunger stuff that's reminiscent of jazz in its earlier days, while Henry Sloan gets a fine kick to the few solos he takes. Tonally, the section does not match the trumpets' sparkle, but as a unit in itself it's an impressive group that fits into the scheme of things nobly. . . .

Good phrasing and intonation are much in evidence among Hampton's reeds. The men get a wonderful, full-bodied beat, and almost everything they play is in tune. Marshall Royal, who's sort of the band's musical director, plays a stolid lead alto, also producing some savage solos on his horn as well as on his fast-moving but not quite as thrilling clarinet. Both tenor men play fine jazz. Illinois Jacquet gets more of a loose-limbed boot, but young Dexter Gordon, a handsome six-foot-four eighteen-year-old, comes across with some fine melodic ideas as well as a mighty pretty tone. Jack McVea, besides giving plenty of body to the section via his well-toned horn, also gets off some interesting baritone passages. The surprise of the section, however, is Ray Perry, who doesn't play jazz on any reed instrument. Instead, he hauls out an electric fiddle, and gives forth with some of the most knocked-out hot stuff you've ever heard. That goes not only for his solos, but also for his riff-chord backgrounds on the band's septet ("Lionel Hampton *and* His Sextet") offerings.

That very impressive seven-piece affair, which you've probably heard on records, consists of Lionel, Perry, Marshall Royal (playing clarinet) and the rhythm section. You know what a thrilling instrumentalist Lionel is, and perhaps by now you've taken this reviewer's word for Perry's and Royal's capabilities. That leaves just the rhythm section—and what a rhythm section that is!

The men produce a really powerful, superbly coordinated drive. George Jenkins is a steady, building drummer, a man with a strong beat that is never lost by too much overdrumming, by unnecessary, tasteless rim-shots and cymbal slashing. He just sits there and gives with whatever beat he has started to give with. The effect is great. He's aided tremen-

Young Newman later joined Basie and Goodman and is also one of New York's top studio men.

Marshall, nine years older than brother Ernie, later assumed the same sort of father figure among Basie's musicians.

Positively amazing the way Hamp discovered all these future stars. Dexter, who lived in France for many years, broke it up at the 1970 Newport Jazz Festival. Still an exceedingly handsome cat.

Hamp was the forerunner in bringing electronic instruments into jazz bands. He used an electric bass years before any of the others did.

189

dously by Vernon Alley, a powerful, driving bassist, with a full, rich tone and plenty of ideas. Pianist Milton Buckner also gives, and on all-too-few occasions produces some incredible solos. And Irving Ashby is not only a fine rhythm guitarist, but he also kicks off some ingenious solos both on septet numbers and when the big band is giving forth with its full arrangements.

Don't think from all of this that Lionel's band plays only kick music all night long. It doesn't. It also plays some mighty pretty ballads, and it's on these that men like Karl George and Marshall Royal show what makes them such fine all-around musicians. The way they lead their sections is really beautiful. George, especially, deserves one rave after another, for his consistently fine performances. And when it comes to ballads, don't overlook Rubel Blakely, a lad who sings with plenty of feeling. . . .

Lionel also sings (besides grunting, of course). His attempts are on faster tunes, and they make refreshing interludes. But it's Lionel, the vibraphonist, and Lionel, the happy-looking leader, who is most impressive. They don't make front men any more spontaneous than he is.

Talking about spontaneity, it's just that sort of jazz on which the band is most effective. A good deal of it sounds like glorified head arrangements. The twenty-minute version of *Flying Home* is a good example. At times, however, the boys trot out stuff that gets too involved for rhythmic comfort. So much is happening in and between sections that the total drive, instead of being concentrated, tends to become dissociated. All that makes for a lot of sound and interesting harmonics, but when applied to rhythm numbers, it doesn't make for the best beat.

Also, it's on that spontaneous-sounding stuff that the band looks its happiest. And this is really one happy-looking crew, too. And a good clean-cut-looking one, as well. The lads seem to be having much fun up there on the stand and they want the folks out front to know it, too. They shout encouragement to one another and they toss horns in the air (a la Lunceford). It's not only smart commercial showmanship, but it also helps to convince you that the boys are enjoying all that's going on just as much as you are.

And if you happen to be this reviewer, or anyone with tastes and standards at all like his, that enjoyment is very likely to reach mountainous proportions. For Lionel Hampton has come across with a thrilling, musical, commercial, rhythmic dance band. Simon says A minus-1.

Hamp was also way ahead in introducing new sounds and arrangers into bands. He'd try just about anything and has rarely received the credit he deserves for his daring and imagination. (And I'm not being swayed by that nice note his wife, Gladys, sent when I asked Hamp to comment on this review—which he didn't: "Lionel is so pleased with what you have done for him he says it's too bad we don't have critics like you now.")

TOMMY DORSEY

(A-1)

Tommy Dorsey and His Orchestra. Astor Roof, Hotel Astor, New York. Saxes: (1) Freddy Stulce, (2) Dom Lodice, (3) Heinie Beau, (4) Harry Schuckman, (5) Bruce Snyder. Trumpets: Ziggy Elman, Chuck Peterson, Jimmy Zito, Jimmy Blake. Trombones: Dave Jacobs, George Arus, Jimmy Skyles. Violins: George Arus, Raoul Poliakine, Al Beller, Bernard Tinterow, William Ehrenkrantz, Leonard Posner, Seymour Miroff. Violas: Leonard Atkins, Sam Ross. Cello: Harold Bemko. Harp: Ruth Hill. Piano: Milton Raskin. Guitar: Clark Yocum. Bass: Phil Stephens. Drums: Buddy Rich. Vocals: Jo Stafford, Frank Sinatra, Peterson, the Pied Pipers. Leader, trombone and occasional vocals: Tommy Dorsey.

Tommy and Frank

191

It's wonderful, this enlarged Tommy Dorsey band! It's really wonderful! It does all sorts of things, and it does all sorts of things so well, too! It can rock the joint with the mightiest sort of blasting jazz, and then it can turn right around and play the soothingest sort of cradle music that'll rock any little babe fast asleep.

The strings have made a difference, a very pleasant one, too. Figuratively speaking, they've added another musical dimension to the Dorsey aggregation—as well as to the Dorsey payroll, of course. And that's not "figuratively" speaking. Credit the creations of arrangers Axel Stordahl and Freddie Woolston for the effectiveness of the bowers. They have supplied them with gorgeous bits of manuscript, none of it overwritten, all of it scored with simplicity, charm and excellent taste. That the strings carry off their assignments so well is a result of their inherent musicianship and the many weeks of playing together (for the majority of them) in Artie Shaw's band, Edition No. 3A.

The strings are used primarily on ballads, a wise move, since nobody has been able to incorporate those instruments effectively into a steady jazz diet, and chances are pretty certain that nobody ever will. They're used in foreground, and in background (note some of the lovely obbligatos) for vocal effects and for Tommy's trombone.

That Dorsey vocal department is important because it is used so often and because it is so good. No need telling you about Frank Sinatra. His easy way of phrasing a song is a truly convincing bit of salesmanship. When he lets out and when he overclowns, he's less convincing. Jo Stafford is finally coming into her own. She sings purely, unaffectedly, from the heart, and always on the nose, lending tremendous distinction not only to her solo efforts, but to those of the Pied Pipers as well. The group, with and without Sinatra, is still this reviewer's favorite among all vocal units, what with its natural and musical approach towards all it does.

Tommy spots his singers wisely. He is spotting himself with more restraint, which in some ways is smart, and in others a bit disappointing. His pretty horn is still immense, and when he emotes he sets musical moods that no other trombonist, and very few other instrumentalists, can duplicate. In past days, a series of his solos used to become monotonous, if only because of background cliches. Now, however, with the strings, Tommy has an opportunity to vary background tone colorings to such an extent that similar solo doses will become tremendously more palatable.

Whereas the sweet stuff revolves around the strings, the singers and the leader, the jazz is depend-

Artie had just gone into the Navy, leaving available, among other things, this well-integrated string section. Tommy had the acumen to grab it.

Frank's still at his least effective when he goes overboard with his comedy.

ent primarily upon the trumpets and rhythm. That the Dorsey brand of jazz is as excellent as it is can be attributed to the efficiency of both the sections.

Dancebandom has probably never heard a more brilliant trumpet section than this one, composed of Messrs. Elman, Peterson, Zito and Blake. It's positively immense! It can bite and blast like the most bombastic Big Bertha, and it can soften right up and become as soothing as a neat shot of cocaine. You don't find trumpeters more powerful and more consistent than Ziggy and Chuck. You aleady know what a fine hot man the former is. The latter's becoming a revelation in that department, batting out stuff you'd never expect to hear from a man you'd always been led to believe was strictly a leadman. And in young Jimmy Zito, Tommy has himself a real find, a trumpeter with an exciting, aggressive tone, and an amazingly versatile range. "Forgotten-man" Jimmy Blake rounds out the section very capably. Not a high-noter, he's still an able, consistent trumpeter with fine conceptions plus an unexploited talent for playing some lovely, melodic ad lib bits.

As a trio, the trombones are entirely capable, playing ensemble bits with proper precision and good blend. When Tommy joins them for quartet spottings, they are, of course, more impressive as they play straight men for one of the world's greatest straight trombonists.

The saxes are a fine section. Spotted less frequently than the trumpets, they still impress with their fluent phrasing, excellent blend, and ditto intonation. Good overall tone there, too, for which much credit must go to young Bruce Snyder, who plays a baritone with both a lovely tone and requisite boot. Freddy Stulce, oldest in point of service in the entire orchestra, is a capable and consistent leadman in the Hymie Schertzer tradition. The effect of having played next to that man for as long as he did has obviously had the desired and desirable results.

The reeds also contain several impressive soloists. One is Heinie Beau, a brilliant-toned clarinetist with a boot who heretofore had been relegated to unstarred tenor sax duties, but who's now taking very fine advantage of opportunities afforded him. Star tenor assignments go to Dom Lodice, a vastly improved hot-man, who comes across with many more ideas of his own (good ones, too) and whose tone is so much better than it used to be that it's hard at times to realize he is himself.

As for the rhythm section—it's great. Buddy Rich paces it. The lad is wonderful! He propels a tremendous, natural beat under the impetus of one of the most magnificent drum techniques dancebandom has ever known. And as he continues to mature, his taste continues to improve, with less emphasis being paid

For years I wrote about him as "Dom" Lodice and for years he didn't say anything. Then, a few years ago, when I was talking in Hollywood's NBC studios with a group of musicians, Lodice included, somebody asked we why I always called him "Dom." "Because that's his name, isn't it?" I said, turning to Lodice. "No," he said, "it's Don." When I asked him why he had never corrected me he said it just didn't matter that much. Come to think of it, I never wrote very glowingly about him, so perhaps he figured some people might have thought I was writing about someone else. Bright cat!

to flash and rim-shots and interpolated rudimental tricks, and more and more being paid to giving the men a beat and holding the entire entourage together. That last job is no snap in this enlarged Dorsey outfit, either, for a big fiddle section, no matter how hard it tries, gives the impression of dragging. Consequently, if a drummer permits himself to be impressed, thereby laxing up on the reins, time is likely to go to pot. That it never does is a credit to Buddy and, of course, to his three cohorts.

Those three are all good. Phil Stephens is an exceptional bassist with a prodigious beat and a full, rich tone. Milton Raskin is playing better than ever, his solos especially showing much more ingenuity than those he had contributed to other name bands in the past. And Clark Yocum, when he's not singing (or getting ready to) with the Pied Pipers, rounds out the quartet in thoroughly workmanlike and beautiful fashion.

The routine of the Dorsey band is still impressive, if not always danceable. Tommy relies primarily on the contrast motif, though he's not making that quite as obvious as he used to, not *always* following a rhythm tune with a ballad, or v.v. His pretty moods are especially mellow when he allows them to grow through the course of two and sometimes even three slower songs, and, obviously, set off his faster attempts that much more effectively. Complaints about the brashness, and the inability to dance to an unhealthy portion of any Dorsey set, aren't without plausible foundation. Successive bombardments are appropriate for stage-show presentations, but a good deal less so for hotel rooms where not *all* patrons come primarily to *hear* the Dorsey band.

With the recent addition of the fiddles, Tommy can afford to be less sensational in his treatment of numbers, while still producing an impressiveness that can be matched by very, very few other outfits in the land. For he now has himself one of the most thoroughly musical and commercial orchestras, per se, that dancebandom has ever known, one that by its very stature will impress anyone who comes to hear, see, or dance to it. Add to that the excellent taste and all-around magnificent musicianship, and you've really got yourself something! Simon says A-1.

I never saw much pot around that band.

Those drawn-out ballad periods stand out in my memories of the big bands. They were right when they tabbed Tommy the *Sentimental* Gentleman of Swing.

HARRY JAMES

(A-1)

Harry James and His Orchestra. Astor Roof, New York City. Saxes: Altos: Johnny McAfee, Sam Marowitz, Claude Lakey. Tenors: Corky Corcoran, Hugo Lowenstein. Trumpets: Jimmy Campbell, Nick Buono, Vincent Badale, Al Cuozzo. Trombones: Murray MacEachern, Don Boyd, Harry Rodgers. French horn: Philip Palmer. Violins: Sam Caplan, Leo Zorn, John de Voogdt, Al Neiman, Bill Spear, Jack Gootkin. Violas: Victor Stern, Herschel Gilbert. Cello: Al Friede. Piano: Al Lerner. Guitar: Benny Heller. Bass: Thurman Teague. Drums: Mickey Scrima. Vocals: Helen Forrest, Johnny McAfee, Buddy Moreno.

Leader James and his prime concentration on the Astor Roof: Miss Betty Grable. Question No. 1: Is the band playing on the stand? Question No. 2: Would Harry know?

This Harry James band can really move. This Harry James band can really play pretty music. This Harry James band has some fine instrumentalists and excellent singers. This Harry James band has power and body and a tremendous amount of commercial appeal.

You're expecting the word "but" by now. Right. BUT this Harry James band is not the most consistent group in the world, and it certainly does not pack the consistent wallop his smaller band did.

Surprisingly enough, the band is most impressive at dinner sets. Early in the evening it just plays, getting a light, buoyant bounce. I don't think I ever heard Harry play with any more rhythmic spirit and more soulful feeling (he used far less vibrato than usual) than he did at a dinner session I caught. It was really beautiful trumpeting. So was what he was trumpeting at. Betty Grable was in the room.

But later in the evening, when bands open up and exhibit what is supposed to be their flash and all their wares, the James tribe was not as impressive. It was basically a matter of pushing too hard, and the more I tried to analyze the cause, the more answers I got.

Most noticeable difference between the band today and the band in those days, three or four years ago, when it never stopped jumping, is in the arrangements. Harry's writers have gradually arrived at a very full style, one in which much of the jazz, instead of going to individual soloists, is written for entire sections, usually the trumpets and fairly often the trombones. The stuff instead of sounding solid, sounds stolid, on the pompous side. You get the feeling that the men are plodding through the notes—and there are often too many notes in a given phrase—so that there's no real rhythmic freedom. With all due respect to his compatriots—and Harry's brass, with additions like Jimmy Campbell and Murray MacEachern, today is better, man for man, than it ever was—the trumpet quintet doesn't get nearly the beat and give nearly the thrills that Harry's solos do and did. For my money, Harry still gets as magnificent a beat as any trumpeter in the business, and so it seems a shame that he has to feature himself on lots of schmaltzy ballads instead of the jump stuff that he does so sensationally.

Not only are many of the arrangements heavy sounding, but the way some of the men try to play jazz makes them just that much more weighty. I don't know whether it's because they are living too well, or because they just aren't capable of playing more rhythmically, but the ensembles, as a whole, don't often show much spirit nor an A-1 conception of time. It's especially true of the strings, who, despite their maturity as a group, still don't play cleanly together.

This was during the period when Harry was still romancing Betty, prior to their marriage.

196

With drags (literally and figuratively) like that, it's hard for the rhythm section, even with as strong a guitarist as Benny Heller and as steady a bassist as Thurman Teague, to keep a healthy beat going. Dragging tempos are no rarity, especially as medium tempos, which are likely to wind up medium-slow. What's more, the rhythm section has to pound out so loud (note Mickey Scrima's bass drum) to assert itself, that it's often pretty difficult for it to produce a natural swing.

There are still plenty of real thrills in the band, however. Harry, of course, is one, though I must admit that the man looks very tired. He's obviously been working mighty hard; the few fluffs (I'd never heard any before this season) alone prove that.

With the exception of Helen Forrest, the other thrills don't get much play. Helen is absolutely stupendous! But that's sort of redundant talk for these pages. (Any of you catch the raves back in 1935 when she was heard on New York's WNEW?) One thing to point out, though, is that Harry's sympathetic tempos and the pretty backgrounds have helped to give her work more depth than it had when she sang with Goodman and Shaw and was appreciated not so much for feeling (a quality difficult to get with the kinds of arrangements those leaders fed her) as for the beat she got.

Re the other singers, Johnny McAfee has a unique style and vibrato, which, if you like it, will hand you as much of a kick as it does me. The man sings with a lot of natural feeling, which is the way you should sing.

Buddy Moreno is a recent addition to the band and a potent personality, visually. He's got about as infectious a grin as ever pervaded a bandstand. As for his singing—well, the guy just got out of Dick Jurgens' band and Dick Jurgens' band used to have a beat like a grandfather's clock. Maybe Buddy'll start forcing less and fall into a more natural and relaxed groove soon. Let's hope so, anyway.

Rare Kicks

As for the kicks that are seldom heard, one is the tromboning of Don Boyd. Here's a lad who's a rare find among men on his horn—a fellow with a great conception of jazz and an elegant tone with which to reproduce his ideas. But only once in a great while does he get a chance, and then it's only for short passages with heavy backgrounds.

Backgrounds also hamper Corky Corcoran's work. He, by the way, is a vastly improved tenor man, who has evolved ideas of his own and who no longer can be referred to as "The Magnificent Aper." But so much is often going on behind him that it's pretty difficult for the lad to play freely.

"As for looking tired," Harry explains, "we were playing seven shows a day at the Paramount Theatre, six 15-minute Chesterfield shows at CBS weekly, and working five hours a night at the Astor Roof." (Not to mention time spent wooing la belle Grable.) "Wow! I get tired now just thinking about it."

Helen has remained eternally grateful. "I've got to thank Harry for letting me really develop as a singer. He gave me the right sort of arrangements and setting that fit a singer. It wasn't just a matter of getting up, singing a chorus, and sitting down again."

Twenty-eight years after this review was written, Corky was still with Harry.

Much of the ensemble work is written for the brass. Too bad not more "written-out" solos are assigned to the saxes, for in that group is one of my favorite lead altos, Johnny McAfee. Plenty of rhythmic guts in his playing, plus a phenomenal upper register that just sings out, much the way Charlie Spivak does on trumpet.

Claude Ignored

The saxes also have a good jazz soloist in Claude Lakey, who is being heard less and less on alto. He plays good hot trumpet, by the way, too.

Don't get from all of this that Harry's band doesn't produce any kicks. It does. But they're by no means as frequent as they could and should be, and I'm fully cognizant of the importance of commercialism and the standards Harry is trying to maintain in order to maintain the gold he has attained. Not a soul can blame him for that, either, for the man had a tough time arriving where he is and ought to be given all the chances in the world to stay there just as long as he possibly can.

Harried Harry

One additional kick, by the way, I got came from Harry himself. It was a new one, too, consisting of his playing a ballad passage way down low on his horn, in the trombone register. I never realized before what fine feeling the man puts into his work down there and I kept wishing all evening for more of the same sort of thing. But I guess the arrangement was the only one for that style that he has in the books. It'd be a good formula to exploit more often.

Yes, there's still plenty that's wonderful in this Harry James band. Once it all is brought out a little more and the less wonderful things, like the tired strings and the muddy-sounding "written-out" jazz, thrown out a little more, this will again be as consistently thrilling a band as this reviewer has been raving about ever since its inception, the kind of band you want to stand in front of night after night (which is just what I used to do at the World's Fair, at Roseland and at the Fiesta Ballroom), thrilled by the beat and the feeling and the spirit of Harry and all the guys in his band. Simon says A-1.

James: "This review at the Astor Roof is very frank and true, but if you would have stopped to think a moment, you would have realized playing Roseland Ballroom for a crowd of jitterbugs, I play different sets than I do at the Astor Roof, where most people are dressed in dinner jackets, and the boss keeps saying, 'Not too fast, and not too loud!' "

WOODY HERMAN

Great is the word to rate Woody's remarkable A-1 band

Reviewed at Pleasure Beach, Bridgeport, Conn. Saxes: Sam Marowitz, Bill Shine, altos; Joe Flip, Pete Mondello, tenors; Skippy DeSair, baritone. Trumpets: Ray Wetzel, Pete Candoli, Neal Hefti, Condi Candoli, Dick Munson. Trombones: Bill Harris, Ralph Pfiffner, Ed Kiefer. Piano: Ralph Burns. Guitar: Bill Bauer. Bass: Chubby Jackson. Drums: Dave Tough. Vocals: Frances Wayne. Leader, vocals, clarinet and alto: Woody Herman.

Fate, or at least the draft, led me to one of this band's first performances. I was stationed in New Haven with the remnants of Glenn Miller's band, and one night a few of us went down to Pleasure Beach and there was Woody. I had no idea he had reorganized a band like this, so you can imagine the thrills I got that night. This bit of luck also made it possible for me to be the first writer to rave about this Herd.

"Before you can have a really great band," Woody Herman once told me, "you've got to be able to play really fine music all night long. You can't just coast along on a few good arrangements and then just play average stuff for the rest of the evening."

The Herman Herd soon after its Pleasure Beach engagement:
FRONT ROW: vibraphonist Margie Hyams, guitarist Billy Bauer, leader Herman, saxists Flip Phillips, John LaPorta, Sam Marowitz, Pete Mondello, Skippy DeSair
MIDDLE ROW: bassist Chubby Jackson, drummer Davey Tough, trombonists Ralph Pfiffner, Bill Harris, Ed Kiefer
BACK ROW: trumpeters Neal Hefti, Charlie Frankhauser, Ray Wetzel, Pete Candoli, Carl "Bama" Warwick

A young Woody and a younger Judy Garland

Today Woody Herman's Herd qualifies in terms of Woody Herman's own exacting requirements, with no reservations whatsoever, as "a really great band." So far as I'm concerned it is, with the possible exception of Duke Ellington's outfit, the most consistently thrilling band among all dance bands.

It can and does do everything. It can jump like mad, with either a soloist in the lead or the entire group attacking riffs en masse. And it can play really pretty, moodful ballads, featuring either its leader or else arrangements that spot interesting, modern chords and voicings, played by seventeen men who produce good tones and fine intra- and intersectional blends.

Most exciting portion of the band is the rhythm section. Led by Davey Tough, who, I realize now, is my favorite of all drummers, this quartet just never lets up. Tough, drumming forcefully and never interrupting rhythmic sequences and moods, is assisted by Chubby Jackson, a powerful and highly imaginative

It was amazing how little Davey, all 97 pounds of him, drove this machine, cutting right through some of the complicated arrangements to keep the swing going at all times.

bassist with a colossal tone, Bill Bauer, an extremely strong guitarist, and Ralph Burns, the band's chief arranger, who plays brilliantly tasty and rhythmic piano.

And the rhythm section alone doesn't carry the band, either. For both the saxes and the brass get mountainous beats by themselves, so strong that they could, if the rhythm section suddenly desired to go out for a short beer, still produce a pretty decent brand of swing on their own.

In the sax section, Sam Marowitz, James alumnus, continues to prove himself a fine leadman, strong, steady, dependable and with a proper feeling for phrasing. Newcomer Bill Shine, recently discharged from the Army, plays some wonderful alto passages (not much has been written about him yet), while Joe Flip easily proves himself worthy of all the raves other critics have been tossing his way. Pete Mondello, a pretty-toned tenor-man, and Skippy DeSair, extremely capable baritonist, round out a section that's fast becoming one of the best in the business.

Shine and Flip aren't the only top soloists in the band. The trombone section spots two. One is the amazing Bill Harris, featured with Goodman before Benny broke up his band and spotted as the behind-the-camera trombonist in the forthcoming movie, *Sweet and Lowdown*. Bill not only plays bootful, original jazz, but he also plays lovely sweet passages, reminiscent, as Woody remarked, of Lawrence Brown. Ralph Pfiffner, who played like Jenney in his Jerry Wald days, emotes even more forcefully these days with some very good passages. Unfeatured Ed Kiefer, Herman veteran, helps make the trombones an outstanding trio.

There are no really brilliant jazz soloists among the trumpets, the only feature even bordering on disappointment in the band. But there are several brilliant men. Roy Wetzel plays a good portion of the high-written lead with amazing consistency and potent punch, while Pete Candoli, unlike many other high-note trumpeters, screeches effectively. His sixteen-year-old brother deserves much watching for the future (he returns to high school any day now), while Dick Munson also aids the section. Neal Hefti plays most of the ad lib solos. He's a Dizzy Gillespie disciple, playing a style I have never been able to appreciate, what with its lagging beat and plethora of notes. Like Dizzy, however, Hefti has an abundance of good ideas, with which he has aided arranger Ralph Burns immensely in the production of riff arrangements that possess all the freedom of head works.

Burns, by the way, can't be praised too highly for his contribution to the organization. The soft-spoken twenty-one-year-old, who looks young even for his age, is one of the greatest arrangers to come along in

I always expected Shine to emerge as a star, but he never did.

"Joe Flip," full name Joseph Edward Phillips, soon became "Flip" Phillips.

Harris had developed into a much better reader by this time, so he was able to hold onto this job for as long as he wanted to. They tell me he's still playing great horn in Las Vegas.

Too bad Harris was all that exciting, because in Pfiffner the band had another exceptional trombone soloist who never got the breaks he deserved.

I grew up musically shortly hereafter, though some of the playing of Dizzy's imitators still distresses me because of their lack of time.

years. Woody can thank him time and again for what he has done and is doing.

As for Woody, all the men in the band can and should thank him. Not only is he a great leader, a fine front man and a sympathetic and intelligent executive, but he's also, so far as I'm concerned, the greatest all-around singer in the business today. The feeling he puts into a ballad (he credits Red McKenzie for anything good that appears in his phrasing) and the beat and humor he gets into other efforts are a combination no other singer possesses. His clarineting continues to improve steadily, as does the singing of sultry Frances Wayne, an extremely smooth-working stage performer who is gradually adapting herself to the band vocalist's medium.

Yes, this is truly a great all-around band, this Woody Herman Herd. The night I heard it at Bridgeport, there wasn't a single letup, and the pace continued right on through the various Old Gold broadcasts during the ensuing weeks. Never once did it coast. The power was on all the way, all the time, and so long as it stays on, nothing can possibly stop Woody Herman. Simon says A-1.

I did let my enthusiasm about Woody's singing run away with me at times, didn't I!

Who could sum up this review better than Woody himself, who recently wrote: "George said it all. I couldn't have written a better review. Love, Woody." Maybe I should ask Woody to review this book!

RAY McKINLEY

Eddie Sauter's brilliant arrangements spark improving band that jumps, rates B plus musically, 2 commercially

Ray McKinley's new band is new in age, maturity and ideas. Therein lie its assets and liabilities with the former far exceeding the latter.

Distinguishing feature of the band is its book of Eddie Sauter arrangements, far advanced in their use of dynamics, chords and intersectional innovations. For, as Glenn Miller once told me, "Eddie Sauter is just about ten years ahead of every other arranger in the business!"

Sauter's great writings are, however, not easy to play, for they require great musical concentration and extremely exact interpretations. And it is because of these requirements that the McKinley band may sound a bit sloppier to you than other bands do. Rest assured, though, that it's not because the men aren't able or trying, but rather because perfecting any Sauter arrangement takes time!

Ray has himself some top musicians, such as Charlie Genduso, a sensational lead trumpeter with tone, range and a beat, Peanuts Hucko, a great clarinetist of the Goodman school, Mundell Lowe, a brilliant guitarist discovered by John Hammond who plays great rhythm and also superb electrified solos, Irv Dinkins, a trombonist with a gorgeous tone, and Ward Irwin, a really fine all-around bassist.

Toppest of the musicians is, of course, Ray himself, who, besides acting as a fine front man and an amusing singer, is playing simpler, cleaner, more effective drums than at any other time in his career. Besides sticking close to the rhythmic provision department, he also spends time behind a battery of tympani (five-volt size, they're so small), which the ingenious Mr. McKinley has utilized, along with the help of the masterful Mr. Sauter, to lend a "different" (you should pardon the expression) tone color to the sound of the band. When the emphasis is upon rhythm, Rollo Laylen attends handsomely to the tymp. jrs.

The entire library is not Sauter's. There's some Henderson and Henderson-type manuscript tossed in, too, which, if nothing else, lends variety. It also gives the band, which has only five brass, added chance to jump, though "chance" is probably the wrong word when you stop to consider the jumpability of the rhythm section, the band's strongest department.

McKinley, long associated with the blues and two-beat jazz, with which he felt very much at home, took a courageous musical jump when he teamed up with Sauter and his much more modern concepts. Eventually, this turned out to be one of the most thoroughly musical bands of all time—but it did take time. "I wish you could have reviewed the band just three months later," notes McKinley, "when we had seven instead of just five brass. Nick Travis and Curley Broyles (he could have been one of the greats if he'd hung around) played jazz trumpets; Vern Friley was on trombone, and we had Deane Kincaide playing crazy baritone sax and Pete Terry on tenor."

Lowe became a top N.Y. studio man, then moved to Hollywood to arrange and produce.

The reed department, ably led by Ray Beller, a strong, assured, not always loose saxist, features Hucko, both on clarinet and on tenor, and Charlie Grant, an average tenor man, and receives versatility from Larry Molinelli, who doubles on flute and bary. The two trumpets don't measure up to Genduso, often resulting in an empty sectional sound, but Rusty Diedrick does play some highly listenable hot and Jack Steele gets a beat as does trombonist Jim Harwood.

The vocal department, in addition to McKinley, spots a fine new singer, Ted Norman, and an attractive lass, Evelyn Stallings, who's at her best when singing with just the rhythm section, sparked by Lowe's great electric guitar, and Hucko's clarinet.

All in all, there's much that works well in McKinley's band and, with the combined brains of Ray, Sauter and manager Willard Alexander, the outfit should be working in top spots and successfully for a long time to come. Simon says B-plus-2.

McKinley: "You're dead wrong, George. Ray was very loose—the best lead alto man I ever heard."

The versatile Mr. McKinley

204

CLAUDE THORNHILL

I'm sold—completely sold! I was scared that maybe when Claude Thornhill got out of the Navy he wouldn't be able to get himself a band as marvelous as the one he gave up. But his new one, which completed a record-breaking engagement at the Post Lodge in Larchmont, is as good and potentially greater, and certainly better than its badly-balanced MBS airings indicated.

Claude's band has superb color, wonderful over-all tone, great arrangements and an array of magnificent soloists. Add to that a tremendous commercial appeal that keeps dancers and listeners interested throughout every minute of an evening and you've got one of the really great bands in all of popular music history.

The arrangements, with their great intersectional voicings, their fine use of French horns, their emphasis upon various phases of dynamics (all meticulously adhered to by the musicians), set the style. Claude, Gil Evans and Bill Borden rate the bows here.

Among the musicians, all rate plaudits, some rate even more. Thus, in the trumpet trio, as excellently blended a section as you'll ever hear, there's leader Louis Mucci with his warm, big tone and fine conception, flanked by two really thrilling soloists, Rusty Diedrick, who plays gorgeous notes with much more spark than he did with McKinley, and Jakie Koven, probably the closest living musical image of Bunny Berigan. His tone is sensational; too bad he hides it too often behind mutes.

The trombones are led by warm-toned Tasso Harris, with Bob Jenney's jazz adding additional

This was truly a fantastic band that kept getting better and better all the time. A year or so later it was playing brilliant Gil Evans arrangements of Charlie Parker originals and also still producing those lovely sounds on its ballads. I could and should have written a much longer review than this—the band certainly deserved much more attention than I'd given to too many other bands—but for some reason or other we decided during this period to cut way down on band reviews. In this particular case, that was a big mistake.

Claude and arrangers Gil Evans and Bill Borden

sparkle, while in Fred Schmitt and Sandy Spiegel-stern, Claude has two modern-sounding French horn players.

The sax sextet is a beautifully blended section. It has two outstanding soloists. One is Bob Walters, the only clarinetist I can think of who could make you forget the great Fazola. His big, warm tone, his fine shading are really things of beauty. The other great soloist is Ted Goddard—but not on tenor! Why a man who plays such magnificent alto should lower himself to playing such average tenor is a mystery.

Rhythmically, Claude's band is way above its pre-war standards. In the first place, Claude is more seri-ous about his section work; in the second place he has a strong, sure bass player with a gorgeous tone and a spectacular name, Iggy Shevak, while guitarist Zeb Julian and drummer Billy Exiner complete a splendidly blended team.

The vocal team of Betty Bennett and Buddy Hughes has warmth, character, good looks, inexperi-ence, but may very easily reach the band's standard. That's high shooting, because Claude Thornhill's really going to make it this time!

SAUTER-FINEGAN
AT MEADOWBROOK

The Sauter-Finegan band at Meadowbrook was an amazing revelation! Previously confined to recording studios, where it benefited from all that such conditions could provide, such as multi-mike setups and as many takes as necessary to produce the desired results, the big outfit on opening night knocked off arrangement after arrangement with amazing precision while displaying all the sounds generally heard on its recordings.

And what sounds! You've heard them on wax, but you've never really heard them till you've heard them in person. All the ingenuity, all the humor, all the fantastic voicing and thrilling harmonies are just so much more impressive when blown straight at you. This evening was just one succession of musical thrills.

There were changes from the studio-born lineup. The rhythm section was entirely new, and if it suffered from anything, it was from an inability to be heard. Doubtlessly the quartet felt a bit restrained, because the parts are by no means easy, and it's pretty hard to swing out uninhibitedly when you're not sure of what you're supposed to do next. But Mousey Alexander, formerly with Marion McPartland, and playing his first date with a big name band, did a surprisingly fine job, keeping good time, showing innate good taste, a firm but not ponderous touch, plus an ability to play the complicated parts. Bassist Bob Peterson, though not always audible, also fit, as did Billy Bauer, who was subbing for Mundell Lowe, and new pianist Dan Finton.

Behind them stood percussionists Walter Rosenberger and Buster Bailey, both borrowed from the New York Philharmonic, both exhibiting uncanny techniques, plus a feeling for a beat seldom associated with classical musicians.

Both the brass and sax sections showed amazing cohesion for groups as new as these. The trumpets had two mainstays, Bobby Nichols and Nick Travis, who along with Al Dirisi blew powerfully well, with both Bobby and Nick emitting some fine solos. Ditto Sonny Russo among the bones.

The reeds, full of doubles, sounded fine too, as a sax team and as a team of any one of dozens of different instrumental combinations. Doris Johnson and Bill Barber (since replaced by Harvey Phillips) played the difficult harp and tuba parts well, while Sally Sweetland sounded fine on the ballads that suited her soprano voice, while Andy Roberts did well with his few assignments.

In front of the band, both Eddie and Bill give surprisingly good accounts of themselves—a bit embarrassed but thoroughly gracious personalities.

One thing the band's appearance did, in addition to proving that all its component parts can be heard (the special S-F audio equipment behaved beautifully), was to prove its danceability. There were times when the audience was asked to participate only by listening, but for the most part Messrs. S. and F. produced thoroughly danceable tempos, which at times required a bit more concentration for beat-following than simple Lombardo and Kaye music do, but which, on the whole, didn't seem to foul up any feet. And the consistent applause after every number (there was not a trade crowd present, either), plus the dozens of enthusiasts crowding around the bandstand, were added proof that the Meadowbrookians loved this great new band, which, so far as this reviewer and probably thousands of satisfied customers are concerned, has as definitely arrived in person as it has on wax.

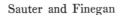

Sauter and Finegan

207

DORSEY BROTHERS

It was a warm sound, a pleasant sound, a rich sound, that pervaded the confines of the Cafe Rouge last month. It was the sound of not one but two Dorsey Brothers as Tommy and Jimmy returned with a combined band to the spot where both had starred for so many seasons.

Technically—and the billing had it that way—it was Tommy Dorsey and his Orchestra, featuring Jimmy Dorsey. And, to be sure, the band was Tommy's, pretty much the same band that was reviewed here a year or less ago. But it didn't play only the TD book. When the younger Dorsey (that's Tommy, in case you didn't know) led the band, it played tunes out of his library. When Jimmy took over, it played from his book. Consequently, you had two band styles for the price of one, though the difference wasn't radical enough to confuse anyone.

The band was good, as all Dorsey bands are. It had a great ensemble sound, and it had disciplined attack and routining that would put almost all of the newer bands to shame. The trumpets were especially sparkling, and in their midst Paulie Cohen blew an outstanding lead. Lee Castle was in there, playing his Dixieland jazz, which was featured more in a small combination that starred the brothers. The brass also sported the very big, lush trombone sound of Tak Takvorian's horn, giving the section a strong, round bottom that you usually don't hear nowadays. And the reeds were, as Dorsey reeds usually are, well matched and consistently in tune.

In some ways, the band was the equal of those that TD and JD used to front fifteen years ago. But in one way it wasn't—in the vocal department. There was no Sinatra, no Eberly, no Stafford, no O'Connell, though Lynn Roberts did venture a couple of Helen's standards and Johnny Amoroso did sing in a big voice. There was Gordon Polk, too, overacting as though his life, and the band's too, depended upon his every grimace. In this section, especially, was the class missing that stamped the various outfits fronted by both brothers.

The rhythm section, too, was not outstanding, but rather stiff in its beating out arrangements that were meant to swing more. It was nice to see Bob Varney back, but he has played looser drums, if my memory serves me right.

Otherwise, though, it was a rewarding performance, especially to those of us who still number such qualities as tone, intonation and ensemble precision among things worth listening to and for. And, of

It seems fitting to close these reprints of band reviews with this one, sort of a coda for all the reviews. Even if the band lacked much of the excitement and enthusiasm that had once pervaded the dance band scene, it, nevertheless, still reflected the fundamentals of good musicianship that had always characterized all of the Dorseys' contributions. It was sort of sad, seeing these two elder statesmen hanging on, hanging on together because apparently there wasn't enough work for them to function independently. It was sad, but it was also a warm feeling, seeing them together again—even if they didn't hit it off well personally— sort of like a family reunion for old times' sake. But within three years, both the band and the two Dorseys had left us—forever. And a wonderful era was really—but really—finished.

Tommy and Jimmy

course, there was always Tommy's amazing trombone, the Rock of Gibraltar among all dance band sounds.

On the set of *The Fabulous Dorseys:* Jimmy and Tommy, with Paul Whiteman flanked by alumni Henry Busse and Mike Pingatore

On the set of *The Fabulous Dorseys:* Tommy and Jimmy joined by ex-vocalists Connie Haines and Helen O'Connell

May, 1935

JOE WRITES PETE ON CRASHING SOCIETY

Wants to Know What It Takes to Play Dances for the Blue Bloods, Does His Own Investigating and Uncovers Some Surprises

NOT SO SNOOTY AS YOU'D THINK

Dear Pete:

This society dance band biz is lots different than I thought. It always seemed to me that those society people, with all their dough, hired only big name bands, like Whiteman and Casa Loma and Kemp and that bunch, to play for their snooty parties.

They don't, though. Instead they use a certain bunch all the time; bands like Meyer Davis, Emil Coleman, Ruby Newman, Mike Markels and others. So, pronto, I hied me up to the offices of some of these guys to find out just what's with the blue bloods.

Naturally what interested me most was how come these guys got all the money parties. They all told me the same thing—it's just a habit with society, and a habit that works both ways. The folks have gotten so used to the type music that Davis and Coleman and all the rest play that they never think of hiring anybody else. Probably they couldn't even dance to anybody else. You see, these leaders have been playing at society dances for years; they play for a crowd at its high school dancing classes, and they're still playing for them at their kids' weddings. Mike Markels has been around New York circles since 1913. Meyer Davis and Emil Coleman came along a little later; they spread out to Philly and Washington and Florida. In those cities it's always Davis or Cole-

man; in New York, Markels joins in the business; up in New England it's all Ruby Newman. And so it goes.

The kind of music (or should I say "dansapation" like all the fancy magazine writers?) society wants is all simple; no fancy frills and mixed-up arrangements. They've been used to this simple stuff and they want only that. Mike Markels said that a few years ago he sent Ted Fiorito out on a job for him. You know yourself what a swank band he's got, with all the arrangements and stuff. But they certainly didn't click at the party. The people who hired him got sore as hell at Markels and told him to send out a dance band and not a bunch of acrobats. That just wasn't in their line.

What They Really Do

You know what they really do, these society bands. They sit themselves down on their fannies and play mostly choruses all night. Seems like a cinch, doesn't it? No featuring stocks and specials the way we did down at the ballroom last summer and at the college dances last year. Not even dignified stuff like Paul and his band pull at the hotel. When they do have arrangements it's practically always on tunes like *Blue Danube* or *Vilia* or stuff like that which sounds lousy faked or on which you can't play choruses. They have quite a few of those semi-classics, because after all there are lots of old fogies in the parties who wouldn't know the difference between *Stardust* and *China Boy*. (Do you? Heh, heh.) But, according to Newman and Markels, they play one arrangement out of every five tunes. Davis and Happy Reis (he's Coleman's right-hand man whom I saw) say that it may go as high as two out of five.

Seems to me that I mentioned something about the job seeming like a cinch. Forget that, colonel, forget that. It's a tough assignment. In the first place you've got to have an iron lip or wrist (depending upon what you play), because at those parties you just forget anything you ever heard about sets and intermissions. You're there to play. You set up, say at ten, and often go right through until four without a letup.

Like a six-day bike race. But you've got to be able to do more than that; you've got to be able to read anything at sight and read it right. These bands don't rehearse much, but if there's one thing they do it's keep up with all the latest tunes. Society knows them all and expects them. No getting away with such old gags as, "The publishers were all out of stock on that today," or "Oh, that's so old we threw it out of the books." And on top of all that, you've got to be able to fake anything, because the class folks know not only all the new tunes but all the old ones, and they expect them, too. The stuff they dig up is almost uncanny. Newman and Davis both said that recently they got requests for polkas and quadrilles. I didn't want to seem like a dumb bloke in front of them, but what in the hell are polkas and quadrilles, anyway? On top of such fluky stuff, you've also got to know foreign numbers and all the old show tunes. Some fun!

Besides all that you've got to be a thorough musician. No floozy tones. If you're a melody man you can't get by with anything but a legitimate tone. Those money men go to lots of concerts and recitals and get to know their instruments. They appreciate a really beautiful tone, and they'll turn thumbs down on anything else. You don't have to worry so much about your hot—so long as it's in good taste and not too corny it will get by—they don't know much about that part of it. But you've got to be a legitimate man who not only has good tone, but who can fit into a section and make it sound like something.

If you're a rhythm man you've got to be good and steady. What the dancers want is a good solid beat that's accented. More or less of the good old-fashioned oom-pah with plenty of sock on the sock cymbal. Almost military in its stiffness. But then so are most of the dancers. And this oom-pah stuff is played at a pretty regular tempo, especially when it comes to dancers above twenty-five or thirty. They're all used to that pretty definite tempo, about the way most bands play *I Get a Kick Out of You*. It's the tempo the older crowd is used to, and if you make it much faster or slower they can't dance, and, of course, blame it all on the band.

With the younger society crowd it's somewhat different. All the leaders told me that within the last few years they've noticed that the younger ones want their tempos mixed more. In moderation they go for the old contrast theory we always used, you know, first something like *Stormy Weather* followed by *I Got Rhythm*. That's something new for society. Newman offered a good explanation. He blames it on the depression. He pointed out that in the good old days there were all the private parties to go to. Now there are fewer, and so the kids go to hotels to dance.

There they get used to the change in tempos and so when they go to parties they want that sort of stuff. Sounds logical. The depression has given the rich youngsters a chance to get used to styles different from the stereotyped Davis, Coleman, etc., stuff.

All this may make it sound like a pretty punk field to get into. It has its good points, though. Not the least is the pay; you're always sure of at least union scale, and usually more. The leaders get the best men and want to keep them.

Another thing in its favor is that the leaders—at least those I met—are all gentlemen. You can see yourself that they have to be in order to get anywhere with society folk. It comes to them naturally, and they treat you accordingly.

And the society folks are generally right there, too. There's little of those up-in-the-air-with-my-schnozzola stuff which you hear about. They talk with you, and kid around with you, and keep you happy with food and drinks, and when they're not around you can have plenty of fun yourself watching them. And some of those gals are worth watching.

All in all, you can see how different this society angle is. It surprised me when I heard about it. I think I'd like it. Guess I'll take out the old horn, practice my tone and reading, take a course in memory, and then run up to those offices and ask them for a job. Maybe next time you write you can send your letter in care of Meyer Davis or one of those guys. Who knows!

Yours,
Joe

January, 1936

PICKIN' THEME SONGS

All the Bands on the Air Need Trade Marks So They Pick Theme Songs. But Why Certain Tunes? You'd Be Surprised

Theme songs—they open and close bands' radio broadcasts; they are the identifying marks of dance orchestras; it's because of them that you know you're about to listen to Zimmerman Blotz and his Blotzers, or that you know you've been listening to O'Shaughnessy Marblehead and his Ten Ears of Corn. You don't need any announcer to tell you, for after all, isn't that the band's theme song? Isn't that what identifies the band? (In case you're one of those guys who must have an answer to even a rhetorical question, your answer is "Yes!")

But what has caused the band to choose that certain tune as its theme? There are four reasons: (1) the leader wrote it and either wants it plugged or else realizes that the song is pretty closely identified with him; at any rate he's pretty proud of the fact that it's his song, and judging from the high caliber of theme songs in general, he usually has pretty good reasons for feeling proud.

Here They Are

Look for yourself at this fine array: The Duke's *East St. Louis Toodle-oo;* Isham Jones's *You're Just a Dream Come True;* Will Hudson's *Hobo on Park Avenue;* Charley Boulanger's *Meet Me Tonight in My Dreams;* Dick Himber's *It Isn't Fair;* Bill Scotti's *Moonlight Madonna;* Claude Hopkins' *I Would Do Most Anything for You;* Ray Noble's *The Very Thought of You* and *Good Night Sweetheart;* Eddy Farley's and Mike Riley's *Music Goes Round;* Frank Dailey's *Gypsy Violin;* Emery Deutsch's *When a Gypsy Makes His Violin Cry;* Felix Ferdinando's *Dream a Beautiful Dream;* Johnny Green's *Hello, My Lover, Goodbye;* Joe Haymes's *Midnight;* Eugene Jelesnik's *Silhouette in the Moon;* Al Kavelin's *Love Has Gone;* Chick Webb's *Get Together*, and so on and on. There must be more—as a matter of fact, because it's "an original composition by Maestro So-and-so" is the most common cause for using a song as a theme.

Closely allied to the above is reason number two: the band introduced it, made it popular, and it has been identified with the band ever since. A few typical examples: Rudy Vallee's *My Time Is Your Time;* Paul Whiteman's *Rhapsody in Blue;* Casa Loma's *Smoke Rings;* Jimmy Dorsey's *Sandman;* Benny Goodman's *Let's Dance;* Cab Calloway's *Minnie the Moocher;* Hal Kemp's *How I Miss You,* and Wingy Manone's unique version of *Isle of Capri.* Some of those tunes, you'll notice, were written by arrangers with the bands —note Gene Gifford's *Smoke Rings*, as well as Bernie Mayer's *Sandman.*

Sentiment

Sentiment has a lot to do with choosing the theme song. That's reason number three. Note the following, who chose their themes mainly because those songs bring back fond memories or something like that: Louis Armstrong's *Sleepy Time Down South*—the lower part of the Mason and Dixon Line still beckons Ol' Satchmo; Al Donahue's *Dream of Bermuda*—the Boston lad made a big success down there, and liked the place so much he wrote a theme about it—and by the time this gets into print he'll probably be back there again; Tal Henry's *Carolina Moon*—Henry being a Carolinian, in case you haven't caught on yet; Oliver Naylor's *On the Alamo*—Naylor came from Alabama and the Alamo is in Texas, but that's close enough for jazz; Ozzie Nelson's *Loyal Sons of Rutgers,* the Nelsonian alma mater. Lucky Millinder chose the tune that brings sentiment to the hearts of most dancers, *Stardust.* Reggie Childs took *I Love You* because he was the first person to play it for composer Harry Archer. Joe Rines selected *Waters of Minnetonka* because he played it so well and often at his first job at Hunter's Cabin. Benny Meroff reversed things a bit; he liked his theme, *Diane,* so much that he named his first daughter after it! Now who's going to play his daughter?

Trick Reasons

The fourth and final reason is the trick reason. That takes a bit of ingenuity, and since not all the bandleaders are ingenious, or else don't want to be known for that, there aren't so many trick themes. But note these: Louis Breese's *Breezin' Along with the Breeze;* Little Jack Little's *Little by Little;* Johnny Hamp's Kentuckians' *My Old Kentucky Home.* And (with explanations) Jolly Coburn's *Music in the Stars,* because he was the first to play way up in the high Rainbow Room; Bob Crosby's *I Think of You With Every Breath I Take* (his first commercial was for a perfume sponsor); Teddy Hill's *Swingin' Uptown* (the band swings uptown in Harlem). But perhaps the whackiest example of all is a band in Massachusetts, led by one John Gunn, whose theme is merely the first two measures of the verse of *Over There*!

It's a lot of fun, this game of trying to figure out just why a band uses a theme. There are probably more examples, so why don't you try to figure them out? There's a radio playing non-theme songs too loud next door anyway, and it's getting hard to concentrate.

212

THE DIARY OF OUR OWN JIMMY BRACKEN

Life was so exciting—there was so much to do and to see and to hear during the Swing Era—that I decided to let our readers in on the exciting times I was enjoying. This I did at irregular intervals over a several years' span via "The Diary of Our Own Jimmy Bracken" columns. And who was Jimmy Bracken? I only knew him as the fictional character to whom studio jazz musicians would refer whenever anyone from the fire department, which prohibited smoking in the studios, would walk in. The first musician to spy him would merely call out "Jimmy Bracken," and immediately all the guys would douse their cigarettes. And so, since he was such an "in" character with so many top musicians, I decided to latch on to his name. Soon those who were "in" knew who *Metronome's* Jimmy Bracken really was, though all the references to George Simon, Gordon Wright and my other pen names must have confused many readers. At times, they even confused me!

September, 1939

WEDNESDAY—We put the August issue to bed around five this afternoon. So to the McAlpin Roof for dinner. First person I met was Leonard Joy of Victor, with publisher Sol Bornstein. Leonard went into raptures about the date Bud Freeman did for them. Six standards; all much better than he'd ever dreamed they'd turn out. I'm anxious to hear them, 'cause when Bud's right, they don't come more exciting. Later Al Zugsmith passed my table. Hadn't seen him since he was in that ill-fated CBS band department. He's now running a paper and dabbling in politics, besides doing publicity work in Atlantic City. After Al came a pretty lengthy talk with band manager Gordette and Messner. Seems they've hit upon a new idea: risque jazz. That and their softball team, which hasn't been beaten yet, are their two big interests right now. The band sounds bigger than nine men and a girl—and a fine girl, that Jeanne D'Arcy—sings well and looks like a million.

One of the Freeman sides turned out to be his umpteenth version of *The Eel*, whether he called the others that or not.

Off at nine to catch the last Woody Herman show at the Parliament. Woody's got a swell band and personality, and that Jerry Colonna guy really knocks me out. After the theatre I went down to Tommy Dorsey's. Big surprise: Colonna was there too. He did some really whacky dancing with his pretty wife out on the floor; thought nobody was looking, I bet. I sat with Ward Sillaway's wife, Kay Weber. (You remember her when she sang with the Dorsey Bros. and with Crosby.) Kay looks better than ever, and still has that marvelous sense of humor. Before I went home I talked with Mrs. Dorsey for a few minutes about tennis at the Dorseys'. What a wonderful lady she is!

An Evening with Glenn Miller and a New Clarinetist

THURSDAY—Dinner at the Casino with Glenn, his mother, and his wife, who's in the Mrs. Dorsey classification. The band sounded the nuts. Glenn, though, was looking for another clarinetist and started asking me about this fellow, Jerry Yelverton, whom George Simon had raved about in his review of Barry Wood's band. After a little talking, Miller got his manager, Tommy Mack, to call Yelverton and have him come out after work. He did, and let me tell you, that guy's really a find! Should have seen the reaction of the guys in the band when he started to get off on Stardust. Glenn signaled him to take one chorus after another. He was sitting with Larry Binyon, fine NBC saxman.

Jimmy Bracken and George Simon were the same person, so Glenn was actually asking me about what I wrote.

Drove Yelverton back to town. A mighty intelligent and modest chap. Just graduated from Auburn last June. He told me Glenn would let him know whether he got the job. Left him at 114th St., and a few blocks later stopped at a red light right next to Van Alexander's car. He was driving some of his band home. They all looked weary. Phyliss Kenny, Ray Barr and Joel Livingston shifted into my car, because I was driving further downtown. Ray's still the good-natured whack of old. The other two weren't in very good moods. After they left, Ray told me they were engaged to be married.

He got the job. He was intelligent and modest, all right. Also quite naive. His favorite curse words were "Christmas Turkey!" Beneke and McIntyre, who flanked him in the sax section, would put him on by trying to outdo one another with startling epithets. Jerry managed to survive.

Pluggers' Union; Old Ben Pollackers Reminisce

FRIDAY—Had lunch with Jack Philbin, Famous' contact man who's in town for a month or so. Jack was telling me what a tough pace pluggers had here compared with out of town, when Larry Shayne of Paramount Music joined us. Seems Larry's pretty active in the attempt to unionize song-pluggers. Said the scheme looks as if it'll go through, even though some of the publishers won't cooperate. Gee, those poor guys sure deserve some sort of a break—they work much too damn hard.

Jerry Colonna and Woody Herman

The very pretty Kay Weber

Had a drug-store-between-stage-shows dinner with some of the guys in Woody Herman's band. Could this be a romance between vocalist Mary Ann McCall and drummer Frankie Carlson? Neal Reid, band manager, said they're adding a fifth sax, who'll take most of the hot tenor, and a third trombone.

MONDAY—Stopped in to see the Crosby band at rehearsal at Nola Studios. After rehearsals, Gil Rodin, band prexy, Dorothy Claire, their new singer, and I were taken to Glen Island by publisher Jack Robbins and Chuck Rinker. Robbins a humorous guy. He and Gil reminisced most of the way up about the old Ben Pollack days. Seems Jack's known all these swing guys for years and years, and helped a lot of them through some pretty lean days.

It was a kick at the Casino seeing Gil and Glenn together again. They were close buddies in the old Pollack band, and they hadn't seen each other in a long time. As you can imagine, they rode one another pretty much about being rivals who really shouldn't talk to each other, but you could tell that each one was crazy about the other.

Visitors at the Convention; Bobby Hackett Brought Down

TUESDAY—The Instrument Manufacturers and Dealers Convention started today so I had to spend most of my time there. Hal Kemp dropped in to say hello. Looking fine. He's tickled pink with Nan Wynn, he said, but rumors have it that Nan is leaving the band soon. I hope not. Later on I went up to see Jack Williams at the RCA Victor exhibit: what a sweet disposition! Gil Rodin was listening to some records of Kathleen Lane and Dinah Shore—"just because some people wanted me to hear them," he said. Crosby and Eddie Miller and Joe Kearney were also there, and Bob and Eddie were televised. That Crosby's got one helluva sense of humor.

WEDNESDAY—More Convention. There was a good jam session in the Rudy Muck studios featuring Frankie Newton. Otherwise the day was strictly business. In the evening to the Tommy Dorsey broadcast. Really fine; Yank Lausen played some stuff that knocked me clean out. Afterwards had a long talk with Dick Jones, who arranges for Casa Loma, and Axel Stordahl, who dittoes for T. D. Dick told me that he'd taken a METRONOME suggestion and written a swing arrangement of For You, *the ballad that Kenny Sargent always slays 'em with. He said Glen had written in from the midwest that the band was crazy about it.*

Later on that night I dropped in to see Bobby Hackett at his closing at the Troc. Jimmy Monaco, whose band used to broadcast coast-to-coast, is the band's new manager. Place was pretty empty and Bobby was pretty brought down. I kept wondering

Those were the days when I (the "some people" here) was trying to get various bands, including Crosby's, to hire Dinah who had recently arrived in town. No luck, which turned out to be a big break for her, because she went directly into network radio and then NBC's "Chamber Music Society of Lower Basin Street" series.

Hey, television back in 1939 yet!

Maybe they were, but I never heard them play it. Later I made the same suggestion to Sy Oliver, and he arranged it for Tommy Dorsey with a Jo Stafford vocal. Remember?

216

why he insisted upon having an 802 band, when he could probably get many more enthusiastic guys from out of town. He's got a good rhythm section, though, especially that Zeb Julian guy on guitar. We left the place between sets to hear the Count across the street at the Famous Door. Band kicked plenty and the place was packed. Coleman Hawkins was due to come in later on but we couldn't wait that long. Back to the Troc and a seat at Jack Robbins' table with Jack, David Breckman, coast leader who had been in the NYC studios for a few weeks, and their wives. Breckman couldn't understand why classical musicians couldn't play better jazz. "Such awful tempos!" he exclaimed, and then related how some guys were laughing at him these days because he, formerly strictly a symphony man, would beat off a few bars to himself in strict swing-bandleader style, before turning over the beat to his orchestra. He didn't care though; said he found much better tempos that way.

Crosby's One-Night Stand; Dope on the Bernie Lads

THURSDAY—Last day of the Convention today. Short, too. In the evening went way out on Long Island some place to Roadside Rest to hear the Crosby band. Almost smashed into Bob's car on the way out. The band sounded especially fine that night. Lots of publishers there. Talked for quite a while with Frank Herz and Milton Ebbins of Jack Jenney's band which plays there regularly and suggested that as long as they were looking for a boy vocalist they try Tom Eldridge, who's a page at NBC. Allen Hanlon, Red Norvo's guitarist, was there, getting a big boot out of the band. So was Bobby Hackett. Wonder why Bobby never got into that band?

FRIDAY—Lunch with Gray Rains, who runs and arranges for Ben Bernie's band. Gray is dying to have his own outfit again and says that he may start any day now with Ben's support. High in praise of his boss. Says the whole band feels the same way. Dinner with Bob Haggart. He says he's going to make an arrangement for the next issue.

MONDAY—Dropped in to see Milton Gabler at his Commodore Music Shop. He's discontinuing those fine releases of his until the fall. Some kid was thumbing through various music magazines. "Which one do you like best?" asked I in my most disarming manner (the old fox!). "They're all bad—not enough swing!" An extremist, no doubt. . . . Then on to Rockwell General Amusements to see publicity lass Ceil Campbell smile. Frank Dailey was at her desk. "Hmm," he muttered, pointing to an article in last month's issue, "I see Clinton's got some of my old boys. Good for him." (Funny, did you ever notice how Frank and his Meadowbrook spot seems to be the new place for "making" bands?) Will Osborne's

A Xavier Cugat caricature of Ben Bernie

manager, Harry Romm, peered in; said Will's going great on the coast; likes singer Jean O'Neill, whom METRONOME got for the band. . . . Next stop Willard Alexander at the Wm. Morris Agency. Jerry Livingston (né Levinson), who wrote *Talk of the Town* and *Under a Blanket of Blue*, was in the waiting room; he now has a society band at a swank 58th St. spot called Mother Kelly's; said it's better than the jazz band he had. Walter Bloom was also there trying to interest the office in the Schnickelfritzers. In his office Willard was still hot on the Wilbur Schwichtenberg band. "Need some hot tenor men." He got Wilbur on the phone for me to spiel off a list. After that we went into an audition room to hear the new Bob Zurke records. "Never thought they'd be that good," exclaimed Willard. (I'll leave the official METRONOME verdict to G. Wright.) . . . From there on to CRA to see Christine Edwards and then home. On the way I ran into David Sternberg, who's mighty hot on that electric band he's publicizing. He'd also been up to see the Duke in Boston. "The best!" he ejaculated. "You oughta hear how soft they're playing, too. Going over really big." Who deserves a better break? was all I could think. Before plunging into the subway I met Ginger Johnson, lately of NBC; he's starting his own recording company for spot announcements. "Catch Eric Siday on the Waring show at seven," he called as he rushed into his Leo Feist haunt. . . . Caught Eric at seven. That's one of the greatest fiddlers of all time! Honest!

In the evening some friends and I drove up to see Glenn Miller and talk with him about the column he's starting for us. It should be the nuts. You can read about it elsewhere in these pages. The big surprise of the evening was Claude Thornhill, Maxine Sullivan's and Skinnay Ennis' arranger, just back from the coast, minus forty pounds, plus a mustache, and looking wonderful. He's going to start his own band. "Won't be ready for six months, anyway," murmured Claude modestly. "I'm not sure just what style I want yet—if any." Whatever Claude does, though, it'll be good; he's such a fine musician. Glenn's band was its usual self. By the way, did you ever notice trumpeter Lee Knowles and the way he hardly ever reads music? Memorizes almost all his parts. Amazing!

A Hep Agency Executive; Busy Office Hours

TUESDAY—At the Crosby rehearsal most of the afternoon. Freddy Goodman, Benny's older trumpet-playing frere, was there. He's now with Hackett's band. Seemed to think that Bobby'd do better with a traveling outfit too. The dress rehearsal was interesting. Wonderful the way Bob Crosby ad libs. Surprise was Dick Marvin, head of the Wm. Esty radio dept., and his knowledge of the finer points and better

That was before Wilbur changed his name to Will Bradley, for obvious reasons.

G. Wright=Gordon Wright=George Simon=Jimmy Bracken.

Ginger (Austen-Croom Johnson) created some gorgeous radio spots. Remember "The Prince George Hotel?" The first truly tasteful musical commercials I can recall.

The rehearsal was for the Camel Caravan program which the band had taken over from Benny Goodman.

218

records of the Crosby band. Unusual for an ad exec to be that well-versed. . . . Dinner with Gil Rodin. Don't be surprised if one of these days Kit Reid, the Texas trumpeter whom everybody's been trying to lure away, but who hasn't been north since his Dick Stabile days (1936), joins the Crosby Crew.

Big turnout for the show in the evening. Tennis star Gene Mako, Ray Bauduc's greatest admirer, sat backstage throughout. Before the show began Faz played some really knocked-out—but good—piano. Said he and his brother and sister all took lessons, but each wound up doing something else. . . . The show itself went off smoother than the rehearsal. Some of us listened in a side room. Husband Albert Marx and song-publisher Jack Bregman vied for top smile-of-pleasure honors when Helen Ward sang Day In, Day Out. . . . After the show we took pictures of the band for this month's cover. All the boys played real corn—but still it made action shots.

Reaction to NBC Bands; Meeting Charlie Barnet

THURSDAY—Lunch with Les Zimmerman, Artie Shaw's publicity man, who just returned from hearing the band in Detroit. Don't be surprised if Artie makes a couple of changes in his brass. . . . Later on to NBC to sit in on one of their vocal sustainings. They finally got some young men who can play jazz in one of their studio band units. Now if the guys could only get some modern arrangements that would make them give a bit of damn those NBC bands might begin to sound like something, especially when they've got trombonists like Al Philburn and Russ Jenner, a tenorman like Johnny Sedola, and a drummer like Neil Marshall. . . . In the evening to Harry James's reopening at Roseland. Band looked and played tired. They had a new girl singer named Blue Drake, there just temporarily. Harry was asking about others. No bright ideas present. There's now a third trombone in the James brass, Dalton Rizzotti, formerly of Gene Krupa. The James guys are plenty excited about their softball team and are sure they'll lick that unvanquished Johnny Messner outfit.

FRIDAY—Ran into Charlie Barnet on the street this p.m. Handsome guy. His last full day in town before leaving for the coast. "Gee," he exclaimed, "I used to have just a band; now I've got a complete organization to move—twenty people!"

SATURDAY—Took in the World's Fair. Tommy Dorsey was there. Tremendous gang watching. Edythe Wright's tan the object of much comment. Band seems to be getting a big kick. Its morale is high these days.

SUNDAY—Spent the p.m. at Roseland listening to Harry James. Brought him a chick to hear warble. She was too scared. Band suddenly started playing

I'm still waiting. Kit never did join. He was a great trumpeter, just the same, but I think he didn't want to leave Texas. Sort of the Peck Kelley of the trumpet.

The very pretty Helen Ward

rumbas, with Harry on drums. "Harry Gomez!" jeered the crowd. That name should stick.

Harry James's New Commercial; Another Pianist for Crosby?

MONDAY—Interesting visitors at the office today. Guy Smith and Jimmy Campbell of Jan Savitt's band dropped in to say hello. Then came Terry Allen, who's now singing with Clinton, with a very pretty Miss Parker. Romance Dept.? Wonderful guy, modest as they come, that Allen! Just before closing Bud Elliot and Dave Faulkner of the Modern Rhythm Corp. stepped in with some ideas anent a radio show. Sounds good. Discussions of records, etc., on small stations. . . . Then supper and to a preview of Columbia Record Corp. radio show. Harry James featured. Some good ideas. Johnny Hammond supposed to m. c., but he was on coast making Goodman records. Afterwards a whole bunch of us went to Roseland to catch more of Harry. Suddenly, from out of nowhere, a gal got up on the stand and started to sing with the band. Sounded fine. Everybody impressed. Found out her name was Margie Carroll; she'd been singing with Paul Martel at the Arcadia. Wouldn't be surprised if Harry took her. That Harry Gomez name, by the way, is beginning to stick! . . . Before going to bed I dropped in at the New Yorker to see Seger Ellis and wife (Irene Taylor) and band, there on a one-nighter. That Choir of Brass idea is fine. Band's rhythm section was weak, but Seger was already looking for a new drummer and pianist.

TUESDAY—Much work at the office. Saw proofs of the swing chapter in Sigmund Spaeth's new book. It's intelligent stuff. Before closing, dropped over to Nola Studios to catch rehearsal of Bob Chester's band. Glenn Miller in no disguise! Good, though. Fine pianist, hot trumpeter and lead trumpeter. And Kitty Lane sings a swell song. Bob makes a fine front too.

October, 1939

In Which Jimmy Sees All Sorts Of People and Does All Sorts of Things in the Music Business— Does He Meet Up With You or Your Friends?

TUESDAY—Got a big kick hearing Ray McKinley play drums in the Crosby band. What a wonderful, all-around man! Later in the evening, Gil Rodin

> Harry took her. She sang for awhile with the band when Sinatra was in it, but didn't last very long.

The elegantly tanned Edythe Wright

and I ran into Benny Goodman at Teddy Powell's opening. Everybody was there. Benny, Gil and I left with Helen Ward, Johnny Mercer and sundry escorts and departed for Harry Goodman's Pick-a-rib place. Benny, despite rumors, was in excellent spirits. Tried to get Charlie Christian at his hotel to come down and play (this was 2 a. m.) but couldn't find him. Jess Stacy dropped in; he and B. G. were surprisingly curt. What a shame. On the way home, I ran into Johnny McGhee, a great hot trumpeter, whose "corn" band, he claims, is going over big at Donahue's in New Jersey. Then a short talk with Chick Reeves, ex-Woody Herman guitarist and arranger, who says he's starting a band that'll be "different!" New idea?

WEDNESDAY—Had some talks today with Eli Oberstein about his U. S. Record Co. He claims to have Dorsey, Miller, Clinton, Himber, Kaye, Eldridge, Stuff Smith and others on contract. Lunch with Xavier Cugat, Herb Marks (what a fine guy!) and Frank Hennigs at Enoch Light's Taft room. Cugat kept longing for three brass too. Enoch's band sounds good, especially that Max Chamitov on piano. Later on heard some good solos Roy Eldridge did for Marks and then on to Tommy Dorsey's rehearsal. Johnny Green was there—still the same happy-go-lucky guy of years back. From there to the Crosby recording date, on which Don Carter was playing drums. A walk from the studio with songsters Jimmy Van Heusen and Eddie DeLange, the latter extremely enthusiastic about his band.

Zinn Arthur's Voice; Drummers at the Fair

THURSDAY—Lunch with Al Brackman of Robbins, Zinn Arthur, and several rival scribes. Zinn played me some records of his band's broadcasts later and they were plenty fine. That guy sings the nuts. On the street I finally found Red Norvo, back from a New England tour. He was looking for men. A few blocks later on I found Leighton Noble, arranger Chick Floyd and warbler Edith Caldwell, all of whom had just collected shekels from MCA. Band's going back to Boston's Statler where they made such a hit last year. But they were brought down for other obvious reasons. Then an evening out at the Fair listening to the Crosby band. Warbler Dorothy Claire's sister, Debby, all decked out to audition for the band, but time-schedules got balled up and she never did sing. After the band left, we walked around with Ray McKinley and heard some marvelous African tom-tommers at an exhibit whose name I forget, but which is supposed to show the world's largest waterfall, in Africa.

FRIDAY—Irving Riskin, Allen Hanlon and I went to hear Zinn Arthur's band play on Buddy Wagner's electric instruments. Band tried playing with ampli-

Quite a claim! He didn't have them, of course. Oberstein was one of the real characters of the recording field. Brilliant as an a. & r. man, but never seemed satisfied with his role and too often reached too far for his own good.

The nucleus of the band of Orville Knapp, who had been killed flying his own plane.

A very blowing Roy Eldridge

fiers off and on. Sounded better (truer) the first way. In the evening out to Glen Island to hear Woody Herman. Fine guys, fine band. They're expecting a swell trumpeter from Milwaukee, Wisc., any day now. Business good, despite tremendous rainstorm.

SUNDAY—Spent the evening with Jess Stacy. He bought all the Crosby jazz records and most of their stocks so that he'd know just what was what when he joins the band. Smart beanwork. In his small hotel room he's crowded a piano (stuffed with towels so he can play at six a. m.) plus a celeste and a practice keyboard!

MONDAY—This turned out to be a record day! In the afternoon to the Decca studios to Woody's date at which they were shooting gag pictures; then to Eli Oberstein to discover that he may use Zinn Arthur. In the evening to Victor to catch Glenn Miller's dates, at which time I met another Simon discovery, Jimmy Abato, who's taking Jerry Yelverton's place on hot clarinet. Johnny Best seemed tickled to be in the band, even though he's playing more lead than hot. I suggested to Glenn that he get Bruce Squires, who was leaving Benny, for that vacant trombone chair. Then up to Decca to the Crosby date. Ray Bauduc was back. After that over to the Famous Door to catch Anne DuPont's not-bad band on a one-nighter. She's interesting to watch and has a fine young trumpeter named Bobby Sprackles. Then some more roaming, including talks with Eddie Condon at the Pick-a-rib and Andy Ferretti and extremely attractive wife outside the place, after which a sojourn in the Forrest Hotel lobby, where I met Squires and told him to contact Miller pronto. Funny coincidence.

Dorsey Tells Tales; Return of Norvo

TUESDAY—A full evening. First the Crosby broadcast. Then to Jan Savitt's, where George Jessel danced with my girl. After that to Manhattan Center to catch the WNEW swing show. Missed Benny, but heard Teddy Wilson's band play some mighty fine jazz. After that over to see Tommy Dorsey who was in rare storytelling form. Poor Cliff Leeman had an awful cold. Yank Lausen was still strutting after having been presented with twins by his wife, Harriet. Peewee Erwin was there, too—just visiting the boys after a two months' absence. Then a ride home with Bob Bach of WNEW.

WEDNESDAY—Spent a good part of the day with Red Norvo, who has stopped worrying and again is the sweet-dispositioned guy he was years ago when he had that great, "soft, subtle swing" group. Mildred had to leave us to go apartment hunting in Greenwich Village. Later in the afternoon I dropped in to hear more of the Will Bradley band, which is really shaping into something, and then played a record of tenor-

222

The nonelectric superiority stills holds for me, providing, of course, that the musicians can get good sounds legitimately from their instruments.

That was Cappy Lewis, who joined the band and became a star.

The Bracken-Simon bit again. I (either Simon or Bracken, take your choice) discovered Abato quite by accident while driving through Baltimore and hearing him on station WBAL. I told Glenn about him and he took him.

Squires and Miller never did get together.

man King Guion for Will and Ray McKinley. They liked him but can't use him. Late in the evening up to the Rainbow Room to chat with Al Donahue and to catch the new show; fine, especially that group called The Revuers.

THURSDAY—Bud Freeman and a gang woke me at 5:15 this morning—all clamoring to be let in to hear records. Nix. Later in the day I made the rounds of the booking offices. Had a lot of fun gagging with Ronnie Lanthier and Bill Burnham at CRA. Met lanky Dick Mansfield at MCA; he's been doing ok as a leader but claims he'd just as soon settle down singing with a name band. On the way out I ran into Bunny Berigan. That recent bankruptcy trouble hasn't worried him noticeably. Spent the evening with Woody Herman and his wife (what a prize pair!). Listened to records for a while—Woody wanted to hear all Hawkins tenor and Red McKenzie singing. Later on dropped into Nick's to repay Freeman's visit. That Peewee Russell guy's marvelous. Brad Gowans was playing fine valve trombone, too. Spotted with craniums close together were Dorothy Claire and Joe Kearney, both of the Crosby crew. Ended the eve at El Chico, a Spanish spot. Give me swing!

November, 1939

MONDAY—Dropped in to see Jan Savitt at the Lincoln. He showed an awfully pretty new gal, Margaret McCall, who sings well also. The new sax section isn't what it should be yet; can't get used to Gabe Gelinas on tenor.

TUESDAY—Heard parts of the record date Jess Stacy did for U. S. Records. Hank D'Amico was playing clarinet and I've never realized how wonderful he is! Carlotta Dale sang well and Noni Bernardi did good arrangements.

WEDNESDAY—Heard Dean Hudson's band rehearse this afternoon. It has a good hot trumpeter named Ray Linn, and three more new men: George Kinnon, alto; Dick Hummer, piano; Torchy Cleyments, bass. Then up to the Goodman apartment for dinner with brothers Harry, Irving, Gene and Jerry and publisher Larry Shayne. After that to the Audubon Theatre with Harry and Larry to catch Jimmy Dorsey's stage show, and then dressing and barroom chatter with Jimmy, manager Billy Burton, songwriter Jimmy Van Heusen and publisher Herb Reese. Jimmy was in fine storytelling form re his early days. We left that group and went to the Fat Man's rib place in Harlem, where Charlie Turner (former bandleader) gave us a grand welcome. I met Coleman

The then little-known Revuers consisted of Judy Holliday, Betty Comden and Adolph Green.

Bud and several Condon-type guys from Nick's kept yelling, "We want Woody Herman! We want Woody Herman!" probably because I'd been writing so much about him and so little about them. Coincidentally, I'd already invited Woody and his wife to dinner for the next night, so, after we'd eaten, I granted Bud and his henchmen their wish by bringing Woody into Nick's. Naturally this embarrassed them, quite an achievement in itself, because embarrassing those guys wasn't easy. Woody got a big kick out of the whole thing.

Gabe was an especially fine alto saxist who later wound up in Glenn Miller's AAF band.

Of course I heard parts of the date—in fact, I heard all of it. As George Simon, I produced it.

That's the same Ray Linn who later made it so big with Tommy Dorsey, Woody Herman, Artie Shaw, Boyd Raeburn and the west coast studios. Recognizing and writing about unknowns like this was one of my biggest kicks. Of course, there were many who were never heard from again. But at least my enthusiasm was consistent.

223

Hawkins for the first time, a quiet, reserved chap. What a band we could have assembled in that place— The Hawk, Benny Carter, Teddy Wilson, and trumpeters Russell Smith of the old Henderson band, and Adolphus Cheatham, and Irving Randolph of Calloway's bunch! Teddy looks thin and tired these days.

So Publishers Fight with Fists!
Brazilian Jazz: Air Mail Stomp

THURSDAY—Lunch today with English jazz-hound Leonard Feather who says he was caught in Sweden when the war began and consequently had to come over here. Busy looking for a job. Publicist Al Brackman and Lunceford manager Harold Oxley

Another great band that could have been assembled for another great date: Coleman Hawkins is again the saxist, Lawrence Brown the trombonist, Buster Bailey the clarinetist, and the pianist is a guy named Leonard Bernstein!

in the party also. Latter tickled pink that Jimmie and boys weren't caught on the other side as per plan. On the way back to the office I met pretty Kitty Lane, who had just left Bob Chester and is now with Red Norvo, and husband Jerry Johnson. We Coked. Did any of you see the near fistfight between the heads of two publishing houses in front of 799 7th? One accused the other of trying to steal a plugger—which is better than swiping a plug these days, thought I. In the evening to Lombardo's Roosevelt opening. Just about everybody turned out, proving again that there is one thoroughly well-liked guy!

FRIDAY—Heard some unnamed tunes by Benny Carter this p.m. Good. In the evening to the fair where I heard a swell band in the Brazilian Building: Romeo Silva. Strictly Latin stuff, but I never realized till then what a tremendous swing they can get also. They've got a wonderful drummer.

MONDAY—Heard the Bob Crosby date at Decca. Watch for an original (which George Simon named Air Mail Stomp) that really goes. After that a bunch of us went to the Pick-a-rib where we met Benny, Harry and Irving Goodman, producer Tom Bernard, Jess Stacy, and publishers Jack Bregman and L. Shayne. Benny's in marvelous spirits these days—we had a long discussion on drummers—you'd be surprised what he really thinks!

Taking Lots of Good Pictures; Benny and Jimmy Open

TUESDAY—Saw the new Carl Fischer record store today. Glenn Miller, Benny, Al Donahue and Dinah Shore helped the inauguration. Went down to Victor with Dinah to hear her first record date. Mighty fine—that gal's really the find of 1939! Jess Stacy came down to my house late in the afternoon to play me the tests of his date—they're good. Dinner with Matty Matlock, who's really dying to play clarinet again instead of doing only arrangements. Then with him to the Crosby show, on which Joe Sullivan, playing his last job with the band, copped all honors.

WEDNESDAY—Benny opened at the Waldorf this evening. What a turnout! Leaders Glenn Miller, Artie Shaw, Larry Clinton, Henry Busse, Xavier Cugat, Will Bradley, Ben Bernie, Sammy Kaye, Matty Malneck, bookers Willard Alexander, Mike Nidorf, Sonny Werblin, Jimmy Peppe, record-men Joe Higgins, John Hammond, Eli Oberstein, Morty Palitz; composers Johnny Mercer, Dave Franklin; singer Helen Ward; arrangers Eddie Sauter and Bill Finegan. The band, especially the sextet, really broke up the swank crowd, which also included glamour-deb Brenda Frazier. Some of us METRONOMERS *got Benny and Artie together for a picture.*

THURSDAY—Out to Jimmy Dorsey's Meadowbrook opening—another fine turnout. That's when we took those pictures for this front cover. That Jerry Rosa guy who took Byrne's place is really a fine trombonist. And trumpeter Johnny Mendel's fitting in nicely too.

Best of the Society Pianists;
Unknowns on Great Jam Session

SATURDAY—Met Glenn and Helen Miller after the last Paramount show and with them and Charlie Spivak, critic Dan Richman and wife to hear Gerry Morton at the Warwick. A fine society band: Morton puts all pianists of his class to complete shame. Glenn

I did, too, but never got composer credit. Never tried to, for that matter. I was a very idealistic pauper in those days.

I can't for the life of me remember what he really thought. Maybe I'd be surprised now, too, if I knew.

Openings like those were a ball. Gave you a chance to table-hop and see a lot of guys at one time—quite a break for a journalist, but it used to bug my deserted dates. Interesting that Sauter and Finegan were there. They didn't start their band until 13 years later.

Must admit I may have been slightly prejudiced in favor of Gerry Morton who, as college classmate Morty Kahn, had played piano in a five-piece group I'd organized for a trip to Europe. He was awfully good, though, and had fine musical taste. In college he had turned me onto Fletcher Henderson while I was buying Clyde McCoy's record of *Sugar Blues*.

225

Artie Shaw and Benny Goodman in another of their
rare photographic get-togethers, this one with Maria
Kramer, patron saint and owner of the Blue Room
and Green Room of the Lincoln and Edison Hotels

was in fine spirits, feeling especially happy about
Spivak's company; they've been close friends for
years.

*MONDAY—Heard a good transcription date at
World Broadcasting: Jerry Sears leading a swing
string quintet plus harp. Spoke smooth words with
headman Charlie Gaines in the control room, who
was especially delighted with the date. Then with
Stewie McKay (tenorman who just left Jones) to
hear pianist Bill Clifton and his friend, guitarist
Danny Perri. Those two are wonderful—so great that
we got together a jam session for the evening with
Murray MacEachern, trumpeter Bill Graham and
clarinetist Jerry Yelverton as additions. That Mac-
Eachern guy is amazing—plays fine trombone, trumpet, alto, clarinet, piano, fiddle and bass!*

TUESDAY—Arranger Eddie Sauter dropped in
this afternoon; we went over to say goodbye to Glenn
Miller, then off to the Crosby rehearsal. Dinner with
Gil Rodin. Jess Stacy starred in the show. Hot penny-
whistler Les Lieber wowed 'em with a post-broadcast
recital. Later Jess and I went to catch Casa Loma
on its Arcadia one-nighter. Boys went over really
big, despite an 83 degree temperature, and manager
Hughie Corrigan was all smiles about the big turnout and the personality of the band. What was Joe
Glaser doing there with band manager Cork O'Keefe?

I was always organizing sessions like these so
that I could play drums with good musicians. Otherwise I wouldn't have had the opportunities. Because
of my influence as a critic, I guess they never objected
too strenuously.

December, 1939

TUESDAY—Heard Jack Teagarden close the
World's Fair in the rain. Last performance for brother

Cubby and Charlie Spivak. That Allen Reuss guy on guitar is astounding; Jack's featuring him more too. And Mr. T's developing a much easier personality.

THURSDAY—Went over to WMCA with Simon to hold his hand on his first weekly spiel for Maurice Hart on his p.m. record show. Down to Shaw's for the evening; he sat at the table with us most of the time and despite what you may hear he's exactly as he's always been. Sid Weiss was bemoaning Buddy Rich's coming departure; said the guy's been playing too wonderfully for the last week. Artie agreed. Asst. mgr. Frank Nichols paying strict attention to his mike-guarding job during the broadcast. Mgr. Ben Cole paying strict attention to my girl.

FRIDAY—Lunch with fine gal-warbling pianist Vi Mele, who's now doubling at the New Yorker and the new Mercer-Morris publishing firm. Then over to 802 to catch some talk between Messrs. Rosenberg, Feinberg and heads of other unions, and then behind scenes to present treasurer Harry Suber with royalty check for that record date we did on Victor. In the evening over to the St. George in Brooklyn to catch Mitch Ayres and band. Mgr. Goldmark switched from fiddle to bass. Band's a great hotel unit; fine novelties; peach of a tenorman in Phil Zolkind. Wound up at Lindy's; saw Peg La Centra and Paul Stewart (Mr. and Mrs.) and Jack Rosenberg.

SATURDAY—Visited various spots tonight. Tried originally to hear Johnny Messner at the McAlpin, but table-trouble intervened. Saw Shaw for a short while; not on the stand at the beginning; feeling lousy again, he said. His tremendous Pennsy Room completely packed with ropes up. Later to spend the rest of the evening with Jan Savitt, a truly cheering chap. His saxes sound much better. Too bad he's losing drummer Isaacs. Jan especially elated because entire band becomes 802 in time to play the Paramount. Savitt continuing his praises of Lincoln, etc., boss Maria Kramer.

SUNDAY—Dropped in at Glenn Miller's Victor record date. More of Miller in the evening at Bobby Byrne's New Yorker debut. Shaw was there too, as was the entire General Amusement booking staff. Band shows a helluva lot of promise; Byrne makes a grand appearance and of course plays wonderful trombone. He's got a neat jazz trumpeter. Rhythm section is stiff, though.

MONDAY—Guitarists Guy Smith (with wife) and Allen Hanlon dropped in at the office. Latter begged us not to drop in on Norvo's rehearsal; wants to give the band more time. Said that Ralph (Sieg-

My right hand held my left hand.

Yes, but Artie was beginning to get mighty itchy about cutting out from the band.

That was a funny scene. I'd just been suspended a few months previously because I'd written something against a drummer in Richard Himber's band who was a friend of the guys on the Trial Board (a ridiculous move on the part of 802), and here I walk in, all smiles and nice and friendly, with a check for something like $1,000 I'd raised for them from the first Metronome All-Star sides. Naturally they mumbled something about "another trial." Eventually they held one and withdrew the suspension. So I immediately resigned.

Can't you see it all building up inside of Artie? The explosion was coming.

fried Schlagenfeld) Connors, the bassist we recommended, is turning out the nuts. The pretty Claire sisters came in for a short while too. Later to the Crosby record session and then an audition for a girl singer for the band: too many badly overschooled things. Dinner and the evening with pres. Gil Rodin. First to catch Dinah Shore's fine NBC show; then to Benny at the Waldorf, sitting with booker Sonny Werblin and pretty wife (formerly Leah Ray) who had just done a guest shot on the Tommy Riggs show, and Lou Mindling. A gal named Kay Foster was trying out with the band; pretty creature. Nick Fatool sounded especially fine. Then some sidewalk talk with Les Brown who's all hepped up about his new pianist and who's as unassuming as ever, after which down to the Pennsylvania. Gil was especially delighted at seeing headwaiter John, whom he, like almost every bandleader who's ever been in the hotel, thinks the best man of his kind in the world. We sat with Mr. and Mrs. Jimmy Dorsey, Rocco Vocco and Mousey Warren. Jimmy especially high in his praises of Artie's clarineting and band. Herbie Haymer and Milt Yaner of Jimmy's band there sporting attractive lassies. Ditto for Mr. and Mrs. Gary (Three Cent Stamp) Rains and Zeke Zarchy, who went into a long consultation with Gil on insurance. Tony Pastor dropped by at the close to divulge plans for his coming (?) band. I gave Ben Cole her phone no. (cf. last Thursday).

TUESDAY—Rabson's big, new store opened this afternoon. Lots of celebs there. Afterwards to the tail-end of Crosby rehearsal, followed by some mighty fine pianoplaying by Helen Ward. You'd be surprised what she can do! Spent the evening with Carlotta Dale, who spilled her version of the Savitt split-up.

That's the same Sonny Werblin of the Jets, Joe Namath and Silent Screen triple fame.

Not the same girl I was there with this night. My job, despite its something like $35 a week pay, did get me to places where the tab would be picked up by the leader and where I would be accorded a great deal of attention because of METRONOME's importance. All this impressed the girls, of course.

Plan-divulger Tony Pastor

WEDNESDAY—Bumped into Eddie (*Music Goes Round*) Farley in the subway. Don't be surprised to hear him and Riley on the air soon. He introed me to Ray Nichols, whose Jersey band I used to admire as a kid. Nichols now doing NJ tax work. Lunch with Herb (of E.B.) Marks, at which Bert Block dropped in. He's now helping run Stabile's band. Back to the office to meet Gary Rains who says he's leaving Bernie. May join Pastor.

THURSDAY—More METRONOME *jive on Maurice Hart's WMCA p.m. show. Got a big kick later in the evening meeting Vincent Youmans for the first time: what an unassuming chap! That was at Whiteman's New Yorker spot. Pops himself appears mighty het up about his new swing band; so are the guys in it! There was talk of Andy Ferretti coming in on the first trumpet chair. Don't be surprised if Joan Edwards gets through this month. (P.S.—Bob Taylor was there, much to songstress Vi Mele's and Dinah Shore's obvious delight.)*

FRIDAY—The Crosbys opened at the Strand today. Band thrilled with singing of Kitty Lane, whom they'd just hired the day before. Jess Stacy in much glee about the way his records turned out. Crosby in a sour mood on critics. At night, a bunch of us helped the dancers review Shaw's band at the Pennsylvania. Artie in the same mood about critics as Crosby was. (Blue Friday.)

(Note: For some reason that I can't recall I stopped writing the Jimmy Bracken column for 10 months. Apparently I got the urge again after that and so, in November, 1940, Jimmy again popped up in the pages of METRONOME.)

November, 1940

SUNDAY—Davey Tough looks wonderful these days. He *sounded* good, too, with Joe Marsala at the Hickory House tonight. Peanuts Hucko, who used to be with Will Bradley, is playing lots of fine tenor for Joe also. Stewie McKay, Eddy Duchin's hot tenorman, who plays a smoking bassoon, got a big boot out of Peanuts. Later to Teddy Powell's Famous Door. Gigi Bohn and Danny Perri, lead sax and guitar with Savitt, were also getting a big boot from Teddy's new band. That Buddy Weed sure plays fine piano.

MONDAY—Kitty Lane, who used to be with Miller, Crosby, Berigan and Ish Jones, auditioned for NBC's Basin St. Show this p.m. Ditto Phyllis Myles, who's with Nat Brandwynne. They say the job, though, is practically set for Louise Wallace, who sang with that good Frank Dailey band in 1937.

Dinah soon replaced Joan for a couple of weeks: the only big name band job she ever held.

A few days later it happened: Artie got so fed up with it all, critics and all the rest, that he jumped the band and flew down to Mexico.

Davey came back periodically from his dry-out periods looking and acting just great, with all of us rooting for him. One of the finest, most intelligent men I've ever known.

Tonight after the program there was a farewell party at the Famous Door for Dinah Shore and lots of folks showed up. Dinah sang a few numbers and knocked us out. Charlie Barnet and Benny Carter wanted to sit in and back her up, but they couldn't find the kind of saxes they advertise, so no go. Charlie was very much impressed with sixteen-year-old Connie Russell, who sings in the show at the Door. So am I. She's a fine showman. Too bad she has to hide her good vocal qualities under some atrocious arrangements!

Benny Begins Band; Byrne Brought Down

TUESDAY—Benny Goodman called up bright and early this morning to see if we could help him find some men for his band. Spent most of the a.m. contacting Bozo at 802 for phone numbers of fellows we thought would do. Had lunch with Benny. He looks wonderful. He has put on weight and a healthy complexion, and he's in great spirits.

Bobby Byrne this afternoon at the Strand wasn't in such good spirits. He was worrying about his appendix, especially because doctors said he could expect an acute attack any time. Then on to the Bob Chester rehearsal. Al Stuart dropped in to see the band he had left. Alec Fila and I helped drummer Bob Bass pick out some new high-hat cymbals later. Bob thinks they're going to make a world of difference in his drumming.

At dinner tonight Gray Gordon's band sounded much better than I'd ever heard it. Dorothy Claire, who eats lefthanded when she isn't singing for Bobby Byrne, thought so too. After dinner, Dolores O'Neill and Alec Fila (romance dept.?) came to the house to listen to records. They got a big kick out of some old Red McKenzies and also from hearing *A Strange Loneliness*, which Dolores made with Artie Shaw.

Ben Cutler's band at the Rainbow Room was impressive later on in the evening. What a lot of doubling the boys do—and well, too! Most of the saxes and trumpets haul out fiddles when you least expect them to. There's a girl who sings with the band and plays fine piano. Name is Virginia Hayes. Most exciting thing of the evening, though, was Elvira Reos, a Mexican lass, who is featured in the floor show. What a gorgeous voice and with what Latinesque feeling she sings! She honestly put me right out.

WEDNESDAY—The first Eddie Cantor commercial went off well this evening. Bobby Sherwood has himself a good band. Toots Mondello plays lead sax; Paul Ricci is on tenor; Russ Case on a trumpet; Wes Heins (remember him with Norvo?) on a trombone, and Chauncey Morehouse play drums. Bobby and Carl Kress combine for some fine guitar duos. Dinah Shore sang as wonderfully as ever. Later on down to Woody's, but the ice show was just going on, so I beat it.

There were quite a few girls like Connie who couldn't decide if they wanted to sing well or work in musical comedies, and who too often would resort to tasteless, unnecessary melodramatics that detracted completely from their singing.

This was the start of the great new band he formed, the one that played Eddie Sauter arrangements. Benny still calls me on occasions for musicians—sort of a standing gag at home: when he phones, somebody in the family will invariably ask me what kind of musician he was looking for this time. But we love him.

Good reason for worrying: it burst soon thereafter.

Romance dept.? Hell, yes! They wound up having five kids. One of them, Alexa Fila, is a helluva good singer and lovely looking, too.

Dinah Shore's farewell party at the Famous Door: Leonard Feather, Carol Asher, whose left hand dangles in front of Jimmy Bracken's (?) face, Charlie Barnet, Herb Reis and Dinah

THURSDAY—Gene Krupa opened at Glen Island tonight. Loads of people there, they say. I wasn't though.

FRIDAY—That Johnny Long band is getting better all the time at Roseland. They're working out some good glee club effects, like their arrangement of Shanty in Old Shanty Town, *that should cause much comment. If you want to get a kick, listen to Johnny fiddle lefthanded through an entire waltz contest.*

Shanty turned out to be the band's biggest hit. None of the other glee club arrangements ever made it, though.

Cafe Society, Miller Open; Goodman Rehearses

MONDAY—Two big openings tonight. First a press preview of the new uptown Cafe Society, with a live broadcast of NBC's Basin Street Show as an added attraction. Teddy Wilson's band sounded swell.

Another Teddy Wilson band with Teddy at the piano, J. C. Heard on drums, John Williams on bass, and trombonist Benny Morton, trumpeter Emmett Berry and clarinetist Edmond Hall

Clarinetist Jimmy Hamilton played some wonderful stuff. Louise Wallace, who's going to use the name of Dixie Mason on Basin Street, sang. So did Dinah Shore. Tom Bennett, Basin Street's busy production man, Barney Josephson, who runs Cafe Society, and Ivan Black, who press-agents the place, were the busiest men of the evening. By the way, is that misplaced m.c. a necessity?

Seems just about the whole town turned up for Glenn Miller's opening at the Pennsylvania. There were the three Duke University grads, Les Brown, Johnny Long, and Sonny Burke, as well as Woody

Herman, Jan Savitt, Gray Gordon, Eddie DeLange, Cecil Golly, and lots of other leaders who should blame omission of their names on poor eyesight rather than poor foresight. Leonard Joy showed up with both his Bluebird singing stars, Dinah Shore and Yvette, just to show no partiality. Glenn's band of course sounded good. Bassist Trigger Alpert has helped the rhythm section loads. But that South American floor show doesn't fit in with the room and its environment.

WEDNESDAY—Goodman held a closed rehearsal this afternoon, using some men who'll be with the band and others who were there strictly on a trial basis. Fletcher Henderson was awfully excited about Harry Jaeger, whom he described as the best white drummer he had ever heard. The man's back with Pollack now, but will be with B. G. later on. I also got a big kick out of Bernie Leighton's piano. Benny was wonderful to all the fellows; nothing at all big-shot about him. Whereas most leaders get some stooge to take down the fellows' names, addresses and phone numbers, Benny personally called each fellow aside, talked to him, and wrote down all the information. Just like a leader beginning from scratch. It was a splendid example of Benny Goodman, the person!

John Hammond had some people at his apartment to hear first pressings of the Columbia jazz reissues. I finally met George Avakian, the writer, who seems like a swell guy. A photographer was taking shots for some picture magazine. Later to Woody Herman's with Sonny Burke and wife. It was closing night there at the New Yorker and everybody had a lot of fun.

Avakian finally wound up heading the entire jazz reissue program for Columbia and turned in an outstanding job.

With James in Boston; Football Notes

FRIDAY—Another Goodman rehearsal before catching a Boston train. Yank Porter of Teddy Wilson's band was in on drums. Jaeger had to return to Pollack temporarily. Brother Irving filled in on trumpet and sounded wonderful. By the time this is read, he may be with Jack Teagarden.

Heard Harry James's band at the Brunswick in Boston this evening. It still gets its great beat despite the new men. Benny Heller on guitar has helped a lot. Instrument caretaker-par-excellence Al Monte was in the midst of blushes because Miss Florence Lewis just became Mrs. Monte. Don't be surprised if Miss Marge McGuire becomes Mrs. Jerry Barrett (James road mgr.) before long.

SATURDAY—Different kind of music today—the University of Michigan football band. Supposed to be the land's finest. It is great. It'd be interesting to find out exactly how many of its members are stu-

The Michigan band even outblew the Harvard band, which may have been why I suspected ringers. Or did they just offer musical scholarships to guys with exceptional trumpet and trombone ranges? Anyway, I didn't like seeing the Harvard band pushed around like that. Tom Harmon was bad enough.

dents, though. Non-musical Note: Tom Harmon is the most amazing thing I've ever seen on a football field.

SUNDAY—Made the Boston to Bridgeport jump with Harry James and the boys. What whacky senses of humor Truett Jones and Benny Heller have. Spent miles discussing how they were going to sell detours to unsuspecting drivers. Finally Jones asked Heller if he'd like to share a nervous breakdown with him! There was a grand reunion and halfway through (in Hartford) between the James boys and Woody Herman's Herd, which was playing the State Theatre there. A good act Woody had, too, with saxist Sid Robin providing good comedy. Frankie Carlson was cursing because he had just split his pet cymbal.

Powell's Commercial? With Some Vocalists

MONDAY—Helen Forrest got in from Washington for Benny's rehearsal today. Looks healthy and happy. Hubby Al Spieldock now heads a small jam band in D. C. Heard several moments of a Cab Calloway record date. How come that band does so badly on wax and sounds so fine in person and on the air? Must be because of its self-conscious novelties. Hoyt Bohannon, the new trombonist from the west coast, joined Harry James's band at rehearsal at Nola's. We took pictures for the front cover of this issue. Harry Goodman and I then galloped down to Radio City where Teddy Powell did an audition show for Raleighs. He was plenty excited, but everything went off fine.

Benny Carter's band attracted a big crowd to the Famous Door tonight. Everybody seemed to get a big kick out of the bunch. Is that a big romance between singers Connie Russell and Terry Allen? Publisher Jack Robbins again in an enthusiastic mood

Hot diggety-dog and twenty-three skidoo. Impressionable young lad, wasn't I!

How about this generation gap! Hoyt's son, Steve Bohannon, was the star drummer (a brilliant musician) in the Don Ellis band until he was killed in an auto accident.

Everything went fine, except he didn't get the job.

Famous Door opener: the talented Benny Carter

about Latin rhythms with bandleader Fausto Curbello backing him with violent head shaking.

TUESDAY—Heard a young girl singer named Ruth Vale audition for Willard Alexander at the Wm. Morris office. They're still looking for somebody for the Bradley band. The lass is going to bear very much watching.

December, 1940

Swell seeing Bobby Byrne open at Meadowbrook so soon after his appendix yankage. He couldn't blow much (doctor's orders), so Moe Zudecoff sat in and played most of the first trombone. He sure blows fine. Ditto clarinetist Jerry Yelverton. Chalk up Dorothy Claire as the year's most improved vocalist. Bobby looks thin, but relieved and happy.

SATURDAY—Dinner with Charlotte and Woody Herman—what senses of humor. Afterwards Mrs. tried to exchange Mr.'s shirt for a negligee, but no luck. Then up to WMCA to catch more of Maurice Hart's whacky record show, after which over to Brooklyn Roseland to pay respects to Mgr. Nate Fagin (the band boys like him) and to listen to Sonny Burke's band. Ira Mangel, who managed the Dancing Campus at the World's Fair, admitted Krupa and Barnet had done best business at his spot, but that the most musical band all season was Les Brown's.

Krupa's Seven Ride Men; Wilson Wins a Radio Show

SUNDAY—Krupa, who played Roseland in N. Y. tonight, now lets all four trumpets and all three trombones play jazz choruses. Good idea the way they battle each other. Bet you never knew what fine hot Torg Halton, who most folks think plays just lead trumpet, gets off—sounds lots like Rex Stewart. Rudy Novak sure blows too. For sheer belly-kicks, though, catch Babe Wagner on trombone—he just lets out and really hits you.

MONDAY—It was fun watching NBC's True or False quiz show between six bandleaders and six singers tonight. Teddy Wilson won it. Tops in the show, though, was Hazel Scott—what a cute gal that is. Biggest laugh came when they asked Teddy if it was true or false that the planet Pluto was discovered 500 years ago. "False," said Wilson. "Right," said the judge. "By the way," he added, "do you know when Pluto was discovered?" "I'm not sure," admitted Teddy, "but it wasn't 500 years ago—it was either before or after!"

TUESDAY—Charlie Spivak's band got back into town. Rehearsed assiduously at Nola Studios this p.m. Speehunk has lost 22 lbs. Dropped by later to see his wife and son. Joel, the boy, wants to learn every

McKinley, Bradley's co-leader, must have watched her for quite awhile, because six years later she joined *his* band.

Moe Zudecoff later became Muni Morrow and then Buddy Morrow. Always a top-notch trombonist.

Good new singer Phyllis Myles with leader Will Bradley

Jo-jo Huffman is the saxist, Ray McKinley the drummer

instrument, except trumpet! Later to hear a new band Alan Grieve, a trumpeter with good ideas, is starting. Roosevelt won today.

WEDNESDAY—Spivak opened at Glen Island tonight. Made quite a hit with everybody, with all the scribes preferring his open horn to his muted. Dave Dexter, Jr., was there—he's in the midst of doing a Kansas City album for Decca, about which he knows more than probably anybody else in the business.

Benny's Rehearsal; Woody's Show; Hallett's Opening

THURSDAY—Heard Goodman rehearse this p.m. Alec Fila, who just left Chester, tried out and went over really big. It looks as if Benny will take him. Band's getting better quickly. That Sauter writes terrific arrangements. Later to Woody Herman at the Strand to fetch a cymbal Frankie Carlson had borrowed. Caught the show. Kitty Lane is singing with the band and sounds as good as ever. Woody's *Somebody Loves Me* is the best thing in the show. Ran into Billy Schultz, who just joined Teddy Powell on drums. Like Carlson, he's also looking for a good 15-inch Zildjian.

FRIDAY—Mal Hallett opened at the Edison to-night. Good to see him back, even though he looks bare without his waxed mustache. Mgr. Charlie Schribman seeming very pleased—rightfully so, too, because there is some good stuff in the band. Dick Wise is really a fine trombone player.

SATURDAY—Benny's band made its first New York appearance tonight at Manhattan Center. Sounded great! Cootie killed 'em. Lots of friends backstage, all getting sent. Among 'em: critics Irving Kolodin, Barry Ulanov, plus Helen Oakley, Sam Donahue, Bob Bach, and Goodman brothers Harry, Freddy and Gene. With Irving and Benny on the stand that made five on the stage at one time!

SUNDAY—Heard Spivak again. Nice bunch of fellows in that band. Young and eager. Bill Downer, who organized it originally, now manages it. He seems to know what it's all about. Frank Howard sure sings fine.

MONDAY—Big opening for Will Bradley at the Biltmore tonight. Band sounds good, but that's an awfully tough room to play in—high ceiling, live walls and no bandstand accommodations excepting a platform. A canopy sure would help. New singer Phyllis Myles is good. Band manager Willard Alexander beaming, but also wincing because of a badly infected toe.

TUESDAY—Bob Hartsell, a really good pianist from Freddy Johnson's band in North Carolina, came to town today and was featured in a jam session tonight that included trombonist Lou McGarity, Alec

Goodman did take Fila, who played such potent lead that Fletcher Henderson used him on his own record dates as well.

Woody still sings the same song. He claims he can't do a ballad well. He's crazy.

That was the night I offered Barry a job with METRONOME. He took it, even though my brother, Henry, music editor of *PM*, then a relatively new newspaper, also wanted him. At this writing, Barry, a full professor, heads the English department at Barnard College.

Fila, Skippy Martin and Sam Donahue. That Mc-Garity is about the closest thing to Teagarden going. Got a big kick out of a CBS house band rehearsal this afternoon, what with guys like Howard Smith on piano, Peewee Erwin and Bill Graham on trumpets, and Johnny Blowers on drums. Heard Benny Carter late tonight, but he was closing at the Famous Door and less inspired than usual. Carter spent most of the time chatting with Jimmie Lunceford, which to an outsider isn't as exciting as hearing him play those wondrous horns.

WEDNESDAY—Les Brown opened at Arcadia tonight. Really good band. Then to George Hall's Famous Door opening with Peter Dean. Sat with a lot of guys in Teddy Powell's band—that new trombonist, Johnny Grassi, is one helluva funny guy. Hall's band was a pleasant surprise, with bass player Biddy Bastien's brother on tenor, drummer Phil Sillman, and the lead alto especially impressive. Wound up at Kelly's Stables listening to Hawk. What can you say about that guy? Tenormen Stewie McKay and Wolffe Tanenbaum, who used to battle each other in Brown's band, were being sent with Les. Hal Gordon, Johnny Long's asst. mgr., also raves about Bob Hartsell (cf. yesterday).

THURSDAY—Glenn Miller's satisfied with his trumpets now. Said so tonight, while raving especially about Billy May, both musically and personally. Also disturbed about the Barnet expulsion episode; very fond of the band.

FRIDAY—Amy Lee got four of the Memphis Five into the office today and took pictures of them. Quite a kick seeing those old-timers together. What a greeting Phil Napoleon, Frankie Signorelli, and Jimmy Lytell gave Miff Mole! What a guy that Miff is!

Too Much Brooklyn; A Weird Jam Session

SATURDAY—Out to the Majestic Theatre in Brooklyn to hear Dinah Shore sing. Caught Jack Denny, too, who has a nice-sounding band these days. Dinah really went over big. Then on to hear Sonny Burke again, but that Brooklyn Saturday-night mob really got the better of us this time.

TUESDAY—Jam session tonight at Jerry Newman's apartment. Standout was a young tenor find named Herbie Fields, about whom you're going to hear plenty henceforth. Plays like the Hawk. Knocked out Willie (Lunceford) Smith, Roy Eldridge, Buddy Weed, Tony D'Amore and Mike (I forget his last name), Benny's new, good guitarist. About two somebody complained and the cops came, and everybody seemed pretty scared. Fields finished his chorus of Body and Soul, *after which one of the cops called out, "Hey, can't you guys play something a little livelier!" Which really broke up the session.*

Just like that November, 1939 session. This one was held in a recording studio with a woman engineer. Midway through one of the takes, she stopped us with "Hold it, George, I think your cymbals are out of tune!" I fell right in with the idiocy of the thing, turned the screw a few times on top of the holder that kept the cymbal from falling off, and asked her if it sounded better. She said "Yes," and I apologized with "Sorry, but these are circus cymbals and they're hard to keep in tune," and on we went.

Barnet had been kicked out of the union by Petrillo because of a fight he had had with his booking agency. Later, when Charlie explained his side in person to Petrillo, he was immediately reinstated and the booking agency got hell.

Jerry was a pretty wealthy jazz fan who'd use his folks' apartment when they were out of town for some pretty wild sessions. The reason we were scared was that the grass was really growing that night, but fortunately the cops, less hip than today's, didn't recognize the pervading odor. That "Mike Somebody" was Mike Bryan.

TUESDAY—Paul Whiteman phoned this morning to say he was starting a band and to ask us if we could help him find men. Had an interesting lunch with him. Met Whiff Roberts of NBC, who's thinking of bringing Red McKenzie in from St. Louis for the Basin Street show. Then on to see Toots Camaratta, who's helping Whiteman form the band in addition to supplying arrangements.

WEDNESDAY—Manie Sacks, new Columbia Record executive, was much impressed with some Henry Wells and Zinn Arthur acetates this afternoon. Also hopes to have Dolores O'Neill make some records with Teddy Wilson's all-star bunch. Claims his pleasantest surprise since joining Columbia was Les Brown's first record date—never realized the band was that good. In the evening to the Famous Door to hear Joe Sullivan—Claude Jones was playing some fine trombone for him.

THURSDAY—Good Goodman rehearsal today. The band did a new tune by Fletcher Henderson and Leonard Feather that you should hear about. Other arranger, Eddie Sauter, also has some songs up his sleeve. Sam Donahue was rehearsing the old Sonny Burke band in the next studio. Sounded good through the wall.

FRIDAY—Burke himself dropped into the office this afternoon. Says he's extremely happy working for Charlie Spivak. Bill Clifton played piano for him and was just about offered the job on the spot. Zinn Arthur dropped by later. Too bad more folks don't get wise to this lad's singing potentialities.

SATURDAY—Lunch with Willard Alexander, Wm. Morris band head, who's still suffering much from an infected toe. Later on with him to hear Les Brown at the Arcadia. He was impressed muchly. Band keeps looking for that missing 1% (see last month's review). Found a wonderful mellow mood this evening listening to some of those old Norvo records. You try a succession of his, like *Remember, It Can Happen to You, Smoke Dreams,* etc., and see what happens!

SUNDAY—Big jam session consisting of six saxes, one clarinet and two rhythm at Jerry Newman's. Lunceford's Joe Thomas and Willie Smith, Millinder's Skippy Williams and Tab Smith, Basie's Buddy Tate, leader Herb Fields, and a good clarinetist from Noo Ohlins named Cus Meyer all cutting each other. Some magnificent piano by Bill Clifton that chilled all the guys.

MONDAY—Three Eberle brothers all showed up at Glenn Miller's tonight. Ray had to be there at the Pennsy; Bob dropped in with Walter, the youngest,

Sacks really revitalized Columbia with singers like Frank Sinatra, Dinah Shore and Doris Day. But he didn't use any of the singers I tried to interest him in; probably had no intention of doing so. Trouble with Manie, one of the most important executives in the field, was that he found it terribly hard to say no to anyone, and so he would eventually disappoint those he hadn't had the heart to discourage in the first place.

Soon hereafter, Les found the lightness his band needed in Butch Stone.

Those records still hold up today and I still play them and achieve the same sort of mellow mood.

Those three Eberle Brothers: Walter, Bob and Ray

who, they say, can also sing really good. Mrs. Tommy Dorsey got in from the coast and said that Tommy's been ill with the flu. She's brown. Clarinetists Jimmy Lytell and Larry Binyon and trombonist Moe Zudecoff were discussing how they were going to get brown in Bermuda next month. Bride Harriet (Clark) Barnet looking very radiant, awaiting hubby's return from his job at Harlem's Apollo Theatre.

TUESDAY—Another interesting lunch with Whiteman and then down to Victor to sit in on a Dinah Shore record date. Former Dorseyites Andy Ferretti, Gene Traxler, Tony Zimmers, Sid Stoneburn and Sammy Weiss, former Clintonians Fletcher Hereford and Sam Mineo, former Nobleman Johnny Sedola, and former Roxy Gangman Freddy Fradkin backed her up. Freddy, the engineer, has a superb ear—you'd think they came only on musicians. In the evening to Les Brown's closing. Doris Day was sick again, poor kid.

WEDNESDAY—Publisher Abe Olman was at Decca studios this afternoon with one of those "BMI Worry" looks on his face. Heard some Andy Kirk tests. Watch for *Or Have I*, which returns vocalist Henry Wells to the band. Blackhawk (Chi) head Roth and his wife sat with us at Willard Alexander's table this evening in an impromptu party for Will Bradley at the Biltmore. Nice, quiet gent. Sam Donahue (now Don Hughes) also there, quite enthusiastic about his band. Milt (Basie mgr.) Ebbins and Lynne (soon Mrs. Ebbins?) Sherman glowing. The Bradley band gets better all the time. That Phyllis Myles sings and looks great. Jimmy Valentine's getting too fat.

A lot of ASCAP publishers had that look then. They couldn't get their tunes played on the air, because of a fight with the networks about usage rates. So BMI, set up to take up the slack, was beating their brains in.

He must have stayed Don Hughes for all of one day. Agents sometimes had funny ideas that leaders should have really WASP-like names. Charlie Spivak was Charlie Sinclair for about a day too, and Charlie Margolis was Charlie Marlowe.

Lynne soon became Mrs. Ebbins and stayed that way for a long time. Very attractive gal, and he was a very bright guy.

238

Ray McKinley's using two small bass drums on the trio numbers—unique effect.

THURSDAY—Heard more of the new Herb Fields band at Nola Studios—it shows even more promise. Leader plays exciting tenor and Hal Greene emotes great first trumpet. There's also a good jazz trumpeter —just a kid, too. Fields also plays swell clarinet.

FRIDAY—Got a big bang out of Teagarden at the Arcadia tonight. Too bad the guys have to play so many tangos, rumbas and waltzes. You'd think they'd give all of them to Saxie Dowell, who seems to specialize in that sort of thing, on the other stand, and let the crowd hear the kind of things Jack's band does best. Dowell has a lot of novelties but no intonation whatsoever.

SATURDAY—Gene King started a new record show idea for WOR this p.m. Had Bradley and Sammy Kaye to discuss differences in their bands. Will said his plays eight to a bar and Sammy's four to a bar, offering to split the difference with Kaye any time he wanted to. Show looks awfully good and will be better once King can put on ASCAP tunes again. Ran into Hal (Glenn Miller) McIntyre later—he was wondering what to get his wife for Christmas and also if he could dig up some more toy trains for Bill May, who's bugs on the subject. Heard Hackett's band at Nick's in the evening—this is swing you can listen to and talk through. Bobby's wonderful as ever. He has Nick Caiazza playing that pretty Eddie Millerian tenor for him now. Jimmy Blake was there looking fine—never think a lung had collapsed on him a few months ago. Plans to have rejoined Tommy Dorsey by the time this gets into print.

MONDAY—Bandleaders' phone call day. Charlie Spivak called in from his hospital bed in New Rochelle to say he was feeling fine at last and would rejoin the band at Glen Island soon. Sonny Burke phoned later to report on more events. In the evening Red Norvo called home to say he's back in town (great reports on his band from the midwest), and after that Claude Thornhill rang up to ask our opinion on a couple of musicians before he returned to New England to rejoin his outfit. Tommy Mack, Miller's former band manager, dropped by. He's working in Boston now. We had a chat with Johnny O'Leary, who's now breathlessly performing Tommy's Millerian duties. A closed session with Mike Nidorf (GAC executive) who has some secret plans up his big sleeve.

February, 1941

SATURDAY—Sat in on George Simon's and Dick Gilbert's WNEW shows—the former subbed for

Ten or fifteen years later other drummers got the same idea. Bet they thought they were first. McKinley was always thinking ahead.

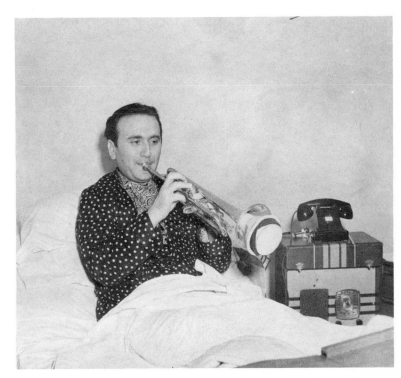

A recuperating Charlie Spivak

Before the chat with O'Leary, who'd just joined the band, Glenn warned me that "this is the only man I've ever met who speaks without any punctuation at all." He was right. I think Johnny inspired Stan Kenton's speech habits.

Martin Block on Make Believe Ballroom, playing only good records, and the latter did his daily, intimately pleasing vocal stint. He has a good band behind him—directed by Merle Pitt and featuring a great fiddler named Mac Ceppos and a ditto pianist, Frankie Froeba, who used to play for Goodman. Later on to see Eugene King on his WOR Danceland program. He interviewed Tony Pastor and Leo Reisman. Had a big argument with the latter, who thinks fast but has some queer ideas about credits for musicians. Red Norvo dropped by the house in the evening and we listened to records. He seems excited about his new band.

SUNDAY—Mr. and Mrs. Norvo (Mildred Bailey) gave a small party this evening. Alec Wilder, a fellow with a lot of personal as well as musical charm, told lots of interesting tales. Had a long talk with 802 secretary Willie Feinberg. Funny how much more real a person is when he's not behind a desk. Howard Smith and his wife were there—he's now CBS staff pianist—and Eddie South and his band dropped in around three.

MONDAY—Will Bradley made some good records at Columbia this p.m. Later on Manie Sacks, recording head, confided that he's looking for new talent. Very interested in getting out a Hal Kemp Memorial Album. Dinner with Glenn Miller, who spent a good part of the time in serious talk with Michael DeZutter, Glen Island Casino head.

TUESDAY—Lunch with Merle Pitt, who's planning to augment his Shades of Blue with clarinet, guitar and drums. He's writing tunes now. Then to Goodman's rehearsal, at which the Four Modernaires were singing. In the evening over to the Lincoln to help take cover pictures of Tony Pastor and to talk with hotel head Mrs. Kramer, who's much enthused about the five Lincolnaires. It's a relief outfit that features Johnny Austin playing both trumpet and drums.

WEDNESDAY—Breakfast up at Benny Goodman's duplex. Don't be too surprised if he makes a few changes in the band before long and releases other plans. Harry James recorded at Columbia this p.m. Band sounded great on swing—not so on ballads—saxes toneless. Morty Palitz is still a great supervisor. Then down to visit Tommy and the Dorseyites at the Paramount. Lee Castaldo says he still isn't feeling well. In the evening up to Child's 103rd St. with Irving Riskin, who's now tune-detectiving for CBS. The Hodes band has some good things, mostly George Brunis and Rod Cless. Met Eugene Williams of *Jazz Information* who really follows this quintet. Then down to Miller's to hear Dorothy Claire open with the band—she's going to fit fine. Talked with Glenn's mother again—she makes New York regularly from

Funny, I have no recollection of having taken over for Block on that top show, but if Jimmy says I did, I guess I did.

What bugged me about Reisman was that he refused to give any credits to his sidemen—all he seemed interested in was Reisman.

I found that to be true of several other officious-seeming union executives. Theirs can be a tough role.

The Modernaires didn't last long with Benny. A few days later they joined Glenn Miller. (See next Monday, to be exact.)

Dorothy never really did fit in too well with the band. But later on she developed into a star of Broadway musicals.

240

Denver and gets really excited about the band, staying up all nights till closing. Knowing her makes it easy to see why Glenn is such a gentleman.

THURSDAY—Teddy Powell recorded at Victor this p.m. Leonard Joy seems immensely impressed with the band—it sounded awfully good. Joy had a tough time supervising the date and taking care of Sammy Kaye in another studio. Pete Terry joined the band on tenor and was featured on some pretty passages. Jimmy Morreale blew great trumpet lead. Back to the office to get a call from fine tenorman Roy Hamerslag to say he'd left Al Donahue and was available. Funny thing happened then—got home a few hours later when a long-distance phone call came in from Norvo asking for a tenorman in a hurry. Contacted Roy, who's now with the band—should fit great there.

FRIDAY—Dean Hudson called this p.m. for names of any good, available girl singers. Suggested Ruthie Vale, who dropped into the office later, but Dean never showed up. Out to hear Alvino Rey, at the Rustic Cabin in Jersey this evening. What a surprise band! They seem to have lots of fun, too, with most of them living in a big, rambling house—sort of a one, big family idea with Rey and Dick Morgan as papas.

SATURDAY—More coincidences: spoke to Ruthie Vale on the phone—she said she bumped into Hudson at BMI right after she left our office, sang for him, and was to work with the band tonight more or less on trial. In the p.m. to Eugene King's WOR show again, this time to chat with Johnny Long and Dorothy Claire. In the evening up to Armonk to hear Hudson's band. Bob Hartsell, who came up from North Carolina a couple of months ago to audition for Goodman, is now playing piano and arranging for the band. Miss Vale, by the way, got the job right on the spot.

SUNDAY—Mostly rest today, though in the evening to hear Red Allen's band at Cafe Society. There is really something! Met Art Tatum for the first time and was greatly impressed, though a prospective phone call at home from Bunny Berigan in Cleveland made it impossible to stay to hear him play.

MONDAY—Much excitement at GAC today because of Dick Rogers' taking over the Will Osborne band. Lunch with Mike Nidorf at Toots Shor's, after which a lengthy gabfest with bookers Nidorf, Willard Alexander, and Harry Squires. Despite the really intense rivalry existing between those men, there's also a certain amount of openness and friendliness that's really refreshing in this business. Plenty of bandleaders at Glenn Miller's tonight—Woody Herman, Les Brown, Charlie Spivak, Sammy Kaye and Larry Clinton helped to inaugurate some gorgeous music stands. Frankie Carlson and wife Dillagene were

Dick Rogers, also called "Stinky" Rogers, was the band's vocalist. I was sorry to see Will depart. He was one of the most human and also one of the most witty leaders I'd ever met.

241

The launching ceremony of the new Glenn Miller stands at the Cafe Rouge: (l. to r.) Miller, publicist George Evans, Tommy Dorsey road manager Bobby Burns, Charlie Spivak, Les Brown, Larry Clinton, Woody Herman and Sammy Kaye

there along with Frank's brother Tony, a good bassist. Frank Dailey was having a good time. Had another interesting talk with Glenn's mother and also with Charlie Spivak's wife, Woody's and Sammy's ditto, and with Les Brown's father, who runs a successful music store in Pennsylvania and looks just like Les's trombone-playing frere, Warren. The Modernaires, who were rehearsing with Goodman last week, started with Glenn tonight.

TUESDAY—Heard Sam Donahue's much-improved band up at Commercial Studios. Benny was rehearsing up there also, running through an Eddie Sauter arrangement with which Eddie, for a change, was satisfied. Then over to the Paramount to catch Harry James and band rehearse—some of Dorsey's boys were eavesdropping. Played a little basketball with Ziggy. In the evening to Pastor's once more to take a few extra pictures. Where were Mrs. Kramer and the Lincolnaires?

Eddie was always a terribly self-critical arranger.

Basketball? Yes, they had a basket backstage, upstairs, in a little old gym built for two.

242

FRIDAY—Heard the Thornhill band tonight. Allen Hanlon, who used to be with Norvo, in on guitar trial. Betcha anything he sticks. The kids go for the band. Claude plays a couple of notes of a tune they know; then they start to sing and the band accompanies with just rhythm. Good effect. Mike Nidorf called from Chicago this afternoon. He's looking for a good, young band to follow a prescribed leader. Suggested Freddy Johnson in North Carolina, Kit Reid in Texas, or Stan Kenton on the coast.

SATURDAY—Saw Dinah Shore backstage at the Paramount this afternoon. Lots of folks there to welcome her back after her illness. Charlie Barnet was having Ticker Freeman rehearse a girls' quartet that included ex-Tommy Dorsey singers Mary Ann Mc-Call and Marie McDonald.

SUNDAY—Listened to Jimmy McPartland at Nick's tonight with saxist Dave Leavitt, well-known Boston tooter, who was in town with Ruby Newman's traveling group. Wettling's playing awfully good drums these days. Hear he's going with Muggsy, though. That pianist, Charlie Bourne, who plays between sets, sure has much technique.

MONDAY—Bandleader Zinn Arthur dropped into the office today. He goes into the army next week. It's the army's gain, for, besides being a fine singer, the man's an excellent organizer and great guy, too. Kay Little dropped in also. Said she'd just left Byrne and didn't seem too happy. She may go with one of the Michaud-Peppe units. Gil Rodin called in from Chicago just to say how happy he was that his Crosby band was beginning to sound the way he wants it to. We spoke for about twenty minutes. Les Brown wired from the same city; wanted trumpeter Randy Brooks. Found Brooks, thanks to Harold Mooney, but Randy wants to stay in town a while.

Bunny Shawker Breaks Up Spivak's Stage Show; Dunham's and Spanier's New Bands Aren't Bad

TUESDAY—Dropped by the Strand to see and hear Charlie Spivak and boys. Bunny Shawker broke up the stage show. That Garry Stevens sings better all the time. Too bad the band didn't play more numbers the folks out front knew. Charlie seems happy, if a little tired from the strain. Ben Long, his first trombonist, has written a new tune that Charlie will probably plug.

WEDNESDAY—Pops Whiteman called in from Florida to say that he'd be back in town the second week in May and was contemplating a few changes before opening in Chicago. He's very happy with Frank Howard, Spivak's old singer, who's killing 'em on stage shows. Ditto with his sax section and the way Alvin Weisfeld leads it. In the evening out to

Hanlon stuck.

Mary Ann could really sing. Marie looked really great when she inhaled deeply.

Dave really wasn't that well-known. But he had played in my band at college for several years, so he was well-known to me, at least. (Slightly dishonest writers sometimes use tricks like that.)

And then there were some who didn't seem too happy staying with the band.

Alvin later struck out on his own as Alvy West and did very well with his Little Band. Remember?

Brooklyn to catch Sonny Dunham's band at Roseland there. It's rough still and Sonny said he's going to make more changes before opening at Meadowbrook. Howard Smith, who used to drum for Les Brown, now with Dunham and proving himself to be a tremendously improved swing-man. Roseland manager Nate Fagin his usually wide-eyed, jovial self.

THURSDAY—Met Paul Kapp on a Sixth Ave. bus. He's all hepped up about his Delta Rhythm Boys, the vocal crew that's backing Mildred on records these days. In the evening, down to the New Yorker for Woody's closing. Many pressmen there, all of them

The Muggsy Spanier band in New York's Arcadia Ballroom. IN FRONT: pianist Dave Bowman, guitarist Ken Broadhurst, saxists Nick Caiazza and Tony Martell, Muggsy, saxists Joe Herde, Benny Goodman, Johnny Smith, singers Dick Stone and Jeanie Ryan. IN BACK: bassist Jack Kelliher, drummer Don Carter, trumpeters Red Schwartz, Ralph Muzzillo and Franke Bruno, trombonists Vernon Brown and Bud Smith

mighty sorry to see this popular bunch leave. Ever know of a band that, as a group of men, is liked better than this? Marion Hutton and husband Jack Philbin there, both looking mighty rosy and anticipatory.

FRIDAY—Heard Muggsy's band this afternoon. It sounds as if it's going to be good. He's wonderful, of course. The rhythm section is excellent, while Vernon Brown's playing some great trombone. Up to Thornhill at Glen Island and then down to the Forrest Hotel to see a few guys. Vic Angel was feeling blue. Ever hear him tell about his Venuti ventures? Some band could use him, if it wants a good dixieland drummer. And is this a romance between a Reggie Childs singer and an Ina Ray Hutton trumpeter?

SATURDAY—Former bandleader and Teddy Powell manager Peter Dean dropped by in full army uniform. Looks good and claims he's having a really fine time. Raved about the piano of Gerry Morton, bandleader, who's in the draft with him. Hopes to help start a band at Camp Jay.

MONDAY—Ran into radio-saxist Floyd Tottle on the street. He's dead set against all band reviews; claims that if you say a guy doesn't fit in a band, you're doing a lot of harm. I wonder. On to Benny's rehearsal and a long talk with la belle Bailey. She's mighty happy these days. Goodman's giving Lou McGarity plenty to play on trombone. He rocks a studio. Ditto the entire band. Davey Tough said he may start writing again, and if he does, you METRONOMERS will be reading his wit.

TUESDAY—Heard Shep Fields's new band. A surprise. Dick Stabile dropped into rehearsal and wanted to know if he could sit in. Shep said he'd give him a job copying arrangements at five bucks per. Dick said his own copyist would take care of that. Bert Block there also. Teddy Powell phoned. Looking for a good jazz clarinet and a girl singer. Ruthie Gaylor doesn't want to leave town and new hubby, both. Harold Dankers phoned too. He's looking for a pianist, trombonist, and alto saxist for the Jarrett band, which'll contain a lot of former Hal Kempians. Ray Conniff phoned also. He's very excited about his new ten-piece outfit. Says MCA many book it. A card came in from Zinn Arthur. He's at Camp Upton on Long Island, and he says he'll be there awhile perhaps to help them organize a band. Those bands in training camps sure are a godsend, both for the musicians and for the rest of the guys there who'll get a chance to hear some fine music.

Shep's new band featured ten saxes, all doubling on various reeds—a total of thirty-five horns. It made some gorgeous noises, but it wasn't commercial and so Shep had to go back to his rippling rhythm. Too bad.

June, 1941

MONDAY—To Providence, R. I., in a strictly non-pro capacity, to catch "Brown-brokers," the annual college show put on jointly by Brown and Pembroke. Definitely the best thing of its kind I've yet seen. Fine tunes and some good singing, especially by a gal named Ginger Bowman, who stands a fine chance of becoming something big in radio. Ed Drew's band, which is an institution around there, turned in an excellent pit job. The outfit's getting a lot of radio work.

She never made it.

TUESDAY—To Boston, in a strictly pro capacity, to hear what was going on. First stop the Shribman office, which gave me the lowdown on what was about. Then out to see Phil Boone, who used to book all those college bands on European boats, and who is now, among other things, conducting various high-school units in the territory. He has a girl singer up his sleeve. In the evening to the Raymor to catch Red Nichols. Another band there, O'Leary's Irish Minstrels, is cause for much wonderment—so different from anything most of us ever catch. Nichols' Penny Banks is the former Penny Parker, the name being changed to fit in with the Nichols and Five Pennies gag. Later on to Roseland-State to catch Tony Pastor's one-nighter and to marvel once more at Johnny McAfee's alto. Tony in fine spirits: a sign that the band is clicking. Sounded good, too. Some fellows from Sam Donahue's band, namely, Wayne Herdell, Paul Petrilla, John Forys, and Mitchell Paul, seemed to feel ditto. They were a bit disturbed about the sickness that laid their leader and drummer Harold Hahn so low.

WEDNESDAY—The "laid-low" leader popped up in the Shribman office today. Sam looked wan, but he was his usual cheery self. Seems mighty excited about his band, which has been getting good receptions in this territory. Lunch with Si Shribman, self-effacing gentleman No. 1, who likes to toss all credit for any office success toward his brother Charlie. In the evening to a club at No. Zero Hereford St. (what an address!) to hear Ruth Bryant, the young singer about whom so many folks were raving. The lass has loads of charm and should be tremendous with a big band soon. She was with Al Zimmerman's four-piece group, which did a good job for four pieces. Nice seeing Warren Hookway, who used to play with the best of them, out of his chiropodist's shroud again. He claims it's just one last fling, though.

Ruth made it even bigger as a night club singer.

THURSDAY—Just a quiet day driving down from Boston to New York in the rain. Musical abstinence like that is good for you once in a while.

See Shore Record; Whiteman Comes to Town

FRIDAY—In the evening up to Glen Island with Olie Neidlinger, a fine pianist from Hartford, Conn., who also enjoyed Thornhill's group. After everyone had gone, Jack Jenney, who had been around all evening, sat on the stand with Claude, and the two of them played some of the most gorgeous duets you've ever heard in your life. Really mellow, no-light stuff. Jack says he's going to start another band soon, only this one is likely to be a small group that will play just soft stuff. Morty Palitz, popular Columbia recorder, was with him and the two were doing the little hatching act.

SATURDAY—Paul Whiteman came into town from his long trek through the south and started on his band reorganization process. Frantic for a girl

246

singer, so he listened to a slew of them and took none. Miriam Shaw was very impressive; ditto a pretty, young lass named Laraine Day, who may soon go with what name band?

MONDAY—Much ado at Whiteman's day of rehearsing, with lots of people dropping by. Joe Mooney, the fine arranger who's starting a band with Frank Dailey's help, around for a long time, listening to the boys run through his stuff. Same for Margie Gibson and Jimmy Mundy. Band just about set now, with trumpeters Rudy Novak, G. B. Wallace, trombonist Red Ginzler, saxist Jack Henderson, and violinist Dave Newman impressive additions. Pops is going to take on Dolly Mitchell, Al ditto's daughter. He used to work for Whiteman. Funny what time will do. Dinner at Longchamps and a short gab with Dick Gilbert, who's now very happy at WOV with his recorded radio shows. The public seems to be elated with him as well. Later on to hear Alfred Simon, who wrote Spivak's theme, play a few songs in that soft, musical way of his, and to note that Whiteman intends using a gorgeous thing, now called Champagne Lady, *for his non-ASCAP theme.*

TUESDAY—John Hammond phoned today. Had lots of fun judging a swing band concert down in North Carolina. Was very much impressed with tenorman Willie Hargreaves. He used to play with King Oliver, and, according to those who have heard him, possesses a tremendous soul. Final farewells in the evening to the Whiteman gang. How about that romance between Buddy Weed and the beautiful, debish-looking girl?

She never did go with a name band, but later she did go with Leo Durocher and married him.

Nice, friendly plug for my brother. Actually, Spivak didn't use the song, because Al balked when Charlie wanted to put his name on it as co-composer. Very idealistic, these Simon bothers. Also not very rich. Oh yes, Whiteman may have had good intentions, but he didn't use that song either.

I'd heard Hargreaves the year before and was so impressed with him that I took him into a studio at Durham, recorded him, and then played the acetate for Hammond, who wasn't at all impressed. But then John went down to North Carolina and discovered Willie for himself.

Amy Arnell and Tommy Tucker in a typical press-agentry pose publicizing Tommy's hit record of *I Don't Want to Set the World on Fire.* Here they're setting a clock and a phony record, neither of which will ignite

WEDNESDAY—Lunch with Dinah Shore, who has yet to change one iota as a really fine person. Her biggest problem appears to be to let people know just that, for they're constantly looking for signs of a big head. That's what always happens when somebody gets suddenly big. In the evening, ran into Paul Wimbish, who came back from the coast with raves about the successes of his Jack Teagarden outfit. Joined Tommy Tucker, a fine fellow, his mother and wife and manager Joe Galkin, and singer Amy Arnell for a short, pleasant snack, and then on to the Lincoln to hear Harry James play and rave about Dolf Camilli of the Brooklyn Dodgers. Harry tried to get the guys to come out for baseball practice next day, but they weren't as enthusiastic as he was.

Harry and I'd sit in the room and talk baseball all night, and then we'd go out to Ebbets Field for a ball game and talk music all afternoon.

Crosby Band Changes? Fun in Philadelphia

THURSDAY—With Gil Rodin part of the afternoon. He was in from the west for a day or so to complete various plans for his Crosby band. Watch for a change or so! In the evening to Frankie Masters at the Taft and a lot of table-fun with him and Phyllis Myles. That sure is a happy-appearing group he's leading. That's a healthy job, too—through every night at nine-thirty.

FRIDAY—Down in Philadelphia this evening, Tommy Dorsey confessed that his band wasn't any more enthusiastic about baseball than Harry's was, only in this case the attitude reflected that of the leader. Tommy says he's not going to play actively this year (for better or for worse?), and that he's also given up the idea of keeping on Grover Cleveland Alexander, former big league star, because of lack of enthusiasm. It was a pleasant evening down there, with the windup a birthday party for Woody Herman at four a.m. Trombonist Jerry Rosa, the proudest person in the place as he beamed at his pretty, just-married. Looks as if Sam Rubinwitch will have to go into the army soon. Shorty Sherock grew very sentimental anent the idea. Herbie Haymer still not over his pleurisy attack and thinking seriously of taking a day or more rest.

SUNDAY—A huge crowd at Glen Island tonight to say goodbye to Claude Thornhill. Gene Lemen feeling sad because he'll have to leave soon for army service. Les Brown suddenly appeared with arranger Abe Osser. Seems his Chicago spot changed management and he went out sooner than he had expected to. Very excited about his forthcoming two weeks at the New York Strand, but quite upset (still) over having lost Doris Day, about whose singing he raves incessantly. Very much pleased with drummer Nat Polen and a new trumpeter he picked up when Joe Bogart joined Duchin, also very optimistic about his new girl singer, Betty Bonney.

Polen is now a top actor in TV soap operas, and Bogart was music chief of radio station WMCA, concentrating almost exclusively on contemporary rock.

THURSDAY—Lots of fun with three Brooklyn Dodgers this afternoon. Dixie Walker, Peewee Reese and Pete Reiser came over to the house, and, along with Louise Tobin, they cut a fifteen-minute show on my home-recorder. That Walker man sings fine, by the way—high tenor with much feeling. In the evening out to Jackson Heights for a cozy, quiet time with the Morty Palitzes—he's the recording-man at Columbia so many leaders are always raving about.

FRIDAY—Up to Charlie Spivak's at Glen Island this evening. That band sounds better all the time, thanks a great deal to Sonny Burke's arrangements. Charlie's taking the mute out more, thus giving the band more variety and a lot richer tonal quality. He has three good-looking girls with him now, who don't sing badly, either. Harry James's father, who's in town for a few weeks, went up with us. He's a swell gent— he taught Harry how to play, by the way—and he got a big boot out of Charlie's blowing.

MONDAY—Big mob at Madison Square Garden tonight, it being some sort of Victor record dealers' get-together. Recording-supervisor Leonard Joy smiling bountifully. Lanny Ross, Barry Wood and Dick Todd showed up for him. Will Hudson was there, too, and he's getting pretty excited about the new band he and Eddie DeLange are putting together. Benny's bunch sounded especially polished

Dixie sort of made it as a singer-actor, but Peewee and Pete were definitely low bush league. Since then, Peewee has progressed, of course, and now does major league broadcasts for NBC. Dixie's wife, by the way, got very sore at me; thought I was trying to fix up her husband with Louise. It was all strictly business, though come to think of it, Louise was awfully cute. Still looks great today.

The mob was also attending the opening of an abortive attempt by producer Monte Proser to bring name bands into Madison Square Garden. But the acoustics were terrible, and on opening night they didn't even have platforms for the three bands, Goodman's, Barnet's and Clinton's. Eventually they had them playing in boxing arenas, but the cold, bare atmosphere was totally inappropriate, and Proser soon junked the idea.

Benny Goodman, Larry Clinton and Helen Forrest help John Reed Kilpatrick, president of Madison Square Garden, and producer Monte Proser publicize the latter's Dance Carnival. (Neither this photo nor anything else helped very much: the venture proved to be a disaster)

tonight. Good to see Jimmy Maxwell back among the trumpets after that siege, though it's too bad that they lost Irving Goodman to the Army. Javanese Harry Lim, back from Chicago, showed up. Everybody got a big kick out of Peggy Mann and the way she was singing for Larry Clinton. And Barnet's bootings slayed the kids. Truly a good setup of bands. Too bad they're bringing in stuff the kids won't appreciate as much.

Later in the evening over to Bobby Byrne's opening with Les Brown. Bobby pulled a unique stunt, taking up all the song-pluggers' checks. Jerry Bittick dropped by the table—he's one of the main men in the new Dick Rogers band, and seems terribly earnest and sincere about it all.

TUESDAY—Dixie Walker dropped in again today to cut more sides. These are so good I think I'll take 'em to some radio station and see if they'd like to put him on. In the evening to Johnny Long's opening at the New Yorker: a well-run affair with the Longfellows in fine fettle. New drummer Floyd Sullivan helps the band a lot.

WEDNESDAY—The Mutual network's interested in Walker, it seems. More later. Big crowd this evening at Vaughn Monroe's Meadowbrook opening. Poor Willard Alexander, band's booker, who had so much one-toe trouble last year, now has two-toe ditto. It's a toss-up whether Monroe has more press agents and managers or musicians scurrying around!

THURSDAY—Back to hear Bobby Byrne again. He's got himself a whale of a fine singer named Stuart Wade. What with Dorothy Claire, that makes his vocal dept. mighty strong. Some of those Don Redman arrangements sound mighty good. But Bob Burnet isn't as relaxed in this outfit as he was in Barnet's. Don't be surprised if he returns to the latter. The addition of a fifth sax gives the band more body than it used to have. But Bobby isn't satisfied yet—says he's going to work hard and within the month hopes to get what he's been striving for.

FRIDAY—Lunch with Benny Goodman today. He's very serious about those rhythm section changes. We heard Mel Powell on piano later in the afternoon, and B. G. seemed very much impressed. Another pianist, Lionel Prouting of Bob Chester's band, and a mighty fine one, by the way, dropped by at the office to say hello between one-nighters.

SATURDAY—Fun backstage at the Strand this afternoon with Bea Wain and the guys in Les Brown's band. Catch those glasses Bea wears! In the evening out to Blue Gardens in Armonk to hear Carl Hoff. What a mob! Sat with Hal Hackett of MCA and publisher Mousey Warren, Hoff's biggest boosters. What you could hear of the band above the mob's din sounded good.

It was unique, because it was the custom for song-pluggers to pack the rooms at openings, bringing in big parties, building up huge tabs, and thereby endearing themselves to the bandleaders whom they'd then ask to plug their tunes. A generous gesture on Bobby's part. I'll have to ask him sometime why he did it—if he's still speaking to me, that is.

This band probably got a bigger buildup than any other band I can recall. It wasn't terribly good, but Vaughn did make a great impression, as my opening night review elsewhere attests.

Burnet's attitude was understandable. Few bands were as relaxed as Barnet's; few as tense as Byrne's.

That bit about "hearing" Mel is some understatement. I (Simon) insisted that Benny listen to him. A very frightened 17-year-old, Powell auditioned in the offices of MCA, where I'd arranged for the audition, and impressed Benny just so-so. But that night Benny had him sit in with the band at Madison Square Garden and I guess he must have impressed Benny and the guys in the band, because he got the job. For weeks thereafter, whenever he saw me, Mel would say thanks—one of the few musicians who bothered to show his appreciation that openly.

250

The young and very talented Mel Powell

SUNDAY—Spent the evening listening to bands on the air. What a boon a good receiving set can be! Especially big kicks pulling in bands doing remotes on out-of-town stations. For examples, did you catch any of the informal fun over New Orleans' WWL when Joe Venuti was playing at the Roosevelt there? Or did you happen to hear Wingy's bigger band on its west coast shots? You really learn a lot about present day bands by sticking close to home once in a while.

MONDAY—Van Alexander dropped by the office today. Seems to be happy in what he's doing: playing jobs now and then (but not taking too many broad jumps) and commencing to teach arranging. In the evening over to Palisades Amusement Park to hear the McFarland Twins. Funny spot they're playing in. With a 12:45 broadcast coming up, the place turns out all lights at 12:30, automatically shooing customers and inspiration home, and then has the guys blow their air program in the dark! Weird effect.

TUESDAY—That singer, Ginger Bowman, you may have read about in last month's column, came to town for auditions today. She's great material for musical comedy and so forth. Ran into Claude Thornhill having a coke at Liggett's, and then accompanied him on a Cadillac-buying venture. Arranger Bill Borden, along too, is disappointed about having to

Ginger still didn't make it.

leave the band just when it's going so strong, but intends to send in arrangements from his army post. Saxist George Paulsen, who's being drafted, dropped by to say goodbye. Late tonight WOR started its all-night broadcasting series. Jerry Lawrence looks like surefire up there. Tommy Tucker, his usual happy self, on for an interview. Mitchell Benson, Mutual man, completely knocked out by Tommy Dorsey's record of *Yes Indeed*, and grabbing all into his office to hear it—from which we emerged a half-hour later for home and sleep.

August, 1941

MONDAY—Ran into Louise Tobin on the way up to the office. We dropped in to see Larry Shayne at Famous Music and listen to some fine acetates a girl named Judy Abbott had made—a white girl with a real beat. Bumped into Mario Maccaferri on the street, who was all set to show me his new reeds till I convinced him I didn't play clarinet. Dinner at the Astor with Gil Rodin, who's mighty excited about the changes to take place in his Crosby band, but who's really brought down about the Chicago Cubs. Then over to NBC to catch the Kirby band on that Basin Street show. That thing they did called *Close Shave* was an awfully close shave from being *I Got Rhythm* —or was it? It's a shame that NBC building is so large, because somewhere within its recesses must be the beat that the Basin St. band lost several years ago—once they discover it, they'll have a semblance of a legitimate excuse for themselves. After the show, down to Johnny Long's at the New Yorker, for a very pleasant evening. Jimmy Farr's trumpet sure helps that band. His younger brother, Tommy, a trombone find who recently joined Pastor, was listening with Hicks Henderson.

TUESDAY—Dick Gilbert, WOV's 5th Ave. Troubador, dropped in to say hello to his former compatriots. He's doing fine over there. Seemed a little lost when we didn't have any records for him to sing with. To Claude Thornhill's rehearsal later in the afternoon. Nick Fatool helps the band lots. Fazola is still with him, despite lots of foolish rumors. Van Alexander was rehearsing his new band in the next studio. It sounded good, through closed doors. After rehearsal with Claude to Glenn Miller's office, to be greeted with the usual sunny Polly Davis smile. Al Simon dropped in to play his new tune, called Still, *and it seemed to impress Claude no little. Young, and getting successful, song-writers Jean Barry and Leah Worth also on the premises. Dinner at Sardi's with Will Bradley, who revealed the contemplated changes*

Judy also happened to be a girl friend of George Simon's. Gorgeous chick.

Dick had been a METRONOME editor but left to sing with the records and talk on the radio.

Polly was one of the truly fine people in the business. She had been married to Claude Thornhill; later she married Don Haynes, Glenn's manager. Through the years, she has remained one of those rare human beings who make everybody feel great by just being around.

in his personnel. Didn't see the stage show, because of the usual inefficiency and general stupidity of the Paramount house crew—how much they could learn from the Strand! So to Roseland to witness ceremonies at which George Hall was officially turning over his band to Dolly Dawn. Bobby Byrne, Johnny Long, Vincent Lopez and Martin Block, who talks too long at affairs such as these, all there to help make proceedings that much more glamorous. Then over to Dempsey's to catch Irv Carroll's band for a few minutes. He's got himself a fine boy singer, a potentially good clarinetist, and a really knocked-out trombonist.

WEDNESDAY—Lunch with Willard Alexander and Ira Steiner of the Wm. Morris office who said that the review we ran of Vaughn Monroe last month spoiled all their fun—whatever that may mean. Out to Charlie Spivak's house in New Rochelle for dinner with the charm of the evening emanating from young Joel, Charlie's six-year old, who's really a hep lad. Over to Glen Island after dinner to listen to an evening of Spivak music (hardly a hardship) and then back to New York with Charlie and wife Fritzie to drop into WOR's Moonlight Saving Man, Jerry Lawrence, and kid over the air for a while. That program's getting an immense listening audience. Jerry, by the way, is one of the few announcers in the business who sounds good-looking and is.

Kicks at Cafe Societys

THURSDAY—Cafe Society evening. First to the uptown branch to hear how well Linda Keene was doing—and she was doing well—and also to get the usual kicks out of Teddy Wilson's playing and from his band. Then, later in the evening, to the downtown branch to hear Lena Horne, than whom they don't come any more beautiful, and Henry Allen's band, which is still getting that fine beat. Miss Horne and Jay Higginbotham seemed a bit bewildered by the record date they had recently made with Artie Shaw and a lot of strings. Paul Robeson was there —what an impressive, gigantic gentleman he is!

FRIDAY—Caught Cab's stage show with Barry Ulanov and George Simon and then backstage to talk to Cab while he was taking a steam bath. Seems he had had his tenth anniversary the night before and was trying to sweat out the effects thereof and therein. Dizzy Gillespie, great kidder on the stage, kidding just as much behind, and slowly driving Tyree Glenn into a coma. Back to the office and a long phone conversation with Bob Chester, whose main worry these days seems to be his male singer department and how to lick his wife at gin rummy. Ran into Paul Laval on the way home, who's all enthused about the second Basin St. album that's due to come along and on which he'll do more woodwind novelties. In the eve-

Steiner was one of Monroe's PR men. Later he headed one of the top TV talent agencies, Ashley-Steiner. I was told that the review bugged them because it was too analytical of the band and they feared that other reviewers, less capable of discerning its faults, might be influenced.

The tunes they recorded on that bewildering date: *Don't Take Your Love from Me* and *Love Me a Little Little*.

253

The very pretty Lena Horne

J. C. Higginbotham

ning up to Rye to catch Duke Daly's band, but it had been raining and the bandsmen outnumbered the customers, so nobody played very long. Tried coming home by way of Brooklyn and K. K. Hansen's directions, which is like trying to get to letter "B" in an arrangement via the coda. It didn't work, either.

SATURDAY—A tennis match this p.m. with Les Brown, his first trumpeter, Bob Thorne, and Peter Dean, who gets out of uniform and off Governor's Island now and then. Discovered that a guy can't lead a band and play a five-set match too. In the evening up to the Log Cabin in Armonk for an evening of Les's music, which gets more thrilling all the time. Jimmy Gardiner, Texas' No. 1 jazz enthusiast, there along with the Misses Miriam Spier and Rosemarie Smith. John Hammond around, too, only nobody could locate him in the record-breaking crowd.

SUNDAY—Still in the Armonk district, so over to a party by the Richmans for the Brown band, feature of which was a softball game. Les's side got licked by brother Warren's. Didn't stick around long enough to see what that would mean on the stand that night, deeming it safer to drive over to Rye and listen to Daly. More people this time.

MONDAY—Over to the union to present them with another royalty check on the All-Star Band (1940 METRONOME version) record date. Harry Suber the gracious recipient. Then into Willie Feinberg's (802 sec.) waiting room, to be charmed, whilst waiting, by the Misses Kessler and Marvin, later to be joined by Prexy Jack ("I-like-my-iced-coffee-iced") Rosenberg, who was on his way out to get a drink of same. Pleasant chatter with Feinberg, who's lost too much weight since his illness, and who's one guy who really deserves the vacation he's about to take. Seems everybody burdens him with troubles with nobody getting lack of understanding. Here's a model union man. Then over to wander around NBC, eventually winding up in drug store with bookers Joe Glaser and Moe Gale, and Les Brown. Then home, later to be joined there by Andy Kirk, Henry Wells, Dell Trice, Guy Wood, a girl trio and sundry wives and arrangers. Got a lot of kicks waxing on my home recorder, most of them coming from the wondrous way Wells warbles. Didn't break up till about three in the morning at that.

The Harry Jameses and the Dixie Walkers

TUESDAY—To a Dodger doubleheader this p.m. with Mr. and Mrs. Harry James (Louise Tobin), the former the most rabid of fans. Rode back with Mr. and Mrs. Dixie Walker, the former a surprisingly good singer. Then out to Bob Chester's opening at the Chatterbox in Jersey, only I got the date all wrong and there wasn't any opening after all. Chapter One

K. K. Hansen was one of the few thoroughly respected band publicity men, but obviously not one of its better travel agents.

Jimmy was so wealthy that he used to import big name bands across the country just to play at his private parties. The musicians liked him, despite his money.

A repeat of that December, 1939, $1,000 scene.

of Frustration Dept. So over to Meadowbrook to catch Sonny Dunham's new band. Bobby Burns there in a huddle with owner Frank Dailey, which leads you to believe that there may be something cooking between the Cork O'Keefe office, for whom Bobby now works, and which is going to handle Peewee Erwin's band, and Meadowbrook.

WEDNESDAY—Caught the Bradley show at the Paramount and then had another confab backstage with Will. Plenty of excitement, what with the Astor opening due for the evening. Things went smoothly, though, at night, with plenty of celebrities helping to make things successful. Band shared the spotlight with Ina Ray Hutton's, a vastly improved group, which spots fine George Paxton arrangements, and a really excellent trumpeter. Spent a good part of the evening chatting with Irving Kolodin, the New York Sun's *music critic, whose fascination lies in the fact that he's one of the few writers who has a thorough understanding of both classical music and jazz. Additional delight added by the personality of Alec Wilder, who beams all the more now that his* It's So Peaceful in the Country *is catching on so nicely.*

THURSDAY—Out to Bob Chester's opening this evening. He did open this time, too. Trying out boy singers also. Dick Lawrence was on the spot this time. Lots of ASCAP publishers out there, despite the NBC wire. Then back to town to catch Bobby Byrne at the New Yorker. Long table talk with Glenn Hardman and wife Alice O'Connell. She's Helen's sister and sings really wonderfully. Finale of the evening with Eddie Masters, Bobby's astute lawyer and

Glenn played fine organ and Alice sang less affectedly than Helen.

Ina Ray Hutton was really much prettier and brighter than this publicity-posed photo could possibly indicate

with Dorothy Claire's family. Watch out for that youngest sister of all!

September, 1941

TUESDAY—Singer Al Nobel dropped by to say thanks for the job we'd gotten him with Carl Hoff's band and to state his happiness thereof. To Johnny Long's for dinner and to watch them take the picture you see on the cover of this issue. Milton Karle in his usual bubbling spirits. Helen Young looking prettier all the time. Then to the Glenn Miller broadcast, to see Bobby Hackett looking wonderful and all the guys in their usual high spirits. Hal McIntyre at his heftiest best. Caught the show with Mrs. Miller, who still gets thrilled at every fine thing her husband does. Later, out for a short malted with Glenn, to find that he's very happy about Marion Hutton's returning to the band. Then up to Will Bradley at the Astor to find his new saxes sounding fine and the band clicking. Everybody a bit upset about the brass changes to come and not quite sure what to expect in that department. Gene Mako, the tennis star, getting a big kick out of Ray McKinley, who, he claims, plays the best breaks of any guy in the business. Tommy Dorsey and Edythe Wright were there, too. He looks well after his operation. She looks healthy, too.

WEDNESDAY—Breakfast with Dinah Shore this morning. She sure is welcoming the vacation she's getting these days. Had to work hard and long to get where she is and is finally getting a chance to relax and go around and hear a few bands. Bill Reynolds, who just left the singing dept. of Bob Chester's band, dropped into the office to point out that he is available. Later to catch the Thornhill band on its first day at the Paramount. Backstage to Claude's room later on to find a big conference going on between him, Glenn Miller and Paramount mgr. Bob Weitman. Tommy Mack was completing his last day before shifting over as Charlie Spivak's band manager. Murray Albert, former Clinton and Powell ditto, moving in to help Claude. Thornhill was pooped, as you might expect, but in his usual cheerful frame of mind. In the evening out to hear Teddy Powell at the Rustic Cabin and to be pleasantly surprised by the band and entertained by Teddy, Ruth Gaylor and sundry others.

THURSDAY—Dick Mansfield, who used to front his own band and then helped to manage others, dropped into the office to discuss the insurance situation. I turned him over to the editors, and the result may be a column to aid musicians this month. Seems like a fine idea. Bobby Hackett dropped by later on and we both had Cokes at the drugstore, after which

I kept plugging that youngest sister, mostly because Dorothy kept insisting she was the best of all of them. Nothing happened.

Karle was the most bubbling of all press agents. Sometimes he even frothed. He's still on the New York scene.

Mako and his close friend, Don Budge, were avid big bands fans. Both liked to play drums, but I don't think either was even as mediocre as I was.

Tommy, former Miller trombonist and then band manager, was a top a. & r. man at Dot Records for years.

I turned him over to me, which wasn't too difficult a trick.

Ruthie Gaylor sings with Teddy Powell's band at the Famous Door, preceding the Rustic Cabin gig. The saxists are Dom Lodice, George Koenig and Gus Bivona. Felix Giobbe is the bassist, Red French is on drums, and Benny Heller is the guitarist. It was reported that Powell was so impressed with getting Heller from the Benny Goodman band that he would stare intently at him as he beat off tempos and call out, "One, and two?"

we dropped up to see Alan Courtney on his WOV show. Bobby, along with Les Brown and others, helped judge the new releases. It was all very much fun.

FRIDAY—Lunch with Teddy Powell, who seems to have plenty of intelligent plans for his band. We ran into Bernice Byers, Harry James's original vocalist, who still looks great and is doing fine. Then up to see Willard Alexander at Wm. Morris and to play some acetates of girl singers for him. He's mighty thrilled about having booked Count Basie into Cafe Society. Back to the office and a fine talk with Paul Laval, who's all het up on the subject of woodwinds in dance bands—claims that they're really coming in in a big way. Later in the evening, up to WMCA to catch Bob Bach's clever Platterbrains show, which is a jazz record version of Information Please. Then up to Glen Island with Mr. and Mrs. (We Have Twins) Sonny Burke to catch Charlie Spivak and cohorts. About half the Thornhill band was there, also. Could this be a romance between ex-vocalist Betty Claire and first trumpeter Conrad Gozzo?

SATURDAY—Backstage at the Paramount this afternoon to gab with some of the Thornhill fellows. Bob Jenney seems awfully worried about a possible army induction any day now. His would be a great loss to that band, too. Charlie Shribman and Huck Rooney, famous Bostonians, dropped by to pay re-

It sure could be—they got married too.

258

The Les Brown band at the Log Cabin in Armonk, New York during the summer of 1941. OUT FRONT: Les, singers Ralph Young and Betty Bonney
FRONT ROW: trombonists Warren Brown, Si Zentner and Bob Fischel, Butch Stone's right ear, saxists Abe Most and Steve Madrick, Eddie Scheer's right ear
BACK ROW: trumpeters Bob Thorne and Eddie Bailey, drummer Nat Polen, guitarist Joe Petrone and bassist Johnny Knepper's left eye and left hand. Vocalist Young later became one-half of the famous night club team of Saddler and Young, Miss Bonney became Judy Johnson, and Polen developed into a top television actor

spects to Claude. Claude told Huck he was beautiful, so the veteran Irishman beamed out of the room. Later in the afternoon up to White Plains to visit the Les Brown household and then to join them for the evening at the Log Cabin. Mr. and Mrs. Jack Robbins, Mr. and Mrs. Peter DeRose (May Singhi Breen), Mr. and Mrs. Alan Courtney and arranger Ben Homer, who's responsible for so much of the fine Brown manuscript, at the table with us. Mrs. Robbins seemed the most completely knocked out by the band.

SUNDAY—A late day today, with not too much effort expended, but lots of fun had at the Cab Calloway, Mutual network, quiz show rehearsal. Have you caught it? It's much laughter. Tyree Glenn, Cab's hot trombonist, has blossomed forth as a fine character actor. Cab makes a ditto m.c. Eugene King, who used to do that all-night record show on WEVD, is producing this opus.

MONDAY—Interesting time up at Columbia records listening to a group of test pressings. George

Avakian, who got out most of those jazz classic albums, wearing that "the-army's-about-to-get-me" look. Henry Nemo banged out some new tunes of his, one of which, called *'Tis Autumn*, is likely to knock you clear out. Then to the Victoria with Jimmy Lytell and to hear him explode on the wondrous merits of Walter Gross's piano-playing and the nerve of anybody else to say anything else. In the evening, out to Teddy Powell with Buddy Weed, Whiteman's brilliant arranger and pianist, who used to ditto for this band. He sat in and lifted the boys right out of their collective chairs. Wound up the evening at Nick's listening to Joe Marsala's band (which was auditioning drummers) and to Johnny Guarnieri's piano. Buddy got an especially big boot out of the latter.

TUESDAY—Ruthie Vale, who just left Dean Hudson, dropped by the office to say hello and nice things about the band from which she had just resigned. Wants to study, which is a commendable attitude for a girl singer. Why didn't more of them do that in the first place? Had a fine telephonic talk with Pops Whiteman, who right now would love to find a great first trumpeter. Seems to be a scarcity of them around town right now. Later in the evening joined the Bill Fredericks table at the Log Cabin in company with Mrs. Maria Kramer, Mr. and Mrs. Charley Agnew, Mr. and Mrs. Sol Zatt, and Bernie Woods. All there to hear Lawrence Welk. The band had a tremendous turnout with music publishers and band leaders there to pay tribute to the North Dakotan who's been doing so well.

WEDNESDAY—Caught two new bands today: Artie Shaw's and Hudson-DeLange's. Artie's sure is a mammoth aggregation with a beautiful tone quality. He himself looks better than he's looked in years and seems far, far more relaxed. Herman (Scoops) Rosenberg introing everybody and keeping spectators happy. Will's and Eddie's outfit looks as if it's going to be good, too. They're both the way they always were, which, in this case, is a happy way to find two guys.

"Likely to?" It's been knocking me out for years. Remember Woody's great record of this?

That was Welk's eastern debut.

This second edition of the Hudson-DeLange band never made it, even though it had some good young musicians like guitarist Barry Galbraith.

The Hudson-DeLange band at its height with Eddie and singer Nan Wynn in front. The pianist is Mark Hyams, the bassist is Doc Goldberg, the guitarist is Bus Etri. The saxes are Gigi Bohn, Ted Duane, Gus Bivona and Pete Brendel. Nat Polen is on drums. The brass are Howard Schaumberger, Charles Mitchell, Jimmy Blake and Eddie Kolyer

(When George Simon went to the west coast last month, Jimmy Bracken went along too. Therefore the locale of his diary this month is in and around Los Angeles, California.)

THURSDAY—Got into L.A. this morning. Bob Laughlin, our west coast representative, called for us at the station and cabbed us to a hotel room. How that traffic moves out here! Later in the morning over to the Decca studios to catch the Bob Crosby band on a record date. Dave Kapp in from New York helping Joe Perry, the Hollywood recorder. Martha Tilton dropped in during the day to keep an ear on sister Liz, now warbling with the Dixielanders. Martha looks wonderful and is the biggest thing in girl singers out here, doing around seven NBC shows per week. After the date, Shirley Ross, who appears to know her jazz, came in to discuss tunes for the forthcoming commercial she and the band are going to do. Then Allen Bode of KFWB dropped over with Dave Hyltone, jazz expert out here, and took us over to the radio studio, whence we went to the Hollywood House of Music to listen to records—funny thing to do on your first day in an eye-opening town! Seems discs get out here as much as two weeks after they hit the eastern stores. From the store over to the

Twenty-seven years later, on a trip in a limousine from Kennedy Airport to Connecticut, a complete stranger in the seat ahead of me turned around and asked, "Aren't you George Simon?" I said, "Yes, but how did you know?" He replied, "I recognized your voice." It was the same Bob Laughlin, whom I hadn't seen in twenty-seven years, who's now Rob Laughlin and a very successful business man in London. How's that for an ear?

Wonderful-lookin' liltin' Martha Tilton

Palladium to catch Woody Herman's Herd rehearsing. Fun surprising them the way we did. Sorry to have missed Mike Vetrano, who left the band as road manager the day before. Jack Archer, west coast contact man, is the replacement. Dinner with songwriters Arthur Schwartz and Gus Kahn and their very charming wives. Greer Garson sat at the next table, but the Schwartz-Kahn conversations were more interesting. Then back to the Palladium for a full Herman evening with Martha Tilton, Charlie Dant, well-known NBC bandleader out here, Skitch Henderson, ditto pianist, and Paul Wetstein, the Crosby arranger. The band was in its usual fine form. Charlie Margolis, whom they know as bandleader Charles Marlowe out here, dropped by the table to reminisce about his famous radio days in N. Y. Songwriters Jimmy Van Heusen and Johnny Burke also table-visitors. To bed around two, completely pooped from a terribly exciting first day in the wild west. That traffic!

FRIDAY—Finally heard that Stan Kenton band, about which correspondents have been writing so vociferously and musicians out here yell about. Lots of good stuff there. Kenton's a great big guy, as enthusiastic as they come. Band was broadcasting out of the KHJ studio, though the announcer spoke as though it were coming in from its Balboa Beach spot. Almost broke the boys up. Ralph Yaw, who's writing some specials for the bunch, but who wants it known that Kenton does much more, an interested spectator. Later on to another recording date at Decca, this one by the Herman band, with Woody so excited about being a papa that he spoiled one master after another. Dinner at Arthur Schwartz's house. He's as interested in writing movie scripts as he is in songs these days. Has had several accepted so far, too.

SATURDAY—Caught Al Jarvis's KFWB Make Believe Ballroom show. This is supposed to be the original program of its kind. Freddy Slack, whose new band is just getting started, was featured on the show along with drummer Spike Jones, who, they told us, has most of the good work sewed up around here—he's that good and that much in demand. Then on over to Catalina Island, a twenty mile or so sail, to see the Crosby band and spend several days there. On the boat we bumped into Joe (Red) Kearney, who used to be the band's road manager, but who's now studying for the priesthood. He was bent on our mission too. Gil Rodin met us at the dock, and from there on started a delightful and whacky week. Besides the band's music and the scenic effects of the isle itself, the highlight was a ball game between the regular Crosby team and an outfit collected by trumpeter Lyman Vunk (called "The Senator" by the band). The latter consisted of twenty-four men and

I was Schwartz's house guest for a week or so. A charming gent. His very young son, Jono, was always playing disc jockey; had a complete fake set-up. He's now Jonathan Schwartz, a top d.j. on New York's big-time WNEW-FM.

Martha, who'd already sung with Goodman and had become a housewife, looked so young that some matron insisted that she show her I. D. card before they would seat and serve us.

It was the Herman's only child, daughter Ingrid, for whom the Woodchoppers' later instrumental, *Ingie Speaks*, was named, and the same child who has long since made Woody a grandfather.

one girl, the gal being songstress Liz Tilton, who pitched. The males were scattered all over; four playing second, three on first, nine in the outfield, and so on. Floyd O'Brien played deep center with a catcher's mitt and mask. Vunk's team lost by around 20 to 3, despite the fact that its leader rode in on a beer truck and supplied both teams with plenty of that beverage.

SUNDAY—Went to the Cocoanut Grove (an awfully pretty spot) with Ruell Freeman of MCA to hear Freddy Martin's band. George Simon went along, too, so you can read about the band's musical proclivities elsewhere. It was fun seeing Freddy again, and also Eddie Stone and Eddie Bergman. Eddie's terribly happy with Martin (he used to be with Isham Jones for years) and goes over big. He still raves about that old Jones band, however, and keeps heaping praises upon the shoulders of Gordon Jenkins, who used to arrange for it. Later on we went to hear C. P. Johnson's fine colored band. He plays great tom-toms (tuned) and he features a brilliant trumpeter and an exciting altoist. I'll have to go back and hear that band some more soon. Things close much earlier out here than they do in the East—or in New York, anyway.

MONDAY—Down to catch Duke Ellington's *Jump for Joy* show and then to see Duke backstage. He's very intent on making this thing go over in a big

The show, basically a revue, relegated Duke's men to the pit, featured some original Ellington music, most successful of which was *I Got It Bad and That Ain't Good*, sung by Ivy Anderson, introduced Herb Jeffries and *Flamingo*, and reached its high point when blues shouter Joe Turner took over.

way. Eventually he wants to bring it east, but not for quite awhile. Charlie Carpenter, Earl Hines's mgr., was there too, and bubbling in his usual spirited way about how well the Father is doing out here on the coast. Wants everybody to watch out for his record of *It Had To Be You*.

TUESDAY—Out to Ozzie Nelson's at the Casa Manana this evening. Had a lengthy discussion with Hollie Humphreys on dixieland. He claims that one of the most authentic groups in the business is Henry Levine's on the Basin Street show (NBC). Ozzie was quite enthused about Don Ferris, his new pianist. Sandy Wolf dropped by—he's Ozzie's righthand receptionist, and does a swell job of it, too.

WEDNESDAY—Another Crosby band record date. Johnny Desmond, who used to sing with the band's Bob-o-links, and who's now soloing with Krupa, dropped by and got a grand welcome. Lunch with Perry Botkin, the guitarist, who's doing so well out here. Then up to the KHJ studios with Skitch Henderson (the pianist), who introduced me to Dave Rose. Heard the rehearsal. What amazing stuff that is—and with only two brass at that! Then down to the airport to see the Crosbians fly back to Catalina. That's really getting to be some romance between songstress Lee Wiley and one of the gentlemen of the orchestra—isn't it!

The gentleman was Jess Stacy, whom Lee later married.

Lee Wiley with Maxie Kaminsky and Joey Bushkin, neither of the gentlemen to whom Bracken refers.

FRIEND (next week)—Back to Hollywood. The Crosby band's first program for Ballantine Ale, with Charles Laughton, Milton Berle, Shirley Ross and Bill Goodwin, went over really big, despite some hectic last-minute rehearsing. Jimmy Lamare, Nappy's brother who plays sax for Barnet, showing off his latest kid at rehearsal. In the evening to Gene Krupa's opening at the Palladium, an affair that was little short of sensational. Roy Eldridge broke it absolutely wide open time after time, while Gene's drumming had the kids yelling too. It was a tremendous ovation, with usually complacent Larry Barnett (head of MCA's Hollywood office) visibly excited. Bandleaders Al Donahue and Lou Bring also in evidence. The latter is out here for a rest, having brought himself a comfortable place to live in. Lou, who used to lead a small group in the Rainbow Grill (N. Y.) is now doing much bigger things in the movie studios. He and wife Frances Hunt (former Goodman singer) now sport a son.

SATURDAY—Caught Freddy Slack's new band at a community dance in Glendale. Not fair to judge it from this first showing, for Freddy had to use a lot of last-minute replacements. He had two former Artie Shawers, guitarist Al Hendrickson and bassist Judd De Naut, as well as Jo-jo Huffman, who used to play jazz clarinet for Will Bradley. The man plays a fine first sax. Bruce Squires, former Goodman and Jimmy Dorsey trombonist, stole the show with that big, fat tone of his. Songwriter Don Raye came along to sing some of his tunes as a help to Freddy. Larry Kent, whose band was reviewed about four years ago in METRONOME, was also there, only this time he's a booker for General Amusement Corp.

November, 1941

SUNDAY—Still out on the west coast. Dropped in on Hank the Night Watchman's all-night recording show with Gene Krupa, Anita O'Day and accomplices. Hank gives you the impression of knowing lots more about music than most record-spielers do. Later on in the day, over to Gus Kahn's house to spend a typical, restful, west coast p.m., and then down to Wilmington to meet the Crosby band on its return from its Catalina Island season. Back to Hollywood with them and then to the Palladium with Gil Rodin to catch Krupa's gang. Plenty of musicians at the table, including Toots Camarata, Milt Yaner and Bill Burton of Jimmy Dorsey's band, and Neal Reid, Jerry Rosa and Vic Hamman, Woody's trombone section.

MONDAY—Down to see Dave Hyltone at the Hollywood House of Music to try to catch up on records I'd missed hearing by not being home. Then to meet Eddie Miller and Nappy Lamare and trying to help them arrange a west coast sequence for Chattanooga Choo Choo, *after which Eddie Stone of Freddy Martin's band called for me and we went to the Palladium again. That's really the hangout place of the coast. Dinner there while the three of us (Eddie's wife was along also) were being pestered by a tactless song-plugger. After that to the It Cafe, for what Hollywood calls a jam session. Highlights were Don Bonnee's clarinet (he's with Ray Noble) and Phil (Charlie Barnet) Stephens' bass. Tommy Reo (Barnet) also played, as did bandleader Bobby Sherwood. He usually plays guitar, but tonight he gave Dave Forrester, the It Cafe maestro, a fine run on trumpet. Additional interested spectators included Freddy Martin and Nat Brandwynne, who was there with an awfully attractive lass, Dorothy Martin, who used to sing.*

TUESDAY—Lunch with Larry Kent of General Amusement Corp., and then to meet Eddie Stone at NBC, who introed me to Gordon Jenkins. The two of them had lots of fun reminiscing about the old Isham Jones band. Then to catch a Jenkins rehearsal, which featured little Peggy Goodwin, doing her first NBC show. She's about the best of the white Billie Holiday imitators: a dubious sort of compliment, at that. In the evening, dinner at King Guion's house (a fine tenorman, by the way), and then over to a place called Bourstens, for a really fine jam session. Dick Peterson's band plays there (rhythm section and clarinet), and Guion and trumpeter Clyde Hurley, who's now a well-known lead instead of hot man on the coast, supplied great kicks. Ditto Al Hendrickson, who used to guitar for Shaw, and who produced some amazing conceptions. There was also a pianist, fresh out of Seattle, named Jimmy Rowles, who bears plenty of eying and earing.

Jimmy Dorsey Makes a Paramount Movie

WEDNESDAY—Spent all day on the Paramount Pictures lot watching them take shots of Jimmy Dorsey's band for The Fleet's In *picture. They were playing back parts of the sound track, while the lads mugged. Some of that music sounds really fine, and a lot of you are going to be pleasantly surprised by the way Helen O'Connell sings in this picture. In the evening—guess where—the Palladium, of course. Is that a romance between arranger Paul Wetstein and pretty Betty Alexander? Much later over to the Rhumboogie to catch C. P. Johnson's fine colored band. He's rightfully featured on tom-toms, while there's also a good hot trumpeter and a ditto altoist.*

Rowles eventually wound up with Goodman, Herman, Les Brown and Tommy Dorsey, before emerging as one of the most admired and most successful pianists in the Hollywood studios.

At least I was consistent. I said precisely the same thing about this band last month.

Highlight of the show was a dance team, Stump and Stumpy, whom you shouldn't miss if they ever come 'round your way.

THURSDAY—Caught the Kraft show, and especially John Scott Trotter's band, definitely one of the most musical of commercial show aggregations. Had lots of fun talking with Andy Secrest, who used to play in the chair next to Bix and who openly admits his sympathy for that style of playing. So does his horn. Later, over to a musicians' hangout to bump into former New Yorkers Mickey Bloom, Lyle Bowen and Sid Brokaw, all of whom are doing fine in Hollywood. Also an intro to Jimmy Simpson, who's running the Lockie store, and who seems to be tremendously respected by the musicians out there. Dinner with Spike Jones, the drummer who's doing so well not only as a beater, but also as the leader of a hillbilly recording outfit. Then into Los Angeles to catch the Crosby band at its Paramount Theatre opening and to be told about the band's assets by MCA's Larry Barnett.

FRIDAY—Dropped in to see Al Jarvis on his record show this morning. He says he's going to borrow Alan Courtney's WOV idea of reviewing weekly releases with experts. Lunch with Alan Bode of KFWB at the Brown Derby, and then out to MGM studios to see producer Sam Marx and to run into Lennie Hayton. Easterners will be glad to know that Lennie's getting healthily tubby (or was it the Hollywood sweater?) and that he's doing a fine job arranging for pictures. He was aiding Frank Morgan. Then over to the RKO studios to find out what was going to take place in Satchmo's Orson Welles picture, but they knew nothing, shunting me over to Dave Stuart's record store. He knew more. A pleasant guy, by the way. Then a rush to catch the Crosby (Bob) commercial, and then out to hear Stan Kenton once more at Balboa. On the way home, we dropped in to hear a young colored outfit led by Jake Porter, which has loads of good, original material, plus plenty of potentialities. Jake plays a fine cornet, and he's got himself good saxes and an exceptional bassist, who's cursed with an exceptionally bad instrument. That's sort of depressing, isn't it?

SATURDAY—Met Glenn Wallick, who's running a spacious, important music store in Hollywood with huge success. The east could stand a place as comfortable and impressive as this. An afternoon of Hollywood tennis, and then down to L.A. for dinner, after which a long ride (should have been short) out to Glendale with Bob Laughlin to catch Ben Pollack's band—newest version. Some fine stuff there, including an amazing trombonist named Joe Howard, who not only plays great jazz but also gets off lovely sweet passages. Clyde Hurley played great lead and King

It was called Music City and it's still very much in business. Glenn moved on to bigger things. He founded Capitol Records and ran it for years and years.

267

Guion emoted some good tenor. It was also a big kick hearing Pollack playing drums, something which I'd never experienced before, and which I want to experience again. The man has an innate, rhythmic drive that's hard to match. Wound up the evening at Krupa's with Alyce King and Jack Egan of Alvino Rey's band, which, by the way, had just arrived to make a picture. They're a west coast pride.

SUNDAY—Listened to records again with Dave Hyltone, and then dropped by to see Woody (Herman) at the hospital. Looks fine after his operation and insists he wants to have one every year, just for the relaxation thereof. He was raving about trombonist Howard, too, whom he heard on the air the night before. Also excited about the mustache he was growing for the sole purpose of shocking his wife. Later in the evening out to the Capri to catch Teddy Bunn, who's still an amazing guitarist, and Leo Watson, who's still a ditto mugger. Lee Young had a band there, too, that featured brother Lester on tenor. He was getting one helluva run for his money, though, from a tooter named Bumps (I think that's what they called him) Myers. Biggest kick of all, though, came when Rex Stewart sat in with the bunch and really tore up everything!

Great mugger and scatter Leo Watson

MONDAY—Dropped in to Local 47 to meet officers Spike Wallace and Frank Pendleton and publicity-man K. J. Shugart. A funny thing happened. Everybody seemed pretty frantic, because a big leak had sprung in the cellar and water was running wild. The building superintendent wasn't around, however, and though there were plenty of plumbers around, they couldn't seem to locate a *union man* in the neighborhood. They were still phoning madly, trying to locate a brother, or at least a cousin, when I left in order to make arrangements for the trip back east, which started a few hours later.

MONDAY night-THURSDAY morning—On the train. Relaxed mostly. Heard some good radio material, especially Ed Stoker's (that's what it sounded like) band from Salt Lake over NBC, which featured a fine trumpeter. Then there was a girl, Joan Brooks, who came in over KSL sounding plenty smart.

THURSDAY—In Chicago. Stopped by to see Les Brown, wife Claire, and son Butch. Then for a haircut, to find Dick Jurgens sitting in the next chair. Later on bumped into a whole slew of Charlie Spivak's guys, including manager Tommy Mack, who's sprouted hairs beneath his proboscis. To the Blackhawk for dinner, and then over to the Chicago Theatre to catch Lionel Hampton's stage show. Wound up the night at the Brass Rail, where Mike Riley's band knocked out everybody, including me, with its totally insane antics. Johnny Guarnieri's brother played bass standing on the bar. What a slaphappy performance and what business! Riley, in case you've never realized it, plays some really stupendous trombone.

FRIDAY—Ran into arrangers Margie Gibson and Bill Gray while calling for Will Bradley. She's now also running a record shop on the South Side, and is completely baffled by the number of race records which she sells and which she's never heard about before. Long talk with Will about the band, which was ended when trombonist Don Ruppersberg dropped in to say farewell before his return trip to New York. To Bradley's for dinner with Linda Keene. The band sounded good, especially Will and McKinley and Terry Allen. And that young Mahlon Clark is really turning into one helluva fine clarinet player! Then out to hear Dick Jurgens, after which a stop-off at the Chez Paree to pay Lou Breese and his fine show band respects upon their reopening. Had a fine talk with Ben Bernie, one of the most lovable and least big-headed guys in the entire music industry. Lots of leaders could afford to try to emulate the Ole Maestro.

SATURDAY—Spent almost all evening listening to the Spivak band, which has been doing fine business at the Palladium (formerly Michael Todd's Theatre

Race records is what they called rhythm and blues records in those days, though most of them sounded less slick and more genuine than today's efforts.

Restaurant). The band's improving regularly, and, as always, it's a huge thrill hearing that brilliant Spivak trumpet tone. Peanuts Hucko's tenor and the Stardusters' singing have upped the outfit's stock plenty, too.

MONDAY—Back in New York at last—really a kick getting here, too! Saw the Dodgers lose, which wasn't a kick, but later on dropped in for Glenn Miller's opening at the Pennsylvania Hotel with Mr. and Mrs. Alan Courtney. Glenn's band was in fine fettle, with Bobby Hackett being an especially welcome addition. Great having bubbling Marion Hutton back on the stand also! The opening, as you'd suspect, was stupendous. This was Hal McIntyre's last night with the band, which, to those who have been close to the outfit since its beginning (Hal's been with it since then) made this a very sentimental occasion. What a wonderful guy!

TUESDAY—Zinn Arthur dropped by today—back from the army. He's starting to rehearse a new band with a fine idea behind it. In the evening over to hear Harry James at the Lincoln Hotel. That bunch gets better all the time. It's wonderful how the fiddles are fitting in. Harry was especially excited about the prospects of Helen Forrest and Corky Corcoran joining the band, though it'd be difficult to improve on the way Dave Matthews was playing tenor—that's really something! Harry Walker, who was the star of the Little World Series, went along with us. He's a music enthusiast with a fine voice, some say even better than that of his more famous brother, Dixie. Keep an eye on him.

February, 1942

SATURDAY—Dropped in to hear Muggsy Spanier at the recently redecorated Arcadia. Russ Isaacs bowing in on drums and sounding fine. Fazola in on clarinet, too, but not getting much of a chance because there's not much stuff in the books for him as yet. Dick Stone feeling blue about leaving the band. Jeanie Ryan less so, because she's leaving to get married. Mgr. Eisendrath beaming because Vernon Brown's remaining on trombone instead of shifting over to Shaw. Brownie's wife, Edith Harper, will be the new gal singer.

SUNDAY—Heard one of Harry Lim's jam sessions at the Village Vanguard. Fine air of informality about the thing. Ken Kersey played some great piano, but Lips Page broke it up on trumpet and with his final announcement about having to leave the session because he had a date uptown to play with a "ukulele-

Hal wasn't fired or anything like that. He was merely leaving to start his own band, with Glenn's backing.

The heat was off the draft for awhile and guys like Zinn and Jack Leonard, after having served some time, were temporarily released. But, of course, Pearl Harbor a few months later changed all that and all of them went right back in again.

Harry later went on to lead the National League in hitting and to manage at least three major league teams, St. Louis, Pittsburgh and Houston. So he *was* a good guy to keep an eye on—but not as a singer!

Lim, a cute little guy from Java, was very popular with musicians for his enthusiasm, integrity and dry wit. Just before I went into the Army he took me aside and said, completely dead-pan, "George, if you ever get to Java and you find some Japanese there playing my Louis Armstrong records, do me a favor, won't you, and ask them *please* to change the needle now and then."

player." He meant Condon. Sat with Mr. and Mrs. J. C. Higginbotham, a fine couple, and Willie Smith (the altoist) who amused everybody with tales about the wild antics of Elmer Crumbley, fellow Luncefordian, who has a mania for cutting off Dan Grissom's undershirt. Surprise of the session was Joe Guy's trumpeting; he really gets an exciting tone.

MONDAY—To Wurlitzer's this evening with Gene Krupa, H. H. Slingerland and Frank Verniere to catch the finals of the Amateur Drum Contest. That kid, Louis Bellson of Chicago, who won it, is one helluva fine drummer: not only amazing technique, but also a good beat and excellent taste. Almost any big band could hire him as an improvement—he's that good. Cozy Cole met us after the affair and we went back to the Paramount to kibitz with Gene and Dinah Shore. She got a big kick out of Cozy, who's always been one of her favorites. Ditto the other way around, too. Down to Benny's at the New Yorker after that, to join Bill Clifton and Eddie Fuerst. Irving Goodman being much fussed over by an attractive lass and being much embarrassed. Squirrel Ashcraft, Chicago's Squire of Swing, at a table with Eddie Condon, Brad Gowans and Ernie Anderson, trying to stir up excitment and B.G. interest in the Waller/Chicago-jazz concert. Surprising, in the light of lots of things, that they should ask Benny to play at the affair.

Bellson was great even then. I immediately told Benny Goodman about him, who eventually made up his mind and hired him. So did Tommy Dorsey, Harry James and Duke Ellington. A very modest, retiring, talented guy then. Ditto to this day.

The blood between the Goodman and Condon camps was not good. But Anderson was a helluva promoter.

Gene Krupa-contest winner Louis Bellson

TUESDAY—*Dropped up to Columbia to hear the tests of the* METRONOME *All-Star Band date. Back to the office and a visit from Jack Torrance, who's starting a small band and looking for young musicians who'd like to spend a winter in Florida without much recompense. Over to Otto Hess's place to look through a lot of wonderful pictures of swing greats and then back to Columbia to watch John Hammond supervise a race date. After that to meet songwriters Jean Barry and Leah Worth and then home and an early evening.*

WEDNESDAY—More tests up at Columbia, including some fine results of a Harry James date. Lunch with Claude Thornhill, who's not at all upset by the changes in his band, and some interesting post-meal talk with Goddard Lieberson, Columbia's classical record personality. Back to the Paramount again, this time conversing with Howie Richmond, Gene's press agent, who's in the army, and listening in on the Mutual Admiration Society confab between Dinah and Roy Eldridge. Windup was Anita O'Day lindying all around her room while catching the All-Star Band's pressing of *Royal Flush.*

THURSDAY—*Plenty of activity at Charlie Spivak's Pennsylvania opening. All the publishers there in full force, of course. Band went over big. Alec Wilder spied at a table working away furiously on a Benny Goodman arrangement; later on conversing with many gesticulations with Kay Thompson. Ran into Garry Stevens on the way home, who's plenty enthusiastic about Charlie's band and especially about the Stardusters, who, he modestly claims, have really taught him how to sing.*

FRIDAY—To Morty Palitz (ace Columbia recording supervisor) and wife's abode for a fine dinner and then a long bull session with them and Sonny Burke, Spivak's arranger. Much later back into town to catch Benny at the New Yorker. Peggy Lee's first boss, Barney Lavin of WDAY, Fargo, N. D., popped up. Swell guy. He's all het up about a kid duo he has discovered out there. Still later on home with Jimmy Maxwell and Will Rowland (Benny's mgr.). It was Jimmy's birthday.

SATURDAY—*Caught Bob Bach's Platterbrains show on WMCA, which is always a lot of fun. Leonard Feather starred as he picked soloists out of some real hazes. Then to catch Johnny Long at Roseland, where the whole band was surprised by the sudden appearance of Paul Harmon, its former vocalist and saxist, who's now in the army. Nice table-talk with Dolly Dawn, George Hall and vocal-teacher Mimi Spier. Then over to the Arcadia and Muggsy, after which some early breakfast with him, while he and a proprietor worked out the entire war between*

Hess covered everything. His collection of photos was colossal.

Lieberson, the "classical record personality," brought into Columbia by John Hammond, eventually became top man in the company. And Richmond, then a budding press agent, now heads one of the most successful music publishing ventures of all time.

272

helpings of Grape-Nuts. Mike Bryan of Artie Shaw's band and Sammy Sachelle there too.

MONDAY—Some interesting, informal talk with secretary's secretaries up at 802. In the evening over to the Roosevelt to catch Lombardo, who, as usual on Mondays, was surrounded by hosts of song-pluggers, who like him not only because he's an important plug, but even more so because he's such a regular guy. Ran into Ray McKinley early in the morning and got into a long discussion about his new band. He doesn't see mat all brought down by his split-up with Bradley—instead, he's looking forward to having himself a great band on his own. Too bad that split had to happen though.

March, 1942

*TUESDAY—*Saw Carl Hoff backstage at Loew's State. Publicity man George Evans busy trying to figure out all sorts of angles to tie Carl up with a lot of Chinese as a tie-in for his anti-Japanese song. Then over to Martin Block's seventh anniversary party for his Make Believe Ballroom, and like all his other parties, it was a big, pleasant, roaming affair. Roamed all around and bumped into Glenn Miller, Shep Fields, Charlie Spivak, Johnny Long, Vaughn Monroe, Freddy Martin, Bob and Edna Chester, Dinah Shore (who was her usual hour and a half late for an appointment) and Helen Young, who seemed cutely bewildered by her sudden marriage to Oggie Davis, Johnny Long's guitarist, and his just-as-sudden departure for Fort Knox in Kentucky.

WEDNESDAY—Today's first backstage visit was with Bob Chester at the Strand, which finally settled down into a gin-rummy game between the Chesters (Mr. & Mrs.), Irving Windish and your roving gin-rummier. The Chesters aren't so hot. So to Center Theatre backstage for a long and exciting chat with David Mendoza, who has many ideas about everything. He is very much enthused about the work he and the others on a citizens' committee are doing for the purpose of getting musical instruments to the fellows in training camps. Much later on at night down to Cafe Society with Muggsy to hear Teddy Wilson's band. He also got a big boot out of trumpeter Emmett Berry's mammoth tone and neat delivery.

*THURSDAY—*Lunch today at the Astor, at Manie Sacks's invitation, to listen to a talk given by John B. Kelly, Director of Physical Fitness of the Office of Civilian Defense. There's an article about that talk somewhere else in this issue that you shouldn't miss. Lots of bandleaders and music publishers at the affair, making it an unexpected field day for the latter.

Kelly was Grace's father.

273

Had a long and fine chat with Johnny Green, to me one of the very greatest of popular songwriters, who says he has been writing a lot of stuff recently. Sure would like to hear them! Alec Wilder, Lyn Murray, Goddard Lieberson and Harry Goodman also at our table. In the evening down to the Pennsylvania to hear Charlie Spivak. Biggest thrill was hearing him play open trumpet on *I Wonder What's Become of Sally*. Ask him to blow it at you sometime, too. Artie Baker has just joined the band, and the way he's playing clarinet these days is really fine. First-Lieutenant-Going-On-Captain Ed Flynn dropped by, en route to camp from North Carolina to Oklahoma, via New York!

FRIDAY—A bit of a change for a few days. Down to Washington with Randy Mergentroid to see how he and his F. O. N. committee were making out. Highlight of the long weekend was being entertained at the Turkish Embassy by Neshui Ertegun and his brother, Adrian. They've traveled all over the country, hearing all kinds of jazz, and still keep raving about the Lu Watters band in San Francisco. They have some acetates of a broadcast, which they played, along with lots of other records. Funny feeling, going into one's first Embassy and winding up getting jazz kicks. The Turkish coffee is wonderful also.

TUESDAY—Back to New York again. In the morning, down to Victor and a Dinah Shore record date. Lots of good men in that background band. Andy Ferretti, Sid Stoneburn and Gene Traxler, from Tommy's original group, for example. Later in the afternoon to a Claude Thornhill rehearsal at Nola's. Lots of new faces in the band, especially in his army-hit brass section. Georgie Auld rehearsing his new bunch next door. Then down to Child's Paramount to hear Henry Jerome and his new and very fast drummer. Henry's playing more and better trumpet this year, but those verbal introductions he still gives each number lend an amateurish tinge to his outfit that doesn't do its music justice. Ran into a couple of Modernaires on the street, and then ran down the aisle of the Strand to catch the Frankie Masters stage show. Had pleasant chats with Frankie and Phyllis "Rusty" Myles later on. Mike Doty's playing lead sax with the band now and Dave Rose is arranging for it. The fellows claim the latter is making a whale of a difference in the quality of the music. And they're probably right, too. Wound up the evening listening to a fine jam-band session over at Kelly's Stables. Jerry Jerome's leading the outfit there Tuesday nights. Biggest kick was hearing George Van Eps play his seven-string guitar! That man is still the greatest on his instrument! Jerry played fine tenor and Billy Graham got off some really tasty trumpet. Same for Johnny Guarnieri's piano. Arthur Herbert sat in and

Know who Randy Mergentroid was? Right . . . Me. If I only could have collected all those salaries!

Ahmet (not Adrian) and Nesuhi (not Neshui) have emerged as two of the recording field's leaders, president and vice-president, respectively, of Atlantic Records. Nesuhi, one of my current tennis partners, also taught jazz at UCLA.

Dave Rose and Hollywood's Dave Rose are not the same.

The Van Eps thrill still holds, almost thirty years later! He broke it up when he appeared at the Down Beat in New York late in 1969. Just about every top guitarist in town dropped in to marvel.

played some great drums—what a left hand that man has! Who, though, was that "critic-of-sorts" who sat in?

WEDNESDAY—Lunch with Les Brown, who flew into town for the day for the express purpose of getting Billy Butterfield to join his band. Billy joined us at lunch. He and Les seemed to hit it off wonderfully, and he'll be with the orchestra by the time this gets into print. Les is mighty enthused, of course—not only because it's Billy, but also because it'll give him a chance to use four trumpets.

THURSDAY—Fine entertainment this afternoon at Larry Adler's house, first listening to classical music, and then listening to his two-year-old daughter sing. Later in the evening over to the Waldorf-Astoria to catch Dinah Shore on her first nightclub job. She went over tremendously—couldn't get her off the floor. Got a big kick out of that Hartman dancing act, which you may or may not have seen by now. And Freddy Martin's band does a fine job for that sort of hotel room.

FRIDAY—Lunch with Claude Thornhill, who's happy about his group and is looking forward to his coast engagement. In the evening up to the Rainbow Room to be charmed by Elsie Houston, not only musically but personally, as well. And then down to the Pennsylvania again, this time to listen in on a ribbing duel between Helen O'Connell and Bob Eberly. These two singers are two very funny people. Get them to try to explain to you what each one does in their forthcoming movie. You'll learn a total of nothing also.

SATURDAY—A total of nothing.

SUNDAY—Zinn Arthur phoned today. In town for a few hours, on leave from the army. Says that they've really got themselves one fine band out at Camp Upton (Long Island) these days. In the afternoon up to the Paramount for a lengthy talk with Glenn Miller, mostly on the subject of critics and why they're not so good. Good cups of Marion-Hutton-made coffee during breathing spells. And then down to the Village Vanguard to catch another one of Harry Lim's fine jam sessions. Earl Hines and Red Allen and Benny Carter really carried it to a new high for the series. Biggest surprise of all, though, was Jimmy Maxwell, of Benny Goodman's band, who sat in and really blew some potent trumpet. There's a man not nearly enough of us know nearly enough about. In the evening out to Glen Island Casino to hear Hal McIntyre's band. Poor Don Ruppersburg is pretty broken up about having to leave the bunch at this stage, but he got that Uncle Sam call the other day. Some army band will profit.

Let's not be THAT coy. The "critic-of-sorts" was the "drummer-of-sorts" named George Simon, Jimmy Bracken, Gordon Wright, Randy Mergentroid, etc.

Hal McIntyre and Helen Ward, who sang with his band for a brief period

Glenn, despite his apparent serenity, wasn't exactly the most thick-skinned gent when it came to criticism. He resented critics who focused almost entirely on his band's jazz, or lack of it (Leonard Feather was a pet peeve), and also those who didn't agree with him that Tex Beneke was a giant among tenor saxists (me included).

TUESDAY—Down to Gordon Wright's home to listen to a fine jam session among guys who aren't too well known. You might keep an ear open, though, for guys like pianist Bob Hartsell, who's got a lot of wonderful ideas and a fine beat, clarinetist Sid Barbato (just joined Dick Rogers) who plays jazz with a kick and who doesn't have the usual phony tone or unreasonable facsimile thereof, tenorman Vincent Francescone, who plays with lots of heart, and trombonist Bob Alexander, who's got plenty of good ideas. Then to catch a preview of the Woody Herman, Andrews Sisters picture, *What's Cookin'*, which has plenty of laughs and quite a bit of the Herman Herd, after which over to Kelly's Stables to listen to the second jam session of the evening. Jerry Jerome's bunch was shelling it out, with George Van Eps again amazing on his seven-string guitar, and Sanford Gold showing off a host of amusing piano ideas. Carol Kay (she sang with Woody and Sonny Dunham before becoming Mrs. Billy Robbins) produced a young brother, Stanley, who produced some good drumming on a short sit-in.

WEDNESDAY—Dropped in to see publisher Herb Marks, who's running everything while famed pa "E. B." is vacationing, and then over to NBC to engage in the usual interesting conversation with transcription producer Ben Selvin. Caught the Basin Street show later on. Paul Laval's group did some entertaining stuff, and little Mary Lou Howard's turning out to be a real asset. Later on up to Star Record Co. to listen to some interesting off-the-air waxes.

Impressive Harry James and a Bartender

THURSDAY—Lunch with Axel Stordahl, who returned from the west coast ahead of the Tommy Dorsey band he's arranging for, publisher Mickey Goldsen, and songwriters Ace Laramee and Buck Pincus. They've just penned *While I'm Crying on Your Shoulder, You're Laughing up Your Sleeve*. Only thing is, their right names aren't Laramee and Pincus. Anybody know? In the evening out to Meadowbrook to find Harry James playing to a prodigious crowd. It was plenty obvious how this band has finally caught on. The trumpet addition has helped a good deal. Harry, though, still would rather discuss the Dodgers. Much bar fun with Rudy, who tends same, while pulling gags on band-fellows. He broke up Helen Forrest, while she was singing, more than just once. They tell me the guy's really become an institution out there.

Friday—An afternoon session up at Billy Burton's penthouse apartment, with the Dorsey mgr. reminiscing about the gags the Boswell Sisters used

Another opportunity for Simon-Wright-Bracken-Mergentroid to play with better musicians. Bob Alexander did become a very successful musician, much in demand in New York studios.

Hey, here's proof that there was a "Herman Herd" in METRONOME long before late 1944, the year people seem to think the "Herd" bit of magnificent alliteration was created for Herman's so-called "First Herd."

Hate to do this to you, but do you know who Buck Pincus really was? That's right: Simon-Wright-Bracken-Mergentroid-etc. Ace Laramee was Alec Wilder, that highly-admired songwriter who had good reason for using a nom de plume on the hokey things we wrote together. A couple of other titles: *Keep the Home Boys Firing* (a patriotic song) and *A Mother-in-Law Is a Mother Too*.

to pull on him and how other bandleaders used to try to yank Artie Shaw out of his Cleveland band. In the evening up to Ina Ray Hutton at the Paramount. Later, a session with arranger and tenorman George Paxton, whose ambition is to sing Honeysuckle *a la composer Fats Waller.*

SATURDAY—Dinner with Muggsy Spanier, who still raves about the Crosby band and big-man Gil Rodin, and who's making arrangements to add a third trombone. Ran into songstress Mary Lou Howard later on, knitting away, and trying to shake off the effects of the flu.

SUNDAY—Quiet day, topped by attendance at the party of Barbara Benedict's, who's celebrating her return to the Fredericks Brothers office. Otherwise mostly gin rummy.

MONDAY—Lunch with Teddy Powell and new vocalist Tommy Taylor. Then a table switch to hear from Jack Philbin anent the changed trumpet situation in his Bob Chester band. Then another switch to talk with Willie Feinberg, 802 executive, who has more modern, straight-thinking ideas about musicians and unionism than most labor leaders ever hoped to have. His ability to think entirely in terms of the men who have selected him for his important post gives you a wonderful feeling of confidence in unionism not only as a theory but as a marvelously practicable scheme. Teddy Wilson dropped into the house later in the evening, spending several interesting hours discoursing the merits of Benny Carter (who's one of his idols) and the possibilities contained in quarter, eighth and sixteenth tones.

An Almost Closing and an Opening

TUESDAY—Dropped by the Pennsylvania to see Jimmy Dorsey, but he was out of town because of his father's illness, so just said "hello" to popular head-waiter John, and pogo-sticked on over to see Benny Goodman. The band closes in a few days and is going to take a vacation. Don't be too surprised to find several changes when it goes back to work early in April. Then out to the Top Hat in New Jersey to a very impressive Dick Stabile opening. Billy Burton, who's also managing this outfit, went on a gardenia buying spree, much to everyone's amusement. Gracie Barrie went over wonderfully in her floor show routine. It's great seeing her combine with husband Dick like that. Two wonderful people!

WEDNESDAY—Dropped up to Bruno's to help Ina Ray Hutton select the cover picture for this edition. Then to a Teddy Powell rehearsal, to catch the guys going over a Henry Wells arrangement which they seemed to enjoy a lot. Here's a writer who still hasn't achieved his due in that department. Dinner with Peggy Mann, coach Miriam Spier, and Eddie

Cunningham, Teddy's new, fine bassist, at the Taft, while holding interesting table talk with various members of Vincent Lopez's outfit. That Grill Room does stupendous business all the time, it seems. After that over to Mecca Temple to catch Alan Courtney's shindig, plus a refusal to engage Benny Goodman bassist and ace checkershark Sid Weiss in the game of his calling. Stan Kenton had just come off the stand as I got there and his appearance proved once and for all that there isn't a bandleader who works any harder than he does. There just couldn't be. After that down to George Simon's house with trumpeter Dick Mains, trombonist Jack Satterfield, tenorman Roy Hamerslag, pianist Tony Aless, bassist Cunningham and vocalist Mann to cut some gag sides and a few good ones, too. Hamerslag proved himself to be the country's "No. 1 Croakalist."

THURSDAY—Heard a young lass up at Coach Spier's studio this p.m. about whom you're likely to hear a great deal one of these months. A really natural radio voice. Name's Rosalind Schachtel, or something complex like that. In the evening out to the Log Cabin in Armonk to catch a Teddy Powell opening that wasn't at all well attended. This Dick Mains kid, though, whom Teddy picked up in Ohio, is a real trumpet find. What a wonderful tone, and what fine ideas, even if there may be a few too many that came direct from Harry James. But he's only seventeen, so there's no telling how great he's going to turn out! Regent Music head Harry Goodman there raving— no, not about any of his plug tunes—but about the new Georgie Auld band which he plans to accompany on several road trips.

Committee Lunch and Songstress Dinner

FRIDAY—Sat in at a luncheon of that citizens' committee that's raising instruments for volunteer army groups. What a fine, quiet job they're doing! John Torrance dropped into the office later on to report some amazingly queer deals he had gotten from some people you wouldn't think would pull stuff like that. After that over to the Strand to say hello to Charlie and Fritzie Spivak and to engage in drum conversation with Dave Tough, one of dancebandom's most engaging and intelligent personages. Then down to Greenwich Village to a dinner Peggy Lee was giving to inaugurate her new home.

SATURDAY—Dropped in to see Les Brown at the Paramount, talking backstage with him while his father waited patiently for his son to stop the gab and engage him in a game of pinochle. So up to see Muggsy at the Arcadia, first hearing Mgr. Hughie Corrigan extol the merits of a Met. scribe's rumba dancing, and then listening to the full tones and fine beat of the band. It leaves the spot soon for the road,

Wonder when one of these months is coming along. It's been only about thirty years so far.

Mains was magnificent. How famous he might have become, we'll never know, because, after being drafted, he made the United States Army Band his career.

Could they have been trying to get draft deferments in exchange for large contributions of musical instruments? Seems to me I recall some attempted hanky-panky along those lines.

Peggy and her friend Jane Leslie (now Mrs. Leonard Feather) lived in a real "Sister Eileen" apartment. Their enthusiastic Greek cook that night was Benny Goodman's bandboy, "Popsie," who has since become a very successful photographer.

with a few personnel changes here and there. *Muggsy seems pretty happy about conditions. What couple, closely connected with the outfit, seems even happier than that about natal conditions to come?*

SUNDAY—Dinner with Mr. and Mrs. Tommy Mack—the former's Glenn Miller's and now Teddy Wilson's mgr.; the latter's a fine cook. Then to a Harry Lim jam session at the Village Vanguard, with interesting notes coming from the harmonica of a young colored lad named Peter Fisher. After that over to Cafe Society to listen to the fine Wilson band and that amazing Emmett Berry trumpet. Charlie Spivak couldn't contain himself about that man's blowing, either. Bar-talk with trombonist Brad Gowans, who seems mighty happy about his intended joining of the new Ray McKinley band and who also tossed in a few raves for Teddy's little outfit.

MONDAY—A p.m. session with songwriters Alec Wilder and Alfred Simon, who are mutual admirers of each other's writings. Later in the evening up to Woody Herman's well-attended official New Yorker opening, at which the band sounded fine. Turned out to be reunion evening for the lads, what with Joe Bishop, Saxey Mansfield and Vic Hamman all very much in evidence. There's a refreshing, almost family-like spirit in this group that makes you want to be around it an awful lot.

TUESDAY—Dropped in to catch Leonard Keller's new band at the Edison Hotel. It's a young outfit, but it's got a lot of fine material, especially a couple of alto saxes and a first trumpeter. Leonard's sane enough not to want to rush things. Then over to the Paramount to gab with Les Brown and wife Claire, and then the three of us went down to the Pennsylvania to engage in table conversation with Dorsey mgr. Burton. Les seems a bit perturbed about the coming loss of Abe Most, his great clarinetist, to the navy, and also the possible loss of recently-added drummer Bunny Shawker to the army, not to mention his own brother, Warren, going to the army, too.

WEDNESDAY—Lunch with Mrs. Bob Chester, who's equally excited about her A.W.V.S. uniform and about the number of defense bonds she has sold and is trying to sell. Phone call at the office from Arcadia mgr. Hughie Corrigan to state how tickled he was with the job Muggsy had done for him and how he hoped for more big things from Johnny McGee, who's due to come in soon. In the evening over to Roseland to engage in tabletalk with Clyde Lucas. He's planning quite a few changes in his band. The fiddles are out already, you know. GAC biggie, Milton Krasny, there looking over two of his prides, Lucas and young Jerry Wald, whom he's priming for a Lincoln Hotel opening this month.

"Here and there" was a gross understatement. Just about all the key men left when Muggsy decided to hit the road. Too bad, because during its weeks in the Arcadia, it was an exciting outfit. But by this time, those musicians who hadn't been drafted could call their shots, and if they didn't feel like traveling (as most didn't) and were well-enough known, they'd grab the most attractive offers. Unfortunately, for his road trip Muggsy had already staffed his band with too many established stars who could call their shots.

Mr. and Mrs. Les Brown dance to the music of Jimmy Dorsey

Edna Chester was a delight, a witty and energetic gal. As a member of the American Women's Volunteer Service she talked an awful lot of us in the business into buying an awful lot of war bonds.

THURSDAY—Dropped into Mike Vallon's office to enter a discussion on how his charge, Woody Herman, might best play *The Star Spangled Banner* at the Paramount. Arranger Lowell Martin had some good ideas about singing, but wasn't so sure of the band's voices. Then a short listen to a few late Herman releases and down to Leeds Music to see Ceil Campbell smile. In the evening over to the Commodore Hotel to hear headwaiter Leon rave about his Yankees and to listen to Ray McKinley's band. Thornhill tenorman Johnny Fresco and drum teacher Bill West tremendously impressed with the outfit. After work, down to Nick's with Ray to catch a load of Bill Davison's dixieland group. That Davison plays great rhythmic trumpet; tremendous beat, plus a pretty melodic conception, too. And they don't make dixieland trombonists any finer than George (Philadelphia-commuting) Brunis.

FRIDAY—Les Brown called from Boston. He's having drummer trouble because Bunny Shawker was called into the army. Think I got him somebody ok. Warren Palmertier, alto saxist, dropped by. He was caught in the reshuffling of Denny Thompson's forces. He's a Nyack, N. Y. resident, and he brought much reassuring news about great arranger Eddie Sauter, who's recuperating nicely up that way after a pretty tough illness. In the evening, up to catch Hal McIntyre at Glen Island Casino. Band manager Don Haynes has something up his sleeve anent the Randy Mergentroid situation, though he isn't talking for public consumption. Hal's got himself some impressive-sounding singers, but it's too bad that Penny Parker is leaving the bunch. She's a gal who sings with plenty of feeling, which isn't something you can say for most thrushes these days. Billy Robbins was playing some fine trumpet, while Jimmy Emert was pulling a huge surprise with that kicking trombone of his. Used to be strictly a pretty man. The band's still great.

SATURDAY and SUNDAY—Relaxation period mostly, though Freddy Goodman's interesting phone call from Akron, Ohio, requesting help for Benny in the alto sax and drum dept. livened things up. Suggested Johnny McAfee and Russ Isaacs, who'd just left Pastor and Muggsy respectively. Hear they got the jobs.

MONDAY—Caught the first of the Monday eve jam sessions at the Village Vanguard. Harry Lim's running them. Some good stuff going on. Bill Coleman got off some great trumpeting with the band; same for Sonny White's piano. And Don Frye tinkled neatly between sets. The man's plenty het up about

Great rhythmic trumpeter Wild Bill Davison

Strictly a manufactured rumor.

Johnny did; Russ didn't.

some new tunes he has written. Left the session for a while to catch Charlie Spivak at his Hotel Pennsylvania opening. Davey Tough has made a colossal difference in the band's beat, getting fine aid from Jimmy Middleton on bass. The whole outfit, as a matter of fact, sounds far ahead of any of its earlier efforts. Opening was big, too, with bandleaders Thornhill, McIntyre, Herbeck and other notables in obvious evidence. GAC executives Tommy Rockwell and Milt Krasny had good things to say about last month's METRONOME *editorial. Did you catch it? Much later on back to the Vanguard session, this time to hear Ben Thigpen, Andy Kirk's man, get off some neat drumming. The man's got a wonderful foot.*

TUESDAY—Interesting session this afternoon up at WRUL, the short-wave station. Songstress Peggy Mann and pianist Bill Clifton put on a fifteen-minute show directed towards the fellows in the armed forces around Iceland and Greenland. What a combination of great talents! In the evening, up to Henry Wells's house for a wondrous dinner from the stove of Mrs. Wells.

WEDNESDAY—*Dropped by the union this afternoon to turn over a check for almost four hundred dollars. It was from the 1941* METRONOME *All-Star Band record of* Bugle Call Rag *and* One O'Clock Jump *on Victor. That makes close to three thousand dollars from the disc alone that has gone to New York's unemployed musicians. Harry Suber, as usual, the gracious accepter. In the evening out to Meadowbrook to catch Ray McKinley on his one-nighter there. Frank Dailey very enthusiastic about the outfit. Ditto Willard Alexander, its manager, though that's somewhat more expected. Roc Hillman, who used to play guitar with McKinley in the Dorsey Brothers' band, dropped by, resulting in much table reminiscing between the two.*

THURSDAY—Sort of sad to see Woody Herman's band closing at the New Yorker this evening. They seem to fit so perfectly into that room. Peewee Hunt was there. Casa Loma had an evening off. He's tremendously enthused about the changes in the outfit and the fact that it has captured the Hotel Pennsylvania spot starting in July. Had only raves for Don Boyd, the trombonist, who has taken over his hot duties. Many contact men in evidence to wish Woody and the lads plenty of good luck. Noted right near by were Honest John Bregman, Juggy Gayle, Julie Stern, Mike Sukin, Solly Cohen, and former English publishers Reg Connelly and Irwin Dash.

FRIDAY—*Henry Adler dropped into the office for final discussion on his new drum column, which you should see on some later page in this issue. Caught Lee Castle's band at Roseland in the evening. The trumpeter's making plenty of changes, so it's not quite*

The editorial was a blast against booking offices that hired territorial offices to represent them, paid them 10% and then added that 10% on to their own 20% commission, so that bands shelled out much too much to them.

Ben Thigpen was the father of Ed Thigpen, long-time Oscar Peterson drummer.

fair to pass much final judgment on the group. There's a good kid trombonist you should keep your ears open for, though. Heard Clyde Lucas, too, whose bunch is doing a fine job entertaining the Roseland bunch. . . .

SATURDAY—Tommy Mack and wife dropped by the house, right in the midst of a fine Lionel Hampton broadcast from the Savoy. On their way to catch Teddy Wilson's band rehearse. Bet you thought a lot of those six-piece outfits didn't bother much with that sort of thing. So did I. In the evening, over to George Simon's house to hear Henry Wells cut some fine waxes. Then all of us down to the Vanguard to catch Eddie Heywood's fine little trio.

SUNDAY—Caught Claude Thornhill's Paramount show this evening. It was highlighted by a couple of ten-year-olds smoking cigars in the front row, being tossed out by the ushers, and breaking up Carol Bruce completely. She handled the situation neatly. Then over to the Astor bar for interesting table-talk with singer Dick Harding, and then down to the house with Claude to listen to records. Amazing thing, but every time any good musician comes down to listen, he always wants to hear the latest stuff by the Duke. That never fails and didn't tonight, either.

MONDAY—'Twas Johnny Long's official opening tonight at the New Yorker, though the bunch actually had been playing there since Friday of last week. But that's the way press-agents do things—helps spread the crowd. The band was in good hotel-room fettle, with improvement in the brass especially and enlargement in the vocal department. Johnny has added a quartet (is there a name band that hasn't?) called the Four Teens. They've been well rehearsed by Kay Thompson and sound it. Helen Young, who sure misses husband Oggie (army) Davis, dropped by the table, to head the evening's charm dept. Later on in the night down to the Vanguard for another Lim session. Most talk centered around Hoake Robert's bass, not because it was the lad's final appearance before going into the army, but because his bassing knocked out all the guys. Other highlights were Joe (Roy's brother) Eldridge's altoing, Joe Thomas' trumpeting and both Arthur Herbert's and Jimmy Hoskins' drumming.

TUESDAY—Went down to Army 2nd Corps Area Headquarters for a while to watch the good work they were doing on Morale Minutes, *the corps area newspaper. Had good news from Harry Suber about a donation Local 802 was making for instruments for the men in the armed forces. In the evening up to New Pelham Heath Inn for Bob Allen's opening. Didn't know that Herman Shubert, who used to be head man in the Edison's Green Room, owned the spot. Bob's band had some good stuff, especially his singing, but it seemed to have difficulty getting used*

Not again!

282

Maestro Bob Allen at the Cafe Rouge with another ex-Kemp vocalist,
Janet Blair. Mrs. Allen, at far left, enjoys the reunion

to the bandstand after doing a lot of one-nighters in
big ballrooms.

WEDNESDAY—Good waxing session this afternoon over at Gordon Wright's home. Pianist Bill
Clifton stole the show, though there was additional
fine playing from Ray Extrand on clarinet (he usually
toots bass sax for Shep Fields), tenorman Birj Vaughn
and trumpeter Tiger Poole. Stayed home in the evening to catch some radio shows for a change. Teddy
Powell's and Bob Chester's shots were especially impressive, while Walter Gross played some fine piano
on a show that starred Vera Barton.

THURSDAY—Interesting record date over at
Columbia. The Goodman band. Some new faces since
its last N. Y. appearance, including trumpeter Paul
Geil, trombonist Charlie Castaldo and saxist Johnny
McAfee. Amazing thing is that Benny has McAfee,
who's about as thrilling a lead altoer as you can find
in the country, playing baritone parts. The band
sounded awfully fine, just the same. Gene Goodman,
Benny's younger brother in khaki, watching the ses-
sion with much interest. Mrs. BG dropped by later
on, a truly gracious lady. Out for some late lunch
with songwriter, arranger, octet-leader Alec Wilder,
who's much too modest for his own good. Then back
to the office to engage in some engaging talk with
young Frances Fare, who just left Jerry Wald, and
who'd be one smart addition to most any band around
town. In the evening up to Glen Island to catch Claude
Thornhill's opening. Like Long's outfit, the biggest
improvement in Claude's is among the trumpets, who
now have two colossal lead men in Conrad Gozzo and
Randy Brooks. Lillian Lane is at last singing as good

Again, not again! Poole developed into a top
studio man.

283

as all those advance reports which you heard before she joined last summer—and that must be good! Ben Pollack at the next table watching the band with much interest and appearing slightly bewildered that his pet tenorman, Johnny Fresco, wasn't getting anything to play. Claude walking around in that bewildered style—only don't let that toss you—the man doesn't miss a trick!

Ted Goddard was blowing all the jazz tenor.

July, 1942

FRIDAY—Caught Frankie Masters' band on an Okeh record date this afternoon, supervised by brilliant supervisor Morty Palitz. Arranger Dave Rose has made lots of difference in the band; so has the revamped rhythm section. And Phyllis Myles sure is singing fine. Then over to the Strand for backstage talk with several of the Jimmy Dorsey band, which was just ready to polish off an amazing run at the theatre. Coked with Linda Keene for awhile and then back to the office. In the evening out to hear Teddy Powell at the Log Cabin, where business was brisk despite the gas situation. Tommy Taylor's singing better than he ever did and living up to all those raves Dinah Shore has been giving his work for such a long time.

Gas rationing was really beginning to catch up with the bands and their patrons.

SATURDAY—Tennis this afternoon with George Simon and a gang and in the evening over to Leonard Feather's WMCA Platterbrains show. Randy Mergentroid appeared as a contestant and came through with some amazing knowledge. You'd never expect a leader of his calibre to dish out stuff like that. Then to La Conga with George Hall to hear Dolly Dawn as a single. She's going to do fine.

If these two days didn't produce some sort of schizophrenic catastrophe, nothing could. Three guys playing tennis against each other, and all of them me!

SUNDAY—A day of tennis in Westchester, this time with Gordon Wright. He can cut Simon any day, though you'll have a tough time convincing the latter about that!

MONDAY—Lunch with music critic Irving Kolodin, who's busying himself with a rebuttal to that recent article about Benny Goodman that shocked the entire music world a good deal more than it did Benny. Later on, into Paramount dressing quarters to engage Swing's King and his wife in some bridge and then down to the Stage Door Canteen to hear his sextet and Peggy Lee and Dick Haymes give the soldiers and sailors a big thrill. After which more backstage bridge till one a.m., after which down to another Harry Lim Village Vanguard jam session. Clyde Hart played some good piano and Jimmy Maxwell emitted some potent trumpeting.

Benny Goodman entertains servicemen at one of several jam sessions arranged by our own Jimmy Bracken (far left). Jerry Jerome is the tenor saxist, Cozy Cole the drummer, and Teddy Wilson is at the piano

Record Session; Band Opening; Jam Session

TUESDAY—Heard Hal McIntyre record at Victor. Wonderful band! Ruth Gaylor did her first side; she's a gal who's going to impress you lots. Where do all these new stars come from, anyway? Alvino Rey recording in the next studio and also putting in some impressive sides. Nick Fatool has helped the band, which now has all sorts of doubles. Pineapple soda with Penny Parker, who apparently is going to stick with the McIntyre band, but in a different role. She said she'll soon be Mrs. Vic Hamman. Later in the afternoon up to WRUL to hear Peggy Lee, Dick Haymes and the Clark Sisters, a fine new girl trio, do a swell short-wave show for the soldiers. Helen O'Connell and Bob Eberly had put through a ditto here the week before. In the evening up to Bobby Byrne's opening at the Edison. Interesting talk with Abe Siegel, former Byrne bassist, and Johnny Mince, ace clarinetist, who are in the pit band of Irving Berlin's army show and getting one tremendous boot out of it, too, and with Ina Ray Hutton managers Charlie Yates and George Paxton. Then over to say hello to Lennie Hayton, in town just for a few days, who was due to return to his fine MGM job in Hollywood next morning. A short stop to say good-evening to Mrs. Kramer and to meet Una Mae Carlisle. Then interesting table-talk with Mr. and Mrs. Harold Mooney, after which over to the Jerry Jerome jam session at Kelly's Stables with them, vocalist Dotty Reid, and Byrne manager Frank Henshaw. Remember Annette?

The same Clark Sisters who later joined Tommy Dorsey and made that great recording of *On the Sunny Side of the Street.*

Annette "Henshaw" (it was really Hanshaw) was one of the best singers when radio was really catching on in the late twenties and early thirties.

He's her brother. The Stables session was great. There's a gal guitarist named Mary Osborne you should run to hear the first chance you get. Not only does she play fine rhythm and solos, but she sings murder out of a song. Don Crosby of Lou Breese's band played impressive tenor and trumpeter Joe Thomas and pianist Don Frye knocked 'em all out. "All" included Al Hendrickson, Louis Mitchell and several other guys who had come into town with Skinnay Ennis' radio band. Don't be surprised if a few of them stick, Hendrickson possibly going with Goodman.

WEDNESDAY—Lunch with Willard Alexander, who has some very definite ideas anent evils in the music business and how and why they should be cured. Over to Don Haynes's office after that to see how his Randy Mergentroid plans were coming along and then a pleasant chat with Charlie and Fritzie Spivak. They're all enthused about their new New Jersey home, and, of course, about Joel, their son, than whom there is none any brighter. Left them to go over and see Glenn Miller between rehearsal and radio performances. Much serious talk with him about the national situation and its effect on the band business and how that business can best serve its country. Then back to his Chesterfield broadcast, including backstage small-talk with the many fine guys in his band. To the Arcadia later in the evening to catch the vastly improved Georgie Auld bunch. Manager Corrigan and asst. mgr. O'Brien claim they've never known a leader who works as hard and as diligently with his boys as Georgie does. Tremendously impressed with his zeal and definition of purpose. They're reflected, too, in the band's fast strides in the right direction. Later in the morning up to Jerry Lawrence's Moonlight Saving Time show to catch a quiz show starring Dick Robertson.

THURSDAY—Up to Decca this afternoon to see Leonard Schneider and promotion man Manning about the record-reviewers' situation and discovering that it's a mighty tough problem. Decca, quite frankly, doesn't give too too much of a hang about the critics and whether they get their discs or not. Which ought to solve a lot of mysteries for a lot of reviewers all over the country. The company's primarily interested in getting sides to dealers to sell, figuring those guys'll always sell them no matter what people write about them. Dinner with Mr. and Mrs. Dick Haymes, who have important plans that include a third person. Then back home to catch some bands on the air, for a change.

FRIDAY—Stopped by Joe Glaser's office to wish him a pleasant coastward journey. Two of us talked with Les Brown in Washington, who's immensely pleased with drummer Shelly Manne and singer

Glenn was deeply concerned and patriotic, as witness his application for a commission, even though he already had been exempted from the draft.

Jimmy Carroll, as well as Billy Butterfield's rejoining him in time for his picture. A bit worried about certain marriage possibilities and their effect upon his band. On the way home bumped into Toots Camaratta and Cork O'Keefe. Don't be surprised if Toots starts arranging for Casa Loma. Cork raving about a gal singer named Betty Bennett, who both he and Toots claim is ready for a big band job. In the evening up to hear Claude Thornhill at Glen Island and to be bowled over once again by his trumpets. Both Terry Allen and Dick Harding, whom Terry replaced, working with the band and sounding fine. Too bad Dick only began to realize his great potentialities such a short time before he had to return to the west coast to prepare either for the army or an important defense job! Terry sounded fine with the band. Claude excited about Jackie Koven's joining, though he admittedly hates to see Randy Brooks leave.

SATURDAY—Spent most of the evening playing records for Henry Simon, music expert for *PM*, who doesn't listen to much jazz, but who couldn't get enough of Goodman's clarineting. Interesting to catch long-hair reactions. Thought Dolores O'Neill immense, for example, and tremendously impressed with some Bill Clifton piano acetates. Couldn't see the Shaw band, or several other top-notchers, though.

SUNDAY—Day of rest in the country. To Cafe Society, after a late return to urbanity, to catch Teddy Wilson and to run into Paul Wetstein, who had just returned from the coast. He's been doing great work out there arranging for many movies, while also penning most of the manuscript for the Bob Crosby band.

That New Jersey Character Pops Up for Dinner

MONDAY—Ran into a whole flock of varied people around Broadway this afternoon. First, Irving Goodman, who has just left Vaughn Monroe and hasn't decided what to do yet. Then Willie "The Lion" Smith, who still knew what to do with the cigar he's always handling. Then Seger Ellis, who's now writing some fine songs instead of leading a ditto band, and Frank Ryerson, who had been doing some arranging, but who now has a mighty yen to blow some more of that good lead trumpet he used to be famous for. Then Dick Stabile and Louis Zito and Clyde Newcomb of his band giving Jack Dempsey's the daylight once-over before their evening opening inside. Gene Goodman showed up, too, looking wonderful after his army training period. He's now a songplugger for the Irving Berlin show and getting to look more like Benny every day. Then some 49th St. chatter with Gigi Bohn, Pete Mondello and Larry Molinelli, which was promptly halted by a truck splashing all four of us with mud. In a much bespattered condition down to the Strand to see Cab, Cozy Cole, Hilton Jefferson and several others in stage-door vicinity. A short Paramount backstage talk with BG to hear that the movie is pretty well set for his band, and then out to dinner with Freddy G. and Mr. and Mrs. Bullets Durgom of the T. Dorsey band. That New Jersey Character and that Mrs. N. J. Character make one happy couple, all right! Later in the evening to a magnificent jam session at the Stage Door Canteen. It started off with Billy Maxted on piano, Ralph Collier drums, George Berg tenor, Bernie Privin trumpet. It wound up with Benny on clarinet, Teddy Wilson on piano, Cozy Cole on drums, Jimmy Maxwell on trumpet, Jerry Jerome on tenor and Sandy Block, that fine Alvino Rey bassist. The guys knocked themselves out. Benny got a tremendous kick out of working with Teddy and Cozy again and was absolutely wonderful in his personal treatment of the soldiers and sailors. Then, to top everything, along came Bob Hope and Jerry Colonna with their knocked-out fun. Climax was Jerry singing *On the Road to Mandalay* and Benny playing corn clarinet behind him. Finally down to the Vanguard for more fine jam, this time with Teddy, Cozy, Maxwell, Jerome, Milton Hinton, Tyree Glenn and Hilton Jefferson. It turned out to be the greatest of all the Harry Lim efforts to date, and, quite naturally, a fine wind-up for what proved to be one of the most thrilling evenings of my young life.

The same Bullets Durgom who started off as a bandboy, became a personal manager, took over Jackie Gleason's career, helped it zoom, and is now a big wheel in Hollywood. A delightful character, always.

The jam session produced by Simon-Wright-Bracken-Mergentroid & Co. These were truly great, because the musicians seemed to want to play for the servicemen and we rounded up enough top name volunteers so that monotony never set in, and there were always surprises taking place.

Jerry Colonna pops a high note

BAND HISTORIES

Various events were responsible for the five band histories included in this section. The one about Glen Gray and the Casa Loma Orchestra celebrated the group's tenth anniversary. The one about Hal Kemp was occasioned by a much sadder event: his tragic death in an automobile crash. The two about the Dorsey Brothers and Glenn Miller—the "Real" exposes—were meant somehow to counteract some of the errors in their filmed biographies, while also paying respects to all three men. And, finally, the long piece, that ran in three consecutive issues, about the Ben-Pollack-to-Bob-Crosby band, came about simply because I had been spending so much time with the Crosby band, heard its members talk so much about their past, and found their history so fascinating that I wanted to pass it on along to our readers.

April, 1939

GLEN GRAY'S GANG KEEPS AHEAD OF CRAZES

Swung Back in '30 . . . Barometer Showing Shift to Sweet

The Casa Loma band is a pretty good barometer of dance music crazes. And if you believe implicitly in barometers, you can be one of those "I-told-you-so" guys if, within the next few years, swing is succeeded by sweet.

Those of you who lived in the east around 1930 might recall the arrival of the Casa Lomans and their tremendous success as they toured the Shribman circuit in New England. They came with a combination almost unheard of in those days: five brass (when almost all bands had three), four saxes (a trio sufficed for others), and a rhythm section.

Around Boston, people raved. Gray and the boys would give out at sensational but undanceable tempos, and the dancers would howl their approval.

"What sort of music is that?" they'd ask. And Gray and his boys would reply, "Why, that's swing!"

Killer-Dillers

Soon the rest of the country began to hear *Casa Loma Stomp*, and breakneck bits like *White Jazz*, *Black Jazz*, *Dance of the Lame Duck*, and so on.

It was on the strength of such swing numbers that the band became a national jazz institution and copped coveted spots like the Glen Island Casino, commercial programs like the Camel Caravan, and caused stampedes whenever they played a dance or a theatre.

But today the Casa Loma band doesn't emphasize those "flag-wavers." Instead, it's feeding its public all sorts of richly-scored, slow-moving, dreamy ballads.

Once in a while, to be sure, it hits a few faster tempos (never as fast as those undanceable old ones, though), but they're included only to break the monotony and to serve as contrast for the more emphasized sweet renditions.

"We're Not Best Swingers"

Critics have said that the Casa Lomans were never really any great shakes when it came to swing. They've pointed out that the rhythm section has always been stiff, that the saxes phrase unrhythmically, and that there aren't enough outstanding take-off men in the band to qualify it among the best swing has to offer.

And the Casa Loma lads have admitted, in their more unguarded moments, that they've never considered themselves a terriffic bunch of swingsters and that they know as well as anybody that they can't shell out the way the colored lads do.

Competition in swing gets keener day by day. Seems almost every well-known soloist is starting his swing band. And here's where the Casa Loma barometrical logic comes in for, back in 1931, wasn't almost every band featuring either a pianist like Eddy Duchin or a sax section like Lombardo's? And wasn't the dancing public getting awfully fed up with them, too?

You go on from here. What's going to be the reaction with every band trying to outblast the other? And what's more, what chance has a band that self-admittedly can't kick as high as Lunceford or Basie?

All the Limitations

Yes, the Casa Lomans are using their beans again. They know their limitations. And even more important than that, they feel that by this time they know the public's limitations! They started the pendulum swinging, so far as the country's dancers are concerned, and now they're edging off while it's still swinging high. According to current popularity polls their "Shift to Sweet" is being accepted by their listeners. Three years ago in METRONOME they finished second in swing and seventh in sweet. In the most recent contest, they wound up sixth in swing but second in sweet!

They have just one more step to go. It's not at all impossible that by the time they make that step, the rest of the country will start stepping with them, too. Better keep your eyes on that 10-year-old barometer!

The seven-man Casa Loma sax section of Dan D'Andrea, trombonist Murray McEachern, Clarence Hutchinrider, Glen Gray, Art Ralston, Pat Davis and Kenny Sargent

April, 1939

CASA LOMA CREW GREW FROM ORANGE BLOSSOMS

Left Biagini After a Year to Incorporate; Clinton Once Chief Arranger . . . Dunham Came, Went and Came . . . Complete Chronology

The origin of the Casa Loma band was really a group called the Orange Blossoms, which bloomed all around the middle west in the middle twenties under the direction of Henry Biagini. The Blossoms flowered in two seasons. The first started in 1924 and contained just one present Casa Loman, lead altoist Glen Gray. The second budding season was 1927, with trombonist Peewee Hunt, pianist Howard (Joe) Hall, and trombonist Billy Rauch arriving in that order. And then came the Casa Loma band. Here's how it all happened, from then until now.

APRIL, 1929—Start of Casa Loma band: Henry Biagini, leader; Glen Gray, Pat Davis, Les Arquette, saxes; Larry Sloat, Chink Dougherty, trumpets; Billy Rauch, Peewee Hunt, trombones; Joe Hall, piano; Gene Gifford, guitar and arranger; Harold George, bass; Walter Urban, drums; Jack Richmond, singer: Cork O'Keefe, manager.

New Rhythm Men

FALL, 1929—Bassist Stan Dennis for George. Band goes east. Tony Briglia for drummer Urban. Joe Hostetter added as third trumpet. Trumpeter Bobby Jones for Dougherty. Trumpeter Dub Shoffner for Sloat.

FEBRUARY, 1930—Band leaves Biagini in Ohio. Plans to incorporate. Ray Eberle for saxist Arquette. Frank Martinez for trumpeter Shoffner.

MARCH, 1930—Mel Jensen, violinist, hired to front band.

Band Incorporates

APRIL, 1930—Casa Loma band incorporated. Eberle, Martinez, Jensen only ones not in corporation.

SUMMER, 1930—Bobby Maron hired to take care of instruments, etc. Band barnstorms.

FALL, 1930—Into Lido Venice, Boston. Shoffner returns in place of trumpeter Martinez.

WINTER, 1931—Barnstorming.

Kenny Comes In

SPRING, 1931—Kenny Sargent replaces vocalist Jack Richmond; also plays fourth sax. Bo Ashford for trumpeter Shoffner.

SEPTEMBER, 1931—Engagement at Steel Pier—first important stay in the east.

OCTOBER, 1931—Grady Watts for trumpeter Ashford, Clarence Hutchinrider on third sax and clarinet for Eberle.

Enter: Mr. Dunham

JANUARY, 1932—Sonny Dunham on third trumpet for Hostetter.

SPRING-SUMMER, 1932—Barnstorming, college dates, Steel Pier again.

FALL, 1932—Belle Rieve in Kansas City; Hotel Lowrey in St. Paul. East for college dates around Christmas. Manager of Glen Island Casino hears band at Yale; immediately hires it for 1933 summer season.

SUMMER, 1933—Glen Island Casino in New Rochelle; band on air regularly; popularity really begins.

FALL, 1933—Essex House, New York.

Radio Commercial

WINTER, 1933-34—Starts Camel Caravan radio commercial. Cecil Stover added as copyist. Jacques Blanchette for guitarist Gifford who now spends all time arranging.

SUMMER, 1934—Glen Island Casino again.

FALL, 1934—Back to Essex House.

WINTER, 1934-35—Art Ralston added on fifth sax and Fritz Hummel on third trombone. Fiddle section of Jensen, Blanchette and Hummel begins. Eddie MacHarg on as new manager.

Enter: Mr. Clinton

SPRING, 1935—Larry Clinton replaces arranger Gifford.

SUMMER, 1935—Barnstorming.

FALL, 1935—Appears as first stage band at Paramount Theatre, N. Y.

WINTER, 1936—Rainbow Room, N. Y. theatres. End of Camel Caravan commercial engagement.

FALL, 1936—Congress Casino, Chicago. Frankie Zullo for first trumpeter Bobby Jones. Back to Paramount for Christmas weeks.

JANUARY, 1937—Back to Rainbow Room.

"Spike" Leads

MARCH, 1937—Glen Gray leaves sax section to stand up front as leader. Jensen leaves, replaced by

Dan D'Andrea, saxist and violinist. Sonny Dunham leaves to start own band, Walter Smith replacing.

SUMMER, 1937—West coast.

OCTOBER, 1937—New Yorker Hotel. Murray MacEachern leaves Goodman trombone section to replace Hummel. Arranger Dick Jones leaves Tommy Dorsey to replace Clinton.

NOVEMBER, 1937—Sonny Dunham calls quits as bandleader; returns, replacing Smith.

MARCH, 1938—Beginning of long trek westward.

JULY, 1938—Palomar, Los Angeles. Start of Burns and Allen radio commercial.

OCTOBER, 1938—Theatres.

DECEMBER, 1938—Christmas weeks at Paramount again.

JANUARY, 1939—Waldorf-Astoria Hotel, New York.

MARCH 28, 1939—End of Waldorf engagement.

APRIL, 1939—Celebration of ten years as Casa Loma band.

Chronological Breakdown of Casa Loma—April, 1939

	Name	Joined	Vocation in Band	Birth Place	Age	Marital State	Vocation Out of Band
1	Glen Gray	1929	Sax	Roanoke, Ill.	35	Married	Shooting, traveling
2	Francis C. O'Keefe	1929	Manager	Montville, Conn.	38	Married	Golf, Gray books and V
3	Walter Hunt	1929	Hot trombone, vocals	Mt. Healthy, O.	31	Married	Food, golf, radio
4	Howard Hall	1929	Piano, celeste	Stratford, Ontario	32	Married	Sports
5	William Rauch	1929	Sweet trombone	Dayton, Ohio	29	Married	Golf, cameras
6	Pat Davis	1929	Hot tenor sax	Little Rock, Ark.	29	Married	Golf, aviation
7	Stanley Dennis	1929	Bass	New York City	32	Married	Golf, cameras
8	Tony Briglia	1929	Drums	London, Ontario	32	Married	Sports, etc.
9	Bobby Maron	1930	Custodian	Peabody, Mass.	29	On the loose	Horses and cards
10	Kenny Sargent	1931	Sax, vocals	Centralia, Ill.	29	Married	Golf, building radios
11	Clarence Hutchinrider	1931	Hot clarinet, sax, vocals	Waco, Texas	30	Rooms single	Photography
12	Grady Watts	1931	Hot trumpet	Texarkana, Tex.	28	Married	Songwriting, horsebac riding, cameras
13	Sonny Dunham	1932	Hot trumpet, trmb., vocal	Brockton, Mass.	27	Single	Aviation
14	Jacques Blanchette	1933	Guitar and violin	Napoleon, N. D.	28	Married	Large airplanes, autos
15	Art Ralston	1934	All reeds	Beatrice, Nebr.	33	Married	Photography, bowling
16	Eddie MacHarg	1934	Road manager, very etc.	Philadelphia	32	Married	Trapping
17	Frank Zullo	1936	Lead trumpet	McAdoo, Pa.	26	Free	Sports
18	Dan D'Andrea	1937	Sax, violin	McDonald, Pa.	29	Married	Woodwork, golf
19	Murray MacEachern	1937	Trombone, trumpet, violin, saxes, clarinet	Toronto, Can.	23	Married	Flying, cameras
20	Dick Jones	1937	Arranger	Como, Miss.	30	Married	Drama and Beverly Hill
21	Larry Wagner	1938	Arranger	Ashland, Ore.	31	Married	Pipes

Everybody got into the act when the Casa Lomans posed for this gag shot in the Terrace Room of the Hotel New Yorker. Leader Glen Gray and drummer Tony Briglia swapped places, Kenny Sargent took up the bass, and Peewee Hunt assumed his own personable stance at the piano

HAL KEMP HAD A SWING BAND BEFORE HIS SWEET OUTFIT!

Tall, lanky, slow-moving, always relaxed—that was Hal Kemp, southerner in every one of his six feet four inches.

He was born in the deep south, Marion, Alabama. His first instrument was a jew's harp, but later he switched to clarinet and saxophone. He organized his first band when he was fourteen years old, attending Graham High School in Charlotte, N.C. After that he went to the University of North Carolina in Chapel Hill, where he started a group that included Skinnay Ennis, John Scott Trotter, and Saxie Dowell, all of whom remained with him for years, and who are now leading their own orchestras.

That band was successful around the south. Strangely enough it was a swing unit, and really broke into prominence via an extremely successful European tour.

Upon its return to America, it played at the Manger Hotel (now the Taft) in New York, in the days when no lesser trumpeters than Bunny Berigan and Jack Purvis used to blast out jazz choruses for the Kempians. Record collectors are referred to *Navy Blues* and *Whistles* (Brunswick Records, Nos. 4676 and 6110) for samples of the kind of good swing the band played in those days.

Then in the early thirties the group went to Chicago, and largely through arranger Trotter's imagination, created the soft, staccato trumpet and unison clarinet style that was to lead it to the top of the country's sweet groups. Skinnay Ennis' breathless vocals used to murder 'em out front, while Earl Geiger's tightly muted trumpet that sounded almost like a violin used to help create some of the mellowest moods dance music has ever known.

Loads of Brunswick Records portray the Hal Kemp band in those days. There was *Heart of Stone, I Nearly Let Love Go Slipping Through My Fingers, Hands Across the Table, It's Easy to Remember, The Touch of Your Lips, I've Got an Invitation to a Dance,* and *Am I To Blame*—just to mention a few of the really moody ones. Then there were gayer bits, such as *Got a Date With an Angel* and *Love and a Dime.*

Hal Kemp, near the end of his career, with Nan Wynn, one of his many fine vocalists

The group probably reached its zenith when it played the Pennsylvania Hotel in New York in 1934. A few years later, after it had enjoyed tremendous popularity everywhere, John Scott Trotter decided to try his hand at arranging out on the coast. Shortly after that, Hal magnanimously decided to back Skinnay Ennis, his biggest asset, with his own band. Later he did the same for Saxie Dowell.

At the time that Trotter, who built the style of the band, and Ennis, around whom it was built, left the group, swing was just becoming popular as a craze. Hal had had experience with that type of music before, and so he brightened his band's style accordingly. Unfortunately, the move wasn't too wise. The public had come to know the sentimental kind of Kemp music, and didn't take so kindly to the switch from tightly muted four brass to open five, and from subtone unison clarinets to full, rich saxes. It wasn't Hal Kemp.

Somewhat over a year ago, Hal decided to return to his sweet style. He engaged Nan Wynn, the feminine counterpart of Ennis, and with the aid of her voice, managed to reincarnate some of those old mellow moods. Try his Victor record of *What's New* for an example. She left him several months ago. Lately the band was hovering between the original mellow style and a richer, more rhythmic but less intimate mode of playing.

Which way they will turn now that they have lost their leader, nobody knows. What everybody does know is that they, as well as dance music, have lost one of the homiest, most loving fellows of all. Friendly and unruffled, his "H'ya all?" was one of dancebandom's warmest and most cordial greetings. There was never anything "big shot" about him. He treated people the way most southerners do—everybody was his friend, and anything he could do to make you happy, he did. Needless to say, that included the fellows in the band, all of whom had both great musical (Hal played a pretty fair sax and was blessed with an excellent ear) and personal respect for their leader. And Hal Kemp demanded every bit of that. Those who knew him well will always remember him as a fine leader, a fine musician, a fine gentleman, and a fine friend.

Shelly Manne on Joining Benny Goodman (April, 1949)—

It was a funny thing with Benny. You know what he told me? He said: "You don't have to bother reading the arrangements. You've been listening to my records for five years!" I lasted exactly four days.

294

THE REAL DORSEY BROTHERS

They fought and made up, and made jazz history

Jimmy and Tommy Dorsey are about as much alike as Jimmy and Tommy Dorsey, and that's not much! Periodic friends and foes, these two sons of a Pennsylvania music teacher blow as hot and cold toward each other as they do through their horns.

They've been like that since they were children. There are stories such as the one about Tommy sliding down the banister full speed and plowing feet-on into Jimmy, on purpose of course, and then a couple of hours later the two of them playing happily side-by-side, in the local band.

The successful careers of the Dorsey brothers ran closely parallel to each other for quite a while. They played in the Scranton Sirens, with Jean Goldkette, and with Paul Whiteman together. They recorded with Red Nichols together. Eventually they both settled in New York and played radio dates. And then finally, in 1934, they started their own band together.

Tommy was the leader and one of the three trombones, the others being Glenn Miller and Don Matteson. Jimmy sat in the sax trio along with altoist Jack Stacey and tenorman Skeets Herfurt. Jerry Neary was the lone trumpeter, then George Thow, while the rhythm section had Ray McKinley, Bobby Van Eps on piano, Roc Hillman on guitar and Delmar Kaplan on bass. Kay Weber was the girl vocalist and Bob Crosby joined a little later. It was a great band for that time, thanks largely to Glenn's arrangements, full of humor and pushing a beat that few other outfits had.

But the brothers didn't stay together long. At rehearsal one day Jimmy and Tommy squabbled

about a tempo. It was just one of those little things that would have meant nothing had not the underlying antagonism between the brothers existed. The result was a big blow-up, with Tommy pulling out of the band and Jimmy assuming its leadership.

Tommy, who's much more aggressive and a more dynamic leader than Jimmy, soon started his own outfit. From Bert Block's band he took a vocal trio called The Esquires that consisted of Jack Leonard, Axel Stordahl and Joe Bauer. The last-named remained in the Dorsey trumpet section, Axel stuck to arranging and Jack became the band's featured vocalist. Tommy also garnered such swing stars as Dave Tough, Carmen Mastren, Bud Freeman and the late Bunny Berigan and it wasn't long before his new band was cutting that of his older brother.

Quick action like that is pretty typical of Tommy. He's impetuous, very impetuous. He gets an idea and he'll follow through on it fast. There was the time when he heard of a chance for the guys in his band to make a lot of money in an oil well and he rushed himself and his men into it. You guess whether or not it panned out. There was another time when he decided he wanted his own music magazine. We talked about it. He wanted to start immediately. The fact that it was sure to be a losing proposition if he didn't wait never bothered him. He started his magazine. It folded after a few issues.

Tommy is strong-willed and quick-tempered. If he doesn't like something or somebody he holds back no punches. He's famous in the trade for telling off anybody at all, from the newest and most scared member of his band to the most important MCA executive. His language is often vicious. In his early studio days he took more than one punch at guys who riled him, and those punches weren't held back, either! Today he gives the appearance of having mellowed somewhat, but don't be fooled by appearances. His hair may be graying, but he still sees red just as clearly, and when he does he's murderous!

Jimmy is a less colorful character. When Tommy walked out of the band in 1935, he wasn't too upset. He got a kid named Bobby Byrne to take his brother's place and went along as before. The band didn't make the impression Tommy's did, primarily because it went out to Hollywood to play on Bing Crosby's show and consequently became pretty well buried so far as the rest of the country went.

Whereas Tommy is strong-willed and quick-tempered, Jimmy is more easygoing, more cognizant of other people's feelings. It's difficult to find a musician who has ever worked for him who'll say anything against the man. Being in the Jimmy Dorsey band may mean playing some great and some not so great music (depending upon the year), but it always means having kicks. Jimmy, in his quiet, almost shy

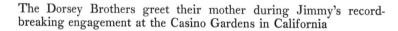

The Dorsey Brothers greet their mother during Jimmy's record-breaking engagement at the Casino Gardens in California

way, gives out with a flock of subtle cracks. Given a few drinks (and, like Tommy, he has been given and has given more than a few), he'll be even more direct, as in the greeting he gave Charlie Barnet when the latter opened at the 400 Restaurant last year. "Good evening, Charles," said Jimmy, with sincerity dripping from each word, "it is nice to see you. May I say that your band sounds very ponderous tonight—as usual!"

Ponderous music is nothing foreign to Jimmy, whose band during the late thirties had all the impact of a subway train flattening a chewing gum wrapper. But Jimmy had Bob Eberly and Helen O'Connell to sustain him. After they left, he again paid attention to choosing better sidemen and lighter arrangements, so that soon he had a band that was as good for its time as the original band had been for the middle thirties. As a matter of fact, the band that Jimmy fronts today is probably the best he's ever had. It jumps lightly, it plays ballads excellently and it spots consistently tasteful arrangements.

Tommy has no band today. He has a forty-foot motor boat which he bought in one of his impulsive moments and while you're reading this he's probably somewhere in the Atlantic or the Pacific sailing it from New York to California on its maiden voyage.

Tommy has had some great bands. Reputed for a time to be the most prolific raider in the business, he has never been at a loss for good sidemen. And though the band may have lowered its standards musically here and there, it has always been a tremendous success commercially, for there just isn't a shrewder bandleader in the business today than Tommy Dorsey. His pacing of sets, his ability to gauge his audiences, his picking of material and personnel have probably never been equaled. When Jack Leonard left him, he got Frank Sinatra. When Davey Tough left, he grabbed Buddy Rich. When Bunny Berigan left he got Peewee Erwin, then Yank Lawson, followed by Ziggy Elman and Charlie Shavers. And when both Axel Stordahl and Paul Wetstein (now Weston) went to Hollywood, he signed up Sy Oliver. It would surprise nobody if he hired Guy Lombardo to captain his new boat!

Though they've been leading different bands and though they haven't been playing together for the past dozen years, the Dorsey brothers haven't been as consistently apart as most folks think. True, they didn't talk for some time after their band busted up, but it was several years before their father's death, the event that supposedly brought them together again, that they appeared publicly. The occasion was one brother's band closing the same night at the New Yorker Hotel on which the other brother's band opened there. From there on in they were together on various occasions and eventually went into business with their own music publishing house. Eventually they appeared in *The Fabulous Dorseys*, and since then they have been together a great deal, Tommy spending many evenings at the Hotel Pennsylvania during Jimmy's recent engagement there.

That's the way the Dorsey brothers stand today. There's nothing too fantastic or fabulous about them right now. They talk together and they play together, and, even though some people will have you believe that jazz is dying, they still blow pretty hot at each other. And yet, each retains his distinctive personality. Tommy the obvious extrovert, Jimmy the more subtle introvert. When they will clash next is anybody's guess. Tommy doesn't think it'll happen again. Jimmy doesn't think it'll happen again. But then, they're so different that one of them is bound to be wrong. You figure it out for yourself, if you please.

Friends and mutual admirers for many years, Tommy and Jimmy and Joe Venuti

297

THE REAL GLENN MILLER

It's now almost ten years later since we saw Glenn Miller for the last time, since he was reported missing in action in the European Theatre.

During those years, his tremendous influence, as a stylist and as a person, on the American music scene has gone on unabated. Others have tried to pick up the threads. Some have tasted success they never would have known without the help of those threads.

This month, Universal-International Pictures offers us THE GLENN MILLER STORY, a moving motion picture about this great man of American music. Though many liberties have been taken to make this a more attractive movie, it still retains the flavor and feel of this great man and his music, and is highly recommended to all who knew him and/or know his music.

Glenn Miller was a very real man, a very vital man. He was dynamic. He was also highly sensitive. I was privileged to know him well for almost ten years. The story that follows will, I hope, give you a greater insight into the man, will help you to understand him and his actions and to admire Glenn Miller as much as I did, do, and always will.

The news hit me a few hours before Christmas, 1944. I was just starting down the stairs of the subway at Broadway and 50th Street when I saw those headlines:

GLENN MILLER MISSING IN ACTION

I bought the paper and read the complete sketchy report, about how Glenn had taken off in a plane on December 15th to go to Paris and how he hadn't been heard from since and was presumed to be lost. Of course it didn't give the complete story. Even today nobody knows the complete story. There's a lot to it that the newspapers couldn't print. That's because they never knew the real Glenn Miller.

I knew him. I knew him well. I was with him when he organized his first band. I was with him when it played its very first job as a substitute band at the Hotel New Yorker and I was with him the night he fronted his civilian band for the last time in a theatre in Passaic, New Jersey. I was with him in the army too. But I wasn't with him overseas.

Why I was left behind, after having been a member of his outfit, I'll never know. I was thinking about that as I walked through the snow that Christmas Eve, after getting off the subway in Greenwich Village. They were singing carols, as they always do in Washington Square, and I thought maybe the spirit of Christmas might soften the shock of that short newspaper story. It didn't. I could only feel the spirit of Glenn Miller. Intensely.

I was back here in the States, still in the army, making V Discs, no longer a part of the greatest morale-building effort of the war. This had been Glenn's big dream when he had enlisted: it was now in the process of completion. He was intensely proud of it, proud of the soldiers who formed this great venture. This pride is exemplified in a letter he had written to me less than two months previously, in which he complained bitterly about an appraisal of his band by an English soldier which had been published in METRONOME. It also shows splendidly just what he felt his role was in the war effort. To quote in part:

". . . We (the band) didn't come here to set any fashions in music—we came merely to bring a much-needed touch of home to some lads who have been here a couple of years. These lads are doing a hell of a job—they have been starved for real, live American music and they know and appreciate only those tunes that were popular before they left the States. For their sake, we play only the old tunes. You know enough about musicians to know that *we* would certainly enjoy playing new tunes and plenty of them. I expect the 'critic' who wrote the article expected to hear mainly new arrangements featuring a bunch of guys taking choruses a la Town Hall Concert . . .

"This lad missed the boat completely on the conditions and our purpose for being here. I'm surprised that the METRONOME editorial staff printed the thing because they should realize the needs over here, even though this 'hot soldier' over here doesn't seem to. While he listened for things which he opined were musically 'wrong,' he failed to hear the most important sound that can possibly come out of such concerts— the sound of thousands of G.I.'s reacting with an earsplitting, almost hysterical happy yell after each number. That's for us, Brother, even if it doesn't happen to be for METRONOME . . .

"What they print about any civilian band of mine is O.K. with me and they are certainly entitled to print anything they like without me taking any action to defend my position, but when they take cracks at a wonderful bunch of G.I. musicians who are doing a great job, that's too much . . .

"I am so firmly convinced that these boys over here ARE great that, should I have a band after the war, and should any of them desire a job, I would gladly give it to him regardless of his musical proficiencies."

It was a strong letter, a very strong letter, from one of the most forceful, dogmatic men the entertainment world has ever known. Glenn was always a man of intense likes and dislikes. He was a man of snap judgments. He was intuitive. You were either on his list or off it. I think that above all he admired honesty. He couldn't stand even a hint of fakery. The phonies in the music business knew it. They learned to stay away from him.

An Impression of Himself

As he became more successful Glenn, in one sense, lost some self-respect, as he felt himself losing a portion of a quality he admired so much in others. He told me about it one day backstage in his dressing room in the Paramount Theatre. "I don't quite know how to handle it," he said. "I'm really beginning to be one helluva ————. I can't help it, though. So many people are asking me to do so many things and I really want to do some of them, but I just don't have the time. It's murder. I find myself doing things I'm ashamed of doing, and yet I know people would never understand if I told them just the plain, simple truth. I'm not the kind of guy I really want to be."

Glenn was practical, extremely so. He knew what he wanted and knew how to get in. In the army, one of his big concerns was to provide inspiring music for marching. With the help of Ray McKinley and Jerry Gray, he produced some great marching versions of standards like *St. Louis Blues* and *Blues in the Night*, which his band played for the AAF cadets in training during reviews on the New Haven Green. The reaction, which I witnessed while beating a street drum, was invariably immense. The cadets always marched ever so much better, alert and spirited.

But there was a major in charge of the training program who didn't approve. It all wound up with a showdown in the post commander's office. The major was vehement, as vehement as any West Pointer, steeped in army tradition, could be. "What sort of junk is this, anyway?" he complained. "What is this jazzed-up music doing in the army? We've been playing straight military music for years, and we've been turning out some pretty fair soldiers. After all, we won the last war, didn't we, without any of this jazz music!"

Glenn eyed the major scornfully, so I'm told, then emitted this thoroughly cutting and convincing reply. "Tell me just one thing, Major. Are you still flying the same planes in this war that you flew in the last one?"

In a relaxed mood at one of the early Chesterfield radio-commercial rehearsals, Glenn sits with saxists Tex Beneke, Hal McIntyre, Willie Schwartz, Hal Tennyson

The Miller brass team recording in the RCA Victor studio in New York. FRONT ROW: Paul Tanner, Jimmy Priddy, Glenn, Frankie D'Anolfo. BACK ROW: Charlie Frankhauser, Zeke Zarchy, Mickey McMickle, Johnny Best

The band continued to blow *St. Louis Blues* and *Blues in the Night*.

Practical common sense had prevailed in Glenn's civilian days. At first perhaps, he had organized his band so that he could express himself and his music—the way it says he did in the picture of his life, *The Glenn Miller Story*. But once he had achieved success, his was strictly a practical, dollars and cents approach. His dance band was, I always felt, primarily a business and secondarily an art form.

A Biographical Suggestion

One incident, more than any other, convinced me of this. Glenn called me one day at the office and asked if I could hurry on down to the Victoria Barber Shop, where he was getting a shave and a haircut, and where he knew we wouldn't be interrupted by phone calls, etc. (He used to transact quite a bit of business in that chair, by the way.) As soon as I arrived, I sensed his enthusiasm. "How would you like to write my story?" he asked. I was knocked out. Here was a story I felt I really knew, a man I really knew, a cause I really knew. I'd watched him struggle for everything he believed in and now that he had the greatest band in the world I figured there'd be a great angle to his story: how a musician fights for his ideals, sticks with them through great hardships, and emerges triumphant! What a great object lesson for every honest, aspiring musician.

"I got the title already," exclaimed Glenn from behind his lather. "Listen: 'My Dance Band Gave Me $748,564!'" I'm not sure of the exact figures. They were somewhere in that vicinity. Immediately my enthusiasm waned. I sensed that this wasn't to be a music story. It was to be a business success saga. Our consequent discussions and my reasons for never having written the story don't make much difference here. But I think the incident indicates rather aptly just how Glenn did feel about the importance of his band and his success.

I suspect that one of the reasons Glenn had asked me to write his biography was loyalty. I'd been his staunchest supporter in print since the very beginning, so much so that I used to take quite a ribbing from other leaders and musicians because I insisted from February of 1937 on, when the band first started rehearsing, that this would be the country's next number one band. Glenn always remembered.

He Wanted to Join the Army

Of course, it was loyalty, in a much larger sense, that prompted him to make the most fateful decision of his life. That was when he decided that he wanted to enlist in the army so that he could play for the men overseas. Glenn's love of his country was amazingly unselfish. He never would have been drafted. He could easily have remained at the top of his profession, perhaps playing in camps and even taking a safe trip overseas, and everybody would have looked upon him as a loyal, war-effort-aiding citizen. But from the start he felt that wasn't enough. His burning ambition became to serve his country firsthand.

This ambition received numerous restrictions in the army, however. Like so many of its members, he found himself constantly being hampered by red tape. Glenn was a man who liked to face problems head on, who was at his best when he could solve them quickly and directly. But, oh, those channels!

Frustrations hounded him in every phase of his army career. For the first year he did little more than desk work. He had all sorts of plans for organizing great dance bands throughout the air force, but other army men had had all sorts of other plans which they had been following for years and years, and they didn't relish the innovations suggested by this new captain.

Finally, after more than a year, he got what he wanted: a complete unit, composed of top-notch musicians, which he could mold into a great marching band and an equally great entertaining unit. This he did, on the Yale campus in New Haven, Conn., starting in March, 1943. Even there he was restricted by men like the major who didn't approve

of his style of marching music. The tip-off on the kind of inefficiency he had to put up with is illustrated by the story of an inspection of his great band by a lieutenant, sent from command headquarters, whose duty it was to supervise and report on all AAF musical unit bands in that particular command.

This lieutenant, whose only previous association with music, so far as I could ascertain, was his last name, which happened to be the same as that of a well-known society bandleader, only spelled differently, came to New Haven to review the Miller band as it played retreat. His opinion, given to Glenn after the parade, was a beaut. Said he: "You know, Glenn, you have a wonderful organization. Simply wonderful! Musically, that is. But, Captain, there's one thing it lacks and that's showmanship. Showmanship. You know, I was standing there, watching the band as it passed by, and, you know, in the front row, those four trombone players. Well, I noticed that they weren't together. One man had his slide way out, and another had his near his mouth, and the other two were doing something else again. I wish you could get them all to do the same thing together at the same time. I think it would look much snappier."

There is no record of Glenn's reply.

The famed Miller sax section on the stand of the Cafe Rouge of the Hotel Pennsylvania: Al Klink, Willie Schwartz, Hal McIntyre, Ernie Caceres, Tex Beneke. Leigh Knowles is the trumpeter, Maurice Purtill the drummer, Rollie Bundock the bassist, and Marion Hutton the girl singer down front

Ray McKinley and Trigger Alpert at a World War II European Army base. John Halliburton and Jimmy Priddy are the two trombonists

How Strained the Leash?

Glenn's frustrations continued throughout his stay in New Haven. His big ambition was to go overseas, but several times, when he felt he and the band were all set to make the jump, another brand of red tape would hold him back again. By the time he broke the leash well over a year later, and more than two years after he had enlisted, the strain was beginning to tell on him. To me and to others who had known him over the years, he had changed in many ways.

He was much more serious in every way. Matters that he used to pass off lightly assumed too much importance. As time wore on, he became more and more G.I. I always had the feeling that he hated the cleavage that existed between officers and enlisted men, that he never knew quite how to reconcile the two different relationships between him and men he had been pals with in civilian days but who were now, rankly speaking, in a lower stratum. He became so strict at one point that he ordered, without offering any explanation, every musician in his outfit to shave off his mustache. For several of the brass men, especially, this meant great hardship, for they had been used to blowing for years with their mustaches on. With them off, it meant almost new embouchures and looks.

As a matter of fact, some of the musicians looked pretty ridiculous, especially to those who had known them with their mustaches on for many years. I doubt, though, if Glenn thought it humorous.

So frustrated and so upset was he in those days that, I'm afraid, he retained little of the great sense of humor that was once his. I think that if he had been able to look at life a little more lightly, he might well still be with us today.

That Last Flight Toward Paris

I'm referring to the circumstance surrounding that last flight. Don Haynes, his close friend and manager, and AAF assistant, wrote me in part a few months later as follows: "Regardless of all the rumors, there's been no trace of Glenn, the other passenger (a colonel attached to the VIIIth Air Force), the pilot, or the plane, since that foggy Friday afternoon I alone saw them off (15 December) . . . Glenn took the trip that I was to make—decided to the day before—and as I had made all the arrangements, it only necessitated cancelling the orders that had been cut for me, and getting orders cut for him. I brought the outfit over three days later (after having been 'weathered in' for two days) only to find that Glenn had not arrived. Our trip was uneventful, but not his."

302

Glenn hated to fly. Why he decided at the last minute to sit in for Haynes on the plane nobody knows. Perhaps it was his sense of duty. Perhaps it was because of the same frustrations that had been plaguing him throughout his Army life. He wanted to get things done, and so, rather than have somebody else hop over to Paris to start things going for his band, he may have decided that he wanted to do it himself. Whatever the cause for his wanting to go may have been, I still feel that if he had retained his sense of humor he might have resisted the dare which, so I'm told, he accepted that foggy Friday afternoon.

The weather must have been truly miserable. All of the AAF Transport Command planes had been grounded. But that colonel and Glenn were all set to go. From all I can gather, Glenn was kidded into going. A less frustrated, a better adjusted man could have taken the purported riding about his fear of flying in his stride. This Glenn did not do. He accepted what amounted to a dare to take off with the colonel and the pilot in a general's small plane on an unchartered flight under obviously unsafe flying conditions. They took off. Nobody knows what happened after that.

Glenn Had Fun Back in 1934

The Miller sense of humor was one of the first things I noticed about the guy. The first time I saw him was in 1934 when he played, as a member of the Dorsey Brothers band, at Nuttings-on-the-Charles just outside of Boston. He sang the last of several verses of his own comedy song called *Annie's Cousin Fanny*, and this studious-looking man looked even funnier than the other musicians as he sang. Later he told me that he and Ray McKinley used to keep each other awake, driving on one-nighters, by making up additional verses for the song. "Glenn made up most of them," McKinley said recently. "I slept most of the time."

The Miller sense of humor didn't desert him when he was requested to leave the Dixie Hotel under slightly ridiculous conditions. It was in 1937, and he and I had gone into the supper room there to listen to a tenorman we'd gotten a tip on. We ordered sandwiches and coffee, listened to the band, then watched our waiter perform in the floor show. His act completed, he returned to our table and asked us what we'd like to drink. We ordered more coffee. "No, I mean *drink* . . . Liquor . . . Whiskey," he explained. We explained, too, that we didn't want to drink. He conferred with the headwaiter. "If you don't order drinks, you can't stay in the room," he told us. So we left. And we took the tenorman with us. "First time," laughed Glenn outside, "I've ever been kicked out of a place for NOT drinking!"

Even when Glenn was struggling with inferior musicians in his early band, trying desperately to keep a band together, his sense of humor didn't desert him. On his first trip he was having a tough time trying to find a drummer he liked. His band had always been plagued by bad rhythm. But, he wrote on October 12th, 1937 from the Hotel Nicollet in Minneapolis, "we are getting a new drummer (thank God) in a couple of weeks . . . about two hundred and fifty pounds of solid rhythm—I hope. This boy we have is pretty bad and MacGregor says outside of being a bad drummer he has a quarter beat rest between each tooth which doesn't enhance the romantic assets of the band . . ."

Another part of the same letter seems strangely prophetic in the light of future events. "I don't know just where we are going from here—I guess no one else does either. We are hoping for some sort of a radio setup that will let more than three people hear us at a time. If this drummer only works out there will be nothing to stop us from now on. (Barring mishaps, of course.)"

Glenn's enthusiasm for musicians, young and old, appears later in the letter. Irving Fazola had recently joined the band. "I sincerely believe," wrote Glenn, "that Faz is the only clarinet player with a chance these days. Shaw, Mince, and all of them play like Benny and they will not live long enough to cut him. Faz like Ole Man River jes' keeps rollin' along and he doesn't want to know from anyone. I doubt if he has heard more than a few Goodman records and up until Dallas had never met or heard Benny personally. Benny listened very closely when Faz was playing.

"While on Benny, he was his usual swell self to us in Dallas and that band, George, is without doubt the greatest thing in the history of jazz. I thought they were good at the Pennsylvania but they have improved 100% since then. That cornet section is the Marvel of the Age and Krupa is more of a genius than ever to me. He drums with his head which is a real rarity . . ."

Nobody Knew Glenn Miller

Glenn may have been enthusiastic about Goodman and his musicians, but too few people in those days were enthusiastic about Glenn Miller and his musicians. In fact, things were very tough.

The Minneapolis band was the second of three Miller editions. The first had been a combination string quartet-jazz band which had been organized solely for making a set of Columbia records and which was never heard from again thereafter.

Edition #2 was organized in 1937, after Glenn had left Ray Noble's wonderful band, which he had organized for the English leader on assignment. It had been a stellar crew. Glenn and Will Bradley were the trombones. Charlie Spivak and Peewee Erwin played trumpets. Bud Freeman and Johnny Mince were among the saxes. Claude Thornhill was the pianist; George Van Eps the guitarist.

Assembling groups was nothing new to Miller. He had helped the Dorsey Brothers put together their great outfit in the mid-thirties by bringing over several musicians, including Ray McKinley and Skeets Herfurt, from Smith Ballew's fine band. And who had organized Smith Ballew's fine band? Glenn Miller, of course.

Before then he had done both studio and jazz tromboning. His first name band had been Ben Pollack's, for which he arranged and played. He had also been an important arranging and playing penny among the numerous Red Nichols coins which made so many great jazz records in the early thirties. Most of the jazz greats blew with the crew. On records it was listed as "Red Nichols and his Five Pennies." I recall one of the first talks I had with Glenn. I asked him about the Five Pennies. The records had always sounded amazingly rich for so few musicians. "The labels said 'Five Pennies'—that's right," said Glenn. "That's all they mentioned. But there were always a few playing behind curtains or something," he added wryly.

The Start of Everything

Glenn let me in on his big secret one day at our house while we were playing records. "I'm going to start a band," he confessed. "And if you can help me find some young, good musicians, I'd appreciate it. Right now all I have is a theme song." He had written *Moonlight Serenade*, based on a Schillinger exercise, and the men in the Noble band were all raving about the song. At the time it was called *Now I Lay Me Down to Weep*, and it had a set of beautiful lyrics by Eddie Heyman (all of which I still remember, in case Eddie is reading this). Later on some publishers convinced Glenn that it should have a more grandiose title, if it were to serve as his theme, so he had Mitch Parrish write lyrics to *Moonlight Serenade*.

The first man Glenn hired (on a tip from John Hammond) was Hal McIntyre, whom we found in Meriden, Conn., after a trip through a snowstorm. Hal wanted Glenn to take on some of the other men in his band up there, but they didn't suit Miller's tastes, so Mac became the band's first musician himself.

Back in New York Glenn held many rehearsals, often aided by several of the many studio musicians who admired and liked him so much. Chief among these were Spivak (then Glenn's closest friend) and saxist Toots Mondello. On Miller's first record date (for Decca in March, 1937) he had to use mostly studio men. Spivak, Mannie Klein and Sterling Bose blew trumpets; the saxists had George Siravo (the arranger), McIntyre and Jerry Jerome, while the rhythm section boasted the late Dick McDonough on guitar and pianist Howard Smith. (There was also a drummer named George Simon who now writes for METRONOME.)

The band's first date, a relief session at the New Yorker Hotel, was heard by the late Ralph Hitz, who owned a chain of hotels. He was greatly impressed, hired the band for several dates, on one of which, the Roosevelt in New Orleans, the group broke all records for that room.

In the late fall the band came back east, playing at the Raymor Ballroom in Boston, where it had its first coast-to-coast air-shots. Until that date, the band had not found a set style. Glenn was experimenting constantly. One day he remembered that happy accident that had occurred in Ray Noble's band. Glenn had been voicing Peewee Erwin's trumpet as lead above the saxes. The musician who replaced Erwin had a more limited range and, so that the arrangements shouldn't be a total loss, Glenn reassigned Peewee's trumpet part to a clarinet. The new sound was pleasant.

Glenn remembered the pleasant sound and, despite opposition from advisors, dropped the guitar from his band and added a fifth sax. That was the start of the now famous Miller style.

But it didn't do him too much good in those days. He had trouble in his band, mostly with drinkers. The morale was very low and when Glenn's wonderful wife, Helen, was stricken with a severe illness, his spirits reached the depths also. By the middle of January, 1938, Glenn had had enough. He disbanded and went back into the studios, even playing trombone in friend Tommy Dorsey's band for a while.

The Start of THE Band

Glenn had learned a lesson. No more prima donnas. No more problem musicians. With just four hold-overs (McIntyre, close friend Chummy MacGregor, bassist Rollie Bundock and trumpeter Bob Price) he started Edition #3 two months later. From Detroit he brought in the tenor saxist he considered "the greatest of them all!" Tex Beneke. Booker Si Shribman was now one of Glenn's managers, and he found work for the group. One of the jobs was the Paradise Restaurant in New York (later Bop City), which it played several times. During one of the band's return visits to Boston, Glenn heard two sisters, Betty and Marion Hutton, singing in Vincent Lopez's band.

The 1938 Glenn Miller band during its scufflingest days (note condition of bandstands). FRONT ROW: Miller, Paul Tanner, Al Mastren, Marion Hutton, Ray Eberle. BACK ROW: Jack Kimbal, Bob Price, Johnny Austin

Glenn could have hired either. He chose Marion, because he felt she was more mature, because her personality seemed to fit the clean-cut, All-American approach for which Glenn always strove.

But despite improved morale in the band, it still wasn't making it. It tried very hard, but the frequent Paradise engagements were a drag, because the band had to play three shows a night, and, after running through them, the guys seldom had lips left for their broadcasts.

By February, 1939, the band had hit another low. I accompanied Glenn on a trip to North Carolina. Everything went wrong. On the way back he had made up his mind. Bandleading was not for him. He was going to chuck it all again, he told me, and return to the studios.

But then came March 1st, 1939. The band was rehearsing that afternoon in its usual spot, the Haven studio on West 54th Street. It was Glenn's thirty-fourth birthday. And then somebody brought in the news. The Glen Island Casino, which had sprung such bands as Casa Loma, Ozzie Nelson, the Dorseys and Charlie Barnet had decided it wanted Miller's for the summer season. And Frank Dailey, after hearing of the pick, decided to book the band for the period prior to Glen Island.

From then on it was all up, including everybody's spirits. Glenn prepared many new arrangements. Some he wrote or sketched himself. Others were produced by young Bill Finegan, fresh from New Jersey, who always remained Miller's particular pet. Later on Jerry Gray, who had been writing for Shaw, also joined.

How did things look? Here's a quote from the December, 1939, issue of METRONOME: "Well, January is coming up, and it looks like a different kind of January for the Glenn Miller band this time. For, after a week or so more at its present Meadowbrook spot, it goes on another tour (on its last one it broke records in almost every spot it played), starts doing the Chesterfield show on December 27th, and then about January 5th goes into the much coveted Cafe Rouge spot in New York's Pennsylvania Hotel."

Then Came Rewards—for Many

Success had come at last. Success had come to one of the really great dance band leaders of all time—for my dough, the *greatest* all-around leader of all time. Personally, I've never known any man who knew so exactly just what he wanted, and what's even more important, knew exactly how to get what he wanted. His moral standards were just as high as his musical standards, and for those of us who stood by him during his difficult years—well, the things that followed were just immense!

The one person who should be cited above all others is Mrs. Glenn Miller. To me, Helen's and Glenn's was the finest, the most admirable marital relationship I have ever known in the entire business. I won't go into details of what an understanding and devoted wife she was. All I can say is that in the picture, *The Glenn Miller Story*, she is admirably portrayed by June Allyson, except that Helen is even greater than that!

Chummy MacGregor, too, was a happy stalwart in those days. Today he still remains a wonderful friend to Helen, who now lives on the west coast with her and Glenn's two adopted kids, the younger of whom arrived in the Miller household while Glenn was overseas and whom, therefore, he never knew.

The late Si Shribman, the big, bluff, hearty, honest man from Boston, was also happy. So was Don Haynes, Glenn's close friend and manager, who came on the scene later. So was I.

Many of us still wonder what Glenn would be doing if he were with us today. Paul Dudley, the radio-TV producer and writer, who served with Glenn overseas and who became a very close friend, told me recently that Glenn had great plans for the future, plans that went much further than just fronting a band. He wanted to do even bigger things, for more people, to expand in his recording, publishing and other activities.

It never happened, of course. But, whatever he had in mind, I'm sure that whatever would have happened would have been another great credit not only to a wonderful leader and person, not only to those closely associated with him, but also to the music and to the country to which Glenn was so intensely devoted, a devotion which, had it been a little less intense, might never have taken him away from us.

FROM BEN POLLACK TO BOB CROSBY

A History of Two Great Bands

Part I

CROSBY BAND WAS POLLACK'S OVER AGAIN

Drummer Ben with Immortals in Outfit Provided Impetus for Dixielanders; Jazz Kicks and Human Kicks Tell Story

There's a long story behind the Bob Crosby band—an awfully long one. It goes way back, long before Bob had even thought of going to Gonzaga College or of singing with Anson Weeks and the Dorsey Brothers. Certainly long, long before he even knew there might some day be such a thing as "The Best Dixieland Band in the Land," and that he'd be the guy waving a stick in front of such wondrous musicians as Eddie Miller and Matty Matlock and Yank Lausen and Jess Stacy and Bob Haggart and Ray Bauduc and a lot more men of their calibre.

The story goes back even before anybody outside of his family had heard much of *Bing* Crosby.

It started in Crosby territory, though—way out there on the west coast in the very middle twenties. Ben Pollack was playing drums in a band led by a fellow named Harry Baisden in a ballroom named the Venice, which was in Venice, which isn't far from Los Angeles. Gil Rodin, who was later destined to become the president of the Bob Crosby band (but that's coming much later) happened to be out on the coast. He had just left Art Kahn's band in Chicago and he felt he needed a rest. So he did the unoriginal thing (it may have been original in those days, but it certainly isn't in these) of taking a trip to California. And so, just to make this story a little easier and lots more convenient, so far as the plot is concerned, he walked one night down the streets of Venice, came to the Venice ballroom, walked in, and saw his old friend Ben Pollack, with whom he used to play in Chicago.

"Why, hello, Gil!" said Ben.

"Hello, Ben!" said Gil.

Little did they know this was the beginning of the Bob Crosby band. But it was. (More of that lots later too.)

"What are you doing out here?" asked Ben.

"Aw, just vacationing."

"Why don't you move in with me?" invited Pollack.

"Aw, shucks, do you mean it?"

"Sure."

"O.K."

Gil and Ben Share Rooms

So they lived together. Not for too long, right away, though. Pollack got Gil a job with Carl Allen's band at the Rendezvous. He wanted to get Gil into the Baisden band at once, but Jack Garrity, who ran

An early photo of the Ben Pollack band in Atlantic City during the summer of 1928. (L. to r.) a page, Larry Binyon, Harry Goodman, Vic Breidis, Pollack, Al Harris, Earl Baker, Dick Morgan, Benny Goodman, Jack Teagarden and Gil Rodin

307

Ben Pollack, still playing in the 60's

the ballroom, had had trouble with leaders Abe Lyman and Max Fisher and wasn't to be approached for a while. Besides, Pollack wasn't the leader—not yet.

Rodin and Pollack didn't live together for long because Ben decided to go back to Chicago for some reason or other. Shortly after Ben left, however, leader Baisden got mentally ill, had to leave the band, and everything started going haywire. So Garrity, who had noticed that Pollack was a darned good organizer, sent for him right away. Ben came back right away. He tried to bring Muggsy Spanier back with him right away too. The union said no right away.

Now that Pollack was leader he could go ahead and bring in friend Rodin. The union couldn't kick, since Gil was a member there. The only guy who might mind would be Garrity. He paid all the men, and Pollack knew Rodin well enough to rest assured that the guy wouldn't come in and play for nothing. Who would?

So Pollack played wise. "I know a good sax player," he told boss Garrity one day.

"Where?"

"Over at the Rendezvous with Carl Allen. I don't know if you'd like him, though."

"I can't tell if I don't hear him," replied Garrity.

They went to hear Rodin.

Garrity liked Rodin.

Rodin joined Pollack's hand.

Things went swell for a while. Gil played lead sax. In the section with him was Fud Livingston, who was playing tenor as well as jazz clarinet. It was strictly a jazz band, by the way. So were all of Pollack's outfits. "The man was primarily 'beat-conscious,'" says Rodin today. "As long as the band had a good beat, he never really worried."

Of course, personal matters might worry Ben. Around this time he had just cause, for his brother passed away suddenly in Chicago. Gil hurried back on the train with Ben—to keep him company, more than anything else. While they were riding eastward, they started figuring out ways of bringing the band to Chicago. After all, that was their territory. And, who knows, they might have been feeling a little homesick, too.

One thing they knew that they had to do was get another clarinet player. Fud and the trombone player in the band had had a big blowoff about some woman. There was an awful lot of friction, and it could never be stopped until one of the men left. All the guys knew that Fud had been in the wrong. "So," figured Pollack and Rodin, "we'd better start looking for another clarinet man."

They knew of a few around town. Gil went to the union and asked the fellows there. "Art Kassel's got a fine guy at Midway Gardens," he was told.

Benny Goodman

Pollack wanted to stay close to his family, so Gil did the scouting all alone. He went to the Gardens to hear the clarinetist. He was just a little kid. Name was Benny Goodman. But he knocked Gil clean out. Rodin went up to introduce himself. Benny had heard of him.

"Yeah, I'd like to go west," he said.

The two of them didn't go west that night. But they did go all over town, listening to bands. King Oliver's was one of them.

Later on Rodin also heard a trumpeter named Harry Greenberg, who played like Muggsy. Gil thought he was wonderful, too.

Meanwhile the friction in the Pollack band out on the west coast had mounted so much that it was starting electric storms in Chicago. Gil heeded the call and rushed right out, even before Pollack was ready to leave. He had to let Fud go. What's more, the jazz trumpeter was having terrible lip trouble. So Gil sent for Benny and Harry at once. Out they came. And the band began to sound even more wonderful.

Pollack remained in Chicago for several weeks more. Meanwhile, Gil and Garrity became close friends. The leader pro tem explained to the boss pro permanent just what he and Pollack had in mind. Garrity, who by this time loved the fellows, told him to go ahead and build. Then, whenever they decided they'd like to head back east, they could go.

The band stayed at the Venice for another half year. Towards the end of the period, Ben told his men about the future plans. Those who didn't feel like going east didn't have to, of course. Only Pollack wanted to know then and there, so that he could start making replacements.

The bass, the guitar, the tenor sax, and the trombone didn't think they wanted to leave their homes. Anyway, they'd heard about the rain in the east. Californians are naive.

Glenn Miller

So Pollack started listening to men. One day a trombone player came in who said he could also arrange. With Fud out, the band needed someone to write stuff. So they went over to the Forum Theatre to hear the guy play with Max Fisher's band. He wasn't too great a trombone player, but his arrangements were fine. And he was deadly serious about his music. Pollack seemed to admire that approach, too. So he hired Glenn Miller.

Shortly after that, the Pollack band began its first invasion of the east. It had new men. It had Glenn Miller. It had Harry Goodman on bass (picked up in Chicago). And Fud Livingston was back. The old trombone player wasn't around, so there wasn't any danger of friction. And there was a new piano player named Wayne Allen who could arrange. So, besides a flock of new men, the band had a flock of classy arrangements.

Only one trouble.

The band didn't have a job.

Yet they rehearsed together regularly in Chicago. Most of the men succeeded in getting placed with various outfits, but their hearts were with Pollack and his lads. Finally the break came.

They were showing the band to Billy Goodheart, who used to be a piano player around town, but who was now with MCA. Goodheart liked it, but so did another fellow, the manager of the Castle Farms in Cincinnati, who happened to be at the audition at the time. Funny, isn't it, how spot managers always *happen* to be at auditions.

Anyway, the manager offered the lads several weeks at Castle Farms. He didn't say exactly how many, but he intimated a long run. The guys were thrilled. Of course, they all gave up their jobs. Imagine, then, how unthrilled they suddenly became when, upon walking into the Ohio spot for the first night, they discovered cards on all the tables announcing the gala opening of another band—just two weeks hence. There was nothing they could do about it except be sore as hell—which, when you come right down to it, still amounts to doing nothing about it. Of course, they could go back to Chicago—which is exactly what they did do—after the two weeks.

Back in Chicago, most of the guys got their jobs back. They still kept on rehearsing, though. One day a booker called up with what he thought was a whale of an idea. That was to have Paul Ash (easily the biggest name leader in Chicago at that time) present the band—you know, "Paul Ash presents Ben Pollack and his Orchestra!" Pollack didn't think it a *whale* of an idea, but he thought it was a pretty good one. He consented, and so Paul Ash presented the band (through his booker) to and at the Southmoor Hotel. It was an instantaneous smash!

Yes, it was an instantaneous smash, even without Benny Goodman. The young clarinetist, who was supporting his family, and who still remembered all the horrible details about the Castle Farms job, and who wasn't at all sure that he could get his old job back if and when the Pollack band folded at the Southmoor, wouldn't offer at the bait. So Pollack hired Lenny Cohen, a fine clarinetist, whom nobody seems to know much about these days.

Things went great for a year and a half at the Southmoor. All the musicians used to come in to hear the band, for it was the only outfit around those parts that played arranged jazz. Benny Krueger, then an extremely successful bandleader, dropped in one night. Pollack spied him. He also spied Benny Goodman, who had come in with Krueger. But he didn't seem to let on to that. He was sore at Benny for having left the band—perhaps for other causes too. For some reason or other Pollack and Goodman never did hit it off too well together, anyway. That's the way it always was. Nobody ever seemed to know exactly why, either.

So Pollack went ahead and introduced Krueger—called on him to come up and play with the band. Krueger came up. Gil had nothing against Goodman, though, so he asked Benny to come up too. Benny did. And how he played! He was greater than ever. Right then and there, Gil knew he'd have to get him back into the band.

Afterwards he spoke with Benny.

"Nothing doing!" grouched the future King.

"Oh, come on, Benny," pleaded Gil. "You know this is the only band for you and we need you."

"Nothing doing!" repeated Benny.

"Oh, come on," repeated Rodin.

"O.K." said Benny.

Gil had just one thing more to do. He had to get Pollack to take Goodman back. Leaders are that way. They like to know who's in their band. Gil convinced Pollack, though, and so Benny returned.

It was a helluva band by then. Everybody around there knew it, too. Jack Kapp (now head of Decca) tried to sign it up for Brunswick Records, for whom he was working, but the fellows liked Victor's offer more and took it.

The way the rest of the country heard it on wax for the first time wasn't the way the band had always sounded. Glenn Miller was a great admirer of Roger Wolfe Kahn's band, which was really a huge thing in that period, and wanted to get the Pollack band to sound something like that on wax. The Kahn band had fiddles, so Glenn got Pollack to add two of them for the session. Ben got his cousin, Al Beller, and a lantern-jawed chap named Victor Young, who's done fine on his own since then. But the versions of *Deed I Do* and *He's the Last Word* by Ben Pollack's Orchestra, which, if you're an avid enough record collector, you may have in your files, don't sound very much like the Ben Pollack band whose jazz was killing 'em at the Southmoor.

Pollack Jazz

It was a strong kind of jazz—especially strong rhythmically. Pollack was a powerful drummer who set wonderful, driving tempos, and held them. To this day Glenn Miller still raves about the man's basic beat. And, of course, the Miller and Livingston arrangements were fine. Then there was Goodman's clarinet and Greenberg's trumpet. Glenn, too, was playing pretty fair jazz trombone by this time. And Livingston let loose plenty of tenor.

The outfit created loads of talk. And when you're being talked about, that means the public wants to hear you, too. And when they want to hear you that much, you're going to be worth just that much more money.

Little wonder, then, that Pollack got an offer from a spot called the Rendezvous for $1,850 a week. For ten men, that was plenty of cabbage. It seemed even more, for the Southmoor was paying them only $1,250 per.

But they didn't stay at the Rendezvous long. Jules Stein, the headman at MCA, which was managing the band by then, thought it should go into a spot that attracted kids instead of a night club. So he moved it over to the Blackhawk, where it stayed for about a year.

Then Pollack heard of a place named The Bagdad that would give the band still more money. And just about the same time, Benny Goodman heard of a leader named Isham Jones who would give him still more money. So Benny, who, you recall, had those heavy family responsibilities, left Pollack for more dough. And Pollack left the Blackhawk for more dough.

Only difference was, Goodman's thing didn't fall through.

But Pollack, hustling business man that he was, wasn't to be denied. He investigated a lead on a night club in New York. After all, that was the place for real dough!

The band went into Gotham's Little Club a little later. Rodin, meanwhile, had pulled another one of his persuasive induction acts, and had gotten Goodman to come back with the band once more. The fact that Benny had always wanted to go to New York helped, of course.

Not all the other men wanted to go east, however. Fud was offered a job by Nat Shilkret at $250, which he grabbed, pronto. Trumpeter Greenberg didn't want to leave and neither did the guitar player.

It just so happened (and how wonderful those "just so happened" incidents often turn out, too!) that about a block away from where Rodin lived there were two fine jazz musicians whom Gil used to like to listen to. He heard them in the spot, and he also heard them on the McKenzie-Condon recording of *Sugar* and *China Boy*, two sides considered by many experts to be among the finest ever grooved into Okeh or any other brand of wax. They were Jimmy McPartland and Bud Freeman.

Jimmy joined right away, but Bud didn't come on until several weeks later when Larry Binyon (now a well-known New York radio musician), who had been hired as soon as Fud had left, decided he'd had enough for the time being. Also making the trek to New York with the band was Dick Morgan, who's now playing guitar in as well as co-directing Alvino Rey's orchestra.

New York Raves

The band bowled 'em over in New York, too. The musicians all fell before its onslaught, for it was the first white band playing organized hot ever to appear in the city.

The band caused so much comment that the producers of a legitimate show, *Say When*, signed it up. However, Local 802 nixed the deal at once, for Pollack's was a traveling band, and it had already wrested one job away from New York musicians.

But Pollack wanted that show job. If he couldn't play both, he'd get away from the Little Club—even if the spot was swank and charged a three dollar cover. Anyway, they made the band rehearse acts every day, and that was asking a little too much. So Pollack handed in the band's notice. Somehow or other, though, things never did get thoroughly straightened out, and the band never appeared in *Say When*. As a matter of fact, it appeared no place for a while.

The fellows didn't mind that much. The fact that the show turned out to be a dismal flop might have caused them to take it all a bit more philosophically. But they were musicians, not philosophers. Musicians have bigger stomachs.

Glenn Miller got himself a good job shortly thereafter. It was with Paul Ash, who was getting as big at New York's Paramount as he had been in Chicago a few years before. It was a swell job, in fact. It was so good that Glenn wouldn't leave with the band when it was offered an engagement at the Million Dollar Pier in Atlantic City. He wanted to get married soon, anyway, to a girl he'd been going around with in Colorado for years. If you should happen to know Mr. and Mrs. Glenn Miller today, you'll know what a wise move that was.

Jack Teagarden

Gil had been hearing Jack Teagarden play at jam sessions at the Louisiana Apartments. He thought he was the greatest trombone player he'd ever heard and he told Pollack as much. Ben heard J. T. play, but he wasn't convinced—not until he heard him in the band. And then he suddenly caught on—and how he agreed with Scout Rodin!

Before the band left for Atlantic City, it did four one-nighters. Gil, who'd had his tonsils yanked at the beginning of the layoff, hadn't quite recuperated at its end. So he got a substitute, a guy who many argue played greater clarinet than Goodman ever hoped to. It's a funny way to argue. Anway, the sub's name was Frank Teschemaker, and whether he was greater than Benny ever hoped to be or worse than Benny ever feared he might become, doesn't make too much difference. However, it's interesting to note that Pollack really had himself an all-star sax section, with Goodman, Teschemaker and Bud Freeman.

He didn't have the last two very long, though, and it wasn't going to be much longer before he lost the first—and this time for good.

Frank, of course, left when Gil's throat had healed, which was the first day of the Atlantic City job. Shortly after that, Freeman and McPartland and Pollack had a fight. Nobody seems to know exactly what caused it, but it did evolve around Ben's reactions towards Bud's love for acting, a love, by the way, which still exists this very day. Freeman is Jazz's Gift to Shakespeare, and v.v. Anyway, Bud gave notice, and since Jimmy was his pal, he quit

Cohesive catalyst Gil Rodin

also. Larry Binyon came back into the band in Bud's place, and a fellow named Earl Baker came in for McPartland. The name doesn't matter much, because Jimmy was back in three weeks. He had avenged Bud enough.

Following Atlantic City, the boys played four weeks at the Oakmont in Pittsburgh, after which they were informed that a layoff was in store. They all went back to New York, which is an exciting place as any to spend a layoff, while Pollack went home to Chicago for a while. He usually went home whenever the band wasn't working.

Pollack, however, told Rodin to keep in touch with Ed Scheuing of NBC. The network was booking the band by then. Gil contacted Ed, who immediately arranged an audition for the Park Central Hotel, which was then playing Arnold Johnson's band. Gil wired Pollack to come right back—almost before Ben had arrived home. The audition was such a rush, however, that the band had to make it without its leader and without its arrangements. But the manager liked it just the same and said the job was theirs, if they'd add two fiddles and a cello. It was a queer request, but they added Eddie Bergman and Al Beller and Bill Schuman, didn't use them much, and had a big winter at the hotel.

Lots of Work

The band always went over . . . when it worked.

It worked a lot then. The boys belonged to the local by now, and so when they had an offer to go into another legitimate show (*Hello Daddy*) they were able to grab it, and did. You can imagine the money they were making by this time.

One night at the Park Central Pollack sprang a startling announcement on his men.

"I'm not going to play drums any more," he stated simply.

"Why not?" asked all the lads in about the best unison ensemble they'd ever produced.

"Because I'm sick and tired of having people come up to the band and asking when Ben Pollack's going to come in."

Nobody knows to this day whether that was the actual reason or whether Ben had some other motive. It's true, he did need a drummer to play in the show at intermissions, which was when he led the band. But it didn't mean he couldn't play on the dance job any more. The fellows teased, begged, cajoled, and any other synonyms you can think of, but it didn't do any good.

That's when Ray Bauduc joined the band.

He was the second of the present Crosby Crew. Rodin, of course, was the first. More current incumbents were soon to come, though.

Matty Matlock was No. 3. He came in the fall, while the band was playing in a theatre, after having done seven weeks on the Fleischmann's Yeast radio commercial.

The two Bennys—Pollack and Goodman—never did hit it off too well, you remember. As long as they didn't have too much to say to one another, everything was all right. But if they ever got close, you'd never know when the lid was going to pop.

The blowoff was actually over a triviality. But the extenuating circumstances turned it into a major catastrophe.

Before one of the shows, Goodman and McPartland were playing handball on the roof. They weren't late for the show, but they did appear on the stage with good old-fashioned handball court dust on their shoes.

And Pollack didn't like that one bit.

Maybe he was burned up about something else that day and just had to let off steam. Anyway, after the show, he got the band in the dressing room and unleashed a lecture on the subject of dress and especially that of unpolished shoes. And he wound it up with "and anybody who doesn't like it can get out!"

The challenge was much too obvious. Goodman and McPartland were the only ones affected. If you know Goodman and McPartland, you know that they're both pretty headstrong guys who are likely to accept any reasonable sort of a challenge.

Pollack's was reasonable.

Exit: Jimmy McPartland.

Exit: Benny Goodman (but for keeps!).

Jack Teagarden got brother Charlie into the band in place of McPartland and Jack recommended Matty Matlock, then playing with the Tracy-Brown band in Pittsburgh, in place of the only fair clarinet player who had hurriedly been hired to take Goodman's chair. Matty came in.

Oh—That Silver Slipper

By this time the band was playing the Silver Slipper in New York for $2,500. It was a good night club in every way except that it was run by a bunch of gangsters. That mightn't have been so bad at that, if the owner hadn't gotten himself murdered, and his spot a lot of subsequent notoriety that resulted in the air wire being yanked out. Since radio time was becoming important by then, Pollack quit.

The band was very big. It had plenty of offers. Pollack selected one in Baltimore. But by this time, Rodin had had enough traveling. He wanted to settle down in New York. Why he changed his mind at the last minute, he himself doesn't know to this day, but the fact remains that if he hadn't, Eddie Miller might never have become the great national tenor sax figure that he is today.

It happened more or less this way: Gil decided to leave, so Bauduc and Nappy Lamare (whom the band had taken out of a small Park Central relief band when Dick Morgan quit) asked Pollack and him to go over to Roseland and hear their fellow-townsman, Eddie Miller, playing alto with Julie Wintz's band. They went, and were tremendously impressed. Then, suddenly, Gil unquit. But Babe Russin, who was in the band for a short time in place of Binyon, decided he didn't want to leave town.

"Can you play tenor?" they asked Miller.

"I don't know, I can try," replied Eddie.

"Have you got one?"

"No."

So Pollack contacted Mort Davis of Conn's and laid out the money for a horn for Miller. Eddie wanted a brass one, but Ben insisted upon gold. "You can pay me back as we go along," he told Eddie. But to this day a battle rages between the two about how many times Eddie did pay Benny back. The claim runs all the way from five to no times. That may have something to do with Miller being labeled "Chief Undercurrent Man," in the Pollack band.

There were changes in the trumpets, too, before the band went to Baltimore. Neither first-man Al Harris nor Charlie Teagarden wanted to leave. So Pollack hauled in a brilliant leadman who had been hanging around admiring the band for a long time. He had been playing alternate lead with Paul Specht at the Ansonia Hotel on uptown Broadway. His name was Charles Spivak.

Teagarden's replacement never became as well known, but he certainly got plenty of attention from the fellows in the band. His name was Tommy Thunen, which probably doesn't mean much to you. He was one of those fellows who tried terribly hard all the time to please everybody all the time. He bent over backwards to make good. Ray Bauduc never liked the fellow's style of playing. One night, after Tommy had finished a chorus, Ray yelled out in disgust, "What you need is a herring!"

The next set Thunen walked on the stand with a herring! Nobody knows to this day whether he was kidding or not.

Pianist Gil Bowers joined the band right after the Baltimore date. The band was at the Hollywood Restaurant in Cleveland, the spot in which Lombardo had made his name.

Part II

POLLACK'S BAND BROKE UP SLOWLY

Ben's Mixed Interests and Layoffs Discouraged Band of Star Musicians Who Reassembled After Disbanding

It was truly a brilliant band that Ben Pollack got together in the early twenties! Last month you must have read about its inception, and how the grand drummer gathered together such notables as Benny Goodman, Glenn Miller, Jack and Charlie Teagarden, Eddie Miller, Matty Matlock and loads of others, and how they laid the cats low wherever they chanced to blow.

They were blowing in Cleveland, when you last heard about them, and a trumpeter named Tommy Thunen had been supplying a lot of interest. But Tommy left the band shortly after it opened at the Hollywood Restaurant, and so Pollack sent for Sterling Bose. Bozo arrived on the job waving a huge bottle of liquor which he offered to all the boys, but from which he refused to take a drop.

"A guy on the train gave it to me," he explained. "I don't drink."

Bozo joined the band in reverse.

Then, after being paid for only ten weeks of a twelve-week engagement, the band embarked on a series of successful location dates. It went to the Blossom Heath Inn in Detroit, and from there down to the Forrest Club in New Orleans, where the band's native sons had an especially fine time. Then it went up to St. Paul, where Harry Goodman left and was replaced by a fellow named something-or-other Johnson, and where it proved to be such a smash hit at the Lowrey Hotel that it was offered a better job by the Streets of Paris, which it accepted, thereby promptly ruining the Lowrey's business. St. Paul in days to come was to prove an exceptionally happy hunting ground for the Pollack band.

Ralph Copsey, a huge man, came in around this time for the band's first enlargement in years. The trombones swelled from one to two. That was a big section in those days of the early thirties.

From St. Paul the band went to Elitch's Gardens in Denver for five weeks, being called back hurriedly by the Streets of Paris owner when some Chicago bunch flopped badly at his summer spot, the Plantations, at White Bear Lake, Minn.

Enter: A Woman!

It was while the band was playing at the Plantations that it met a girl who was destined to play an important role in its future. She was an attractive lass who sang in the floor show. Her name was Doris Robbins, and, more than anybody else, she attracted Ben Pollack. It was real love at first sight—all of which may or may not have had something to do with Ben's putting her on the air from that spot.

The manager of the Lowrey was still smarting from the licking he'd received when the Streets of Paris grabbed the Pollack band away from him. Unable to use the band himself, he succeeded in getting it a job at the Belle Rieve in Kansas City for more money than the Streets of Paris had to offer. Pollack accepted, and so the Lowrey was at least rid of its stiffest competition.

Romance was still rampant in the Pollack breast, and it wasn't long before he sent for his love, not to appear in the floor show, as before, but to become a full-fledged member of the organization.

For the first time in its history, the Ben Pollack band had a girl singer.

Some of the fellows didn't like it one bit.

It wasn't only because they didn't like the way she sang.

They just resented the intrusion.

The band stayed at the Belle Rieve for eight weeks or so, during which time it used Barry Weinstein (now well known as bandleader Barry Winton) on violin. He left, though, shortly after the outfit opened at the Chez Paree in Chicago, at which time Eddie Sheesby, formerly of Jean Goldkette's great band, joined them until such time as he was found wound up inside a bureau drawer!

Exit: Two Stars

Bozo left during the Chez Paree engagement. He got Jack Teagarden to leave, too, which was unfortunate, for the man had become one of the most important men in the band and was extremely well liked by all the fellows. But Bozo had gotten wind of some rich fellow who was going to put a band into a fine spot at the Chicago World's Fair and he had convinced the fellow that Jack was his man and Jack that the man was his fellow—or something like that. Anyway, Jack left for a job that took an Alka-Seltzerian fizzle and Joe Harris, who played good jazz trombone and sang something like Teagarden, came in from Frankie Trumbauer's bunch.

The band left the Chez Paree after nine months of what looked like an indefinite engagement. But the story goes that Pollack got pretty peeved when they decided to leave Doris out of the floor show one time, and so he pulled the band out.

Anyway, a layoff followed. Pollack and Miss Robbins went east and the fellows all went home for a while. They reassembled later in New England for some one-nighters and then went back to trusty St. Paul—back to the Plantation Club where Deane Kincaide joined as non-sax-playing arranger. But this time the Lowrey was on its toes, and soon the band was back in the hotel. It stayed there for eight weeks, during which time Harry Greenberg, who had again joined the band when Bose left, again left the band.

Enter: One Fixture

The hot trumpet chair this time was filled by a young fellow from Missouri, a great big guy, with whom Eddie and Matty had been doing a lot of jamming, and whom Kincaide had been crazy about too, ever since he'd played with him in Slats Randall's band. They told Pollack and Gil about him, and that's how Yank Lausen joined the band.

Late in November of that year, the Pollackers reinvaded New York. This time they went into Billy Rose's mammoth Casino de Paree. Again there were personnel changes, though none had much bearing on the band's future. The band did very well with both trumpeters, Ruby Weinstein and Chelsea Quealey, who swelled, at different times, the band's growing brass section to five.

Following the Casino de Paree (Benny Goodman had just started his band and was playing at Billy Rose's Music Hall close by), Pollack took the band way down to the Hollywood Dinner Club in Galveston, Texas. That's where Deane Kincaide pulled the first of his changes of heart—this one known as the famous "Midnight Creep." It seems that for no reason or other, he suddenly got fed up with just arranging and not playing, so he just yanked up stakes, left a note revealing his gripe, and gone he was. To this day, nobody (including Deane himself, probably) knows just what he likes to do best, because when he's writing and playing, he'll come to the point where he'd just rather write, and if he's writing and not playing, he'll suddenly realize that he'd rather be playing. It's like trying to decide which came first, the sax or the reed.

Coming: The End!

That Hollywood Dinner Club was the beginning of the end of the great Ben Pollack band. Not that the job itself had much to do with it, though the morale of the band wasn't at its highest by any means. It's what happened afterwards.

After the four week Galveston stint, Ben and Doris went to California. He was beginning to show a desire to get her into the movies, which was, according to some of the fellows, where she belonged. He told the boys to proceed to the Forrest Club in New Orleans and that he'd fly right back and join them there for the job.

The fellows went, all right. They expected a big welcome, for they'd gone over so big before. But all they got was a short telegram from Pollack, saying that there wasn't any job there after all, and that they'd be smart to continue their layoff. To this day, it amazes people, including the veterans of the group, that a band as successful as this one could find time for so many layoffs. This one lasted six weeks, during which time most of the fellows were on the point of giving it all up.

Then suddenly Pollack went into action, with the aid of Western Union. The wire he sent read something like this:

"We go into Cotton Club. Hall of Fame radio show in the bag. Come right out."

The fellows came right out, though Spivak and Bauduc hesitated a long time. They were fed up. And the band went into the Cotton Club (now the Casa

Manana), all right. But all the fellows are still looking for the bag in which Pollack or somebody else hid the Hall of Fame show.

Pollack, who for years had been building the band, decided after four weeks that he'd have to cut down on the brass and let two men go. The fellows didn't like it. What's more, they felt that Ben was no longer as interested in the band, and that Doris (Mrs. Pollack) and her career in the movies were occupying most of his thoughts. You can't tell what a guy's thinking about from the outside, of course, but that seemed logical enough, especially when Ben stated he wanted to settle down in California.

And so, a few days before the November 1st closing at the Cotton Club, and with nothing in view, Spivak, Bauduc and Lausen handed in their notices.

Pollack called a meeting.
The fellows could see no future.
So they all left.
Ben Pollack had lost his band.

Goodman to the Rescue

The saddest part of all this was that it wasn't done under the friendliest conditions. There had been bickering, occasioned in part by the long layoffs, in part by Pollack's split interests, and probably by other reasons which nobody will ever know about. At any rate, as soon as he found out what was happening, Harry Goodman wired brother Benny in New York and told him the news. Benny immediately wired back and offered jobs on his Let's Dance commercial to his brother, to Spivak and to Rodin.

The Crosby band-to-come, with young Bob on an early broadcast

The Crosby band-to-come poses in the Silver Grill of New York's Hotel Lexington.
FRONT ROW: guitarist Nappy Lamare, trombonist Mark Bennett, clarinetist Matty
Matlock, Crosby, saxists Gil Rodin and Eddie Miller, trumpeter Andy Ferretti
BACK ROW: trombonist Ward Sillaway, pianist Gil Bowers, bassist Bob Haggart,
trumpeter Yank Lawson, violinist Eddie Bergman, drummer Ray Bauduc, saxist
Noni Bernardi

Pollack, though, never believed that story. He claimed that it was a put-up job; that the fellows left him because Benny had offered them the jobs.

If you recall the constant friction that existed between the two Bennys, you can readily understand why Pollack should have entertained such thoughts.

It was just unfortunate.

At this point the fellows were really in a pickle. They had nothing whatever in view and no Ben Pollack to look out for future bookings. In fact, so far as the general public was concerned, they were no longer a band.

The general public be damned—they knew that they were still a band; that they had much too much to offer; that you could never break up a bunch that thought, played and lived so much as one. They'd get together soon again—in fact, before they parted, they vowed to meet soon in New York.

First, though, they separated. Only Joe Harris stayed in California.

Lausen and Bauduc went to Minnesota.

Miller and Lamare went home to New Orleans.

Matlock went home to Nashville.

Rodin, Spivak, Goodman and Bowers went to New York.

It's hard to play together when you're that far apart. So they got together again—in New York.

Different Ways

Gil and Harry joined Goodman at once, but Spivak and Benny had different ideas on music, so Charlie never did play with the bunch. Instead, he joined the Dorsey Brothers. Ray Bauduc played with—of all things—society bands, and he didn't like it one bit, either. Eddie Miller and Matty Matlock worked with Smith Ballew, from whose band Glenn Miller had

316

taken a host of men to form the Dorsey Brothers outfit. Yank, who was having the hardest time, because he didn't have an 802 card, did occasional guest shots with Ballew, a wonderful guy, who sang plenty well. The others did odd jobbing, making enough dough to keep themselves alive.

Meanwhile, they kept rehearsing together. As soon as Gil arrived in New York, he started getting offers from bookers and leaders who wanted to take over or front the band. But the fellows were taking their time. They had learned from experience.

The morale was high. Phil Harris offered Ray Bauduc a fine job, but Ray refused. Like the others, he wanted to rehearse at the Jackson Heights studio, near which they all lived, and build for the future.

Then came break #1. Roy Wilson booked Red Nichols for the Kellogg College Prom commercial, and he wanted Gil to organize a band to play behind Red.

That was easy. The guys were right there. Only Yank didn't have a card, so they used Charlie Teagarden instead. Little Gate played all the jazz, except when they'd use some of Red's own arrangements. Actually, Nichols had little to do with running the band, coming in only on the day of the show, after everything had been rehearsed.

Of course, there had to be a couple of other changes. In the first place, Joe Harris was out on the coast. So Jack Teagarden played the show. Harry was with brother Benny, so Artie Bernstein bassed. Deane Kincaide was playing fourth sax by this time— at some period or other he'd had one of his changes of heart and done a "Midnight Creep" back into the band.

The show was a lot of fun and produced really inspiring music. METRONOME even said so—that was in April, 1935.

The fellows got even more enthused and rehearsed all the harder. Glenn Miller worked with them, along with Spivak, for the Dorseys were in town at the Palais Royale in those days. Jack Jenney and Neal Reid used to alternate on the other trombone.

The former appeared with the band on its record dates. The best of these consisted of six sides made under the name of "Clark Randall" for Brunswick. Randall was actually Frank Tennille, a handsome vocalist, son of a wealthy Alabama family, whom Pollack had picked up at the Cotton Club and who had stuck with the guys. He was featured singer on these records, one of which was a tune Glenn had written about Dick Morgan, called *When Ickey Morgan Plays the Organ, Look Out*. There was also a Rodin original entitled *If You're Looking for Someone to Love You a Little Bit, Why Don't You Give Me a Chance*. The best side of the six, however, was *Here Comes Your Pappy With the Wrong Kind of Load*, which showed the band with a wonderful beat, plus thrilling solos by Miller, Matlock, and Lausen.

There were also some Melotone labeled works, under Rodin's name. Pete Peterson, now in the army, but formerly a Red Norvo mainstay, played bass on these.

Pete, though, was having a lot of trouble with his instrument, which must have belonged to a dancer at one time, judging from the number of splits. So Rodin started asking about other bass players around town.

The Crosby band at a midwestern ballroom.
IN FRONT: Bob Zurke, Crosby, Kay Weber, Gil Rodin, Joey Kearns, Matty Matlock, Eddie Miller
IN BACK: Bob Haggart, Nappy Lamare, Yank Lawson, Charlie Spivak, Billy Butterfield, Warren Smith, Ward Sillaway

Glenn said: "There's a wonderful bass player somewhere out on the island named Bob Haggart."

Goodman said: "John Hammond brought me a wonderful bass player from somewhere out on the island. His name is Bob Haggart." (Remember, Harry was playing bass for Benny at the time.)

George Van Eps, the ace guitarist, said: "I made some duet records with a fine bass player from out on Long Island the other day. His name is Bob Haggart."

You're crazy if you think Gil hired Candy Candido.

Enter: More Arrangements

Haggart not only played bass, but he also started giving the band more arrangements. With Matlock and Kincaide also writing regularly, the bunch was building up a whale of a library.

Don't think people didn't sit up and take notice. Irving Mills and other bookers tried to sign the band up. But it was still waiting.

Then one day song publisher Jack Bregman ("Honest John" to his friends) told Cork O'Keefe of Rockwell-O'Keefe all about the band. Interested, Cork contacted Rodin, who one day went up to the R-O'K office and found himself confronted with O'Keefe, Mike Nidorf and several propositions.

The first was to incorporate the group, with shares for office, band and leader. That sounded great. Only thing missing was a leader.

"We can fix that," explained the soft-spoken O'Keefe. "I know three guys you can have. There's Johnny Davis. Then there's Goldie of Whiteman's band. And we've got Bing Crosby's brother, Bob, singing in our Dorsey Brothers band. He might do, too."

Gil took it up with the fellows.

Davis wasn't bad, but he sang just the way Nappy did, and the fellows weren't too enthusiastic, anyway.

Goldie was too corny, they thought.

They didn't know much about Bob Crosby.

Gil did, though. He had met him often at the Palais Royale. Rodin used to hang out there a lot with his very close friends, Glenn Miller and Charlie Spivak. He liked young Bob Crosby. The guy impressed him with his personality. He was a likable sort of fellow, very sincere, modest, and he didn't go around trying to trade in on his brother's name. He was young and he looked good, too.

And so, at that Jackson Heights rehearsal, the boys voted for Bob Crosby.

And they've never regretted it —never!

318

Part III

CROSBY BAND HAD MANY UPS AND DOWNS

Clicked at Once when Bob Took Over; Office, T. Dorsey, Switch to Sweet Caused Headaches; Back to Dixieland

Ben Pollack did an awful lot for the success of the Bob Crosby band. If you read the first two installments of this series, you'll realize that if it hadn't been for his organizing powers, his ability to find men, his tenacity of purpose, and several other Pollack attributes (both good and bad), there'd never have been a Bob Crosby band in the first place. And if you haven't got something in the first place, it's impossible to make it successful.

So no matter what disagreements the men may have had with their original leader; no matter how much they may have argued with him, the Crosby Crew must be eternally grateful to Ben Pollack, that spunky, chunky little man who's still unearthing sensational musicians, coming up with one surprise band after another, and who is destined to go down in dance band history as probably the greatest organizer the field has ever known.

Ben's out on the west coast now. He recently organized another new band and he's trying to gain some recognition for it. He has some wonderful musicians—guys nobody ever heard of before—and he's hoping that this time the established big-shots will leave him alone and not try to grab the budding stars away from him.

He's still playing plenty of drums. And his wife, Doris Robbins, is still singing. And they're batting away, hoping to mold another great group that will startle and thrill the dance music world as much as the Bob Crosby band is doing these days. Maybe even more. Who knows?

It was in June, 1935, that Bob took over the remnants of Ben's band and v. v. Rockwell-O'Keefe (now General Amusement Corp.) had brought the two together, but they were handling the whole thing with much caution. Tommy Rockwell warned the fellows not to rush into it, even though he did happen to have a personal interest in Bob. He had brought him from the west coast, where he had been singing (and making records, too) with Anson Weeks's band, and he had taken mighty good care of him around New York. "But," said Tommy, "why not try it out for four weeks? If it works, fine. If it doesn't, forget about it."

A young Billy Butterfield patiently sits and waits as Yank Lawson and Charlie Spivak blow their solos

Spivak, Miller Out

It worked—fine. Right from the start, too. In June, 1935, the band played its first job under Bob Crosby —at a country club in Greensboro, N. C. A booker named Jack Mason took it through that territory, spotting it every night for two weeks at $5,000 for the term. Not bad for a new outfit!

It wasn't quite the same band that had been rehearsing together so assiduously. Spivak and Glenn Miller had gone with Ray Noble's new band by then, so Phil Hart came in on first trumpet and Joe Harris, who'd come back from the coast, returned on trombone.

But the morale and the reaction were equally high. In fact, the owner of Savannah Beach, Ga., liked the outfit so much he offered it two weeks at his spot.

Before they took the job, though, they returned to New York and made their first record date. For Decca, naturally. R-O'K and Decca were very close in those days.

Artie Foster came in on additional trombone before the date and Eddie Bergman rejoined on fiddle. Foster was a funny fellow. Every time he took a chorus, he'd turn to the fellows and ask, "Did you hear me play that?" "It's wonderful" was never said, but the fellows sure thought it was always implied. Maybe it was.

Foster helped the band sound better than ever on its first date. So did Harris, who sang the fine vocals on *Dixieland Band* and *Beale Street Blues*. Bob emoted on the second of the other two sides, *Flowers for Madame* and *In a Little Gypsy Tea Room*. The band was one of the first to record that last tune, which turned out to be a big hit. And so, believe it or not, the Bob Crosby Crew had a best seller on its first record date.

Hits with Hitz

Rockwell-O'Keefe at that time had the Hitz Hotels pretty solidly tied up. So they tied the Crosby band down to the Adolphus in Dallas. It was originally a four-week contract, depending upon how well the band did. It was going to be its first steady job, and, though the office had lots of confidence in the boys' musical ability, it wasn't sure of how (1) the Texans would like it, and (2, and more important) how well Ralph Hitz would like it.

The Texans liked it so much that the opposition Baker Hotel had to yank the sissified music of Henry King and try to get a jazz band to compete with the new dixieland band.

As for Hitz—well, any hotel man likes any band that does good business—especially when it's for his hotel.

Hitz came down on the fly.

He was nuts about the band. As long as he lived, he was one of its biggest boosters and staunchest friends. He immediately promoted them to the Netherlands-Plaza in Cincinnati.

That fitted in nicely with plans Bob had made before taking over the lads' leadership. He had auditioned for the Roger Gallet commercial with Vic Young's orchestra and had copped the show. So the band played the Netherlands-Plaza and did the commercial, too.

Quite a start for a new band!

The show shifted after six weeks to New York. So did the Crosby Crew. Phil Hart's lip went bad all of a sudden, so Joe Barone came in on first trumpet. And Ward Sillaway quit Phil Harris and came in on second trombone. The band was doing so well around New York that Hitz told it it could soon go into the New Yorker.

Before they opened at that spot, though, they went down and played the Biscayne Kennel Club in Florida, where they just had a lot of fun and got healthy. And then to the New Yorker.

When they opened there, Andy Ferretti came over from the first trumpet chair of another band that had just been organized, Tommy Dorsey's, to be exact. The Crosby brand of dixieland proved very successful in the New Yorker. At that time, they used to mix it up with a lot of schmaltz, featuring Eddie Miller's tenor and Gil Rodin's baritone and flute, and lots of medleys of old show tunes. For some reason or other, though, they discarded that style right then and there, and they've never been able to achieve the same sort of intimacy since. Maybe they don't want to. Who knows?

Their Favorite Room

The band stayed around New York for a long time and got plenty of air-shots. After eleven weeks at the New Yorker, they copped the Hotel Lexington job away from Will Osborne, who'd been a big success there the summer before. According to the boys themselves, the room (since gone Hawaiian) had the best acoustics and atmosphere of any they've ever played in.

That Lexington job was fun. The band made a lot of friends, and it used to draw many of the big musicians almost every night. Glenn Miller and Charlie Spivak were almost steady customers, Glenn at that time considering this the finest jazz band in the business.

There were personnel changes. Deane Kincaide pulled a usual switch and decided he didn't want to play—just arrange. So they got Noni Bernardi from the Dorsey band, put him on the lead sax chair, while Gil shifted over to fourth. Mark Bennett came in on second trombone in place of Artie Foster and never once asked the guys if they had heard what he had just

The Crosbyites picked by *Collier's* Magazine as "The All-American Four" clown with the Andrews Sisters. Left to right: Patti A., the Bobs Haggart and Zurke, La-Verne A., Ray Bauduc, Maxene A., Eddie Miller

played. And right at the close of the engagement, the lads landed a guy they'd always wanted to have with them, Joe Sullivan. Gil Bowers wanted to remain in New York to study classical piano, so the switch was easy to make.

And before they left, the fellows also augmented the singing department. Kay Weber, who had been with Bob in the Dorsey Brothers band, came in as the girl vocalist.

As a matter of fact, that was a big move in itself. At first the guys definitely didn't want a gal. They remembered all those Doris Robbins repercussions, and they didn't feel like taking any chances when they were going so well.

But they took Kay anyway. And she proved to be a fine investment—especially for Ward Sillaway, whom she later married.

Aid for Crosby

The band also took on another male vocalist. Frank Tennille had run into some unfavorable publicity via the neat trick of remembering one night that he had been in a nightclub and waking up the next morning and finding himself married to the hatcheck girl, who already had one child. Frank's wealthy parents rushed up from Alabama and yanked their handsome son

home. So the Crosby band yanked in a fellow named Bob Wacker, but after a while they realized that Crosby would do on his own, and so they let Wacker go.

Then followed a long traveling term.

When you're traveling and you're not on the air, people are likely to forget you. That's what happened to the Crosby band. They did the Hitz circuit, and though they were heard and admired by people in those hotels, the rest of the country began to pay attention to Tommy Dorsey, and of course Benny Goodman, and several other young bands.

It was while they were in the hinterlands that two important men left them. Matty Matlock, because of family conditions, didn't want to leave New York, so Gil engineered a switch with Ray Noble, giving him Matty and getting Johnny Mince in return.

The other loss was both more serious and more dramatic. It was while they were at the Adolphus in Dallas that Joe Sullivan started feeling pretty bad. As the engagement went on, he grew worse and worse, and finally, when he collapsed completely, they all found out that he had contracted the dreaded t.b.

Of course Joe had to leave the band. He was taken to the west coast, to a sanitarium there, and everybody was terribly blue. It was at this point that Bob Zurke, who had been creating a lot of talk up in Detroit, joined the band.

And it was several months later that the Bob Crosby orchestra did one of the grandest things any organization ever did. At the Congress Hotel in Chicago, where they had been playing for a few months, they put on a mammoth swing concert and donated all proceeds to Joe. It was a magnificent gesture, and it did lots towards eventually bringing Sullivan back to the jazz world and even to the Crosby band again for a short time.

They made more personnel changes at the Congress. Matty came back and Johnny Mince went to Tommy Dorsey. Zeke Zarchy came over from Benny Goodman's band and replaced Andy Ferretti on first trumpet, while Warren Smith took over Mark Bennett's trombone chair, and immediately proceeded to blow some potent hot.

Merry Widow Fox-Trot

It was while they were at the Congress that the band met one of the finest and yet one of the most mysterious persons it had ever known. An attractive widow, Mrs. Rene LeBrosi, became tremendously at-tached to the men. Just about every night she'd come into the Congress Casino, usually bringing a bevy of friends with her. Not only did she entertain them lavishly, but she also insisted that all the fellows in the band make her table their headquarters and consume all the food and drinks that they possibly could. Never had the fellows (nor probably anyone else) seen a person so genuinely generous.

Mrs. LeBrosi followed the band all that spring and summer. Her young son was made assistant to the assistant manager, which actually amounted to taking care of some instruments, which somebody else was already taking care of, while his mother paid the band $35 a week which the band in turn paid him. It was a neat plan, for it enabled the jazz enthusiast to follow the band on the pretext of watching over her son. Which made everything perfectly all right to her fellow blue bloods.

She gave the band a huge party at her Long Island home when they stopped in New York for a record date, and she went with them up to Boston for the Ritz-Carlton engagement. There she outdid her Congress efforts. Every night she'd have a huge table on the roof, right next to the bandstand, which was re-

Arranger Matty Matlock (rear) supervises the rehearsal of his four-clarinet, one-sax voicing as played by Gil Rodin, Bill Stegmeyer, Joey Kearns, Fazola and Eddie Miller

served just for her friends, the band, and all its friends, too. Then, every night after work, the fellows would trek en masse down to her suite, where she'd have all sorts of sandwiches and drinks decked out on a big row of tables. The fellows relate that during their first week up there, Mrs. LeBrosi ran up a hotel bill of over eleven hundred dollars.

Not only was she wonderfully generous, but she was as loyal as they come. To this day, she hasn't forgiven John Hammond for reading his newspaper in the Congress Casino while the band was playing. Other leaders, jealous in numerous ways, tried to woo her away with all sorts of attentions, but Mrs. LeBrosi stood fast by the Crosby Crew.

When they went to the coast in September of 1937, she followed with her family, including a stepdaughter who later married Bob Haggart, a chauffeur, a limousine and a baggage trailer. She rented a huge mansion in Beverly Hills, where she was always entertaining the boys. The address was 802 Alpine Drive and it didn't take the fellows long to catch on to the numerical similarity and call the place "The Local."

Coast Cacophony

That west coast jaunt was a memorable one.

Billy Butterfield joined them, coming from Austin Wylie's band and giving the band a brand of pretty hot it had never before enjoyed.

Jerry Colonna used to come around and listen.

Bing entertained all the fellows royally, while ending a long feud with his younger brother.

MCA started to pay a lot of attention to the band.

The band went over every place in Hollywood.

Every place, with the possible exception of one; the Palomar, where it was playing.

It had started off well there, but business didn't continue. Still, the band was so individual, both musically and personally, that an awful lot of people became attached to it.

Before the band started back east on a string of one-nighters, Charlie Spivak came back. He hadn't been with the lads since the Pollack days, and in all that time, despite jobs with the Dorsey Brothers, Ray Noble and a great deal of radio work, cheery, chubby Charlie had never been really happy. Now he was.

The Crosby Crew's Charm

If you've ever spent much time with the Crosby Crew, you can appreciate exactly why. For there's a certain atmosphere around this band that you won't find in any other. It's something you can't explain, either, for there are other bands that comprise a bunch of really fine fellows, too. But there's a unanimity of purpose, of thought, both musical and otherwise, plus a sense of freedom and play—all combined with an air of maturity—that you won't find in any other orchestra. The nearest thing exists, perhaps, in Woody Herman's, and, according to those close to the band, in Ted Weems's outfit. Both those groups have been together for years, too, but not for nearly so many years as have the mainstays in the Bob Crosby band. What's more, the Crosby boys have a dogged belief in their music, strengthened after years and years of constant playing. It's really a unique spirit within this great organization, a spirit that, possibly more than anything else, has helped it to keep its head above water, no matter how hard the going may have been.

And the going for a half year or more after the Palomar date wasn't at all easy. The first tough break (literally) took place in a midwestern town.

The Bobs, Haggart and Zurke, were fooling around on a sidewalk.

"Ever show you this trick?" asked Haggart.

"Which one?" asked Zurke.

"This one," explained Haggart, said explanation being some sort of a tripping act that landed Zurke on the cement.

"No," shouted Zurke as he fell.

"Get up," said Haggart.

"No," continued Zurke.

"Why?"

"You busted my leg in two places."

Which was correct.

So Zurke, whose playing had been drawing much public acclaim, couldn't play with the band for quite a while. They got a very fine pianist named Lester Ludke who didn't stay long, but long enough until Zurke could crawl on to a stool again. Deane Kincaide also floated back in around this time, while Joey Kearns came in on lead sax in place of Bill Depew, who had replaced Bernardi when the latter was taken ill at the Ritz-Carlton in Boston.

The troubles went further—into financial and managerial departments. For a long time the band had been dissatisfied with Rockwell-O'Keefe. There were all sorts of gripes, on the parts of both the band and the office, with the former's chief claims being that they weren't allowed to see their own books and that they felt they were being and had been charged too much money for various services in the past. The payoff came, though, when they found out that the man who was secretary of their corporation was also Rockwell-O'Keefe's lawyer in the litigation.

Death of Corporation

So the fellows dissolved their corporation, formed a new one, and signed with MCA. The result was years and years of legal wrangling and unpleasantness, with the whole thing finally winding up two and

Nappy Lamare, Bob Crosby and Gil Rodin examine a contract as an oblivious Bob
Zurke pays attention to the music

a half years later by MCA paying the Rockwell office $4000 for the contract. So today, MCA still books the band and nobody up at Rockwell's has too much use for the boys and the boys haven't too much use for anybody up at Rockwell's.

But the bad luck wasn't over. MCA's first big move was to book the band into the Pennsylvania Hotel in New York, following Benny Goodman's most successful engagement. Why the guys, especially the usually astute Gil Rodin, were ever foolish enough to consent to a thing like this, nobody to this day can explain. For there was bound to be tremendous contrast, after the highriding, screeching Goodman band that had Krupa and James and Elman, and, of course, a consequent letdown.

There was.

Even Mrs. LeBrosi was brought down.

And when Matty decided he didn't want to leave New York again, things looked even blacker.

Fortunately, though, the band was able to procure the services of a human butter tub named Fazola, who right then and there proceeded to convince everybody that he was one of the really great jazz clarinetists of all time.

Things got better after that, too. The band did a successful tour, highlighted by Deane Kincaide's famous late date. It seems that Deane found a very attractive lass at a dance and asked her if he could drive her home afterwards. She said "Sure." So Deane started to drive her home.

On the way they parked.

Deane didn't know she was married to a milkman.

And she didn't know they were parking on her husband's route.

You guessed the answer. The guys still keep talking about it.

After the milkman, they went into the Blackhawk in Chicago, probably their most successful engagement of all. It was one of those things where the band clicked right off and clicked even more after that. Business and interest were stupendous. The kids used to flock into the place. Mgr. Roth put on Sunday afternoon sessions, which soon became known as Meetings of the Bob Cat Club. It was at one of these sessions that Ray Bauduc and Bob Haggart put on an impromptu duet, which could hardly be heard above the big noise the kids, many from suburban Winnetka, used to make. Ergo, *The Big Noise from Winnetka*, probably the greatest attention-drawer the band has ever possessed.

324

Dorsey Starts Slump

Tommy Dorsey played a theatre engagement towards the close of the Blackhawk sojourn and when he left he took Spivak, Lausen and Kincaide with him. That was probably the greatest individual blow the band ever suffered and to this day some of the fellows bear plenty of resentment towards Tommy for his high-salaried, wholesale offers.

That Dorsey raid made a big difference. For a long time after that the band wasn't the same, chiefly because it couldn't put together a brass section as brilliant as that of Spivak, Lausen and Butterfield. There were days to follow in which even the band's staunchest admirers were ready to talk mostly in the past tense and shake their heads and murmur things about "remembering when" and so forth.

Chances are you know pretty much what happened from then until now. You probably recall that four of the men, Miller, Haggart, Bauduc and Zurke, made the METRONOME All-Star record date in January of 1939, the biggest number from one band ever to appear on that charity disc. Then you probably remember that Zurke, bitten by a bandleader bug, left after the band went back to the Blackhawk and that Pete Viera replaced him, after which Joe Sullivan, recovered from his illness, came in, and that the band copped the Camel commercial and spotted two singers, Helen Ward and Dorothy Claire.

Bad Stuff

But even though the band had a commercial and was working a lot, chances are you don't know that the morale was at a new low during that summer of 1939. Zeke Zarchy and Fazola had a fistfight in Atlantic City that nobody knew about and Zeke left the band shortly thereafter. And the return of Sullivan wasn't as great as the fellows had anticipated it would be, so that the big fellow left in August and Jess Stacy came in.

Jess was very much in demand at that time. To use his own words, he had just left "Benny Badman," and had good offers from "Tommy Doorstep" and "Jan Savage." But he chose the Crosby band.

There were lots of other changes during the next year, proving that all wasn't too well within the ranks. In and out came good musicians like Shorty Sherock, Ray Conniff, Billy Graham, Sterling Bose, Eddie Wade, Bob Peck, Hank D'Amico and Muggsy Spanier.

Of all those, only Muggsy has publicly raved about his days with the Crosby Crew. Just the other day he claimed that they were the happiest he has ever known. And like so many others, he thinks Gil Rodin is without any qualifications the finest guy the dance band business has ever known.

Gil's standing in the band is unique. You know, if you read the earlier installments of this story, that he was mainly responsible for keeping the band together, not only after it left Pollack, but often during some turbulent Pollack days, as well. Little wonder, then, that to the guys in the band he's the headman. They call him "Pops" and they call him that with all the devotion and respect that the name implies. For they trust in him, implicitly, knowing he's honest, genuine, and all for them. Such trust is probably the greatest respect ever accorded any man in dance-bandom. And all those who are close to the band know full well that every bit of it is deserved.

The happy part of all this is that Bob Crosby, who is nominally the leader of the orchestra, bears no resentment towards Gil or towards the fellows for this attitude. Few people know what a fine guy Crosby is. When he started, he used to act big-shotish, and he antagonized folks. It wasn't done maliciously, though, but rather with too much of a desire to prove himself. That Bob soon caught on and became the great fellow he is, is all the more to his everlasting credit. Today, he and Gil get along wonderfully, rooming together on the road, always discussing the band's problems together, and all in all forming two halves of a great Mutual Admiration Society.

Rodin's Error?

Neither man is infallible. Gil proved that a year and a half ago when he suddenly decided to change the band's style and went out and hired a vocal quartet called the Bob-O-Links and put in orders for a lot of dull, schmaltzy arrangements. And, as a further deemphasis upon the band's dixieland style, he also got some killer-diller arrangements.

Commercially, the move wasn't bad. In fact, the band went ahead and made some movies and a lot of money. But after about a year of this, the monotony began to tell on Messrs. Miller, Bauduc, Matlock (who had rejoined), Haggart, and others, and the band began to sound worse and worse. Come to think of it, it began to sound downright terrible.

Gil wised up in time, however. He's a firm believer in adding new blood to a band every once in a while—just as a tonic. And if ever the Crosby band needed a tonic, it was last spring.

Gil must have realized that the band had never been the same since Tommy Dorsey had raided that trumpet section. And last spring, the Crosby trumpets were about as unimpressive as they've ever been.

It's a strong statement to say that one man can make a band. And yet, if one man ever remade the Bob Crosby band, that man was Yank Lausen. You all know what a powerful, direct beat that man gets. What you probably don't know is the effect it has upon Ray Bauduc. And what you might also not know is the effect Ray has upon the rest of the band.

For Ray, life, until the day Yank returned, had been a constant succession of gripes. He had threatend to quit more than just once. And then Yank came back.

And Ray grinned and grinned and began to feel the beat once more.

And the whole band began to feel the beat once more.

And Bob Crosby's band began to play really wonderful jazz once more.

The addition of a brilliant trumpet like Lyman Vunk's and a powerful trombone like Moe Zudecoff's helped lots, too. And so did the return of Matty Matlock to full-time clarinet duties. There never was a tenor-clarinet team like that of Miller and Matlock, anyway.

Last spring it was, then, that the Bob Crosby band began to come back into its own. A lot of you may not appreciate the return as yet, for you've probably heard it only on Decca Records, and the Decca company has for some reason or other given the boys a whole batch of dog tunes to record.

But all you've got to do is catch the band in person. You'll be convinced. For here's a band that not only plays great jazz again, but has also recaptured an esprit de corps that it had found years and years ago, when it was first being whipped into shape by the one and only Ben Pollack, and carried through all the hardships of its earliest and darkest days.

And what a spirit that was in those days!
And what a spirit that is today!!
And what a band that is today!!!
Boy!!!!

Rosemary Clooney on Children (before having a gang of her own; July, 1949)—

You know what I like to sing most of all? . . . No, not like Ella; . . . I like to do children's songs. . . . You know why? Because I think that kids have the most completely honest approach toward everything, including music. They haven't learned to be phony yet. They either like it or they don't.

Child-admirer Rosemary Clooney at a record session with pianist Stan Freeman. (Since the session, Rosey created five kids of her own)

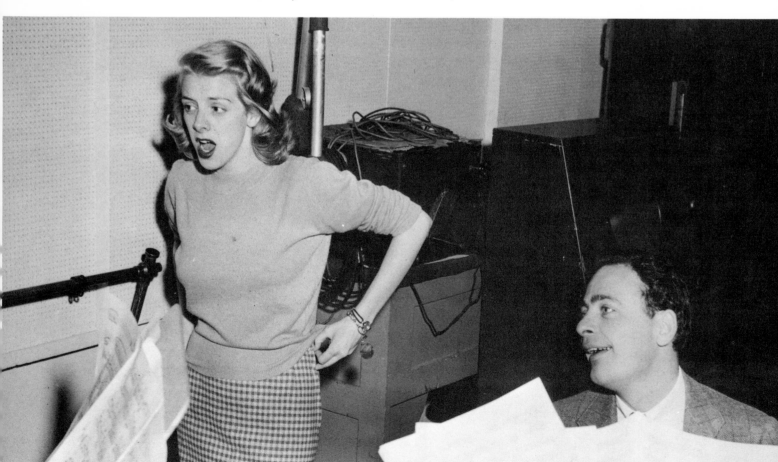

BIX AND BUNNY

Bix Beiderbecke and Bunny Berigan had more in common than just their initials. Each was an astounding trumpeter, a totally original stylist, immensely musical and intensely dedicated. Each was idolized by countless musicians around him for his playing; each was loved by his many friends for his warmth, his generosity and his good-fellowship. Each was with us for much too short a period; each a victim of an extraordinarily exciting, thrill-filled, nondisciplined existence. Bix was only twenty-eight when he died; Bunny was only thirty-three.

In November, 1938, we devoted a good portion of the issue to Bix. As the lone jazz writer on the magazine, I naturally wrote most of that portion, filling it with reminiscences by many of his friends of a man I had never known. In July, 1942, a few weeks after Bunny had died, I wrote an article about a man and a career that I had known. The following pages contain some of the more interesting portions of the Bix section, plus the entire article on Bunny.

BIX

"THE GREATEST GENT I'VE EVER KNOWN" —PAUL WHITEMAN

"Not only that, but also the greatest musician," avers Pops as he describes true character of ethereal Bix

"Bix was not only the greatest musician I've ever known, but also the greatest gentleman I've ever known!"

Those are the words of Paul Whiteman, who's probably known more musicians and more gentle-men than anybody else in dancebandom. Mr. Whiteman, thoroughly aroused on the subject of his pet musician, Mr. Beiderbecke, was keen to continue the discussion.

"But hang it," he muttered as a completion to a short pause, "I can't tell you why!" Another pause apparently carried Leader Whiteman into another bit of reminiscence on the personal and musical attributes of the cornetist whose thrilling passages graced the renditions of so many Whiteman works.

Marvelous ... Polite

"Looking at him as a person, he was just one marvelous guy: quiet, unassuming, never worrying much about anything, and taking everything just as it came. He was reserved and extremely polite. I remember his stock greeting to any kid or kids who'd greet him as he came off the stand. With that warm,

Pops Whiteman was often sent by Bix

Whiteman swings with Henry Busse

The Whiteman band plays it cool in Florida during the mid-twenties.
Bix Beiderbecke had not yet submerged into the ensemble

almost bashful smile of his, he'd exclaim to each one: 'Well, how's everything down there?' and then a minute later he'd be off with: 'Well, I'll see you down there!' Chances are he never knew where 'down there' was, but he just wanted to be and was nice to everybody—despite his greatness he was anything but a big-headed, fluff-you-off fellow!

"But there was more than just mere politeness and common decency in Bix. His musicianship alone reflected that. Yes, you know I'd say that there was a sort of ethereal quality about him; you had the feeling that he was always in the air (especially when he was close to music). Somehow or other he gave you the impression that he was constantly striving for something that was just out of his reach. His continual searching for some sort of ultimate created almost a mystic halo about him—it gave you the feeling that here was a genius who knew of something beautiful to strive for and that, even though he might never reach it, he was far above you merely because he could sense that beauty for which he was reaching."

Relaxation

"You'd note that quality especially after jobs at night. Then Bix would lay aside his cornet and, with almost nobody around, sit himself at the piano and play just chords. Sometimes he'd sit there for hours in a musical trance, obviously far off in the distance. That was his relaxation, and, I'd dare say, the closest he ever got to his ultimate Utopia."

It was suggested to Leader Paul that Bix, according to reports now current, relaxed most when he drank. That pricked Pops Whiteman.

"That drinking business about Bix (and musicians in general) has been much exaggerated. Sure, Bix drank, and I'll bet you he got far more out of imbibing the stuff than any of us ever did or will. Drinking to him was an emotional release: apparently he felt that he was getting closer to that other world of his which he could never find, merely because he was getting further away from our reality."

The Fatalist

"You know, he had a terribly fatalistic attitude about our world: he couldn't see any future in it. It even got to the point when he was convinced that everything wrong had to happen to him. I remember one time on a train when Bix had been sleeping in his chair for hours. Suddenly he awoke, still quite unsteady. He got up quickly, but his legs weren't quite ready. He lost his balance. 'Doggone it!' exclaimed Bix, 'why does it always have to happen to me? We go along straight for hours, but the minute I want to get up the train has to take a curve and throw me!'

"But I guess a guy like Bix had a right to a fatalistic attitude. With a soul like his, he must have been awfully disappointed in his ordinary fellow creatures and the world in general. They say that's the way every genius is: he has such a wonderful conception of the future that he's bound to be dissatisfied with his present surroundings. I guess about the only time that Bix wasn't frustrated was when he played that horn of his. And I'm sorry, gentlemen, but I just can't describe that tone, those notes and phrases, and, least of all, the feeling with which he played. To me, there's never been a soloist like him, and let me tell you, I'd give my right arm if I could live to hear another Bix. I think my arm's safe, though!" concluded Paul Whiteman.

ROOMMATE IRVING RISKIN:

"Bix's heart was ahead of his lips . . . I never heard him say a bad word about anybody."

Bix Was Never a Great Reader, Avers His Roomie . . . Was Fooled By Own Chorus Put on Paper . . . Played Piano in Key of C Only

"Bix was a much greater musician than he was a cornetist!"

That almost conflicting bit of comparison has been drawn by Irving (Itzey) Riskin, brilliant pianist and now chief B. A. Rolfe arranger, who roomed with Bix from 1924 through 1927. "Yes," went on Itzey, "there were probably scores of cornetists who technically speaking could play rings around Bix, but there never has been one or will be one who can approach him when it comes to innate musicianship on his horn. After all, there's a big difference between being a straight, perhaps almost soulless instrumentalist, and a person whose very soul breathes music that's translated so beautifully through the medium of a horn. Bix's heart was far ahead of his lips."

"Duck That Chair!"

"That Bixian feeling pervaded through the man's piano playing as well. His improvisations were the most moving passages I've ever heard. I remember one night in an Indiana cafe after work when Bix hit a chord that was so beautiful that somebody (I think it was Hoagy Carmichael) became so excited that he threw a chair at him!

A rare photo of Bix taken by his friend, Irving Riskin, in Atlantic City

"Funny thing about Bix's piano playing: he could play only in the key of C and he had great difficulty in reading—something which he seldom bothered to do anyway. And don't get the idea that Bix was the greatest reader in the world when it came to cornet, either. He was, I should say, only an average reader, if that."

"I Can't Read Me!"

"Once when we were with Goldkette, in Cincinnnati, we were invited to listen to a kid's band that was patterned pretty much on ours. They had an arranger with a marvelous ear. He'd copy out our arrangements note for note. Well, after we had been listening for a while, the kids asked Bix to sit in, and he, in his usual gracious manner, acquiesced. Everything went along great until they got to the hot trumpet passage which was written out note for note. Then an astrounding thing happened:

"Bix faltered!

"He tried to read 'at sight,' but he couldn't make it!

"The band had to stop! Amateurs couldn't go ahead because the great Bix couldn't keep up with them!

"But the most amazing part of all this is that the passage Bix had such great difficulty in reading was the one he had faked spontaneously on the record of this arrangement and which had been copied down note for note by the brilliant kid arranger!

"But to those of us listening that surprise was nothing to what happened later in the same arrangement—something which didn't concern Bix at all, by the way. On the original record, Jimmy Dorsey had taken a clarinet break in which he got all balled up and played some very bad notes. He always had objected to the company's having released that particular master. Imagine how it broke us up when the kid clarinet player got to Jimmy's break and, reading from the arrangement, played Jimmy's version—bad note for bad note!"

That Stravinsky Moan

"But to return to Bix and his musicianship—he was a great admirer of the modern classicists. Debussy, MacDowell, Eastwood Lane and Stravinsky were his favorites. I remember many a night when I'd have to play the works of one of these four to lull Bix to sleep. To complete the mood, he'd ask me to play by red light. It became pretty eerie at times, especially when I'd strike an especially screwy Stravinsky chord and Bix would commence to moan—a moan of delight, if you can imagine such a thing.

"Those, though, were just about the only groans I ever heard come from Bix in all the years that I knew him. He was the most easygoing guy I ever met. Nothing ever bothered him much—or if anything did, he'd never let on. As long as I knew him, *I never heard Bix say a bad word about anybody!* Even without his playing you could love him and admire him for that characteristic alone. If you'll pardon the superlatives, I'd say that he certainly was the greatest natural musician and the grandest guy any of us will ever know. . . . I rest my case!"

And Irving Riskin, a scholarly, partially bald chap, who now looks more like the studious arranger that he is than the wild and woolly pianist who accompanied Bix all over the country, caught his breath and smiled. "What a man," he murmured softly to himself and smiled some more.

FRIEND EDDIE CONDON:

"Little things didn't bother Bix much— none of them made any difference, just so long as he could play."

The End, Not the Means, Interested Bix

"Bix never bothered much about his horn or embouchure or any stuff like that, the way so many trumpeters do too much nowadays," opines Eddie Condon, guitarist with Bobby Hackett, who played with Beiderbecke during many of his earlier years.

"He was always losing his cornet or stepping on it. I can't remember how many horns he'd run through. But they were all the same to him—he just played."

(Irving Riskin has pointed out that Bix never knew or cared much what notes he hit. He didn't go up into the higher register much—in fact, once he was quite surprised when somebody pointed out to him that he had just hit a high C sharp!)

"Yeah, Bix was that way about all his belongings," Condon continued. "I remember the first time I met him. It was in a railroad station where I was meeting a band I was going to join. The leader had told me in advance about this wonderful cornetist he'd picked up named Beiderbecke. I looked at all the guys in the band, and the last guy I'd ever suspect of being the star of the band was a guy with a nonchalant, almost vacant look on his face, with his hat way back on his head, just about ready to topple down on his shoulders, and his coat resting so far back on his back that I thought it would fall off any second.

"It wasn't because Bix was just a kid or anything. I remember years later when Bix opened at the Chicago Theatre with Paul Whiteman. He was due on the stage, but he couldn't even find his tuxedo or his tie or shirt. He came rushing in to Jimmy McPartland and me and we had to get together some clothes for him in a hurry. He went out wearing Jimmy's much too small tux and my very tight collar and small tie.

"But that's the way he was—he never bothered much about his personal appearance—that wasn't the only time he lost his tux. But little things like that didn't ever bother him much: his horn, his mouthpiece, his clothes—none of them made any difference, just so long as he could play.

"And once he played, you forgot all about those things too!"

"Let's Shoot the Ickies!"

The jitterbugs followed Bix as much as they do Benny and the Dorseys today. And what an influence he had over them!

Towards the end of Bix's career he was in such poor health that he could play only half notes—his lips wouldn't function any faster than that. But that didn't perturb the jitterbugs.

"Gee whiz," they'd exclaim, obviously overcome, "listen to that, will you? Why, nobody plays like him—he has a style all of his own!"

Bix, on the other hand, was never too fond of the gapers. When he'd see some especially ickey couple dancing out on the floor, he'd cock his horn to his shoulder, simulating a gun, point it at the jittery duo, and then, as he'd "click the trigger," the drummer would "fire the shot" via a rim shot. These occasions were some of the few when Bix displayed any disdain for any person or persons.

BIX ON HIGH

Poor Health in Later Life and Early Death Caused by Excessive Imbibing . . . Friends Relate Wild Experiences

Many stories have been written about Bix's drinking and the crazy things he did in his tighter moments. Though one hates to admit it (let alone write it) about a musician and person as great as Bix, the fact that he imbibed frequently and almost passionately cannot be overlooked in a cross-sectional approach to his life.

It should be pointed out that it wasn't until his later years that drink and Bix became so close, and also that in the "flapper" age in which Bix was famous, it was considered smart, especially among musicians, to drink a lot.

However, it can't be denied that Bix's early death was attributable in no small measure to his love of alcohol. A few years before his passing, he had been sent home for a twelve-months' rest cure by Whiteman, and during that time he was treated at a hospital in Dwight, Illinois, for alcoholism. When he returned from his vacation, he was, according to friends, in much better health, but apparently the old routine brought back old habits, and Bix was soon far off the wagon. When in August, 1931, he collapsed in the street, he had little or no strength to combat the disease (supposedly pneumonia), and he passed away in a very few days.

For Example

Probably nothing could serve as a better example of Bix's pitiable condition before his death than the following incident, described by guitarist Frank Victor:

"Al Duffy, Vic Irwin, Mike Riley, Lou Schoobe, I, and some others were playing a spot in Pelham, New York. One night Bix came in to see us. He'd been ill, as you know, off and on, and when we invited him up to the stand he seemed reluctant. It was the first time we'd ever seen him stand back."

"Yes" . . . But

"The boys crowded around him, and after we had coaxed and handed him a horn, he began to play his chorus of *Sweet Sue*.

"Well, it was an awful shock to us. He tried, but he just couldn't make the music he felt. It was one of the saddest moments I've ever experienced—Bix wanting to make his horn talk and not getting the response he'd always known. We all felt for him and were mighty sorry we'd insisted on his playing for us. He died soon after that."

That Buick!

But sadness wasn't the only note struck by Bix's liquor love. Most of it was gladness—good, wholesome fun. For example, there are all sorts of funny ancedotes about the 1899 Buick Bix bought when playing for Goldkette's unit at Hudson Lake, Indiana. He was mighty proud of the car and lived in it almost all the time. It got so that Eddie Condon nicknamed it "The Shaving Stand."

Goldkette used to come every few weeks to check up on his band. On one particular evening, according to Peewee Russell, Goldkette arrived but Beiderbecke and Russell were not to be seen. Suddenly there was a tremendous roar in front of the place. The band rushed out to find Peewee and Bix seated very unsteadily in their car—which had been towed all the way in by another machine!

"Charles—Chuck"

Paul Whiteman recalls the night when the band was playing at Nuttings-on-the-Charles—near Boston. The dance started, but no Bix. All of a sudden at about eleven o'clock Bix rushed up on the stand.

"What's the name of this place, anyway?" he asked with a big grin.

"Nuttings-on-the-Charles," snapped back Whiteman.

"Nuttings-on-the-Charles?" queried Bix. "My God, and here I was bawling out that cab driver because he couldn't find Muttings on the Chuck!"

That misunderstanding, intentional or otherwise, cost Bix $38 in taxi fare.

No Jitterbugs

Adrian Rollini tells this one about Bix in his lighter and tighter moments:

"Late one night he and I were going home together from the Colonial Club. We were passing Loew's State (then new) on the Forty-fifth Street side and he noticed that the side entrance was open and the lights on.

"Bix spied the stage and made for it. He climbed up and took his cornet out of an old paper bag he was using for a case. We were having a wonderful little jam session on that stage all by ourselves, Bix on cornet and me on my goofus, when the night watchman came and started yelling at us. But Bix kept right on playing at the empty seats. Finally the watchman sneaked behind Bix, grabbed him by his neck, and commenced shaking him like a rat, at the same

The Jean Goldkette Band in 1926 at the Hillcrest Inn, Southboro, Mass.
FRONT ROW: Ray Ludwig, Bill Challis, Spiegle Wilcox, Fuzzy Farrar, Bill Rank, Bix
BACK ROW: Howdy Quicksell, Chauncey Morehouse, Irving "Itzey" Riskin, Doc Ryker, Don Murray, Frankie Trumbauer, Steve Brown

Bix gets a stranglehold on clarinetist Don Murray

time whistling for the cops. But somehow or other we managed to run away in time."

Trunk, Not Drunk

Even in his sober moments, Bix did whacky things. It must have been l'Artist in him. Once on a Whiteman tour, according to Rollini, discipline was suddenly tightened and Bix, intending to cooperate, got up bright and early the next morning, bathed, shaved, and packed his trunk while still in his pajamas. Then, to get the jump on the other boys, he sent the trunk to the depot ahead of time.

Came the hour of departure and time to stop lolling around in pajamas and to get dressed. Suddenly Bix realized that he had packed all his clothes, including those he had intended wearing that day—and his trunk was already well on its way.

There are loads of other stories about Bix's antics, but those just related by men who knew him pretty well should serve pretty well as examples of the wholesome whackiness that was part of this immortal's character.

BIX ON SLEEP

There have been all sorts of stories on Bixian idiosyncrasies making the rounds, but none has had more tellings, or incorrect renditions, than the one about Bix's famous sleep.

It seems the Whiteman band was playing down in Oklahoma. At that time it didn't have much competition—it could command and get almost any price. As a result, discipline in the band was just about nil. Everybody was getting so blotto that it became ludicrous.

The Awakening

At this point the managers decided to do something drastic. They started a system imposing a twenty-five-dollar fine on anybody missing an afternoon session and a fifty-buck penalty for missing the night shot.

Bix immediately went into action: he'd be the Model Child. And so the first night he went to bed early, got up at the crack of dawn, feeling fine and healthy, and beat it down to the railroad station to catch the train that was to carry the band to the next town. Imagine his surprise when he saw a string of passenger cars pulling slowly out of the station.

He ran as fast as he could and with an heroic gesture pulled himself up on the last car. He wended his way forward until he met the conductor.

"Which way to Mr. Whiteman's car, please?" he asked.

"Mr. Whiteman's car!" ejaculated the conductor. "Why, that train doesn't leave for another hour and, what's more, it goes in the opposite direction. You're heading west, son, and you should be going east!"

Back Again

"Oh well," murmured Bix in his easy way, and he waited until the train stopped at the next station. There he got somebody to drive him back to the original town. They raced in, but the Whiteman train had already gone.

Now Bix was really up against it. Only one way he could get to that afternoon town in time to avoid a twenty-five buck fine, and that was to take a plane. Bix was scared stiff of flying, but fines were fines, and so, fortified with some liquor as a bracer for going up, Bix and a chartered plane headed for the next town.

Beiderbecke had wired ahead to the band to be met at the airport. Imagine the surprise at the airport when the plane came in with the wind (instead of against it, as is customary), and Bix stepped out with an excited "Whee, here I am!" A moment later the pilot appeared, only to fall down flat on his face, out cold. The liquor had had its effect.

No Awakening

Bix, thoroughly high, was rushed to the theater and played the afternoon show. But his efforts were taking their toll, and after the show Bix went to his room for a sleep out of which nobody could wake him. And so what did he do but sleep right through the night show!

Somebody in the band figured it all out later on. Bix, in order to save a $25 fine, had paid $85 for a plane ride and then had fallen into the clutches of a double fine for missing the night show. The whole affair cost him $135! But Bix didn't care, and it sure gave the guys in the band one swell story to tell when they got back home.

BIX'S ALL-STAR BAND

He was such a nice guy, this Beiderbecke, that he could never bear to hurt anybody's feelings, relates Peewee Russell. As a result, when Victor finally got Bix to organize his own band for recording purposes, he showed up at the first and only date with the following included (among others) in his band:

Clarinets: Benny Goodman, Jimmy Dorsey, Peewee Russell.
Tenor sax: Bud Freeman.
Trombone: Tommy Dorsey.
Violin: Joe Venuti.
Guitar: Eddie Lang.
Drums: Gene Krupa.

All in all, there were so many stars and friends of Bix in the band that nobody could play more than a few measures. The records weren't successful, but at least Bix hadn't hurt anybody's feelings!

DID BIX REALLY ADLIB?

Contrary to general belief, Bix very often *did* play the same chorus the same way! That was especially true in his later years. Paul Whiteman claims that Bix would never play a chorus the same way *until* he got just what he wanted. Then he'd stick to that chorus and play it that same way over and over again. Once in a while he'd try to improve on his finished product, but most of the time he didn't distort his new composition.

Itzey Riskin points out that once Bix found a cornet chorus he really liked, he'd have it written out for three trumpets. In that connection note the three-part trumpet chorus in the Whiteman record of *San*, quite obviously a Bixian masterpiece. What's more, the three trumpets on that record are Bix, and Tommy and Jimmy Dorsey!

THE BEIDERBECKES
DIDN'T KNOW!

"We never knew our Bix was famous!"

Those are the astounding words uttered by Bix's parents to Marshall Stearns, when that student of swing went out to Davenport, Iowa, to interview them three years ago.

Mr. and Mrs. Bismark Beiderbecke, stolid, cheerful, typical midwestern folks, living far away from their late son's swing world, had no way of knowing the great respect in which Bix was and still is held. Mrs. Beiderbecke, to be sure, was proud of her son,

but that pride was little more than the natural pride a mother takes in her offspring.

At home, Bix had never been considered an especially brilliant musician. He had an older brother whose musical qualities were always thought of much more highly. By the time Stearns had finished telling them about their son, Leon, and his great reputation, though, Ma and Pa Beiderbecke were almost on the verge of changing their minds!

HIGHLIGHTS IN THE
LIFE OF BIX

1903—Born in Davenport, Iowa.
1922—Left swank Lake Forest Academy (near Chicago) to play club dates and on excursion boats.
1923—Attended University of Iowa for short time. Went to New York to hear Original Dixieland Jazz Band. Joined Wolverines there.
1925—Left Wolverines in Hammond, Indiana. Played in relief band for Charley Straight at Rendezvous Cafe, Chicago; then joined Straight.
1926—Joined Frankie Trumbauer's band at Arcadia Ballroom in St. Louis. Played in Jean Goldkette unit under Trumbauer at Hudson Lake, Indiana—wrote *In a Mist*. Joined Goldkette's main band in Detroit.
1928—Goldkette band broke up at Roseland, New York. Joined Whiteman's band.
1930—Home for a year: ill but receiving full salary from Whiteman.
1931—Returned to Whiteman for a short while. Left Whiteman to do few radio jobs. Died suddenly in summer after short illness.

BIX RECORDS

Milton Gabler, noted swing record authority and head of the Commodore Music Shop, herewith submits a list of recordings featuring the best bits Bix Beiderbeck ever put on wax.

BIX—with FRANK TRUMBAUER Orch.
Riverboat Shuffle
Ostrich Walk
Com. Music Shop, CMS 29-30
I'm Coming, Virginia
Singing the Blues
Brunswick 7703
Way Down Yonder in New Orleans
Clarinet Marmalade
Vocalion 4412

BIX AND HIS GANG
Jazz Me Blues
At the Jazz Band Ball
Vocalion 3042
Sorry
Since My Best Gal Turned Me Down
Vocalion 3149

BIX—with PAUL WHITEMAN Orch.
Lonely Melody
Mississippi Mud
Victor 25366
Louisiana
You Took Advantage of Me
Victor 25389
Changes
Victor 25370

BIX with JEAN GOLDKETTE Orch.
Clementine
Victor 25283

BIX BEIDERBECKE (piano solo)
In a Mist
Vocalion 3150

October, 1937

(Note: This extra piece about Bix appeared as part of a column called "From the Dorsey Dome," which I ghostwrote for several months for Tommy.)

FRIEND TOMMY DORSEY:

"All that I can recollect through the haze is we did two tunes."

However, if you fellahs want to know who I am just take a look at the accompanying picture. I'm the guy with the twisted licorice stick glasses who really needs a shine. We had the picture taken in 1924 when under the name of "The Rhythm Jugglers" we made some Gennett Records. "We" in this picture stands for Bix in the sweater, Don Murray with the clarinet, Paul Mertz with the bow tie, Tommy Gargano with the drums and Howdy Quicksell, who missed the entire record date but who arrived just in time to get himself and his banjo into the picture.

The Rhythm Jugglers (left to right): Howdy Quicksell, Tommy Gargano, Paul Mertz, Don Murray, Bix, Tommy Dorsey

What a crazy date that was! We all got blind on prohibition gin on the way down to the studios in Richmond, Indiana. We were playing with Jean Goldkette in Detroit at the time, and Bix, knowing the Gennett recording director, a fellow by the name of Wickermeyer, had arranged the date.

Well, we may have been blind on the train coming down, but that was nothing compared to our condition once we started cutting some wax! All that I can recollect through the haze is that we did two tunes*: *Davenport Blues*, in which Bix played a chorus that's still considered one of the greatest in the annals of jazz corneting, and a tune that had something about *Toddlin* in the title.† I do remember pretty vividly, though, that sometime during the session Hoagy Carmichael walked in with a tremendous jug (filled) in one hand and a new manuscript in the other. After inspecting the jug, etc., we looked at the manuscript. It was his famous *Washboard Blues!* We must have fooled with that piece for hours, but we never could get to play it right. And, I might add now in a much soberer state, what a shame! You've probably heard it done lots of times, so that you know what we missed by not being the first band to record it. Incidentally, if you look very hard at that picture you might find Hoagy someplace under the piano!

In defense of all of us at the date, I should add that it wasn't entirely our fault that we cut only two sides. It seems that the studios were right next to the Starr piano factory and that at the time we were making the records the piano business was awfully good. That in itself wouldn't have been so bad were it not for the fact that railroad trains used to back up to the factory right beneath the Gennett studio. And with business booming, the trains went zooming, and what a terrific racket they made! So it was the combination of gin and enGINe that made matters sort of tough. Still, believe it or not, I get a big kick whenever I hear either of those two sides!

---

* They actually did four, but two, *Magic Blues* and *Nobody Knows What It's All About*, were rejected—no doubt the victims of that alcoholic haze.—*G.S.*

† *Toddlin Blues.*—*G.S.*

BUNNY, LIKE BIX, WILL SOON BE A MYTH

Star Trumpeter, Who Died Last Month, Helped Bring Swing to Present Heights

One of these years they're going to start talking about Bunny Berigan the way they now talk about Bix Beiderbecke. They're going to rave about his trumpeting feats; they're going to dig out his records, and they're going to play them for the next generation, pointing out this passage and that passage to prove that Bunny was one of the true Greats of All Jazz.

And they'll be right, of course.

Bunny Berigan, who passed away as only a shadow of his former self in New York's Polyclinic Hospital, June 2nd, was truly one of the Greats of Jazz. His thrilling, imaginative, fat-toned trumpet, more than anybody else's, blazed the trail that brought swing into its heyday during the middle thirties.

The public first started hearing him and knowing who he was when he made records with Benny Goodman's up-and-coming band in 1935. The more discerning jazz enthusiasts might have noticed his work on several early Dorsey Brothers records, as well as many other studio groups like Red Norvo's and Red Nichols', and if they had discerned even further, around that time, they could have heard him on CBS sustainings when he used to lead various jazz-band units, most famous of which, perhaps, was the group known as Bunny's Blue Boys.

Bunny had played with name bands before that CBS and record studio stretch. Hal Kemp, passing through Berigan's native Wisconsin in 1928, heard him, and a year or two later hired him. Paul Whiteman also used him at the Biltmore in his early thirties sojourn there. That, too, was shortly after Bunny had migrated from Fox Lake, Wisconsin, where he had been born late in 1908. (That made him 33 at the time of his death.)

Bunny's childhood wasn't musically startling. His explanation of how he started to play trumpet is quite simple. One day his granddad came home with a trumpet, handed it to him, and said, "Here, this is you. Play you!" Which was a pretty matter-of-fact way to start on one of the greatest trumpet-blowing careers jazzdom has ever known.

The public started to appreciate Bunny in 1935. At that time he was a pretty stolid, serious-looking

Bunny Berigan in an impromptu jam session with friends Tommy Dorsey, Gene Krupa, Jimmy Dorsey and Carmen Mastren

fellow, a characteristic not at all reflected in his playing. Red McKenzie once made a very pertinent remark about Bunny's playing, right after Berigan had left Goodman's band. Said the much-respected one: "If that man wasn't such a gambler, everybody'd say he was the greatest that ever blew. But the man's got such nerve and likes his horn so much that he'll go ahead and try stuff that nobody else'd ever think of trying."

At that time Bunny was playing around 52nd Street in a club run by McKenzie. He was doing radio work, too, and was just beginning to record under his own name. With a pickup band, he waxed one side for Vocalion that was destined to stick. It was *I Can't Get Started*, his identification tag.

Shortly after that, Tommy Dorsey was looking around for someone to spark his brand new band. Like all the other top-notch musicians of that time, he had played with Bunny on all sorts of studio dates, and like all those other top-notchers, Tommy considered Berigan the greatest of the white jazz trumpeters. To know what happened, all you have to do is listen to the brilliant trumpet passages on Dorsey records like *Marie*, *Song of India* and others which are listed in the Berigan discography below.

Wins *Metronome* Poll

Jazz followers the world over also considered Bunny top man. In the METRONOME All-Star Band Poll of 1936, Bunny came in first by a stupendous margin.

Shortly after that he started his own band. It made its New York debut at the Pennsylvania Hotel in April. Featured, besides Bunny, was a young tenorman he had discovered. His name was Georgie Auld.

There were other kicks in that band, too. Joe Lippman arranged and played piano. George Wettling, switching from Jack Hylton, was the drummer. Tommy Morgan played guitar and there was a fine young first trumpeter named Steve Lipkins. Ford Leary was in the band also.

Bunny did quite well with that group for a while. He recorded for Brunswick and Victor and played lots of choice spots and theatres. He himself was playing sensationally, and he appeared to have a brilliant future ahead of him.

He made improvements, too. In 1937, Irving Goodman and Sonny Lee joined the brass section, and the following year he added two splendid trombonists, Ray Conniff and Nat LeBovski, and a fine young clarinetist, Gus Bivona. And his rhythm section was a really jumping affair. Veteran Hank Wayland was on bass, and on piano and drums were two Berigan discoveries. The pianist was Joe Bushkin. The drummer was Buddy Rich.

But the Berigan band didn't do too well from 1938 on. It had its share of tough breaks, like the time when an eastern hurricane just about blew the roof off

Boston's swank Ritz-Carlton Hotel just at the time Bunny was due to click there. Another time the band showed up for a Sunday night date at Bristol, Conn., only to find Gene Krupa's bunch on the bandstand. Consequently Berigan and boys missed their scheduled Bridgeport date that night.

Very late in 1938 Bunny had a run-in with Arthur Michaud, his guiding manager, and the two split. Almost all the stars left the band around this time and when New Year's came around Bunny was busy vehemently denying all reports that he was about to give up his band.

1939

Nineteen thirty-nine saw a different Berigan. He was still capable of playing great horn, but he didn't lift the rest of his men to previous heights. Maybe it was because the men weren't capable of being lifted that high. And maybe it was because Bunny was no longer as consistent an inspiration. Probably it was both. Bunny used to drink a lot, but it never affected him the way it started to in 1939. He carried on with his band, but everybody knew it was a losing proposition, Bunny included.

In February, 1940, two things happened at the same time. Bunny junked his band and Bunny joined Tommy Dorsey.

It looked like the comeback of Berigan. He started playing magnificent horn once more. Some folks claim he never played better than he did in that last sojourn with Tommy. He sparked not only the brass section, but the entire band, and Tommy, who wasn't riding as high as he had been, came roaring back to popularity heights.

That lasted just six months. And then—boom— Dorsey and Berigan parted. Tommy claimed he fired Bunny; Bunny claimed he quit Tommy. Those close to both didn't say much, but they did know that Berigan hadn't been in the best of physical condition at the time of the blowoff.

Back to Leading

So Bunny went back to bandleading again. Those last months were the most dismal of his career. Every once in a while he would perk up, but the strain of constant one-nighters and not keeping in good condition soon began to tell. This writer went to hear the band on a Connecticut one-nighter last year, and it proved to be one of the most depressing experiences in his life. The band was just nothing. And, compared with Berigan standards, Bunny's blowing was just pitiful. He sounded like a man trying to imitate himself, a man with none of the inspiration and none of the technique of the real Berigan.

He looked awful, too. He must have lost at least thirty pounds. His clothes were loose-fitting; even his collar looked as if it were a couple of sizes too large for him.

Apparently, though, he was in good spirits. He joked with friends and talked about the great future he thought his band had. But you had a feeling it would never be. And when, after intermission, Bunny left the bandstand, not to return for a long time, and some trumpeter you'd never heard of before came down to front the band, play Bunny's parts, and spark the outfit more than its leader had, you realized this was enough, and you left the place at once, feeling simply awful.

Bunny with his band early in 1939

Tough Times

Yes, those last months weren't good. Bunny went into bankruptcy, too. That didn't help matters, certainly not his mental state.

And yet he carried on with dogged grit. The guys in his band realized how hard he was actually trying. He proved it to them on many a night by getting up and blowing when he should have been flat on his back in a bed. He broke down several times and, only a few weeks before the end, he had been released from a Pennsylvania hospital after a pneumonia siege.

On June 1st of this year his band played a job at Manhattan Center in New York. It played without Bunny, though. He was in Polyclinic Hospital, very sick. He had cirrhosis of the liver and complications, an illness much like that of John Barrymore, who had died just a short while before. His band played the job without him. Benny Goodman brought his sextet over from the Paramount and they helped out their fellow-musicians.

The next day word started seeping around Manhattan that Bunny was really sick. Bassist Sid Weiss, a close friend, went over to the hospital to see him. Bunny grinned when he saw Sid's slight figure. "And they tell me *I'm* sick," he joked. "Looks like you should be here instead of me!"

Later on that night, Tommy Dorsey, playing at the Astor, got a call to come over to the hospital right away. He left the band at once. The minute he saw Bunny he knew there was no hope.

Tommy was right.

And now Bunny Berigan, like another great horn player with the same initials, is gone. Naturally, people are going to remark how great he was. And how right they are, too! There's too much proof to dispute the fact, recorded proof as well as the words of the many who heard him in person.

And those who knew him, know what a great person they have lost, too. That goes not only for his wife, Donna, and his children, but also for men like the Dorseys and Goodman and Shaw and Glenn Miller and Mannie Klein and Carl Kress and Toots Mondello and Eddie Miller and Gene Krupa and Jack Teagarden and Jack Jenney and Charlie Barnet and Teddy Wilson and Red Norvo, and just about all the greats of jazz who some time or other played with and got to know Bunny Berigan.

Most of them will claim he's the greatest. If you had asked Bunny, he probably would have called each of them the greatest, even though such appraisals of each would have been logical impossibilities. But Bunny always spoke well of everybody. You'd never hear him tearing down any musician. He'd build them up, whether they were already established stars, or whether they were discoveries of his, like Auld and Rich and Bushkin.

But he is gone now, gone much too soon. Undoubtedly excessive drinking had much to do with it, just the way it undoubtedly had with Bix, too. For some constitutions can stand such punishment. Others can't. Bunny's happened to be one of those others.

Bunny is gone now. Fortunately, for most of us, he has left memories via the many phonograph records he made. Others of us, those who knew him as a person, don't even need such recorded evidence. We can remember Bunny Berigan, the person. You don't forget a man like that.

Bunny Berigan Records

that show him off, and which are still at least somewhat available, include the following:

with **HIS OWN BAND** (Victor)
Mahogany Hall Stomp
Davenport Blues
I Can't Get Started

with **BENNY GOODMAN** (Victor)
Jingle Bells
Blue Skies
King Porter Stomp

with **TOMMY DORSEY** (Victor)
—first time—
Marie
Song of India
Melody in F
Who'll Buy My Violets
Liebestraum
Mendelsohn's Spring Song
—second time—
I'm Nobody's Baby

with **DORSEY BROTHERS** (Columbia)
Mood Hollywood
Shim-Sham-Shimmy

METRONOME ALL-STARS (Victor)
Blue Lou (band included Goodman, E. Miller, T. Dorsey, J. Teagarden, Spivak, Dunham, Haggart, Bauduc, etc.).

JAM SESSION AT VICTOR
Blues
Honeysuckle Rose (with T. Dorsey, Fats Waller, Dick McDonough and George Wettling).

with **RED NORVO** (Columbia)
Blues in E Flat
Bughouse
With All My Heart and Soul
—in this group, besides Norvo and Berigan, were Chu Berry, Johnny Mince, Jack Jenney, Teddy Wilson, George Van Eps, Artie Bernstein and Gene Krupa.

with **MILDRED BAILEY** (Decca)
Squeeze Me
Honeysuckle Rose
Downhearted Blues

with **GLENN MILLER** (Columbia)
In a Little Spanish Town
Solo Hop

with **HAL KEMP** (Brunswick)
Whistles
Navy Blues

Bunny also played on countless "date" sides, especially on early Deccas, when he used to pop up behind all sorts of singers, including one of his favorites, Red McKenzie.

July, 1943

It took me awhile to become convinced that Sinatra was really as great as he was, primarily because I couldn't believe anyone could phrase more prettily than Henry Wells did. Eventually, though, I grew more objective, influenced, no doubt, by observing Frank in the kind of action reported here.

SINATRA

The success of Frank Sinatra is really sensational! And deservedly so, too. I sat through one of his recent Paramount stage shows, and the man really chilled me, more than he'd ever done before. He's so absolutely relaxed, both in voice and demeanor, and he uses such impeccable taste all the time.

The effect he had on the audience was at the same time gratifying and amusing. It was a kick to see a bunch of people appreciate something as good as Frank, but the way they appreciated some of his mannerisms was really funny. He'd just have to gliss down a bit, and the girls would giggle and scream and yell "o-o-o-h-h-h," with exactly the same downward inflection. They say that Valentino was probably the greatest matinee idol of them all, but I have a hunch that a dilated Valentino nostril never had any more effect upon feminine hearts than a downward Sinatra gliss.

Frank's success made me reminisce a bit, too. It made me think of the first time I ever heard him. He had just joined Harry James's band at Roseland, and I was up there doing a review of the outfit. As you may remember, I always got a big boot out of it. Harry always knew I did, too, so that if I was up there to review his bunch, he usually had a pretty fair hunch that the next issue of METRONOME would entail some boost.

Reviewer Intercepted

But I'll never forget what happened as I was leaving that evening. Harry had a manager named Jerry Barrett, a fellow he'd taken fresh from the MCA stockroom or some such place, and who used to run around with a very businesslike-looking briefcase, a new managerial mustache, and a habit of always calling the James band "MY band."

As I was walking down the steps from Roseland, Jerry came running after me. "Listen," he said, "everything all right? The band o.k.?" (This is the usual manager's routine towards a visiting reviewer. They always want to know if everything's o.k. and you always answer a polite "yes" and then tell them what you really think in print afterwards. You'd think some of them would have more tact than to try to pin you down right then and there. You're never going to tell them it's lousy, just like that, because [1] it'd create an uncomfortable situation, and [2] after the embarrassment has worn off he'd start telling you about all the attributes that he says the band has and which it usually doesn't have.)

But back to Barrett and the Sinatra episode. After I told him "Sure," he came across with this: "Look," he said, "did you like this new singer I picked up?"

"Yeah, he's fine," I answered truthfully, though it might not have sounded too convincing.

"Well, give him a good write-up then, will you?" I must have given Jerry a surprised look, because that wasn't the usual method of his attack. He caught it, I guess, because he immediately began to explain.

"I think the boy is wonderful and I want to keep

him with my band. But there's one thing about him, and that is he wants a good write-up more than anybody I've ever seen. So give him a good write-up, will you, because we want to keep him happy and that's the only thing that'll make him happy."

I don't remember exactly what I did write afterwards, but I know that I gave Frank the good write-up he deserved and which I'd, of course, have given him anyway.

But that impression Jerry gave me of Frank lingered, and so I wasn't surprised, as I got to know Sinatra better as the years went by, to find under that boyish naturalness, an amazing amount of cockiness.

I'll never forget, for example, the time he came up to me backstage at the Paramount—he was with Tommy Dorsey by this time—and asked me to put his picture on the front cover of METRONOME. There wasn't any doubt about it, I could see, in the Sinatra mind. He wasn't as big then as he is now, but he must have had a hunch he was going to be—and, I guess, he figured that a break, such as a front cover on a national magazine, wasn't going to hurt a bit.

And so, whereas other singers would just hang in the background, depending upon their band's publicity man to make the break for them, Frank, with his self-assurance, dove right in. (He didn't get the cover, because we weren't using vocalists in those days, but that doesn't affect the significance of the incident.)

That cockiness of Frank's is a wonderful thing for him. For the fellow had plenty of tough breaks, and chances are most of the country would never have heard of him if he hadn't had that amazing confidence in himself.

And that Sinatra cockiness is likely to keep him on top longer than the usual matinee idol stays on top, provided, of course, that he doesn't let it get too far.

For now that he is where he is, he doesn't have to go around selling himself anymore; he's already very well sold. Now it's just a matter of keeping his own self-confidence and keeping it to himself rather than letting it loose on anybody who happens to come his way.

Frank, who, though slight in build, knows how to and does take care of himself handily, never shirked a fistfight, nor so far as I know, never came out on the short end of any, either.

The reason I, for one, am glad that Frank is so sure of himself, is that there's just that much less chance of his being talked into doing the wrong thing, musically speaking, of course. For, now that he is right on top, plenty of folks, including managers, are going to try to tell him how to sing and what to sing and how he should put an act across and all that sort of stuff. They're going to hammer him with ideas of stage presence and mike presence and all other forms of salesmanship.

But Frank Sinatra, being the kind of guy he is, will just keep on going the way he has. And for me, that's great. For, of all the men singers in the business today, I don't know of one who shows any better musical taste and musical feeling in everything that he does than Frank Sinatra. And as such, he's been a distinct boon to one phase of the field that has become cluttered with artificialism during the past years, filled up with men whose bosoms are all filled up with words that they can't get out, because, in order to sound romantic and masculine, they close their throats and mouths and make everything sound as if it's the greatest effort in the world, as though they were singing and changing a tire at the same time.

Frank does just one thing when he sings. He sings. And to me, brothers and sisters, the way he does it is plenty!

Nothing in this book marks me more clearly as a sentimentalist than this article about Red McKenzie. Red's been gone for years, but I still play his records and I still feel the same unabashed, warm glow I felt when I first heard him in the early thirties. And I still remember what I think was the very last time I saw Red. We were standing on a street corner and he was telling me once again how much he appreciated my waging what seemed to be a losing battle for his recognition. "Georgie," he said slowly and very emphatically in that deep, resonant voice, "if I ever do make it, I'm telling you, you're going to get the most beautiful Buick any man ever had!" Obviously, Red was also a true sentimentalist.

RED McKENZIE

Red McKenzie's a name that mightn't mean much to many of you people, especially you younger people. For he retired from the music business a good many years ago, and, besides, even when he was in it, he wasn't overly well known.

That lack of appreciation is something that always bothered me tremendously, because Red McKenzie was my favorite of all singers. And I have a pretty firm hunch that that same lack of appreciation is one reason for Red McKenzie never reaching the popularity he deserved.

Before I go any further, I ought to mention that McKenzie isn't just one of those comparative unknowns a writer happens to pick upon because he heard him once or twice and nobody else ever heard him and so nobody can ever question his judgment. Believe it or not, that's just what does happen when some of those so-called critics (they write just one article that's ever published and every other word in it is "stink") comes across some three-fingered piano-playing fool. No, McKenzie was tremendously appreciated by the comparative few who really paid some attention to him. Bing Crosby, for example, has stated often that he thinks Red was the greatest of them all and that Red offered him tremendous inspiration. And next time you see Woody Herman, just mention McKenzie's name. Woody worships the guy, and, incidentally, more than anyone else, phrases a great deal like him.

Phrasing

Phrasing is the key to McKenzie's greatness. He has a very resonant quality to his voice, but still, technically, he's no singer. He doesn't breathe correctly and he can't sustain a tone and he's got a vibrato at times a mile long and two miles wide. But all that doesn't mean a thing when it comes to McKenzie's phrasing. That comes from way down—deep down from the bottom of what must be a huge heart. It's absolutely immense, so far as I'm concerned.

But still, Red wasn't appreciated the way he should have been. And it wasn't because people couldn't catch on to his very individual style too readily, though I did find from trying to sell the man to disbelievers that he does grow on you. I think the reason Red McKenzie was never the national sensation he should have been was, to put it tritely, Red McKenzie.

See, Red was primarily a musician. He didn't play an instrument, unless you can call a comb with a piece of tissue paper across it an instrument. But as long as he was in the music business he lived like and he lived with musicians. Before he ever made any records on his own—long before, in fact—he had waxed discs with all-star groups that he assembled. They used to be known as the Mound City Blue Blowers. And what wonderful records they were, too! There was one on Okeh I'll never forget. The coupling was *I Can't Believe That You're in Love with Me* and *Georgia on My Mind*, and included in the personnel, as I recall, were Coleman Hawkins, Jimmy Dorsey, Muggsy Spanier, Jack Russin (a great pianist whom not many people know about), Eddie Condon and, I think, Gene

Krupa. [I thought wrong; the drummer was Frank "Josh" Billings.] There were other groups of his whose works were recently reissued on Bluebird that featured more Hawkins, Jack Teagarden, Glenn Miller, Peewee Russell and others. Listen to *One Hour* and *Tailspin Blues* especially.

Red thought like most of these men—musically. He wanted to sing the way he felt. And he did. If songs were poorly constructed, as so many of them were and still are, so that to phrase them musically would mean to sacrifice the meaning of the lyrics, it never occurred to Red to compromise. He'd make it sound like a trumpet or like a tenor, and to hell with whether or not the words made sense to Joe Blow out there in the audience. I don't think Red ever considered the public much—not that he looked down on it, but rather that he could think first only in terms of what he felt was *musically* right.

The fact is that the public wasn't ready for the kind of stuff McKenzie was shelling out. Remember, this was twelve and fifteen years ago. And, because the right kind of reaction wasn't forthcoming, Red, I think, built sort of a protective shell around himself. And so when his big chance came to make himself the great commercial success he should have been, he muffed it.

That chance was around 1932 and 1933, when he went with Paul Whiteman. "Pops" was big then. He had Mildred Bailey and then he had Ramona. In fact, the latter and McKenzie used to do a radio show. But nothing ever happened, and one of the reasons, it struck me later, was that Red could never unbend sufficiently. He was by no means a gracious, smiling personality up there on the stand.

Relaxation

When you get to know the guy, you'll find he's wonderful. He's sincere and honest and despite what appears to be a certain hard quality, one of the most considerate and sentimental souls you'll ever meet. But by the time he'd gone with Whiteman, Red had been buffeted around a lot, and he wasn't going to let himself be buffeted anymore. Thus developed what appeared to be a chip on the shoulder, and which actually grew so big that at times McKenzie would readily admit that he thought the world was just set against him.

He left Whiteman after not too long a time, and relaxed back into the groove he knew and loved—with jazz musicians. He made quite a few records for Decca and some for Vocalion. Most of the former featured Bunny Berigan and a tenorman named For-

Red McKenzie with singer Stella Brooks and pianist and friend Joe Sullivan

345

rest Crawford, who, Red used to swear, was the greatest of them all. He wasn't far from wrong, but unfortunately, Crawford became quite ill and had to give up playing.

Red's last venture of any note in the music business was running a nightclub on 52nd Street, which was alternately known as the Yacht Club and the Club McKenzie. But Red proved again that he was no commercial success. I remember going into the place time and again and finding just about nobody except Red's musician friends. They'd drink and play and play and drink—but mostly drink; and I still think to this date that Red never let them pay a tab. Once in a while some customers would come in, but the musicians would go on just as before, playing when and what they felt like playing, kidding among themselves. Sometimes the music was good and sometimes it was horrible, but I'll say this for it: even the tripe was spontaneous tripe. It was always loud, and I doubt if the guys ever played a request, unless it was for something they liked anyway. I know a bunch of us used to ask for *I've Got the World on a String* and *Sweet Lorraine* and *I Cried for You* (numbers which Red sang especially well), and we'd always get them, even though they were interspersed with constant *Muskrat Ramble*s and *Jazz Me Blues*es and other Eddie Condon standards.

The two last recollections I have of Red are the two most vivid. The first was a month or two before he left New York. We were at the bar in the Club McKenzie. It was late afternoon. I suggested to Red that we go someplace—I forget whether it was for dinner or for what. I could see he wanted to go. "But, George," he said, "the wife and kid are waiting at home for me for dinner, and I love them too much not to show up."

Last Meeting

The last recollection I had was standing on a curb with him on Sixth Avenue between 52nd and 53rd Streets. I've never seen a man so blue and lost in my life. He was going to leave New York for good. His wife, to whom he had always been so terribly devoted, had passed away. "There's only one thing left for me in this world now," he said, "and that's the kid. I'm going back to St. Louis with him and see to it that he gets a good bringing-up so he can amount to something. I want to be with him always, and I want him to have some good feminine care, too. He'll get that from the women in the family back there."

"And how about you, Red?" I asked. "You're not going to give up the business, are you?"

"I certainly am. It's never been too kind to me, you know. I'm going to take a job in St. Louis, a daytime job, and earn a good steady income, and be near the kid, and be a really good father."

And that's just what Red McKenzie did. Latest reports have him out there now—I hear he's selling liquor. He has given up his singing career so that he can make a success of another career—that of being a father. And a fellow as fine and sincere and honest and sympathetic as Red McKenzie just can't miss. That's going to be a whale of a fine kid.

But I, for one, still sure do wish he could take a little time off to do some singing. He'd do wonderfully in radio or on records (if they ever make 'em again) today, much better than he ever did before. For I think that the general public is much wiser musically now and would be much more likely to accept Red. What a thrill it would be for so many of us, including, I suspect pretty strongly, for Red McKenzie and that kid of his.

Notes on Red McKenzie Records

I doubt if you can find that Okeh coupling I mentioned, but Columbia has reissued *Darktown Strutters' Ball*, which was made on the same date. . . . For a different type of McKenzie, listen to *Three on a Match*, with Whiteman's band on Victor. . . . Red did fine rhythm vocals too and sang excellent blues. For examples of these, catch Red Nichols' *Fan It* and *How Long Blues* which came out on Brunswick and which Decca could revive. . . . For an earlier McKenzie, dig in your attic for an old Columbia of *Indiana* by the Mound City Blue Blowers. . . . The best of the Decca sides are those he made with the Spirits of Rhythm, *I've Got the World on a String* and *Way Down Yonder in New Orleans* especially, and also one solo called *What's the Use of Getting Used to You*. . . . The McKenzie voice is likely to pop out of any old record you might happen to have around the house. For example, I recently discovered a wonderful vocal by him on some old tune called *I Got to Have You*, waxed for Columbia by a group called the Hot Air Men, or something like that. . . . Columbia, by the way, issued the most sentimental of all McKenzie sides, about eight sides ten or so years ago, of which I remember most vividly *Just Friends*, *Time on My Hands* and *I Found You*. The backing on these, by Red's friends, is absolutely immense.

How did band vocalists ever get their jobs in the first place? And how did they feel once they got the kind of a job they'd always been dreaming about? This interview with Stuart Foster, a truly talented and highly respected guy who worked for Tommy Dorsey, Guy Lombardo and others, offers some good samples of the problems and emotions of many of the era's band singers. I still remember Stuart well, and I felt very sad when he died a few years ago.

Stuart Foster with singer Martha Wright and upcoming disc jockey William B. Williams

FOUR STAR FOSTER

Stuart Sang in the Church Choir, Then Joined Ina Ray and Lombardo before Achieving Real Fame with Dorsey

This is the story of Stuart Foster, the guy who sings with Tommy Dorsey, the guy who starts where Frank Sinatra left off with *Old Man River*, the guy who's the most talked-of band singer in the country today. It's the story, just as he told it to me over a couple of cakes a la mode with fudge sauce the other afternoon in an ice cream parlor to which we two nondrinking nonsmokers had retired.

The story starts with Pat Ruggles, the bass player and arranger, who dropped into the George F. Pavillion in Binghamton, N. Y., Stu's home town, on either a Wednesday or Saturday because those were the two nights when Len Fennell's band played there and Stu sang. "Come to New York with me and join Hank D'Amico's band," said Ruggles. "Who is Hank D'Amico?" asked Stu. "He is a great clarinetist who's being backed in a new band by Richard Himber and I'm supposed to help him organize," "Oh," said Stu. "Well, I'll phone you when I get to New York and speak to Hank," said Pat.

So Stu got word a few days later to come to New York. That was big stuff in Binghamton and it made the church choir sad because Stu was the soloist on *Come to Jesus*, singing those good whole notes so fine. But the choir gave him a big send-off and a beautiful gladstone bag, anyway, and Stu left. D'Amico's band had just one rehearsal, folded, and

347

Stu came back to Binghamton. "I was awfully embarrassed. I didn't know what to do with the bag. I offered to give it back but they wouldn't take it and I felt more foolish than ever. Finally I gave it to Jim Chronic, who led the choir, played organ, and coached me in singing. I felt better."

A year later Pat Ruggles joined Ina Ray Hutton and one midnight Stu got a frantic phone call. "We'll be through Binghamton at six this morning. Meet our bus at the corner of Court and Chenango and ride on to New York with us. We open at the Astor Roof. Okay?" "Er," said Stu slowly, "I think that . . ." But Pat had hung up.

At six in the morning, Stu met the bus at Court and Chenango. "The inside of that bus was the most gruesome sight I'd ever seen," says Stu, who hadn't been away from the family hearth much at this time and who certainly wasn't used to musicians in the raw. "Guys were lying in every direction, mouths open, snoring, and the smell was awful." So Stu climbed in gingerly, found an empty seat next to Ruggles and sat there "scared to death. I was still scared when I got to New York, so scared that I started thinking up excuses to go back home. I told 'em I had to go back to get my clothes. But they said I had to stay. So I stayed."

And Foster stayed for four years. The band broadcast the opening night. After the air-shot he phoned his folks in Binghamton. "How was it?" he asked. "Why, you weren't on the air." said his mother. "Sure I was," insisted Stu. "No, Tamer," said his mother, calling him by his right first name, "We heard a singer named Stuart Foster." So Stuart investigated and found that Ina Ray had changed his name from Tamer Aswad (honest, that's his real name) to Stuart Foster but had forgotten to tell him.

What sort of a name is Tamer Aswad? It's Syrian. Tamer's father was born in Syria, his mother in Albany, N. Y. Tamer was born in Binghamton, June 30, 1918, the oldest and smallest of five kids. His mother still calls him "The Pullet," which is the first egg, a small one, that a hen lays. Tamer worked in his Dad's furniture store and studied singing at the Ithaca Conservatory. His sister liked Bob Eberly and Jack Leonard and wanted her brother to sing like them. "But I wanted to imitate Dick Powell!"

Stuart's sister won out because when Foster sang with Ina Ray he sounded just like Eberly. George Paxton, arranger, manager and tenorman in the band, helped Stu a great deal, roomed with him, went to church with him every Sunday, encouraged him, too, especially after Foster's first write-up. "It was in Madison, Wisconsin, and it was horrible! It was a little better in Chicago, where we played next." Ina Ray stuck by him too. Stu says she's a much better leader than she is given credit for. She's no great technician, but she knows what she wants to hear, she's very astute, she follows an act wonderfully and she has a great conception of time. She worked awfully hard, too hard, in fact, so that during a theatre tour in Texas during 1944 she collapsed and the doctors told her she'd have to quit or else. So she quit, the band broke up and Stu went back to Binghamton for a vacation he'd been looking forward to for four years.

He'd been home less than a week when Charlie Yates, Ina's manager who also handles Tommy Reynolds, phoned and asked him to sing with Reynolds for a week at the Apollo Theatre in Harlem. "I was awfully tired, but Charlie was so persistent that I went. I had a great time there, too!" During that week he also did one radio show with Paxton's band (George had left Ina about a year before), subbing for Alan Dale. Music publisher Stan Stanley, noting that Stu was back in town and that Guy Lombardo needed a singer badly, phoned Guy and Guy phoned Stu backstage at the Apollo next day. "Want to join my band?" he asked. "I'm sorry, I'm tired," said Stu as politely as any music lover could to a question of this sort. "Oh, come on, I like your singing," said Guy. "No, I want to take a couple of months off. Besides, I sing too heavy for your band. Thanks just the same." Lombardo persisted. He phoned again the next day. Same thing happened, except it sounded a little bit better to Stu, because Guy talked about a six-month location and Stu hated the road by now and there was more talk about records and commercials. But Foster still didn't like the idea. So Guy came on up to the Apollo, a pretty incongruous combination. His wife came along, too, wearing, another incongruity, an ermine coat. Carmen came along, too, apparently to prove there were no hard feelings toward a possible successor. They broke Stu down quicker than you can say "Tamer Aswad."

"It did me no harm, I guess," says Foster today. "It was a big, happy family affair. I'd sit on the bandstand all night, sing maybe four songs. The rest of the time I'd be listening to Rosemarie asking me what time it was (she'd do that at least a dozen times a night), or else work the p.a. system. The brothers and I couldn't get together on phrasing. They wanted me to chop everything and I couldn't sing that way. It was pretty much of a bringdown altogether, especially when they'd do things like making me chop a phrase so that a flute in the background could come out. Finally Jimmy Brown came into the band. He'd been with Sammy Kaye and Blue Barron so naturally he knew the style. That was my cue to get out, so I did."

Stu emerged a better singer than when he'd joined,

however. "One thing the brothers did teach me to do was to sing on the beat. They broke me of that habit of singing way behind it, the way I did when I used to sing like Eberly. That was a good thing for me."

Before he left, Stu planned to take that vacation at last. But a lot of folks had told Tommy Dorsey, who was playing at the 400 Restaurant just a block and a half away, about Foster. "My morale was way low. I was scared to audition or even to go to see Tommy. But finally one night I went over. Who should be there but Carmen! He was wonderful. He paved the way. But when Tommy asked me to sing I was still too scared. Next day, though, I came to rehearsal and Tommy took me. You know the rest."

The rest is simple. Stuart Foster has caught on tremendously with Tommy as a singer. He has also caused a great deal of comment with his exhibitions of dialect on Dorsey's radio shows. "Picked it up listening to so many comedians. In all those theatres we used to play with Ina, I used to go on first for a number or so. After that I'd rush right out front and catch the rest of the acts. I picked up all that dialect stuff just by listening. Guess I've always been a ham at heart!"

As for me, after listening to Tamer Aswad confess everything, after seeing firsthand what a natural, unaffected guy he is, still admitting that he gets scared, that's he's got a lot to learn, that he's grateful—well, if that's what a ham is like, pass me that meat, son. That's for me!

Fostography

You can hear Stuart Foster on many Tommy Dorsey RCA Victor records. Soon to be issued are *There's No One but You* and *Like a Leaf in the Wind*. Other TD-SF sides recommended include *It's Never Too Late to Pray*, *A Door Will Open*, *That Went Out with High Button Shoes*, *Where Did You Learn to Love?*, *Aren't You Glad You're You?*, *You Are Love*, *Nobody Else but Me*, and, of course, Foster's great rendition of *Old Man River*.

Jerry Gray on the Rash of Glenn Miller Imitators
(June, 1950)—

I can't understand why certain bandleaders who had nothing at all to do with the development of the Glenn Miller style have suddenly taken it upon themselves to adopt this style and to cash in on the work of other people. Ralph Flanagan did not have the slightest connection with the Miller band, except, of course, that his name sounds like Bill Finegan, who did some very fine arranging for Glenn. As for Ray Anthony, I just remember him as having been a trumpeter who did not play with the band for too long a time.

I first met Dinah Shore late in 1938 when a mutual friend worked out a date for me with her roommate. I don't remember the mate, but I do remember Dinah, at the urging of her date (a big six-footer named Tiny Freeman), singing a cappella down there in my little Greenwich Village house while I provided some light backing with brushes on cymbals. She knocked me out, and I did what I could to help her get started, including publishing my far-out prediction for her success (printed elsewhere), and arranging auditions for her with numerous bandleaders, none of whom took her. Nevertheless, she soon made it big in radio on her own, thanks not only to her singing talent, but also because, as this interview as well as most of her interviews show, Dinah was (and still is) an extremely bright, intelligent and practical human being.

Dinah Shore, of NBC's Chamber Music Society of Lower Basin Street radio series, at a May, 1940 party at Cafe Society honoring Joe Sullivan, at the piano

DINAH SHORE

"Gee, that's wonderful. I like it lots. It's Boyd Raeburn, you say. I've heard a lot about him. I wonder if maybe it isn't a little too far advanced for the general public, though."

Dinah Shore Montgomery (that's how she signs all autographs) was catching up on her jazz via a phonograph and records in her dressing room backstage at the Paramount in New York. Out in Hollywood, it seems, the movie set doesn't stay up late, consequently doesn't get too much of a chance to maintain an interest in things like swing. Besides, George Montgomery's not an addict. He prefers tinkering with houses and walls and cars. And Dinah Shore Montgomery's a George Montgomery addict. Could be the reason why she hasn't been tinkering with jazz much of late.

"But, you know that Raeburn stuff—the public may catch onto it in time." Dinah is smart, shrewd, knows her public. Her words mean something. "I don't think the general public's ready for anything quite as advanced as this, but it's surprising how much more good jazz they'll take now than they did before—better music, too."

Dinah had a reason for that statement. "The way they've reduced prices in classical phonograph records has a lot to do with it. So many more people can get to hear really good music nowadays—and all they've got to do is to hear it once and they'll like it. It's no longer just the rich man's music. Good classical music's for everybody now."

A couple of days later Dinah was down at the Cafe Rouge of the Pennsylvania Hotel listening to Elliot Lawrence, fellow Columbia artist, about whom she had heard so much. "This is it!" she explained. "This is it!" she repeated. "He's going to reeducate the American public."

More clear, commercial logic. If the public won't take it the hard, abrupt, more advanced way like Raeburn, they'll become inoculated by the sweet, danceable, moody music of Lawrence. Maybe Lawrence isn't so dumb, either!

Dinah's a smart girl, a very smart girl. I've known that ever since her tenure on WNEW when she sang five days a week for free and we were trying to do something about her future. She wanted to sing with a band very badly. She worked with Mitch Ayres at Murray's in Westchester, with Johnny Gart, who had a Hammond organ unit at the Shelton Hotel, for a short while, and she sang with Peter Dean's band at

Dinah visits Bing on his show. Or was it Bing visiting Dinah on her show?

351

Nick's for two weeks. She auditioned for Benny Goodman twice, for Tommy Dorsey twice, for Jimmy Dorsey, for Bob Crosby and for other bands, but nobody wanted her. She sang great then, too—in fact she was better for bands because she was less stylized. But you know the way so many bandleaders are.

Finally Dinah got her break. She switched from WNEW to NBC sustaining. The future wasn't too bright there, especially with the terrible backings she got from strictly studio musicians and arrangers. And so when Tommy Dorsey changed his mind and wired her from the midwest to come join his band, but quick, all of us friends got pretty excited. I urged her to hop the first plane.

"Nothing doing," said Dinah, with cold, clear, commercial logic. "I'm in radio now. There's a much better future for me here on my own. If I don't make good with Tommy there's no telling where I'll wind up." So Dinah wound up her good, right voice by herself and—well, look where she tossed herself—right on the top of the heap.

Dinah Shore, just in case you haven't read these basic facts in some movie-fan magazine, was born in Nashville, ran away for one evening at the tender age of twelve or so to sing in a nightclub, only to wind up larynx to larynx with her parents who were sitting at a ringside table, went to Vanderbilt University, where she was a cheerleader and where the Governor of Tennessee used to do her homework for her (and not too well) while she went out and campaigned for his reelection (both she and he didn't do too well again). She sang on local radio station WSM, where she used to have to stand six feet from a mike because she chirped so loud, finally came to New York in 1938, first reinforced by money from her family, hung around singing but not earning, had her allowance cut off till—boom—it happened on New Year's Eve, 1939.

She was supposed to do a club job on Long Island for $25. She had just a dime left to her name, but she felt so good about the job that she took a ten-cent bus home instead of the nickel subway. She arrived to find the note that said the job had been canceled. She busted out in tears, borrowed a nickel, called her family in Nashville, collect, and said, "Please wire me some money. It's New Year's Eve and I'm alone and I'm hungry and I haven't a cent left." Her family, who thought cutting her off her

Dinah returns to New York and the Paramount

352

allowance would bring her home, was so impressed with the way she was sticking it out down to her last nickel, that they sent her $25 plus an assurance that they'd keep on sending more till she made good.

Shortly after that, thanks to Peter Dean and Ginger Johnson, she made good on NBC and the financial angle lost its acuteness. She was a big pet around the studios, for Dinah was cute, vivacious and very real. She had a wonderful knack of getting along with everybody. She used to run around in sloppy sweaters and woolly skirts, a happy relief from many of the pseudo-glamour chicks who tried to impress folks with their voice by means of other and usually more advanced attributes.

It's a wonderful thing to be able to report that Dinah, today, has lost none of that natural charm, that sincerity, that ability to be interested in other people, in their problems, in their attitude toward life. If Dinah ever started to enter the phony world that engulfs some of the stars of today, I'm sure she did the neatest and quickest backstep it ever saw. Undoubtedly there were times when some folks tried to push her into it. Undoubtedly Dinah pushed back just twice as hard.

To get back to that career. . . . She had a commercial for a few weeks with the late Ben Bernie, but got canned because she wasn't what the sponsor wanted. The hucksters were working even then. Her next commercial was with Eddie Cantor, who, wisely enough, grabbed her after she had achieved so much fame on the Chamber Music Society of Lower Basin Street radio shows and on Victor Records that she couldn't miss.

Next month Dinah starts her new commercial for the Ford Company. It has only one drawback. Mr. Montgomery, after a long wait, recently surprised Dinah with a Chrysler convertible station wagon. You know sponsors. Anybody wanta buy a Chrysler convertible station wagon?

Dinah's going to continue recording for Columbia. She thinks Manie Sacks, its recording director, is the greatest guy in the entire music business. As for her musical favorites, she's not decided between Frank and Perry. She loves the former's shading and phrasing and the latter's quality and control. "Too many singers don't pay enough attention to dynamics," she says. "And they're so important. You know the kind of a singer who really thrills me? The kind who gives you the feeling that he's always got a lot in reserve and makes it exciting for you while you're sort of waiting for him to let out all the way. That element of surprise, of suspense, is terribly important when you're an artist. Once you show 'em everything right away, you're licked, because they have nothing more to look forward to."

As for the girls in her field, the one who has impressed her most of late is Peggy Lee. Dinah likes her simplicity, her sincerity, her style. "You know what she sounds like to me? Like a nice little girl who's trying to be tough. She's so great!" Dinah also leans toward Maxine Sullivan, the way she sang on those records, especially *Nice Work If You Can Get It*. She admits that Maxine had a big influence on her style when she was still back in Nashville. She also likes Carlotta Dale, who used to sing with Savitt and Bradley, because more than just about any other singer she gave one the feeling that she had a great deal in reserve. "And then, of course, there's Ella. I love her!" Dinah wants a copy of the V-Disc of *That's Rich* on which Ella riffed breaks and a coda on *Bugle Call Rag*. "And why hasn't Pearl Bailey made any more records like *Tired*? What a style she has!"

As for bands, Dinah hasn't been listening to them too avidly. She got a big boot out of Elliot Lawrence and she has been a Duke fan from way back. She also likes Thornhill and Herman. She follows soloists and records pretty closely. One of the first things she asked me when we saw each other after a number of years was, "Do you still have that wonderful record of Coleman Hawkins, *Talk of the Town*—you know, the one that was broken on the outside and I could never hear the first couple of bars? Gee, I'd like to hear that again. I'd also like to hear those first few bars sometime!"

There's one singer, though, she raves about more than anybody else. His name is John Raitt and he was the star of *Carousel*, the Broadway musical. He made a record called *Soliloquy* on Decca "that," says Dinah, "gives George and me goose bumps every time we play it. John's a lyric baritone, he has a legitimate voice, to me the greatest voice in America, but he's not at all stiff or pompous. As a matter of fact he loves to listen to Frankie. I have a feeling he'd like to phrase like Frankie, too."

Number One on the list of favorites in any and all fields, though, is George, the Montgomery, former Montana sheepherder, present movie star. He's not too interested in jazz; he likes it enough, but that's about all. But that relationship between Dinah and George! "Well, I can say only one thing," and Mrs. M. goes right ahead and says it. "If he asked me tomorrow to give up singing, I'd give it up tomorrow."

Here's hoping that that tomorrow never comes!

353

Dick Haymes, for me, had the greatest natural voice of any of the band singers. He was likable, well-educated, seemingly dogmatic but, I suspect, never too sure of himself. If only he'd had better control of himself, he might have realized some of the laudable ambitions he talked about here.

Dick with right arm Gordon Jenkins

DICK HAYMES PLANS

As soon as Dick Haymes had finished his first show with Tommy Dorsey he told Tommy off. Not in any belligerent, bullheaded way, but strictly in man-to-man fashion. "Tommy," he said, "I appreciate what you're telling me about how you want me to sing. But I don't want to sound like Frank or like Jack Leonard. Besides, you must have taken me because you liked the way I sing. So let me sing that way, won't you? I want to be me and nobody else."

Dorsey respected Haymes for this. It was good common sense, and, besides, it was straightforward and right to the point. You can't get mad at a guy for believing in himself and letting you know about it.

Today, a distinct Hollywood, radio and phonograph record success, Dick maintains the same philosophy. "Be what you are. Affectations aren't for me. If you're going to be a male singer, don't be half a man. Don't use a lot of cooing tricks. Sing out, big, strong and virile. And if you're a woman, be feminine and sing like one.

"The world's too full of phonies who are trying to get by with a lot of synthetic tricks. If you're going to do something, do it the right way. If you're going to be a singer, sing and don't spend all your time showing off your knowledge of chords and forgetting all about the song. If the melody isn't important enough, why sing it at all?"

Haymes has been that direct and that outspoken all his life. Even back in his prep school days, he eschewed affectations, which meant that he limited himself to a pretty small circle of friends. And that form of selectivity still holds today, though it has sometimes been mistaken as a form of snobbishness. "No, I got a pretty good idea of who my friends were in the music business back in the days when I got my first big break with Harry's band and then later on with Benny and Tommy. I've still got them and some more, of course, whom we made out here in Hollywood, but that's all. We're not interested in the rest."

"We" refers to himself and to Joanie, his exceptionally pretty wife, who used to double between the Copacabana and the Lincoln Hotel in New York, working at the former and gazing adoringly at her future husband in the latter while he sang for Harry James. Today, besides appearing under the name of Joanne Dru in movies like *Abie's Irish Rose* and *Red River*, she shares his comfortable home with him and their two children, Skipper and Pigeon, said home consisting of three houses, a stable, a riding ring, a swimming pool and a tennis court. It's all located in the San Fernando Valley, far enough away from Hollywood so that Dick can beg off pretty easily from the social life out there which he dislikes so much. "Ever go to one of those parties?" he asks. "Everybody's trying to cut everybody else, just like a jam session, and if you don't get up to perform, they think you're a snob. When I go to a party, I want to have fun and I don't want to work."

Work is a very serious thing with Dick. "Singing is being thrown away by too many people. They don't take it seriously enough. I'm making a career of it, not only of singing, but of all of show business. To me it's just like any other career, like law and like medicine. You study and you learn and you apply yourself and after a good long while you become a success."

Dick isn't satisfied with what he's doing. He wasn't satisfied singing with bands, though "it gave me great experience. Harry was a great friend, Benny was a good taskmaster, and Tommy Dorsey was the greatest leader in the world to work for. Not only did he insist on right backgrounds for a singer that didn't drown him out, but do you know that he actually knew all the words of every song I sang? But band singing is so limited—that one-chorus-and-sit-down routine, always in tempo. And anyway, the guys almost always play too loud."

Singing, in itself, is too limited for Dick. He wants to act in a few more movies, preferably opposite Jane Wyatt, Ann Sheridan or Martha Scott, sing in a Broadway musical, then eventually become a movie

Dick and the Andrews Sisters

director and a producer. "It's amazing how little progress they've made in the movies. It's strictly a business with them. They work out cut-and-dried, foolproof formulas and work them to death, over and over again. I'd like to get in there and be given the chance to create something original. The movies, after all, are the greatest medium for advancement we've ever had, and yet what are we doing about it?

"Actually, I guess the trouble is that we have so few real leaders in the entertainment field. That goes for jazz, too. Outside of Woody and Duke, what bands have really tried to improve music? The others are just trying to keep a dead art alive. It's the same old tenor and trumpet chorus routine, always playing the same stale old riffs.

"Of course there are a few musicians I'll always like: Benny and Tommy and Bill Harris and Mel Powell and Chubby Jackson, just the way there are some singers, the sincere kind, who always thrill me —singers like Bing and Frank (Frank, by the way, is the only real creator we've had in our field in the last ten years) and Buddy Clark, who has a great natural voice, and Herb Jeffries. Then, among the girls, there are Margaret Whiting and Ella Fitzgerald, who never use any of that overrated schmaltz, and a girl whom nobody talks about much but who's great by me, Pauline Byrne. But most of the others always seem to be trying too hard to impress."

Dick tries hard too, but it's to satisfy himself rather than to attract attention. He's not sure that he'll ever be satisfied, and he's sort of hoping he won't be because to him "satisfaction is a dangerous thing. It makes you stop working and that's no good."

Some of the things Dick has never been completely satisfied with are his movies: *Diamond Horseshoe*, *State Fair* ("though I liked making it more than the others because I had to play the part of an eighteen-year old boy and to a guy who's almost thirty that's a real challenge"), *Do You Love Me*, *The Shocking Miss Pilgrim* and his latest, *Carnival in Costa Rica*. As for his Decca records, he thinks the best are *Easy to Love* and *The Lord's Been Good to Me*, the latter from his *State Fair* album, though it wasn't in the movie.

Come to think of it, the Lord's been pretty good to Dick Haymes, who was born into a family where music and adventure were abundant and where financial security was not exactly scarce. Dick's mother was a concert singer who started her oldest son on his career at a very early age. Though the family traveled a lot (Dick's father was a writer and a cattleman), Marguerite Haymes insisted that Dick practice as much as possible, a part of his training which he still retains. The fact that Dick was gifted with a naturally resonant voice, more so than that of his brother Bob who also became a singer (he's now known as Bob Stanton), undoubtedly encouraged him and made him stick with it despite a decided tendency to indulge in outdoor activities. Now that he has more free time on his hands, a condition that has become identified with life in Hollywood, Dick rides a great deal, plays tennis often, swims a lot and is trying to figure out some way of holding his nightly movie sessions outdoors. That the life agrees with him is obvious: he has jumped from a hundred and thirty to a hundred and seventy-five pounds since he left Harry James.

"Maybe I have been lucky. I know I owe Mother a great deal. And what a break when I got Gordon Jenkins as musical supervisor! When it comes to music, that guy's both my arms."

How long Dick and Gordy will work together is conjectural. The combination should last as long as Dick lasts as a singer, but nobody knows, Dick least of all, when he's going to forsake that art form. For Dick is ambitious, he's intelligent, and he's a man's man who wants to go ahead, straight and fast, to whatever goal he sets for himself. Right now he's looking forward more and more to goals outside of radio and record singing, first, perhaps, to musical comedy ("just so I can really sing out for once"). But eventually he hopes and he expects to branch out into broader fields, to a position where he can convince more and more of the world that the right way to live is to work hard, not to be too easily satisfied, to think straight and, above all, to be honest with yourself and with your fellowmen.

This is the second of several interviews I had with Frank Sinatra, on neither of which he held back any punches. At the time of this one, Frank was having his troubles with Mitch Miller, his recording chief at Columbia, as well as with music in general. Here he disdains any attack on Miller, but he does unburden himself about what to him seem to be decadent, almost immoral conditions taking over the field of music—much to the like of the commercially-oriented executives and to the disgust of some idealistic artists like Sinatra. Times haven't changed too much, have they?

FRANK SINATRA

When Tommy Dorsey's band was playing the Astor Roof several years ago, a young girl approached his vocalist, Frank Sinatra, and asked him for his autograph. After he'd given it to her, she smiled sweetly and murmured, "Thanks. Now all I need is three more of these and I can trade them in for one of Bob Eberly!"

It was all a rib, of course, but Sinatra, who was a mighty touchy lad in those days, full of ambition and the suspicions that usually go with it, didn't like it. It was instigated by Buddy Rich, Dorsey's drummer and probably the guy Frank hated most in the whole world. And so, just to prove to everyone how much he hated Rich, when Buddy cut out of the Dorsey band to start his own group, Frank put a whole hunk of thousand dollar bills into his band, and lost them. Which also proves how Sinatra changes.

Right now his biggest interest, outside of his family and career (perhaps even bigger than the latter), seems to be boxing. He's backing a fighter and according to reports, for several weeks he was considered very much in the running as promoter for the Joe Louis-Joe Walcott return bout. Few people know that he's at least partially responsible for the latter's comeback, having promoted the Walcott-Gans fight which started Joe on the road to Louis. Sinatra lost another hunk of thousand dollar bills there.

You'd think, of course, that the guy would stick to music, especially because he always wanted so terribly hard to become a success and because he worked so hard to be one. But if you know Frank real well, know how much he likes good stuff, know what basically good taste he has in everything artistic (he's recently started to draw and paint, has turned out some impressive stuff, and now plans to study intensively under a private teacher), you can begin to understand why he's pretty fed up with the music business and why his thoughts and his ever-prevalent ambition go roaming off into other fields.

Right now certain conditions in the music business really have him down. Chances are that he can't stand *Your Hit Parade* any more than most of us can. He hates almost all agents savagely, so much so that he's planning to start his own agency just so he can be rid of them, and also because he feels that good young talent deserves more attention than it has been getting.

But his biggest gripe of all right now is the terrible trash turned out by Tin Pan Alley. Frank was a pretty weary guy when he sounded off during a short break on a recording date on what was wrong with music, but it seems that when you're really pooped you relax more, you lose your inhibitions, and you say what you want to say. Some of the stuff Sinatra passed along was so libelous that it's not printable, but all the rest is something The Voice feels just as strongly about, even though the language may be more pianissimo.

"About the popular songs of the day," pet-peeves Frankie, "they've become so decadent, they're so bloodless. As a singer of popular songs, I've been looking for wonderful pieces of music in the popular vein— what they call Tin Pan Alley songs. You can *not* find a thing. All you get is a couple of songs like *Apple Blossom Wedding* and *Near You* . . . [censored]. . . .

"If the music business is to lead the public—and actually we do lead it as to the things it likes—we must give people things that move them emotionally, make them laugh, too. But we're not doing it and there's something wrong someplace.

"I don't think the music business has progressed enough. There are a lot of people to blame for this. The songwriter in most cases finds he has to prostitute his talents if he wants to make a buck. That's because not enough publishers are buying the better kind of music. The publisher is usually a fly-by-night guy anyway and so to make a few fast bucks he buys a very bad song, very badly written. And the recording companies are helping those guys by recording such songs. I don't think the few extra bucks in a song that becomes a fast hit make a difference in the existence of a big recording company or a big publishing firm. If they turned them down, it wouldn't do them any harm and it would do music some good.

"I'm not talking about songs like *Peg of My Heart*. It's a pretty song, a love story. But some of those other songs are absolutely pointless. They go no place. You can't get your teeth into them. You can't find a way to dress them up . . . [censored]. . . .

"You know, I talk to a lot of kids. They're pretty smart; they've been around, buying records and listening to bands. They don't like those bad songs, at least not the kids with whom I speak individually. They know all the great Glenn Miller things, they constantly mention songs like *When You're Awake, Polka Dots and Moonbeams*—wonderful pieces of music the publisher took because they sounded good to him. But he never pressed the point and they never became hits. They just don't seem to work on songs like that. Instead, they'd rather take an easy song, one that's a novelty. It's a very short shot that will click right away, but over the years it doesn't last. Most publishers don't think that far ahead, though.

"I'm not classing all novelties as bad. *Civilization* is a novelty and it makes a lot of sense. At least the guy tells a story. I don't care where a happening takes place so long as the writer tells a story about it. But when a guy writes a song called *Apple Blossom*

Wedding! What the hell does that MEAN? And you may quote me. I don't understand it, and I've been singing a lot of songs."

Sinatra's not the kind of guy who'll just sound off on what's wrong with music without offering some pretty constructive ideas about how to right those wrongs. As he has preached in his racial tolerance pleas in movies, on the air, and very often in person, education is probably the greatest remedy. Teach the kids what it's all about and as they grow older they'll refuse to accept the tripe that Tin Pan Alley feeds them. "I'd like to see popular music brought into grammar and high schools as part of the education, if the proper people were teaching it. Or possibly people in the music business could make appearances in schools and discuss these things. With all the people in the music business, we could get enough people to go to so many schools each year and explain the inner intricacies of making a song hit, the type of song that is bought, one that is considered a good song and one that is considered a poor song. Show the progress that jazz has made the past few years; explain where jazz is going, for instance jazz like Alvy West's Little Band, which is tasty and wonderful, or Joe Mooney's, which is interesting."

Surprisingly, Frankie has not kept up with most of the newer bands. He seems to be more interested in songs than in their instrumental interpretation. He remembers some Sauter, however, the stuff Eddie wrote for Goodman. "Actually, I haven't heard too much of Eddie's stuff recently," explains Sintra, "because I've been so busy that I haven't heard anything.

But the stuff I've heard Sauter write for years is wonderful because it goes someplace. Dizzy's and Raeburn's stuff I don't understand. Maybe it's a little too far ahead of me. I don't think, though, that as a national liking it has much of a future."

Altogether, then, the future of music doesn't look too bright to Frank. The song publishing business is beset by commercialism, apparently by people incapable of recognizing good songs and certainly incapable of promoting and selling them. Some progressive music, for him, has a good chance of becoming accepted. But he admits that he hasn't kept up with the times, so far as bands go. Chances are that if he ever did take time out from his various outside interests, he'd become progressive jazz's most powerful champion. Right now, though, he's much more interested in his new house, in painting, in boxing and, of course, in his championing the cause of all minorities. And so he'll even sing on *Your Hit Parade* and record things like *The Dum Dot Song*.

But Frankie, much like Tommy Dorsey, his former boss who influenced him more than just musically, is liable to blow up and off at the most unexpected moments. He feels things very keenly, just as all really sensitive people do, and after a while they affect him so much that he just has to do something about them. And so don't be too surprised if Sinatra should suddenly go ahead and open up a modern, progressive school of music, or something like that—anything to alleviate his pent-up emotions about what, to this progressive, far-thinking and thoroughly honest guy, is so very, very wrong with music.

Peggy Lee, whom I used to date during her Goodman band days, had begun to find her niche when this interview appeared. An extremely sensitive, sentimental and warm human being, turned inward for too many years, she began to blossom as a singer, songwriter and woman after she met and married guitarist Dave Barbour, "the only man I ever really loved," as she later told me. Dave, who was still living when this interview took place, also has some interesting things to say about the love and music which he and Peggy shared so beautifully.

HOORAY FOR LOVE!

Peggy Lee Would Like to Find Its Magic Spell Everywhere; Lets Dave Do All the Talking about Armstrong, Bop and Critics

If she could just remember everybody's birthday and could spend all of her Thanksgivings at home, Peggy Lee would be an extremely happy girl. For it's the little things like that which count most in the life of one who is recognized by many as the biggest singer in the business today. Born and raised in North Dakota, part of a large family in which the parents just didn't have enough time to spread affection as thickly as Peggy wanted it, the soft, kind sort of love now means more than anything else to this loving mother and wife. Sure, she's interested in her career, in her singing, in her songwriting, but most of all she wants and expects to find her happiness through associating with people.

"It would help everything if people loved each other more," she says. For a time, Peggy was a seemingly cold, calculating performer. She did her job all right, but you had the feeling that she was just up there singing and not much more. There wasn't a really warm feeling emanating from this gorgeous blonde. Maybe she just didn't know how to project. Maybe she just was scared. But for quite a time those who knew Peggy well, who knew her as a sensitive, sentimental, love-seeking girl, kept hoping that she would be able to transmit some of that inner warmth to the rest of the world around her.

When Peggy's boss, Benny Goodman, took on a guitarist named Dave Barbour, Peggy started coming out of her shell. It was a gradual transition until now "when I get out on a stage I feel as if I know people so well that I can say to any one of them, 'How's your family?' and I wouldn't feel foolish. And that attitude comes from being around Durante and Crosby. Jimmy is so wonderful. He's interested in big things and in little things. And he's interested in people, especially in little people. I can't say enough fine things about him as a person," a rave, by the way, which appears to be shared by just about everybody else in show business.

Bing was another inspiration. "The first time I met him," Peggy recalls, "he knew all the little things about me, about my house, even about Dave's health, which wasn't too good at the time. He asked me about them, just as if he'd always known me. Bing wants to know about people, all about them. I think that's why he's so happy."

Peggy admires a couple of other men, too. They're Alec Wilder and Willard Robison, both of whom write songs "in the direction I'd like to see vocal music progress. They're sort of poems set to music, little character sketches. This is nothing new, I know, but it hasn't been done enough."

Music is good to Peggy so long as it does no bad to people. Progress to her is "a big turmoil. To make progress, you have to make a mess." She feels, however, that she's not qualified to talk about technical progress in music, though she does feel that bop has had "a dangerous effect on young musicians, not as musicians but as people. . . . But let Dave talk about that; he knows much more about it."

Dave thinks, quote, that "bop is sensational, the

Dave and Peggy

damnedest thing that ever happened, a terrific stride forward. But the actions of some of the cultists are too much for effect. Some of them stand and gape like idiots or they stare right through you. As for those ties and hats, they're sort of childish, so you can't be too disturbed about that."

What does disturb Dave, though, is the fact that prettiness, sentiment and emotion are being lost. Though he likes bop, still to Dave "Louis can do no wrong. He can play just a straight, simple lead line on a song and it's great with me. But why can't these young kids see that? Is it because they were raised in a generation when Louis was supposedly through because he didn't win any polls or anything?

"Another thing: the guys who were hot men some years ago but who are now considered fools by some of the young, cultish kids, are really thorough musicians, guys like Babe Russin, Herbie Haymer, Will Bradley, Chris Griffin and so on. Yet most of these cats today can't sustain a note. It seems to me that outside of what they're doing, the bop world finds music in general a pretty abstract thing."

The coming music for Dave is Afro-Cuban. "That's really going to happen!" he predicts. All those intricate rhythms knock him out and for an experienced guitarist who's played in many a topflight rhythm section, that's quite a feat. "My big ambition now is to have a band with about five men in the front line, a regular rhythm section and then about four extra rhythm guys."

Reminded that such music is a far cry from the Armstrong type about which he had just been raving, Dave promptly admitted that "I like all kinds of music, except maybe Hawaiian. Which reminds me, those record reviews in METRONOME, they're almost like a cult. They sound as though they're afraid to admit to a little sentimentality in music." This is a subject, by the way, on which Dave and Peggy Barbour concur completely. It reflects a mutual philosophy, expressed by Mr. Barbour by "You're not being a boob or an idiot to want to like people. That's the way it's supposed to be. That's a positive type of thinking!"

Mrs. Barbour puts it even more personally. "When you see unloveliness in others, it's because you have some unloveliness in yourself." Which seems straight and to the point.

There's a great deal of oneness between Peggy and Dave. Not only do they think alike musically and philosophically, but they also share another major interest, their cute daughter, Nicki. Then there's their home, an unpretentious, rambling house in North Hollywood, from which they don't roam very much. It's pretty obvious why. Bop, *Manana*, Afro-Cuban rhythms, Durante, Crosby, Armstrong, Wilder and Robison—they're all fine, extra added attractions. But there are bigger things for Peggy and Dave and they've found them, recognize them and hope to be able to cherish them forever.

Gene Krupa on a Common Jazz Cause
(September, 1948)—

We all like jazz, so why not pull together instead of one faction always trying to tear down the other? I like bop and I like dixie. If a guy or a band plays one musical style well, then let's encourage him. But let's discourage bad musicianship, and I mean by that mickey-mouse bands. By merely fighting among ourselves, we've giving those no-goods just that much more of a chance to get ahead of us.

Few people appear to believe less in the greatness of Ella Fitzgerald than Ella Fitzgerald herself. This interview is typical. I had talked with Ella many times before and I have talked with her many times since, and the graciousness, the kindness, the enthusiasm have always been there. But so has the self-doubt. I keep wondering why.

ELLA FITZGERALD

Ella

More girl singers today think that the best girl singer in the world is Ella Fitzgerald. This sounds like a slogan that could have been written by the copy department of Decca Records, for whom Ella records, by Gale Associates, who manage and book her, by Virginia Wicks, her press agent, or even by Ray Brown, her personal representative and husband.

Actually it is being written by a Fitzgerald admirer of long standing, by a guy who was completely knocked out when he first heard Ella with Chick Webb's band at the Savoy Ballroom late in 1935, who predicted at that time that she would be the greatest of them all and who, since then, has interviewed countless other singers, the majority of whom have assured him that, so far as they were concerned, his prediction was absolutely correct.

His most recent interviewee would say no such thing. I don't think the idea ever even occurred to her. For, you see, modesty is one of Ella Fitzgerald's prime virtues, a type of real, unphony modesty that graces the character of few people in this business of ours. In that recent interview she talked enthusiastically about the many good singers she thinks there are in this world and how very wrong she thinks it is for anybody, including herself, to tear down others. She was particularly irked by the remarks of one of our youngish boy singers during a recent radio interview in which he proceeded to air his opinions (and they were very strong ones) about how bad this and that singer (Ella escaped) sounded to him.

Ella has always had a fear of being considered big-headed. That is why she owns very few of her own records, why she is invariably pleased and surprised when somebody tells her he has one of the things she did way back with Chick, and why she seems to get such a big boot out of reviving songs she had forgotten all about. "I used to think," she told me, "that people would think I was bigheaded if I went into a record store and asked for my own records. So I never went for them and now I find I have very few records of my own."

363

Some of the old Ella Fitzgerald records are really exciting things. There's that first hit she had with Chick, *Sing Me a Swing Song*, and one that came out a little bit later on called *A Little Bit Later On*. Then there's her record of *Tain't What You Do, It's the Way That You Do It*, in which she scatted a bit and wound up (she doesn't know exactly why) singing the word "rebop," which as a word didn't get any further than that record for many years. (Now watch somebody, not Miss F., announce that Ella invented rebop!) Then there are those sides she made on Victor with Benny Goodman, *Take Another Guess, Goodnight, My Love* and *Did You Mean It?* which had to be recalled because of previous contractual agreements. And then there was that great *Undecided* bit, which she is reviving these days, and three fine things she did for V-Discs, *I'll Always Be in Love with You, That's Rich* and *I'll See You in My Dreams*.

Ella loves the old tunes, loves them more than the new things she too often is pressured into doing, despite her better judgment. She wants very much to do an album of such standards as *Ill Wind* and *I've Got the World on a String*. She also likes especially *The Boy Next Door, Easy to Love* and Benny Carter's *My Kind of Trouble Is You*, which she wants to wax.

You can see from this sort of selection that Ella likes pretty things and is also pretty much of a sentimentalist. After all, she loves ballads and when it comes to dancing (she started as a dancer, got scared when she was supposed to hoof it that famous night at the Harlem Opera House when she won the amateur show and on the spur of the moment started to sing), you're most likely to get Ella and her handsome, pleasant husband, bassist Ray Brown, out on the floor by feeding them a waltz. "That's such a beautiful dance," she says. "Remember how they used to dance it up at the Savoy? They don't dance like that much any more. Now everything is so fast and you hardly ever hear a waltz. If you don't Lindy Hop, what happens?

"Maybe it's just a trend. I hope so. We have a lot of bands to listen to, but not enough to dance to. Before, most of your listening bands could be danced to, but now. . . . It's not entirely the musicians' fault, either. Maybe people just don't like to dance any more, I don't know."

Dancing appeals to Ella so much that now she wants to learn a Latin number, "just so I can go through all those motions," she grins. "I also want to do a French number. They're so cute," thinks the gal with the warmest, cutest grin in captivity. Her success as a novelty singer (she insists that she doesn't like to do only ballads but definitely prefers a variety) has been reassured by the country's reaction to her record of *Basin Street Blues*. She's especially tickled with the question put to her by one of her fans who didn't recognize his idol and asked her, "How did you and Louis Armstrong come to make a record together?" If you've heard the record, you'll know that the "Louis Armstrong" on that side is actually Ella imitating one of her idols. She has had several occasions to regret that night when for some reason or other she first decided to do her Satchmo stunt, for though it has gone over big ever since, it has wreaked havoc on her vocal chords, almost as much as the front-row people in nightclubs who invariably start smoking when she starts to sing.

Armstrong isn't the only trumpeter whom Ella admires. She is intensely fond of Dizzy's work. "I like him just the way he is," she says. And the bands of Les Brown, Tex Beneke and Ray McKinley are among her pets, "especially Brown's because they play a variety and sound like bands used to sound."

As noted before, Ella isn't discouraged about the future of the dance band. She is, however, pretty discouraged about her own future, not as a singer, of course, but as a songwriter. "I used to love to write," she says. "I had big ambitions. But I got into ASCAP and that's as far as I've gotten and probably as far as I'll go." It seems that Ella hasn't lost faith in her ability to write songs (she penned, among others, *You Showed Me the Way, A-Tisket A-Tasket, My Little Yellow Basket* and *Oh, But I Do*, which King Cole recorded), but she gets a little weary when she realizes what happens to some of her efforts. She feels almost bitter about the fact that she wrote the lyrics she sings on her record of *Robbins' Nest*, yet they were never published and she gets no credit for them. She has just completed lyrics for Duke's pretty *In a Mellotone* and hopes for more recognition there. "All that ever happens when I write a song is that a publisher says, 'Why don't you record it and then maybe we can do some business?' There's always an angle." Ella, you can see, doesn't like those angles.

It's really quite amazing how different this Fitzgerald gal is from most of those in the business in which she is such a leader. The things she doesn't like are the things too many people stand for and the things she does like are so straight and simple that to many people they may seem either corny or foreign. So far as I'm concerned, the music business would do well to look up to Ella Fitzgerald not only as its leader among all of its great girl singers, but also as one of its finest human beings, an unspoiled, unselfish, unaffected, understanding and wonderful woman!

The first song Tony Bennett ever recorded (under the name of Joe Bari) was one I wrote called *Vieni Qui*. On the date, he confided that he'd much rather sing jazz, and after I'd heard how he performed my ballad, I wished he had tried something else. But despite all this, Tony and I managed to maintain a cordial friendship, probably because of our mutual love of jazz. When this interview appeared, Tony was beginning to really make it as a ballad singer, thanks to the same Mitch Miller whom Sinatra couldn't get along with. But was he happy? Read on.

TONY BENNETT

A Hot Commercial Bet Likes Hot Jazz Better

The hottest singer in the business, as this is being written, likes the hottest sort of music, perferably unwritten. He is Tony Bennett, whose renditions of ballads like *Because of You, Cold, Cold Heart* and *Blue Velvet*, have brought lumps to people's throats and to Tony's wallet, but which aren't at all the kind of songs that Tony wanted to sing when he first started in the business.

I happened to know him then, just about three years ago. Freddy Katz, who is Lena Horne's accompanist, used to go to an obscure club out on Long Island to hear Tony, who was then known as Joe Bari. Another friend of Freddy's was Ray Muscarella, who used to manage Vic Damone and who was looking for another singer to build. After a lot of persuasion, Freddy got Ray to listen to Tony by bringing him over to the Muscarella home. Joe, or Tony, was then, as he still is, a wonderful, modest, shy guy. He also had a musical style. Ray liked him and started him off on a record label in which he was interested. But the company flopped, despite a good jazz side that Tony cut, and so Ray put his boy into clubs. He was singing at La Comedia when Herb Jeffries heard him. Herb was recording for Columbia then, but he still kept after Mitch Miller, the company's a. and r. head, to catch Tony. Addenda: Tony is now the biggest thing on Columbia; Herb now records for Coral.

Tony, who has great respect for great jazz men, raves about Jeffries. "He has it all the way, both as a singer and as a person." Tony also likes Ella and Billie and Mabel Mercer, but his favorites of all are two relatively obscure singers, about whom many other knowing musicians and singers also rave, David Allen and Sylvia Sims.

Tony still feels close to jazz. He used to be a big jazz shouter, sort of in the Frankie Laine medium. Now that he has established himself, he'd like to cut some jazz sides, but he doesn't want to sing the way he used to. "I've been listening to the singers who really jump, men like Louis Armstrong and Nat Cole and Frank Sinatra. I've been experimenting a great deal, and I've found that I should tone down. Once I get it right, I hope they'll let me make some jazz sides."

Tony realizes that becoming a top record star takes a lot of time, and that that time is represented in much experimenting. "Some of those first sides I made just didn't feel right. The keys were all wrong and they were filled with gimmicks. Now, though, I think we have hit the right approach. It's the soft sound that has really done it—that and the right keys.

"You know, one thing I've found out—and this is very important—and that is that you can't fool the public. The more I feel what I am doing, the better response I get. In theatres, for example, the minute I stop thinking about the audience and about what I'm singing, I start losing them.

"Taking it a step further back: unless I feel that I am singing a song sincerely and honestly, I feel insecure. But as soon as I feel secure, then I know that my audience will be with me. You just can't fool them.

The more correctly you interpret a song, the more an audience will listen to you."

They're really listening to Tony these days, all over the country, on wax and wherever he chooses to play in person. He used to be a scared guy, hoping he'd make it, working very hard, but hardly an assured performer. Now, though, he has no more fears. "I'm happy and I feel at home. I'm not going to worry. I'm just going to go out and sing my head off each time."

Columbia will probably keep him on the kind of material with which he has succeeded so handsomely. But just as soon as that craze starts tapering off, Tony'll be rarin' to jump onto the jump wagon. Maybe he'll do so even before then. For there's no getting away from it, this Bennett boy loves his jazz. He's been listening to it for so long now that he's just got to have his say one day. And when he does, it'll be because of Herb, Nat, Louis, Frankie, Ella, Billie, Mabel, David, Sylvia and other jazz idols, and NOT because of you!

Every once in a while a writer comes up with a piece which he feels is truly inspired. This interview with Frankie Laine was one of mine. The inspiration came solely from Frankie himself. I can't remember ever having left an interview session feeling more enthused and inspired (especially amazing because I was not a fan of his singing). I think it all shows—for which my thanks again to him!

FRANKIE LAINE

The guy with one of the biggest hearts in the music business is also the guy with one of the smallest heads. I'd heard about it before and I had begun to suspect it when every time, despite some uncomplimentary things I had been writing about him in the record review section, he always greeted me with complete enthusiasm, unstintingly friendly, with never a sign of one of those pseudo-hurt looks, those "why-did-you-have-to-do-that-to-me?" glances that so many artists in these fields toss at their critic "friends."

But I never saw it so obviously in action as the day I took down the notes for this interview—and if this is beginning to sound like a fan story, so be it, because few people in my seventeen years in this business have impressed me as much as Frankie Laine did that morning we had breakfast together. When I rang his hotel room there was no intercepting flunky's voice asking, "Who's calling?" Frankie picked up the phone himself, said he'd be right down and, unlike most other stars, *came right down*. On the way over to Sardi's, there were none of those furtive "boy-I-hope-I'm-not-recognized-but-if-I-am-I-love-it-though-I-shouldn't-admit-it" looks. Instead it was Frankie who approached some of the backstage guys at the Paramount lolling outside and who asked them how things were, about their families, etc. At Sardi's, with the captain and the waiters, it was the same thing, sincerely interested in other people rather than in making an impression.

And so it was in our story, which was prefaced with some talk about how funny it is, but often little things you forget about completely come back and in some cases may turn out to be the turning point in your career. The way Frankie told it, with complete candor, and never trying to build up Frankie Laine, it encompasses a big part of his career. It made such interesting listening for me that I thought you'd like to read it, in Frankie's own words, transplanted as best I could from the quick notes I took:

I was in New York in the middle thirties. I wanted to sing. You remember me, George. I used to come down to Nick's when Bobby Hackett was there and I'd hang around till he let me sing a chorus with the band. Well, Danny Alvin was playing with Joe Marsala at the Hickory House and he was one of the few people who liked the way I sang. Joe was wailing pretty good then. They used to have jam sessions every Sunday afternoon and Danny told me to come around and Joe would put me on. Well, I hung around all afternoon and by closing time nothing had happened. I remember Red Allen was playing *Stardust* when I finally managed to catch Joe's eye. So Joe nodded for me to come up and sing a chorus. I got a tremendous hand so he let me sing the last half of the last chorus, too. That's all we had time for.

As I got off the stand, a guy at the end of the bar stopped me. He told me he was with *Downbeat* and he gave me a big pitch and a note to Glenn Burrs who was the owner then and told me if and when I got to Chicago I should look up Glenn and he'd do something for me.

I was a real green kid then. Real gullible. But I finally got back to Chicago, which is my hometown, you know, and I went up to *Downbeat* with the note. You should have seen the expression on his face when Glenn read it. He looked at me and back at the note and at me and then he finally wanted to know where in the world I'd gotten it. I told him the story and then he told me that this guy who had written the note was an ex-con who used to work for him and who had absconded with fifteen hundred bucks and they were

Frankie and some backstage admirers

looking all over the country for him! I didn't know what to do and I guess Glenn, who's a real regular guy, must have realized I had nothing to do with all this, because after he got over the shock he started talking with me about myself and finally he told me to come over to the Congress Hotel next Sunday afternoon where they were running a benefit for Jimmy Cannon, a sax player who had gotten t.b., and he'd see that I got to sing. All the big people in the music business would be there, he said.

All the people were there all right, and I just kept fidgeting around waiting to sing for them. Five minutes before closing Glenn told me I should get ready to go on, but right then and there Roy Eldridge decided to go into *Body and Soul* and who'd dare interrupt that for a punk kid nobody even knew? All might have been all right, but they had to clear the room promptly at five because they had to set it up again for another party at five-thirty. Well, Glenn argued and argued with the maître, and it finally wound up with Glenn slugging the guy. But I still didn't get to sing. I remember crying all the way on my long walk back home.

Eddie Gilmartin, who originally started me in this business in 1937, introduced me to Perry Como around this time. I was teaching dancing at the Aragon Ballroom so that I could get in free to hear

Ted Weems's band—that's how broke I was. Nobody would listen to me sing. But Perry—and this shows you what a great guy he was even then—wanted to help me out and so when that big thing started about Perry going with Whiteman, he took me aside and said, "Frankie, you try out for the job." So I took the audition. I remember I sang *Never in a Million Years* and I guess it was a pretty prophetic song because Ted said right away, "You got a great style, kid, but it's not for ballads." So Perry took me aside again and asked me if I wanted to go to Cleveland to work there and when I said sure he made a phone call and got me the job. Do you know, to this day he still won't let me repay him the buck and a quarter it cost him to make that phone call!

The band I worked with in Cleveland was Freddie Carlone's, a Lombardo band but all great guys. But you can imagine how my style fitted theirs! I don't remember who closed first, me or the club, but I was out of work very soon. Then I worked at a spot called the Ace of Clubs. Murray Arnold was in the band, but the club burnt down a week later. Then I went to Lindsey's Sky Bar and there I met a great jazz pianist named Art Cutlip. He taught me all the great songs. We used to play a game where he'd play a couple of bars and say "Remember this?" and then I'd sing a couple and I'd ask him the same question.

Frankie with Mr. and Mrs. Dean Martin

In that way I acquired a knowledge of over two thousand songs and that's the basis of my library today.

After that job I met another fine pianist, Ray Raysor, and he got me into Cleveland's jazz clique. There was a fellow there named Hoyt Klein and he suggested I go to New York and try it there. He gave me letters to Earle Ferris, who was a big publicity man then, and to Jane Froman and her husband, Don Ross.

Ferris was a great guy, but he couldn't do much for me until I could be heard. That meant getting a job and I had no luck at all. I hardly had any money either. Then one day I ran into Nita Moore, who used to work in a music store in Cleveland and who had just come to town to go to work as Jimmy Dorsey's secretary. She took me to breakfast and while we were eating she told me that Jimmy was looking for a singer, only it was a girl not a boy. It just happened that the night before I'd been in the Village Barn and I'd heard a girl who looked great and who knew how to sell a song. I told Nita about her and that night she and Jimmy went down to hear her and that's how they got Helen O'Connell.

As for me, I finally got a job on WINS singing for just about nothing. I remember my first program. I sang *Shine*, *Rosetta* and *Marie*. I don't think the station approved. They didn't want a jazz singer. I stayed a little while, though, and then I met Art Hodes. We used to rehearse every day. There was a guy then who owned a spot called the New Paramount Grill over in Passaic and he was looking for two guys, a singer and a pianist, only he wanted them both to be Italian. He must have had a tough time, because he finally took us, after being told that only one of us was Italian, the other Jewish. The guy made a big fuss over Art because all the time he kept thinking that Art was the Italian and I was Jewish! What an amazed guy when he found out it was the other way around!

We were booked for one night but we stayed eight weeks. Then we got a job at the Crawford House in Boston but Art couldn't stay because it turned out the band was nonunion. It was all right for me, though, because I was just a singer. We had to do three one-and-a-half-hour shows a night and I not only sang but they also made me m.c. By the end of the date I was a pretty good talker.

In a little while I was back in New York again and one day on the street I saw a gal who looked awfully familiar to me. I must have looked the same way to her because she sort of stopped and stared, too. Well, it turned out that she was a girl singer named Phyllis Usher whom I'd never seen before in my life. And she'd never seen me either. I realized later that

I thought she was Ginger Rogers and she told me that she thought I was Mitch Ayres and that maybe I— Mitch, that is—could get *her* a job!

Phyllis introduced me to Jean Goldkette. He was trying to make a comeback at that time and he flipped when he heard me sing. But he was spending all his time then on a swing concert he was to put on at Carnegie Hall. He asked me to go to work with him as sort of librarian and assistant and he invited me to live with him. It was an interesting arrangement. Jean was a great guy. The only trouble was that he used to stay up all night long listening to recordings of the numbers he was going to conduct. That's the only way he could learn to conduct them. I never could get any sleep. The concert turned out to be a big flop. Jean took an awful beating and when it was all over he somehow managed to scrape up a little cash and gave it to me and told me I'd better go on home and he'd send for me when he could find something.

I didn't stay home too long. There was nothing for me there and I was dying to come back to New York. So, when a young couple offered me a free ride in exchange for doing the driving I jumped at the chance. We got to be very chummy and when they decided, after being in New York for awhile, to go to California to start some big business there, they asked me to go along and offered me what sounded like a great job. I turned them down. Shortly afterwards I heard that the guy really cleaned up. And I would have been in on the deal, too.

My big reason for staying in New York was because Jean had cooked up a job for me singing sustaining on NBC. But the day that I was supposed to start, England declared war on Germany, and that was the end of my NBC job.

I worked at the Pirate's Den in the Village with Gene Schroeder, another great pianist, for awhile and then I went back to Chicago for my brother's wedding and from there into the hospital to fix up a torn cartilage in my knee. When I got home there was a postcard there for me from Art Cutlip in Cleveland telling me to rush there because he had a fine job for me. A week later I had scraped up enough cash for the trip. But by the time I got there, Art had lost the job and there I was stranded. I decided to hitchhike back to Chicago, but on the road going out of town I noticed the College Inn and remembered that a girl I knew told me that if I ever needed a job to go see her girl friend who was working there and maybe she could fix it for me. I'm now getting to the point of this whole story.

Well, I got the job and after I'd been there for a short time I got a call from Ray Raysor who told me he was sending out a girl singer he knew who had just come in from Detroit, that she was really great. The gal, her name was June Hart, walked in about eleven. What she needed most of all was food, so first I fed her and then I got up to the mike and gave her a really great big buildup. Mind you, I'd never even heard her sing yet! Well, that girl really knocked me out. She had a sensational beat and a wonderful wistful quality. She was simply great, that's all there was to it. She was so great, in fact, that the boss hired her and fired me! But I still hung around the place just to hear her sing. One number especially used to kill me. It was a tune I'd never heard before called *That's My Desire*.

Shortly after that I began to think about quitting the business. I was pretty low. I used to do fine with musicians and jazz followers, but nobody wanted to give me a job. So I went into a defense plant and when I got that first paycheck for sixty-eight bucks I gave up singing altogether. I worked there for two and a half years.

There was a gal trio in Cleveland then called the Three Barries and I fell in love with one of them. When they went to Hollywood to record for Capitol, I got myself transferred and went with them.

The only guy who gave me any sort of a tumble at first was Al Jarvis, the disc jockey. He used to take me around to the hospitals to sing for the wounded service men. I met Carl Fischer shortly after that and of course you know what that meant then and has always meant to me. He's my right arm. Soon the Barries brushed me off completely and the only thing I had left was Carl.

Carl introduced me to some people and finally Slim Gaillard worked it for me to sing a little at Billy Berg's. One night when I was singing *Rockin' Chair* some guy jumped up and acted real excited. I could see him talking with Billy and I could feel he liked what I was doing. It turned out the guy was Hoagy Carmichael, who only wrote the song, and he liked the way I did it so much that he got Billy to give me a regular job.

Edgar Hayes was the pianist there and you can imagine what a kick I got when I found out that he knew *That's My Desire*. One night I decided to try it out. I introduced it as a brand new song—I don't know why I did that—and it broke up the joint. It was the greatest hand I'd ever gotten. In fact, from then on the place was mine.

I'd made a record shortly before that of *I May Be Wrong* and Al Jarvis used to play the hell out of it. Milt Krasny's daughter (he's vice-president at GAC) heard it and kept telling her dad about it. He got to Berle Adams, who was then head of Mercury, and Berle decided to record me. But he wanted me to do pops and I didn't want to do them. Finally when *That's My Desire* began to break up the Berg crowd every night, Berle saw it my way, and—well, you know the rest of the story from there.

It's funny, though, what one little favor can do for you, isn't it? Just to think that if I'd never tried to get June Hart that job in Cleveland and had never heard her sing *That's My Desire*—who knows where I'd be. Maybe begging Joe Marsala at the Hickory House to please let me sing a number!

Tommy Dorsey's Advice to Other Bandleaders
(November, 1948)—

Use your head. Try to figure out what they want out front. Look around the place. And don't look just at the few who are right in front of the bandstand. You know that *they* like you, or else they wouldn't be there. But look back farther. See what happens when the band jumps. It's all just common sense.

As you can read in this interview, soul was a very big thing at least a generation ago. It permeated jazz as well as gospel, but there was and still is a difference, as one of the great Soul Sisters of all time tells us here.

MAHALIA JACKSON

A Veteran Gospel Singer Thinks Jazz Should Have a Soul but "Gospels Penetrate Deeper"

It was an incongruous setting. It was an Indian summer's day in New York. It was World Series time and the Columbia Records public relations man was holding a portable radio to his ear, trying to hear above the swank Madison Avenue din, when I met him outside the fashionable hotel.

I had heard Mahalia Jackson and I had heard about Mahalia Jackson. But I had never met her. I'd never even seen her, and I was wondering what she was like. "Let's go right on upstairs; she's expecting us," said the Columbia man, as he switched off his radio and left the Indians in the lead, for the time being. (Such a sacrifice I considered almost beyond the call of duty.)

In the elevator I wondered even more. I knew that gospel singers didn't usually stop at such chic East Side hotels. But I'd been told that Mahalia was something quite different. I recalled her picture on the front of an Apollo Record album, complete with flowing gown, and I pictured some sort of a flowery setting and interview.

The maid met us at the door to the suite and took our hats. In the living room three men were busy talking business. The Columbia man introduced us, and we'd just started discussing what the Giants had been doing during our elevator ride, when Mahalia came in the room.

She wore a different dress this time. It was a simple cotton house dress, the kind any wife might wear any morning. And from her warm, straightforward greeting, I sensed immediately that Mahalia was as simple and as disarming as the garment she wore. Her frankness in the interview that followed complemented my initial sensory perception.

Gospel and jazz: Mahalia and the Duke

From listening to her records, I knew that Mahaila had a real, honest, old-fashioned feeling for real, honest, old-fashioned jazz. I knew, too, that she was actually more of a religious singer than a jazz singer, though, of course, the two have a good deal in common. So I hit her directly. "What do you think of jazz today?" I asked.

She looked at me—a little startled at first, I thought, and then almost condescendingly. "It ain't jazz," she answered simply. "It's nothing much—just a lot of noise. You know, when you take a real jazz player, like a trombone, he's supposed to sound like a real voice. They don't sound that way now.

"It hurts me. I was brought up in the south. I know sound. I knew Louis and Papa Celestin and King Oliver. It's a bringdown up here in the north. Louis is great, of course, and I liked that Bob Crosby band, but most of the stuff that's supposed to be dixieland is just plain hideous. It sounds like the way some of the English did when they first tried to play jazz years ago. It's terrible.

"Good jazz has to have a soul and feeling, like the blues. If it has to be loud, let it sound round and full . . . But maybe I shouldn't be talking about all this, because I'm a gospel singer. I sing Divine songs and they have more to offer than jazz does."

I asked her to elaborate further. She hesitated a bit because she didn't want to hurt anybody—and, anyway, jazz wasn't exactly her field. She was, after all, primarily a gospel singer, she kept insisting. I asked her if the two really weren't almost the same thing.

"Well, they are and they aren't," she said. "The blues and spirituals are closely related, but the big difference is that a spiritual has hope, whereas the blues is sad all the way through and stays that way. Another thing about jazz—it makes people happy on the surface, but when it's over, it's through. But a gospel song lasts—it penetrates much deeper and stays with you."

Gospel singing and jazz have one common factor, however, according to Mahalia. Both depend greatly upon the performer's emotional projection. "You can't write jazz, and when I sing I don't go by the score. I lose something when I do. I don't want to be told I can sing just so long. I make it till that passion is passed. When I become conscious, I can't do it good."

Mahalia, who has just been signed by Columbia Records (she is also doing a radio show for the CBS network), feels that her singing has never been captured properly on records because she has had to pay too much attention to timing, etc. "It all disgusts me. You don't really get my feeling till you hear me in person." CBS gave her a press party at a swank Park Avenue apartment recently, and they say that when Mahalia really let loose, many people many floors below on the street stopped, and stood enchanted at the awesome sound that emanated from far above.

Recording session restrictions also hamper jazz performances, she feels. "Jazz is all in the bounce. All that production is all wrong."

She likes most of the jazz singers of today. Ella, Billie, Sarah, "they all come from Ethel Waters. Dinah Washington's like Mamie Smith. Annie Laurie, she *really* sings the blues, the old kind of blues, primitive, in a sulky, mournful voice."

There are others she likes. Kay Starr was the first one of all she named. Then, surprisingly, came Jo Stafford, "soulful, deep feeling." Then, among the men, were Billy, Nat and Perry and another surprise, "that Tennessee Johnny, or Ernie—he's good, too!"

The hint that she had had enough interviewing for the time being came when she brought out her Bible and started to read through it. First it was a bit to herself. "There's something here that tells how I feel about all this," she said. "It's from the Sixty-Sixth Psalm where David said 'Make a joyful noise unto the Lord.' And then he said, 'Sing with a loud voice.'

"That's how they sing in the cotton fields. They sing for faith and for courage to go on, for deliverance, for freedom."

She didn't say it, but the implication was obvious. Mahalia Jackson doesn't sing to fracture any cats, or to capture any *Billboard* polls, or because she wants her recording contract renewed. She sings the way she does for the most basic of singing reasons, for the most honest of them all, without any frills, flourishes or phoniness.

Sounds sort of incongruous in this day and age, doesn't it? But there's nothing incongruous about it when Mahalia Jackson tells it.

I left the chic East side hotel with the Columbia man and for awhile I'd forgotten all about the Indians and the Giants. There are, after all, giants in other fields, too!

 RECORDS OF THE YEAR

For five years, from 1936 through 1940, I was *Metronome's* only record reviewer. Mostly, I used the name of Gordon Wright (where it came from I have no idea), though once in a while, in order to relieve the monotony, I'd substitute Henry S. Cummings for Wright. During that period, Wright (or Cummings) commented on many thousands of recorded performances. Then, at the end of each year, I would list and comment upon those I considered to have been the Year's Best. It would be interesting to see if you agree with the comments that follow. I'm not sure I always do.

BEST RECORD SIDES OF 1936

BUNNY BERIGAN—*I Can't Get Started* (Vo 3225)—Inspirational Berigan blowing and singing of his favorite song, plus great Dave Tough drums* and Forrest Crawford tenor sax.

BOB CROSBY—*Muskrat Ramble* and *Dixieland Shuffle* (De 825)—Two swell, orthodox dixieland sides by the best of the modern dixielanders with great choruses by Eddie Miller, Matty Matlock and Yank Lausen.

TOMMY DORSEY—*I'm Getting Sentimental Over You* (Vi 25236)—Tommy trombonistics guaranteed to raise goose pimples all over you with a great Noni Bernardi lead sax passage to push them even higher.

DUKE ELLINGTON—*Echoes of Harlem* (Br 7650)—Cootie Williams' trumpet concerto that just swings like nobody's business, and in which Cootie's trumpeting should be everybody's ditto.

*Others say it's Stan King.—*Ed.*

BENNY GOODMAN—*When Buddha Smiles*, a wonderful Henderson arrangement, elegantly played and highlighted by some bursting brass unison (Vi 25258)—*Between the Devil and the Deep Blue Sea*, fine relaxation, Benny clarinet, and the best of the Helen Ward vocals backed superbly by Frank Froeba's piano (Vi 25268)—*Swingtime in the Rockies* the most sensational Goodman record and clarineting of the year, featuring astounding ensemble attack and Krupa drums (Vi 25355)—*Take Another Guess*, the band in its greatest recorded groove aided by a fine studio setup and Ella Fitzgerald's vocal (Vi 25461).

BENNY GOODMAN TRIO—*Lady Be Good* and *China Boy* (Vi 25333)—The most parlorish of the Trio or Quartet sides, propelling great, but intimate swing.

HAL KEMP—*The Touch of Your Lips* (Br 7626)—Wonderful Kempian subduation throughout with some Skinnay Ennis vibratoing that's guaranteed to get you into a genuine perambulative mood.

ANDY KIRK—*Froggy Bottom* (De 729)—Real, relaxed black swing; quite the best of the band's many good sides, with great passages by Mary Lou Williams and Dick Wilson.

JIMMIE LUNCEFORD—*My Blue Heaven* (De 712)—Even more relaxed black swing; likewise the best of the band's many good sides, with a stupendous vocal trio passage.

RAY NOBLE—*Yours Truly Is Truly Yours* (Vi 25277)—Lovely, delicate Noble scoring, daintily played in fine taste and featuring fine work by vocalist Al Bowlly and guitarist George Van Eps.

RED NORVO—*Lady Be Good*, the greatest example of soft, subtle swing in its smaller stages in which Red's xylophone, Herbie Haymer, Dave Barbour and Howard Smith share honors for brilliant solo passages, and Eddie Sauter deserves a bow for the orchestrating (De 779)—*Porter's Love Song*, a great example of soft, subtle swing with a larger unit and with Mildred Bailey's vocal to help (Br 7744).

CHICK WEBB—*A Little Bit Later On* (De 831)—Terrific bite and sock by the most underrated of bands, with fine drumming by Chick and swinging by Ella Fitzgerald.

TEDDY WILSON—*Blues in C Sharp Minor*, in which Teddy plays a stupendous chorus and Israel Crosby contributes some remarkable bassing (Br 7684)—*My Melancholy Baby*, in which Teddy plays just about the greatest chorus of his career.

Loch Lomond's Maxine Sullivan

BEST RECORDS OF 1937

In Which Tommy Dorsey and Maxine Sullivan Cop Top Honors

PERFORMER	TUNE	RECORD	WHY
Mildred Bailey	More Than You Know	Vo3378	Heartfelt rendition of the ballad closest to Mildred's heart.
Calif. Ramblers	Take My Word	Va577	Soul-stirring version of great tune with Charlie Barnet's tenor for chief stirrer.
Bing Crosby	I Never Realized	De1186	Prettiest Bing singing of the year of fine Cole Porter tune plus grand Victor Young accompaniment.
	Peckin'	De1301	Heap of fun and swing with Jimmy Dorsey band.
	Bob White	De1451	Ditto stuff with Connie Boswell.
Bob Crosby	Sugar Foot Strut	De1094	The dispensers' most dixieland swing side.
	Between Devil and Sea	De1196	As exciting as above if only because of Eddie Miller's tenor.
Tommy Dorsey	Who'll Buy My Violets	Vi25519	Swing classic; fine arrangement and Berigan trumpet passages.
	Song of India	Vi25523	Swing classic; fine arrangement and Berigan trumpet passages.
	Marie	Vi25523	(You should know why by now!)
	Posin'	Vi25605	The Clambake Seven's best side: fun and swing.
	Are All My Favorite Bands Playing?	Vi25632	The whackiest record of the year.
	Once in a While	Vi25686	Quartet and trombone make this the band's prettiest side.
	Stop, Look and Listen	Vi36207	Twelve inches of great swing; Bud Freeman especially.
Benny Goodman	Bugle Call Rag	Vi25467	The most typical killer-diller.
	Sing, Sing, Sing	Vi36207	Twenty-four inches of great swing, featuring fine format, Krupa, Benny, Vido, and Harry James.
Goodman Quartet	Vibraphone Blues	Vi25521	Pretty blues with outstanding Benny and Wilson passages.
	Man I Love	Vi25644	Wonderful interpretation of Gershwin's mournful classic with Wilson's piano starring.
Woody Herman	Doctor Jazz	De1307	Great dixieland swing, arrangement, and fun.
	Don't You Know?	De1397	Really beautiful ensemble phrasing throughout.
Hudson-DeLange	If We Never Meet Again	Br7795	Loose swing plus terrific Fredda Gibson vocal.
Frank Marks	Quicksand	Va658	Extremely musicianly composition and interpretation plus grand Toots Mondello alto chorus.
Ray McKinley	Shack in the Back	De1020	The best of the four greatest dixieland sides (all by McKinley) of the year; note leader's drums especially.
Glenn Miller	Moonlight Bay	De1239	Wonderful Miller arrangement and trumpet section composed of Spivak, Klein and Bose.
Red Norvo	Remember	Br7896	Slow, undulating swing with special merit to sax inflection and Pletcher's trumpet.
	Do You Ever Think of Me?	Br7932	Most soft, subtle swing of the year, made so by Eddie Sauter's arrangement and fine inflections.
Leo Reisman	Have You Met Miss Jones?	Vi25687	Definitely the prettiest schmaltz side waxed in many years.
Artie Shaw	No More Tears	Br7835	Stringy Shaw with colossal Peg La Centra vocal.
	Tipperary	Br7975	Swingy Shaw with great brass biting a great arrangement.
Maxine Sullivan and Claude Thornhill	Gone with the Wind	Vo3595	Most mellow and bedroomy of all of Maxine's vocals plus beautiful band backing.
	Loch Lomond	Vo3654	Colossal swing of voice and arrangement.
	I'm Coming, Virginia	Vo3654	Ditto, but in a bit sadder vein.
	Blue Skies	Vo3679	Maxine shines in an almost melancholy gladness.
	Nice Work If You Can Get It	Vo3848	A real, slow, beautiful seducer; magnificent backgrounds, as usual.
Teddy Wilson	I Must Have That Man	Br7859	Slow swing; featuring Benny's clarinet, Lester Young's tenor, Billie Holiday's vocal.
	I'm Coming, Virginia	Br7893	Socker swing featuring Teddy and Harry James.
	I'll Get By	Br7903	Tremendous Teddy chorus and Artie Bernstein bassing.
Wilson Quartet	Just a Mood	Br7973	Two sides of grand blues with magnificent passages by Teddy, Red Norvo, and Harry James.

BEST RECORDED SIDES OF 1938

LOUIS ARMSTRONG (De)—*Strutting with Some Barbecue*—Louis' most inspired 1938 trumpeting; that's plenty!

BUSTER BAILEY (Vo)—*Planter's Punch*—Extremely mellow swing featuring Buster, Shavers' trumpet, Kyle's piano and Brown's alto—it moves!

MILDRED BAILEY (Vo)—*Lonesome Road*—Mildred at her most relaxed and best. Awfully pretty. —*Now It Can Be Told*—Mildred fine, backed by a Sauter arrangement that'll make you gasp.

COUNT BASIE (De)—*Every Tub*—Band's best 1938 kick; great arrangement; great swing; great passages from Young, Clayton, and Evans.

LARRY CLINTON (Vi)—*My Reverie*—Pretty scoring and Bea Wain vocal; mellow mood creator.—*Old Folks*—Sincere Bea Wain vocal of a tune that might have been written just for her; nice backing too.

JERRY COLONNA (Vo)—*Sonny Boy*—Funniest record of the year, the century. (Unquote.)

EDDIE CONDON (CMS)—*Love Is Just Around the Corner*—Sincere, effective jam with inspired Russell clarinet.

BOB CROSBY (De)—*At the Jazz Band Ball*—Good dixieland highlighted by brilliant Matlock clarinet.—*Dogtown Blues*—Twelve inches of honest-to-goodness blues, but well-scored.—*Louise, Louise*—more fine blues with Fazola clarinet and thrilling rideout.—*Panama*—Good two-beat swing, marvelous Miller tenor plus fine Smith trombone.—*Royal Garden Blues*—Most obvious two-beat dixieland of 1938.—*South Rampart St. Parade*—Twelve inches of thrilling dixieland march with great ensemble and solos. Band's most brilliant side. *Squeeze Me*—Another great Haggart work with good Miller.

BOB CROSBY BOB CATS (De)—*Can't We Be Friends*—Slow, moving dixieland with soulful Miller tenor chorus.—*You're Driving Me Crazy*—Greatest dixieland swing of 1938 plus fine Matlock clarinet.

JIMMY DORSEY (De)—*Darktown Strutters' Ball*—Fine arrangement, ensemble, Dorsey clarinet.—*Dusk In Upper Sandusky*—Ray McKinley doing the greatest drumming of 1938.

TOMMY DORSEY (Vi)—*Carolina Moon*—Band's best 1938 swing: two-beat, relaxed style.—*Music, Maestro, Please*—Band's best 1938 ballad: soulful Dorsey trombone and Leonard vocal.

DUKE ELLINGTON (Br)—*Steppin' into Swing Society*—Colossal swing propelled from muted trumpets, sax section inflection and unpretentious rhythm section.

Louis

ELLA FITZGERALD (De)—*What Do You Know About Love?*—Grand phrasing from Ella plus simple, sensible Webb support; Ella's 1938 best.

BUD FREEMAN (CMS)—*What's the Use*—Slow and pretty with moving passages from Bud, Hackett and Russell.

GLEN GRAY (De)—*Drifting Apart*—Extremely pretty revival (12 inches) of ditto tune.—*I Cried for You*—Four trombones highlighting another neat revival (10 in.).—*Sleepy Time Gal*—Twelve more fine revival inches plus lovely MacEachern trombone.

BENNY GOODMAN (Vi)—*Life Goes to a Party*—Benny's clarinet and James's trumpet make this side kick more than any other by the band in 1938.

Three-quarters of the Goodman Quartet, Benny, Lionel Hampton
and Teddy Wilson, being watched by pianist Jess Stacy

BENNY GOODMAN QUARTET (Vi)—*Blues in Your Flat; Blues in My Flat*—Two colossal sides, producing a mellow mood, and proving Benny's right to whatever clarinet honors he desires.—*Sweet Lorraine* (Trio)—More mellow stuff, with Teddy rivaling Benny.

JOHNNY HODGES (Vo)—*Jeep Is Jumpin'*—Great swing propelled greatly by Hodges' alto, best of 1938.—*Prelude to a Kiss*—Slow, lovely but never saccharine: Hodges and Mary McHugh shine.

JAM SESSION AT COMMODORE (CMS)—*Embraceable You*—Pretty and easy 12 inches with Hackett's trumpet tops.

HARRY JAMES (Br)—*Life Goes to a Party*—Harry's horn, Evans' tenor and Stacy's piano make great swing.

KANSAS CITY SIX (CMS)—*I Want a Little Girl*—Pretty but plenty swing; Young's clarinet swell.—*Pagin' the Devil*—Softest insinuating swing of 1938 with colossal rhythm figures by part of Basie's Bunch.

ANDY KIRK (De)—*I'll Get By*—Featuring the best male vocal of 1938—by Henry Wells.

GENE KRUPA (Br)—*Nagasaki*—Arrangements, Gene's drums, Watson's whackiness make this the best of the band's sides.

JIMMIE LUNCEFORD (De)—*Down by the Old Mill Stream*—Typical Sy Oliver offbeat swing featuring Ted Buckner's alto and stupendous ride-out passages.—*Margie*—More light swing and Buckner blowing. Band's best 1938 side.

GLENN MILLER (Br)—*Silhouetted in the Moonlight*—Especially pretty five-sax arrangement, Fazola clarinet and vocal by the unappreciated Kathleen Lane.

TOOTS MONDELLO (Br)—*I'll See You in My Dreams*—Toots' impressive alto drives the entire band to a fine side.

RAY NOBLE (Br)—*I Hadn't Anyone Till You*—Best schmaltz of 1938; typical of Noble's English works.

RED NORVO (Br)—*After Dinner Speech*—Pretty tune, arrangement, Bailey, band.—*More Than Ever*—Band's closest 1938 approach to its forgotten soft, subtle swing.

BEN POLLACK (De)—*Sing a Song of Sixpence*—Stupendous two-beat drive featuring fine drumming and Bob Anderson lead trumpeting.—*So Unexpectedly*—More solid drive, featuring great get-off by trumpeter Clyde Hurley. (Two biggest surprise sides of 1938).

ARTIE SHAW (Bl)—*Back Bay Shuffle*—Great swing thanks to great sax tonguing.—*Nightmare*—Eerie swing and great Shaw clarineting.—*What Is This Thing Called Love?*—Fine sock, brass, Shaw arrangement of grand tune.—*Yesterdays*—Lovely tune swung, yet unspoiled.

CHICK WEBB (De)—*Liza*—Best 1938 example of band's solid drive and Chick's drums.—*A-Tisket, A-Tasket*—(You should know by now!)

378

ELLINGTON COPS 1939 RECORD HONORS

His Men Supply Six Sides of Wax, Basie, Crosby, Miller Four Each, as Wright Picks Year's Best Fifty

Red Norvo and Mildred Bailey ready for that After Dinner Speech?

COOTIE WILLIAMS (Vo)—*Swingtime in Honolulu*—Perfect example of what soft, well-phrased sax passages mean to swing; Williams' trumpet helps greatly.

MIDGE WILLIAMS (Vo)—*Mama's Gone Goodbye*—Insinuating swing made so by Midge and supporters.

TEDDY WILSON (Br)—*Laugh and Call It Love*—Best swing of all Teddy's 1938 sides, with his piano, Carter's alto, Websters' tenor and Nan Wynn sharing glories.

Tops among record-makers for 1939 is Duke Ellington! In a summation of all the records reviewed during the year, METRONOME's discographer, Gordon Wright, has placed six Dukian sides on the list of the year's fifty finest offerings. Four of these works were by a small unit taken from the band under Johnny Hodges, while two were waxed by the entire entourage.

In second place on the honored list were three bands: Count Basie, Bob Crosby and Glenn Miller, each with four sides, with the Count's two-sided version of *Miss Thing* giving him a slight edge over the other two.

The selections, chosen only from those actually appearing in Wright's 1939 DISCussions, covered nine labels. Vocalion led with 13. Decca had 12, Bluebird 9, Victor 7, and Blue Note, Brunswick, Columbia, Commodore Music Shop two each, and Varsity one.

On the alphabetical list that follows, asterisk (*) on one side means that it is strongly recommended as a "must" for every swing collection.

ALL-STAR BAND—*The Blues*—Fine passages and ensemble by the greatest group of all time (assembled by METRONOME), including Goodman, Dorsey, James, Berigan, Teagarden, Miller, Zurke, Haggart, Bauduc and others (Vi).*

MILDRED BAILEY—*Slumbertime Along the Swanee*—Most sincere and relaxed work of the year by this wonderful singer (Vo).

CHARLIE BARNET—*Cherokee*—Tremendous Barnet tenor bite with fine background riding (Bl).

Fives Sides of Really Great Swing

COUNT BASIE—*How Long Blues*—Swell relaxed swing, building to a magnificent ride-out (Vo).—*If I Could Be with You*—Excellent medium-groove kick, made deeper by Helen Humes's singing. (Vo).—*Jumpin' at the Woodside*—The classic Basie jump opus, highlighting Lester Young on tenor and the late Herschel Evans on clarinet (De).*—*Miss Thing*—Two sides of rhythm figures building to a great climax (Vo).

SIDNEY BECHET—*Summertime*—Mournful soprano sax blowing of the old school, effectively sincere (Blue Note).*

CASA LOMA—*Heaven Can Wait*—Best of a number of great pop renditions in which the band does more than just read notes to make money (De)—*Tumbling Tumbleweeds*—The exquisite Casa Loma coloring tone, and ensemble at its moodiest best (De).

Real Cheer on Crosby Wax

BING CROSBY—*Yodelin' Jive*—One of the cheeriest records of the age with the Andrews Sisters as additional rays (De).

BOB CROSBY—*Big Noise from Winnetka*—The bass and drum duet that defies imitation or description (De).*—*I Hear You Talkin'*—Quartet excitement, reaching fever pitch, by Eddie Miller, Ray Bauduc and Bobs Haggart and Zurke (De).—*I'm Free*—Gorgeous trumpeting by Billy Butterfield of Haggart's tune now known as *What's New* (De).*—*Smokey Mary*—Typical band drive and brilliant solos, with the Bob Cats starting and giving way to the full outfit (De).

JIMMY DORSEY—*Deep Purple*—Best of many pretty band sides and great Bob Eberly vocals, chiefly because of the wonderful Don Redman arrangement (De).

Here's How Pretty Music Should Be Played

TOMMY DORSEY—*Davenport Blues*—Clever arrangement with the great Yank Lausen trumpet at its best (Vi).—*Baby, What Else Can I Do?*—The perfect pop side: gorgeous shading, scoring and passages by Tommy and Anita Boyer (Vi).

DUKE ELLINGTON—*Boy Meets Horn*—Highly imaginative Rex Stewart trumpeting at its best (Br).*—*I'm Checkin' Out, Goom Bye*—Tremendous band ensemble drive with Ivy Anderson's best vocal (Co).

Under name of JOHNNY HODGES—*Dance of the Goon*—A goony figure, straightened into swing by Hodges' alto and Cootie Williams' trumpet (Vo).—*Hodge-Podge*—Hodges, Cootie, Harry Carney and all the boys just swing like mad with no letup in sight (Vo).*—*Wanderlust*—Weird, plaintive blues that moves, nevertheless; Hodges again stands out, this time on soprano (Vo).—*You Can Depend on Me*—Beautiful Hodges altoing and backgrounds at a very slow tempo (Vo).

BENNY GOODMAN—*Bach Goes to Town*—Alec Templeton's satirical masterpiece, swung daintily by Goodman's reeds (Vi).—*Pick-a-rib*—Benny's Quintet in a delicate mood, not delicate enough to prohibit exciting blowing by its leader, however (Vi).*

LIONEL HAMPTON—*Sweethearts on Parade*—The greatest rolling swing on wax, with Chu Berry's

The Duke of Ellington holds an early court, surrounded by such notable subjects as vocalist Ivy Anderson, trombonist Juan Tizol (second from left), and (from far right) drummer Sonny Greer, trombonist Lawrence Brown and saxist Johnny Hodges

prodigious tenor and the rhythm section that gathers no moss (Vi).*

WOODY HERMAN—*Indian Boogie Woogie*—The year's best humor in swing, which really swings, by the way! (De)

The Epitome of True, Soulful Jazz

J. C. HIGGINBOTHAM—*Weary Land Blues*—Most moving instrumental passage of the year—what soulful tromboning—what impeccable taste! (Blue Note).*

BILLIE HOLIDAY—*Strange Fruit*—Most moving song of the year in which Billie cries out against injustices to her race (Commodore Music Shop).

HAL KEMP—*What's New*—The Kemp Krew at its musical best, with an unexpected brass climax (Vi).

JOHN KIRBY—*The Turf*—Fine medium-pace swing, with great solos by various members of this sextet (Vo).—*Royal Garden Blues*—Faster, even more exciting swing, showing a marvelous blend, and an exceptionally brilliant passage by trumpeter Charlie Shavers (Vo).*

Real Musical Imagination, Electrified

ANDY KIRK—*Floyd's Guitar Blues*—Magnificent, full orchestral conceptions swung prodigiously on an electric guitar by Floyd Smith (De).*

JERRY KRUGER—*Summertime*—A classic example of swinging and singing with your tongue in your cheek, all of which sounds impossible till you hear Miss Kruger (Vo).

GENE KRUPA—*Sweetheart, Honey, Darling, Dear*—The band falls into a great tempo; Irene Daye gets the idea of swing nobly (Co).

JIMMIE LUNCEFORD—*Cheatin' on Me*—Fine, slow, mean, insinuating swing (Vo).*—*Tain't What You Do*—Tremendous drive with a ride-out that out-basies Basie (Vo).

GLENN MILLER—*Isle of Golden Dreams*—Gorgeous arrangement, showing the Miller reeds and fine taste at their best (Bl).—*Little Brown Jug*—Best Miller swing of the year, made so in part by solos of Tex Beneke and Clyde Hurley (Bl).—*Moonlight Serenade*—Glenn's theme—that's enough (Bl).—*Sunrise Serenade*—Extremely musical, yet delicate, arrangement, faultlessly played (Bl).

FRANKIE NEWTON—*Rosetta*—Free, exciting swing, highlighted by Pete Brown's spirited and highly amusing altoing (Bl).

Here's How Girls with Bands Should Sing Ballads!

JAN SAVITT—*Twilight Interlude*—One of the finest dance band vocals of all time—by Carlotta Dale—height of simplicity and good taste (De).

ARTIE SHAW—*Copenhagen*—Band's biggest boot of the year—very little restraint by all and very much fine drumming by Cliff Leeman (Bl).—*Out of Nowhere*—Subdued, medium-tempoed, easy swing, with soulful solos by Tony Pastor and Artie (Bl).

DINAH SHORE—*I Thought About You*—A really mellow mood, as created by the year's best new voice (Bl).

JESS STACY—*Ec-stacy*—The prettiest, most relaxed piano solo recorded all year, and possibly in many, many years—twelve inches of it, too! (Commodore Music Shop).*—*Jess Stay*—Slow blues by an all-star group, with Jess and clarinetist Hank D'Amico supplying the best of many brilliant solos (Varsity).*

JACK TEAGARDEN—*Octoroon*—A mournful theme, gorgeously scored, and played and sung with great feeling by leader Jackson T. (Br).*

Pianist-leader Jess Stacy with Varsity Records chief Eli Oberstein

DUKE ELLINGTON TOPS ALL 1940 DISCS

Places Eight Sides on Record Honor List; Woody Herman Second with Four; Satchmo, Tommy Dorsey and Muggsy Spanier Follow

Duke Ellington had it all over the rest of the country's popular recording artists so far as 1940 discs are concerned. That's the way Gordon Wright, METRONOME's discographer, feels in his annual summation of the Fifty Favorite Sides he reviewed during the past year.

On this preferred list, Duke placed eight sides, twice as many as his closest rival. Whereas Ellington's victory was totally expected (he placed first in 1939, too), the identity of the runner-up band was more of a surprise. The band: Woody Herman's, four of whose sides went on Wright's list of favorites.

Three other artists followed Woody: Louis Armstrong, Tommy Dorsey, and Muggsy Spanier. Each placed three sides.

Largely through Ellington's efforts, Victor led the label list with 12; Bluebird and Decca tied for second with 10 each; Columbia had 9; Okeh (and Vocalion) 4; Blue Note and Varsity two each, and General had one side.

Here's the complete list of Wright's Fifty Favorites of 1940, arranged alphabetically by artist:

LOUIS ARMSTRONG—*Bye and Bye*—Satchmo blows and sings with much inspiration, but he's almost overshadowed by J. C. Higginbotham's trombone (De).—*Cherry*—Typically great Satchmo trumpeting, with good Mills Brothers backing (De).—*Marie*—Same as *Cherry* (De).

MILDRED BAILEY—*There'll Be Some Changes Made*—Nobody sings like Mildred when she's as soft and relaxed as she is on this—the fine Floyd Smith guitar and Mary Lou Williams piano must have helped her plenty, too (Vo).

CHARLIE BARNET—*It's a Wonderful World*—Cheery swing with a grand ensemble beat that grows on you with each playing (Bl).—*Wings over Manhattan*—A great two-sided instrumental by Billy May, showing much melodic and harmonic feeling, plus soulful trumpeting by the writer, and tenoring by the leader (Bl).

CONNIE BOSWELL—*They Can't Take That Away from Me*—The finest vocal background of the year, as supplied by Victor Young, for some of Connie's best singing (De).

Not Beat Me Daddy Eight to the Bar

WILL BRADLEY—*Celery Stalks at Midnight*—The entire band really moves, with Joe Weidman's trumpet leading the way (C).—*In a Little Spanish Town*—The great rhythm section at its best, with McKinley and Goldberg especially brilliant—good Bradley jazz trombone, too (C).

TEDDY BUNN—*Blues Without Words*—Really sincere, informal blues, that might have been made when Teddy didn't even know the machine was going. His guitaring is stupendous (Blue Note).

BOB CHESTER—*Don't Let It Get You Down*—A gorgeous arrangement that's both musical and mellow, plus good Dolores O'Neill singing (Bl).—*Don't Make Me Laugh*—The most soulful of Miss O'Neill's numerous great vocals, plus brilliant lead trumpeting by Alec Fila (Bl).

Soulful singer Dolores O'Neill with bandleader Bob Chester

BOB CROSBY BOB CATS—*Spain*—Best side of the year by the octet or the band, featuring gorgeous Fazola clarinet, relaxed Miller, crisp Stacy, melodic and rhythmic Butterfield, and solid Haggart (De).

TOMMY DORSEY—*I'll Never Smile Again*—The classic mood-creator, featuring Tommy, Frank Sinatra and the Pied Pipers (Vi).—*Polka Dots and Moonbeams*—A perfect example of how effective musical simplicity can be—wonderfully relaxed (Vi).—*We Three*—An intimate ballad version with a beat—everything in front is simple and straight, but how that Sy Oliver background moves (Vi)!

Octet of Brilliant Sides

DUKE ELLINGTON—*Bojangles*—Forceful kicks with Blanton and Greer leading the rhythm section in a terrific attack and Webster's tenor stealing solo honors (Vi).—*Conga Brava*—Biting swing at an up tempo, magnificent ensemble, fine muted brass, breathless Webster tenor, and pretty Tizol trombone (Vi).—*Cotton Tail*—A charging Joe Louisian brass attack, plus two wild Webster tenor choruses and a ditto ride-out (Vi).—*In a Mellotone*—Slow, deeply grooved melancholia with fine solos by Hodges, Williams and Carney, and great Blanton bassing (Vi).—*I've Never Felt This Way Before*—A mellow masterpiece with gorgeous Bigard clarineting and soulful Brown tromboning (C).—*Morning Glory*—A lovely, moody opus, featuring astounding trumpeting by Rex Stewart (Vi).—*Never No Lament*—Easy-tempoed swing propelled by magnificent backgrounds and highlighting Hodges, Blanton, Brown, and an astounding, concerted attack (Vi).—*Sepia Panorama*—A medium beat that really moves, this time showing off Webster, Carney and Blanton more than any of the other equally greats (Vi).

ELLA FITZGERALD—*Gulf Coast Blues*—Ella proves that she can really sing blues with feeling and conviction while her band gets a surprisingly fine beat (De).

Singer-leader Ella Fitzgerald visited by fellow bandleader Russ Morgan, as trumpeter Taft Jordan leads her crew

BENNY GOODMAN—*Dreaming Out Loud*—Eddie Sauter supplies the most interesting pop arrangement of the year, with Benny playing his usual, fine clarinet, and Helen Forrest singing one of her relaxed vocals (Co).—*Hour of Parting*—Sauter can also arrange great swing: the band hits a swell tempo, Toots Mondello's alto vies with Benny's impregnable clarinet, while a trumpet and trombone engage in interesting conversation (Co).

LIONEL HAMPTON—*I'm on My Way from You*—J. C. Higginbotham's trombone steals a well-tempoed show, with Henry Allen blowing exciting trumpet and Artie Bernstein beating a prodigous bass (Vi).

HORACE HENDERSON—*Chloe*—A surprise record, showing the band better than anybody thought it to be and featuring a magnificent, mournful-sounding Emmett Berry trumpet plus a unique Henderson arrangement (O).

Quartet of Intelligent Sides

WOODY HERMAN—*Bessie's Blues*—Great tempo, rhythm section, and rhythm figure produce an undulating beat that moves all the way through Joe Bishop's concluding, soulful flugelhorn passage (De).—*Frenesi*—A sympathetic ballad rendition, musical in all respects, played at an intimate tempo and sung with much Herman feeling (De).—*It's My Turn Now*—A good ballad beat (not v.v.), great Cappy Lewis trumpeting, sincere Herman singing, and an unexpected, thrilling ensemble ride-out (De).—*I Wouldn't Take a Million*—A classic example of how a pop tune should be played: simple, unaffected, at an easy tempo. Woody sings another fine vocal (De).

HARRY JAMES—*Flash*—The best recorded example of this band's great beat, with a repeated rhythm figure and Harry's kicking trumpet leading the way (Co).—*Maybe*—A unique example of kicking hell out of a ballad, with the entire band and Harry's trumpet getting the right feel of Jack Mathias' excellent arrangement (Va).

JOHN KIRBY—*One Alone*—Daintiest and lightest swing of the year with solo honors going to Charlie Shavers' neat trumpet and Billy Kyle's ditto piano (Vo).

JIMMIE LUNCEFORD—*Uptown Blues*—Slow, moving blues, propelled mightily by a tenacious background and showing off Willie's Smith's alto and Snooky Young's trumpet (Vo).—*What's Your Story, Morning Glory?*—Smith and Young again at another soulful, slow tempo, this time joined by Joe Thomas and his heart-pouring-out tenor sax (Co).

JOE MARSALA—*Reunion in Harlem*—Joe plays clarinet with immense feeling, backed by Pete Brown's alto, Bill Coleman's trumpet, Carmen Mastren and Gene Traxler (General).

METRONOME ALL-STAR BAND—*King Porter Stomp*—The year's greatest assemblage of jazz stars, with magnificent ensemble passages and brilliant solos by James, Goodman, Barnet, Teagarden, Mondello, Stacy and Elman (Co).—*All-Star Strut*—Nine stars jamming like mad: Goodman, Carter, Eddie Miller, James, Teagarden, Stacy, Christian, Haggart and Krupa. Each takes a solo, too (Co).

Fellow trombonists Jack Teagarden and Jack Jenney

GLENN MILLER—*Danny Boy*—Probably the most beautiful arrangement ever played by this technically faultless aggregation—slow, with much heart (Bl).

NEW FRIENDS OF RHYTHM—*Foster Chile*—Soothing music by a unique instrumental group, featuring gorgeous tones, chords, and tone colorings (Vi).

PORT OF HARLEM JAZZ MEN—*Port of Harlem Blues*—Unpretentious, thoroughbred jazz in the form of slow, soft, soulful blues, with fine solos from Frankie Newton's trumpet, Teddy Bunn's guitar, J. C. Higginbotham's trombone, and Albert Ammons' piano (Blue Note).

DINAH SHORE—*How Come You Do Me Like You Do Do Do*—The year's singing find, who achieved her rep via ballads, shows that she knows how to sing good blues and emote a fine beat too (Bl).—*Smoke Gets in Your Eyes*—The most relaxed side by this wondrous lass who doesn't strain on a difficult tune the way so many other singers do (Bl).

MUGGSY SPANIER—*Livery Stable Blues*—Best crisp two-beat sides of the year are Muggsy's small band works, made so mostly by its leader's rhythmic cornet—George Brunis' trombone helps him most on this (Bl).—*Riverboat Shuffle*—Same as above, except that Joe Bushkin's tasty piano helps Muggsy most (Bl).—*I Wish I Could Shimmy Like My Sister Kate*—Another two-beat kick, probably Muggsy's best, with his horn and Joe Bushkin taking top honors (Bl).

VARSITY SEVEN—*Easy Rider*—Coleman Hawkins tenor leads an all-star group that hits a fine tempo and boasts of a magnificent vocal by Jeanne Burns and some good Danny Polo clarineting (Va).

Coleman Hawkins

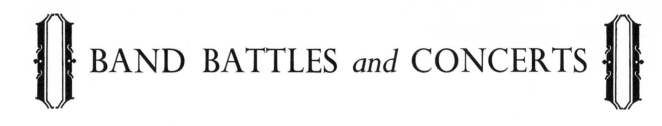

BAND BATTLES *and* CONCERTS

The early swing years featured some exciting battles of bands as well as some impressive debuts. This section presents on-the-scene reports of four of the most famous band battles and of the debut of Benny Goodman's band at Carnegie Hall.

June, 1937

CHICK WEBB DEFEATS BEN GOODMAN

Takes Decision of 4,000 In Hometown Battle

Outside Harlem's Savoy Ballroom at midnight of May 11th swarmed about 5,000 folks. Mounted police reserves and fire department reserves kept them in check. No more room inside.

Inside Harlem's Savoy Ballroom over 4,000 folk tried to get close to two bandstands. On the left platform was Benny Goodman, white King of Swing. On the right was Chick Webb, idol of Harlem, defendant in the great battle of music that was raging there this night of May 11th.

With five policemen on the platform to scare the crowd from rising onto the stand, Benny's boys fired the first shot. The crowd went wild. Its white idol was really shelling out with Harry James's outstanding arrangement of *Peckin'*.

Came the end of the first barrage. It was little Chick's turn. When that Webb man opened up on his drums the wildly excited crowd screamed its applause.

From then on Chick fought Benny every inch of the way, and Benny fought Chick every inch of the same way. It was really a torrid battle. Nip and tuck.

Came the first break, and it was all in Chick's favor. Benny, famous for his version of *Jam Session*, blasted it out. The Men of Webb came right back and literally blew the roof off the Savoy. The crowd screamed, yelled, whistled with delirium. On the stand Chick grinned. He grinned because he felt victory. And he was right. For at that point the sentiment began to lean more and more towards Chick, and before the evening was over it was the general consensus of opinion among Savoy folks that, though Benny leads the greatest swing bunch among the white tribe, he must take second place when it comes to battling one of the greatest of all swing bands in its own territory.

HIGHLIGHTS: Krupa picking up *Big John Special* after the Chicks had completed it, and the entire Goodman Gang picking up Krupa and really blasting their guts out on the piece . . . the surprise failure of the Goodman Quartet to really click, due, no doubt, to the size of the place and the continual crowd noises . . . Ella Fitzgerald's singing, with the crowd locking arms and just swaying to and fro before her.

386

BENNY AND CATS MAKE CARNEGIE DEBUT REAL HOWLING SUCCESS

Shorthairs Shag, Longhairs Wag, Walls Sag, as Goodman's Gang Transforms Ancient Hall Into Modern Swing Emporium

The first formal swing concert is history. It was made so Sunday, January 16, by Benny Goodman's band, which, taking full possession of sedate, solid Carnegie Hall for the evening, proceeded to enthrall several thousand bristling and whistling swing cats and mystify several hundred long-haired symphony hounds who deigned to put in a rather smug appearance. Since several thousand enthusiastic cats can be, and in this case were willing to be, much more vociferous in voicing their approval than a few hundred mesmerized hounds could be, but weren't, in admitting their mystification, the Goodman concert was considered to be literally a howling success.

It started off a bit gingerly. Benny, quite nervous, beat off *Don't Be That Way* a bit too slow, and for one chorus it was quite obvious that his men were neither relaxed nor in any sort of a groove. Suddenly, though, Gene Krupa emitted a tremendous break on drums. The crowd cheered, yelled, howled. Gene's hair fell into his eyes. The band fell into a groove, and when it had finished this fine Edgar Sampson opus, received tumultuous applause. Now the concert was in a groove, too.

For contrast, Benny next offered *Sometimes I'm Happy*. The nervous brass softened; the saxes flowed through that truly beautiful Fletcher Henderson chorus; Harry Goodman, heretofore white as a sheet, grinned broadly. Everything was fine.

Found: One Groove

As a finale in the first group came Count Basie's *One O'Clock Jump*. To be sure of finding a groove this time, Benny began beating off to himself during the applause of the previous number. When he had hit upon the right tempo, he handed it over to pianist Jess Stacy, who, tense in his first solo recital in Carnegie Hall, became even more flustered when the audience applauded his two choruses. There followed fine passages by Babe Russin and Vernon Brown, the latter being unusually relaxed. Next Benny himself started building from a low register beginning, and as he played louder and higher the crowd began to beat its feet in (what it thought was)

Maestro Benjamin Goodman, whose cats replaced those of Maestro John Barbirolli on the Carnegie Hall bandstand

Preparing for the concert's jam session: pianist Jess Stacy, guitarist Freddie Green, clarinetist Goodman, tenor saxist Lester Young, drummer Gene Krupa, trumpeter Harry James and trombonist Vernon Brown

rhythm. Benny, grinning, handed it over to the entire band, which commenced to build on the brilliant ride-out figure. Before the men had completed their job, they had been drowned out by applause and cat-calls. The cats were surely having their evening.

Came a short history of jazz which provided a lull to the sensational stuff. First Benny, Harry James, Vernon Brown, and the rhythm section doing the *Original Dixieland One-Step*, and presenting the unique sight of Gene playing dixieland drums. Bobby Hackett strode coolly on and off the stage, sandwiching a fine imitation of Bix's chorus of *I'm Comin'*, *Virginia* between his entrance and exit, after which the crowd showed that it was beginning to catch on by laughing at Benny's satirical exposé of the Ted Lewis school of clarinet. The history lesson ended with Harry James's short but effective parallel of Louis Armstrong's *Shine* choruses.

Tribute to Duke

Apparently feeling that no swing concert would be complete without at least some semblance of Ellingtonism, Benny trotted out Johnny Hodges, Cootie Williams, and Harry Carney of the Duke's band, who, after receiving a grand ovation, proceeded to do a

bit of pleasant lulling with their soft *Blue Reverie*. Cootie was cocky, grinning and grumbling into his mute; Hodges and his soprano sax were thrilling; young Carney, obviously a bit abashed, played well and ran off the stage. Throughout, Benny played and grinned at the moving soloists.

Then the entire Goodman group returned to the stage, and almost blasted itself off with Harry James's *Life Goes to a Party*. Harry himself, as well as Gene, led the devastating attack upon Carnegie walls, which, by the way, held nobly.

Sticky Jam

The jam session was next and proved to be the weakest part of the program. Jam sessions can't be forced upon musicians successfully, as Benny undoubtedly well knew before the concert, and realized even more so after it. This jam stuck too long. Though there were some good passages from Lester Young, Buck Clayton, Count Basie, Harry Carney, Walter Page, and Benny, the twenty-minute version of *Honeysuckle Rose* was uninspired, uninspiring, and lagged pretty sadly until Harry James bit into a few choice figures towards its close. Even then, the listeners, including the most thoroughbred cats, were

388

quite obviously restless and didn't tend the jammers any smaller ovation than they deserved. The setting was just unfortunate, that was all.

The Trio and then the Quartet came on for the finale of the first half. Teddy received a grand ovation as he replaced Stacy at the keys and responded with some beautiful passages in *Body and Soul*. Just one number for the Trio; then Lionel grinned onto the stage to do his bit in *Avalon*, after which he got off to a wrong start on *The Man I Love*, with the continued applause for the previous number covering up his mistake. Both he and Teddy came through with some lovely note picking. The four galloped through *I Got Rhythm* for a windup, with Gene pretty pooped by the time, and Benny showing his good nature by grinning knowingly at a few ickies who were being overcome. It was quite obvious that all in all the King, instead of being nervous, was just having himself one helluva good time. Nevertheless he probably made good use of the ensuing respite.

The Jitters Again

The start of the second half was similar to that of the first. Again nervous, this time for no apparent reason, the men didn't get together through *Blue Skies*, its rhythm being choppy and the ensemble execution pretty ragged. Chris Griffin bit out some sock trumpet, Arthur Rollini made good his first tenor solo passage of the evening, and Gene grinned a lot, but still nothing much happened worthy of being set down in swing history.

Martha Tilton, very cute in a pink dress, but plainly even more nervous than the band (which was commencing to settle down) appeared to do *Loch Lomond* sans a mike. She garnered tremendous applause that held up proceedings for almost five full minutes. The ovation apparently helped to settle the band, for it dug itself a nice groove behind Benny in Fletcher's arrangement of *Blue Room* and once more began the rocking of Carnegie Hall. The brass bit notably on this opus, though poor Chris Griffin, unused to facing so many faces, didn't do his best on his short solo passage.

The Breakdown

Then followed the real breakdown of the evening. As soon as the band hit the first few strains of Jim Mundy's *Swingtime in the Rockies*, the crowd let loose. Gene turned in some particularly fancy drumming behind Benny. All of a sudden, blasting like hell, riding on high out of the ancient alcoves came Ziggy Elman with a trumpet passage that absolutely broke everything up. Emotionally this was the high spot of the concert. The crowd commenced to yell; the band began to dig and blast at a pace it had never

approached before Ziggy's outburst, and by the time the boys had wended their way out of the Rockies they had created a ruckus that must have been heard way out there.

It didn't let up much, either, as the band snuck into the initial strains of *Bei Mir Bist Du Schön*—proving, if nothing else, that New York isn't inhabited entirely by Irishmen. The Gothamites commenced to do all sorts of clapping here and seemed to enjoy immensely Ziggy Elman's Ghetto Get-off.

After much applause for Ziggy and Martha, Messrs. Goodman, Krupa, Wilson, and Hampton came to the fore for their final parlor touch of the evening. This time they were much more relaxed, and even went so far as to kid among themselves as they swung through *China Boy*, *Stompin' at the Savoy*, and an original composition. Strictly upon musical merits, Teddy stole the show, though Lionel and Gene went through plenty of contortions that amused the crowd.

Sending Sing

Then came the real finale of the evening. Gene, hanging on for dear life by now, started the tom-tom-tomming that started *Sing, Sing, Sing*. It was the occasion for a wild outburst. After many choruses the band began to build toward a climax. As it did

389

so, one kid after another commenced to create a new dance: trucking and shagging while sitting down. Older, penguin-looking men in traditional boxes on the sides went them one better and proceeded to shag standing up. Finally Benny and Gene alone—just clarinet and drums—hit the musical highlight of the concert with both of them playing stupendous stuff. Came the full band, and then suddenly soft, church music from Jess Stacy at the piano. It was wonderful contrast. Benny started to laugh. Everybody started to laugh. And then everybody started to applaud, stamp, cheer, yell, as the band went into the number's final outburst. And long after it was completed they kept on yelling, until Benny satisfied them with a couple of encores.

That move may conceivably have been necessary, but it wasn't smart. Anything was bound to be an anticlimax, and Sampson's *When Dreams Come True* and Henderson's *Big John Special*, despite the brilliance of their composition and of the Goodman entourage that evening, couldn't overcome that tremendous psychological obstacle. They proved to be fearful letdowns.

The concert wasn't, though. From an objective view, that was self-evident. And it wasn't a letdown to this reviewer either, filled up as he is almost every day and night with swing, and often damned sick of it, too. It wasn't because he didn't expect too much and got lots more than he expected. It wasn't because of an audience's enthusiasm that helped to carry him on; an enthusiasm that, coupled with the very nature of the occasion, helped to carry Benny's band to really great heights. It wasn't, because for intelligent followers of swing this was a great, a thrilling triumph. Benny Goodman and his veritable, virile vipers had, in the opinion of a record gate, cut to the core Jack Barbirolli and his Philharmonic Cats. The shorthair had triumphed over the long. Time and tempo march on!

PICKETS, CAMERAS ATTEND CONCERT

Soloists Get Big Ovations . . . Ickies Make Noise . . . Old Men Dance

The concert was picketed. Nobody knew by whom. Nobody cared much either. Except the picketers. It was a cold night. Their signs said something about Benny being a Red from Spain. That's not true. He's a clarinet player from Chicago. But not to picketers. They didn't like him because he once played at a benefit for Spanish Communists. Hitler wasn't at the concert, anyway.

The crowd was slow in filing in. When everything had been packed into all available seats and standing room, the estimated total was 3,100. Not bad. The Philharmonic usually doesn't do that well. Not nearly that well, in fact.

Benny received a real Toscanini ovation. He bowed three times. Still they kept cheering. So he tapped his foot a couple of times, and his band proceeded to drown out his audience. Not polite, but thoroughly expedient.

Big Hands

Harry James got a big hand when he got off his chair to get off the first time. So did Teddy Wilson and Martha Tilton upon their initial appearances later on. Seems the crowd was well prepared in advance. Irving Kolodin, music critic of the New York *Sun*, helped it a lot with some illuminating program notes.

Harry Goodman looked all white, drawn, and scared stiff during the first number. By the second tune, though, the color came back into his face and he was grinning his usual broad grin.

A movie camera man was loudly shhhd when he indiscreetly started his machine during the soft passages of *Sometimes I'm Happy*. He just kept on grinding annoyingly away for the better part of the concert.

As Gene came down front for the first dixieland number, a genuine ickey yelled: "Come on, drummer, go to town!" There were numerous of that ilk spattered generously through the audience. They managed to make themselves much more obnoxious than the longhairs, who at least had the courtesy to shut up. Fortunately, much clapping of hands out of time didn't seem to disturb the band a great deal.

The biggest grin of the evening was supplied by Cootie Williams; the most awed expression by Harry Carney.

"You First, Gaston"

When the men came out for the jam session, they couldn't make up their minds as to who should sit where and how. Finally Benny in the role of leader and host seated them all.

The dead stops in the middle of *I Got Rhythm* fooled the crowd every time. Each one drew quickly hushed applause.

Reflected Glory

Ethel Krupa received all sorts of congratulations during intermission for her husband's fine performance. Helen Ward received much attention too. She's been paying most of hers to her six-weeks-old child.

During the time-out one wit was heard to remark: "This is the first audience in Carnegie Hall that ever really seemed to enjoy the music it was listening to!" Rather a broad statement.

Gene Gives

Gene gave the eighty-five-cent gallery a broad grin when it commenced to beat its hands all out of time during *Blue Skies*. Apparently he liked its spirit, anyway.

Benny refused to sing his solo passage in *Loch Lomond*. His only display of temperament during the evening. When the audience refused to stop cheering and yelling for more at the close of the number, Benny simply walked front stage and graciously murmured: "I'm sorry, we are not prepared for any encores." The crowd believed him and let the concert go ahead.

"One More"

All through the final set of Quartet numbers Gene delighted the audience with cries of "Take one more, Jack!" "Give me one more!" and "One more, gang!" But the biggest kick came when Gene conked his cymbal so hard that it fell off its stand on to the floor. Lionel picked it up, hit it a few times with his vibre hammer, and returned it to Gene. Whereupon Gene hit it off the stand again. It was like a Ping-Pong match.

As was expected, *Sing, Sing, Sing* brought down the house. It didn't bring it out, though. Almost everybody hung around for two encores. Finally Benny and the boys just walked informally off the stand. They, as well as some of the audience, were in a hurry to get uptown to hear the Savoy battle between Chick Webb and Count Basie.

February, 1938

BASIE'S BRILLIANT BAND CONQUERS CHICK'S

Newspapermen Give Decision to Count Over Webb in Savoy Battle . . . Solid Swings to Heart Triumph Over Sensational Blows to Head

Count Basie did it! For years nobody was able to lick Chick Webb and his Chicks within the walls of his home Savoy Ballroom, but on January 16, right after Benny Goodman's concert further downtown in Carnegie Hall, a milling throng that included such notables as Duke Ellington, Red Norvo, Mildred Bailey, Eddy Duchin, Gene Krupa, Lionel Hampton and the Benny Goodman family jammed into Harlem's Hottest Hot House to see and hear the Count gain a newspapermen's decision over the famed Chick.

Basie had everything that night! Seldom has any band, anyplace, cut loose with such unmitigated swing the way the Count's Cohorts did that memorable eve. METRONOME, usually proud of its predictions, completed a complete turn-about-face that eve, and right now goes publicly into print with apologies to backers of the band who have been singing its potential praises for many months now, but with whom METRONOME, unimpressed until Basie's recent upheaval, could never bring itself to agree. (Such an apology is doubly hard to make because Chick Webb has so often been referred to as the least appreciated band in the country within these same pages.)

Sincerity vs. Showmanship

To put it briefly, the battle was one of solid swing versus sensational swing, both brilliantly swung, but with the sincerity of the former triumphing over the showmanship of the latter. Basie's, a bluesplaying (with variations) band if there ever was one, devoted its attack to the body, to the heart, with a steady hammering of truly sending rhythm figures behind the truly sensational solos of trumpeter Buck Clayton, tenor saxists Herschel Evans and Lester Young, and its piano-playing leader, and with an ensemble

391

The Conquering Count

and steady rhythmic attack (led by drummer Jo Jones) that was truly devastating.

Webb's sensational, whirlwind barrage was aimed chiefly at the ears and head with resounding arrangements played at breakneck tempos, and including within them all sorts of screeching and even novelty effects. At times it was turned more to the heart via the extremely effective and soul-lifting vocals of Ella Fitzgerald, but for the most part Chick's weapons were crushers to the head and ears, led by some brilliant trumpeting from Bobby Stark, exciting tromboning from Sandy Williams, and, of course, the always effective and thrilling drumming from little Chick himself.

Crowd's Verdict

Apparently the Savoy crowd, loyal at it always has been to its idol, was forced to admit that Basie was doing his little bit of cutting. When, at about one in the morning, master of ceremonies Martin Block asked for the dancers' verdict, the yelling and cheering for Basie appeared to overshadow a bit that for Webb. And in home quarters, where in past battles the yelling and screams of approval have always been for Chick, such a demonstration was indicative of just one thing. The Chick had met at least his equal!

The Count can credit his victory both to himself and to Chick's band. There's no question of a doubt that Basie's band is a surprisingly improved unit: entirely different from the mediocre group he carted into a downtown ballroom last year. On top of that, all the men settled into one unbeatable groove after another, and were held there fast by the stupendous drumming of Jo Jones as well as by the otherwise brilliant rhythm section. Moreover, coming to blows with Webb's famed aggregation at last filled the boys with an incentive and enthusiasm that could not be denied.

No Groove

The Chick, on the other hand, suffered from an inability to settle into a rhythmic groove that could be shared with his judges. As a matter of fact, he seldom tried to do that, but instead attempted to lift them suddenly to the ceiling with electrifying rhythm attacks, attacks which suffered by comparison through their lack of stability. The Chicks were obviously an arrangement- rather than a swing-conscious band that night, playing all sorts of brilliant but intricate stuff that at times became so involved as to be almost humanly incapable of producing swing.

Had the battle been on a theatre stage before the usual un-hep public audience, Webb would undoubtedly have won by a wide margin. But his judges at the Savoy comprised swingsters who know their swing, who feel their swing, who get into real grooves, and who no longer are fooled by too many breakneck tempos offered as true swing. They knew the Count was swinging, they felt he was swinging, and they got into the real grooves with him. And they didn't accept the breakneck tempos.

Rumor has it that there will soon be a return engagement between these two terrific bands, with Chick ready to carve out the Count's heart, or vice versa.

ICKIES' ANTICS SUBMERGE GOODMAN-BASIE BATTLE

Madison Square Garden Swing Fiesta Becomes Fiasco as Jitterbugs Knock Themselves Out And Few Appreciate Bands' Brilliant Work

The bug-eyed jitterbugs jittered and the ickies icked all through huge Madison Square Garden in New York on Sunday night, June 12th, while Benny Goodman's and Count Basie's boys helped them to make what a lot of people got a kick out of calling "swing history."

Maybe it was.

Maybe it wasn't.

Chances are it wasn't.

But it was lots of fun. The music was marvelous and everybody seemed to have a wonderful time. Most of the assembled didn't know why—in fact, most of the assembled gave pretty good proof that they didn't know from nothin'.

Basically the affair was just like any big dance featuring two name bands, held at an armory. New York not being used to that sort of an affair, and Madison Square Garden being noted more for punch-drunk boxers, instead of Coca-Cola-drunk shaggers, the affair was supposed to be something different—or at least the jitterbugs tried to make it so.

They danced all over the place. Cute college boys shagged and trucked by themselves; Big Apple parties started and usually soured into cider; sharpies, with collars unbuttoned and neckties flopping sloppily on their stomachs, and who thought they had to show everybody that they caught on, trucked (?) around the door by themselves, and a lot of semi-amused and/or semi-bored people sat back in boxes and just looked.

The next day the daily press gave the jitterbugs and ickies a lot of space. Why?

The next day the daily press didn't give the Goodman and Basie bands a lot of space. Why not? The answer is pretty obvious.

Too bad, too, because Goodman's Gang and Basie's Boys really turned in thrilling performances in what turned out to be more of an exhibition than a battle of music. Benny's band has seldom, if ever, sounded so good; it hit upon one of its relaxed periods, and just shelled out. Benny himself was marvelous; Davey Tough played by far the best drums heard since he joined the band; Harry James was his usual brilliant self; Bud Freeman really dug, and Lionel Hampton played such fast drums that you'll have to hear him do it again to believe that what you heard the first time was really true. This last bit of sensationalism, by the way, *broke it up*. Without detracting from Lionel's performance, the fact that it took speed and noise to make an impression proves pretty conclusively the low standard of music appreciation possessed by the so-called *hepcats*.

Basie's Bunch was every bit as good. What a rhythm section! You'll never find a cleaner drummer than Jo Jones. And those tenor men! That night, at least, Herschel Evans cut the more famed Lester Young. Buck Clayton was brilliant on trumpet and Benny Morton got off some great stuff on trombone. The improvement, as well as the swing, in this band is almost unbelievable.

It was swell music. And it was all much fun, too. Fun for the jitterbugs and ickies because it gave them another opportunity to show off, and fun for the others because they heard some really grand swing.

The only people it wasn't fun for, were the promoters, who lost about $5,000 on the show. That was unfortunate, too, because proceeds were supposed to benefit the Los Angeles Sanitorium.

ARTIE SHAW COLLAPSES IN SWING BATTLE

Contest at New York Benefit Reaches Sad Anti-Climax as Exhaustion Rather Than Dorsey Overcomes Clarinetist . . . Tommy Impressive

A rigorous one-night schedule caught up with Artie Shaw, while he and his bandsmen were in the midst of battling Tommy Dorsey's boys in a benefit show at New York's 105th Regiment Armory, September 16, and laid him so low that he was forced to cancel the final portion of his program. Artie, suffering from a cold in the head and a pain in the stomach, had to be assisted from the battle-ground by friends and rushed home to bed and doctor's care.

Prior to the unfortunate collapse, Shaw's Solid Senders had been outswinging Tommy's lads in no uncertain terms, though for all-around good dance music, the Dorseyers stood out among the four bands WNEW's Martin Block had assembled for the occasion (Claude Hopkins and Merle Pitt ended third and fourth respectively). Holding back nothing, Artie and his men shelled out as few white bands have ever shelled before. Their rhythmic attack was devastating; their pace scorching; their effect upon the assembled jitterbugs downright murderous. It was an awful shame that the first to succumb to this band's terrific barrage was its leader.

Tommy's Greatest Swing

To keep up the pace, Dorsey's bunch had to swing as it never swung before—and it did! The new brass team, paced by trumpeters Charlie Spivak and Yank Lausen, and aided by trombonist Moe Zudecoff, added a punch to the ensemble (and to the soloists, too, when Lausen was playing) that the band heretofore had never been able to attain. The effect of the brass drive was mirrored in the work of the rhythm section with the improved lift being especially noticeable in the drumming of Maurice Purtill, whose nonchalant, uninspired drumming of late had been threatening this potentially great percussionist with an early swing-star death.

The Collapsing Shaw

Shaw's brass, though not composed of such great soloists, also possessed a terrific drive, but more than that it was an indefinable ensemble feel, plus simply effective arrangements and great clarineting from Artie, that propelled this rising band to such great swing heights. And as a quartet, the rhythm section surpassed Dorsey's, with Sid Weiss's prodigious bass, Al Avola's strong guitar, and Cliff Leeman's driving drums leading the attack. Leeman (despite what you may have read elsewhere) is a good drummer: he may be a bit short on experience, but he possesses a natural swing which he's able to impart through his drums and which certainly lifts the entire band.

Saxes Star

The Dorsey band was at its best during the final hour. (Original plans had called for Artie and Tommy splitting this period, but when Shaw became ill, Dorsey and his boys graciously offered to play his final half hour for him: a gesture typical of the generosity of Tommy and of his boys.) During that last period, besides shelling out, the band exhibited a gorgeous brand of sweet with the new five-man sax team, ably led by Hymie Schertzer, as well as Tommy's trombone becoming the chief mood creators. It was an hour's contrast of fine swing and sweet.

Guest artists included Ozzie Nelson, who sang one song and was immediately mobbed, and Glenn Miller, who played some swell jazz trombone before Tommy's band. The jazz trombonists were well represented: besides Glenn and Tommy, George Arus of Shaw's band and Les Jenkins of the Dorsey outfit slipped off a big number of fine licks.

Musical celebrities were everywhere: spotted besides Nelson and Miller were Count Basie, Peewee Erwin, Bill Harty, Al Mastren, Kay and Sue Werner, Randy Mergentroid, and Tommy Rockwell, Cork O'Keefe, and Mike Nidorf on obviously very good terms. Gene Mako jitterbugged for a while, but had to leave early so as to get much sleep before his semifinal match in the Men's National Tennis Singles Championships.

The letdown when Merle Pitt's band played could be attributed not to the fact that Pitt doesn't have good men, but more to the lack of good arrangements, good section work, and interest. In some ways it was truly a Pitt band.

April, 1948

A CONCERT TO END ALL CONCERTS

Stan Kenton Forgot to Take Himself Seriously at Carnegie Hall; Result: Vaudeville

I've never been a Kenton band enthusiast. I've appreciated what Stan has been trying to do all these years, and I've admired him for his tenacity and for his qualities as a leader of men. I've tried to mitigate all criticisms, because I've felt the man deserves to be encouraged in his attempts to produce what he sincerely believes is progressive jazz, when just about every other band in the business has been willing to settle for a status quo or else slide backward with the rest of popular music.

Stan often asked me to wait. His wouldn't be a dance band much longer. He was going to play concerts and he'd appreciate my withholding judgment until after his New York debut in that field. There'd be a lot of new and interesting material for me to hear.

So I waited. And finally I went to the concert.

I'm less of a Kenton band enthusiast than ever before!

You'd think that during a concert as important as this one must have been to Stan, he and Pete Rugolo would have presented some new and exciting material for the affair. The band played thirty-two numbers at this concert. Thirty-one of them were things it had played before, in theatres and in hotels. Of these, twenty were instrumentals, seven were songs by June Christy (all in one section thereby detracting considerably from her improved singing) and three were novelties, the last of which, Stan's gag version of *St. James Infirmary*, plus comic introductions of various men in the band, lasted fully ten minutes and served as the climax of a supposedly serious concert!

The one new number was a four-part *Prologue Suite*, written and conducted by Rugolo. Starting with a stentorian introduction, it went into a Kenton piano passage, reminiscent of *Intermission Riff*. Part two showed off the high trumpets, who unfortunately weren't in tune here, and then resolved into some cute byplay between Stan and bongo drummer Jack Costanza. The third portion, a rather martial-sounding affair, featured some squeals by George Weidler, whom I recall as a very able, well-toned alto saxist,

The End?

but who has been overblowing his horn dreadfully since he joined Stan. The finale was wild and high, somewhat like *Machito*, interspersed with some good, legitimate electric guitaring. *Prologue Suite* is an interesting bit of work, somewhat lacking in continuity (at least on the basis of a single hearing), but certainly worthy of being presented at a Kenton concert and obviously a sincere attempt to present progressive jazz in concert form.

But the rest of the instrumentals! Well, how would you feel if you had gone to a concert, prepared to hear at least a few new compositions which would be indicative of what Kenton had stated he was trying to do, bring progressive jazz into the concert hall and present it in its proper medium, and you had, instead, been bombarded with the same things you'd heard the band do before: *Artistry Jumps, Collaboration, Intermission Riff, Artistry in Percussion, Opus in Pastel, Machito, Artistry in Boogie, I Get a Kick Out of You, Safranski, Concerto to End all Concertos*, etc., etc.

Even that program mightn't have been too disappointing, for the band played well that night, as it almost always does, and there were, in addition, some lesser-known instrumentals, like the pretty *Elegy for Alto* with its very exciting climax, *Message to Harlem* which spotted some excellent tromboning by Eddie Bert, the lovely *Interlude*, marred slightly by the rough blend of the trombones, Bob Graettinger's interesting *Thermopolae* and the intriguing *Impressionism*.

But you expected more, because of all the talk you had heard about how terribly sincere Stan was and about how truly interested and thrilled he was to be able to produce in a concert hall for the first time this really true great American art form this medium of expression this emotional pictorial pattern of young emotional America presented through the medium of a progressive group of musicians who felt and believed the same way about jazz and about its place as a true American art form and as the best medium of expressing the pulse and the drive and all the emotions of young America striving to find its place in this wild unsettled chaotic world of ours. (Absence of punctuation influenced by Kenton.) You expected lots more new material.

But what you surely didn't expect was a dressed-up version of Kenton's vaudeville appearances, which, in the final analysis, is all that his Carnegie Hall appearance turned out to be. The guys hammed it up much too much. Stan pulled off gag after gag. Ray Wetzel, who shouldn't even sing in a gin-mill, did *Now He Tells Me* and followed it with an off-color parody of *Trees*. Bart Varsalona, sitting in the front row and showing off all through the evening, was featured in a comedy routine titled *Invention for Bass Trombone* which might well have been subtitled, *Low Man in a Minstrel Show*. In addition to Stan's gagging, the repetitive cracks about how little the men were paid, and so forth, there was the lengthy *St. James Infirmary* routine, replete with references to homosexuals and Superman, and finally individual comedy routines by several band members, none of which bore any relationship to music and which certainly had no place whatsoever in a concert hall.

Stan has complained bitterly to me about METRONOME's attitude toward his music. He has been so vexed by what has appeared in these pages that he has told me point-blank that he wants to have nothing to do with the magazine, whatsoever. He has taken that "I-wouldn't-lower-myself-to-your-level" attitude. In all fairness to Kenton's viewpoint I must state that he has not complained as much about the fact that Barry [Ulanov] and I have never been too enthusiastic about his music as he has about what he considers a too flippant and too belittling approach that he feels we have toward his music. He has complained much more about what he considers to have been merely wisecracks in our record reviews than he has about any analytical criticisms we have made.

Whether our attitude was right or whether it was wrong in the past would necessitate another article of at least this size for adequate discussion. However, what our attitude was in the past seems to me to count very little in the light of what Kenton has shown his attitude to be at present. Though he continues to talk on and on with unmitigated intensity and though I believe very certainly that the man is absolutely sincere, I think that his behavior at the concert, his own flippant, hammy attitude, plus the nonfulfillment of his promise to produce interesting new concert music, disqualifies him and his band from any really serious consideration as concert artists. As a dance band and as a vaudeville act, the Kenton aggregation is still one of the finest in the business. But I'm afraid, at least for the present, that's all that it is.

 MEET THE BAND

December, 1935

WHO PLAYED IN NOBLE'S ENGLISH BAND?

It's the Recording Outfit That Made Ray Noble as Well as Dance History, but, Strangely Enough, Personnel Remained Unknown until Now

HERE PUBLISHED FOR THE FIRST TIME

Much has been heard of Ray Noble's English recording orchestra over here. That's the outfit which Ray Noble started, and which, in turn, started Ray Noble. For it was that smart aggregation, playing the equally smart arrangements of its leader, which introduced Noble's music to the record-following world. The rest is dance-musical history.

Yet surprisingly little is known about this English recording outfit. Every once in a while you hear people discussing it; they say: "Oh, it's wonderful"; or "Don't be silly, it's not nearly so good as his American orchestra"; or "That bunch he has playing in the Rainbow Room can't touch his English record outfit." And so it goes on.

But this is not to be an article discussing the relative merits of the two orchestras—rather it's an informative article, telling you just who the chaps are who comprised Noble's English band and who were so instrumental in spreading his fame over all sorts of maps.

First of all, many thanks to Bill Harty, Noble's sidekick, manager and drummer, for most of the information in this article. Without the aid of this popular and busy Britisher, this article would have been an impossibility.

Ray Noble's English orchestra was strictly a recording outfit. It was an all-star aggregation consisting of most of the leading instrumentalists in England—men who played nightly with one or another of England's leading dance orchestras, but who popped up at the H. M. V. studios long enough, and often enough, to rehearse thoroughly the fine arrangements of Ray Noble and then to wax them for posterity and record buyers.

Much credit goes, of course, to the individual men. Just as much, though, must go to Ray Noble. For it was the combination of the great musical ability of the men and the consistently exquisite arrangements of Ray Noble that resulted in the fine set of recordings labeled "Ray Noble and his New Mayfair Orchestra, (Recorded in England)."

But on to the men themselves. To begin with, the lineup: Saxes: (1) Freddy Gardner (2) George Smith, (3) Ernest Ritte or Bob Wise, (4) Laurie Payne. Trumpets: (1) Maxie Goldberg, (2) Bill Shakespeare. Trombones: (1) Lew Davis, (2) Tony Thorpe. Violins: (1) Reg Pursglove, (2) Jean Pougnet, (3) Eric Siday. Viola and sax: Harry Berly. Piano: Harry Jacobson. Guitar: Bert Thomas. Bass: Jack Fretts or Tiny Winters. Drums: Bill Harty. Vocals: Al Bowlly.

Freddy Gardner (now with Reg Pursglove), considered to be England's greatest sax man . . . of the Ellington alto tone and school . . . discovered in a small cafe by Bill Harty . . . outstanding hot recording work near the end of *You Ought to See Sally on Sunday.*

George Smith (with Carroll Gibbons): a thoroughly reliable tenorman . . . very solid . . . excellent tenor lead when required . . . more of a legitimate than a hot man.

Ernest Ritte (with Lew Stone): beautifully toned alto . . . an outstanding leadman, playing lead on many of the records . . . very reliable and solid.

Bob Wise (with Maurice Winnick): equally as reliable as Ritte . . . not as good a leadman but still mighty fine . . . spent more time in the air in his own planes than in the studios with Noble.

Ray Noble's English orchestra: (l. to r.) Max Goldberg, George Smith, Tony Thorpe, Bill Shakespeare, Laurie Payne, Bert Thomas, Harry Jacobson, Jack Evetts, Bill Harty, Al Bowlly (seated on floor), Noble, Reg Pursglove, Bob Wise, Eric Siday, Ernest Ritte, Jean Pougnet. Not in photo: Freddy Gardner, Lew Davis, Harry Berly

Laurie Payne (with Carroll Gibbons): plays one of the prettiest, if not the prettiest, baritone sax in captivity . . . note recordings of *Love Locked Out* and *By the Fireside*, especially final ensemble chorus of latter . . . also an exceptionally sweet alto man . . . lend an ear to *Blues in My Heart*.

Maxie Goldberg (with Bert Ambrose): a terrific lead trumpeter as well as one of the finest hot tooters of all time . . . for hot note him on *Brighter Than the Sun* and *Sally on Sunday* . . . for equally brilliant smooth get a load of the first chorus of *Hold My Hand* . . . also noted as the only living Canadian with a cockney accent.

Bill Shakespeare (with Carroll Gibbons): a good all-around trumpeter . . . solid work behind Goldberg plus great technique on hitting high notes . . . never threw a pass for Notre Dame or wrote a play for Queen Elizabeth.

Lew Davis (with Lew Stone): considered to play the greatest dance trombone in England . . . style a cross between Teagarden and Mole, if that's possible . . . note hot on *Who Walks In When I Walk Out* . . . very pretty smooth, too . . . pay attention to opening high chorus of *This Is Romance* and closing chorus of Lew Stone's record of *Don't Change*.

Tony Thorpe (with Jack Jackson): very pretty trombone . . . also very valuable for his fine work on third trumpet.

Reg Pursglove (now leading his own orchestra at the Embassy Club in London): considered to possess the finest fiddle recording tone in England . . . listen to his pretty solo on *Mad About the Boy* . . . a great first chair artist.

Jean Pougnet (free lance): noted for his great technical work . . . a thorough artist . . . first violinist for the London Symphony . . . note his introduction on *Love Is the Sweetest Thing*.

Eric Siday (formerly with Henry Hall; now touring someplace in South America): a terrific modern hot fiddler . . . considered by some to out-Venuti

Venuti . . . great ideas, technique and four-string work . . . listen to background of *Driftin' Tide*.

Harry Berly (free lance and with Lew Stone): noted as the finest viola player in England . . . gives own recitals . . . plays both in London Symphony and London Philharmonic . . . has solo spots on British Broadcasting Company . . . surprisingly enough a fine hot tenor sax man.

Harry Jacobson (with Carroll Gibbons): possessor of a beautiful piano touch and exquisite taste . . . featured on innumerable records . . . note especially *The Very Thought of You* and *Hold My Hand* . . . not a hot tinkler but a fine dance band man.

Bert Thomas (with Howard Jacobs): a strong, steady guitar . . . English style with perhaps a bit less heavy plunking than most English guitar men.

Jack Evetts (with Carroll Gibbons): fine, legitimate bassist with great tone . . . listen to *Mad About the Boy* and *Ich Liebe Dich, My Dear*.

Tiny Winters (with Lew Stone): perhaps not quite as legitimate as Evetts, but a better hot man . . . also a Bill Harty discovery.

Bill Harty (Lew Stone): considered to be one of the greatest living drummers . . . refuses to admit it . . . very solid with great technique . . . listen to *Sailing on the Robert E. Lee* . . . also possessor of fine taste on smooth tunes.

Al Bowlly (Lew Stone): recording with Noble ever since *Lady of Madrid* and now with him over here . . . a great stylist and personality . . . plays much guitar in his own quiet way.

And that's that so far as the men in Ray Noble's English band are concerned. Of course, you know, there's an entirely different group playing now for Noble in the Rainbow Room. That outfit was discussed in some detail in the Dance Band Review columns of the July METRONOME.

What you may not know, though, is that Ray Noble has led a third band, known as the Holland orchestra. It's an all-star outfit of Britishers which Noble collected to make a European tour. They made a few records, including the much discussed *Tiger Rag*. Unfortunately space does not permit a discussion of that fine outfit; perhaps in time to come there'll be an article about it in these pages. What say you?

OZZIE NELSON

●

Ozzie Nelson—nickname: Randy . . . real name: Oswald George . . . a Rutgers University graduate and lawyer . . . a super-mediocre malted-milk-with-two-scoops-of-ice-cream drinker . . . doesn't drink anything else . . . doesn't smoke or wear a hat . . . nuts about wife Harriet Hilliard, son, son's picture, and tennis . . . a fine athlete who played on his college football, boxing, lacrosse and swimming teams . . . keeps in condition via penthouse exercises, walking a mile and a half home from work each night, and running ad lib through crowded city streets . . . knows how to win friends and influence people . . . a very earnest and thoroughly sincere fellow whom anybody'd be proud to have as a friend . . . talks intelligent shop . . . biggest ambition is to do a great truck . . . his attempts prove he's a pretty good rumba dancer.

●

Charlie Bubeck (1st sax)—nickname: Little Butch . . . a great mechanic . . . member of the Amalgamated-P. A.-On-One-Night-Stand-Fiddlers Association . . . official card-loser of the Nelson Indoor A. C. . . . usually thinking of his red-headed baby (boy) . . . the IRT subway's biggest headache . . . commutes twenty-four miles a day for a dime . . . alternate nickname: Randy.

●

Bill Stone (2nd sax)—nickname: Big Butch . . . strong man of the Nelson A. C. . . . a willing hand lender, making it tough for him to play sax until somebody returns one of his hands . . . a breeder of dogs that do very well in shows . . . another extensive commuter . . . official checker champ of the Nelson Semi-Indoor A. C. . . . alternate nickname: Randy.

●

Bill Nelson (3rd sax)—nickname: Slippery . . . not a boss's relative though an original member of the band . . . a great philosopher whose prime conception of life is that eight bottles a day of Guinness' Stout make a swell tonic . . . consequently very quiet . . . never wears a hat . . . commutes to Pelham every night . . . alternate nickname: Randy.

●

Hollingsworth Humphreys (1st trumpet)—nickname: Holly . . . star member of the Amateur Cinema League . . . makes entire movies alone, even playing all parts himself . . . a writer of ability . . . fine dog raiser

The Ozzie Nelson band (even before 1937). Front row: Harriet Hilliard, Sid Brokaw, Bill Stone, Charlie Bubeck, Bill Nelson, Sandy Wolf and Ozzie. Back row: possibly Irving Gellers, Joe Bohan, possibly Holly Humphreys, Bo Ashford, Fred Whiteside, Harry Johnson, Harry Murphy. Trombonist Smithers had not yet joined

but an even greater golf score lowerer (when nobody's peeking) . . . possessor of a perennially embryonic mustache . . . alternate nickname: Randy.

●

Bo Ashford (2nd trumpet)—nickname: Toughie . . . a Casa Loma importee . . . best and fastest driver in the Nelson Outdoor A. C. . . . very much in love but worries even more about his embouchure . . . referred to in Arkansas history books as the Original "Mass o' Muscle Man" . . . the Nelson hot chorus man . . . alternate nickname: Randy.

●

Harry Johnson (3rd trumpet)—nickname: Heiress Snatcher . . . the band's Beau Brummel . . . the original What Will I Tell My Heart man . . . an easy-going Georgian . . . candid-camera crackpot who concentrates on snapping unsuspecting soup-eaters . . . a fine Ping-Ponger . . . prefers blondes, brunettes and redheads . . . alternate nickname: Randy.

●

Elmer Smithers (trombone)—nickname: Indiana Terror . . . can't differentiate between towns and states because he comes from Indiana, Pennsylvania . . . quiet . . . best Ping-Pong player, second best checker man, and worst golfer in Nelson Indoor And Outdoor A. C., Inc. . . . owns two dogs . . . practices horn

three hours a day . . . insists that friend wife consider his embouchure first in all closeup scenes . . . alternate nickname: Randy.

●

Sid Brokaw (violin)—nickname: The Sarge . . . Nelson's right-hand man, substitute tempo-setter, on-the-stand caller, and between-sets timekeeper . . . now studying tenor sax . . . will play with section . . . can play two notes but can't decide on what kind of horn, mouthpiece, reed, straps or stands to buy . . . proud husband of attractive warbler Martha Mears . . . alternate nickname: Randy.

●

Irving Gellers (piano)—nickname: The Killer . . . greatest defense attorney in the Nelson Legal Society . . . a Bronx double papa . . . newest member of the band . . . alternate nickname: Randy.

●

Harry Murphy (piano)—nickname: Joe Hollywood . . . the flash dresser of the Nelson Young Men's Wholesale Clothing Union . . . quiet . . . original pianist of the band . . . proud possessor of a super-colossal, super-British, superbutterfly black bow tie . . . a 52nd Street inhabitant . . . attends four cocktail parties every two and a half days . . . alternate nickname: Randy.

Sandy Wolf (guitar)—nickname: Grave Digger . . . always speaking for the entire band . . . another original member who always reminisces about those Glen Island Casino days . . . a social lion who keeps waiters waiting for forty-three minutes after closing time every two and a half days . . . most dishes don't tempt him but kidney stew . . . alternate nickname: Randy.

Fred Whiteside (bass)—nickname: Dale Carnegie . . . a philosopher of no mean merit . . . a collector and lover of classical records . . . commutes every day from and to Maplewood, New Jersey . . . will walk eight miles every two and a half days to get: (1) a dish of chow mein; (2) two dishes of sauerbraten . . . alternate nickname: Randy.

Joe Bohan (drums)—nickname: Joe . . . recently voted as the best burglar-off-fire-escape-chaser in the world . . . official band statistician and newspaper reader . . . alternate nickname: Joe.

The Duke and the most expansive spread

April, 1937

DUKE ELLINGTON

Duke Ellington (leader and piano)—God's greatest gift to jazz . . . tremendously popular and exceedingly modest . . . world's greatest jive artist and protagonist of Ellingtonian chivalry . . . hates peanuts on pianos, whistling on stage, three on a match, dangling buttons . . . consequently the inventor of wraparound coats . . . rabid bridge player . . . calls his slight, slender wife "Tubby" . . . always orders last so that the stuff he swipes from other people's plates will agree with what he's eating . . . deadly serious only about his music . . . his colossal feats in that department are too well known to bear repetition.

Otto Hardwick (1st sax)—bald at 19 . . . now 32 . . . looks older . . . used to fiddle bass in Washington . . . dad carried it to work for him . . . got his first sax job from Duke . . . very amiable and exceedingly sociable with drinkers . . . biggest ambition is to beat Duke "pulling those two-a-day gags."

Barney Bigard (2nd sax and featured clarinet)—hates playing tenor but dotes on clarinet . . . wants Duke to get a straight tenorman . . . a Noo Ohlins Creole who used to play with King Oliver and who's blessed with thousands of French relatives who drag him off all trains to kiss him . . . unlimited hot, cold, sweet or bitter coffee drinker . . . a bridge fanatic who's devoted to his wife and three kids too . . . described as a yard wide and a yard and one inch tall in stature.

Johnny Hodges (3rd sax and featured alto)—one of those small men who loves his night life and the wing of any chicken . . . always has a box of food that's quickly devoured by the sea-gullic Ellingtonians . . . perpetual gambler who always stays the full limit . . . spends his winnings on lamb chops and peas.

Harry Carney (4th sax and featured baritone)—a big, bashful Bostonian who used to play with Toots Mondello . . . very easygoing . . . partner with Hardwick in Amateur Photography Co. . . . has two trunkloads full of all kinds of stuff . . . one of those very lovable guys . . . charter member of the new vocal trio.

Artie Whetsol (1st trumpet)—went to Howard University to become a doctor but the call of the wild, in the form of Ellington, got him . . . very loyal . . . always on job even when not well . . . intellectual . . . tender personality . . . a press agent's pet love . . . a bridge fanatic . . . a press agent's pet hate.

Cootie Williams (trumpet)—a statuesque figure with great esprit de corps who just gives and gives in whoops . . . terrific overeater and chronic gambler . . . but a smart one . . . good advisor on both music and commercialism . . . another bridge fiend . . . always borrowing somebody's trombone to emit the best gutbucket slide choruses in the band.

Rex Stewart (trumpet)—round guy: sort of a five-cent scoop of ice cream on top of a ten-cent scoop figure . . . a graduate of Wilberforce University . . . loves his horn best of all . . . tries all different styles . . . can hit E above C above high C . . . another gambler and trio man.

Freddy Jenkins (trumpet)—back in the band after years' absence due to illness . . . nickname "Posey" because of his posing ways . . . showman all the time . . . a solid jive man, maladjusted New Jersey real estate agent and another Wiberforce grad . . . always writing letters in the world's fanciest hand.

Joe Nanton (trombone)—strictly gutbucket . . . a fine storyteller . . . used to carry tricks around in his pocket (thus nicknamed "Tricky") . . . now always carries *Time* magazine in his pocket and an almanac in his berth to answer all arguments he bets on . . . a fine connoisseur of liquors.

Lawrence Brown (trombone)—a crooner at heart . . . has played symphony . . . his dad, a Topeka minister, taught him every instrument except trombone . . . excellent ideas on arrangements . . . disagrees in all arguments but in a gentlemanly way . . . used to be a policeman in Los Angeles . . . husband of famed dramatic actress, Freddie Washington . . . always explains the straight and narrow path idea to all young girls.

Juan Tizol (trombone)—musically the most thoroughly educated man in the band . . . arrived from Puerto Rico to play symphony . . . still plays valve trombone . . . goes into raptures over Spanish music . . . dances a plenty solid rumba.

Freddy Guy (guitar)—close pal of Duke's who's been with him since 1923 when he joined as a "fly banjo" player . . . in bed most of the day . . . one of the bridge players . . . claims to have the most perfect watch in the world upon which the sun depends entirely.

Billy Taylor (bass)—a real family man . . . three kids . . . world's greatest five-and-ten shopper . . . always sending novelties and electric stuff home . . . famous for putting dimmers in Pullman car lights . . . very sincere sort of chap . . . conservative too.

Hayes Alvis (bass)—Chicagoan who used to play with Jelly Roll Morton . . . mystery man when it comes to age . . . outstanding amateur photographer . . . has passed his first aviator's test . . . a member of the new trio . . . used to have charge of Mills Blue Rhythm bunch . . . possesses some sort of a mysterious office in California.

Sonny Greer (drums)—with Duke since 1920 . . . oldest but youngest-looking man in band . . . spends all his money buying drums and all his time making sure they're shined . . . a great belly-laugh provoker . . . two drinks and he's knocked out "thereby," in the words of Duke, "saving the wear and tear on the body" . . . loves to look at high buildings and to be two hours early for every show . . . has friends everywhere . . . leads a heavy night life . . . a grandfather at the age of 37!

TOMMY DORSEY

Tommy Dorsey—The Original Bernardsville, N. J., Farmhand . . . checks up on each of his 165 chicks each night before hitting his own hay . . . talks golfdom's greatest thirty-over-par-game . . . self-named God's Gift to Bus Drivers . . . continually worrying about financial affairs, cracking his knuckles, and bending all fingers way back . . . kills all the many guests at his estate with funny stories . . . reminisces about the time his old man made him toot in the town band from a tree stump so he'd look like something.

Mike Doty (1st sax)—Former University of Minnesota All-American thirty-third sub right tackle . . . eats a lot (viz., 8½ eggs per breakfast) but certainly is hefty (viz., down to 320 lbs.) . . . happily married . . . jolly, except when vetoing all Johnny Mince suggestions . . . used to front (in a big way) Doty's Ding Dong Daddies.

Bud Freeman (2nd sax)—Shakespeare behind a mouthpiece . . . the greatest golf-stroke-chopper-downer east of San Antonio, wherein resides a long-lost love . . . continually mooning about and composing new licks . . . can't stop talking about "those beautiful changes."

Johnny Mince (3rd sax)—The official *In a Mist* man . . . always missing a 0.25 note while dreaming about an f1.5 camera lens . . . his female admirers languish everywhere . . . good golfer . . . vetoes all Mike Doty suggestions . . . proud of his Lloyd Hamilton cap . . . up at 7 each a.m to take exercises for "breath conservation."

Fred Stulce (4th sax)—A Texas Ranger who's forsaken steers for steering wheels . . . continually looking for a newfangled supercharger and for a female date for breakfast . . . holds a mean wheel and any gal's hand . . . soft disposition . . . graduated from S. M. U.

Andy Ferretti (1st trpt.)—The Original Griping Bringdown Man . . . likes nothing and wants to eat babies all day . . . The Boston Onyx Club Dandy . . . hates Minneapolis . . . "sure would like to get a girl!" . . . has a mania for watching for Buicks.

Peewee Erwin (2nd trpt.)—No. 2 Gripe Man . . . recently and happily hitched . . . a great astrologist who'd just as soon be hitched to a star . . . always looking for things through a telescope and building little garages on the stand . . . loves to roller-skate downhill . . . busy inventing a mechanical trumpet.

Joe Bauer (3rd trpt.)—Strictly a slow-moving guy from Green-pernt, Brooklyn . . . can hit anything driving in and out of traffic—and does . . . a tinkler . . . sure would like to learn to dance . . . always dopes

Jack Leonard, Edythe Wright and Tommy observe guitarist Carmen Mastren

the horses wrong . . . can't figure out why he always borrows tablecloths from restaurants.

•

Les Jenkins (trmb.)—The One and Only Powter-waterbwee-County-Oklahoma-Flash . . . intimates know him as Few Clothes and as Curly . . . fond of golf . . . shoots a much better rifle . . . tortoise-tempoed . . . grabs at fantastically colored shirts.

•

E. W. Bone (trmb.)—The man with no first name . . . his loving wife knows but won't tell what it used to be . . . won't admit his 84 makes him the best golfer in the band . . . always running after ballplayers to tell them their averages . . . a finger-licker . . . can get you one-third off on anything at all.

•

Howard Smith (piano)—Another of those happily married men . . . goes for Canadians . . . world's champion French toastmaker and eater . . . worried stiff about gaining weight . . . practices scales backwards and inside out all day . . . no drinkee—no smokee.

•

Carmen Mastren (guitar)—Le Detective Incomparable . . . always finding everybody's wrong notes and returning right ones . . . worried stiff about his health . . . incumbent of last month's METRONOME Hall of Fame.

•

Gene Traxler (bass)—The band's big, handsome athlete . . . great tenniser . . . extremely quiet and happily married . . . his baby's greatest admirer . . . sings and shim-shams while he plays.

•

Dave Tough (drums)—The band's mental wizard . . . extremely intellectual and able at writing . . . plays good golf, too . . . would rather quit drums entirely than have to sock a chime, a triangle, or a temple-block.

•

Edythe Wright (vocals)—The Warbling Outdoor Girl Scout and Camp Fire Girl all in one . . . great sport, swimmer, tenniser and cook . . . gets all upset when you mention the word Mergentroid.

•

Jack Leonard (vocals)—Doesn't believe in all the love stuff he sings about . . . still looking for ideal girl, though . . . can't seem to find her . . . very near-sighted (explanation?) . . . a great admirer of the Dorsey brand of phrasing.

•

Odd (Axel) Stordahl (vocals and arranger)—A Whacky Swede . . . can spot any ickey a mile off and imitate him perfectly before he arrives . . . a great symphony fan and record collector . . . makes many rye faces but drinks more milk and eats more apple pie . . . happily enamored of and by pretty songstress Gail Reese.

Gene Krupa on Buddy Rich (July, 1954)—

Buddy Rich, to me, is the greatest drummer of all time, bar none. Actually, I wouldn't be surprised if studying might hurt him, because Buddy is both the most natural and the most uninhibited drummer I've ever heard, and if he tried to figure out how and why he did certain things, he might lose some of that amazing freedom that characterizes his work.

September, 1939

BOB CROSBY

The Leader Man

Bob Crosby came into his own as a bandleader in 1936, when Tommy Rockwell took him from the Dorsey Brothers' band and stuck him in front of what used to be the Ben Pollack outfit. Then he was a modest chap, anxious to learn, carried on by a rare sense of humor. Today he's still the same, except, perhaps, that he's learned some things.

Crosby is far more concerned with the band than he is with himself. Singing to him is something that he *has* to do, but it doesn't interest him nearly so much as fronting the band and trying to make it get somewhere. In which undertaking he has been eminently successful.

Obviously the social go-between for the Dixieland Dispensers and the rest of the world, Bob has done a fine job. At first shy, and often quite misunderstood, he rapidly gained the requisite poise, till now he makes one of the finest front men in the business. Throughout, his quick wit has been of tremendous importance, with his ability to keep his head down to an extremely normal size running a close second on the Asset List.

Recently he became a proud papa—his few-months-old daughter already writes him regularly, something which he can't explain. He's a good golfer, a fine tennis player, and follows the horses as closely as those of his brother, Bing, do.

President "Pops"

The guys in the Crosby band call him "Pops." Business associates refer to him as the president of the Crosby band. Friends outside the business nest call him Gil. Gil Rodin is his full name.

Together he and Ben Pollack ran the old Pollack band that harbored such greats as Benny Goodman, Jack Teagarden, Glenn Miller, Sterling Bose, Bud Freeman. When the Pollack band broke up, many of the men gathered under "Pops'" wing for a while before Bob Crosby came along to front for them, and when he did the boys rewarded "Pops" by electing him president of their band corporation, of which Crosby became vice-president.

Today everything, both in music and business, that the band does depends upon Rodin. People on the inside and out come to him. Even Crosby consults him on all matters.

But the casual outsider never would suspect all this. To them, Gil Rodin is just the second tenorman, who never takes a chorus, and who might even be replaced in the band quite easily. They never suspect, because Gil never lets them. Extremely self-effacing, he lives for the band instead of for himself.

The less casual insider knows all this, however, and those closest to the band have come to respect and love Gil Rodin as few men in the business have ever been respected and loved. To most of them he is, without any qualification whatsoever, the finest guy in the entire music business: the most honest, the decentest, the sincerest of all. Than which there can be no higher praise!

RAY BAUDUC (drums)—Band's chief worrier: always sure the boys get on the stand on time . . . constantly creating stuff: anything from a foot pedal spring to an arrangement . . . admits never having studied much drums: just picked it up from an older brother in hometown Noo Ohlins . . . now acknowledged as the greateast dixieland drummer in the world.

BILLY BUTTERFIELD (trumpet)—Plays most of the lead and most of the hot . . . a chubby lad in his early twenties who expects to be the father of something even chubbier any day now . . . very easygoing . . . constantly turning down offers from other bandleaders.

SHORTY SHEROCK (trumpet)—A recent importation from Jimmy Dorsey's band who before that had been imported from Gary, Ind. . . . waitresses consider him an ickey . . . young and impressionable . . . goes in for outlandish clothes . . . possessor of a brilliant future.

RAY CONNIFF (trombone)—Another recent importation, Bunny Berigan having been the previous owner . . . a young, quiet New Englander whose pretty style and tone amazes the entire band constantly . . . sports a beautiful girl friend named "Dixie," and a rabbit's foot on his trombone . . . writes pretty melodies.

IRVING FAZOLA (clarinet)—Known as "Fun-Loving Tom" . . . real name, Irving Prestopnik . . . plays typical hometown Noo Ohlins style plus a knockout piano . . . formerly with Ben Pollack and Glenn Miller, who still wants him back . . . fat and easy-going, except when aroused—then watch out!

BOB HAGGART (Bass)—To many, the musical brains behind the band, his arrangements setting a merry pace . . . gets the dixieland idea perfectly, despite hailing from Douglaston, Long Island . . . a graphic artist, too, with a keen sense of humor . . . plays guitar, trumpet and piano . . . the band's chief lady-killer.

JOE KEARNS (lead sax)—Quietest man in the band . . . used to play plenty of hot clarinet with Jan Savitt and still longs to get off more often . . . from the deep South, though Philly's now his home town . . . mighty proud of the trumpet played by his brother, "Buddy."

NAPPY LAMARE (guitar)—Personality lad of the band, in his own impy way . . . his high voice and laugh pop up at all crucial moments . . . sports three-year-old son who knows just about every great in dancebandom . . . the band's chief "Scooper," both editorially and cinemagraphically.

MATTY MATLOCK (arranger)—Played all the jazz clarinet till Fazola came along . . . now only arranging, though still ranking as one of the world's greats on the stick . . . always smiling and good-natured . . . together wtih Haggart has been responsible for the band's finest arrangements . . . Eddie Miller's inseparable buddy.

EDDIE MILLER (hot tenor sax)—Noo Ohlins personified in talk and in playing . . . blows a great clarinet and sings a fine song . . . in his middle twenties with an eleven-year-old son . . . worships Leon Rappolo . . . smiles almost as much as Matlock . . . musicians vote him the best hot tenor in the land.

GIL RODIN (tenor sax)—Band prexy . . . always worrying about the outfit's musical and financial affairs . . . only diversions are golf and the Chicago Cubs . . . from Chicago . . . graduate of Northwestern University there.

WARREN SMITH (trombone)—Plays most of the hot, as well as in the Bob Cats . . . another quiet guy with a ditto smile . . . joined the band a couple of years ago from Michigan . . . married and papa.

BILL STEGMEYER (alto sax)—Another Michiganian . . . latest addition and latest papa in the band . . . plays fine hot alto and makes good arrangements . . . helps Crosby find keys for new tunes . . . formerly with Glenn Miller.

JOE SULLIVAN (piano)—The Prodigal Son returns . . . famous for years as a brilliant pianist, but cut down while with the Crosbians almost three years ago by a serious disease . . . still taking it easy, perhaps because of an additional sixty pounds . . . composer of *Little Rock Getaway, Onyx Breakdown,* etc. . . . grand sense of humor.

ZEKE ZARCHY (trumpet)—"Reuben From Brooklyn" . . . has played with just about every big swing band in the country . . . plays some lead for Crosby and can play pretty fair jazz . . . a whacky sense of humor and a transient mustache . . . one of the band's few singles.

HELEN WARD—Though not officially a member of the band, since she sings with it only on its Camel commercial, she rates plenty high musically and personally with all the boys . . . you remember her from her Goodman days . . . now really Mrs. Albert Marx . . . a real musician, who plays fine piano and always shows impeccable taste . . . extremely sweet and gracious towards all.

DOROTHY CLAIRE—Band's regular gal warbler . . . started off as a specialty act at the Blackhawk, but her potentialities were too great to let her remain there . . . extremely eager to learn all about the business and as sincere a girl as the band business has ever known . . . plenty of personality . . . resents terribly being referred to as a jitterbug.

JOE KEARNS—Rodin's assistant and general man of much work . . . Redheaded childhood chum of Crosby's, whose equally ready wit has tided over many tough situations . . . watches over all details.

HIX BLUETT—Copyist, part-time arranger, instrument caretaker, truck driver, Bauduc drum-setter-up and tearer-downer . . . an easygoing Texan with a Will Rogers sense of humor and delivery . . . fine artist: his sketches on the arrangements constantly break up the entire band, calling numerous halts to arrangements and record dates.

Lionel Hampton on Grunting While Playing (March, 1938)—

Now, about that noise I make. I guess you could call it a cross between a running grunt and something along a delayed squeal. You know, honestly, the first time I heard it on a record nobody was any more baffled than me. But I never let on. It handed Benny a good laugh from the start, and the more I tried to remember to soft-pedal it, the more I'd grunt. So to 'ell with it.

Crosby boardwalkers: Bob and Dorothy Claire
Joey Kearns and Gil Rodin
Fazola and Bob Haggart
Joe Sullivan and Ray Bauduc
Ray Conniff and Eddie Miller
Billy Butterfield and Bill Stegmeyer
Nappy Lamare and Shorty Sherock

STAN KENTON

BOB AHERN—guitar . . . 27 years old . . . comes from Oakland, Calif. . . . graduated from Washington University, St. Louis . . . used to play piano . . . with Kenton four years.

CHICO ALVAREZ—plays good portion of jazz trumpet . . . one of original members of band . . . rejoined last February after three years in army . . . used to play violin.

JOHNNY ANDERSON—plays all parts in trumpet section . . . loves to jam . . . comes from Fort Smith, Arkansas . . . joined band in April, 1945 . . . hipped on all sports.

AL ANTHONY—claims to be smallest lead alto man in business . . . claims he's only five feet one . . . comes from Brockton, Mass. . . . worships daughter . . . joined band in 1945.

MILTON BERNHART—plays second tram . . . joined Sept., 1946, shortly after discharge from army where he played with Dorris and Forbes . . . from Chicago . . . worships Delius.

BUDDY CHILDERS—splits trumpet lead . . . joined band at 16, only 20 now . . . comes from St. Louis . . . owns an AT 6 plane . . . likes Dizzy, Miles Davis, Hal Baker.

JUNE CHRISTY—succeeded Anita O'Day in band in July, 1945 in Chicago . . . comes from Decatur, Ill. . . . very happy creature . . . 21 years old . . . real name is Shirley Lester.

BOB COOPER—wants to be able to play tenor as well as idols Lucky Thompson and Don Byas . . . avid bebop man . . . comes from Pittsburgh . . . 21 years old . . . haunts 52d St.

RED DORRIS—plays most of jazz tenor . . . rejoined band after two years in army . . . used to be band's vocalist . . . married to Dolly Mitchell, former Stan Kenton singer.

HARRY FORBES—copies music as well as plays trombone in band . . . one of crew's original members . . . comes from California . . . rejoined after army stint in July, 1946.

BOB GIOGA—road manager, baritone saxist, *the* dependable guy in the band . . . with Kenton since outfit started . . . native Los Angelesian . . . goes for sailing and photography.

KEN HANNA—plays 5th trumpet . . . also arranges . . . recently discharged from navy . . . home: Baltimore, Md. . . . married . . . likes to spend time bowling and playing softball.

Stan Kenton leads METRONOME's Band of 1946. Saxists are Red Dorris, Boots Mussilli, Al Anthony, Bob Gioga and Al Cooper. Trombones are Skip Layton, Harry Forbes, Kai Winding, Milt Bernhart and Bart Varsalona. Trumpets are Johnny Anderson, Buddy Childers, Ray Wetzel, Ken Hanna and Chico Alvarez. Bob Ahern is on guitar, Eddie Safranski on bass, Shelly Manne on drums. Photo taken in the Cafe Rouge

SKIP LAYTON—latest addition to band. Joined trombone section during current run at Paramount . . . from Elmira, N. Y. . . . Played in Bobby Sherwood's *Hear That Trumpet.*

SHELLY MANNE—native New Yorker . . . with Kenton nine months . . . 26 years old . . . married . . . loves Italian food . . . wife's name is Flip . . . used to drum for Les Brown.

BOOTS MUSSILLI—featured hot alto man . . . likes Hodges, Parker and Carter . . . comes from Boston . . . married and has three daughters . . . ambition: to settle down with family.

PETE RUGULO—arranger who has set band's present style . . . quiet, modest, intensely interested in music . . . comes from Santa Rosa, Calif. . . . holds several degrees . . . married.

EDDIE SAFRANSKI—first made name for himself playing bass with McIntyre . . . comes from Pittsburgh . . . married . . . has one daughter . . . used to play fiddle . . . flying addict.

BART VARSALONA—one of the few bass trombonists in captivity . . . has been with band four years . . . comes from Bayonne, N. J. . . . considered to be top-flight comedian.

RAY WETZEL—splits 1st trumpet book with Childers . . . played with Herman and Powell . . . comes from Parkersburg, W. Va. . . . only 22 . . . loves all types of food.

KAI WINDING—plays hot trombone and much of lead . . . comes from Copenhagen, Denmark . . . came to America in 1934 . . . joined band a year ago . . . 3 years in Coast Guard.

Frank Sinatra on Why He Decided to Start His Career as a Single (December, 1953)—

I don't think I ever told anybody this before, but the reason I started on my own when I did was because I wanted to make sure I got there as a single before Bob Eberly did. I knew that if that guy ever did it first, I'd never be able to make it the way I did. That Eberly, he sang so rich and so pure, it used to frighten me. Even today, guys who sing in his fashion can't even sit in the same room with him. That guy has always been too much, and I knew he'd be too much for me if he ever got started on his own before I did.

February, 1946

On re-reading this interview, I still can't decide whether Sy was putting me on. He likes to, as you can see by his remarks alongside my review of the Jimmie Lunceford band, and as I've discovered through our close to thirty years of friendship. No, I don't think that anyone with such great talent could really feel about it the way Sy says here he feels about his. What do you think?

SY OLIVER ARRANGES

Sy Oliver's a plain, commercial arranger. Always has been. So says Sy Oliver.

"I'm just plain lucky with the publicity I've gotten. Hell, you're bound to get it when you arrange for Dorsey. My name's just been tossed before the public and so they like it, I guess."

Which is not just second-guessing, it's about nine-hundred-and-fifty-second-guessing. For Sy Oliver's got the reason for his success all wrong. Only he'll never know it or admit it. He's a helluva stubborn guy. But you and I know, so just let the gent rave on. Let his wife, Billie, listen to him. She has to. We can run away.

Billie's been listening to him since 1933 when she stopped using the name of Farnsworth. Like Sy, she came from Zanesville, Ohio, only unlike Sy she wasn't born on December 17, 1910, and her real first name isn't Melvin. Nor is her middle name

Sy Oliver at a METRONOME All-Star record date, surrounded by Tommy Dorsey, Rex Stewart, Tom Whaley, Duke Ellington's music copyist, Johnny Hodges, and the Duke himself

James. Nor was her mother a fine pianist and teacher like Mrs. Oliver. Nor did her father teach music to just about every kid in town except Sy, as Mr. Oliver did. That's 'cause little Melvin wouldn't practice, especially the piano which pa and ma tried to foist on him. But then later on when so many of his friends got out nights so they could play in bands, Sy's commercial side came out and he got his father to teach him trumpet. He learned fast. And good, too.

Only thing, when he'd finished learning Dad said he couldn't go out anyway. And after all that work.

But next year Sy's dad had a stroke and Sy had to go out to earn money. So he joined Al Sears's band and did all right, making fifty and sixty bucks a week. That was good dough for a kid. Still is.

After high school graduation he joined several bands, mostly Zack White's, and while playing in Cincinnati he was heard by Jimmie Lunceford for whom he wrote some arrangements. Several months later Jimmie asked him to join the band. Sy didn't want to very much, but the band was going to New York and Sy and Billie wanted to go to school there (they were married by now), so they went. At least Billie went to school. Sy was too busy.

Sy stayed with Jimmie from 1933 to 1939. His arrangements are generally conceded to have been the making of the band. Stuff like *For Dancers Only, My Blue Heaven, Four or Five Times, Stomp It Off, Cheatin' on Me, Tain't What You Do*, etc.

"Those arrangements," says Sy lightly and slightingly about bits of music that have been gospel to thousands of musicians, "they were all just alike. I couldn't write. It's just that those guys played so well. Anybody could have written for that band."

His enthusiasm can be reflected by the amount of his remuneration. He was so het up about the band that he wrote arrangements for two dollars and fifty cents, and that included copying! Later on he wanted more dough, very, very much more dough and he and Jimmie couldn't get together. So Sy quit. In fact, so he says, he quit the music business.

But the night he quit, Lou Levy of Leeds Music, Andrews Sisters and Harvest Moon fame listened in and he told everybody and soon everybody was calling the Oliver home and asking Sy would he please write some arrangements and Sy was telling them all no dice but Billie happened to be near the phone and she kept saying he could go to school later on but that he ought to take some job now because he seemed to be hot so she talked him into trying it at least.

"So I tried it," says Sy, "chose Tommy and here I am. Some story, huh?" And the tall, roundheaded, barrel-chested, happy-faced guy gives off with one of those "so-you-see-I'm-not-Superman!" looks.

"You know, I can never quite understand it. There are so many better arrangers than me who don't get the reward they deserve. Guys like Eddie Sauter and Billy Finegan can write rings around me. Me, I never even took a lesson in my life. Someday I will, though. Meanwhile, I still never get over being surprised if an arrangement turns out successful. The most surprised party is me!"

February, 1948

This interview with Monk took place in my Greenwich Village living room before he had received major recognition, though he seemed to sense that would soon be coming. One moment of that afternoon stands out in my memory: Monk had left the room after having illustrated a few points on the piano. Immediately, his manager asked me what I thought. Monk's multi-pause style had confused me and I told him so. "Man," he said, "that's just it. It's not so much the notes he plays as the ones he leaves out that mean so much!"

BOP'S DIXIE TO MONK

Thelonious, Responsible for Much Of Modern Jazz, Isn't Satisfied With All That's Happening to It

Bebop should be planned and organized and then blown. Otherwise, according to Monk, "it turns out to be like dixieland, with everybody blowing for themselves." And the trouble with most bop as it's blown today, again according to Monk, is that "too many guys don't know what they're doin'!"

Who's Monk and what's *he* doin'? Monk is Monk, first name Thelonious, if you want to get technical. He has been credited by several leading boppists, including Charlie Parker, with having started this altered chord style of playing jazz during the nights in the early forties when he played piano at Minton's in Harlem. Monk himself doesn't think he actually

413

plays bop, at least not the way it's being played today. "Mine is more original," he says. "They think differently, harmonically. They play mostly stuff that's based on the chords of other things, like the blues and *I Got Rhythm.* I like the whole song, melody and chord structure, to be different. I make up my own chords and melodies."

Monk has been playing his own chords for years. He's a New Yorker, born there in 1918, the only musical member of a family that, so far as he knows, is unmusical. "I never studied. I just experimented arranging. You learn most harmonics by experience. You fool around and listen. Most chord structure is practically arithmetic, anyway. You just have to use common sense."

He first started experimenting with chords and rhythmic effects in a four-piece group with which he used to gig. That was in 1939. Jimmy Wright played tenor, Keg Purnell was the drummer and the bassist was named Masapequha. He could have

Monk

gone with big bands, but "bands never did knock me out. I wanted to play my own chords. I wanted to create and invent on little jobs." So little jobs he played.

Then he landed at Minton's, a Harlem spot run by former bandleader Teddy Hill, who says, "Monk would fall asleep all the time. He'd stay there hours after the place closed, or get there hours before we opened. Sometimes the musicians would appeal to me to see if I could wake him up. Suddenly he might wake up and go into some intricate, tricky little passage, with Kenny Clarke playing those funny, off-beat effects on the drums." (METRONOME, April, 1947.)

Clarke was one of the four regulars at Minton's. Joe Guy played trumpet and Nick Fenton was on bass. A lot of musicians used to hang out up there, Diz and Bird, Charlie Christian, Kermit Scott, Ike Quebec, Ben Webster, King Cole, Mary Lou Williams, Max Roach, Art Blakey, whom Monk considers the best of the modern drummers, and Denzil Best, known to most boppists as a drummer, but who, according to Monk, "was one of the best trumpets I ever heard. He'd outblow everybody in the place, but he had to quit because of his health."

The fact that Best recuperated and then came back in the role of a drummer should be an object lesson to a lot of musicians, feels Monk. "He didn't blow his top because he was frustrated. To me, a true musician is a guy who never gives up, even though he feels like it sometimes." Monk is not in favor of the undisciplined ways of too many modern musicians and can't sympathize with them because they blow their tops when they aren't appreciated. Though many feel that Monk hasn't received the recognition that's due him, he doesn't resent anything. "My time for fame will come." The many sides he recently cut for Blue Note Records should bring that time much nearer, he feels.

He's not too anxious to be associated with most of the bop that's being blown nowadays. Besides accusing some musicians of turning bop into something akin to dixieland, he also upbraids them with phrases like, "they molest," "they magnify," "they exaggerate." "They don't pay any attention to swing, and that goes both for the horns and the rhythm sections. They don't know where to put those bops. When the horns say *bloop*, the drummer shouldn't say *bloop, bloop, bloop* with them. You should throw in your rhythmic bops when a guy's taking a breath.

"Another thing is the chords. I can tell right off when a guy knows what he's doing. Diz and Bird, they know their chords. But too many horns use the flatted fifth where it sounds absurd, instead of where

HITS AND MISSES

One of the joys of a critic-commentator is the opportunities the post gives to discover new, unknown talent, and, at the same time, to encourage it by telling the world about it in print—and for the first time. During my *Metronome* years, especially the earlier ones, I indulged myself fairly regularly —more so than almost any other writer did—for which I often took quite a ribbing. But my enthusiasm remained intact, and almost always my predictions bore fruit, though, sad to state, quite a number of them turned out to be lemons.

What follows is a selection of those descriptions about some of the more famous artists and some of the most complete unknowns. If anyone knows whatever happened to any of the latter, I'd love to hear from you or from them.

The left-hand column contains predictions that hit the mark; the right-hand column contains those that missed.

HITS

Benny Goodman and his "Let's Dance" band are a great medicine . . . whenever this reviewer has a sour taste in his mouth from too many mediocre bands, he runs up to hear the Good-men rehearse . . . truly great outfit . . . fine arrangements, and musicians who are together all the time—they phrase together, they bite together, and they swing together . . . wonderful.—*April, 1935*

Eddie Lane uncovered a nice pianist in *Cy Walter* . . . coming from the Shadowbox in Pittsburgh (NBC), the rest of the band sounded like any average, well-rehearsed unit.—*April, 1935*

MISSES

Boston has a gal singer who rates a rave . . . *Billie Trask* at the Hotel Westminster has more personality than any one femme this reviewer has seen . . . a charmer, with a winning smile, this youngster is a cinch to click on the big stem before long.— *April, 1935*

From a review of radio show, Fox Fur Trappers, WEEI, Boston—Singers are good, with *Buddy Clark*, a local lad, slaying the lassies with a Crosby-Richman style of warbling.—*April, 1935*

From a review of Chick Webb's band—*Miss Fitzgerald* should go places.—*June, 1935*

And still in Philly, a nice toast to *Jan Savitt* and his boys broadcasting over CBS from WCAU . . . an outstanding clean and neat outfit with pretty tones . . . only drawback was a trumpet whose name must be McGee . . . band, as a whole, is certainly worth watching.—*June, 1935*

From a review of Bert Block's band—It's fun listening to the band, and you've got to give plenty of thanks to *Odd* (later "*Axel*") *Stordahl*, who has been turning in some splendid arrangements.—*September, 1935*

From a review of Al Kavelin's band—Be sure to note this lad *Carmen (Cavallaro).* He is positively sensational at the keys. A beautiful touch plus a magnificent technique permit full expression of his really genteel taste. His fill-ins behind the band, his modulations and his solos are the height of dance-musical refinement. Hi, work must be heard to be truly appreciated, And one of the biggest surprises is to hear Carmen, who quite obviously has studied much concert piano, begin to get off on some real swing.—*November, 1935*

The New York indie, WNEW, has started an interesting program a.m.'s . . . it's the Joy-makers (spelled G-L-O-O-M—that's their gag) . . . three really good vocalists who should be heard from soon . . . *Helen Forrest* who sings some hot but who shines more on ballads.—*November, 1935*

During the past year or so, this column has emitted various toasts and raves about various heretofore unknowns . . . some of them have fulfilled their promise . . . others haven't . . . at any rate, this column is continuing the same policy during the current year . . . here's number one for 1936: *Ella Fitzgerald* . . . the seventeen-year-old-gal singing up at Harlem's Savoy Ballroom with Chick Webb's fine band . . . unheralded, and practically unknown right now, but what a future . . . a great natural flair for singing . . . extraordinary intonation and figures . . . as she is right now, she's one of the best of all femme hot warblers . . . and there's no reason why she shouldn't be just about the best in time to come . . . watch her!—*January, 1936*

A singer you must watch out for, who absolutely can't miss going places, is *Jack Plant* . . . recently arrived here from England on what was intended to be merely a vacation . . . this reviewer had the privilege of hearing him at an audition recently . . . he looks like one of the few sure bets in radio today.—*October, 1935*

Tempo King who really sizzles . . . and *Bobby Godet* who has a clear ballad delivery.—*November, 1935*

Clayton (Sunshine) Duerr's taxi-meterlike precision coupled with fine tone and lift should draw him much of that evasive attention.—*January, 1936*

Little *Helen Forrest* is doing some really lovely warbling . . . You can hear her under her own name and a few nom de plumes on New York's WNEW, and as Bonnie Blue on CBS . . . A grand soft style that should be heard on even better spots.—*April, 1936*

In the Pollack band, note first trumpeter *Harry James*, when you get to hear the outfit . . . his lead is good, but it's his attack and soul in his hot style that really impresses you . . . they say he's a lad who's been around Chicago for years, even though he's only in his early twenties, but has never been appreciated in the east as he should be . . . he will be!—*October, 1936*

Apparently the best of the college bands, and it's taken for granted that it is a college band, is *Les Brown's*. The outfit has been coming in via NBC from Cleveland and has flashed some good swing. Most notable are the arrangements and somebody's hot trumpet. There's a vocalist, though, Herb Muse, who'd do much better if he took the cry out of his voice and the potato out of his mouth.—*February, 1937*

THE COUNTRY'S NEWEST COMING BAND?!
—Last month there was a little news item in this magazine to the effect that *Glenn Miller* was organizing his own band. That item inspired this writer to search the rehearsal halls for the Miller embryo. He found it, and what he heard was even more inspiring than the short article that inspired the search. In the first place there are some arrangements in that new Miller library that are (to coin a counterfeit phrase) really out of this world. And Miller, besides great talents as an arranger, possesses other attributes which should help him nicely in what already looks like a pretty easy climb to the top for him. He's a thorough, as well as a thoroughly hep musician; knows what he wants, and, judging from the qualities of his embryo, knows how to get what he wants . . . All of you swing men out there can expect plenty . . . Listen!—*March, 1937*

And watch for *Mickey Barry*, a cute femme vocalist picked up by chance while singing with the Jerry Johnson band up in Albany.—*April, 1936*

Jimmy Littlefield is leading this up-and-coming bunch, which exhibits, besides some smart arrangements and pacing of tunes, a really great trombone find, as well as a second trumpeter and tenorman . . . the boys definitely bear much close watching.—*July, 1936*

It's second trumpeter *Dave Frankel* who really makes the section. The lad has sureness of attack and a truly fine and original style of hot; definitely he bears very much watching.—*September, 1936*

Here's another flyer. Up in Boston there's a totally unknown lad named *Don Frisora*. He was caught playing piano in Hughie Conners' band in a Chinese restaurant in that town. The lad's just seventeen years old, but already he's got more on the ball than most men who have played as long as he's lived! To say that he's a combination of Wilson, Mary Lou Williams and Fats Waller is, of course, as a blunt statement, an absurdity. It's truer to say that he has borrowed some of the fine points of each and is now busy developing a style that one of these days is going to make plenty of you cats out there really sit up and notice. On top of that, the lad is an arranger. Remember the name, and watch!—*July, 1937*

Up in Boston, by the way, there's some fine talent that's very much unheralded. For example, there's a lad named *Eddie Flynn* who's the greatest white Fats Waller yet heard—and when it comes to sheer whackiness (not musicianship, unfortunately) and fun, he can go Thomas even two better. Flynn plays drums, of all things, with a band headed by one Bob Freeman, who in turn is an unusually fine vocalist—along Crosbian-McKenzie lines.—*December, 1938*

Early Ella with Chick and bassist Beverly Peer

Young, unknown Clark Terry back in St. Louis

THE FIND OF 1939?—This column comes forth once more with an extremely long shot whom and about whom you should be hearing a lot. Again, she's a girl singer. Right now she's appearing on a New York indie (WNEW). Her name is *Dinah Shore*.

This lass has a brilliant future because (1) she has a marvelous style of her OWN; (2) she sings perfectly in tune (unusual among femme warblers), and (3 and most important of all) she knows what it's all about musically. If you're lucky enough to be near New York, catch her by all means, so that you can be one of those guys who can brag: "I heard her when—!" And even if you're not the bragging kind, you should get a tremendous boot out of just hearing her sing—as this column has been getting consistently for more than the past month!—*February, 1939*

From Harry James band review at Roseland Ballroom—Featured throughout many (of the ballads) are the very pleasing vocals of *Frank Sinatra*, whose easy phrasing is especially commendable.—*September, 1939*

From record reviews—Frank Sinatra's voice and Claude Lakey's tenor, plus Dave Matthews' alto in the background, combine to make pretty works of Harry James's *From the Bottom of My Heart* and *Melancholy Mood.*—*September, 1939*

March seems to be an auspicious month for this column. It made its first appearance five years ago this month, and three years later it had the good fortune to pick Glenn Miller as the coming band. Which auspiciousness makes it about time for a bit more auspicing. And so, under the auspices of itself, this column hereby goes on record as predicting the Coming of *Charlie Spivak's* band!

Caught at rehearsals in January and at relief session for Miller in February, the young outfit had everything. It played gorgeous ballads, a truly important requisite these days, which featured the non-copyable trumpet of its leader. What beautiful tone and notes come from that horn—and what commercial possibilities it possesses! The full orchestra, itself surprisingly well polished, played wonderful soft stuff and then once in a while for contrast kicked right out . . . Don't forget, the orchestra you should keep your ears on is that of Cheery, Chubby, Charlie Spivak!—*March, 1940*

King Guion, a lad about whom absolutely nothing is known anywhere except, possibly, on the west coast . . . will quite definitely go down as the outstanding hot man discovery of the year.—*June, 1939*

Some of you may recall a rave last month about an unknown tenorman. At the risk of being termed "an habitual tenorman addict," this reviewer proffers another toast anent a similar horn-blower. His name is *Willie Hargreaves* . . . who used to play with King Oliver, but who's now working as a busboy in the University of North Carolina's cafeteria while playing occasionally with a local band, Willie's soul is absolutely glorious. What feeling he puts into and gets out of a 20-year-old, battered, leaky horn! Spiritually and mechanically, Willie is a real musician—another comparatively unknown whom, and about whom, you're going to hear plenty often!—*July, 1939*

Atlantic City, by the way, possesses a sixteen-year-old lass whose voice and looks should carry her far. Her name is *Betty Phillips*, and, according to reports, Rudy Vallee has taken an interest in the girl's future. Unlike most modern maidens, Miss Phillips is able to sing in a full, round voice, without shouting. She has a swell delivery, and if you don't hear her with Vallee soon, chances are you'll be catching her with some other outfit.—*August, 1939*

This column got one of the biggest kicks of its entire listening career late in November. A gal gave it to him. Her name is *Jayne Whitney*, and folks who go into the Roosevelt Hotel in New Orleans this month will be lucky enough to hear her with Johnny Hamp's band.

Miss Whitney is, without any qualifications whatsoever, the finest orchestra ballad singer this column has ever heard. Not only does she sing with musical feeling, but she also sings perfectly in tune with a beautiful soothing quality. . . . This column doesn't expect to experience a similar thrill for a long, long time to come!—*December, 1939*

After judging a talent contest—That kid, *Louis Bel[l]son* of Chicago, who won it, is one helluva fine drummer: not only amazing technique but also a good beat and excellent taste. Almost any big band could hire him as an improvement—he's that good.—*February, 1942*

From a radio review, station WCAU, Philadelphia—The band and the program as a whole were a revelation. Once *(Elliot) Lawrence* cleans up some messy attacks, he's going to have himself an outfit that might well surpass that of his famed Philly predecessor, Jan Savitt.—*March, 1945*

A distinct joy and a definite boon to those who are appalled by the dullness of Chicago's disc shows . . . is *Dave Garroway*, who comes on (and really comes on, too!) at midnight over WMAQ, the NBC station, for fifty-five minutes with not only a host of great musical sides (mostly swing), but also some of the smartest, subtlest, most listenable adlibbing to hit any airlanes in a long time.—*September, 1946*

From a survey of St. Louis jazz—The most amazing man and the one who is just about God to the local swing gentry is a clean-cut, intelligent trumpeter named *Clark Terry*. Like many of the modern young musicians, he has been influenced by bebop, but unlike many of them, he has accepted only the parts of the style which he likes and has discarded others. The result is that Clark Terry plays some weird notes, but plays them with feeling, with a gorgeous tone, and he doesn't play behind the beat. He is a musician who is definitely tabbed for stardom, provided, of course, he gets the breaks that are not easy to get.—*November, 1946*

(Editorializing on news story that Harry James contemplated adding strings) The announcement of the plan, however, has resulted in universal wagging of heads with apparently no other person concurring with James in a plan, tentative as it may be, that would break up his brilliant combination.—*February, 1940*

If you're the kind of person who likes to keep his ears open for budding musicians, keep them peeled in the general direction of . . . trumpeter *Billy Jones*, a lad whose comparative inexperience is cause for a slight lack of polish, but who should be one of the great horn-blowers in days to come. Not only has he fine musical conceptions and a pleasing tone, but he's also blessed with an excellent musical training, responsible for some mighty good arrangements which he has turned out. Just keep those ears of yours wide open, folks!—*May, 1940*

Harry Walker, who was the star of the Little World Series, [is] a music enthusiast with a fine voice . . . Keep an eye on him.—*November, 1941. [Walker did turn out to be a fine big league hitter and a manager, though.]*

From review of Tony Pastor's band—And there was a girl singer who has stardom written all over her, just as Eugenie Baird and Rosemary Clooney did in the same band. Her name: *Marie Johnson*. She sings with fine feeling and taste, and she does something few other band vocalists do: she projects. Keep your eyes and ears on her!—*August, 1953*

428

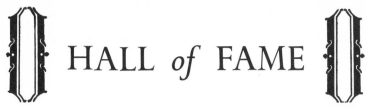

HALL *of* FAME

Many of the pieces that follow may seem pretty incomplete to many of you. That's understandable, for, after all, they were written long before most of these musicians had completed their careers, or even before they had reached their musical maturity. But they do serve as feeders of early factual data and, in several instances, offer a pretty good insight into the early attitudes and ambitions of their talented subjects. The Hall of Fame series, by the way, was designed to recognize sidemen, as opposed to leaders. It's interesting that quite a number of these sidemen eventually wound up as leaders.

May, 1935

GENE KRUPA

METRONOME regards Gene Krupa as just about the best swing drummer in the business. Judging from all the name bands he's played with, you'd think he was at least five years older than he is; just looking at him, you'd think he was at least five years younger.

He's really twenty-six, a Chicago-born boy, the youngest of four children. The three oldest all got musical training, but they were pretty sour, so when it came to Gene his folks decided that they had wasted enough money. Thus, Gene had to wait until he could start on his own hook.

That happened after he was graduated from St. Joseph's College in Indiana. Shortly after that he heard Ben Pollack drum, and, pronto, the unborn swing in Gene started to emerge. His inspiration!

It was while working at a soda fountain in Wisconsin one summer that he got his first break. There was a small-time band there, and every evening Gene would sit in for one set while the drummer danced with his wife. The usual success story: the drummer got sick and Gene got the job.

From then on it was quick work. His natural swing was recognized everywhere he went and before long he got better offers. From Joe Kayser to Thelma Terry and then to the McKenzie-Condon Chicagoans. Gene claims that it was their recordings of *Nobody's Sweetheart* and *China Boy* (on which he played)

that really got him going, for when other bands heard them he was made. Shortly after that he went to New York with Red Nichols, staying with him for a long time and making the majority of his famous recordings. After the Pennies split, Gene went with Irving Aaronson; then to Russ Columbo, Mal Hallett, Buddy Rogers and finally Benny Goodman. You can hear him on the Let's Dance program Saturday nights on NBC.

Gene's quick rise, which he modestly claims is the result of good luck, can be attributed not only to his superabundance of swing, but also to his go-gettiveness. He's a livewire; maybe that's what causes the youthful impression he creates. Right now he's not content to sit back and be recognized as the leader in his field. He's trying to improve his already amazing technique by practicing and by analyzing it via giving lessons to others. And on top of that he's taking lessons in xylophone and tympani for he plans to become a symphony man before long—certainly a loss to dance music.

In his spare moments, Gene manages to stay at home with his charming young wife and their Scottie. Whenever that happens, there's sure to be a lot of company, for the Krupas are one of the most popular young couples in musiciandom. But it seldom lasts long, because up pops Gene, into the next room, and he's back at the drum pad or xylophone again. So far he hasn't been able to convince the superintendent of the building that it will be perfectly okay to bring in a tympani. But you can never tell!

Gene Krupa

BUD FREEMAN

He never played much sax till he was about twenty—he's not even thirty now—yet he's considered by most to be the greatest white tenor sax man today—and he was asked to join the ranks of all-stars and did join the ranks of all-stars assembled by Ray Noble last February. That's Bud Freeman. And ask him what he thinks about it all, and Bud Freeman will reply, "Aw shucks, there are loads of guys much better than I can ever hope to be!"—and in a minute he'll be off to practice clarinet.

A Chicagoan, Freeman had been playing for only two years when he created a recorded sensation via his tooting on the McKenzie-Condon Chicagoans' platters of *Nobody's Sweetheart, Liza,* and *China Boy.* Ben Pollack asked Bud to join his band—after that came sojourns with the Dorsey Brothers, Red Nichols, Zez Confrey, Joe Venuti, Roger Wolfe Kahn, Joe Haymes, and now Bud is still sojourning nightly on the Rainbow Roof with Ray Noble et al.

Because he's so extremely modest in his appearance and demeanor, the terrific swing that emanates from his tenor sax is all the more astounding. For if you haven't heard Bud on the recent Eddie Condon records of *The Eel* or *Home Cooking,* or in the Mezz Mezzrow record of *Thirty-fifth and Calumet* (which Bud considers his greatest piece of work, by the way), you've never really been astounded by swing tenor sax.

Musically speaking, Bud has certain very definite tastes. A study of his style makes his love of Chicago swing quite obvious. But coming down to even more basic fundamentals, Bud is a lover of any kind of real swing. And at the same time he detests imitating and adores inspiration—which, after all, fits right in with any formula of swing. Note, for example, Freeman's list of favorite musicians—you'll find that everyone possesses an original style, and that not one is an imitator: hot trumpeters, Bunny Berigan and Maxie Kaminsky; lead trumpeter, Charlie Spivak; lead sax, Toots Mondello; tenor men, Coleman Hawkins (ten years or so ago), Eddie Miller and Dick Clark; pianists, Jess Stacy, Claude Thornhill and Teddy Wilson as well as Fats Waller and Willie (The Lion) Smith when they feel inspired. He considers George Van Eps the greatest guitar soloist, and Arthur Schutt the greatest legitimate soloist in the dance piano field.

But though Freeman doesn't like imitators, imitators do like Bud Freeman. Note the number of men who have studied Freeman and his style. As for Bud, he's busy studying, too—studying much clarinet as well as men of literature and languages. For Bud is a great intellectual; he's tremendously interested in those two fields and pursues his studies of them whenever the slightest opportunity permits. Which is most unusual for a great hot tenor man. But then Bud Freeman is an unusual great hot tenor man.

Lawrence "Bud" Freeman

431

RED NORVO

It's a generally recognized fact that nobody can touch Red Norvo when it comes to playing swing music on the xylophone (or marimba). In fact, it wasn't until Red suddenly hit upon the idea that you can really swing on a xylophone that anybody had heard anything from that instrument except a lot of runs and notes, a la the style of those rootin-tootin last choruses of the Joseph C. Smith recordings.

Red (born "Kenneth" on March 31, 1908, in Beardstown, Ill.) can't quite explain what got him going on the xylophone in the first place. As a youngster his musical family had supplied him with piano lessons, but teacher gave up in disgust when she discovered little Ken continually faking by ear rather than reading what was writ.

Nothing daunted, Ken went ahead and bought a pony, and then one high school day, for no reason at all, traded it in for a xylophone he had seen in a music store. He taught himself the instrument and then started filling in with a marimba band. After that a discovery of Norvo by Paul Ash and plenty of vandeville stuff.

But everything Red was doing was strictly legitimate. It was tough on him, too, because just about that time he really started to become interested in swing. For years his routine consisted of sitting in awe in his dressing room listening to Bix and Louis and Tram come at him from a squeaky portable, and then suddenly dashing upstairs to the stage to have the audience sit in awe while he pulled stuff he considered corny as hell.

Soon, however, came a chance for him to lead his own dance band at the Eagles Ballroom in Milwaukee, and after that at the Marigold Ballroom in Minneapolis. But Red became fed up with the usual commercial routine, and so one day he handed the band over to Isham Jones and decided to go back to the college he had quit three times before. Jones, incidentally, still has the nucleus of the Norvo outfit.

Red didn't like college any more the fourth time, however, so he decided to go back to radio. He had done much good work on KSTP while he was in Minneapolis, and so he didn't have too much trouble getting into the NBC studios in Chicago. Paul Whiteman heard him about this time and asked him to tour with him—which Red did. Finally into New York, where Red decided to strike out on his own hook.

You've heard Red's recent records of *Blues in E Flat, I Surrender Dear, The Night Is Blue,* etc. But Red had also made some sides before that; in Chicago

Kenneth "Red" Norvo

he had done a beautiful solo waxing of *In a Mist*, released a few years ago by Brunswick.

You have a chance to hear Red in person now, though, for he's organized a really fine swing outfit that's receiving notices everywhere. And when you do hear him, go up and speak to him; you'll find him one of the swellest guys you've ever met, and you won't wonder at all why Teddy Wilson, when he first met Norvo, said to Johnny Hammond later: "John, I thought you were the world's finest gentleman until I met Red Norvo!"

There's a romantic side of Red's life revolving about the lady considered the greatest blues singer of all time, Mildred Bailey. But that's worth another story in itself! Suffice to say Mildred Bailey is Mrs. Kenneth Norvo—which is quite enough reason for both Mr. and Mrs. Norvo's being considered two of the world's happiest people.

GLENN MILLER

There are a lot of men in the music field who aren't appreciated as they should be. You know, arrangers, and their unrequited ilk. Chalk up a double on that score for Glenn Miller, for Glenn is not only an unappreciated arranger, so far as the general public is concerned, but one of the great trombonists in the country today.

And Glenn's arranging identity is kept a double secret, because he's one of those chaps who for years has been turning out specials for various swing bands, specials that have been talked about and admired, but to whose author the due credit has seldom been paid.

Take a look at this list of bands Glenn has arranged and played trombone for. Recall, if you can, some of their very smart arrangements; then thank Glenn Miller: Boyd Senter, Ben Pollack, George Stoll, Charley Straight, Red Nichols, Smith Ballew, Dorsey Brothers, and Ray Noble.

Listen to the swing arrangements and note the definite reversion to the original New Orleans Dixieland style. The Dorsey Brothers' version of *Dippermouth* is an excellent example. That, especially, typifies, as Glenn puts it, the old New Orleans parade style, when the colored lads would march and swing at the same time. That's real swing for Glenn.

That same parade business is what started Glenn on trombone. Though born in Clarinda, Iowa, March 1, 1905, his early life was spent in Colorado. Out there he used to be fascinated by the parades. He wanted to get into them, and following the true adolescent - center - of - attraction psychological theory, he decided to take up trombone, because those slidehorn men always marched in the front row. So his pa got him a horn and Glenn experimented until he had learned how to play it. After that much practice and listening to and talking with and studying trombonists, so that in later years Glenn turned out to be a really finished master of his instrument. After studying at the University of Colorado, he joined Boyd Senter, and then went along with the various bands listed above. Feature bits of Glenn's trombone work can be found in various Red Nichols Five Pennies records (e.g., *Carolina in the Morning*, and others of that period), though his own favorite piece of work is on the Mound City Blue Blowers' versions of *Hello Lola* and *One Hour*.

Glenn is very modest about his own blowing. He doesn't think he should be mentioned in the same paragraph with Tommy Dorsey's tone, with Jack

Alton Glenn Miller

Teagarden's swing style, or with Wilbur Schwichtenberg,* whom he considers the best all-around trombonist of all. He and Schwichtenberg sat side by side for months while playing for Ray Noble, for whom Glenn is still playing and arranging, as well as concertmastering.

Definitely one of the most popular chaps in the field, this Miller man; an easygoing personality, extremely modest, and, so far as swingsters in general are concerned, thoroughly unappreciated.

* Later known as Will Bradley.—*G. S.*

EDDIE MILLER

A group of well-known authorities on swing music was seated one evening at a table in New York's Onyx Club. They were hashing over things in general. From the midst of the hash popped up this question from Critic Number One: "Whom do you rate as the best tenor sax man today?"

Spake Critic Number Two: "Coleman Hawkins, I guess, still."

Retaliated Critic Number Three: "Yes, but he only stands out when he's playing at a slow tempo. He can't touch Bud Freeman when it comes to really swinging out."

Popped up Critic Number One again: "You're both right as far as you go, but what I meant is who do you think is the best swing tenor man in all ways?"

To which question there was much discussion, and, eventually, the unanimous opinion that Eddie Miller was the best all-around swing tenorman today. As one critic said: "He can play gutbucket hot; he can play commercial hot; he can swing at a slow tempo; he can swing at a fast tempo. Besides all that, he plays in exquisite taste with a grand tone. And he never kills that tone to create an effect; instead he creates many of his effects by some very subtle intonations. And besides all that he can play a truly lovely tenor lead in a section."

Right now Eddie is playing with Bob Crosby's band. Originally it was Ben Pollack's, and that's the only name band Eddie's ever played with. He joined them seven years ago, at the age of eighteen, just after he came up north from his hometown of New Orleans.

New Orleans has had a decided effect upon Eddie Miller's life. His idol of idols, Leon Rappolo, used to play clarinet down there, and it was he who has offered Eddie much inspiration. Eddie plays plenty of clarinet too. As a matter of fact that's the instrument he started on when he got his first job playing in the New Orleans Newsboys' Band. All the big guys hogged the saxes, and, though Eddie wanted one, he was too small and had to be satisfied with a clarinet.

All that time Eddie was being enthralled by the New Orleans colored lads playing on parade. As they marched, they used to swing out in true dixieland style. "You know," Eddie says, "that marching dixieland style is still the real swing. You can take ninety per cent of this so-called Harlem swing (not all of it, for some of it is really fine), and you can just swing it into your East River and let it sink there. It was that stuff they used to parade to down in Noo Ohlins that really swung right out."

A pretty good example of the swing Eddie refers to is now being played by Bob Crosby's band. In the Noo Ohlins brogue, "It's just good bass trombone, clarinet routine, and a cornet taking charge of everything, with a good drop beat from the drums and everything played not too fast." Benny Pollack's old

Eddie Miller with fellow townsman Hilton Lamare

band used to play just that, and so did the original New Orleans Rhythm Kings, of course.

Eddie's favorite band would play that style real well. He'd have Chicago's colored pianist, Pinetop Smith; Bob Crosby's guitarist, Nappy Lamare, playing banjo; Bob Haggart (Crosby) or Chink Morton (New Orleans Rhythm Kings) on bass; Benny Pollack or Ray Bauduc (Crosby) on drums. His brass section would include Louis Armstrong (of the old days), Sterling Bose (now with Ray Noble), and from New Orleans a comparative unknown, Bill Padron, on trumpets, with Jack Teagarden tromboning. His reeds would consist of clarinetists Leon Rappolo (unfortunately now committed to an asylum), Matty Matlock (Crosby), and Johnny Dodds (of the old Armstrong records); while on his own instrument, tenor sax, Eddie would choose Bud Freeman, who "really plays with that old Chicago swing and punch."

Choosing Freeman makes the score just about even, for recently in an interview Bud stated that Eddie Miller was his favorite tenor sax man today. Red McKenzie, responsible for digging up scores of swing men, also claims that Eddie's the greatest he's heard yet. "Not only that," says Red, "but you couldn't ask for a finer fellow than little Eddie. That man's so absolutely on the level and so thoroughly decent that it almost hurts."

To which Red forgot to add that Eddie's also a fine family man; he's been married for nine years already, and he beams all over whenever he mentions his seven-year-old boy. In fact that contagious Miller smile puts into appearance plenty; Eddie's grand disposition is known by all swing men. Most of them know his work too, if only because of such recordings as Wingy Manone's *Send Me* and Clark Randall's *Jitterbug* (both Brunswick). But what most of them don't know is that Eddie's so modest that he almost didn't get into this Hall of Fame, simply because he didn't think he rated it. But, quite obviously, he does and so here he is!

Gene Krupa on Characters and Self-Confidence
(July, 1954)—

The well-schooled, studious musician has enough self-confidence to carry him through almost any given setup; he no longer needs to resort to all sorts of extraneous devices to draw attention to himself and to build up his ego. A thorough musician knows he's good; he doesn't feel the need to be a character. If only for that reason alone, I believe wholeheartedly that plenty of studying of whatever you are trying to do is just about the greatest investment a person can make.

TEDDY WILSON

Says Benny Goodman: "Teddy Wilson is the greatest musician in dance music today, irrespective of instrument." Benny Goodman should know; he does know. So do lots of others—Red Norvo, Johnny Hammond, etc.

If you've heard Teddy play piano you'll know just why those men say that—and you'll probably be agreeing with them too. This quiet, unassuming Alabaman has, within the short space of about a year, jumped right into the fore as the ace swing pianist of the day. First came records with other bands (Jimmie Noone's, Benny Carter's, Red Norvo's and Willie Bryant's), and then with his own on Brunswick. Engagements first in Chicago with Jimmie Noone, in New York with Bryant and as his own boss, and now a member of the famed Goodman Trio, playing not only for Victor records, but for a commercial radio program and for dancers in person.

That's the fairly brief summary of Teddy Wilson's meteoric career. The reason it's so comparatively short is not that people didn't get to appreciate Teddy at first, but rather because they didn't know him at all. It wasn't until a few years ago when he was only nineteen that Wilson popped up in Chicago, a refugee from Alabama's Tuskegee Institute, who was pretty fed up on learning all the rules and wanted a chance to show how he could apply them. Within Chicago swing circles he was a sensation, but the thought of an even larger New York circle intrigued him. Thus to Gotham and to work first for Benny Carter on record dates and then right in with Willie Bryant's band in Harlem's Savoy. And then the rest.

In case you haven't met him, you should know that Teddy is one of the most charming and genteel of all swingsters. He never wants to put himself forward; he's not even content to take all his due credit. A year or so ago, for example, a musical publication voted him the best swing pianist of the day. Explained Teddy: "Aw, just a coupla my friends got together and gave me a little boost."

That's pretty typical of Wilson. Not that he's a lazy sort of guy who doesn't get enthused and who just wants to sit back and take things easy. Quite on the contrary—he's very enthusiastic—he'll discuss all aspects of swing with you and discuss them most intelligently, but when it comes to discussing Teddy Wilson his mind becomes very much of a blank.

His picture here shows his good looks. It doesn't show his medium build—about five feet nine and one hundred and thirty-five pounds. It doesn't show his infectious smile or much about his personality in general. You just have to believe all about that.

Nor does the picture show anything about Teddy's pianistics—his colossal technique; the rapid thought transference from brain to fingers; his conception of single finger figures; his solid and tasty bass work. You've got to listen to some of Teddy's record or radio work, or, better still, get to hear him in person. After listening for a while, chances are you'll also be of the Goodman-Norvo-Hammond school—and it will be a pleasure, too!

Teddy Wilson

CHARLIE SPIVAK

Because they aren't commercially sensational, because they don't stand up and look as if they're blowing their guts out, because they don't make a lot of funny faces when they hit high C's and F's right on the button, first trumpeters don't get nearly the amount of public recognition they deserve. Judged by the amount of hard work they do, and the technical accomplishment necessary for them to succeed, first trumpeters, as a class, have just about the hardest job, if not the most important job, of any man in a dance band. To hold down a first chair, they've just got to be good.

Chubby, smiling, good-natured Charlie Spivak, therefore, can be classed as really wonderful, for in dancebandom circles he's generally recognized as the best of all those good men. And if you're the best among a lot of good ones, you really must be wonderful.

You've probably heard much of Charlie's work; though, because he's not a second trumpeter, he might not have chilled you as one of the men he was sitting next to might have. If you haven't paid his work its due attention, make up for it soon—listen to him and note the exquisite phrasing done in such beautiful taste with one of the most brilliant tones and surest attacks in dance music history. True, there may be greater cornet players behind long heards in symphony orchestras, but in dancebandom you won't find a greater technique phrasing both sweet and hot more intelligently than that of Charlie Spivak.

Charlie was born in 1906 and brought up in New Haven, Conn. By the time he was eleven he grew pretty sick and tired of the fiddle, and, dropping it ever so gently out of a top floor window, grabbed hold of the nearest trumpet and started in tooting. He tooted through high school, in bands and semi-classical orchestras, through club jobs, and finally joined John Caballero's band as second trumpeter, and then a jump into bigger time.

In 1925 Paul Specht was passing through Bridgeport and heard Charlie play at a dance. Paul Specht passed right on through Bridgeport, but when he got as far as Hartford he realized that he wanted this Spivak guy, and wired back for him to come along. Charlie was scared stiff that he wasn't good enough, but he stayed with Specht until 1931, so he must have been good enough!

In 1931 Charlie used to listen to the famous Ben Pollack band, playing in the Little Club at the time. Charlie thought it was the nuts and wanted to play

Charlie Spivak, by now a successful leader

with it, of course. Came the break: Charlie met Benny strolling down Musicians' Muse (48th Street in New York). Said Benny: "Come on along to rehearsal; Ruby Weinstein's leaving and I need a first cornet player." Said Charlie: "Sure, but I hardly ever played first." (He was forgetting the Georgian records he made on Columbia!) Said Benny: "That's okay; come on along anyway."

And so to Benny Pollack Charlie Spivak owes his existence as a first trumpeter. And Charlie has never forgotten that. He gives all credit to Patient Pollack, whom he admires more than he does any other man in the business. Charlie still insists that "Benny knows more about handling a dance band, both musically and psychologically, than do any other three leaders I've come across."

Charlie, quite obviously, would have Benny front his all-star band, and play drums, too, if he wanted to. If Benny didn't want to, Charlie would include either Ray McKinley or Ray Bauduc. The rest of the rhythm section would include George Van Eps, or Nappy Lamare for swing, on guitar; either Artie Bernstein, Delmar Kaplan, or Bob Haggart on bass, and Claude Thornhill on piano. As lead sax man he'd have Toots Mondello with either Eddie Miller or Buddy Freeman playing tenor, and Benny Goodman, Matty Matlock, or Johnny Mince on clarinet. Spivak, by the way, regards Mince as the coming hot man of the country. For hot trumpeters he'd have either Bunny Berigan, Sterling Bose or Yank Lausen, while the three trombonists would be Tommy Dorsey for smooth, Jack Teagarden for hot, and Glenn Miller as valuable section man, arranger, rehearser, etc. (Style analysts should find a strong preference for New Orleans Dixieland swing, caused, no doubt, by the years with Pollack's band.)

In 1934 Charlie had to leave Pollack, because the band was out on the west coast, and Charlie's first son was expected any minute on the east coast. And so right into a job with the Dorsey Brothers' outfit in New York's Palais Royale, at the time quite a Dixieland style band, and containing Charlie's buddy, Glenn Miller. Shortly after that Ray Noble set foot on the same east coast. One of the first things he did was to ask Charlie Spivak to play first trumpet for him. Which Spivak did.

Now, though, Charlie has left Noble to concentrate upon radio work. Already in the past he had done many dates with Red Nichols, Al Goodman, and Victor Young; he's now first trumpet with Jack Miller's orchestra. Note the really great music emanating from the first Spivak trumpet. It should chill ya!

Benny Goodman on In-Person vs. Recording-Studio
Performances (January, 1953)—

I can remember many times after we'd done a particular number especially well [in person], or after we had played a good job, how Harry or Gene or Hymie would remark, "If we could only play like that when we're making records!" . . . Those crowds really made you play, whether you felt like it or not, with their contagious enthusiasm. . . . And also, on some of those dates the whiskey flowed a little, shall I say, more freely.

JACK TEAGARDEN

He's Jackson T. He's Mr. T. He's big Mr. T. He's Big Gate. He's the Vocalizing Vamoosing Vernon Virtuoso. He's the Talented Tranquil Texas Thoroughbred of the Tepefying Trombone. He's Jack Teagarden.

You've heard his trombone, his facile way of expressing the lazy blue feeling of his south, on records with all sorts of famous swing units—Benny Goodman's, Red Nichols', Ben Pollack's, Frank Trumbauer's, as well as his own. You've heard him over the air with Paul Whiteman's organization. And if you've been fortunate, you've heard him in person.

To many Jackson T. is the last word in the interpretation of swing, the greatest medium of expression of that sensation. Hughes Panassie, in his *Hot Jazz*, pronounces Jack "the greatest white musician since the death of Bix." A METRONOME critic regards him as his favorite swing man, regardless of instrument or color.

Jackson started playing twenty-seven years ago, at the age of five, in his home town of Vernon, Texas. First it was on a baritone horn—when his arm grew long enough to negotiate a slide, he switched over to trombone. Much playing around his home town was followed by huge success and first tastes of fame with the New Orleans Rhythm Kings and Leon Rappolo. When that famed bunch came north, Jackson T. didn't. Some years later though, the urge got him, and with the aid of the only man he knew in New York, Wingy Manone, Jack became well established with the bands of Red Nichols, Tommy Gott, and eventually Ben Pollack. That Pollack band, now being led by Crosby, is still Jack's idea of the epitome of organized dance music dispensaries.

"Of course," says Jack, "that's the best if you've gotta have an organized bunch. If I had my choice, though, I'd get me a smaller outfit and just fool around with Benny Goodman, Bud Freeman, Frankie Trumbauer, Little Gate [his brother, Charlie, that is], Ray Bauduc, George Van Eps, Artie Miller, and Peck Kelley."

All of the above, you'll note, are famed men on their instruments—that is, all except Peck Kelley. Peck right now is Jack's greatest interest. "Man," he exclaims, "I'll get that piano boy up here from Noo Ohlins if it's the last thing I do. Why, he's the best; they don't come no better—not even Willie the Lion."

Once in a while, though, Mr. T. manages to forget about Peck Kelley. Then he goes into raptures about steam engines. Down in Texas he has the last Stanley

Jackson T

Steamer (that's a car, in case you don't know) ever turned out. Jackson putters around and in it; succeeds in making ninety-three miles an hour (unofficial) as well as his wife the most scared person any side of Vernon, Texas.

When he isn't scaring the wits out of friend wife, Jack is "a mighty good boy," according to the oracle-at-home. To the more objective observer he's a quiet, easy-going fellow with the mannerisms of a bashful but lovable school boy. Seldom does he say much about himself; when he does, he sort of mumbles it, looks a bit embarrassed, and makes you feel so self-conscious that you immediately try to change the subject to the Price of Pitted Prunes in Pelham. Which relieves the general embarrassment but might make you look sort of foolish—especially when your object has been to find out something about the Big Gate. But then, perhaps the best way to let him express himself is to let him bring that sliphorn mouthpiece to his smackers and just blow. It's much easier and you'll love it.

RAY McKINLEY

Ray McKinley may not be a household drum word to many of you, but to many of those who know him and his drumming well he's really the finest of the modern swing men. Admittedly there are some drummers who are better known, but that just makes the score all the more in McKinley's favor, when, after having played in a band with him for a few weeks or so, each musician almost invariably comes out with: "Yeah, that man's the best! Boy, the way he feeds you and sends you in that solid, background way of his can't be beat—even if you haven't got it in you, you gotta swing then!"

McKinley, a Fort Worth, Texas product of 1910 vintage, once had a set of drums presented to him as a Christmas present. They didn't impress him much until one day he happened to hear theatre-drummer John Grimes. "Hm," murmured little Mac into his sweater, "that guy's the nuts and it looks like he's having a lot of fun. Guess I'll try those things."

Fun Man

And so when McKinley came home from the show he tried the things, and he had fun. And he's been having fun with them ever since. He's never had a lesson; he's just taught himself to play what he feels and how he feels. Just watch or listen to Mac and you can see how much fun he's having. Definitely the most original of all swing beat men, with an uncanny conception and execution of new beats and breaks, his style attracts you not only because of its basic solidity and natural swing, but even more so because it's an inspired style of drumming you don't hear any other drummer using. Drumming, quite obviously, is Ray's idea of fun. You'll get the idea when you see him.

But fun and originality aren't limited to drumming alone with McKinley: he enjoys a rep of being one of the whackiest musicians in all whacky musiciandom. There are all sorts of legends about him. One is that just for fun he once made a long soapbox speech in New York's Columbus Circle about the sad state of affairs in general, a speech to which absolutely nobody listened. Another is that while playing in New Orleans he always rode to work in his tuxedo on

Ray McKinley

a bicycle, and that one time he went right over the handle bars into a mud puddle, showing up on the job a few minutes later in a beautifully leopardized stiff-bosom shirt. Then some people swear that he's the man responsible for bursting a balloon dancer's pièce de resistance in New York's Palais Royale via the BB shooting route, though Ray claims it took him three nights to finally burst the damn thing. Mac himself admits that he has an uncanny knack of falling off Christmas trees, though he can't explain how he ever gets into them in the first place.

Break Man

That whackiness is often prevalent in his drum breaks, for which he is so justly famous. In *Old Man Harlem* there's a coda which calls for a break repeated every other two measures. One night, they say, Mac played twenty-three different breaks in succession, each one screwier than the one before, and finally ended up by standing up and whistling the last break through his teeth!

Perhaps you've heard some of those breaks in person. You have if you heard any of the bands of Savage Cummings, Larry Duncan, Smith Ballew, Red Nichols, Milt Shaw, the Dorsey Brothers, or Jimmy Dorsey at the time Ray was playing with them. Doubtlessly you've heard him on all the Dorsey Brothers and Jimmy Dorsey records on Decca, on the Brothers' Brunswick record of *Judy* and *Annie's Cousin Fanny*, and you might even have heard him and his fantastic warbling on the Red Nichols' platter of *Moan You Moaners*.

But in spite of all the surface McKinley whacki-ness and breaks, he's really a pretty serious and level-headed chap when you get him in a straight mood. He's the he-mannish type, tall, a good Texas build that's usually topped by a Texas Ranger hat. He doesn't like to talk much about himself, but he will tell you that he thinks most drummers nowadays are neglecting their bass drum work and the importance of the afterbeat. Solidity depends mostly upon the former; swing (especially the dixieland kind) hinges upon the latter. But no drummer, no matter how good he can be, can really swing unless he has the right men playing with him, says Ray—which ought to encourage some of you bat men.

Mac admits he's single, but apart from that doesn't say much about his life's routine. Intimates, though, say that he's one swell guy, about as kindhearted and thoughtful as they come, who more than anything else thinks about his family in Texas and what he can do for the home folks. He reads a lot, and also writes: right now he's busy preparing a book on the art of drumming, a treatise that should inspire most drummers one way or another. And he writes music, too. Record fans should listen to his recently-issued *New Orleans Parade*, which appears on Decca played by Ray McKinley's Jazz Band. That band has just made four sides, by the way, and Gordon Wright, who has a habit of peering over everybody's shoulder just to find out what's being written, says they're four of the most inspired sides he's ever heard.

All of which makes Ray McKinley a great fellow and a great drummer, a whacky fellow and a whacky drummer, and an inspiration. And that's enough to land in anyone's Hall of Fame!

Rex Stewart on Duke Ellington as a Musician (April, 1955)—

He was and is the all-time genius in jazz. He was able to take all sorts of divergent personalities and mold them into a whole. Duke caused everybody associated with him to think musically.

DAVE TOUGH

When Daddy Tough dropped a lot of dough out in Chicago's famous Wheat Pit some years back, he did a good turn for dancebandom. That bit of droppage started to make son Dave take his drums more seriously, for from then on the offspring's bread and butter would have to come via percussioning instead of via papa.

Not that Dave didn't like to drum—far from that! He can't even remember at what tender age he began to diddle. He does remember that he used to supply rhythm to Benny Goodman's singing, much to the disgust of a common history professor in a common class room, and that somebody gave him a drum for some Christmas or other, and that Ed Straight taught him rudimentals, and that Baby Dodds, then playing with Joe Oliver in Chicago, was the man who really convinced him that beating drums was a thoroughly inspiring occupation.

So he started jobbing around town with men like Bud Freeman (still his closest friend), Frank Teschemaker, Jimmy McPartland, and Floyd O'Brien. They beat out the most uncommercial jazz in existence. Only their intimate followers appreciated them. Everybody else referred to them merely as "That Wild West Side Mob."

Just about the time the Mob began to be appreciated a bit more universally, though, Dave left them. Danny Polo (now Ambrose's featured clarinetist) took a band, including Tough, to England. That was about 1929. Dave was 22 then, and, incidentally, terribly homesick. And so he started to drink—slowly, at first, but finally to a point where, as he now puts it, he "dedicated his life to getting drunk." Some years later he reeled down a U. S. gangplank into the arms of his buddies. He did some unsteady jobbing with Bix, Bud, the Dorseys, Benny, Wingy Manone, and Joe Sullivan. For a time he played and recorded with Red Nichols. Remember the Five Pennies' platters of *Who Cares* and *Basin Street Blues*? Dave made those —with the assistance of Bud Freeman, who shoved him back on the chair after each test was cut—a tedious procedure.

About a year and a half ago Dave grew disgusted with all this drinking stuff. He wants it understood that it wasn't a matter of glorious willpower, or anything as beautiful as that. It was just plain disgust with the Life of a Souse. About the same time Tommy Dorsey made him a conditional offer to join his band. The combination of circumstances was ideal. Dave just said "I'd rather play good drums for Tommy,"

Davey Tough

stopped drinking, and is now recognized as one of the very greatest in the business. His rhythmic conceptions, his good taste, his uncanny perception of fill-ins, his steadiness, and, of course, his lift, make him the favorite drummer of many of our leading swingsters.

Dave likes others much better, though. He thinks Chick Webb is the greatest drummer living today, and that big Sidney Catlett and Gene Krupa aren't far behind. He likes Ray Bauduc, too, and claims that George Wettling is the most unappreciated beater in the business. One of his ambitions is to hear Ray McKinley drum in person: from what he's heard of Mac via wax and rep, he's pretty certain he'd include him in this group.

Looking at and talking with Dave, you'd never think he's the great swingster that he is. From his picture you can see that he's pretty studious-looking. And that's no optical illusion, either. He can probably talk rings around practically anybody in the profession when it comes to intellectual matters. His philosophy of life is straightforward and exceedingly practical, and it doesn't take him long to convince you that he's pretty right. He's an untiring reader who won't give up until he's read all of Ernest Hemingway and William Faulkner. Which is much of a job. Needless to say, all the fellows in Tommy's band look up to him as an intellectual genius of some sort or other. And they're crazy about him, too, for Dave puts on no airs: he's completely at ease, a grand mixer, and possesses a really wonderful sense of humor.

Dave is, of course, nuts about drumming. But, as you'd suspect from the foregoing, he wants to do other things, too. He's already planned his ideal post-percussion life: to live in southern France, lie on the beach, read, play records and golf, and, maybe, take a drink or two. If, and when, he does that, dancebandom will have lost not only a fine drummer, but a truly great person.

February, 1949

THE LIFE AND DEATH OF DAVEY TOUGH

The life of Dave Tough was sketchily summarized in a Hall of Fame article that I wrote for METRONOME *back in June, 1937. After commenting upon Davey as a drummer and as an intellectual being, I concluded with, "He's already planned his ideal, post-percussion life: to live in southern France, lie on the beach, read, play records and golf, and, maybe, take a drink or two. If, and when, he does that, dancebandom will have lost not only a fine drummer, but a truly great person."*

As you know, Davey died early in December. He was just forty, too young to lead that ideal, post-percussion life which he had planned. And yet, the chances are that even if he had lived to be a hundred, Davey would never have achieved that sort of goal. For his life was one of seemingly continual frustration, of one attempt after another to acclimate himself to a society in which he could never seem to find exactly what he wanted.

Society accepted him primarily as a drummer, as a great drummer. Did Davey accept himself as such? Definitely, no! It wasn't uncommon for him to deprecate his own ability, and those who knew him well knew that he wasn't saying so just to hear somebody reply, "Oh, of course you're great, Davey! You're the greatest of them all." He honestly felt that there was something lacking in his work, and when he left the bands of Woody Herman and Tommy Dorsey he seemed to be convinced that he was just no good as a drummer.

It was at times like these that Davey reached his lowest depths, when he tried in all sorts of ways to readjust himself, to find just what he wanted and where he fit. Shortly before he died, he had definite ideas about quitting drumming altogether and starting his career as a writer.

Davey was never satisfied to lead the one-track existence that most musicians follow. His creative mind, always encouraged by his wonderful wife, was constantly seeking other outlets but was just as constantly being thwarted by the restrictions, physical and other kinds, under which jazz musicians must live.

The death of Davey Tough, while reflecting once again the limited lives of jazz musicians and the difficulties they encounter when they try to achieve greater freedom, does more than merely point a moral. It takes from us one of the most sensitive, talented, intelligent, one of the most wonderful guys in the history of jazz. In so doing, it has done too much.

JOHN (YANK) LAUSEN

"You can have your screechers!" So commented a well-known music commentator. "Yes, you can have all of them, and in exchange give me just one really fine cornet player, Bix preferred. As long as that's out of the question, though," continued the commentator, "I'll even settle for one guy who plays something like the way Bix did—Yank Lausen, for example."

That's a big compliment to be paid to tall, quiet, curly-topped Yank Lausen. To some of you it may even be a big surprise. And that, in itself, isn't too surprising, for after all, Yank isn't one of the trumpeters who draw a lot of attention because they bang out a lot of loud, high ones. But listen carefully for a while to the really tasty, rhythmic stuff that Yank's blowing so consistently well with the Bob Crosby Crew, and you'll begin to realize just what that music commentator was driving at. Yank's co-bandsmen honestly believe that he's the last word when it comes to get-off corneting, and they don't just say that because he happens to be one of them. As a matter of fact they ASKED him to become one of them. That happened about four or five years ago in St. Paul. A bit of Lausen biography follows: then you can see just when and why it all happened.

Yank was born in Trenton, Missouri, on May 3, 1911. He followed the usual course of playing cornet in high school military bands and even went so far as to do a bit of dance work on the side. Then he

John "Yank" Lawson with Ray Bauduc

entered the University of Missouri, started his own dance band, and began learning much about cornet playing from Carl Webb. He was mighty successful with his own band, and as soon as he was graduated from college he joined the Slats Randall outfit for a two years' tenure. About that time Bix Beiderbecke did quite some playing in the territories that Yank frequented, and every now and then Yank found himself seated in a trumpet chair next to the one occupied by his idol. Needless to say Yank learned plenty.

Then came the urge to go to Louisiana and to gain some first-hand knowledge of this dixieland business. So to Louisiana went Lausen to do quite a bit of playing with Wingy Manone. There followed a return to the Slats Randall fold, short periods with the bands of Will Osborne and Smith Ballew, and then a sudden desire to be off to Chicago and make good in that town. At the time, remember, most of the best musikers were in that windy city.

But Yank didn't go directly to Chicago. On the way he decided to stop off at St. Paul. Deane Kincaide, arranger par excellence, whom Yank had known down in Shreveport, was there, arranging and playing sax and bass trombone for Ben Pollack's bunch. (Ed. note: The climax is coming; to appreciate it you must know that the present Bob Crosby band used to be Ben Pollack's, Bob having taken Benny's place.) The boys in the band got a load of Yank's playing. First trumpeter Charlie Spivak, tenorman Eddie Miller, and guitarist Nappy Lamare became especially excited, and wouldn't stop plaguing Pollack until he had agreed to take on Lausen. And that's how Yank got with the Crosby (*né* Pollack) Crew.

Since that time, Yank's become a greatly improved player. Time, of course, has had much to do with that, but Yank wants to give much thanks, publicly, to Spivak, who taught him really much.

Yank's very happy right now. He's nuts about the kind of music the Crosby band plays. Note, for example, that his favorite trumpeters are Bix, Sterling Bose, and Muggsy Spanier—all of them definitely of the dixieland, blues-blowing school. And he really gets a big boot from the various soloists he plays with.

Off the musical stage, Yank's a quiet, soft-spoken chap. Nothing seems to ruffle his six feet two inches of masculine pulchritude. He's a great collector of pictures, even going so far as to present musical publications with shots of leading musikers not snapped at leading moments in their lives. He's happily married to an extremely attractive wife, and has already presented the world with a lively daughter who can cover more acreage per minute on a sofa than any kid in captivity. And that, in itself, is something!

HARRY JAMES

What a difference between the way he blows a trumpet and the way he blows about himself!—or *doesn't* blow about himself.

Harry James can and has drawn a colossal amount of attention via his sensational lead and hot trumpeting with the Benny Goodman brass section. And if it weren't for the fact that just about everybody in dancebandom has heard him work and realizes what a colossal musician Harry is, you'd probably never hear about the man. His sincere modesty would prohibit that entirely.

There's not much point in elaborating upon either Harry's musical ability or his fine personal traits. His playing suffices to prove the first point, while all that need be said about the second is that even if Harry were the world's worst musician, you'd still be tickled to death to have him for a friend. His popularity among the Goodman Gang, in which he's second in command, serves as added proof.

And at that, Harry's just twenty-two years old, having been born on March 15, 1916 in Augusta, Georgia. But Ma and Pa James were traveling folks with a circus, and it wasn't until the tent rolled into Beaumont, Texas, that they finally settled down to the task of bringing up Harry.

The musical James upbringing consisted of playing drums in the circus band at the age of five, and blowing a trumpet behind tents until ten. Then came the switch to that instrument. At thirteen came his first dance band work, and shortly thereafter lots of jobs, including one with Joe Gill in Galveston. After that Ben Pollack grabbed him, and Harry created such a sensation playing all the lead and all the hot that Benny Goodman snatched him away from his ex-boss. You know the rest.

What you may not know, though, is that this James man is a helluva fine drummer, having done some swell sub work behind the cymbals when Krupa left Benny. His innate sense of rhythm is obvious in its playing, and his uncanny sense of hitting just the right tempos has been rewarded—he now kicks off on all numbers for the Goodman Gang.

Other things you probably don't know about Harry is that he appears to like both the so-called Chicago and New Orleans styles, as evinced by his ideal band: alto saxists Johnny Hodges and Dave Matthews; tenormen Bud Freeman and Herschel Evans; clarinetist Goodman; trumpeters Louis Armstrong, Henry Allen, Jr., and Bunny Berigan; trombonists Jackson Teagarden, Warren Smith, and Vernon Brown; pianist Jess Stacy; guitarist (no preference); bassist Walter

Ballplayer Harry James loses out to sportscaster Mel Allen

Page, and a drummer consisting of Gene Krupa's left foot, Jo Jones' left hand, Davey Tough's right hand, and Lionel Hampton's right foot.

Harry plays a whale of a game of baseball, having pitched in Beaumont, and having hit around .260, damn good for a pitcher. His ambition is to write a swing symphony, but he intends to spend at least two more years studying arranging. Sometime or other he'd like to have his own band, but he won't do that for at least a year—"Benny's too great a guy to work for!" is one of his explanations. To which Benny would probably respond: "Harry's too great a guy!"

IRVING FAZOLA

It's a toss-up, which is rounder—his tone or his tummy.

Of course, in their respective ways, they both possess a definite amount of attraction, but so far as being the nominative object for any *musical* Hall of Fame, the nod must go to I. Henry Prestopnik's tone.

I. Henry Prestopnik is also Fazola, clarinetist in Claude Thornhill's band. More than possibly you heard that mournful, heartfelt blowing of his during his years with the Bob Crosby Crew, or during his months with Ben Pollack, Glenn Miller, Gus Arnheim, and Jimmy McPartland. And even more probably you were chilled and thrilled by its sincerity, by its warmth, by its complete relaxity, by the way the notes flowed from somewhere way down deep in that tummy, and up through that cherubic but oftimes sombre face.

Irving Henry Prestopnik was born where so many good clarinetists are born: New Orleans. They didn't know him as Fazola when he first burst into this reed-troubled world on December 12, 1912. That happened many years later, even after he took up his first instrument, a C-melody sax, in 1925. Louis Prima called him that—just why, nobody knows.

Louis' brother Leon, a trumpeter, and ditto-man Sharkey Bonano gave Fazola his first real job in New Orleans. Ben Pollack heard him there in 1932 and told him that Matty Matlock was going to leave the band soon and that he wanted I. Henry to join. But for some reason or other Matty stayed with Pollack anyway and so Faz stayed in New Orleans anyway.

Three years later, though, Pollack traipsed through again, this time without Matty. So Faz drove out of town with him. Glenn heard him at a Pollack recording session in 1936 and when he started his band the next year, he sent for Faz. A short while later, Faz rolled back to Pollack, then eventually to the Crosbyites. He dispensed with the Dispensers last year, drifting on to Chicago where he played with McPartland.

Suddenly came the urge for Noo Ohlins and home cooking, so down he went. He was doing radio work there when he got a letter from friend-clarinetist Jack Ferrier, telling him that Thornhill needed a good clarinet bad. Faz gave a listen to the band, thought it sounded really fine, wrote to Claude, of course got the job pronto, and is now terribly happy—so happy, in fact, that he turned down a fine Muggsy Spanier offer with heartfelt definiteness.

Needless to say, Thornhill is also terribly happy

Fazola, *né* Irving Prestopnik

with the man with the round tummy and tone. "Fine guy, too," says the leader-man. "Just sits there and takes it easy and blows. Wonderful, isn't it?"

Most musicians think it is. I. Henry thinks B. Goodman is far more wonderful, though. "Put all other musicians in a class by themselves; put Benny above everybody else. Man, you know, he gets better with age. I don't know how he does it."

Fazola's taste also runs along similar Louis Armstrong and Jack Teagarden lines. That's his kind of music. But he'd never have to tell you that for you to know it. You just have to listen to him blow that mournful blues way of his, that nostalgic, round-bellied clarinet of his. In the words of C. Thornhill, it's "wonderful, isn't it?"

COZY COLE

From the depth of his voice, you'd think Cozy Cole would like nothing better than to hold conversation with his bass drum. That's not so, though. He prefers his snare. As a matter of fact, unlike almost all modern drummers, who'd rather slash a cymbal than anything else, William Randolph Cole would like nothing better than to beat an arrangement from beginning to end with sticks on his snare drum.

"I really feel the beat there!" he exclaims via a wide mouth that's the climax of a long, lean face. "I like to play on one thing as long as possible. When you do that, you're not breaking the rhythm and you're keeping the band in one solid groove!"

Cozy himself has summed up perfectly the reason he's the ideal man for any band, and why so many leaders and other drummers in the business feel just that way. Because for Cozy, the most important thing in drumming is to keep the beat going, without any show-offy interruptions—just steady rhythm that builds and builds by its incessant repetition.

If you want to get an idea of what Cozy is driving at, listen to the press-roll he played from beginning to end on Lionel Hampton's *Sweethearts on Parade*, waxed for Victor in 1938. There's drumming that really builds.

Cozy did that date shortly before joining Cab Calloway's band, with whom he's still playing, by the way. Strangely enough, even though his work is tremendously in demand (for example, he has recorded by request with outfits headed by Hampton, Teddy Wilson, Artie Shaw, Bunny Berigan, Red Allen, Dick McDonough, and has supported the Andrews Sisters and Billie Holiday often), Cozy has played with surprisingly few bands. He didn't start playing professionally till he was 21, joining Wilbur Sweatman's outfit. That was in 1929, three years after his family had moved to New York from his native East Orange, N. J. But, as William Randolph puts it, "Sweatman fired the devil out of me because I couldn't play nothin'—I had a beat but I just couldn't read!"

Joining His Idol

The following year, after learning more about what makes drums and drummers work, he joined Blanche

William "Cozy" Cole

Calloway, remaining for two years. Then, in 1933, came a real thrill. Benny Carter, who, to this day, is Cozy's favorite of all musicians ("I worked for him, so I should know," he adds), gave Cozy a job in an outfit that included Teddy Wilson, Ben Webster, Edgar Battle, Keg Johnson, Big Green, Johnny Russell and Glynn Pacque. Benny went to Europe after that, so Willie Bryant took over the outfit. It remained at the Savoy several years, reaching some fine musical heights. Catch, if you can, the record of *Viper's Moan* which the bunch made for Victor.

Three years later Cozy moved to Stuff Smith and then two years after that to Cab. Ask the boys in the Calloway band about him, and you'll get nothing but raves. He gives them a beat the band never approached before. He'll play on that snare, which he likes to keep tight but not too snary, for a few choruses, and then he may shift to those two Zildjians he has pressed tightly together for thirty-two more bars. He doesn't shift emphasis much. And no matter what he does, the beat's always there, never varying, always being given to the rest of the boys.

Flash in His Pan

Don't think that Cozy isn't flashy, when flash is necessary. Catch the Okeh records of *Paradiddle*, *Ratamacue*, and *Crescendo in Drums* he made for Cab, and you'll get an idea of what a good beat and good technique, combined, sound like.

Finally, take this for what it's worth: Paul Whiteman's come out openly and declared that there's only one drummer for him, and that one of his big ambitions is to have Cozy Cole play drums in his band. Pops, just between you and a hundred other name band leaders, that's truly a notable ambition!

Tommy Dorsey on Bop (November, 1948)—

Maybe some day bop will be accepted by all the kids just the way swing is today. Maybe it won't be such a mystery after awhile. Remember about ten years ago when everybody asked you to define swing? Now they ask the same questions about bop. But swing is now a part of American music, with no questions asked, so maybe the same thing will happen to bop.

ROY ELDRIDGE

They're all talking about him—now that he's with Gene Krupa's band—talking about him plenty. They're telling you to listen to his chorus on Gene's Okeh record of *Green Eyes* and the prodigious horn he screams on *After You've Gone* and the way he sings "Ahhneetahhh!" on *Let Me Off Uptown*.

But folks who know their jazz have been talking about "Little Jazz" Roy Eldridge for years. They may not have started as far back as 1925, when, at the age of 14 he was playing in T.O.B.A. (colored touring unit) pit bands, or in 1928 when he was playing horn in Fletcher Henderson's Stompers (directed by Horace Henderson), or the following year, when he was with McKinney's Chocolate Dandies and then later playing with Teddy Wilson in Speed Webb's band.

No, they didn't know Roy then. Not many of them knew him when he first came to New York ten years ago, either, and planted himself in the midst of Elmer Snowden's band (a John Hammond ravee) at Small's Paradise, only to go a little later with Teddy Hill and then into the Spanish Band of Connie's Hot Chocolates.

In Pittsburgh, which is where he was born, they may have started talking about him when he and brother Joe, who plays alto, organized a seventeen-piece band that sounded pretty good but which was too big to last. But then Pittsburghers may have lost sight of him when he went up to Detroit to play with McKinney's Cotton Pickers.

New Yorkers and true jazz lovers really began to notice Roy around 1934 when he put in his second semester with Teddy Hill's band at the Savoy. Teddy and Cozy Cole and Ben Webster were in that outfit, too, which made several fine sides for Victor. And they noticed him even more when his name was in lights outside the Famous Door on 52nd Street, when he led his own jam band.

The Eldridge name really began to grow after that. He started being featured on a lot of Fletcher Henderson Victor records, and then he went into the Three Deuces, the musicians' hangout in Chicago that burned down when Roy wasn't blowing inside, with one helluva fine little jazz band that used to feature Zutty Singleton. It stayed there for a long time, and everybody around the midwest (that is, everybody who cared anything at all about jazz) used to talk about it.

Roy dropped out of national prominence for a while after that. True, he made some great records for Milton Gabler's Commodore Shop with an all-

Roy Eldridge

star cast—he had made some equally fine stuff on the Vocalion label with his Chicago bunch—but for the most part he was buried beneath a standard-sized band that didn't suit Roy. It was one of those bring-downs that you can't exactly explain. You just have to feel it. And Roy did.

Then came Saviour Krupa. He got Roy into his band and he started featuring him, and before you knew it, everybody, all the way from the guy who taught "Little Jazz" how to play drums when he was ten years old, to the kid next door who's just heard his first jazz band—everybody was talking about Roy Eldridge.

That's what they're doing these days.

Talk, of course, isn't enough to put a man in a Hall of Fame. But when his trumpet talks and screams at you with such a beat and with such a rich tone and with such an amazingly facile technique, then it's about time he got pushed right into that Hall, isn't it?

Roy thinks lots of other fellows should get into it, too. It's amazing the number of musicians this little dynamo thinks are wonderful. He started off by having Rex Stewart and Red Nichols for idols; then, as he grew older, he learned more about Louis, and then, as he grew still older, he started learning about a lot of others. And he started admiring so many of them for so many different things, that he didn't know just which one to like the most.

One guy he's nuts about is Boss Krupa. Sure, he says that because Gene's his boss. If the drummer-man weren't, Roy wouldn't have the opportunity to appreciate him the way he does. That he admires the man's drumming goes without saying, but he also worships Gene for the way he treats him. "Man, he never turns and glares at you if you have a bad lip and you hit a bum note. He just lets you play the way you know best. Never drives you. That's wonderful, too!"

So's Roy Eldridge!

Benny Goodman on Progressive Music (August, 1948)—

That word "progressive" kind of makes me ill. That's a political word. If it's good, it can be re-actionary.

450

 # METRONOME ALL-STAR BANDS, 1939-40

Assembling and producing records by the *Metronome* All-Star Bands was a brainstorm which at times I'd wished I'd never had. It consisted of getting together as many winners of our annual polls as possible (runners-up were substituted for those not available) and supervising them on two recorded sides. As you can well imagine, it always turned out to be a huge job, logistically, and required infinite tact and patience. These reports of the first two sessions (eventually there was a total of ten) reflect quite accurately just what did take place.

February, 1939

GREATEST BAND OF ALL-TIME RECORDS FOR MUSICIANS' CHARITY

Goodman, Dorsey, Berigan, Teagarden Head Group of Thirteen Stars, Assembled by Metronome and Readers to Aid Unemployed Musicians . . . Record Of Magnificent Solos and Ensembles Issued by Victor

The musicians' dream came true—and how it came true! The greatest stars in dancebandom all in one band on one record! For early in the morning of January 12 the METRONOME All-Star Band (comprised of the country's *leading* musicians as chosen by the country's *smartest* musicians) assembled under the magazine's auspices in the Victor studios and batted out two sides, the likes of which will probably never be heard again!

What a stellar gathering. Benny Goodman . . . Tommy Dorsey . . . Bunny Berigan . . . Harry James . . . Jack Teagarden . . . Bob Haggart . . . Eddie Miller . . . and other Greats of Swing—making up one swing band—playing as they've never played before—and getting a tremendous kick out of every minute of it! They made just two sides, but they contained more thrills than you'll hear in a dozen of the year's greatest records.

Those of you who have already obtained your copy will hear on one side *Blue Lou*, and on the other *The Blues*. Tommy led the boys through the Edgar Sampson immortal, while Benny directed and composed the basic figure on the reverse.

Had to Be Good

It was a session in which the men just *had* to be good; had to be at their best. For there was a lot at stake.

In the first place, each man was forced to hold up his end in the galaxy of stars. Competition was terrific, so that each man had to shine not only on his solo passages but on ensemble as well.

In the second place, the men were out to throw the jinx that has always beaten a band of stars tossed together for the first time. And what a job of jinx-tossing they did, too!

Photos of the first METRONOME All-Star record date as they graced the cover of the February, 1939 issue. TOP ROW: Ray Bauduc, Charlie Spivak, Tommy Dorsey, Jack Teagarden. SECOND ROW: Bob Zurke, Harry James, Bunny Berigan, Arthur Rollini, Carmen Mastren. BOTTOM ROW: Eddie Miller, Hymie Schertzer, Benny Goodman (in a rare sax-playing shot), Sonny Dunham, Bob Haggart

Charity

And finally, and most important of all, they were out to make the best sides they possibly could. For this assembly had in mind one common purpose: they wanted to make great music whose sale would benefit their less fortunate brethren. For METRONOME, in sponsoring the date, had made arrangements with Victor to receive royalties from the sale of *every* record (usually royalties commence only after a specified number have been sold) which it, in turn, will turn over to the Unemployment Fund of New York's Musicians' Union. (Associate editor George Simon acted as contractor as well as contactor for the date.)

Benny and Tommy

Little wonder, then, that the entire proceeding was blessed with a feeling of good-fellowship never before paralleled in the meetings of rival stars. Goodman and Dorsey, who, previous to this gathering, hadn't exchanged more than three-and-a-quarter curt "how-do-you-do's" in two years, cooperated magnificently,

forgetting all personal animosity, helping each other all they could, and even going so far as to pull the most natural "Alphonse and Gaston" act in the history of Emily Postdom. The three hot trumpeters graciously pulled for one another. Eddie Miller insisted upon Arthur Rollini playing some jazz on tenor too. And so it went on!

Sacrifices

It was indeed a magnificent gesture on the parts of all concerned. Goodman, due later in the same morning on the stage of the Paramount Theatre and in need of sleep, remained gracious and enthusiastic through the final groove at four a.m. Ditto for the smiling, good-humored Dorsey, on the eve of a lengthy and exhausting road trip. The sacrifices of Crosby's men are told elsewhere.

It was a great evening with great musicians, great men, producing great sides. METRONOME is proud of having had the opportunity to partake of such an event —conceivably the greatest in the history of jazz!

FOGBOUND TRAIN, FOGGY PIANIST, ALMOST KILL DATE

Philly Train Delay Nearly Fatal . . . Zurke Gets Lost . . . Men Arrive in Studio at All Times . . . Blue Lou Trouble . . . Blues Done in 28 Minutes

Here's a timetable story of what happened on the All-Star record date in the Victor studios on the morning of January 12, 1939:

12:40 A.M.—George Simon, contactor and contractor for the date, arrives—one-half hour before anybody else—just to make sure!

1:10—Arthur Rollini comes in. Sees no other band members. Walks out for smoke.

1:14—Jack Teagarden and Charlie Spivak enter. Reminisce about old Ben Pollack days. See no other band members. Walk out for smoke.

1:15—Carmen Mastren, Hymie Schertzer and Mrs. Schertzer arrive. Unwrap themselves. Rollini, sensing support, returns from smokedom.

1:17—Benny Goodman comes in with Harry James. Goodman makes beeline for chair. Sits down. Thinks. James grins at Spivak. Spivak returns grin. Both thinking. "What goes? We can't both play first trumpet."

1:18—Bunny Berigan enters.

1:19—Tom Dorsey strides in followed by Lawyer Gluskin and Assistant Burns. Dorsey spies Goodman. "Hi, Harve!" he shouts good-naturedly. "Hello, Tommy," returns Benny, sincerely but a bit more formally.

1:30—Recording supervisor Eli Oberstein comes in. Looks around. Walks into control room.

1:31—Everybody gets chummy. Session is scheduled to start, but no signs yet of Sonny Dunham or of four Bob Crosby men.

1:35—Dunham arrives. Gets introduced to men he doesn't know.

1:35¼—Somebody notices FOUR trumpeters. More "What goes?" exclamations. Everybody put at rest with explanation that James's contract won't allow him to play under anybody except Goodman, and since Benny is to lead only one side, Spivak will play first trumpet when Dorsey leads.

1:35½—Everybody commencing to worry about four Crosby boys, now over fifteen minutes behind schedule.

1:40—Everybody worrying more.

1:45—And still more.

1:48—Some start thinking about date not coming off at all.

A run-through on the first METRONOME All-Star date. Front row: Eddie Miller, Hymie Schertzer, Arthur Rollini, Carmen Mastren. Middle row: Benny Goodman, Jack Teagarden, Bob Haggart. In back: Tommy Dorsey. Mostly hidden: Bob Zurke

1:50—Simon calls Gil Rodin, manager of Bob Crosby band, in Philadelphia. Rodin, awakened from sleep, insists men left in plenty of time to catch 11:30 train.

1:53—Goodman starts rehearsing sax section without Miller on Dorsey arrangement of *Blue Lou*.

1:53½—Dorsey does ditto with brass—only rhythm comes from Mastren's guitar.

2:00—Everybody really jittery.

2:05—Everybody really more jittery.

2:08—Taxi crashes up to entrance. Out sprawl Miller, Haggart, and Bauduc, hauling instruments after them. "Train was late." No Zurke!

2:10—Zurke reported definitely lost in Pennsylvania Station. Pianist needed.

2:11—Jess Stacy contacted in hotel room. Sick. Very sick. Can't possibly come down.

2:13—Frantic Simon calls Nick's in hopes of catching Dave Bowman. Explains to headwaiter. Mentions Zurke's name. Headwaiter explains Zurke was there but just left for date in taxi.

2:14—Everybody relieved.

2:20—Zurke still missing—overdue again.

2:21—Bowman contacted at Nick's. Rushes out in taxi to make date.

2:21¼—Zurke ambles in. "Taxi driver wouldn't take me where I wanted to go." Simon collapses.

2:21½—Band rehearses *Blue Lou*.

2:22—Band still rehearsing *Blue Lou*.

2:25—Bowman arrives. Goes back.

2:40—Band still rehearsing *Blue Lou*. Choruses assigned by this time.

2:45—Test record made of *Blue Lou*.

2:48—Band listens to playback. Disappointed. Too sloppy. Last 24 bars especially bad.

2:51—Dorsey makes cuts and revisions.

2:55—Band makes a second test.

2:58—Still disappointed.

3:01—Few more minor changes.

3:08—Third test.

3:11—Much better.

3:18—First master. Pretty good.

3:25—Second master. Much better.

3:29—Third master.

3:29¼—Clinkers kill it.

3:30—Fourth master. Fine!

3:34—Goodman takes over leadership of band. Decides to fake the blues. Hits upon rhythm figure. Hums it to saxes. Assigns parts. Asks Dorsey to do same with brass.

3:38—Benny assigns choruses.

3:42—Band runs through blues. Sounds good.

3:45—Test.

3:48—Playback. Fine!

3:52—First master. Very good.

3:56—Second master.

3:56½—Second master ruined by trouble in control room.

3:58—Third master.

4:01—Third master completed. Wonderful!

4:01½—"Go home!" shouts Oberstein.

4:01½—"Burns!" shouts Dorsey.

4:02—Everybody goes home.

Benny Had No Sax

Biggest visual surprise of the METRONOME All-Star record date was seeing Benny Goodman play third alto in the sax section. B.G. had been playing sax so seldom that he had to borrow Dave Matthews' for the date. Consensus of the entire band was that the King can play in any section!

Rex Stewart on Duke Ellington as a Person (April, 1955)—

He's a god who doesn't have feet of clay—oh, maybe just a little toe made of clay—and that's exceptional in these days!

BG, TD MAKE UP
ON ALL-STAR DATE

Bitter Rivals Break Long-Standing Ice in Charitable Venture . . . Goodman Insists upon Featuring Modest Rival

Tommy Dorsey and Benny Goodman actually talk to each other again! The two former close friends, but bitter rivals since their individual successes as bandleaders, got together on the All-Star date where to all intents and purposes they kissed and made up.

It was ticklish at first. Benny was sitting on a high chair in the middle of the studio when Tommy walked in.

"Hi, Harve!" called out Tom, good-naturedly.

"Hello, Tommy," came back Ben, a bit more stiffly, but still sincerely.

Ice Starts to Melt

Neither said much for a while. There was an obvious strain. Spectators watched on the sides to see whether there'd be blows or bows. The late arrival of the Crosby band was a good excuse, so—

Said Benny: "Wonder what's happened to Gil's boys."

Said Tommy: "Yeah, wonder what's happened to them."

And so it continued, the two of them talking peacefully about everything in the music business except themselves. It was a gradual but effective bit of ice-melting.

Ice Breaks Down

The real breakdown came on the date itself, though. There was quite a bit of trouble with *Blue Lou*. It was Tommy's side. Benny made suggestions for the saxes, even for choruses and cuts. Tommy accepted many of them, willingly, too. Came time for the first test—

Called Tommy: "Go ahead, Benny, you kick it off!"

Queried Benny: "Want me to ?"

Replied Tommy: "Sure, Harve, you're up front; they can all see you. I'm just a trombone player back here!"

And so it went on. Little things happened here and there that reminded Goodman and Dorsey of the past days. "Hey, Tom," Benny would call back laughingly, "remember when so-and-so happened like this?"

"Yeah," Tom would come back, "and how about the time we did this and that?"

Benny Pushes Tommy

The high point of all the good fellowship business came when Benny was getting choruses set in *The Blues*. Tommy hadn't played a solo on his own *Blue Lou* side.

"Okay, Tommy," said Benny, "we'll take a guitar and bass intro and then you play the first chorus."

"Oh, no—nix," cried out Tommy, really aroused. "I won't play any jazz when you've got a man like Teagarden here. Jackson should take all the trombone jazz."

"Come on, Tommy," urged Benny, "you haven't played anything yet, and the guys who buy this record want to hear you."

But Tommy continued to refuse. Everybody started begging him, coaxing him, urging him. To no avail, though. "Teagarden plays jazz—I only play pretty," was Tom's answer every time.

"Okay, then," exclaimed Benny, "if you only play pretty, play pretty and Jack'll play jazz around you. Come on, now, I'm the leader, and you play the first chorus."

"All right," acquiesced Tommy, "but Jack plays the jazz!" And that's how that marvelous first chorus was born.

ALL-STARS LOOKED LIKE GOODMAN'S OLD BAND

Spivak, Teagarden Reunited; 11 Leaders in Group; Other Highlights of Session

If you'd looked at some of the men in the [2nd] METRONOME All-Star Band, you'd have thought it was Goodman's All-Time Band. . . . Besides Benny, there were Krupa, Stacy, James, Elman, Christian, and Mondello. . . . And both Teagarden and Jenney had played for him before he'd become famous, too. . . . Making the King pretty much the central figure.

There was another reunion, too. . . . Charlie Spivak and Teagarden, who hadn't been seen together since the former quit the latter's band, talked over old times before the date. . . . "Hey, where did you find the new vocalist?" the guys kidded Jack, referring to those broadcasts from Boston on which he had used Duke's Ivy Anderson. . . . Mr. T. just grinned that good-natured, bashful grin of his.

Only four members of the recording band were not actual first-place winners in the contest. . . . Tony Pastor couldn't make it because his new band was playing in Boston, so Charlie Barnet, who finished after Miller in the hot tenor division, was called in. . . . Jimmy Dorsey and Johnny Hodges were in Chicago, so third best hot alto man, Benny Carter, come along. . . . And both Tommy Dorsey and Carmen Mastren were stuck in Indianapolis on the day of the date.

Leading Leaders

Surprising how many of the winners lead their own outfits: Goodman, Barnet, Carter, Spivak, James, Jenney, Teagarden and Krupa, while Mondello, Elman and Stacy head recording groups. . . . That left just Eddie Miller, Charlie Christian and Bob Haggart as the only legitimate sidemen.

As in last year's date, the Alphonse-Gaston acts cropped up, the two trombonists again getting top billing in that department. . . . Last year Tom Dorsey sincerely exclaimed: "Shucks, I won't play any jazz when you've got Jack Teagarden!". . . This year Jack Jenney also felt he wasn't in the same league with Mr. T. and insisted that Jackson play all the hot. . . . No getting away from it, that Teagarden man is sure the top-notchers' idol!

Bowing Dept.

The A-G feeling appeared in other departments too. . . . Eddie Miller and Charlie Barnet were continually bowing to one another, while James wanted Elman to play most of the hot and Ziggy wanted Harry to. . . . They compromised on *King Porter*, but there was trouble with the lead there, for Spivak wanted each of the others to share it with him—result, they all played some.

The date wasn't delayed nearly so long as last year's when Bob Zurke, coming in from Philadelphia, showed up at Nick's instead of Victor. . . . The guys had to wait for Charlie Barnet to come off his own band's session, which he did surprisingly quickly, and then had to look around for Harry James, who had overslept after riding all night on a bus. . . . The affair, scheduled to commence at twelve noon, was well under way by twelve-thirty. . . . A lot of the guys, especially those in the Crosby Crew (their training must be awfully good) got there a half hour ahead of time.

The full band was originally going to wax *I Can't Believe That You're in Love With Me*, but after running through it a couple of times decided to try something else. . . . Benny and John Hammond simultaneously suggested *King Porter*, which turned out to be a great choice. . . . Hammond, who helped before, during and after the date to make it a success, was there supervising for Columbia along with Morty Palitz. . . . The latter, with his astounding ear, was also a wonderful help. Benny even asked him to lead the band on the first side, that's what a great reputation he has in the field!

There was quite an audience in the studio, uninvited but still welcome, especially since it behaved so well. . . . It included mostly representatives of rival papers, as well as band managers. . . . Goodman's Leonard Vannerson and Peewee Monte, Spivak's Peter Dean, James's Jerry Barrett, Teagarden's Frank (Jumbo) Herz, Jenney's Melcher, and Krupa's Frank Verniere all glowed as their bosses shone. . . . But the biggest glow of all was Benny's, as everybody marveled at the guitaring of his pet, Charles Christian.

The small band side, a Hammond suggestion, was mapped out in advance by METRONOME. . . . George Simon assigned the guys choruses, gave 'em the approximate tempo, and they were off on a simple blues in C. . . . Jess Stacy set the exact tempo via his piano intro. . . . By the way, there wasn't any sign of the expected friction between Jess and Benny, while Krupa and the King acted like long-lost pals. . . . Gene seemed to get especially big kicks out of Charles Christian, Jess and Harry—he hadn't played with the last two for years. . . . Everyone marvelled how softly and with what impeccable taste Gene drummed throughout the entire date—he must have been reading his own METRONOME column!

All the guys seemed to get a big boot out of the date, not only from the music angle, but from getting together personally as well. . . . As Krupa remarked afterwards: "Imagine getting paid for so much fun!" . . . There was plenty of gabbing among the boys before they ever opened an instrument case. . . . Almost everybody knew everybody else beforehand, and a lot of the guys had played together before—in fact, six of 'em (Goodman, Miller, Teagarden, Spivak, James and Haggart) had made last year's METRONOME All-Star Band record together. . . . When it was all over, most of the men hung around to talk some more about what they were doing or had done together in the past and how fine each one thought the other had played on the date. . . . Just real, regular guys, every single one of 'em—musicians who love their work and love to talk about it—exactly like you and me!

On the second METRONOME All-Star date producers George Simon, Gordon Wright and Jimmy Bracken talk things over with leader-clarinetist Benny Goodman

SIMON SAYS

Shortly after I went into the army in 1943, I worked out a deal with *Metronome* whereby I'd write an almost monthly column called "Simon Says" about anything I felt like. Fortunately, my army orders never took me very far from New York—to Fort Dix for induction, to Atlantic City for basic training, to New Haven for the Glenn Miller band, and back to New York for the V-Disc program—so that I was able to keep abreast of much that was happening. Some of those columns had some interesting things to say about some people and some conditions that interested me especially in those days, and might still interest you today.

July, 1944

ON JOINING DUKE ELLINGTON

"It's Like Nothing Else!"

The tenorman in the band came over and sat himself down next to me. Al Sears was both beaming and bewildered. Apparently, the initial shock of working in Duke Ellington's band still hadn't worn off.

Sears, who's as intelligent as he looks (he was graduated from the University of Illinois, by the way), readily admitted that he couldn't get over and couldn't get used to playing with the greatest of all bands.

"It's like nothing else!" he exclaimed. "Really, you've got no idea of what it's like till you've actually tried playing in the band!"

It being my turn to admit readily, I readily admitted I had no idea of what it was like, except that it sounded wonderful to me, as always, and that went for Al's blowing, too.

"Naw," Sears came back. "I'm not playing right—yet. It's going to take me more time to get used to it —more than just a few weeks."

Al Sears's road map interpreter, Johnny Hodges

He grinned. The Sears grin is abnormally broad. "It's not like any other band. In another band you just sit down and read the parts. Here you can sit down and read the parts and suddenly you find you're playing something entirely different from what the rest of the band's playing."

That didn't seem quite logical to me. I said so.

"That's just it—it's not logical," retorted Al. "You start at letter 'A' and go to 'B' and then suddenly, for no reason at all, when *you* go to 'C' the rest of the band's playing something else which you find out later on isn't what's written at 'C' but what's written at 'J' instead. And then on the next number, instead of starting at the top, the entire band starts at 'H'—that is, everybody except me. See, I'm the newest man in the band and I just haven't caught on to the system yet."

Al explained what he considered the solution, or, to be more exact, what he thought was the reason. It seems that the band, whenever it does write out its music, plays through it a few times and then one or two men come up with ideas for changes, and before *you* know it (*they* know it all along, of course), the whole routine is altered and the brass is playing a different figure behind the sax chorus and that part where the trombone is blowing isn't in at all anymore because the baritone's playing a part that wasn't written in the first place for the trumpet from whom it was taken away.

"And if it weren't for Johnny," went on Al, pointing to Hodges, who was at least sitting where he was supposed to be sitting, "I'd be completely lost. He cues me. Sometimes it's a couple of bars before I realize it's my solo. He's wonderful, the way he helps. Why, the other night on a broadcast he practically pushed me into the mike to make sure I'd come in right on my chorus, and then, when it was all over, he actually yanked me back by my coat to make sure I'd stop! I did."

Such are the trials and tribulations of playing with the greatest band in the world. A guy gets pushed into a mike and yanked into his seat by his coat-tails. But, from the way Duke sounded on his last night at the Hurricane, it should easily be worth it—and more. The band was immense, as immense as ever, and that goes all the way from its oldest members, Messrs. Ellington, Greer, and Hardwick, right down to its newest member, who, besides being confused by cues, isn't always certain what tune's up next. Seems nobody says anything; Duke just plays an undetermined number of measures, in which are hidden a few thematic fragments, and then—boom—you're off.

So far Sears hasn't gone into *Perdido* while the rest of the band fell into *Harlem Airshaft*. But maybe that's because Hodges keeps sitting next to him.

November, 1944

DIXIELAND

"He sounds as if he's got a split lip," said the man next to me at Nick's, while the young soldier standing directly in front of Peewee went into ecstacies as Russell finished his clarinet passage of *Muskrat Ramble*.

It struck me as being pretty indicative of the reactions of the majority to dixieland: either you think it's the greatest or you're convinced it's terrible. Nowadays it seems to be fashionable not to tread the middle path: not to classify some of it as good and some of it as not so good. No, it's either the best there is or it's just plain nowhere.

Personally, I don't get either of these dogmatic attitudes. I used to go to Nick's lots more in those days when Hackett first started, around 1938 I guess it was, but that was because it was something new for me for a while. Then it began to pall and so I started going to other spots again. But still, whenever I go back, I'm lucky enough to be able to listen to what goes on with what I consider a pretty unbiased attitude. That's why sometimes I walk out after just a couple of numbers and sometimes I stick around for hours.

Dixieland's something you either get or you don't get. Either you feel that type of beat or you don't feel it. If you don't feel it, there's no sense in your hanging around it, but, on the other hand, there's no sense in your condemning it, either. Because, since you don't feel it, you literally don't know what you're talking about.

But it also strikes me that a lot of people who don't condemn dixieland, but, on the other hand, go around praising it to high heaven as the only kind of jazz, as the real jazz, and tossing aside as pure rubbish anything by the Count or Lionel or even the Duke, merely because it's opposed to dixieland, also don't know what they're talking about. A lot of them hang around Nick's and Jimmy Ryan's religiously, gaping and cheering and acting completely knocked out by anything and everything, whether it's good or not. As long as Condon or Peewee or Muggsy is there, it's got to be good, per se, they figure. No, it couldn't be that one of their idols could be having a bad night of it. No, that's not possible at all. After all, Peewee's playing it and Eddie's there, isn't he, so how could it be anything else but the good, the pure, the righteous jazz?

Yes, and they're the people who laugh at Sinatra's bobby-soxers. Funny they don't realize how close they are to them!

Some of the better dixieland sessions of the thirties and forties took place at Nick's in Greenwich Village, played by such groups as this one of guitarist Eddie Condon, trombonist Brad Gowans, cornetist Bobby Hackett, clarinetist Peewee Russell, drummer Zutty Singleton and pianist Joe Sullivan

It's honestly a shame that dixieland lovers aren't better educated in the field in which they consider themselves experts and worshipers rolled into one. It's a shame they can't tell the good from the bad. For instance, I spent a few nights in a row at Nick's recently. Muggsy was consistently magnificent, and when Muggsy's right, there's no beat like his. But he had some pretty sad backing (I almost said "support," but it wasn't even that) so that the performance, taken over longer stretches, such as a complete number or a complete set, was pretty lethargic. But, still, the followers gaped and applauded and cheered. It was just fair dixieland (and I'm sure any of the participants would agree with me), only spasmodically comparable with some of the great moments at Nick's, but that didn't faze the righteous followers. After all, it was dixieland, wasn't it, or at least a fairly reasonable facsimile thereof?

Having followers of the "you-can't-do-anything-wrong-because-you're-God" ilk must be somewhat satisfying, but it must be awfully annoying at times, too. I don't think that, deep down inside, Condon or Peewee or Muggsy or any of their crowd relish the undisciplined adoration of Nicksielanders who think they know all there is to know about jazz because they can yell *Muskrat Ramble* in one breath.

These kids (perhaps they're not all kids in years, but they're kids so far as any mature outlook toward jazz is concerned) do just as much to make dixieland look foolish as the Paramount audiences do to make other forms of popular music seem ridiculous. They're not as much in the majority because dixieland hasn't been as widely publicized as Sinatra and Crosby, etc., but that's not saying they might not be some day.

The famous Peewee Russell face, this time with Stan Kenton. Who's understanding whom?

460

Life recently ran an article on jazz. Peewee's face as usual was blown up. A few fellows connected with dixieland are pretty astute entrepreneurs, and they've managed to bring to it more than its proportionate share of publicity. At times when Ellington and Goodman and Herman and Hampton are doing things that are new and which advance the scope and hope of swing, the Nicksielanders remain just as they were, producing nothing different, but still cashing in on tradition.

The sad part of it is that when these entrepreneurs and helpers do go ahead and get publicity for dixieland, they don't go ahead and get it on its musical merits. Angles that have nothing at all to do with music are emphasized way out of proportion. It's not honest publicity, honest so far as the good the men actually represent is concerned.

There are some folks who go to hear dixieland because they want to hear good jazz with a fine, decisive beat. They can tell the good from the bad. They're the authentic followers, sometimes perhaps a bit too rabid (occasioned more often than not by a defense mechanism), but they go to hear the music.

On the other hand there are too many young squirts who have been attracted to dixieland not because of the music but because of the glamor they've read about. I'll bet you anything that Peewee's face is far more important to them than what he plays, and, commercially, I daresay, it's probably far more important to Peewee, too!

As a result of all this, there has been little or no progress in dixieland in years. There are still some brilliant sessions going on at Nick's, but there are also some horrible moments, more than ever before. Because, after all, dixieland no longer has to be great to survive. No, Peewee just has to make a few faces, Condon just has to make a few nasty cracks about big bands, Muggsy just has to look sad, and nobody has to keep time anymore if he doesn't feel like it. After all, we dixielanders will always make a living, just so long as *Life* and others keep on telling the world that the way we live is JAZZ, that we're the greatest. So why bother?

LOUIS ARMSTRONG

As the old year draws to a close, nothing impresses me quite as much as something that should have been impressing me much more during the last years. I dwelled upon it in last month's column, but it was impressed upon me even more than that during the past month.

It's the respect, the reverence, the hero worship that top musicians have for the playing of Louis Armstrong. Harry James admitted to me, as I said last month, that he actually cried last time he heard Louis play. That's impressive, but after a while you tend to forget one incident. But since then several things have happened:

I dropped in one night at Nick's to listen to Muggsy. I listened, was thrilled by his playing, then sat down to talk to him. All Muggsy could talk about was Louis. He'd heard him at the Hurricane the night before. And he still couldn't believe it. "The Greatest!" he exclaimed. "Absolutely the Greatest! Why, all those other guys with those peatones, they're just not in the same class with him!"

The next night I happened to be at a midnight all-star jam session for V-Discs. (Note: I'll be honest. I was producing the session.) It was going along swell. Suddenly somebody spied Louis entering the studio. Guys like Teagarden and Butterfield and Hackett and McGarity and Cozy and Johnny Guarnieri were running through a fast blues, rehearsing it before the take. But when Louis entered, they all stopped—automatically. They greeted him, they watched him take off his coat, unpack his horn. And they kept sitting and standing there, not blowing a note, as he warmed up. Then he joined them, and right then was the first time in my life that I'd ever heard the Real Armstrong in person. I've never heard anything like that in all of my days. The way he blew! The feeling, the tone, the phrasing, the heart! It was something that just doesn't come out of anybody else's horn.

When it was over and Louis had rushed back to the Zanzibar, I realized that I wasn't the only one who felt the way I did: completely knocked out. Somebody asked Billy Butterfield to play something with the rest of the band backing him. The idea was to feature each of the stars on the date. But Billy absolutely refused, refused several times. Butterfield, who is one of the Trumpet Greats of All Time, wouldn't even think of playing. "How can I?" he asked with sincerity. "How do you expect me to play after that? It would just be an awful anticlimax."

Louis surrounded by some of his admirers, including Jerry Lewis, Dean Martin, Bob Hope, Meredith Willson, Frankie Laine, Tallulah Bankhead and Deborah Kerr

Meanwhile, over in another part of the studio, little Bobby Hackett, who's playing probably the best trumpet of his career, went around muttering something about "they're all fakes, all of 'em. He's the only *real* thing." And Teagarden and McGarity and all the rest seemed to agree perfectly.

(In a way I hate to add this paragraph to what I've just written, so I'll put it in parenthesis. It concerns Louis and it's quite deprecatory. More exactly, it concerns his broadcasts from the Zanzibar. I've heard several of them and never in my life have I heard anything that does anyone a greater injustice.

The choice of tunes, many of the arrangements, the pacing of the shows, and, in many instances, the band behind him are positively abominable. Nothing could possibly do more harm to such a great artist. It's absolutely murderous. If Louis can't be presented to the radio public in a better light than that, he shouldn't be presented at all. I sincerely hope that by the time this gets into print somebody will have given this subject some thought and rectified the ridiculous conditions, or else that Louis will be spared future embarrassment and the rest of his broadcasts be cancelled.)

GOODMAN AND CORN

Several eves ago this fellow with the Benny Goodman allergy dropped in on a friend of mine and spied several albums of Brunswick reissues. One of them was the one that has Benny and Glenn Miller, Bud Freeman, Dick Morgan, Jimmy McPartland and others. My friend, you see, likes Goodman, which is nice to hear, because my friend knows little about music and it's usually the record collectors who know little about music who take wild, arrogant pokes at the clarinetist ninety-nine out of a hundred musicians will admit is easily the greatest. That takes them out of the realm of ordinary record collectors and makes them experts.

Anyway, this chap spied the album and recognized the records. (Many of these experts recognize records quite readily, just so long as the personnel is plainly printed on the label.)

"There's a record in that album," announced Benny's would-be burier, with a condescending air of authority, "that's the *only* good record he ever made."

My friend looked up and said nothing.

"That's right," said the expert defensively. (Rarely having constructive arguments to offer, many of these experts assume a constant defensive air.) "It's the *only* good record he ever made. Play it for me, will you. It's called *Shirt Tail Stomp*."

The record was played.

"That's really great jazz!" exclaimed Anti-Goodman. "Play it again."

The record was played again.

"That's fine. I've got to buy that record."

When my friend told me this story strictly without prejudice, because he claims to know nothing, I immediately became suspicious. I recalled some things Glenn Miller had told me about some of those sessions he had made with Benny in the early days. So I listened to *Shirt Tail Stomp*.

And I was right!

Just to make sure, though, I asked Benny about the record and then a week later I checked with Dick Morgan and he corroborated what Benny said.

"Sure, I remember *Shirt Tail Stomp*," said Benny. "We made that record as a gag. We all played as corny as we could, on purpose, of course, sort of like Spike Jones, just to see what would happen."

"And," added Dick Morgan the following week, "you want to know what did happen? The record sold so well that Irving Mills had us make a whole batch more, just like it!"

All of which makes me think that maybe some of us are all wrong when we insist that the stuff which some of those purist academicians think is the only acceptable music isn't at all commercial. After all, look at the success of Spike Jones!

I wonder if George Lewis can play corny on purpose, too!

BUNK JOHNSON

I wish I could have heard Bunk Johnson play when he was in his prime. They say he was pretty sensational then. Naturally, at his advanced age, he's somewhat less than that now, but thirty years ago he must have been magnificent because (1) he must have had better control of his horn, and (2) by the standards of thirty years ago he was a modern trumpeter whose playing very likely was unrivaled then.

These nights he's playing not in his native Louisiana but in New York where he is being bravely sponsored by Gene Williams, his most ardent booster, in a magnificently rundown meeting-hall on the Lower East Side called the Stuyvesant Casino, whose atmosphere must be somewhat like that to which Bunk and his compatriots were limited in their heyday.

Bunk's seven-piece band gives you an excellent idea of what jazz must have sounded like twenty, thirty and even forty years ago. And, serving as a museum piece, Bunk and his men must be credited with doing a superb job.

Unfortunately, however, some folks are trying to credit the Bunk Johnson band with much more, and by doing so I think they're missing the idea of its being entirely. While I was listening to the band, some frantic character came up to me, cognizant of the fact that I was reporting for METRONOME, and started insulting not only me but just about every modern swing band. All the others were just nothing: this was "the real thing, the REAL jazz, the ONLY REAL jazz."

To me he was completely wrong on several counts. In the first place I have tremendous respect and admiration for bands like Ellington, Herman, Goodman, etc., and to say that they are "nothing," is a stupid way of dismissing them with prejudice.

In the second place, the Bunk Johnson type is not the ONLY REAL jazz. There are other types of jazz that are every bit as REAL. What my insulter should have said, and what I believe most of the intelligent followers of Bunk Johnson mean, is that his type of music is the only ORIGINAL jazz. With that statement I have no argument because (1) the music Bunk plays certainly sounds about as primitive as anything I've heard in jazz, and (2) I don't profess to know the various origins of jazz anyway and don't believe anyone living today does either.

And, in the final place, I don't think it's either necessary or even possible to compare the two types of jazz and arrive at any sensible conclusion. Columbus, if you'll recall your third grade history, sailed the Atlantic in a sailboat called the *Santa Maria*. Recently most people in traveling across the Atlantic used boats like the *Queen Elizabeth*. The *Santa Maria* and the *Queen Elizabeth* are both ships, one somewhat more modern than the other. For all I know, some people would still prefer sailing across the Atlantic. It's certainly more glamorous. But just because you prefer sailing across, that doesn't mean that the *Queen Elizabeth* isn't a boat.

It's just that sort of fallacious reasoning that has widened the breach between the followers of modern, more advanced jazz and those who prefer the original. And just as man went ahead and discovered steam and other types of engines and put them to use, so have musicians gone ahead and produced more advanced types of music which they have applied to jazz. Personally, my leanings are all toward the latter group, but I must say I have no argument to find with those who honestly and for some sane reason prefer the former type.

I do, however, have much fault to find with most of the Bunk Johnson lovers, who refuse to listen to modern bands, who know nothing at all about the basic ingredients of music, and who worship at his shrine just because they think it's the thing to do. At the Stuyvesant Casino there are so many of those adolescents present that you can't help feeling un-comfortable. Instead of *listening* to Baby Dodds drum, they want to *watch* Baby Dodds drum. They like Lawrence Marrero, not because he happens to play good banjo, but because he plays banjo. Their inability to judge (because they know no music and therefore possess no standards) and their appropriate demonstrations remind me very much, I'm sorry to say, of the antics of the bobby-soxers.

For Bunk Johnson's band, judged musically, is certainly not great. Bunk himself now and then phrases with tremendous feeling and he has a certain drive to his playing but he is handicapped by an inability to get everything through and out of his horn. Baby Dodds, when he plays for the band instead of for the crowd (which is very seldom), is the great drummer I'd always heard he was. But, even more so than Krupa ever did, he goes through all sorts of antics and gyrations, constantly messing up the beat with all sorts of explosions of tom-toms, cowbells, rims, etc., that detract tremendously from the basic drive that characterizes the music Bunk and his band are trying to play. To me, the most impressive man in the band is the banjoist (much as I hate the sound of the instrument), because Lawrence Marrero, more than anyone else in the band, produces a truly infectious, pulsating drive on his instrument. There has been a great deal of talk about clarinetist George Lewis and I give you my word I did my best to like his playing, but he played so consistently flat all night long that despite flashes of real feeling, I couldn't be convinced. It's quite conceivable that playing flat is part of that style, but if it is, then that's one phase of the ORIGINAL jazz that I'll never be able to stomach. The rest of the band impressed me not at all, Slow Drag slapping his bass morbidly and Jim Robinson playing uninspired trombone. In defense of pianist Alton Purnell, I must state he was handicapped by a horrible piano.

That, then, is an appraisal of the musical worth of the Bunk Johnson band. I admit that musical proficiency isn't nearly so important in a band of this type as in those that play more advanced jazz. For the spirit and the feel of the old days is there, and though fifteen-minute versions of the same tune in the same key may pall on people like me, Bunk's group is a genuine museum piece, and as such, worth raving about.

PLAY BALL

Baseball's here again! Baseball, that great "All-American" Game. Note the quotation marks; they're mine; they're important.

What has me started on baseball when this is a music magazine? It's simple. Music, jazz especially, is the most American thing this country owns. Not only does it exemplify the emotional spirit of our people, but it's the freest of all mediums of expression. It knows only one measuring rod, that of the quality of the product, whether it be a sax passage, a blues composition or a crooner's inflections. In jazz, if it's good, it's good, no matter who makes it, no matter if it comes from a man or a woman, from a Christian or a Jew, from a white man or a colored man.

And then there's baseball, that grand "All-American" Game. It typifies America, the American Youth, the American Spirit, the American Sense of Sportsmanship.

Take the great names in baseball: Ted Williams, Stan Musial, Bob Feller, Dixie Walker, Jackie Robinson. But wait, I'm a little premature. Jackie Robinson, did I say? Sorry, I was confused. Jackie isn't really one of the great names in baseball. Not yet, anyway. And there's a good chance that, despite his talents, he will never be, or, more important, never get the chance to be a big name.

For Jackie Robinson is not white, he is a Negro. And baseball, that great "All-American" Game, that great leader of American Youth, that great symbol of the American Spirit, that great example of American Sportsmanship—well, it isn't quite American enough to accept Jackie Robinson without any qualms, without any hesitation, without drawing the color line.

Jackie's talents lie in an unfortunate field. Were he a top-flight musician, he'd be recognized as such, just as Duke Ellington, Benny Goodman, Louis Armstrong, Coleman Hawkins, Gene Krupa, and all the rest are, regardless of whether their skin is white or black. But Jackie's not a musician, he's a ballplayer, and things aren't always so easy for All Americans in that "All-American" Game.

Baseball players and fans will have an opportunity this year to see if they measure up to jazz musicians and fans. Jackie Robinson has been signed by the Brooklyn Dodgers, after a lot of talking back and forth, a lot of knee-shaking and hectic player conferences. Let's hope that baseball comes through the way jazz has.

I'm glad I'm not in baseball!

SIMON BLOWS HIS TOP—ABOUT BOP

Too Many Guys Are Getting Too Infatuated with the Sound of Their Own Notes and Not Paying Enough Attention to Musicianship

It's getting too frantic for me. I'm sorry, but I'm just about fed up to here, good and fed up, too. I've been stringing along with bop and all the guys who blow it, looking for and appreciating the good and trying to overlook the bad. And so I've gotten my kicks from Bird's great alto, from Max Roach's drumming, from the amazing improvement in Miles Davis' trumpeting, from the big-bodied, inventive baritone of Leo Parker. And yet, as I listen more and more, month by month, I become increasingly dismayed by the flagrant faults displayed by so many of bop's greats, by the constant repetition of the same overcute, multinote phrases and by the increasing deemphasis of certain basic factors in the production of good music, whether it be classical, dixieland or bop.

What really made me stand up straight and take stock happened a few weeks ago when I caught two concerts in one night. The first was by Duke and right after that came one by Diz.

Now Duke's band wasn't at its best that night at Carnegie, not by any means. It showed faults, not so much in execution, perhaps, as in the occasional use of overworked, old-fashioned phrasing. And yet there was still an awful lot of good stuff, such as the trumpets of Nance, Baker and Killian, Larry Brown's trombone, Johnny Hodges' alto, and Harry Carney's baritone when he wasn't trying to swing. And the sections almost always played together, phrased together. They had good blends and they paid accurate attention to such niceties as dynamics and matching vibratos. For this was a professional band in which the men knew what they were doing and knew how to do it. They didn't grope or guess, nor did they get up on their solos and blow real mad stuff just to get a rise out of the other guys in the band and out of the folks in the audience who thought they knew what they were trying to play.

And then I went to hear Dizzy's band and the immediate comparison convinced me completely. He was playing one of Freddy Robbins' concerts. They're

The bop cult at its cultiest, with producer Gene Norman and Dizzy Gillespie front and center

pretty informal affairs and Dizzy's followers made it even more so with their atrocious behavior. Maybe if there had been a little more dignity attached to the whole thing, the band might have sounded better, the way it did at its Carnegie Hall concert. But whatever the cause may have been, I can't recall ever having heard a less polished band in the supposedly top bracket than the one Diz fronted that night.

Blend, dynamics, shading, intonation must have been left at Carnegie. The trumpet and sax sections suffered from tones and vibratos that didn't even begin to match, and the trumpets, especially, were often guilty of phrasing that sounded as though each man had rehearsed his own part in a soundproof room, all by himself. The trombones were better, but they didn't have to pay as close attention to one another. There were only two of them. As for the rhythm section, Kenny Clarke drummed so boisterously all night long, even predominating with stick work on ballads, that all I could think of was the old days of Stan King, and if you never heard Stan King bludgeon those drums, then you've never heard really loud, boisterous drumming.

With all this disintegrated stuff going on, it's little wonder that the band swung very little. Once in a while the brass got a beat going, but the ensembles weren't convincing and some of the soloists played so far behind the beat that I began to wonder which concert they thought they were playing, Gillespie's or the just-concluded Ellington one. I don't think the guys felt they were moving either. It's been a pet theory of mine that if a band is swinging, most of the guys in it will be tapping their feet. From time to time I noted the feet of Dizzy's men. I'm afraid very little shoe leather was lost that night.

As for the ballads, they really showed up the band. The intonation was like something you might hear in a nightclub that didn't have enough dough to pay for a union band. And Dizzy's trumpet seemed to exaggerate the boppists' penchant for playing flat, so much so that I felt as though somebody had trapped me in a vise and was just squeezing and squeezing and squeezing till I hollered, "I give up!" As a matter of fact, that's just about when I did give up on Diz.

And then suddenly an awesome thought struck me. This was the band which I, as one of the editors of

52nd Street in the forties. Look at all those big names. But who is Henry Fink? !

METRONOME, had proclaimed The Band of the Year! True, I was in the minority when it came to the selection. I thought that either Ray McKinley or Claude Thornhill deserved the honor, but Barry Ulanov disagreed violently, and if you've ever faced a violent Ulanov disagreement, you know what a fight you've got on your hands! We fought it out for days and then Barbara Hodgkins got into the battle and sided with Barry and I gave in, though with the out that even if it didn't strike me as the best band of the year, it deserved some sort of recognition for what it was trying to do, and for the impression it had created by appearing before a sellout crowd at Carnegie. Anyway, what else could I do; it was two against one.

Now I'll stick with Diz on two counts. First of all, he has made a great contribution to jazz with his ideas. He has tried to incorporate them, as well as some of Bird's, into the music of a big band, possibly because it's easier to gain national recognition with a larger group, possibly because he felt that bop could be presented best that way. And secondly, Diz has never stopped trying. He hasn't remained stagnant, like too many other boppists, enthralled by the sound of a few clichés. Instead, he has continually tried to go ahead, experimenting harmonically and recently more rhythmically, including the use of conga and bongo drums and encouraging the writing of numbers as complicated and intriguing as John Lewis' *Toccata for Trumpet.*

But Dizzy and his band at their last concert crystallized an impression about bebop that I, and I suspect other musicians too, had been forming more and more of late. This is their deemphasis of performance to such an extent that they are beginning to negate the impressive impressions they had created with their new ideas. So infatuated have so many bop musicians

become just with the sound of their own notes and with their ability to play the same phrases that Diz and Bird had originally put down for them, that they seem to have forgotten all about other important things like tone, intonation and playing with a beat.

This is getting dangerous. It's a slovenly attitude that's bound to lead backwards. And its causes, I believe, are basically psychological, for few will deny that the younger, predominantly bop musicians coming up these days are able to get over their horns pretty well.

But, as mentioned in these pages before, in their attempts to emulate Diz and Bird, too many of them have overlooked pretty completely the basic factors that comprise good musicianship. They have tried to take shortcuts. In the old days, kid musicians used to go out and buy "hot lick" books and then read and try to play what the best jazz musicians of their time used to blow. Now, primarily because most of the stuff has been put down for them on wax instead of in print, they don't even have to bother to learn to read. They just copy from the records and much too often they don't know why or what they're copying.

Still, they manage to create some sort of an impression and before you know it they figure that because they can knock out a few cats (most of whom don't know what they're blowing anyway) they don't have to worry too much about learning all the other important phases of blowing a horn, such as blowing in tune, controlling your vibrato, and, above all, getting a good, clear-sounding tone.

Now get this straight. What I'm saying doesn't hold for all boppists. Some of the younger musicians like trumpeters Fats Navarro and Clark Terry and altoists Lee Konitz and Sam Staff are real, serious musicians who don't blow their horns just so they can

467

get a rise out of some fanatic followers. But from the recent sound of things, including Dizzy's band, musicians like these are in the minority.

In addition to the false sense of security engendered by being able to put down a few things that the famous boppers have put down, there's another factor to be reckoned with, namely the tremendous acclaim currently being accorded all boppists. All the plaudits, all the raves, all the written notices about this being the RIGHT kind of music, all the good reviews of records and bands which show good, progressive ideas but are still short on performance, all that adds up to a feeling of complacency that's going to be difficult to penetrate. Many bop musicians, including too many of those on top, are beginning to coast on their reputations and on the reputation of bop itself. They feel that their ideas are right and that ideas are all that count. It's so easy to rationalize like that—after all, as long as you've got the ideas (whether they're yours or Diz's or Bird's doesn't matter too much), you're in there, man, you're gone, you're mad, 'cause you've got the right idea and you're blowing the right stuff and so what difference does it make how you're blowing it! You're puttin' it down and that's all that counts!

Some of the more serious bands, like McKinley's and Thornhill's, don't feel that way. They don't dismiss performance with the old axiom that the end justifies the means. They pay attention to the means, too, and that's why these bands sound so consistently good. Same goes for Stan Kenton's band. I'm not one of its biggest admirers because it often gets too frantic for me but I do have to admire the discipline displayed by Stan and his men and the way all the men in the band are constantly and seriously trying to prove and improve what they're doing. Though theirs isn't the perfect performance either (the rough trombone section bothers me), they do pay attention to and worry about tone, intonation and blend so that listeners will hear everything that Pete Rugolo and Stan have put down on paper for them to hear. Actually, this is probably the best disciplined band in the business today.

How bebop needs discipline like this! Most of us know what frantic lives many of its musicians lead. I think that their degeneracy is reflected in their attitude toward their music. It's getting to the state where they're being governed almost completely by emotion and hardly at all by logic. Their sense of responsibility, their attitudes toward their fellowmen are mirrored in the way they play together, in their lack of regard for blend, for playing in tune, in the way drummers are constantly trying tricks, lousing up the rhythm, in the way soloists are blowing as much as they can, caring little how it fits with what the others are putting down. These men have tasted success, not so much because of their own ability, but rather because they have latched onto something that is now in favor, because they have gained recognition, because they have become a part of that fad.

Bebop right now has assumed many of the qualities of a fad. Granted that many of its contributions will live, I doubt that this style of jazz, in its present form, can last too much longer. There'll always be elements of it creeping into musicians' solos and into arrangements, but I'm afraid that unless there's more logic and less emotion employed by its exponents, it's going to drown in its own juice. Right now the majority of boppists remain too content just to knock each other out and to bask in the glory of being leaders of a cult. And how they resent any form of criticism! Anybody who disagrees with them is automatically labeled a square, a guy who's old-fashioned, a dixielander, even a Moldy Fig. That goes not only for anybody who questions their music, but also for those who laugh at the adolescent way in which boppers copy everything Diz does, from his goatee, his heavy-rimmed glasses, his nanny-goat laugh and his funny little felt cap on down.

Such smugness is bound to lead to disaster. A group that was once progressive and considered the saviour of jazz is slowly turning into a reactionary band of self-satisfied cultists. The change is reflected not only in their behavior but also (and this is more important, of course) in the way they're blowing. Dizzy's band sounded worse at Town Hall than it did at Carnegie. Maybe it could have sounded better. Maybe the men just didn't care as much. The point is, it should have progressed, it should have sounded better and the men should have cared every bit as much. For unless the boppists start to care pretty seriously about what they do and how they blow, about performing well at all times, under all conditions, unless they make a serious attempt to progress and to match their ideas with performances, a lot of other folks are going to tire of them as I have, and bebop, like too many other fads, will be gone, really gone, man!

March, 1949

A WARNING TO TELEVISION

The reason you see good jazz shows on television these days is because television is, for the most part, being run by young people. And young people, for the most part, have young ideas, and, what's more, they don't have set ideas. They're experimenting, for various reasons, artistic, technical, financial and others, and while they're experimenting they're creating something new all the time.

Compare this with what's going on in radio, especially along musical lines. Radio, and I'm referring primarily to big-time, commercial radio, is about as imaginative as the rear of a BMT subway train—and looking just about as far ahead. Many of its programs have all the musical earmarks of the middle twenties —a few have gone as far ahead as the thirties—but I can't think of a single big show that consistently brings forth the music that reflects the musical style of the late forties.

There's a reason for this contrast between modern, smart television and old-fashioned, stagnant radio music. It all reflects upon the people who are running each. The television boys are, as I've said, mostly young, and they are mostly eager, too—eager to make something out of their new baby. But the men who run radio, the network and advertising heads, are older men, too often prematurely older men, many of whom have been in radio since the beginning and who have no idea of ever relinquishing any of the power they attained merely by having been there at the beginning and having obtained that power because of lack of suitable competition. As a result, much of radio is still infested with the styles of the twenties; it still satisfies the tastes, not of the public, but of the stale old men who wield despotic power far out of proportion to their abilities or talents.

Let television take fair warning right now. Sure, everything is great today. We're trying things; we're experimenting; we're young and we're able to bring forth the kind of stuff we know the average listener with today's tastes likes to see and hear. But let's not kid ourselves. As television grows, we're going to get the same reactionary pressure from advertising agencies. What's worse, as television grows older, WE grow older, too! And as we grow older, younger people and younger ideas are going to fight for deserved recognition. Right now is the time for television to make a vow never to close its eyes and ears to the changing times, never to fight artistic progress, never to be arrogantly smug and self-sufficient, never to grow old.

Jazz on Dave Garroway's morning TV show: pianist Marian McPartland, accordionist Art Van Damme, saxist Bud Freeman, clarinetist Buddy DeFranco, trumpeter Roy Eldridge, trombonist J. J. Johnson. Whatever happened to jazz on TV, anyway?

JAZZ *IS* MY BUSINESS

Norman Granz was mad—steaming mad! He phoned in from the coast and he must have talked to me for twenty minutes about my editorial of a couple of months ago, in which I faulted his and several other record companies for issuing so many jazz records at a time.

I argued with him as patiently as I could, for Norman is a very volatile guy, and it's not always easy to relax when you're being bombarded by him. One thing he said, though, burned me, and I'm commenting on it here, because I think the record should be set straight, in case anybody else is laboring under a similar false impression.

"You've got no right to find fault with the way any of us run our business," said Norman in effect. "You're just a jazz critic. If you want to find fault with the jazz on our records, go to it. You've never heard me complain about that. But so far as the industry and its policies are concerned, that's none of your business."

That's what burned me. I think what Norman and possibly other recording company people don't realize is that being an editor of a magazine means much more than just passing on an opinion of whether this record is good or bad and why. I think what Norman has overlooked completely, for example, is the fact that during the many lean jazz years, all of us here at METRONOME were far more than just critics. We kept right on fighting for jazz, even though the record companies were issuing very few records to help us. Of all the publications in the world, ours has remained most consistently in the forefront, battling for the recognition (sometimes even the mere survival) of what we consider to be the greatest art form that this country of ours has contributed to the world.

Ours has been a strong and a vital fight. We have had great opposition. Some of it has come from our advertisers, whose sympathy toward jazz has at times not been heightened by any basic love or understanding of the music, and who certainly couldn't see any commercial gain for themselves during the years when jazz was far less popular than it is today.

We have, during the years, been the sounding board for musicians, arrangers, composers and singers who believe and perform in the jazz medium. We have done this for one reason: because we love and believe in jazz and because we feel an obligation to support those who love and believe as we do, to the best of our individual and combined abilities.

So far as I'm concerned personally, I have given more than twenty years of my life to this cause. I have been vitally interested in jazz all those years, and for many more before I joined the magazine. I have tried to encourage musicians whom I considered especially deserving with encouraging reviews and notices in my critical columns. Even those whom I haven't heard ear to ear with but who I felt were sincere in their efforts to produce good jazz, I have tried to help through the use of our editorial columns, via interviews, news and feature stories and pictures.

In those twenty years I have naturally learned a great deal about the business, as well as the music, of jazz. I have not been so naive to believe that the two are not critically interdependent. And though I may not in that period have made as much money from jazz as have other nonperformers who have been associated with it, I have still made it my business in a much larger sense—made it my business to try to help jazz—made it my business to try to help it with no axes to grind, with no ulterior financial motives. How much I have succeeded I will probably never know, for *I* have no definitive measuring stick with which to measure my success. But I must emphasize —and I hope you will agree with me—despite Norman Granz's, and possibly some others', feeling that I am "just a jazz critic," that jazz is very *much* my business, that when I note practices that might be harming jazz in general for the benefit of a few, I should speak out as forcefully as I can to protect the life of an art form with which, I frankly admit, I am very much in love.

THE LAND OF THE FREE

It was great working regularly on Metronome! Those twenty years were almost a lifetime in themselves, meeting and getting to know all the great people in jazz, finding out why they did what they did, and how they did it, and what sort of people they were.

But that part of it is all over. I'm still with the magazine, as you can see, but it's in a different capacity. Before now, every time I heard a band or a group or a singer, I immediately began to criticize. I listened to everything always with the thought, "Now, let's see, what can I write about them? How am I going to phrase it? What sort of constructive criticism can I make?"

The answer to the last question was always the most difficult. It's the easiest thing in the world to write about what you don't like. In fact, it can be a lot of fun. You can get rid of all your aggressions and you can really let somebody have it right between the eyes, and you can even show the world what a really witty guy you are by getting off some of the funniest, most sarcastic cracks this side of George Jean Nathan.

But criticizing constructively and seriously—that's a different matter. I tried it many, many times over the years. Sometimes perhaps I succeeded. When a bandleader comes up to you and thanks you for pointing out some failing in his band that he, maybe because he was too close to the scene, had overlooked, and then tells you that your constructive criticism helped, that's when you know you've succeeded. But for any critic, occasions like that are not very numerous. And to those critics who have neither understanding nor sympathy for their job and whose only form of criticism is destructive, such a rewarding experience never comes.

I recall an incident some years ago when a band manager lambasted the music editor of an important trade weekly in my presence, pointing out several flaws in the writer's review of the band. But the writer refused to admit anything, though it was pretty obvious to anyone with any sort of a musical background (which the manager had, by the way) that the criticism didn't make very much sense. When it was all over, the editor left the office with me, and when we got out on the street he muttered, "I've got a perfect right to write what I want. Maybe I don't know much about music, but I've got a right to my opinion. And, anyway, this is still the Land of the Free!"

Much too late I thought of a pertinent answer. Since this is the Land of the Free, then certainly bands and musicians should be free of critics who admittedly don't know what they're talking about.

But to get back to what I was writing about a bit earlier. That urgent feeling of having to criticize everything I hear has suddenly left me. The other night I went down to Basin Street and I heard Woody's band, and for the first time I was able to concentrate solely on the things that I liked, while almost closing my ears to those that didn't knock me out especially. I went there to have fun, and fun I did have. No longer did I feel like Dr. George Simon, who used to be so concerned with all the patients he went to visit, wondering if he could do right by what he heard, worried lest something he put into print might make the patient worse.

My wife was with me, and as we left, after having a lot of laughs with Woody, she said to me, "You really had fun tonight, didn't you?"

She was right. And it suddenly dawned on me that after twenty years I had finally entered into my own Land of the Free. I think jazz and life are going to be more fun than ever from now on.

471

APPENDIX: COMPLETE LISTING OF METRONOME BAND REVIEWS, 1935-46

These are the bands I reviewed during my first years with *Metronome,* the twelve years from 1935 through 1946 that cover the era of the big bands. Most of them received ratings from "A" for excellent, "B" for good, "C" for fair, to "D" for poor, though, come to think of it, I never had the heart (or was it the guts?) to give a "D" rating. The plus or minus following many of the letters is there for reasons that are obvious to anyone who went to school.

Sometimes numerical ratings follow the letters. That's because in 1941 we began using a dual system, with the letters indicating the bands' musical worth and the numbers (from "1" for excellent down to "4" for poor) their commercial value.

Some bands received no ratings at all. There were two reasons for this. During the thirties, I was concerned primarily with dance bands, and so, when I reviewed jazz or novelty groups that weren't playing for dancing, I found I couldn't evaluate them as dance bands and therefore didn't rate them at all. Then, in the mid-forties, after incessant insisting by co-editor Barry Ulanov and friend Leonard Feather that ratings were meaningless, we omitted them entirely for awhile. (Later I got my way and the ratings returned.)

Some of these ratings may look pretty weird. And I guess some are. For example, Al Kavelin's society-type band got a straight "A," while Jimmie Lunceford and Charlie Barnet got only "B plus." How come? Well, in those days, perhaps because I had actually worked in bands, I seemed to be more concerned with *how well* a band succeeded in doing what it set out to do, and less concerned whether *what* it was trying to do was really worthwhile. Thus, the emphasis lay perhaps too much on mechanics and not enough on inspiration and creativity. This may have been a good, objective way of reviewing, but I'm sure it annoyed many jazz and swing-oriented musicians and readers—just as it does, at this late date, the guy who wrote them.

BAND LISTING

BAND LISTING

Band	Month	Rating
Van Alexander	July, '39	B plus
Willard Alexander	April, '35	B
Bob Allen	Sept., '42	B plus — 2
Henry Allen	April, '41	A — 2
Leroy Anderson	July, '36	B
Ray Anthony	Sept., '46	———
Harold Arden	Nov. '36	B minus
Gus Arnheim	June, '37	B plus
Zinn Arthur	May, '37	B
Georgie Auld	May, '42	B — 3
" "	Sept., '46	———
Mitchell Ayres	Sept., '38	B plus
Ken Baker	Dec., '37	B plus
Dick Ballou	March, '37	B minus
Charlie Barnet	Aug., '39	B plus
Hughie Barrett	Sept., '35	B plus
Blue Barron	Feb., '38	B minus
George Barry	March, '45	———
Count Basie	Feb., '37	B
Charlie Baum	May, '38	B minus
Leon Belasco	April, '37	B minus
Tex Beneke	July, '46	———
Bunny Berigan	July, '37	B plus
Ben Bernie	April, '39	B plus
Don Bestor	June, '36	B
Henry Biagini	June, '36	B
Jerry Blaine	Feb., '37	B
Bert Block	July, '35	B plus
" "	March, '38	B plus
Sharkey Bonano	Sept., '37	———
Johnny Bothwell	Aug., '46	———
Charlie Boulanger	Dec., '36	B
Will Bradley	April, '40	A minus
Mario Braggiotti	Jan., '37	B
Nat Brandwynne	Oct., '36	B
Lou Breese	Feb., '36	B
" "	July, '42	B — 3
Lou Bring	Sept., '36	B minus
Randy Brooks	June, '45	A minus — 2
" "	May, '46	———
Les Brown	Sept., '37	B
" "	Dec., '40	A minus
" "	Feb., '45	———
Willie Bryant	April, '35	B
Sonny Burke	Dec., '40	B
Henry Busse	Sept., '38	B plus
Bobby Byrne	Aug., '41	B — 2
" "	July, '46	———
Frankie Carle	March, '44	B — 1
Benny Carter	Nov., '40	B plus
Casa Loma	May, '35	A minus
" "	May, '40	A minus
" "	June, '44	B minus — 2
Lee Castle	Oct., '42	B minus — 3
Carmen Cavallaro	Feb., '42	B — 3
Bob Chester	Sept., '40	B plus
Reggie Childs	Aug., '42	B minus — 2
Larry Clinton	Aug., '38	B plus
" "	Aug., '40	B plus
Jolly Coburn	May, '35	B
Christopher Columbus	Nov., '38	B
Del Courtney	Dec., '39	B minus
Bob Crosby	April, '36	A
" "	July, '39	A
" "	Oct., '41	A — 1
Bernie Cummins	May, '35	B minus
Ben Cutler	Aug., '38	B
Frank Dailey	Nov., '37	A minus
Duke Daly	Aug., '41	B — 4
Meyer Davis	April, '35	C
Bobby Day	Oct., '40	B
Jack Denny	July, '35	C minus
Emery Deutsch	March, '37	B

Band	Month	Rating
Al Donahue	Oct., '35	B minus
" "	Oct., '39	B plus
Sam Donahue	Sept., '42	B plus — 2
" "	Dec., '46	———
Charlie Dornberger	June, '36	B
Jimmy Dorsey	May, '38	A minus
" "	April, '39	A
" "	March, '45	———
Tommy Dorsey	May, '36	A minus
" "	Jan., '39	A
" "	July, '42	A — 1
Eddy Duchin	July, '40	B
Sonny Dunham	Aug., '41	B — 2
" "	March, '43	B — 2
Les Elgart	April, '45	———
" "	Dec., '45	———
" "	Nov., '46	———
Duke Ellington	June, '37	A
Seger Ellis	July, '40	B
Willie Farmer	Sept., '39	C plus
Happy Felton	Oct., '37	B plus
Shep Fields	June, '36	B plus
" "	Feb., '42	A — 2
" "	Nov., '45	———
Ted Fio Rito	Jan., '36	A minus
" "	Dec., '43	B — 2
Scott Fisher	March, '35	B minus
Jerry Freeman	Sept., '35	B minus
Rudolph Friml, Jr.	March, '38	B
Jan Garber	Jan., '44	B — 3
Neal Gianinni	Jan., '38	B
Benny Goodman	June, '35	A
" "	May, '38	A
" "	Dec., '41	A — 1
" "	Nov., '43	A — 1
" "	July, '46	———
Gray Gordon	March, '39	B
Johnny Green	March, '35	B
Jimmy Grier	Dec., '37	B
Bobby Hackett	Feb., '38	———
George Haefely	May, '35	B
George Hall	April, '40	B
Mal Hallett	Oct., '35	A minus
Henry Halstead	July, '35	B minus
Hale Hamilton	Aug., '35	B minus
Johnny Hamp	Nov., '36	B minus
Lionel Hampton	May, '42	A minus — 1
Phil Harris	Oct., '35	B
Erskine Hawkins	May, '37	B minus
" "	May '46	———
Ralph Hawkins	March, '42	B — 2
Lenny Hayton	May, '37	B plus
Horace Heidt	Aug., '37	B
" "	Sept., '43	B plus — 1
Ray Herbeck	May, '42	B minus — 2
Woody Herman	Jan., '37	A minus
" "	Jan. '40	A
" "	Sept., '44	A — 1
Teddy Hill	July, '35	B
Richard Himber	Dec., '38	B
Everett Hoagland	March, '40	B
Carl Hoff	July, '41	B — 3
" "	Oct., '42	B plus — 2
Ernie Holst	June, '39	B
Claude Hopkins	May, '36	B minus
Dean Hudson	Feb., '41	B plus
" "	Aug., '44	B — 2
Hudson-DeLange	Aug., '37	B plus
Ina Ray Hutton	Oct., '40	B
Harry James	Sept., '39	A minus
" "	Sept., '40	A
" "	June, '41	A — 2
" "	July, '43	A minus — 1

Band	Month	Rating
Harry James	July, '45	A minus — 1
Henry Jerome	April, '41	C — 2
" "	Oct., '43	B plus — 2
" "	March, '46	———
Johnny Johnson	Dec., '35	B minus
Isham Jones	Dec., '35	B plus
Dick Jurgens	Nov., '41	B — 1
Paul Kain	Oct., '38	B
Gene Kardos	June, '38	B
Al Katz	June, '37	B minus
Al Kavelin	Nov., '35	A
Sammy Kaye	Nov., '38	B minus
Hal Kemp	April, '35	A minus
Larry Kent	Jan, '38	B minus
Stan Kenton	Nov., '41	A — 3
" "	Aug., '42	B plus — 2
Henry King	March, '35	A minus
John Kirby	Nov., '37	———
Andy Kirk	March, '37	A minus
" "	Jan., '43	B plus — 2
Orville Knapp	April, '36	B
Gene Krupa	March, '40	A minus
" "	July, '45	———
" "	June, '46	B plus — 1
Davey Kuttner	Dec., '35	C plus
Kay Kyser	April, '37	B
Howard Lally	Jan., '36	C plus
Frank LaMarr	March, '36	B minus
Eddie Lane	April, '36	B minus
Elliot Lawrence	April, '46	A minus — 1
Allen Leafer	Sept., '35	B minus
Phil Levant	April, '37	B
Enoch Light	Oct., '35	B
" "	May, '39	B plus
Little Jack Little	Nov., '35	B
" " "	Oct., '39	C plus
Guy Lombardo	Feb., '42	C — 1
Johnny Long	May, '40	B plus
" "	April, '44	———
" "	Jan., '46	———
Vincent Lopez	Jan., '42	B — 3
Clyde Lucas	June, '35	B
" "	June, '42	B — 2
Jimmie Lunceford	Sept., '36	B plus
" "	Sept., '38	A
Dick Mansfield	May, '36	B minus
Paul Martell	April, '35	C
Freddy Martin	Feb., '36	B plus
" "	Oct., '41	B — 1
Frankie Masters	Nov., '39	B plus
" "	June, '41	B — 2
Nye Mayhew	Oct., '36	B plus
Bill McCune	Oct., '37	B
McFarland Twins	July, '41	C — 2
" "	Nov., '42	B — 2
Johnny McGee	Nov., '40	B plus
Hal McIntyre	March, '42	A — 2
" "	Feb., '45	———
Red McKenzie	April, '36	———
Ray McKinley	June, '42	A minus — 2
" "	April, '46	B plus — 2
Jimmy McPartland	May, '41	B — 3
Hugh McPherson	Jan., '37	C
Randy Mergentroid	April, '42	D — 1
Benny Meroff	Oct., '37	B
Dick Messner	March, '36	B
Johnny Messner	Feb., '38	B
" "	Jan., '42	B — 2
Marti Michel	April, '35	B minus
Glenn Miller	June, '38	A minus
" "	Feb., '40	A
" "	Jan., '42	A — 1
Herb Miller	June, '46	———

Band	Month	Rating
Lucky Millinder	Dec., '36	B
Vaughn Monroe	July, '41	B — 2
Art Mooney	Sept., '45	B minus — 2
Russ Morgan	March, '36	B plus
Buddy Morrow	Jan., '46	———
Billy Murphy	Feb., '36	B minus
Phil Napoleon	Sept., '37	B
Ozzie Nelson	April, '35	B plus
" "	Oct., '41	B — 2
" "	Dec., '41	B — 3
Henry Nemo	Feb., '36	A minus
Ruby Newman	June, '40	A minus
Red Nichols	June, '41	B — 3
" "	Dec. '38	B plus
Leighton Noble	July, '35	A
Ray Noble	March, '36	A
Red Norvo	Oct., '38	A
" "	Aug., '35	B plus
Will Osborne	June, '40	B plus
" "	Aug., '43	B plus — 2
" "	Feb., '41	A minus
Tony Pastor	June, '46	———
" "	Dec., '44	———
George Paxton	July, '45	———
" "	Aug., '35	C minus
Ted Peters	Nov., '39	B
Teddy Powell	Sept., '41	B — 1
" "	Jan., '43	A — 1
" "	June, '35	———
Louis Prima	May, '44	B minus — 2
" "	March, '46	———
" "	Nov., '42	B minus — 2
Boyd Raeburn	April, '44	A minus — 1
" "	Dec., '35	B minus
Arthur Ravel	July, '37	B
Carl Ravell (Ravazza)	Sept., '36	B
Joe Reichman	Nov., '36	B plus
Harry Reser	April, '41	B — 1
Alvino Rey	July, '46	———
" "	Aug., '40	B
Tommy Reynolds	Sept., '36	B minus
Frank Reysen	Feb., '46	A minus — 2
Buddy Rich	Nov., '44	———
Johnny Richards	Nov., '35	———
Riley–Farley	July, '36	B minus
Joe Rines	Feb., '37	C plus
Rita Rio	May, '39	B plus
Jan Savitt	Oct., '36	A minus
Artie Shaw	Feb., '39	A
" "	Dec., '42	B plus — 2
Bobby Sherwood	March, '35	B plus
Noble Sissle	May, '36	———
Stuff Smith	Sept., '41	B — 2
Phil Sobel	Nov., '41	A — 2
Muggsy Spanier	March, '41	A minus
Charlie Spivak	Feb., '43	A — 1
" "	Feb., '44	A minus — 1
" "	Dec., '45	———
Dick Stabile	July, '36	A minus
" "	April, '42	B plus — 2
Bill Staffon	Nov., '35	B minus
Harold Stern	Jan., '36	B
George Sterney	Dec., '36	B plus
Eddie Stone	Sept., '45	B minus — 1
Bob Strong	Sept., '46	———
Johnny Strouse	Aug., '35	C plus
Billy Swanson	Nov., '37	B
Bob Sylvester	Jan., '36	B
Jack Teagarden	June, '39	A minus
" "	Jan., '41	A minus
Claude Thornhill	May, '41	A — 1
" "	July, '46	———
" "	Dec., '46	———

BAND LISTING

Band	Month	Rating
Three T's	Jan., '37	———
Anthony Trini	July, '37	B
Orrin Tucker	March, '41	B
" "	Sept., '46	———
Tommy Tucker	Dec., '41	C — 2
Joe Venuti	March, '39	B
Jerry Wald	May, '41	B — 3
" "	April, '42	B — 2
" "	May, '46	———
Frankie Ward	Jan., '38	B minus
Chick Webb	June, '35	B plus

BAND LISTING

Band	Month	Rating
Marek Weber	Dec., '37	B plus
Ranny Weeks	Sept., '35	C plus
Lawrence Welk	Sept., '41	C — 2
Paul Whiteman	Dec., '39	A minus
Paul Whiteman's Juniors	June, '35	C plus
Ran Wilde	July, '38	B
Julie Wintz	March, '38	C plus
Barry Wood	July, '39	B minus
Julian Woodworth	Aug., '37	B minus
Lee and Lester Young	Dec., '42	B — 3

Index

Places listed in the index, such as hotels, restaurants, night clubs, dance halls, etc., are identified by city or area if outside of New York (Manhattan). New York listings are not further identified unless there is a special pertinence. Numbers in italics indicate pages on which subject appears in a photograph.

479

490

PICTURE CREDITS

The photos that appear on the following pages are reproduced through the courtesy of METRONOME:

Pp. 9, 10, 11, 12. P. 14, by Arsene. P. 15, by (left) Franklin Worth, (right) by Albert Freeman. Pp. 16, 18, 20, 22. P. 24, by Gary Gray. P. 26, by Gene Howard. Pp. 28, 29. P. 32, by George T. Simon. P. 35, by Edward Ozern. P. 38. P. 39, by NBC. P. 43, by Drucker. Pp. 45, 47, 49, 52, 59, 63, 65, 71, 74, 77. P. 80, by Harold Stein. P. 85, by Miners. P. 86, by Maurice. P. 89, by RCA Victor. Pp. 95, 96, by Otto Hess. Pp. 100, 101, by CBS. Pp. 102, 105, by Pictorial Feature Service. Pp. 106, 114, 122 (left), 129. P. 129 (right), by Otto Hess. P. 131, by Arsene. Pp. 134, 140, 145. P. 147, by Otto Hess. P. 153, by Gary Gray. P. 154. P. 156, by Otto Hess. Pp. 160, 164, 166. P. 173. P. 177, by Ray Levitt. Pp. 183, 185. P. 187, by Ray Levitt. P. 188, by Gene Lester. P. 195 by Press Association. Pp. 199, 200. P. 204, by Zinn Arthur. Pp. 205, 207, 208, 209. P. 215 (top), by Otto Hess, (bottom) by Maurice. Pp. 217, 219, 220, 221, 224, 226. P. 228, by Edward Ozern. P. 230, by Gabriel Benzur. Pp. 231, 233. P. 235, by Ray Levitt. P. 238, by Barry. P. 239. P. 242, by Barry. P. 244, by Ray Levitt. P. 247, by Michael Caputo. P. 249, by Murray Lewis. P. 251, by Otto Hess. P. 254 (top). P. 254 (bottom), by Metropolitan Photo Service. Pp. 256, 258 (left). P. 258 (right), by Arsene. P. 259, by Otto Hess. Pp. 260, 261. P. 263, by Graphic House. P. 264, by Otto Hess. P. 268, by Charlie Mihn. P. 271, by Danny Pucello. P. 275, by Al Hauser. Pp. 279, 280. P. 283, by Benmar Studio. P. 285, by Metropolitan Photo Service. Pp. 288, 290, 292, 293. P. 295, by Cookie Marett. P. 296, by Lew Nichols. P. 299, by Otto Hess. P. 300, by RCA Victor. P. 301, by Arsene. P. 302. Pp. 303, 305, by Otto Hess. Pp. 307, 308, 311, 315, 316, 317, 319. P. 321, by Roger Stern. P. 322, by Otto Hess. P. 324. P. 326, by Ben Greenhaus. Pp. 328, 330, 331. P. 333 (top), courtesy Fuzzy Farrar and Chauncey Morehouse, (bottom) courtesy Irving Riskin. P. 336, courtesy of Tommy Dorsey. P. 338, by Moss Candid Photo. P. 342. P. 345, by Otto Hess. P. 347. P. 350, by Libson-Ehrenberg. P. 351, by NBC. P. 352. P. 354, by Gene Lester. Pp. 355, 358. P. 361, by Charlie Mihn. P. 363, by Newspictures. P. 368, by Barry Kramer. P. 369. P. 372, by Bill Spilka. P. 375. P. 377, by Lew Nichols. Pp. 378, 379, 381. P. 383, by Adrian Boutrelle. Pp. 384, 385. P. 387, by Barry. Pp. 388, 392, 396, 399, 401. P. 402, by Barry Kramer. Pp. 408, 409, by Central Studios. P. 410, by Zinn Arthur. P. 412, by Metropolitan Photo Service. P. 414, by Francis Wolff. P. 417, by George T. Simon. P. 418, by Warren Rothschild. Pp. 421, 426. P. 430, by George Larriew. Pp. 431, 432, 433, 434. P. 436, by Metropolitan Photo Service. P. 437, by Edward Ozern. P. 439, by Otto Hess. P. 440, by Werner Wolff. P. 444. P. 445, by CBS. P. 446, by Werner Wolff. P. 447, by Metropolitan Photo Service. P. 449, by George T. Simon. Pp. 452, 453, by Otto Hess. P. 457. P. 458, by Skippy Adelman. Pp. 460, 462. P. 466, by McLain's Photo Service. P. 467. P. 469, by Maurey Garber.

OTHER CREDITS

P. 13, courtesy of John Scott Trotter. P. 30, by Bert Block. P. 66, NBC. Page 67, courtesy of Shep Fields. P. 91, courtesy of Horace Heidt. P. 110, courtesy of Jimmy Crawford. P. 118, courtesy of Sammy Kaye. P. 124, courtesy of Artie Shaw. P. 124, Central Studios, courtesy of Harry James. P. 170, Metropolitan Photo Service, courtesy of Freddy Martin. P. 191, RCA Victor. P. 297, courtesy of Tino Barzie. Pp. 339, 380, courtesy of Vito Marino. P. 366, CBS. P. 382, courtesy of Dolores O'Neill. P. 389, CBS. P. 394, NBC. P. 404, courtesy of Vito Marino. P. 416, by George T. Simon. P. 442, CBS.